OXFORD REFERENCE

DICTIONARY OF
COMPUTING

DICTIONARY OF
COMPUTING

THIRD EDITION

Oxford   New York
OXFORD UNIVERSITY PRESS
1991

Oxford University Press, Walton Street, Oxford OX2 6DP

Oxford New York Toronto
Delhi Bombay Calcutta Madras Karachi
Petaling Jaya Singapore Hong Kong Tokyo
Nairobi Dar es Salaam Cape Town
Melbourne Auckland
and associated companies in
Berlin Ibadan

Oxford is a trade mark of Oxford University Press

First edition 1983
Second edition 1986
Third edition 1990
First issued as an Oxford University Press paperback 1991

British Library Cataloguing in Publication Data
Dictionary of computing. — 3rd ed. — (Oxford reference).
1. Computer systems
I. Illingworth, Valerie
004
ISBN 0-19-286131-X

Library of Congress Cataloging in Publication Data
Dictionary of computing. — 3rd ed.
p. cm. — (Oxford science publications)
General editor: Valerie Illingworth.
1. Electronic data processing—Dictionaries. 2. Computer—Dictionaries.
I. Illingworth, Valerie. II. Series.
004'.103—dc20 QA76.15.D526 1990 89-26662
ISBN 0-19-286131-X

Text prepared by
Market House Books Ltd., Aylesbury
Printed in Great Britain by
Clays Ltd.
Bungay, Suffolk

Preface

The great advances in the last few years in all aspects of computing—in theory, technology, and applications—have brought about a tremendous growth in the uses to which computers can be put and in the number of people using them. As the computing scene has expanded so has computing terminology. For this third edition of the *Dictionary of Computing*, over 550 new entries have been added and many of the existing entries have been extensively updated. This reflects recent advances in all aspects of computing, especially new approaches to both programming and computer organization and architecture (and the associated new languages), and developments in the software and hardware associated with microcomputing, networking, and information technology. This edition contains, in a single alphabetical listing, nearly 4500 terms used in computing and in the associated fields of electronics, mathematics, and logic. The branches of computing covered in this dictionary include:

  algorithms and their properties
  programming languages and concepts
  program development methods
  data structures and file structures
  operating systems and concepts
  computer organization and architecture, past and present
  hardware, including processors, memory devices, and I/O devices
  computer communications
  information technology
  computer applications and techniques
  major computer manufacturers
  legal aspects of computing

The entries in the dictionary have been written by practitioners in these branches of computing and in the associated fields. The terms described range from basic ideas and equipment to advanced concepts of graduate-level computer science; some entries are supplemented by diagrams and tables. The dictionary should be of use to students and teachers of computer science and of all subjects in which computing plays a part. It should also be a valuable reference book to people employed in the various branches of computing as well as to the interested layman with his own micro.

A major undertaking by over fifty people on both sides of the Atlantic, the dictionary has been compiled and prepared for computer typesetting by Market House Books Ltd. The editors would like to express their thanks and appreciation to the many contributors for their co-operation, time, and effort.

September 1989

Valerie Illingworth
Edward L. Glaser
I. C. Pyle

Consultant Editors

Edward L. Glaser AB, Phi Beta Kappa, Dr.Sc., FIEEE, MNAE
I. C. Pyle MA, Ph.D., FBCS, FIEEE, C.Eng.

General Editor

Valerie Illingworth B.Sc, M.Phil.

Contributors

Guide to the Dictionary

Alphabetical order in this dictionary ignores spaces, punctuation, and numbers in the entry titles.

Synonyms and generally used abbreviations are given either in brackets immediately after the relevant entry title, or occasionally in the text of the entry with some additional information or qualification.

An asterisk (*) used before a word or group of words indicates to the reader that he will find at the entry so marked further information relevant to the entry he is reading. The asterisk is not used before all the words in an article that are themselves entry titles as this would lead to an unhelpful proliferation of asterisks.

Some entries simply cross-refer the reader to other articles. These may be synonyms or abbreviations or terms more conveniently discussed under the article referred to. In the latter case, the relevant term will appear in the entry in italic type.

A distinction is made between an acronym and an abbreviation: an acronym can be pronounced while an abbreviation cannot. The entry for an acronym always appears at the acronym itself whereas the entry for an abbreviation usually appears at the unabbreviated form, unless the abbreviation is in common use.

Some terms listed in the dictionary are used both as nouns and verbs. This is usually indicated in the text of an entry if both forms are in common use. In many cases a noun is also used in an adjectival form to qualify another noun. This occurs too often to be noted.

Typography and Character Set

The typefaces and characters used in the dictionary follow normal conventions for printing mathematical and technical texts (rather than the more rigorous styles used in some specialist computing texts). *Italic type* is used for scalar quantities, variables, functions, and matrices. ***Bold italic type*** is used for vectors.

The special characters shown in the table have been used to express specific logic, set theory, and mathematical operations; for further information, see relevant entry. Letters of the Greek alphabet also occur in some entries.

operation, etc.	symbol	operation, etc.	symbol
AND operation, conjunction	$\wedge$.	equivalence	$\leftrightarrow \equiv$
OR operation, disjunction	$\vee$ +	biconditional	$\leftrightarrow \equiv$
NOT operation, negation	$'\ \neg \sim$	conditional	$\rightarrow \Rightarrow$
NAND operation	$\mid \Delta$	general binary operation	$\circ$
NOR operation	$\uparrow \nabla$	universal quantifier	$\forall$
EXOR operation	$\underline{\vee}$	existential quantifier	$\exists$

For set S and/or set T:

x is a member of S	$x \in S$	union of S and T	$S \cup T$
x is not a member of S	$x \notin S$	intersection of S and T	$S \cap T$
S is a subset of T	$S \subseteq T$	Cartesian product of S and T	$S \times T$
S is a proper subset of T	$S \subset T$		
complement of S	$S' \sim S\ \bar{S}$	set of all x for which $p(x)$ is true	$\{x \mid p(x)\}$

relation	R	greater than	$>$
function of x	$f(x)$, etc.	greater than or equal to	$\geqslant$
function f from set X to set Y	$f\colon X \rightarrow Y$	less than	$<$
		less than or equal to	$\leqslant$
inverse function	f^{-1}	approx. equal to	$\cong$
inverse relation	R^{-1}	not equal to	$\neq$
sum, with limits	$\sum\limits_{i=1}^{n}$	infinity	∞
integral, with limits	$\int_{b}^{a}\ \mathrm{d}x$		

elements of vector v	v_1
elements of matrix A	a_{ij}
transpose of matrix A	A^{T}
inverse of matrix A	A^{-1}

Greek alphabet

alpha	α, A	iota	ι, I	rho	ρ, P
beta	β, B	kappa	κ, K	sigma	σ, Σ
gamma	γ, Γ	lambda	λ, Λ	tau	τ, T
delta	δ, Δ	mu	μ, M	upsilon	υ, Υ
epsilon	ε, E	nu	ν, N	phi	ϕ, Φ
zeta	ζ, Z	xi	ξ, Ξ	chi	χ, X
eta	η, H	omikron	o, O	psi	ψ, Ψ
theta	θ, Θ	pi	π, Π	omega	ω, Ω

A

abelian group (commutative group) *See* group.

ablative An optical recording technique in which the heat generated by the recording beam melts or vaporizes a small area of the recording medium, leaving the underlying layer (with a different reflectivity) exposed.

abnormal termination A termination to a *process brought about by the operating system when the process reaches a point from which it cannot continue, e.g. when the process attempts to obey an undefined instruction. In contrast, a process that reaches a successful conclusion terminates normally by issuing a suitable supervisor call to the operating system. It is common practice to inform the initiator of the process as to whether the termination was normal or abnormal.

abort (of a process) To undergo or cause *abnormal termination. Abortion may be a voluntary act by the process, which realizes that it cannot reach a successful conclusion, or may be brought about by the operating system, which intervenes because the process has failed to observe system constraints. Thus, computationally, the term has a rather similar meaning to its medical meaning of spontaneous or induced fetal death.

absolute address A unique number that specifies a unique location within the *address space where an operand is to be found/deposited, also where an instruction is located. It generally specifies a memory location but in some cases specifies a machine register or an I/O device. In the case of a binary machine, it is an n-bit number specifying one of 2^n locations. The result of calculating an *effective address is usually an absolute address.

absolute code Program code in a form suitable for direct execution by the central processor, i.e. code containing no symbolic references. *See also* machine code.

absorption laws The two self-dual laws
$$x \vee (x \wedge y) = x$$
$$x \wedge (x \vee y) = x$$
(*see* duality) that are satisfied by all elements x,y in a *Boolean algebra possessing the two operations $\vee$ and $\wedge$.

abstract data type A *data type that is defined solely in terms of the operations that apply to objects of the type without commitment as to how the value of such an object is to be represented (*see* data abstraction).

An abstract data type strictly is a triple (D,F,A) consisting of a set of domains D, a set of functions F each with range and domain in D, and a set of axioms A, which specify the properties of the functions in F. By distinguishing one of the domains d in D, a precise characterization is obtained of the *data structure that the abstract data type imposes on d.

For example, the natural numbers comprise an abstract data type, where the domain d is
$$\{0,1,2,\dots\}$$
and there is an auxiliary domain
$$\{TRUE,FALSE\}$$
The functions or operations are ZERO, ISZERO, SUCC, and ADD and the axioms are:
$$ISZERO(0) = TRUE$$
$$ISZERO(SUCC(x)) = FALSE$$
$$ADD(0,y) = y$$
$$ADD(SUCC(x),y) =$$
$$SUCC(ADD(x,y))$$
These axioms specify precisely the laws that must hold for any implementation of the natural numbers. (Note that a practical implementation could not fulfill the axioms because of word length

and overflow.) Such precise characterization is invaluable both to the user and the implementer.

The Ada programmer can obtain many of the benefits of abstract data types by defining *packages.

abstract family of languages (AFL) A class of formal languages that is closed under all the following operations: *union, *concatenation, Kleene-plus (*see* Kleene star), *intersection with *regular set, Λ-free homomorphic image, and inverse homomorphic image (*see* homomorphism). An AFL is *full* if it is also closed under Kleene star and homomorphic image. The motivation for the concept of an AFL is to investigate properties of classes of languages that follow merely from the assumption of certain *closure properties. Each member of the *Chomsky hierarchy is an AFL; all except type 2 are full.

abstraction The principle of ignoring those aspects of a subject that are not relevant to the current purpose in order to concentrate solely on those that are. The application of this principle is essential in the development and understanding of all forms of computer system. *See* data abstraction, procedural abstraction.

abstract machine A machine can be thought of as a collection of resources together with a definition of the ways in which these resources can interact. For a real machine these resources actually exist as tangible objects, each of the type expected; for example, addressable storage on a real machine will actually consist of the appropriate number of words of storage, together with suitable address decoders and access mechanisms. It is possible to define an abstract machine, by listing the resources it contains and the interactions between them, without building the machine. Such abstract machines are often of use in attempting to prove the properties of

programs, since a suitably defined abstract machine may allow the suppression of unneeded detail. *See* virtual machine.

abstract specification A specification for software expressed in a (mathematically) *formal language such that the specification is completely independent of, and does not imply, any design and implementation method and languages. It does not normally express the constraints that the final software must satisfy. *See also* formal specification.

acceleration time (start time) The time taken for a device to reach its operating speed from a quiescent state.

accept (recognize) *See* automaton.

acceptance testing *See* testing. *See also* review.

accepting state *See* finite-state automaton.

access The reading or writing of data, with the connotation that the content of the reading or writing is taken into account. The word is also used as a verb: to gain entry to. It is most commonly used in connection with filed information and is often qualified by an indication as to the types of access that are to be permitted. For example, read-only access means that the contents of the file may be read but not altered or erased.

access arm *See* arm.

access control A *trusted process that limits access to the resources and objects of a computer system in accordance with a *security model. The process can be implemented by reference to a stored table that lists the access rights of subjects to objects, e.g. users to records. Optionally the process may record in an *audit trail any illegal access attempts.

access method Any algorithm used for the storage and retrieval of records in a *data file or *database. An access method determines a set of structural characteristics for the file for which it is used. A *file organization is determined by the set of access methods used for the file. In the simplest case where only one access method is used, the same term may be used interchangeably (and loosely) for both the access method and the file organization. *See* indexed file, ISAM, random access, sequential access, VSAM.

access time The time taken to retrieve an item of information from storage. The access time may be counted in nanoseconds for a semiconductor device or in minutes if the file containing the required data is on magnetic tape.

6

1   3   7

4   2

5   8   9

row-ragged array

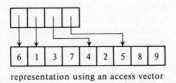

representation using an access vector

Access vector

access vector A vector that is used in the representation of a *ragged array. For example, the elements of a row-ragged array, A, would be stored row by row in a vector B. The ith element of the access vector would then point to the position in B where the first element of the ith row of A was stored (*see* dia-

gram). A column-ragged array would be similarly represented using an access vector referring to the beginning of columns and a listing of the elements column by column.

accountable file A file that will be taken into account when evaluating system usage. An example is a user's permanent file holding the text of a program. Files that have only a transient existence, for example to hold spooled files, will not be accountable.

accounting file A file that contains records of the resources used by individual jobs. These records are required both to regulate the amount of resource used by a job and, in a commercial environment, to manage the charging for use of the system. As each job is started, an entry is opened in the accounting file into which records concerning system utilization are written as the job is processed. *See also* system accounting.

accumulator A *register that is used to contain the results of an operation performed by the *arithmetic and logic unit (ALU). It can normally be one of the inputs to the ALU, thus the results of a number of successive operations may be built up – hence the name. In addition to holding results, the accumulator commonly has the ability to perform the various *shift and *circular shift instructions. It is commonly part of the *processor status word.

accuracy *See* precision.

ACE *Acronym for* Automatic Computing Engine. An electronic stored-program computer designed in 1945–46 by Alan Turing while he was at the National Physical Laboratory (NPL), near London. The prototype version *Pilot ACE* was built at the NPL, ran its first program in 1950, and was in full-time use in 1952. The final version was working by 1957.

ACIA *Abbrev. for* asynchronous communications interface adapter. An integrated circuit that can be used in serial data communication interfaces. The function of the device can be varied by signals applied to its control inputs.

ACK *See* acknowledgment.

Ackermann benchmark A use of the *Ackermann function to provide a *benchmark for computer performance. Typically in excess of 100 000 recursive calls to the function are made and the number of completed calls per second measured. The benchmark gives a good indication of the overhead associated with procedure and function calls.

Ackermann function The *function A defined inductively on pairs of nonnegative integers in the following manner:

$$A(0,n) = n + 1$$
$$A(m+1,0) = A(m,1)$$
$$A(m+1,n+1) = A(m,A(m+1,n))$$

where $m,n \geqslant 0$. Thus

$$A(1,n) = n + 2$$
$$A(2,n) = 2n + 3$$
$$A(3,n) = 2^{n+3} - 3$$

The highly recursive nature of the function makes it a popular choice for testing the ability of *compilers or computers to handle *recursion. Named for W. Ackermann, it provides an example of a function that is general *recursive but not *primitive recursive because of the exceedingly rapid growth in its value as m increases.

The Ackermann function may also be regarded as a function Ack of a single variable:

$$Ack(n) = A(n,n)$$

where A is defined as above.

acknowledgment A message that describes the status of one or more messages sent in the opposite direction. A *positive acknowledgment (ACK)* confirms that the previous messages were received correctly. A *negative acknowledgment (NAK)* indicates that the previ-

ous messages were not received correctly and should be retransmitted. In some *protocols, acknowledgments are also used as a simple form of *flow control: sending an ACK implies that another message may be sent in the same direction as the message being acknowledged.

Piggyback acknowledgments are acknowledgments that are carried in a special field in regular data messages. Thus, as long as there is data ready for both directions of a circuit, no extra messages are needed to carry acknowledgments.

Different layers of a protocol hierarchy may have their own acknowledgment systems operating simultaneously. For example, an end-to-end transport protocol may be used to send a message reliably from one host to another in a packet switching network. When the message reaches its destination, an acknowledgment will be generated and sent in the opposite direction. Both the original message and its acknowledgment will cause data link layer acknowledgments to be generated as they travel from node to node in the network.

See also backward error correction.

ACM Association for Computing Machinery, a US organization founded in 1947 with the following purposes.

"To advance the sciences and arts of information processing including, but not restricted to, the study, design, development, construction, and application of modern machinery, computing techniques, and appropriate languages for general information processing, for scientific computation, for the recognition, storage, retrieval, and processing of data of all kinds, and for the automatic control and simulation of processes.

"To promote the free interchange of information about the sciences and arts of information processing both among specialists and among the public in the best scientific and professional tradition.

"To develop and maintain the integrity and competence of individuals engaged in the practices of the sciences and arts of information processing."

acoustic coupler A type of *modem that converts serial digital data into a *frequency shift keyed sound signal in the audio range for transmission down telephone lines, and decodes similar incoming sound signals. The connection between the acoustic coupler and the telephone system is made by means of a small microphone and loudspeaker held close to the earpiece and mouthpiece of an ordinary telephone handset in a sound-absorbent enclosure.

This system is ideal for connecting portable terminals or data-capture devices to remote computers using any convenient telephone. The lack of any electrical connection between terminal and phone lines is of benefit when obtaining the approval of the PTT for the use of such a device. The quality of ordinary switched voice circuits normally limits the speed of transmission to 300 baud or less.

acoustic delay line See delay line.

actigram See SADT.

active Another term for running.

active star A network topology in which the outer *nodes connect to a single central node. The central node processes all messages in the network, including messages that it forwards from one outer node to another. A failure of the central node causes the entire network to fail. See also passive star, star network, network architecture.

activity network (activity graph) A graphical method for showing dependencies between tasks (activities) in a project. The network consists of *nodes connected by arcs. Nodes denote events and represent the culmination of one or more activities. Arcs represent activities and are labeled with the name of the activity and have an estimated time to complete the activity. Dummy unlabeled arcs with zero completion time are used to fan out from one event to other dependent events. Before progress can be made from one event to another, all activities leading to that event must have been completed. The longest path through the activity network gives the completion time for the project represented by the network. See also critical path method, PERT chart.

actual parameter Information passed to a *subprogram at the *call. See also parameter, argument.

actuator of a disk drive. The mechanism that causes the head carriage and heads to be moved to the desired track. There are two main types: the voice coil and the stepper motor. The former gains its name because its operating principle is similar to that of a moving-coil loudspeaker. This type of actuator invariably forms part of a closed loop servosystem. The reference information is often provided by a disk with a dedicated servosurface. The servohead positions itself symmetrically between two servotracks by sensing positioning information from both tracks (di-bits) and moving in such a way that the amplitudes of the two signals are equal. A recently developed alternative method employs bits recorded on all surfaces that fall between sectors containing stored information; this technique is known as embedded servo.

The second type of actuator is essentially open loop in that it makes use of a stepper motor – a motor that moves in discrete steps when currents of the correct phase relationship are applied to its windings. This type of actuator is only used in low-cost systems where the track density may be as low as 150 tracks per inch.

ACU Abbrev. for automatic calling unit. A device that allows a computer or terminal to originate calls over the public switched telephone network, or in some cases over a private switched network. An ACU is often used in conjunction with a *modem: the ACU is responsible for placing the telephone call, while the modem is responsible for data transfer and call termination. Since the ACU is needed only when the call is being placed, a single ACU can often be shared among multiple modems and phone lines. ACUs are used when the traffic between two nodes (terminals or computers) is too large for manual call origination, but not large enough to justify a dedicated connection. Computer networks that use ACUs usually function as *store-and-forward message switches.

acyclic graph A *graph possessing no *cycles; when the term is applied to directed graphs the direction associated with the edges must be taken into account. *See also* tree.

Ada *Trademark* A programming language developed at the behest of the US Department of Defense for use in embedded systems, i.e. systems in which a computer is used for control purposes. (Aircraft navigation systems are an obvious example.) Such systems require concurrent activity and have severe response-time constraints, thus Ada is a *real-time language.

The design requirements of Ada were elaborated in a sequence of reports, successively more detailed specifications being identified as Strawman, Woodenman, Tinman, Ironman, and Steelman. When the specification was complete, four contractors were invited to implement a language to meet the specification. The language developed by CII-Honeywell-Bull was chosen: originally code-named *Green*, it was renamed Ada in honor of Augusta Ada Lovelace who, as assistant to Charles Babbage, has some claim to be the world's first programmer.

In addition to facilities for real-time concurrent programming, Ada incorporates novel ideas of modular structure and separate compilation to support the development of very large systems. It also introduces the idea of a programming support environment (*APSE) whereby program development tools are specified along with the language as an integrated whole. However, the task of developing a practical support environment has proved to be more difficult than at first anticipated, and this is still an area of active work.

Ada was released in 1980. In 1982 a new definition was published that clarified ambiguities and obscurities, and this new version became an ANSI standard in 1983. It was agreed that this definition would be frozen for five years, and the next revision of Ada is currently under discussion. From 1986 use of Ada was made mandatory for US military applications, and European countries have followed suit. However, it is possible for a contractor to seek a waiver of this requirement if he can show "good cause", and the use of Ada in real applications is still not widespread.

Adams methods *See* linear multistep methods.

adaptation data Data used to adapt a program to a given installation site or to given conditions in its operational environment.

adaptive channel allocation A process by which the capacity of a communication channel is multiplexed (shared) among several sources depending upon their relative requirements. The resource distribution varies with time to match changing requirements. *See* multiplexing.

adaptive-control system An automatic (process) control system that uses adaptation as part of its prediction of process behavior in order to optimize the control. *See* adaptive process.

adaptive maintenance *See* software maintenance.

adaptive process The process of performing computations on a set of measured or presented data (believed to be) from a physical, i.e. natural, source in such a way as to develop a "best" parametric model of that physical source, i.e. one that best fits the observed data according to some error criterion. *See also* adaptive-control system, self-organizing system.

adaptive quadrature *See* numerical integration.

ADC *Abbrev. for* analog-to-digital (A/D) converter.

ADCCP *Abbrev. for* advanced data communication control procedure. A bit-oriented *data link control protocol developed by ANSI and similar to *SDLC and *HDLC.

A/D converter (ADC) *Short for* analog-to-digital converter. A device that can accept an analog, i.e. continuous, signal whose amplitude lies within a given range, and produce an equivalent digital signal, i.e. an n-bit parallel binary word that represents this analog signal. The analog signal is "examined" at discrete fixed intervals of time by means of a *sampling process in order to produce the digital signal. Analog signals originating from devices such as analog sensors or tachogenerators may thus be converted into a form that can then be processed by, say, a microprocessor.

The *resolution* of an A/D converter gives the smallest change in analog input that can be discriminated by the device. If the voltage range of an n-bit A/D converter is V, then its resolution is

$$V(2^n - 1)$$

Since the resolution is finite, the conversion process introduces quantization noise (*see* discrete and continuous systems). A/D converters are available in integrated circuit form. *See also* D/A converter.

adder In its simplest form, a digital electronic device that performs the operation of addition on two binary digits, the *augend* and the number to be added, the *addend*. It is therefore also known as a *binary adder*. This operation is exemplified by the truth table shown in Fig. *a*, where Σ is the sum and C_o is the carry. From this it can be seen that binary addition may generate a carry to subsequent stages.

A *full adder* has provision for inputs of addend, augend, and carry bits and is capable of generating sum and carry outputs. These adders may be cascaded when it is desired to add binary words greater than one bit in length by connecting together the carry inputs and outputs of adjacent stages. The circuit shown in Fig. *b* is a *parallel adder operating on two 3-bit binary words ($A_0A_1A_2$ and $B_0B_1B_2$) to produce a 3-bit result ($D_0D_1D_2$) and a carry. The adder uses a *ripple-carry* technique: the carry at each stage of addition must propagate or ripple through the succeeding stages of addition in order to form the result.

A *half-adder* is an implementation of an adder that has provision only for input of addend and augend bits and is capable of generating sum and carry outputs. These devices cannot directly be cascaded as can full adders but may be made to perform a similar function by including additional logic gating, as shown in Fig. *c*. This type of adder is relatively slow in operation. *See also* BCD adder, serial adder, carry lookahead.

address 1. The term most generally used to refer (in some way) to a location within the computer memory; the word *location* is actually used as a synonym. Such reference is usually made for the purpose of retrieving or storing some information at that location. The refer-

A	B	Σ	C_o
0	0	0	0
0	1	1	0
1	0	1	0
1	1	0	1

Fig. *a* Truth table of binary addition

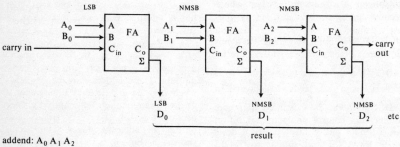

addend: $A_0\,A_1\,A_2$
augend: $B_0\,B_1\,B_2$
result: $D_0\,D_1\,D_2$

LSB : least significant bit
NMSB : next most significant bit

Fig. *b* Parallel 3–bit ripple-carry adder using cascaded full adders

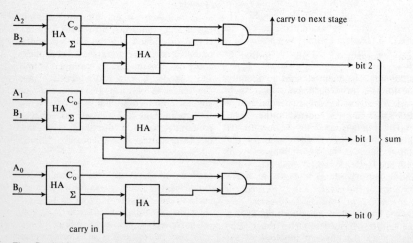

Fig. *c* Parallel 3-bit ripple-carry adder using half adders and additional gating

8

ence may be explicit (*see* direct addressing) or it may be made in any of a number of ways for convenience or brevity (*see* addressing schemes). In some architectures the registers in the CPU and/or the I/O devices are also addressed.

The word address is also used as a verb: to specify a location.

2. In communications, *see* addressing.

addressable location A location whose position in a storage medium is precisely defined and can be accessed. As a safeguard it is usual to arrange that not all memory locations are addressable by all programs.

address bus A *bus that is dedicated to passing address information. It may be a set of conductors that are physically separate from other dedicated buses or it may be a subset of a system bus. The number of conductors is often the same as the maximum allowable number of bits in the address.

address calculation sorting A form of *sorting that uses extra storage space to improve upon a *straight insertion sort. One method employs *n* *list heads, corresponding to *n* different ranges of the sortkey, together with a *link field on each record.

address format *See* instruction format.

addressing The method used to identify the location of a participant in a *network. Ideally, addressing specifies where the participant is located rather than who they are (*see* name) or how to get there (*see* routing). This is true for *flat addressing*, in which addresses are assigned independently of each other and carry no internal structure. More common, however, is *hierarchical addressing*, in which addresses are grouped to reflect relationships among the addressed entities. Often the grouping reflects the physical topology of the network, so addressing and routing are

interrelated. Sometimes the grouping reflects administrative or functional relationships (*logical addressing*), so addressing and naming are interrelated.

In a system employing layered protocols (*see* X.25, seven-layer reference model), different forms of addressing may be used at different levels. The data link level may use addresses that identify specific stations on a multidrop line. The network level uses addresses that identify the source and destination hosts associated with a packet. Higher protocol layers may use addresses that distinguish different connections or processes.

Addresses may be fixed-length or extensible. In *fixed-length addressing* all addresses occupy a fixed number of digits. An example is the Ethernet protocol, which uses 48-bit addresses. In *extensible addressing* the length of an address may vary from case to case. For example, in *X.121 "international data numbers" are defined and these may be from 3 to 14 decimal digits in length.

addressing schemes The wide variety of schemes developed in order to provide compact or convenient *address references in cases where the *absolute address is too large to be comfortably included in an instruction (*see* instruction format) or where it is not possible or even necessary to assign an explicit address. *Augmented, *indirect, *implied, *immediate, and *relative addressing schemes provide compact references. *Indexed, relative, and *symbolic addressing schemes provide convenient references. In the absence of any of these addressing schemes *direct addressing is used.

address mapping Use of one of the *addressing schemes to convert an address that is specified in an instruction into an *absolute address. *Virtual memory and *cache memory use forms of address mapping for additional memory-management functions.

address mark The special code or d.c.-erased area on a magnetic disk track that occurs just prior to the address information of a *sector. In the case of an MFM drive using a special code (*see* disk format), the encoding rules for MFM are broken so that the code is unique. The purpose of the address mark is to bring the drive control electronics into byte synchronization.

The *data mark* fulfills the same function with respect to data as the address mark to the address.

address register A *register in which an *address is stored. *See also* control unit.

address-relative Having or involving a relative address or relative addresses. *See* relative addressing.

address space The number of distinct locations that may be referred to with the *absolute address. For most (i.e. binary) machines it is equal to 2^n, where n is the number of bits in the absolute address. In many large machines the address space is larger than the number of physical or real addresses that are present in the system. Additionally, the number of bits available to specify an address is restricted (*see* instruction format), and some form of *address mapping or *addressing scheme is used to obtain the absolute address from the specified address. The address space embraces the primary memory, the I/O devices, and, in some cases, the registers in the CPU.

address table sorting A form of *sorting that is useful when the information records are long. A table of addresses that point to the records is formed and these addresses, rather than the records themselves, are manipulated.

add-subtract time The time required by a computer to find the sum or difference of two numbers; it may or may not include the time required to obtain the numbers from memory. This is often used as one form of (speed) figure of merit for computers. *See also* computer power.

adjacency list *Another name for* adjacency structure.

adjacency matrix (connectivity matrix; reachability matrix) A *matrix used as a means of representing a *graph. If A is the adjacency matrix corresponding to a given graph G, then
$$a_{ij} = 1$$
if there is an edge from vertex i to vertex j in G; otherwise
$$a_{ij} = 0$$
If G is a directed *graph then
$$a_{ij} = 1$$
if there is an edge directed from vertex i to vertex j; otherwise
$$a_{ij} = 0$$
If the vertices of the graph are numbered $1, 2, \ldots m$, the adjacency matrix is of a type $m \times m$. If
$$A \times A \times \ldots \times A$$
$$(p \text{ terms}, \ p \leqslant m)$$
is evaluated, the nonzero entries indicate those vertices that are joined by a *path of length p; indeed the value of the i, jth entry of A^p gives the number of paths of length p from the vertex i to vertex j. By examining the set of such matrices,
$$p = 1, 2, \ldots, m-1$$
it can be determined whether two vertices are connected.

It is also possible for adjacency matrices to be formed from *Boolean matrices.

adjacency structure (adjacency list) A means of representing a *graph. The adjacency structure corresponding to a *path G is the set
$$\{\text{Adj}(v) \mid v \text{ is a vertex in } G\}$$
If G is an undirected graph, then a vertex w is in $\text{Adj}(v)$ if and only if there is an edge in G between v and w; if G is a directed graph, then w is in $\text{Adj}(v)$ if and only if there is an edge in G directed from v to w.

ADP *Abbrev. for* automatic data processing. *See* data processing.

AED *Acronym for* Algol extended for design. A programming language based on *Algol 60 with extensions for computer-aided design, now obsolete.

AFIPS American Federation of Information Processing Societies, Inc., founded in 1961 to provide a structure for societies and associations interested in information processing to join together in order to advance the state of the art. AFIPS includes: the American Society for Information Science, American Statistical Association, Association for Computing Machinery, Association for Computational Linguistics, Association for Education Data Systems, Data Processing Management Association, IEEE Computer Society, Instrument Society of America, Society for Computer Simulation, Society for Industrial and Applied Mathematics, Society for Information Display. It is the US member of IFIP.

AFL *Abbrev. for* abstract family of languages.

AI *Abbrev. for* artificial intelligence.

Aitken's Δ²-process An *iterative method to find the root of a nonlinear *polynomial, developed by B. Aitken. It uses knowledge of three successive terms of a sequence to increase the rate of convergence to the computed root. *See also* Steffenson iteration.

AIX An IBM version of *UNIX.

aleph null *See* cardinality.

algebra 1. The investigation both of mathematical properties of numbers and of mathematical structure employing the use of symbols.
  2. A collection of *sets together with a collection of *operations over those

sets. Many examples involve only one set, such as the following:

(a) the integers together with, for example, the operations of addition and subtraction, together with multiplication and finding the remainder;

(b) the set {TRUE, FALSE} together with the operations AND, OR, and NOT (*see* Boolean algebra);

(c) strings together with the operation of *concatenation;

(d) sets together with the operations of *union, *intersection, and *complement (*see* set algebra).

In computer science, however, it is natural to consider algebras involving more than one set. For example in programming languages there are different *data types such as integer, Boolean, etc., as well as user-defined types. Operations on elements of these types can then be seen as forming an algebra. By stating axioms that characterize these operations, an *abstract data type is obtained. Operations require names, both in order to write axioms and in order to allow the comparison of different algebras, which are then seen as different associations of operations with the same collection of names, i.e. as different Σ-algebras for the same *signature Σ. *See also* algebraic structure.

algebraic language *Another name for* context-free language.

algebraic semantics A refinement of *denotational semantics that stresses the *algebraic structure on both syntactic and semantic entities. Typically syntactic entities are expressed as elements of some *initial algebra. The mapping from syntax to semantics is then the unique *homomorphism corresponding to some interpretation of the primitive symbols. A feature of this approach is that it seeks, as far as possible, to study properties of programs at the purely syntactic level or, more generally, subject only to some precisely stated assumptions about the range of possible interpretations.

algebraic specification *Another name for* axiomatic specification.

algebraic structure A structure involving *operations taking any finite number of arguments. Such structures are sometimes called "discrete" in contrast with the "smooth" structures found in mathematical analysis and calculus, where discussion of continuous functions involves the notion of limit, which takes an infinite sequence of arguments. Computer science tends to emphasize discrete structures, and is hence inherently algebraic in nature. Exceptions include the study of *analog signals, also Scott's use of the idea of "limit" to capture the *semantics of *recursive definitions.

In considering algebraic structures in computer science, it is usually understood that there exist algorithms for computing the operations involved, i.e. that they are *effectively computable. Indeed such operations are usually represented in terms of algorithms to compute them. Algebraic structures are of direct relevance to *program verification and *program specification. *See also* algebra, discrete structure.

algebraic symbol manipulation language A programming language in which the data are algebraic expressions in symbolic form, and the operations are the operations of algebra. The operations provided usually include multiplying out brackets, simplification, factorization, polynomial division, and differentiation with respect to one or more variables. Such languages are now rare, their function being subsumed into *algebra systems.

algebra system An interactive system that performs the operations of algebra (simplification, factorization, multiplying out brackets, etc.) on algebraic expressions typed in by the user. These sys-

tems are increasingly used in "mathematical assistants", particularly in the field of general relativity. One of the best known systems is MACSYMA. *See also* algebraic symbol manipulation language.

Algol *Acronym for* algorithmic language. The generic name for a family of high-level languages of great significance in the development of computing. In 1958 the Association for Computing Machinery (ACM) in the US and the Gessellschaft für Angewante Mathematik und Mechanik (GAMM) in Europe set up a joint committee to define an *international algorithmic language (IAL)*. The language that was designed became known as Algol, and was later called *Algol 58* to distinguish it from later versions. Algol 58 was not intended to be a viable language, and in 1960 an augmented committee was convened to devise the second iteration, which was published as the language *Algol 60*. *See also* JOVIAL.

Algol 60 was much more popular in Europe than in the US, probably due to the dominance of IBM and FORTRAN in the North American market, and to the extent that it was at all widely used, that use was in Europe. It introduced many new concepts, notably block structure (*see* block-structured languages), nested scopes, modes of parameter passing to procedures, and the definition of the language introduced the now classic *BNF notation for describing syntax. The influence of Algol 60 can be seen in all succeeding languages, and it stands as a milestone in the development of programming languages.

In the years following the publication of the Algol 60 Report, a working group of the International Federation for Information Processing (IFIP – WG2.3) was set up to consider the definition of a successor to Algol 60. There were many dissensions within the group, and eventually a minority report was issued proposing the language *Algol 68*. The first implementation of Algol 68, named ALGOL 68R, was produced at the Royal Radar and Signals Establishment in the UK. ALGOL 68R demonstrated that Algol 68 was a viable language (not at the time a self-evident proposition).

Although Algol 68 introduced many novel concepts of great theoretical interest and significance, its practical application was almost nil. One of the most notable features of Algol 68 is its formal specification using a VW-grammar. Although a very precise definition, it is very difficult to understand, and this difficulty partly accounts for the low acceptance of the language. One of the most significant effects of the split in the Algol 68 working group is that it led indirectly to the development of *Pascal.

algorithm A prescribed set of well-defined rules or instructions for the solution of a problem, e.g. the performance of a calculation, in a finite number of steps. Expressing an algorithm in a formal notation is one of the main parts of a *program; much that is said about programs applies to algorithms, and vice versa. An *effective algorithm* is one that is effectively computable (*see* effective computability). The study of whether effective algorithms exist to compute particular quantities forms the basis of the theory of algorithms.

Save for the simplest of algorithms it is difficult to *prove* that an algorithm is correct (*see* program correctness proof), or even to specify the effect it is intended to achieve. In practice it is usually necessary to be content with *algorithm validation*. This process certifies, or verifies, that an algorithm will perform the calculation required of it. It involves testing the routine against a variety of instances of the problem and ensuring that it performs satisfactorily for these test cases. If the test set is chosen sufficiently well there can then be confidence in the algorithm.

Algorithm analysis is the study of the performance characteristics of a given algorithm. One branch of this study, *average-case analysis*, examines the average behavior of the algorithm. *Worst-case analysis* studies the behavior when all circumstances are as unfavorable as possible. Algorithms can be analyzed in terms of their *complexity and efficiency. The efficiency of an algorithm is characterized by its *order. If two algorithms for the same problem are of the same order then they are approximately as efficient in terms of computation. Algorithm efficiency is useful for quantifying the implementation difficulties of certain problems.

algorithm efficiency A measure of the average execution time necessary for an algorithm to complete work on a set of data. Typically a *bubble sort algorithm will have efficiency in sorting N items proportional to and of the *order of N^2, usually written $O(N^2)$. This is because an average of $N/2$ comparisons are required $N/2$ times, giving $N^2/4$ total comparisons, hence of the order of N^2. In contrast, *quicksort has an efficiency $O(N \log_2 N)$.

algorithmic language A language or notation used to express clearly an algorithm. It is usually part of a programming language.

allocation routine A routine that is responsible for the allocation of resources to a *process. *See* resource allocation.

alphabet An ordered *character set. *See also* formal language.

alphabetic code A code whose target alphabet contains only letters and/or strings of letters from the Roman alphabet.

alphanumeric character Any of the 26 letters of the Roman alphabet, or any of the decimal digits, 0 through to 9.

alphanumeric code A code whose target alphabet contains *alphanumeric characters and/or strings thereof.

ALU *Abbrev. for* arithmetic and logic unit.

Alvey Programme A five-year program of precompetitive collaborative R&D, started in the UK in 1983 as a result of the government-initiated Alvey Report, in response to the Japanese *fifth generation project. The four "enabling technologies" addressed by the Alvey Programme were *VLSI, *software engineering, *IKBS, and the *human-computer interface. In 1988 the Alvey Programme was succeeded by the *IED. IED funds all the Alvey areas plus some new ones, but has reclassified them under the following headings: systems engineering, systems architecture, and devices.

Two derivation trees in an ambiguous grammar

ambiguous grammar A *context-free grammar that derives the same word by different *derivation trees, or equivalently by different leftmost *derivation sequences or by different rightmost derivation sequences. A familiar programming language example is:

S → if C then S else S
S → if C then S

where S and C stand for statement and condition. This grammar is ambiguous since the following compound statement

if c1 then if c2 then s2 else s1

has two derivation trees, as shown in the diagram. *See also* inherently ambiguous language.

amplitude *See* signal.

amplitude modulation (AM) *See* modulation.

amplitude quantization *See* discrete and continuous systems, quantization.

analog computer A computer that performs computations (such as summation, multiplication, integration, and other operations) by manipulating continuous physical variables that are analogs of the quantities being subjected to computation. The most commonly used physical variables are voltage and time. Some analog computers use mechanical components: the physical variables become, for example, angular rotations and linear displacements. *See also* discrete and continuous systems.

analog signal A smoothly varying value of voltage or current, i.e. a signal that varies continuously in amplitude and time. It often represents a measured physical quantity. *See also* A/D converter, D/A converter, analog computer, discrete and continuous systems.

analog-to-digital converter *See* A/D converter.

analysis of variance (ANOVA) A technique, originally developed by R. A. Fisher, whereby the total variation in a vector of numbers $y_1 \ldots y_n$, expressed as the sum of squares about the mean

$$\sum_i (y_i - y_.)^2,$$

is split up into component sums of squares ascribable to the effects of various classifying factors that may index the data. Thus if the data consist of a two-way $m \times n$ array, classified by factors A and B and indexed by

$$i = 1, \ldots, m \qquad j = 1, \ldots, n$$

then the analysis of variance gives the identity

$$\sum_{ij} (y_{ij} - y_{..})^2 \equiv \sum_{ij} (y_{i.} - y_{..})^2 +$$

$$\text{Total} \qquad \begin{array}{c} \text{A} \\ \text{main effect} \end{array}$$

$$\sum_{ij} (y_{.j} - y_{..})^2 + \sum_{ij} (y_{ij} - y_{i.} - y_{.j} + y_{..})^2$$

$$\begin{array}{c} \text{B} \\ \text{main effect} \end{array} \qquad \begin{array}{c} \text{A.B} \\ \text{interaction} \end{array}$$

where dots denote averaging over the suffixes involved.

Geometrically the analysis of variance becomes the successive projections of the vector y, considered as a point in n-dimensional space, onto orthogonal hyperplanes within that space. The dimensions of the hyperplanes give the *degrees of freedom* for each term; in the above example these are

$$mn - 1 \equiv (m-1) + (n-1) + (m-1)(n-1)$$

A statistical model applied to the data allows mean squares, equal to (sum of squares)/(degrees of freedom), to be compared with an error mean square that measures the background "noise". Large mean squares indicate large effects of the factors concerned. The above processes can be much elaborated (*see* experimental design, regression analysis).

Analytical Engine The logic design for a mechanical computer conceived by Charles Babbage around 1833, but never built. The design envisioned a memory of a thousand 50-digit numbers. The machine, which could do addition, subtraction, multiplication, and division, was to be controlled by programs punched into loops of cards; the machine was thus to be directed through a variety of computations, and alternative paths could be taken depending on the values of intermediate results. It was to have included a printer to obtain the results. The design was remarkable in anticipating so many elements of modern computers.

analyzer A program, such as a parser, that determines constituents in a string; the word is rarely used except in the combinations syntax analyzer and lexical analyzer. *See also* static analysis.

ancestor of a node in a *tree. Any node on the unique path from the root of the tree to the node in question. A *proper ancestor* of a node, A, is a node, B, such that B is an ancestor of A and $A \neq B$. *See also* parent.

AND gate An electronic *logic gate whose output is logic 1 (true) only when all (two or more) inputs are logic 1, otherwise it is logic 0 (false). It therefore implements the logical *AND operation on its inputs and has the same *truth table. The diagram shows the usual circuit symbol and the truth table of a two-input gate.

inputs	A1	0	0	1	1
	A2	0	1	0	1
output	B	0	0	0	1

Two-input AND gate, circuit symbol and truth table

P	F	F	T	T
Q	F	T	F	T
$P \wedge Q$	F	F	F	T

Truth table for AND operation

AND operation The logical *connective combining two statements, truth values, or formulas P and Q in such a way that

ANNOTATION

the outcome is true only if both P and Q are true; otherwise the outcome is false (*see* table). The AND operation is usually denoted by $\wedge$, and occasionally by . or by juxtaposition, as in PQ. It is one of the dyadic operations of *Boolean algebra and is both *commutative and *associative.

When implemented as a basic machine operation on computers, the AND operation is usually generalized to operate on complete words. Then the operation described above is applied to the corresponding bits in each word. In this context AND is often used for *masking purposes, i.e. to select parts of words, such as the address field.

annotation Explanation added to a program to assist the reader. This may take the form of manuscript additions to the program listing, but more often takes the form of *comments included in the program text.

ANOVA *Acronym for* analysis of variance.

ANSI American National Standards Institute, an industry-supported standards organization, founded in 1918, that establishes US industrial standards and their correspondence to those set by the *ISO (International Organization for Standardization). ANSI determines hardware-related standards for such items as link-level protocols, pin positions and meaning in chips, and recordings on tape and disk, and some software standards, e.g. the FORTRAN and COBOL standards.

ANSI–SPARC American National Standards Institute/Systems Planning and Requirements Committee. It is best known for its proposed architecture for *databases, according to which they are defined at three levels: conceptual schema, external schema, internal schema. *See* data description language.

antialiasing The removal or subduing of the jagged appearance that can occur when an inclined line or curve is printed or displayed via a fixed array of *pixels. *See also* raster-mode graphic display.

antisymmetric relation A *relation R defined on a set S and having the property that
$$\text{whenever } x \; R \; y \text{ and } y \; R \; x$$
$$\text{then } x = y$$
where x and y are arbitrary members of S. Examples include "is a subset of" defined on sets, and "less than or equal to" defined on the integers. *See also* asymmetric relation, symmetric relation.

API *Abbrev. for* application programmer interface. The specification of the communication between an *applications program and a *utility program. *See also* interface.

APL *Acronym for* a programming language. Originally devised by Iverson as a mathematical notation in the mid-1960s, and only later implemented as a programming language, APL had a meteoric rise in popularity. The main feature of APL is that it provides a rich set of powerful operators for handling multidimensional arrays, together with the capability for the user to define his own operators. The built-in operators are mainly represented by single characters using a special character set. Thus APL programs are very concise and often impenetrable.

Apple A microcomputer system made by Apple Computer Inc., one of the world's top three microcomputer manufacturers (in terms of revenue – 1988 figures). An early market leader, the Apple range has a wide variety of hardware options and software available. The successful and innovative VisiCalc *spreadsheet program was developed for the Apple. The Apple Macintosh microcomputer systems with their *mouse and *window operating system, $3\frac{1}{2}$ inch disk drives, and small *footprint marked an important departure in personal computer development.

application generator *See* fourth generation language.

application layer of network protocol function. *See* seven-layer reference model.

application package (software package) A suite of programs or modules that is directed at some generic application and can be tailored (perhaps with some additions) to the needs of a specific instance of that application.

applications program Any program that is specific to the particular role that a given computer performs within a given organization and makes a direct contribution to performing that role. For example, where a computer handles a company's finances a payroll program would be an applications program. By contrast, an *operating system or a *software tool may both be essential to the effective use of the computer system, but neither makes a direct contribution to meeting the end-user's eventual needs.

applications programmer A person who specializes in writing *applications programs. *Compare* systems programmer.

application terminal A combination of input and output devices configured into a unit to meet the requirements of a particular type of business activity and environment. They usually have some built-in processing capability and are connected to a controlling processor via a data communication link. Examples include point-of-sale terminals and bank teller terminals.

applicative language *Another name for* functional language.

applied robotics *See* process control, robotics.

approximation theory A subject that is concerned with the approximation of a class of objects, say F, by a subclass, say $P \subset F$, that is in some sense simpler. For example, let

$$F = C[a,b],$$

the real continuous functions on $[a,b]$, then a subclass of practical use is P_n, i.e. polynomials of degree n. The means of measuring the closeness or accuracy of the approximation is provided by a metric or *norm*. This is a nonnegative function that is defined on F and measures the size of its elements. Norms of particular value in the approximation of mathematical functions (for computer subroutines, say) are the *Chebyshev norm* and the *2-norm* (or *Euclidean norm*). For functions

$$f \in C[a,b]$$

these norms are given respectively as

$$\|f\| = \max_{a \leqslant x \leqslant b} |f(x)|$$

$$\|f\|_2 = (\int_a^b f(x)^2 \, dx)^{1/2}$$

For approximation of data these norms take the discrete form

$$\|f\| = \max_i |f(x_i)|$$

$$\|f\|_2 = (\sum_i f(x_i)^2)^{1/2}$$

The 2-norm frequently incorporates a weight function (or weights). From these two norms the problems of *Chebyshev approximation* and *least squares approximation* arise. For example, with polynomial approximation we seek

$$p_n \in P_n$$

for which

$$\|f-p_n\| \text{ or } \|f-p_n\|_2$$

are acceptably small. Best approximation problems arise when, for example, we seek

$$p_n \in P_n$$

for which these measures of errors are as small as possible with respect to P_n.

Other examples of norms that are particularly important are *vector* and *matrix norms*. For n-component vectors

$$x = (x_1, x_2, \ldots, x_n)^T$$

important examples are

$$\|x\| = \max_i |x_i|$$

$$\|x\|_2 = (\sum_{i=1}^{n} x_i^2)^{1/2}$$

Corresponding to a given vector norm, a subordinate matrix norm can be defined for $n \times n$ matrices A, by

$$\|A\| = \max_{\|x\| \neq 0} \frac{\|Ax\|}{\|x\|}$$

For the vector norm

$$\|x\| = \max_i |x_i|,$$

this reduces to the expression

$$\|A\| = \max_i \sum_{j=1}^{n} |a_{ij}|$$

where a_{ij} is the i,jth element of A. Vector and matrix norms are indispensible in most areas of numerical analysis.

APSE *Acronym for* Ada programming support environment. The *PSE that is to be an integral part of *Ada processors. The APSE specifies program and system development tools to accompany the Ada language processor. Its facilities (like those of the parent language) were defined in a sequence of progressively more detailed specifications, the latest being Stoneman. Implementation of a practical APSE has proved to be difficult, and work is continuing in this area.

arc of a graph. *See* graph.

architectural design (high-level design) *See* program decomposition, program design, system design.

architecture The specification of a (digital) computer system at a somewhat general level, including description from the programming (user) viewpoint of the instruction set and user interface, memory organization and addressing, I/O operation and control, etc. The implementation of an architecture in members of a given *computer family may be quite different, yet all the members should be capable of running the same program. Implementation differences may occur in actual hardware components or in subsystem implementation (e.g. *microprogramming as opposed to wired control), generally in both. Different implementations may have substantially different performances and costs. An implementation feature – such as a cache memory –that is *transparent to the user does not affect the architecture. Common architecture provides compatibility from the user's viewpoint.

In the context of engineering and hardware design, the term architecture is used to describe the nature, configuration, and interconnection of the major logic organs of a computer (and is thus closer to the general meaning of the word). These devices would normally include the memory and its components, the control unit and the hardware components designed to implement the control strategy, the structure, range, and capability of the arithmetic and logic unit, and the interconnection of the input/output – such as whether star or bus connected – and the nature and capabilities of any channel controllers. A detailed block diagram or schematic of the actual (as distinct from the virtual) machine would normally form part of, or even be central to, such a description.

archived file A file that has been transferred to a lower level in the *memory hierarchy, usually from magnetic disk to magnetic tape. The decision for this transfer to take place may be made as a conscious decision by the owner of the file, or it may arise from the operations of the appropriate resource management.

Arden's rule A rule, used in formal language theory, stating that $A*B$ is the smallest solution for X in the equation
$$X = AX \cup B$$
where X, A, B are sets of strings. (For notation, *see* union, concatenation, Kleene star.) $A*B$ is furthermore the only solution, unless A contains the empty string, in which case $A*B'$ is a solution for any subset B' of B.

Although simple, Arden's rule is significant as one of the earliest fixed-point results in computer science. In conjunction with the normal process of eliminating variables, it can be used to solve any set of simultaneous linear equations over sets of strings. *See also* Kleene's theorem (on regular expressions).

argument A value or address passed to a procedure or function at the time of call. Thus in the BASIC statement
$$Y = SQR(X)$$
X is the argument of the SQR (square root) function. Arguments are sometimes referred to as *actual parameters*.

arithmetic and logic unit (ALU; arithmetic unit, AU) A portion of the *central processor that (generally) forms functions of two input variables and produces a single output variable. These functions usually consist of the common *arithmetic operations, the common *logic operations, and *shift operations. Associated with the ALU is a *qualifier register that holds certain properties of the last output variable.

arithmetic instruction An instruction specifying that one of the *arithmetic operations is to be carried out by the computer.

arithmetic operation An operation that forms a function of two variables. This function is usually one of the class of operations: add, subtract, multiply, and divide. These operations may be carried out as operations on integers, fractional numbers, or floating-point numbers. The

operation is normally performed in the *arithmetic and logic unit.

arithmetic operator A type of *operator appearing in an expression denoting one of the operations of arithmetic, e.g. $+$, $-$, $*$ (multiplication), $/$ (divide).

arithmetic shift *See* shift.

arithmetic unit (AU) *Another name for* arithmetic and logic unit.

arity of an operator. The number of operands to which the *operator applies. *See also* operation.

arm 1. (access arm) A lever or bar that supports and moves the read/write head to the correct track on a disk.
2. (tension arm) A lever or bar that is fitted with rollers or guides and is automatically moved so that it maintains the right tension in a low-speed tape transport. *See also* buffer.
3. To bring a device to a state of readiness.

ARMA *Abbrev. for* autoregressive moving average. *See* time series.

ARPA *See* DARPA.

ARPANET or **Arpanet** *Acronym for* Advanced Research Projects Agency Network. The collection of *host computers plus *backbone network making up the first major *packet-switching network. Begun through research grants provided by ARPA (now *DARPA) to universities and private organizations for computer science, the ARPANET started as a four-node network in December 1969. It now connects many hundreds of host computers throughout the world.

The ARPANET utilizes minicomputers called interface message processors (*IMPs) as a backbone network of message-switching nodes. The IMPs are primarily connected by 56K bps leased lines, although other links are also used (such as the satellite link between the US and Europe). Each IMP takes blocks of data from its hosts, subdivides them into 128 byte packets, and adds a header specifying destination and source addresses. Then, based on a dynamically updated routing table, the packet is routed over whichever line is currently the fastest route to the destination. Upon receiving a packet, the next IMP acknowledges it and repeats the routing process independently.

The ARPANET pioneered many of the network concepts that are in use today. An important contribution is ·the ARPANET routing algorithm, which is completely distributed, is performed on a packet-by-packet basis, and is based on a continuous evaluation of the network's topology, capacity, and utilization. The practical demonstration of distributed routing was viewed as an important step in demonstrating that packet switching networks would be cost-effective and reliable.

The ARPANET technology has been successfully replicated for several other military and intelligence-gathering networks used by the US. The ARPANET itself was transferred to the Defence Communication Agency in 1975, and is no longer the direct responsibility of DARPA. *See also* internet protocol.

array An ordered collection of a number of elements of the same type, the number being fixed unless the array is *flexible. The elements of one array may be of type integer, those of another array may be of type real, while the elements of a third array may be of type character string (if the programming language recognizes compound types).

Each element has a unique set of *index values that determine its position in the ordered collection. Each index is of a discrete type. The number of dimensions in the ordering is fixed.

A one-dimensional array, or *vector, consists of a list of elements distinguished by a single index. If v is a one-

dimensional array and i is an index value, then v_i refers to the ith element of v. If the index ranges from L through U then the value L is called the *lower bound* of v and U is the *upper bound*. Usually in mathematics and often in mathematical computing the index type is taken as integer and the lower bound is taken as one.

In a two-dimensional array, or *matrix, the elements are ordered in the form of a table comprising a fixed number of rows and a fixed number of columns. Each element in such an array is distinguished by a pair of indexes. The first index gives the row and the second gives the column of the array in which the element is located. The element in the ith row and jth column is called the i,jth element of the array. If i ranges from L1 through U1 and j ranges from L2 through U2 then L1 is the *first lower bound* of the array, U1 is the *first upper bound*, L2 is the *second lower bound* and U2 is the *second upper bound*. Again it is common practice to take the indexes as integers and to set both L1 and L2 equal to one. An example of such a two-dimensional array with U1 = m, U2 = n is given in the diagram.

$$\begin{bmatrix} a_{11} & a_{12} & \cdots & a_{1n} \\ a_{21} & a_{22} & \cdots & a_{2n} \\ \vdots & \vdots & & \vdots \\ a_{m1} & a_{m2} & \cdots & a_{mn} \end{bmatrix}$$

Two-dimensional array

In *three-dimensional arrays* the position of each element is distinguished by three indexes. Arrays of higher dimension are similarly defined.

array processor A computer/processor that has an architecture especially designed for processing *arrays (e.g.

matrices) of numbers. The architecture includes a number of processors (say 64 by 64) working simultaneously, each handling one element of the array, so that a single operation can apply to all elements of the array in parallel. To obtain the same effect in a conventional processor, the operation must be applied to each element of the array sequentially, and so consequently much more slowly.

An array processor may be built as a self-contained unit attached to a main computer via an I/O port or internal bus; alternatively, it may be a *distributed array processor* where the processing elements are distributed throughout, and closely linked to, a section of the computer's memory.

Array processors are very powerful tools for handling problems with a high degree of parallelism. They do however demand a modified approach to programming, which has not yet reached full maturity (1989). Conversion of conventional (sequential) programs to serve array processors is not a trivial task, and it is sometimes necessary to select a different (parallel) algorithm to suit the parallel approach.

See also vector processing.

articulation point *Another name for* cut vertex.

artificial intelligence (AI) A discipline concerned with the building of computer programs that perform tasks requiring intelligence when done by humans. However, intelligent tasks for which a *decision procedure is known (e.g. inverting matrices) are generally excluded, whereas perceptual tasks that might seem not to involve intelligence (e.g. seeing) are generally included. For this reason, AI is better defined by indicating its range. Examples of tasks tackled within AI are: game playing, inference, learning, *natural-language understanding, plan formation, speech under-

standing, *theorem proving, and visual perception.

Perceptual tasks (e.g. seeing and hearing) have been found to involve a lot more computation than is apparent from introspection. This computation is unconscious in humans, which has made it hard to simulate. AI has had relatively more success at intellectual tasks (e.g. game playing and theorem proving) than perceptual tasks. Sometimes these computer programs are intended to simulate human behavior (*see* computational psychology). Sometimes they are built for technological application (*see* expert systems, robotics). But in many cases the goal is just to find any technique for doing some task, or to find a technique that does the task better than hitherto.

Computational techniques that have been invented in AI include *augmented transition networks, *means/ends analysis, *production rule systems, *resolution, *semantic nets, and various *line finders.

ASCC *Abbrev. for* Automatic Sequence Controlled Calculator. *See* Harvard Mark I.

ASCII (American standard code for information interchange) A standard character encoding scheme introduced in 1963 and used widely on many machines. It is a 7-bit code with no parity recommendation, providing 128 different bit patterns. The character set is shown in the table, together with the control characters. *See also* character set, ISO-7.

ASIC *Acronym for* applications specific integrated circuit. An integrated circuit designed to carry out one or more specific functions and implemented on a single semiconductor chip in order to reduce the size of a system, reduce the number of interconnections that are required at printed circuit board level, and to reduce the number of components that, at a lower level of integration, might otherwise be used to implement the function. ASICs are economic where production runs in the high hundreds are required and have become viable due to advances in VLSI design, layout, and fabrication technology. *See also* semicustom.

ASM *Abbrev. for* algorithmic state machine. A technique, based upon annotated charts, used in the design of computer hardware.

ASPECT A project within the *Alvey programme of IT research and development in the UK that developed a prototype second-generation *IPSE. The project used the formal language *Z to specify the *object management system and *PTI (portable tool interface).

assembler 1. A program that takes as input a program written in *assembly language and translates it into *machine code or *relocatable code.
  2. *Colloquial* An assembly language.

assembly language A notation for the convenient representation of machine-code programs in human-readable terms. An assembly language allows the programmer to use alphabetic operation codes with mnemonic significance, to use symbolic names of his own choice for machine and memory registers, and to specify *addressing schemes (e.g. indexing, indirection) in a convenient way. It also allows the use of various number bases (e.g. decimal, hexadecimal) for numerical constants, and allows the user to attach *labels to lines of the program so that these lines can be referenced in a symbolic manner from other parts of a program (usually as the destination of a control transfer or jump).

assertion A Boolean formula whose value is claimed to be true. The following are all examples:

$$4 + 5 = 9$$

4 is even and 5 is odd
x is even or y is odd
$$x - y > 15$$
for all relevant i, $x[i] < x[i+1]$

The last assertion states that the array x is sorted into ascending order, with no repeated values.

Assertions are employed extensively in proofs of *program correctness, where they are used to characterize program states.

assertion checker An automated system for checking whether *assertions attached to the text of some program are consistent with the *semantics of that program as given by some formal semantic definition of the programming language. *See also* mechanical verifier.

assignment-free language A programming language that does not include the concept of assigning values to variables. It is usually a *functional language.

assignment statement A fundamental statement of all programming languages (except *declarative languages) that assigns a new value to a variable. The typical form in Algol-like languages is

  variable : = expression

where : = is read as "becomes"; the symbol suggests a left-pointing arrow to signify the conveyance of a value to the variable on the left. Other languages (particularly BASIC, C, and FORTRAN) use = as the assignment operator, e.g.

$$a = b + c$$

This leads to problems in expressing the concept of equality. BASIC, being an unsophisticated language, is able to use = for both purposes; C uses = = for equality and FORTRAN uses .EQ.

associative addressing A method of addressing a location by what is in the memory rather than where it is. This is achieved by specifying something about the contents of the desired location rather than by a normal address. An

b4	b3	b2	b1	row	0	1	2	3	4	5	6	7
0	0	0	0	0	NUL	DLE	space	0	@	P	`	p
0	0	0	1	1	SOH	DC1	!	1	A	Q	a	q
0	0	1	0	2	STX	DC2	"	2	B	R	b	r
0	0	1	1	3	ETX	DC3	#	3	C	S	c	s
0	1	0	0	4	EOT	DC4	$	4	D	T	d	t
0	1	0	1	5	ENQ	NAK	%	5	E	U	e	u
0	1	1	0	6	ACK	SYN	&	6	F	V	f	v
0	1	1	1	7	BEL	ETB	'	7	G	W	g	w
1	0	0	0	8	BS	CAN	(	8	H	X	h	x
1	0	0	1	9	HT	EM	)	9	I	Y	i	y
1	0	1	0	A	LF	SUB	*	:	J	Z	j	z
1	0	1	1	B	VT	ESC	+	;	K	[	k	{
1	1	0	0	C	FF	FS	,	<	L	\	l	|
1	1	0	1	D	CR	GS	-	=	M	]	m	}
1	1	1	0	E	SO	RS	.	>	N	^	n	~
1	1	1	1	F	SI	US	/	?	O	_	o	DEL

ASCII code chart with binary and hex equivalents

NUL	null character	DLE	data link escape
SOH	start of header	DC1	device control 1
STX	start of text	DC2	device control 2
ETX	end of text	DC3	device control 3
EOT	end of transmission	DC4	device control 4
ENQ	enquiry	NAK	negative acknowledge
ACK	acknowledge	SYN	synchronous idle
BEL	bell	ETB	end of transmission block
BS	backspace	CAN	cancel
HT	horiz. tabulation	EM	end of medium
LF	line feed	SUB	substitute
VT	vert. tabulation	ESC	escape
FF	form feed	FS	file separator
CR	carriage return	GS	group separator
SO	shift out	RS	record separator
SI	shift in	US	unit separator
		DEL	delete

ASCII control characters

*associative memory (or content-addressable memory) is used to provide a search mechanism to match on partial memory contents for a word that satisfies the match. In some applications it may be permissible for more than one word to be found. The desired data will be in close association or proximity, most often as an additional field of the retrieved word.

associative computer A computer containing an *associative memory.

associative law *See* associative operation.

associative memory (content-addressable memory, CAM) A memory that is capable of determining whether a given datum – the *search word* – is contained in one of its addresses or locations. This may be accomplished by a number of mechanisms. In some cases parallel combinational logic is applied at each word in the memory and a test is made simultaneously for coincidence with the search word. In other cases the search word and all of the words in the memory are shifted serially in synchronism; a single bit of the search word is then compared to the same bit of all of the memory words using as many single-bit coincidence circuits as there are words in the memory. Amplifications of the associative memory technique allow for *masking the search word or requiring only a "close" match as opposed to an exact match. Small parallel associative memories are used in *cache memory and *virtual memory mapping applications.

Since parallel operations on many words are expensive (in hardware), a variety of stratagems are used to approximate associative memory operation without actually carrying out the full test described here. One of these uses *hashing to generate a "best guess" for a conventional address followed by a test of the contents of that address.

Some associative memories have been built to be accessed conventionally (by words in parallel) and as serial comparison associative memories; these have been called *orthogonal memories*. *See also* associative addressing.

associative operation Any *dyadic operation ∘ that satisfies the law

$$x \circ (y \circ z) = (x \circ y) \circ z$$

for all x, y, and z in the domain of ∘. The law is known as the *associative law*.

An expression involving several adjacent instances of an associative operation can be interpreted unambiguously; the order in which the operations are performed is irrelevant since the effects of different evaluations are identical, though the work involved may differ. Consequently parentheses are unnecessary, even in more complex expressions.

The arithmetic operations of addition and multiplication are associative, though subtraction is not. On a computer the associative law of addition of real numbers fails to hold because of the inherent inaccuracy in the way real numbers are usually represented (*see* floating-point notation), and the addition of integers fails to hold because of the possibility of *overflow.

assurance A measure of the confidence that (a) a system complies with its *security policy or (b) a feature of a system complies with its security requirement. Assurance may be increased by the use of rigorous design techniques and/or by *security evaluation.

A-stability *See* stability.

astable An electronic circuit that has no stable output state and whose output therefore oscillates between two voltage levels. As a result it functions as a square-wave oscillator or a pulse generator. *See also* multivibrator.

asymmetric relation A *relation R defined on a set S and having the property that

whenever $x \ R \ y$

then it is never the case that

$y \ R \ x$

where x and y are arbitrary elements of S. The usual "is less than" ordering defined on the integers is an asymmetric relation. *See also* antisymmetric relation, symmetric relation.

asynchronous Involving or requiring a form of computer control timing protocol in which a specific operation is begun upon receipt of an indication (signal) that the preceding operation has been completed. *See also* interrupt, glitch. *Compare* synchronous.

asynchronous circuit An electronic logic circuit in which logical operations are not performed under the control of a clock signal with the result that logic transitions do not occur (nominally) simultaneously. In asynchronous circuits transitions may follow one another with minimum delay, but at some cost in circuit complexity and risk of incorrect operation.

asynchronous TDM *See* time division multiplexing.

Atanasoff–Berry computer (ABC) The first known attempt at an electronic digital computer, designed in 1936–38 by John Atanasoff, a mathematics professor at Iowa State College, primarily for the solution of linear algebraic equations. It was built by Atanasoff and his assistant Clifford Berry, using vacuum tubes (valves) as the logic elements, but was never fully operational and was abandoned in 1942.

ATL *Abbrev. for* automated (or automatic) tape library.

Atlas The first computer to incorporate many features now considered standard, including: a virtual (logical) address space larger than the actual (physical) address space; a *one-level memory using core backed by drum; an architecture based on the assumption of a software operating system, with hardware features to assist the software (e.g. extracodes). The design commenced in 1956 under Tom Kilburn at the University of Manchester, UK, and the project was supported from 1958 by Ferranti Ltd. The prototype was operating in 1961 and production models appeared in 1963.

ATM *Abbrev. for* automated (bank) teller machine. A computer-controlled machine for issuing banknotes on demand from a holder of a bank account. The account holder inserts a *magnetic card into the ATM and on request types in a *pin as identification. The ATM will then issue banknotes after checking with the computer system of the bank holding the account that the account holder is in credit. ATMs are generally available and accessible 24 hours each day and are located at banks and other public locations such as airports, railway stations, and shopping centers.

Some ATMs also allow the account holder to view account balances, to transfer funds between bank accounts, and to order statements and check books.

atom A value that cannot be decomposed further. In *LISP an atom is a representation of an arbitrary string of characters or the special atom NIL, i.e. nothing. The word is also used as a predicate in LISP-like languages to determine whether an arbitrary value is or is not an atom:

  (atom (cons(h, t)))

always yields FALSE but

  (atom, NIL)

and

  (atom, "word")

evaluate to TRUE.

atomic action An indivisible sequence of primitive operations that must complete without interruption (or that can be expected to do so), or can be considered as instantaneous.

atomic formula *See* propositional calculus.

atomicity A term used in connection with the extent to which a resource can be subdivided. For some resources the amount allocated to a process can be completely arbitrary; an example is processor time (outside *critical sections). For other resources allocations must be in terms of a smallest allowable amount; an example might be memory, which may only be allocated in multiples of, say, 1024 bytes.

attach To make a device available for use by a system. On simple systems this may be achieved by simply engaging the appropriate plug and socket of the interface and putting the device into a state of readiness. In more complex systems it is often necessary to make the operating system aware of the type of device and the address of the connector to which it is attached. It is also necessary to ensure that the operating system has available the appropriate utility program for that device. In some designs the operating system can itself determine the type and address of all the peripherals that are electrically connected.

attenuation The reduction in amplitude of a *signal when it passes through a medium that dissipates its energy. It is usually measured in decibels (attenuation then being negative while *gain* is positive).

attribute A defined property of an entity or object. *See* ERA model, inheritance.

attribute grammar A *context-free grammar that has been augmented with attribute evaluation rules or conditions enabling non-context-free aspects of a language to be specified. Associated with each symbol of the grammar is a finite set of attributes or conditions. Rules for evaluating the attributes are associated with the productions of the grammar. Using these rules the attributes of each node in a *parse tree may be evaluated. The attributes may either be *inherited*, meaning that their values are a function of the attribute of their parent node in the parse tree, or *synthesized*, meaning that their values are a function of the attributes of their children in the parse tree.

The concept of an attribute grammar was introduced by D. E. Knuth who suggested that the semantics of a program could be specified by the attributes of the root node in its parse tree.

AU *Abbrev. for* arithmetic unit. *See* arithmetic and logic unit.

audio response unit An output device that can give a spoken response. The message may be prerecorded phrases, a collation of prerecorded words, or synthesized from digital data. The range of applications includes prompts to operators of application terminals and acknowledgment of input via a telephone keypad.

audit trail A record showing the occurrence of specified events relevant to the security of a computer system. For example, an entry might be made in the audit trail whenever a user logs in or accesses a file. Examination of the audit trail may detect attempts at violating the security of the system and help to identify the violator.

augmented addressing (augmenting) A method of expanding a short specified address by concatenating the specified address (as low-order address bits) with the contents of the *augmented address register* (as high-order bits) to produce an *absolute address. *See also* addressing schemes.

augmented transition network A generalization of *finite-state automata that is used to represent natural-language grammars and hence to parse and generate natural-language text (*see* parsing, natural-language understanding). The grammar is represented as a set of labeled directed *graphs whose labels are word categories, or recursive calls to itself or other graphs, or calls to update or access a set of registers. Procedures can be associated with the arcs to build a *parse tree, to build a semantic representation, to generate text, etc.

authentication A process by which a subject, normally a user, establishes his identity to a system. This may be effected by the use of a *password or possession of a physical device, e.g. a coded token. In *reverse authentication*, the object is required to authenticate to the subject, e.g. to establish confidence in a user before he enters sensitive information into a system.

authentication code An appendage to a message that indicates to the recipient whether the message has been tampered with during transit. Authentication codes can be derived cryptographically as a function of the message and a secret key held by the sender and recipient. *See also* cryptography.

authoring language A *high-level language used for creating CAL (*computer-assisted learning) and other educational and training software packages.

autobaud *Colloquial expression for* automatic baud rate detection. A feature of some communication systems that automatically detect and adapt to the transmission speed of incoming data.

autocode The generic name given to the precursors of modern high-level programming languages. The term is now obsolete.

autodump *See* autoload.

autoload 1. A facility provided on some tape transports whereby a tape reel is automatically located and clamped on the hub and the tape is then automatically threaded. (The word is often wrongly used when *autothread is meant). The term is also used as a verb: to load a tape reel on a tape transport automatically by the use of the autoload.

2. A facility in a magnetic tape subsystem whereby a single unqualified command from the host causes a quantity of data from the tape mounted on a transport, selected according to predetermined rules, to be read and transferred to the host. The function is provided to assist in initial program loading. The corresponding process in which data is written to tape is known as *autodump*.

autoload cartridge *See* magnetic tape cartridge.

autoload success rate The proportion of tape volumes presented to a magnetic tape transport that are successfully autoloaded (or autothreaded) after a defined number of attempts. For open reel ½″ tape about three attempts are usually made and the success rate is typically about 97%; failures are mainly due to the end of the tape being damaged, often as a result of manual threading on another tape transport. The operator should then trim the end of the tape, or load it manually.

automated disk library *See* optical disk library. (In principle, magnetic disk libraries can be used but none is on the market.)

automated tape library (ATL) A peripheral device in which a large number of cartridges or reels of magnetic tape are stored in *cells* in a *storage matrix*. Any chosen cartridge can be transferred mechanically to a tape transport (directly or by way of a further mechanism called a *shuttle*) where it can be accessed by the host system, and then returned to the same or another cell. The device also contains one or more *drawers* that can also be reached by the transfer mechanism: these are accessible to an operator so that cartridges can be introduced to or removed from the library. An ATL is functionally equivalent to a conventional *tape library but without the need for a human operator except to add or remove cartridges. In one brand of ATL, standard reels of ½″ tape are used, but more often the cartridge is specially designed for the purpose and generally contains a single reel with a relatively short length of tape several inches wide.

The virtues of the ATL are the rapidity with which any cartridge can be selected and mounted on the transport, typically a few seconds, and the elimination of human operators. Its disadvantages are cost and mechanical and functional complexity. ATLs have not been widely used.

automatic calling unit *See* ACU.

automatic check Any automatic (as opposed to programmed) computed check on the validity of a segment of data. *See also* error detection, error correction.

automatic coding A term used in the early stages of development of computers to signify the use of a primitive high-level language or *autocode, as contrasted with the more usual "hand coding".

automatic data conversion The conversion of data from one form to another without any direct action by the programmer, e.g. decimal integers on input to stored form of integer. Such facilities are commonly available for individual items of data in modern programming languages. Many database input systems carry out more complex transformations of the data, and at the extreme may translate data from the format of one database system to another.

automatic data processing (ADP) *See* data processing.

automatic programming 1. The use of a high-level programming language. The term in this sense is now obsolete.
2. Generation of programs automatically from a nonprocedural description

of their desired effect. Thus in artificial intelligence we describe the required actions of a robot, and the system generates a program that will cause the required movements to take place. In commercial data processing we describe the various documents – orders, invoices, delivery notes, etc. – and the relationship between the quantities involved, and the system generates a suite · of programs to do the required processing. The term is falling into disuse. *See also* generator.

automatic tape library (ATL) *See* automated tape library.

automaton A general term for a device that mechanically processes an input string with the aim either of deciding whether it belongs to some set of strings, i.e. a *formal language, or of producing an output string.

There are two senses in which an automaton A is said to *recognize* (or *accept*) a language L:

(a) for any input string w, A halts and indicates that it *accepts* or *rejects* w, according to whether or not $w \in L$;

(b) A halts if $w \in L$ and fails to halt otherwise.

In the case of *Turing machines, the languages recognizable in sense (a) and the weaker sense (b) are the *recursive sets and the *recursively enumerable sets respectively. Hence, if a language is recognizable (in either sense) by any kind of automaton, it is so recognizable by a Turing machine.

Turing machines are a particular kind of automaton. Other kinds include the *finite-state automaton, *pushdown automaton, and *linear-bounded automaton. *Sequential machines are automata that produce an output string.

automorphism An *isomorphism from an *algebra to itself.

autoregression *See* time series.

autothread A facility provided on some tape transports whereby magnetic tape is automatically threaded from the file reel through the tape path and secured to the hub of the take-up reel (*see also* autoload).

The first autothreading transports, introduced by IBM in the 1960s, required the tape reels to be placed within an Easyload *magnetic tape cartridge and manually mounted on the transport hub; later designs dispensed with the cartridge but still required the reel to be manually mounted. The most recent types only require the tape reel to be "posted" through a slot in the transport housing; this has the advantage that transports can be mounted horizontally and stacked, giving a very compact layout. The arrangement was pioneered by Cipher in 1980.

auxiliary memory *Another name for* backing store.

availability 1. The probability that a system will be capable of functioning according to specification at any point in time throughout a stated period of time. *Compare* reliability.

2. The ratio of *available time to total time for a system in a given period.

available list (free list) A list of the unallocated parts of a sharable resource. Some resources, such as processors, are shared by being allocated in their entirety to a *process for a period of time. Other resources consist of a number of functionally similar units, e.g. pages within memory, and the resource is shared by units of the total resource being allocated to a process. This allocated share remains with the process until the process releases it. The available list provides the resource controller with a convenient record of which parts of the resource are not allocated to a process. *See also* free-space list.

available time The amount of time in a given period that a computing system can be used by its normal users. During available time the system must be functioning correctly, have power supplied to it, and not be undergoing repair or maintenance. Available time is comprised of *productive time* and *idle time*. Productive time is the amount of time in a given period that a system is performing useful work for the users. Idle time is the amount of time in a given period that a system is performing no useful function. It usually occurs when waiting for completion of some I/O function or backing-store transfer.

average-case analysis *See* algorithm.

AVL tree (height-balanced tree) A *binary search tree such that for each node the *heights of the left and right subtrees differ by at most one. Thus the *balance of each node is -1, 0, or $+1$. During insertion or deletion, a node in an AVL tree may become *critical* or unbalanced and then the tree has to be reorganized to maintain its balanced property. The tree is named for its originators, Adel'son-Vel'skii and Landis.

axiomatic semantics An approach to the *semantics of programming languages in which the meaning of a language is given by describing the true statements that can be made about programs in that language. Typically the statements are written in some suitable formal notation such as *predicate calculus or *modal logic, and concern the states of execution before and after running the program. The approach grew out of the early work of Hoare. Though originally intended as a notation for *program correctness proofs (in particular as an alternative notation for the *Floyd method), it was observed that *Hoare logic could also be viewed as an axiomatic semantics for a very simple programming language. The approach was consequently extended to the description of practically useful languages.

axiomatic specification (algebraic specification) A particular approach to writing *abstract specifications for programs, modules, or data types. What distinguishes this approach is the fact that specifications are expressed purely in terms of the effects of operations, and not in terms of their implementations or of the particular representation of any data involved. A specification in this style consists of a collection of operation names, together with a collection of axioms that express how these operations combine with each other. The operation names can be thought of as comprising a *signature, and an implementation of them as an *algebra over that signature, satisfying the axioms. *See also* formal specification. *Compare* constructive specification.

B

B A programming language derived from *BCPL, developed in 1970 as an implementation language for the PDP-11 version of the *UNIX operating system. Like BCPL, B was a type-free language: it was soon superseded by *C, the main difference being the addition of types.

Babbage A machine-oriented high-level language (*MOHLL) for the GEC 4080 series machines and their derivatives. Particularly noteworthy is the fact that it was supplied by the manufacturer and entirely replaced the assembler for these machines.

backbone network (bearer network) The underlying *nodes of a multilevel distributed network, providing communication services for the rest of the network (the hosts). The backbone network usually consists of dedicated packet, mes-sage, or circuit switches connected by high-capacity trunk circuits, along with some special diagnostic and control equipment. An example is the *ARPANET's *IMP subnet.

An important requirement for backbone networks is that they must be extremely reliable. For this reason they are usually built out of homogeneous (essentially similar) processors and run by a centralized administration, although the rest of the network may be highly heterogeneous and under distributed authority. Distributed procedures are often used to control the operation of the backbone network in order to reduce the possibility that a single failure might disrupt the entire network. When a central control system is used, there is usually a standby system ready to take over when the active system fails.

Backbone networks are often characterized by distributed traffic patterns. *Packet switching may be used internally by backbone networks to take advantage of these traffic patterns, even though the backbone network may present a *circuit-switching appearance to external hosts (*see* virtual connection). Traffic-pattern analysis may be used to construct backbone networks that minimize certain network parameters, such as average delay, circuit costs, etc. Backbone networks may themselves be multilevel, incorporating low-capacity terrestrial links, high-capacity terrestrial links, and satellite links.

back-end processor A processor that is used for some specialized function such as database management, or a special-purpose arithmetic and logic unit. *Compare* front-end processor.

background processing Processing without the opportunity for interaction with the user, within a system that provides for interaction by *foreground processing. The jobs are submitted by users from terminals but are not processed immediately. They are placed into a *background queue* and are run off as resources become available.

backing store (auxiliary memory; bulk memory; secondary memory) The memory on which information is held for reference but not for direct execution. Backing store is the lower part of the *memory hierarchy, in which the speed of access to the information stored is matched to the requirements of the system so as to achieve the greatest economy. The term may be used either in an absolute sense, in which case it usually refers to a disk, or it may be used in a relative sense to refer to the device next down in the memory hierarchy.

backplane A hardware device that may be considered as the physical "plane" by means of which a computer or similar device communicates with its various peripherals. Normally a backplane consists of a series of multiway sockets that are wired in parallel and are connected to the internal wiring, or *buses, of the computer. Peripherals may then be attached to the computer simply by inserting compatible interface cards into any one of these sockets.

backtracking A property of an algorithm that implies some kind of tentative search for a goal, and the possibility that any search path may turn out to be a deadend; the algorithm then retreats back down the search path to try another path. The technique is generally suitable for solving problems where a potentially large but finite number of solutions have to be inspected. It amounts to a systematic tree search, bottom-up.

backup A resource that is, or can be used as, a substitute when a primary resource fails or when a file has been corrupted. The word is also used as a verb, to back up, i.e. to make a copy in anticipation of future failure or corrup-

tion. Thus a *dump forms a backup to be used in cases where a user's file has become unusable; the taking of the dump can be regarded as backing up the version on disk.

Backus normal form, Backus–Naur form *See* BNF.

backward error analysis *See* error analysis.

backward error correction (backward correction) Error correction that occurs in a channel through the detection of errors by the reciever: the receiver responds to any errors in a *block by requesting the transmitter to retransmit the affected block. Backward correction requires a *return channel, by contrast with *forward error correction.

There are two ways in which the return channel can be used to indicate errors: *positive acknowledgment* and *negative acknowledgment*. With positive acknowledgment, the receiver returns confirmation of each block received correctly, and the transmitter is prepared to retransmit a block that is not acknowledged within an appropriate time. With negative acknowledgment, the receiver returns a request to retransmit any block received erroneously, and the transmitter is prepared to retransmit such a block (implying that the transmitter retains a copy of every block sent, indefinitely).

Since the return channel itself may be prone to errors, and to limit the amount of storage necessary at the transmitter, the positive acknowledgment and retransmission (PAR) technique is generally preferred. *See also* error-detecting code.

backward error recovery A mechanism that, on discovery of an error, restores a system to an earlier state (a *recovery point) by undoing the effects of operations that have been performed since that earlier state was last current. This is achieved by saving *recovery data during the execution of operations.

badge reader A device designed to read information encoded into a small plastic card. It is often part of a data collection system in which each operator can be identified by the badge they present to the machine. It can also be used to control access to areas associated with electrically operated door locks, and when built into keyboards and other parts of information systems it can control access to information.

The badge is usually of plastic, or paper laminated between plastic, and may contain a photograph and other information in addition to what is encoded. The encoding takes many forms, some of which are proprietary and complex to achieve greater security. The most common form for data collection systems in an industrial environment was originally the punched badge: there were five standardized formats using the rectangular punched holes common to the 80-column punched card. The punched badge reader has been superseded by devices that sense information encoded by printed marks or characters, by capacitive or magnetic elements embedded within the card, or by magnetic recording on a strip of material on the surface.

bag (multiset) 1. An unordered collection of items where more than one instance of the same item is allowed.
2. Any data structure representing a bag. Representations are similar to those used for *sets. In a set, however, it is only necessary to represent the presence (or absence) of an element whereas in a bag it is also necessary to represent the number of times it occurs.

balance of a node in a *binary tree. A measure of the relative size of the left and right subtrees of the node. Usually, the balance is defined to be the height of the left subtree minus the height of

the right subtree (or the absolute value thereof). However, formulas are also used that measure balance in terms of the total number of nodes in the left and right subtrees.

balanced (height-balanced; depth-balanced) Denoting a tree that has *height (and thus *depth) approximately equal to the logarithm of the number of nodes in the tree. This property is usually achieved in a binary tree by ensuring every node is balanced according to some measure. *See also* AVL tree, B-tree.

band 1. A set of adjacent tracks on a magnetic or optical disk.
2. A loop of flexible material, in particular the loop of steel tape that acts as the font carrier in a *band printer.
3. A section of the frequency spectrum lying between limits that are defined according to some requirement or to some functional aspect of a given signal or transmission channel. When used as a suffix the word is a contraction of *bandwidth, as in narrowband, wideband.

band-limited channel A transmission channel with finite *bandwidth. All physically realizable channels are band-limited. *See also* channel coding theorem, discrete and continuous systems.

band matrix A sparse matrix in which the nonzero elements are located in a band about the main diagonal. If A is a band matrix such that

$$a_{ij} = 0 \text{ if } j - i > p$$
$$\text{or } i - j > q$$

where p and q are the distances above and below the main diagonal, then the *bandwidth* w is given by

$$w = p + q + 1$$

band-pass filter A *filtering device that permits only those components in the *Fourier transform domain whose frequencies lie between two critical values to pass through with little attenuation, all other components being highly attenuated.

band printer (belt printer) A type of *impact *line printer in which the font – characters and timing marks – is etched on a steel band. The operating principle is similar to that of the *chain printer and train printer. Although demonstrated in the mid-1960s it was 1972 before machines with satisfactory print quality and band life were available. Band printers have price/performance advantage over *drum (or barrel) printers and satisfy the preference for printers in which the font moves horizontally: any mistiming of the impact on a horizontal-font machine results in a change in the space between characters, which is less noticeable than the vertical displacement that occurs with mistiming in a drum printer.

The majority of new impact line printers in the late 1970s were band printers. Machines were available at speeds from 300 lpm to 2500 lpm when using a 64 character repertoire. Designs for the lower-speed machines often time-share a print hammer between adjacent print positions. In one implementation this is achieved by having a wide hammer head that spans two columns and in another a bank of single-width hammers is moved – or shuttled – laterally by one or more column pitches. An advantage of some shuttle printers is the ability to print at "compressed pitch", i.e. 15 characters per inch as well as the standard 10 characters per inch.

band-reject filter *Another name for* band-stop filter.

band-stop filter (band-reject filter) A *filtering device that permits only those components in the *Fourier transform domain whose frequencies lie below one critical value or above another (higher) critical value to pass through with little attenuation; all components whose frequencies lie between the critical values are highly attenuated.

If the two critical values are very close together, the device is called a *notch filter*. Notch filters are used, for example, in *modems in order to prevent certain components of the data signal from interfering with equipment in the telephone system.

bandwidth 1. of a transmission *channel. Usually, the range of *frequencies passed by the channel. This will often consist of a single *passband, but may instead consist of several distinct (nonoverlapping) passbands. Each passband contributes to the bandwidth of the channel a quantity equal to the difference between its upper and lower frequency limits; the sum of all such differences gives the total bandwidth.

In these cases bandwidth is measured in frequency units: hertz (Hz) or, colloquially, cycles per second (cps). If the bandwidth is considered in a transform domain other than frequency (such as *sequency) then it is measured in the appropriate units.

There are several loose classifications of frequency bandwidths employed for convenience of description in various areas of technology; one classification is as follows:

narrowband (up to 300 Hz)
voiceband (300–3000 Hz)
wideband (over 3000 Hz)
See also band-limited channel, channel coding theorem (for Shannon–Hartley law), Nyquist's criterion.
2. *See* band matrix.

bank switching A technique for *memory management commonly used in microcomputer systems that require more memory than the microprocessor can directly address. In a bank-switched system, different *banks* of memory are selected by writing different bit patterns to a specified output port. Bank switching is similar in concept to memory segmentation (*see* segment) but does not require the use of a processor that knows about a segmented address space.

bar code (or **barcode**) A printed machine-readable code that consists of parallel bars of varied width and spacing. The application most commonly observed is the coding on food and other goods that is read at the checkout and translated into a line of print on the bill showing product and cost. The information is also used to update stock records and provide sales statistics.

In the US the code used for this purpose is the Universal Product Code (UPC) and in Europe it is the European Article Numbering (EAN) code. The UPC decodes initially into two five-digit numbers. The first five identify the supplier and the next five are the item number within that supplier's range of goods. From this information the checkout terminal can access the details to be printed on the bill. The EAN code has a two-digit number to indicate country of origin, then the two five-digit numbers, followed by a check digit. The EAN arrangement simplifies the allocation of codes to suppliers. Only the two-digit code and the format need to be agreed internationally.

Other codes are used for shop-floor data collection, library systems, and monitoring the circulation of confidential documents. The advantage of bar codes is that they can be produced and read by relatively simple equipment. Codes used for these purposes are Code 39, Codabar, and "2 of 5". *See also* bar code scanner.

bar code scanner A device for scanning a *bar code. It may take the form of a hand-held *wand, a *holographic scanner, a telescope with a sensor, or a slot containing a sensor.

Barker sequence In data communications, a sequence of symbols (binary or *q-ary) that, when embedded in a string of randomly chosen symbols (from the same alphabet), has zero autocorrelation except in the coincidence position. Barker sequences are used to check, and if necessary to correct, the synchronization and framing of received data.

barrel printer *UK name for* drum printer.

base *Another name for* the radix of a positional number system. Hence decimal numbers are base 10 numbers and binary numbers are base 2 numbers. *See* number system.

base addressing *See* relative addressing.

baseband networking Communication in which a digital signal is placed directly on the transmission medium without requiring a carrier, i.e. without modulation. Only one signal may be present on the baseband channel at a time. This type of signaling, *baseband signaling*, is also called *d.c. signaling* because in some baseband networks a continuous d.c. voltage is present when the data does not change. Baseband networks may use twisted pair or coaxial cables for data transmission. The *Ethernet is a prototype *local area network using baseband signaling on a coaxial cable. *Compare* broadband networking.

base-bound register (datum-limit register) Hardware used for *virtual-memory allocation. A base-bound register is associated with each *segment of data or code and defines the position in physical memory of word zero for that segment, the so-called *base* or *datum*, and the number of words available to that segment, the so-called *bound* or *limit* (or alternatively the physical memory address of the next word after the end of the segment, in which case it is a *bounds register). Whenever a process attempts to access the memory segment, the hardware of the system checks that the address of the word lies within the range

$$0 \leqslant \text{word address} < \text{bound}$$

and then adds the address to the value contained in the base register to give the physical address. A restriction on this system is that the storage for the segment must be allocated in a contiguous area of memory (*see* best fit, first fit).

The *base register*, used in the construction of relative addresses, should not be confused with the base of a base-bound system; the result of modifying an address by a base register's contents is still an address within virtual memory space of the process, and is not necessarily a physical address.

base field *See* polynomial.

base-limit register *See* base-bound register.

base register *See* relative addressing.

BASIC or **Basic** *Acronym for* beginners' all-purpose symbolic instruction code. A simple programming language, developed in the mid-1960s to exploit the then novel capability of interactive use of a computer from a remote terminal. BASIC as originally conceived was a very simple language that could be learned very quickly. The BASIC system included crude editing facilities as part of the language so that the user was insulated from the complexities of any underlying operating system. At first BASIC only handled numeric values, but it was later extended to allow string variables and was provided with a set of procedures for simple string manipulation that have become a de facto standard.

The simplicity of BASIC made it a natural choice as a programming language for the early microcomputers, and it became established as a common language for programming personal computers. Unfortunately, almost every machine has its own dialect of BASIC so that programs are not readily portable. The establishment of an ANSI Standard for BASIC has not made any appreciable improvements in this situation. A welcome trend is the incorporation in many dialects of modern control structures, e.g.

REPEAT ... UNTIL

See also Turbo languages.

batch control Correctness checks built into *data-processing systems and applied to batches of input data, particularly in the data-preparation stage. There are two main forms of batch control: *sequence control* involves numbering the records in a batch consecutively so that the presence of each record can be confirmed during the data-vet run; *control totals* involve establishing record counts, or totals of the values in selected fields within each record, and checking these totals during the data-vet run. Control totals may be "meaningful", in the sense that they may have a use (for instance to an auditor) that is additional to their function within the system. Most commonly they are meaningless totals (e.g. of employee numbers), often referred to as *hash totals.

The scope of batch control may extend beyond the data-vet program, for as far into the system as batches retain their separate identities. In particular, they may be used to check that incorrect records, rejected during the data vet, are resubmitted before a batch is released for further processing.

Batcher's parallel method (merge exchange sort) A form of *sorting by selection that chooses nonadjacent parts of sortkeys for comparisons. The sequence of comparisons was discovered by K. E. Batcher in 1964. It is particularly appropriate for *parallel processing.

batch processing 1. Originally, a method of organizing work for a computer system, designed to reduce overheads by grouping together similar jobs. One form avoided reloading *systems software. The jobs were collected into batches, each batch requiring a particular compiler, the compiler was loaded once, and then the jobs submitted in sequence to the compiler. If a job failed to compile it took no further part in the processing, but those jobs that did compile led to the production on magnetic tape or other backing store of an executable binary. At the end of the batch of compilations those jobs that had produced an executable binary form were loaded in sequence and their data presented to the jobs. Another form avoided the time taken to read cards and print on paper by off-line processing, having a batch of jobs on magnetic tape.

The term has also come to be applied to the *background processing of jobs not requiring intervention by the user, which takes place on many multiaccess systems.

2. A method of organizing a *data processing system in which *transactions are input in a batch, sorted, and sequentially processed to update and/or query a *master file. This is the only possible method if magnetic tape is used as backing store; there are applications where it is the most efficient method even using disks. *See also* transaction processing.

baud rate The number of times per second that a system, especially a data transmission *channel, changes state. In the particular case of a binary channel, the baud rate is equal to the bit rate, i.e.

1 baud = 1 bit per second
For a general channel,
1 baud = 1 digit per second
1 baud = 1 symbol per second

or whatever the states of the system represent. The rate was named for J. M. E. Baudot.

Bayesian statistics *Statistical methods that make use of assumed prior information about the *parameters to be estimated. The methods make use of a theorem of Rev. T. Bayes, measuring the change in *probability attributed to observational data. The use of Bayesian statistics is sometimes regarded as controversial.

BCD *Abbrev. for* binary-coded decimal.

BCD adder A 4-bit binary *adder that is capable of adding two 4-bit words having a BCD (*binary-coded decimal) format. The result of the addition is a BCD-format 4-bit output word, representing the decimal sum of the addend and augend, and a carry that is generated if this sum exceeds a decimal value of 10. Decimal addition is thus possible using these devices.

BCH code *Short for* Bose–Chaudhuri–Hocquenghem code.

BCPL A systems programming language that incorporates the control structures needed for *structured programming. Its main distinguishing feature is that it is type-free, i.e. the only type of data object that can be used is a word made up of bits (hence the suitability for systems programming). BCPL has been implemented on many machines, and programs written in the language are readily portable. *See also* CPL, B, C.

BCS British Computer Society, formed in 1957 to further development and use of computer machinery and related techniques and to facilitate exchange of information and views by means of conferences, meetings, and publications. It is the UK member of IFIP.

BDF methods *See* linear multistep methods.

bead A *data structure consisting of several fields, some or all of which are instances of the same data structure. It is now obsolete, having been replaced by the more general concept of a *record.

bearer network *Another name for* backbone network.

Bell Telephone Laboratories The research and development laboratories for American Telephone & Telegraph (AT&T), jointly owned by AT&T and Western Electric Corporation (the manufacturing arm of AT&T). The products of Bell Labs include Shannon's seminal work on information theory, the transistor, and the UNIX operating system.

belt printer *Another name for* band printer, used to describe the early versions of those machines, but also used to describe printers in which the font is carried on plates or fingers attached to a flexible belt. The operating principle is similar to that of the *chain printer but the font carrier is lower in cost. In some designs it was possible to change individual type carriers.

benchmark (benchmark problem) A problem that has been designed to evaluate the performance of a system (hardware and software). In a *benchmark test* a system is subjected to a known workload and the performance of the system against this workload is measured. Typically the purpose is to compare the measured performance with that of other systems that have been subject to the same benchmark test; the performance is then said to be *benchmarked*.

See also Ackermann benchmark, debit-credit benchmark, pi benchmark, Ramp-C benchmark, sieve benchmark, whetstone benchmark.

best fit A method of selecting a contiguous area of memory that is to be allocated for a segment. The available areas are examined in order of increasing size; the area that exceeds the request by the smallest amount is taken and the request met by allocating the amount requested from this area.

beta reduction *See* lambda calculus.

beta test A test of a packaged software system in a small number of normal working (as opposed to development) environments. The beta test is usually performed at carefully selected customer sites. A beta test is carried out following acceptance *testing at the supplier's site (alpha test) and immediately prior to general release of the software as a product. It is a confidence-building exercise that also limits the costs of correcting faults revealed when new or upgraded software is first exposed to its normal working environment and workload.

bias 1. The d.c. component of an a.c. signal.

2. The d.c. voltage used to switch on or off a *bipolar transistor or *diode (*see* forward bias, reverse bias), or the d.c. gate-source voltage used to control the d.c. drain-source current in a *field-effect transistor. The word is also used as a verb: to switch.

3. In statistical usage, a source of error that cannot be reduced by increasing sample size. It is systematic as opposed to random error.

Sources of bias include (a) bias in *sampling, when members of the sample are not fully representative of the population being studied; (b) *nonresponse bias* in sample surveys, when an appreciable proportion of those questioned fail to reply; (c) *question bias*, a tendency for the wording of the question to invite an incorrect reply; (d) *interviewer bias*, a problem of personal interviewing when respondents try to reply in the way the interviewer is thought to expect.

A narrower definition of bias in statistical analysis (*see* statistical methods) is the difference between the mean of an estimating formula and the true value of the quantity being estimated. The estimate

$$\sum_i (x_i - \bar{x})^2 / n$$

for the variance of a population is biased, but is *unbiased* when n is replaced by $(n-1)$.

4. (excess factor) *See* floating-point notation.

biased exponent *Another name for* characteristic. *See* floating-point notation.

bicomponent algorithm A *depth-first search with the addition of tests to check whether a vertex in the tree is a *cut vertex, i.e. to make sure a particular path is not searched twice, which could happen if a vertex could be reached in two different ways.

P	F	F	T	T
Q	F	T	F	T
$P = Q$	T	F	F	T

Truth table for biconditional

biconditional A logical statement combining two statements, truth values, or formulas P and Q in such a way that the outcome is true only if P and Q are both true or both false, as indicated in the table.

The biconditional *connective can be represented by

$$\equiv \quad \leftrightarrow \quad <-> \quad \text{or} \quad <=>$$

and is read as "if and only if" or "iff" or "is equivalent to". Note that $P \equiv Q$ has the same truth table as the conjunction

$$(P \rightarrow Q) \wedge (Q \rightarrow P)$$

where $\rightarrow$ denotes a simple *conditional. The biconditional connective itself is also known as the biconditional.

biconnected graph A *graph G, either directed or undirected, with the property that for every three distinct vertices u, v, and w there is a path from u to w not containing v. For an undirected graph, this is equivalent to the graph having no *cut vertex.

Two edges of an undirected graph are said to be related either if they are identical or if there is a *cycle containing both of them. This is an *equivalence relation and partitions the edges into a set of *equivalence classes, E_1, $E_2, \ldots E_n$, say. Let V_i be the set of vertices of the edges of E_i for $i = 1, 2, \ldots n$. Then each graph G_i formed from the vertices V_i and the edges E_i is a *biconnected component* of G.

bifurcation A splitting in two. The term can be applied in computing in various ways.

1. Bifurcation is the generic name for a collection of algorithms that initially convert a *decision table into a *tree structure, which can then be systematically encoded to produce a program.

The *bifurcation method* involves choosing some condition C and eliminating it from the decision table to produce two subtables, one corresponding to the case when C is true and the other to when C is false. The method is then applied recursively to the two subtables. From this approach a *decision tree can be built, each node of the tree representing a condition and subtrees representing subtables; leaf nodes identify rules.

2. *Bifurcation theory* is the theory of equilibrium solutions of nonlinear differential equations; an equilibrium solution is a steady solution, a time periodic, or a quasi-periodic solution. Generally *bifurcation points* are points at which branches and therefore multiple solutions appear.

bijection (one-to-one onto function) A *function that is both an *injection and a *surjection. If

$$f : X \rightarrow Y$$

is a bijection, then for each y in Y there is a unique x in X with the property that

$$y = f(x)$$

i.e. there is a one-to-one correspondence between the elements in X and the elements in Y. The sets X and Y will have the same number of elements, i.e. the same *cardinality. There will be a unique function

$$f^{-1}: Y \to X$$

such that f and f^{-1} are *inverses to each other; f^{-1} will also be a bijection.

binary adder *See* adder.

binary chop *Informal name for* binary search algorithm.

binary code A *code whose alphabet is restricted to $\{0, 1\}$. In general, any *q-ary code has the important special case $q = 2$. *See* binary system.

binary-coded decimal (BCD) A code in which a string of binary digits represents a decimal digit. In the *natural binary-coded decimal (NBCD)* system, each decimal digit 0 through 9 is represented by the string of four bits whose binary numerical value is equivalent to the decimal digit. For example, 3 is represented by 0011 and 9 is represented by 1001. The NBCD code is the *8421-code such that the weighted sum of the bits in a codeword is equal to the coded decimal digit. *See also* EBCDIC, packed decimal.

binary-coded octal The representation of any octal digit by its three-bit binary equivalent.

binary counter *See* counter.

binary digit *See* bit, binary system.

binary encoding 1. The representation of symbols in a source alphabet by strings of binary digits, i.e. a *binary code. The most commonly occurring source alphabet consists of the set of *alphanumeric characters. *See* code.

2. The encoding of a number into a binary string in which the i th bit from the end carries weight 2^i. For example, 13 is represented by 1101. This encoding of natural numbers can be extended to cover signed integers and fractions. *See*

also radix complement, fixed-point notation, floating-point notation.

3. of a set A. Any assignment of distinctive bit strings to the elements of A. *See also* character encoding, Huffman encoding.

binary-level compatibility *Compatibility that exists when a program in executable binary form may be executed on different computer systems without recompilation. This will normally only be possible between systems with the same operating system and with processors or *emulations of processors capable of executing the same instruction set. *See also* source-level compatibility.

binary logic *Digital logic employing two states. *See also* logic circuit, q-ary logic.

binary notation *See* binary system.

binary number A *binary encoding of a number.

binary operation 1. (dyadic operation) defined on a set S. A *function from the domain $S \times S$ into S itself. Many of the everyday arithmetic and algebraic operations are binary, e.g. the addition of two integers, the union of two sets, and the conjunction of two Boolean expressions.

Although basically functions, binary operations are usually represented using an infix notation, as in

$$3 + 4, \quad U \cup V, \quad P \wedge Q$$

The operation symbol then appears between the left and right operand. A symbol, such as ∘, can be used to represent a generalized binary operation.

When the set S is finite, *Cayley tables and sometimes *truth tables are used to define the meaning of the operation.

2. An operation on binary operands.

binary relation A *relation defined between two sets.

binary search algorithm (logarithmic search algorithm; bisection algorithm) A searching algorithm that uses a file in which the sortkeys are in ascending order. The middle key in the file is examined and, depending upon whether this is less than or greater than the desired key, the top or bottom part of the file is again examined. Continuing in this way the algorithm either finds the desired record or discovers its absence from the file. Thus the algorithm treats the file as though it were a *binary search tree.

```
IF    t is empty THEN v not present
ELSE  case 1:  t = root  →  v present
      case 2:  t < root  →  search left subtree
      case 3:  t > root  →  search right subtree
```

Binary search tree, search algorithm

binary search tree A *binary tree in which the data values stored at the nodes of the tree belong to a *well-ordered set, and the value stored at any nonterminal node, A, is greater than the values stored in the left subtree of A and less than the values stored in the right subtree of A. To search a binary search tree, t, to see if the value, v, is present, the recursive search algorithm shown in the figure is used.

In data-processing applications, the data values stored at the nodes of a binary search tree will be key values with an associated link to the record to be retrieved. The same principle is used in the *binary search algorithm. The concept can be generalized to a *multiway search tree. *See also* AVL tree, optimal binary search tree.

binary sequence A sequence of binary digits. Such a sequence, produced randomly or pseudorandomly (*see* random numbers) and generally of known statistical properties, may be employed either as a model of noise affecting a binary channel or as a means of controlling synchronization between transmitter and receiver.

binary signal *See* digital signal.

binary symmetric channel (BSC) A binary communication channel in which the random errors are such that substitution of a 0 for a 1 occurs with the same probability as substitution of a 1 for a 0. Much of the theory of *error-correcting and *error-detecting codes assumes a BSC.

binary synchronous communications *See* BISYNC.

binary system Usually, the binary number system, i.e. the positional number system with base 2. This is the number system most commonly used in computers. A *binary digit* (or *bit*) is either 0 or 1. The representation of numbers by binary digits is called *binary notation*.

The term binary system is also used to describe any system in which there are just two possible states. For example, each of the elements comprising the memory of any computer is a binary system, one of whose states is used to denote the binary digit 0 and the other to denote the binary digit 1. It is customary to refer to such a storage element, or to the unit of information in any binary system, as a *bit*.

binary tree 1. A finite set of nodes that is either empty or is such that firstly there is a single designated node called the *root* and secondly the remaining nodes are partitioned into *disjoint sets, T_1 and T_r, where each of these sets is itself a binary tree. T_1 is called the *left subtree* and T_r the *right subtree* of the root.

At *level h of a binary tree there is a maximum of 2^h nodes. A binary tree of *depth d thus has at most $(2^{d+1} - 1)$

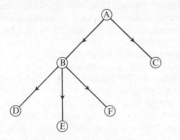 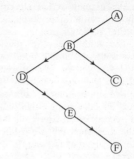

A tree and its binary representation

nodes and one with n nodes has a minimum depth of $\log_2 n$.

The term binary tree is also used to describe any (ordered) tree of *degree two. *See also* tree.

2. Any data structure used to represent a binary tree. Each node would be represented by pointers to the left and right subtrees as well as to the data value associated with the node. The binary tree could then be represented as a pointer to its root node.

binary-tree representation 1. A binary tree constructed to represent a tree of arbitrary *degree. For any node, the root of the left subtree in the binary-tree representation is the eldest child of the node in the original tree and the root of the right subtree is the next eldest sibling (*see* diagram).

2. *See* binary tree (def. 2).

bind To resolve the interpretation of some name used in a system for the remaining lifetime of that instance of the system. For example, upon invocation of a procedure the formal parameters are bound to the actual parameters that are supplied for that invocation, and this binding remains in force throughout the lifetime of that invocation. Similarly, at some time the variables in a program must be bound to particular storage addresses in the computer, and this binding typically remains

in force for as long as the variable continues to exist. In a *virtual memory system, there is further binding between the virtual addresses used in the program and the physical addresses of the hardware.

For an *abstract specification, the implementation will involve *binding* to a language. For example, the *PCTE specification is available in *C and *Ada language bindings, each having a binding to *UNIX.

binding *See* bind.

binding occurrence *See* free variable.

binomial distribution The basic discrete *probability distribution for data in the form of proportions. An event, E, can occur with *probability p. In a sample of n independent trials the probability that E occurs exactly r times is
$$^nC_r\, p^r(1 - p)^{n-r}$$
(*see* combination). The distribution is discrete, taking only the values 0, 1, 2, ..., n. The mean of the binomial distribution is np and the variance is
$$np/(1 - p)$$

BIOS *Acronym for* basic input output system. The *firmware permanently resident in microcomputer systems that is responsible for performing input and output operations when so directed. The BIOS is usually called from the operating system, but can be called directly from applications. Calling the BIOS directly can result in performance gains and loss of portability.

bipartite graph A *graph G whose vertices can be split into two *disjoint sets, U and V, in such a way that the only edges of G join a vertex in U and a vertex in V. Bipartite graphs tend to provide a convenient graphical representation of *relations and therefore *functions.

bipolar integrated circuit *See* integrated circuit.

bipolar signal A signal whose signaling elements consist of both positive and negative voltages. Bipolar signals are used in data-communication systems. *Compare* unipolar signal.

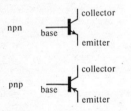

Bipolar transistor circuit symbols

bipolar transistor A semiconductor device having three electrodes: *emitter*, *base*, and *collector*. It is effectively a sandwich of two types of doped *semiconductor, usually p-type and n-type silicon, and so contains two p-n *junctions. When the region common to both junctions is p-type, an *npn transistor* is formed; when it is n-type a *pnp transistor* is formed. This central region forms the base electrode.

Bipolar transistors are so named because both charge carriers, i.e. electrons and holes, contribute to the flow of current. Current flow between collec-

tor and emitter is established by applying a *forward bias between base and emitter. In linear (i.e. *nonsaturated*) operation, the magnitude of this current is proportional to the input current drawn at the base. The directions of current flow are indicated on the circuit symbol by an arrow on the emitter connection (*see* diagram).

If the base current is increased but the collector current is restrained, so that the transistor effectively receives more base current than it would seem to require, the transistor is driven into a state of *saturation*. It then behaves as a very efficient switch since the base-collector junction becomes *reverse-biased and, in saturation, the collector-emitter voltage can fall as low as 20 millivolts. The device thus seems virtually a short circuit. Bipolar transistor switches, working into saturation, are the basis of *TTL circuits. Saturated transistors do however have a fairly low switching speed. The much higher switching speeds of *Schottky TTL and *ECL circuits are achieved by using a nonsaturated mode of operation.

biquinary code (quibinary code) A seven-bit *weighted code, two bits of which are used to indicate whether the encoded number (a decimal digit) is or is not at least 5 in value, the remaining five bits comprising four zeros and a single one whose position is used to determine the number completely. Thus from left to right the weights of the bits are 5, 0, 4, 3, 2, 1, and 0. The weighted sum gives the value of the encoded decimal digit; for example, 3 is represented by

$$0101000$$
and 9 is represented by
$$1010000$$

bisection algorithm *Another name for* binary search algorithm.

bistable An electronic circuit, usually an integrated circuit, whose output has two stable states to which it is directed by the input signal or signals. It is more usually known as a *flip-flop. *See also* multivibrator.

BISYNC (BSC) *Abbrev. for* binary synchronous communications (protocol). A *line protocol created by IBM for synchronized communication between mainframe computers and remote job-entry terminals. BISYNC is a character-oriented protocol: it uses special control characters to mark the beginning and end of a *message, to acknowledge previous messages, to request retransmission of missing or damaged messages, etc. The BISYNC protocol may be used with the 6-bit Transcode, 7-bit ASCII, or 8-bit EBCDIC character codes, and multidrop or point-to-point communication lines.

The protocol is inherently half duplex: a message is sent, a reply is sent, the next message is sent, etc. Thus BISYNC communication usually uses half duplex communication lines and modems. Full duplex communication lines and modems may be used but most of the additional capacity is wasted.

BISYNC has been largely replaced in computer communications by newer data link control protocols, such as *SDLC and *HDLC. BISYNC's retransmission and acknowledgment scheme does not work efficiently over connections with long delay times. This is particularly important in the US and other areas where the telephone system is converting to satellite transmission systems for voice and data traffic.

bit *Short for* binary digit. **1.** Either of the two digits 0 and 1 in the binary number system. Bits are used in computing for the internal representation of numbers, characters, and instructions. The bit is the smallest unit of storage and hence of information in any *binary system within a computer.

2. The fundamental unit of information used in *information theory. It is the quantity of information required to distinguish between a pair of equiprobable events.

bit density The number of bits stored per unit length or area of a magnetic recording medium. The figure is usually calculated as the maximum density achieved, i.e. it does not take account of the unrecorded areas between blocks, tracks, sectors, etc.

bit handling The facility provided in some programming languages to manipulate the individual bits of a byte or word. Operators provided usually include bitwise "and" and "or" between two bytes (or words), bitwise "not" (inversion) of a single byte (or word), and circular shifts. Many of the programming operations traditionally regarded as bit handling can be achieved in Pascal by use of sets.

bit mapping A technique for managing the image displayed on a computer screen such that each pixel (picture element) corresponds to one or more bits in memory. This allows for great flexibility in the display of text or pictorial information. In a monochromatic display the number of bits corresponding to each pixel determines the number of *gray-scale levels supported. If there is one bit per pixel the image will be strictly black-and-white with no shades of gray. In a color display the number of bits per pixel determines how many colors can be displayed. *Compare* hardware character generation.

bit matrix A two-dimensional *array in which each element is equal to 0 or to 1. *Compare* Boolean matrix.

BITNET An IBM-sponsored network, initiated in the academic and research community in the US and Canada in the early 1980s. The original concept was of a purely *message switching network, running only on IBM 370 architecture systems and using the large processors as the *store and forward units. The system was later ported onto other hardware architectures, especially the DEC VAX family, and additional functions were added. The system has been widely copied, helped by support from IBM, and led to *EARN in Europe and a number of other networks.

bitpad A device for digitizing the position of a pen. *See* digitizer.

bit rate The number of bits transmitted or transferred per unit of time. The unit of time is usually one second, thus giving rise to bits per second, bps. *See also* baud rate.

bit-slice architecture A computer architecture or design, used especially for microprocessors, in which the CPU is constructed by concatenating a number of high-performance processing units. Each of these "slice" elements represents a limited width (commonly 2, 4, or 8 bits) of an ALU and CU section; a parallel computer of any desired word size can therefore be constructed. Specific system customization is accomplished by *microprogramming. This form of architecture permits the use of standard (thus low-cost) VLSI elements to produce different computer systems.

bit string A *string of bits.

bit stuffing 1. A means of providing synchronization in a *data link control protocol such as HDLC where, for example, a 0 is automatically inserted whenever a predetermined number of 1s is present in a data stream at the sending end of the link. The receiving equipment automatically deletes the extra 0s before delivering the received message to the receiving terminal.
2. A means of inserting and deleting bits on multiply connected high-speed

digital transmission links that are not synchronously clocked.

black-box testing A style of *testing that considers only the inputs, the outputs, and the relationships specified between them to derive test inputs that will demonstrate that the required outputs occur. Usually the term is applied to software, but is also used for any system component (hence "box") for which no knowledge of the internal structure or processing is used to derive the test (hence "black"). *Compare* glass-box testing.

blank Empty, i.e. not containing meaningful data. In a memory, blank cells may contain a particular bit pattern that has no assigned value.

blank character A character that creates a blank space when displayed or printed.

blast *Another term for* blow.

blink An attribute that causes a character to be intermittently displayed on a screen at a regular rate, usually in the range 1–10 Hz. The technique used for presenting data on a cathode-ray tube inherently causes it to blink at a rate usually in excess of 50 Hz; this is not usually apparent to the eye but when it is it is referred to as *flicker*.

block 1. A collection of data units such as words, characters, or records (generally more than a single word) that are stored in adjacent physical positions in memory or on a peripheral storage device. A block can therefore be treated as a single unit whereby data can be (and usually is) transferred between storage device and memory, using one instruction. Blocks may be fixed or variable in size.

A stream of data to be recorded on magnetic tape is divided into blocks for convenience of handling and particularly of *error recovery. (The equivalent on disks is *sectors.) Successive blocks are separated by *interblock gaps* and often also by control signals introduced by the magnetic tape subsystem and invisible to the host (*see* tape format). It is usual but not essential for the block length to be the same for all blocks of data within a volume or at least within a file, though this may not apply to *labels; where the end of a file occurs partway through a block, the remainder of the block may be filled with *padding characters*.

The choice of block length is largely dependent on *error management considerations. The minimum length of the interblock gap is defined by the standard for the tape format in use; the maximum length is usually undefined, except that a very long stretch (typically 25 feet) of blank tape is taken to mean that there is no more data on the volume. To avoid wastage of tape the gap written is usually fairly close to the minimum but it may be elongated in some circumstances, e.g. by error recovery actions or to leave space for the *editing* of a file (which in this context means its replacement by a new version of the same length).

In conventional magnetic tape subsystems the division of data into blocks is carried out by the host. However some buffered tape subsystems, particularly streaming cartridge tape, accept a continuous data stream from the host, and the subsystem itself divides the data into blocks (in this case often called *blockettes*) in a manner that is not visible to the host. In these subsystems the interblock gap may be very short or absent.

2. In coding theory, an ordered set of symbols, usually of a fixed length. The term is generally synonymous with word or string, but with the implication of fixed length.

3. *See* block-structured languages.

4. In parallel programming, to prevent further execution of one sequence of instructions until another sequence has done whatever is necessary to unblock it. *See also* blocked process.

block code A type of *error-correcting or *error-detecting code in which a fixed number (conventionally k) of digits are taken into the encoder at a time and then output in the form of a *codeword* consisting of a greater number (conventionally n) of digits. It is often specified as an (n, k) *code*, with block length k and codeword length n. The corresponding decoder takes in n digits, and outputs k digits, at a time. Since the codewords are longer than the input words, the possible received words are no more numerous. The codewords are only a selection of all possible words of their length: the selection method gives any code its particular properties. *See also* code.

block compaction *Another name for* memory compaction.

block diagram A diagram that represents graphically the interconnection relationships between elements of an electronic system, e.g. a computer system. These elements may range from circuits to major *functional units; they are described as labeled geometric figures. The whole block diagram may represent any level of computer description from a compound circuit to an overall computer complex.

blocked process A *process for which a process description exists but which is unable to proceed because it lacks some necessary resource. For example, a process may become blocked if it has inadequate memory available to it to allow the loading of the next part of the process.

blockette *See* block.

blocking factor The number of records, words, characters, or bits in a block.

block length 1. *See* block (def. 1).

2. The input word length, k, of an (n, k) *block code. The term is also applied to the codeword length, n, of an (n, k) block code.

3. The input word length (i.e. the *extension of the source) used in a *variable-length code.

block retrieval Fetching a block from backing store as part of a *memory-management process.

block-structured languages A class of high-level languages in which a program is made up of *blocks* – which may include *nested blocks* as components, such nesting being repeated to any depth. A block consists of a sequence of statements and/or blocks, preceded by declarations of variables. Variables declared at the head of a block are visible throughout the block and any nested blocks, unless a variable of the same name is declared at the head of an inner block. In this case the new declaration is effective throughout the inner block, and the outer declaration becomes effective again at the end of the inner block. Variables are said to have *nested scopes*.

The concept of block structure was introduced in the *Algol family of languages, and block-structured languages are sometimes described as *Algol-like*. The concept of nested scopes implicit in block structure contrasts with FORTRAN, where variables are either local to a program unit (subroutine) or global to several program units if declared to be COMMON. Both of these contrast with COBOL, where all data items are visible throughout the entire program.

blow (blast; burn) *Jargon* To program a *PROM, i.e. to record information in a programmable read-only memory using a *PROM programmer.

blue book 1. The *coloured book that defines the file transfer protocol used by the UK academic networking community. *See also* NIFTP.

2. Part of the defining documentation for the *ISDN standards, which further refines the definitions appearing in the earlier *red book.

Blum's axioms Two axioms in complexity theory, formulated by M. Blum. Let
$$M_1, M_2, \ldots, M_n, \ldots$$
be an effective *enumeration of the Turing machines and let f_i be the *partial recursive function of a single variable that is computed by M_i. (For technical reasons it is simpler to think in terms of partial recursive functions than set (or language) recognizers.) If
$$F_1, F_2, \ldots, F_n, \ldots$$
is a sequence of partial recursive functions satisfying
axiom 1:
  $f_i(n)$ is defined if and only if $F_i(n)$ is defined,
and axiom 2:
  $F_i(x) \leqslant y$ is a recursive predicate of i, x, and y,
then $F_i(n)$ can be thought of as the amount of some "resource" consumed by M_i in computing $f_i(n)$. This notion represents a useful abstraction of the more usual resources – time and space – and helps to understand their relationship.

BM algorithm *See* Boyer–Moore algorithm.

BNF *Abbrev. for* Backus normal form, Backus–Naur form. The first widely used formal notation for describing the *syntax of a programming language; it was invented by John Backus. BNF was introduced as a defining mechanism in the Algol 60 Report (editor Peter Naur) to describe the syntax of Algol 60. BNF is capable of describing any *context-free language, and variants of it are still in use today.

A BNF grammar consists of a number of *production rules*, which define syntactic categories in terms of other

$\langle\text{digit}\rangle ::= 0\,|\,1\,|\,2\,|\,3\,|\,4\,|\,5\,|\,6\,|\,7\,|\,8\,|\,9$

$\langle\text{integer}\rangle ::= \langle\text{digit}\rangle\,|\,\langle\text{digit}\rangle\,\langle\text{integer}\rangle$

$\langle\text{fractional number}\rangle ::= \langle\text{integer}\rangle\,|\,\langle\text{integer}\rangle\,.\,\langle\text{integer}\rangle$

$\langle\text{number}\rangle ::= \langle\text{integer}\rangle\,|\,\langle\text{fractional number}\rangle$

$\langle\text{signed number}\rangle ::= \langle\text{number}\rangle\,|+\langle\text{number}\rangle\,|-\langle\text{number}\rangle$

Production rules of a BNF grammar

syntactic categories, and of the *terminal symbols* of the language. Examples are shown in the diagram. The name of the syntactic category that is being defined is placed on the left, its definition on the right; the two are separated by the symbol ::=, read as "is defined to be". The names of syntactic categories are enclosed by angle brackets. The symbol | is read as "or".
See also extended BNF.

board 1. The thin rigid board of insulating material on which a circuit is constructed, often a *printed circuit. *See* circuit board.
2. *Short for* circuit board.

book A term used in connection with the organization of files in Algol 68. A file is regarded as one or more books, each book being composed of numbered pages; within a page data is organized into lines made of individual characters. It is important to distinguish "page" in this context from a *page in memory management systems.

Boolean algebra An *algebra that is particularly important in computing. Formally it is a *complemented *distributive lattice. In a Boolean algebra there is a *set of elements B that consists of only 0 and 1. Further there will be two *dyadic operations, usually denoted by $\wedge$ and $\vee$ (or by . and +) and called *and* and *or* respectively. There is also a *monadic operation, denoted here by ', and known as the *complement operation*.

These operations satisfy a series of laws, given in the table, where x, y, and z denote arbitrary elements of B.

There are two very common examples of Boolean algebras. The first consists of the set

$$B = \{\text{FALSE, TRUE}\}$$

with the dyadic *AND and *OR operations replacing $\wedge$ and $\vee$ respectively, and the *NOT operation producing complements. Thus 1 and 0 are just TRUE and FALSE respectively. This idea can be readily extended to the set of all n-tuples

$$(x_1, x_2, \ldots, x_n)$$

where each x_i is in B. The AND and OR operations are then extended to operate between corresponding pairs of elements in each n-tuple to produce another n-tuple; the NOT operation negates each item of an n-tuple.

The second common example of a Boolean algebra is the set of subsets of a given set S, with the operations of *intersection and *union replacing $\wedge$ and $\vee$ respectively; set *complement fills the role of Boolean algebra complement.

Boolean algebras, named for George Boole, the 19th-century English mathematician, are fundamental to many aspects of computing – logic design, logic itself, and aspects of algorithm design.

Boolean expression (logical expression) An expression in *Boolean algebra, i.e. a well-formed formula of Boolean vari-

idempotent laws:
$$x \vee x = x$$
$$x \wedge x = x$$

distributive laws:
$$x \wedge (y \vee z) = (x \wedge y) \vee (x \wedge z)$$
$$x \vee (y \wedge z) = (x \vee y) \wedge (x \vee z)$$

associative laws:
$$x \vee (y \vee z) = (x \vee y) \vee z$$
$$x \wedge (y \wedge z) = (x \wedge y) \wedge z$$

identity laws:
$$x \vee 0 = x$$
$$x \wedge 1 = x$$

commutative laws:
$$x \vee y = y \vee x$$
$$x \wedge y = y \wedge x$$

null laws:
$$x \vee 1 = 1$$
$$x \wedge 0 = 0$$

absorption laws:
$$x \vee (x \wedge y) = x$$
$$x \wedge (x \vee y) = x$$

complement laws:
$$x \vee x' = 1$$
$$x \wedge x' = 0$$

Laws of Boolean algebra

ables and constants linked by *Boolean operators. An example is
$$a \wedge (b \vee \neg c)$$
Any *combinational circuit can be modeled directly and completely by means of a Boolean expression, but this is not so of *sequential circuits.

Boolean function (logical function) A *function in *Boolean algebra. The function is written as an expression formed with binary variables (taking the value 0 or 1) combined by the dyadic and monadic operations of Boolean algebra, e.g.
$$f = (x \wedge y) \vee (x' \wedge z)$$
For any particular values of its constituent variables, the value of the function is either 0 or 1, depending on the combinations of values assigned to the variables. A Boolean function can be represented in a *truth table. It can also be transformed into a *logic diagram of logic gates.

Boolean matrix A two-dimensional *array in which each element is either TRUE or FALSE. *Compare* bit matrix.

Boolean operator (logical operator) Any one of the logical connectives of *Boolean expressions, i.e.
$$\neg \quad \wedge \quad \vee \quad \bar{\wedge} \quad \bar{\vee} \quad \equiv \quad \not\equiv$$
or, in another notation,

NOT AND OR NAND NOR
EQUIV XOR (or NEQUIV)

See also logic operation.

Boolean type (type Boolean; logical type) A *data type comprising the Boolean values TRUE and FALSE, with legal operations restricted to *logic operations.

Boolean value (logical value) Either of the two values TRUE and FALSE that indicate a truth value.

boot To invoke a *bootstrap process.

bootstrap In general, a means or technique for causing a system to build up from some simple preliminary instruction(s) or information. The preliminary instruction may be hardwired and called by the operation of a switch. The word is used in a number of contexts.

For example, a bootstrap can be a short program, usually held in nonvolatile memory, whose function is to load another longer program. When a computing system is first powered-on, the contents of its memory are in general undefined except for those parts that are fabricated from read-only memory or for the contents of nonvolatile memory. The bootstrap routine is stored in ROM and is capable of reading from backing store the complete operating system, which is loaded into the empty machine.

A bootstrap is also a method by which a compiler is transferred from one machine to another, and which depends on the compiler being written in the language it compiles. To transfer from machine A to machine B, given a compiler that runs on machine A, it is first necessary to make the compiler generate B's machine code. The source code of the compiler is then compiled by this modified compiler, so generating a version of the compiler for machine B. In practice it is usually necessary to recode some machine-dependent portions of the compiler by hand to complete the transfer.

The term originates from a story told by Baron Munchausen who boasted that finding himself trapped and sinking in a swamp, he lifted himself by the bootstraps and carried himself to safety on firm ground.

Bose–Chaudhuri–Hocquenghem codes (BCH codes) An important family of *binary *linear *error-correcting *block codes. They are reasonably efficient and have reasonably good error-correcting abilities, but their importance lies in their ease of encoding (by means of *shift registers) and of decoding. They can be regarded as a generalization of *Hamming codes, and as a special case of *Reed–Solomon codes. BCH codes can be arranged to be *cyclic.

BOT marker *Short for* beginning of tape marker. A physical feature of a magnetic tape by which the tape transport senses on the tape the start of the volume into which data can be recorded, or has been recorded. When the transport senses the marker it commences the logical sequence of recording or reading data. The marker may be, for example, a rectangular strip of reflective material adhering to the tape, a transparent part of the tape, or a hole in the tape, according to the type of tape and transport. The distance of the marker from the physical beginning of the tape allows the tape to be loaded, threaded through the transport, and wound on to a point at which data will be reliably recorded. This distance, and the form of the marker, are defined by the standard pertaining to the type of tape. *See also* EOT marker. *Compare* tape mark.

bottom-up development An approach to program development in which progress is made by composition of available elements, beginning with the primitive elements provided by the implementation language and ending when the desired program is reached. At each stage the available elements are employed in the construction of new elements that are more powerful in the context of the required program. These new elements will in turn be employed at the next stage in the construction of still more powerful elements, and so on until the available elements can be employed directly in the construction of the desired program.

In practice, "pure" bottom-up development is not possible; the construction of new elements must always be guided by a look-ahead to the requirements of the eventual program, and even then it will often be discovered at a later stage that some earlier construction sequence was inappropriate, leading to a need for iteration. *Compare* top-down development.

bottom-up parsing (shift-reduce parsing) A strategy for *parsing sentences of a *context-free grammar that attempts to construct a *parse tree beginning at the leaf nodes and working "bottom-up" toward the root.

Bottom-up (or shift-reduce) parsers work by "shifting" symbols onto a stack until the top of the stack contains a right-hand side of a production. The stack is then "reduced" by replacing the production's right-hand side by its left-hand side. This process continues until the string has been "reduced" to the start symbol of the *grammar.

The string of symbols to be replaced at each stage is called a *handle*. Bottom-up parsers that proceed from left to right in the input string must always replace the leftmost handle and, in so doing, they effectively construct a rightmost *derivation sequence in reverse order. For example, a rightmost derivation of the string *abcde* might be

$$S \Rightarrow ACD \Rightarrow ACde \Rightarrow$$
$$Acde \Rightarrow abcde$$

A bottom-up parser would construct this derivation in reverse, first reducing *abcde* to *Acde*, then to *ACde*, then to *ACD*, and finally to the start symbol *S*. The handle at each stage is respectively *ab*, *c*, *de*, and *ACD*.

See also LR parsing, precedence parsing.

boundary protection *See* bounds registers.

boundary-value problem *See* ordinary differential equations, partial differential equations.

bound occurrence *See* free variable.

bounds registers Two registers whose contents are used to denote an area of memory for which there is *access control. The area may be defined by beginning and ending addresses, or by the beginning address and the area length – in which case it is a *base-bound register. The use of bounds registers is a form of hardware security, and is some-

times known as *boundary protection*. *See also* memory protection.

Box–Jenkins forecasting techniques *See* time series.

Boyer–Moore algorithm (BM algorithm) A string search developed by R. Boyer and J. Moore in 1975. This search compares characters at the end of the pattern rather than at the beginning, until a match is found.

bpi *Abbrev. for* bits per inch.

bps *Abbrev. for* bits per second. *See also* bit rate.

bpt *Abbrev. for* bits per track.

branch 1. A *control structure in which one of two or more alternative sets of program statements is selected for execution. The selection is achieved during execution by means of a *branch instruction*; this instruction thus breaks the normal sequential program flow. (Branch instruction is usually regarded as synonymous with jump instruction.) *See also* jump, if then else statement, case statement, GOTO statement.
2. The set of instructions selected for execution as a result of a branch instruction.
3. To perform such a selection.

branch and bound algorithm An organized and highly structured search of all possible solutions to a problem. It is a general form of the *backtracking methods, and is used extensively in artificial intelligence and operations research.

branch instruction (jump instruction) *See* branch.

branch testing A test strategy seeking to choose test data values that lead to the testing of each *branch in a program at least once (branching occurring at each decision point). It is equivalent to finding a set of paths through the *control flow graph whose union covers all the arcs of the graph. Branch testing normally requires more tests than *statement testing but fewer than *path testing. *See also* test coverage.

breadboard An easily adapted *circuit board on which experimental arrangements of electronic components may be realized. Access to the individual components is simple and hence the overall arrangement may be readily modified. Breadboards are used mainly for the development of prototype circuit designs.

breadth-first search A technique of searching through a tree whereby all nodes in a tree at level k are searched before searching nodes at level $k + 1$. *Compare* depth-first search.

breakpoint *See* debugging.

bridge A device that interconnects two networks and whose presence is usually invisible to network users (as distinct from a *gateway, whose presence is generally visible). A bridge may link two effectively identical networks, where some physical or logical constraint means that a single larger network cannot be used; for example, a bridge may link together two *Ethernets, where the physical length of a single Ethernet would exceed the length limit. A bridge may also link two distinct types of network, using different signaling conventions; for example, a bridge may link together an Ethernet used within a building, and a *Cambridge Ring used between buildings on a single large site.

The terms bridge, gateway, and *relay are among those whose meanings vary between different communities of users at a given time, and within a given community at different times. *See also* filtering bridge.

bridgeware Any software or hardware that eases the transition from use of one computer system to use of another not entirely compatible one. Bridgeware is

normally supplied by a computer manufacturer when a new range of machines does not offer complete upward *compatibility from some previous range. Typically the bridgeware will permit programs developed for the previous range to be executed (perhaps after minor modifications) on the new range of machines.

broadband coaxial systems Communication systems that use *broadband networking techniques on coaxial cable. The 300 megahertz (MHz) bandwidth of a coaxial cable is divided into multiple channels through *frequency division multiplexing. The channels can transmit signals at different data rates, allowing diverse applications to share the cable by means of dedicated channels. Channel bandwidth may range from a few kilohertz to several megahertz. A single cable may carry both digital data and analog data (voice, television) simultaneously. Access to the cable is provided through radio-frequency *transceivers (modems) assigned to a particular channel. *Frequency-agile modems* may be used to communicate on different bands at different times.

There are two classifications of broadband coaxial systems. In a one-way system signals travel in only one direction in the cable. This kind of system is common in cable TV (CATV) systems. In a two-way system signals can travel in both directions on the cable. All traffic that originates from network nodes travels on the inbound channels to the *headend*. The headend is the origin of all traffic on the outbound channels, routing all messages on inbound channels to the proper outbound channel to reach their destination. Network nodes transmit messages on inbound channels and receive messages on outbound channels.

Two-way systems fall into *midsplit* or *subsplit* categories. Midsplit systems divide the cable bandwidth equally between inbound and outbound channels. Subsplit systems put inbound traffic in the 5 – 30 MHz bands and outbound traffic in the 54 – 100 kHz bands. This format is the easiest way to retrofit onto a one-way CATV system, and leaves the VHF TV channels on their normal "off-the-air" frequency assignments.

broadband networking 1. Communication using a modulated carrier (*see* modulation) to apply a data signal to a transmission medium in analog form. Multiple signals can be present simultaneously using *frequency division multiplexing. Different bandwidths may be allocated to different signals, and different kinds of traffic (digital data, analog voice, television) may be carried at the same time. *See also* broadband coaxial systems. *Compare* baseband networking.

2. A term sometimes used for wideband networking, i.e. networking with wideband channels (*see* bandwidth).

broadcasting A message-routing algorithm in which a *message is transmitted to all *nodes in a network. Some data-communication media, such as the *Ethernet, are inherently broadcast in nature. Address filtering is used to restrict the set of messages that any one host actually reads. The network service that delivers the message is known as *broadcast service* and is implemented using a special address, which all stations are prepared to accept. Other communication systems, such as the *ARPANET, may require that a copy of the message be separately addressed to each possible recipient in order to implement broadcasting.

Broadcasting may be used for a variety of purposes. For instance, to find the shortest path to a destination, a message can be broadcast to all intermediate nodes repeatedly until the destination node is reached. If path information is recorded as the message traverses the network, the same path can be used for future messages to the same destination node. As a second example, in local area networks with a tree-like topology, or in satellite communication links with multiple ground stations within a beam radius, broadcasting can be used to simplify addressing. This allows certain messages, such as request for a bootstrap, to be sent to all hosts with the expectation that at least one host will be able to satisfy the request. Thirdly, a broadcast message may be one that carries general information of potential interest to all nodes on the net.

A generalization of broadcasting is *multicasting*, in which special address flags are used to indicate that particular messages are of interest to particular classes of nodes, but not necessarily to all nodes on the net.

brother *Another name for* sibling.

browsing Searching through information often with intent to acquire unauthorized access to sensitive information. As such, browsing constitutes a *threat to a computer system.

BSC 1. *Abbrev. for* binary symmetric channel.
2. *Another abbrev. for* binary synchronous communications. *See* BISYNC.

BSI British Standards Institution, the body founded in 1901 to approve standards for a wide variety of products with a view to establishing minimum standards of quality and avoiding duplication in design, sizes, etc.

B-tree or **b-tree 1. (balanced multiway search tree)** of *degree n (≥ 2). A *multiway search tree of degree n in which the root node has degree ≥ 2, every nonterminal node other than the root has degree k,

$$\text{where } n/2 \leqslant k \leqslant n$$

and every leaf node occurs at the same level. Originally defined by R. Beyer and E. McCreight, the data structure provides an efficient dynamic retrieval device.

An extension to a B-tree is a B+ tree, which is used as a primary index to an *indexed file. It comprises two parts: a sequential index containing an entry for every record in the file; a B-tree acting as a multilevel index to the sequential index entries. B+ trees are used in *VSAM.

2. A binary tree with no nodes of degree one.

BTron *See* Tron.

bubble jet (thermal ink jet) A pulsed *ink jet printer in which the rapid displacement required to eject the ink drop is achieved by surface boiling of the ink within a tube.

bubble memory *See* magnetic bubble memory.

bubble sort (exchange selection) A form of *sorting by exchanging that simply interchanges pairs of elements that are out of order in a sequence of passes through the file, until no such pairs exist. The method is not competitive with *straight insertion.

bucket 1. A subdivision of a *data file, serving as the unit within which records are located. Buckets are specially used in connection with *hashing techniques, and with indexing techniques (*see* index) where index entries point to groups of records. In these circumstances, hashing or indexing will yield the address of the start of the bucket; the location for storage or retrieval within the bucket will then be found by searching.

2. A capacitor whose electric charge is used as a form of dynamic *RAM. A fully charged bucket, or *full* bucket, is equivalent to a logic 1; an uncharged or *empty* bucket is equivalent to a logic 0. The charge may be passed through an array of capacitors and associated electronics, which together form a *bucket brigade*.

bucket sort An external sort in which the records to be sorted are grouped in some way, and each group stored in a distinct *bucket. Different buckets will probably be stored on different storage devices. If searching is to be performed on the data, then each bucket should contain records with the same hash value (*see* hashing). In this way all the records that might contain the required key may be fetched from the external memory at once.

buddy system A method of implementing a *memory management system. The available memory is partitioned into blocks whose sizes are always exact powers of two. A request for m bytes of memory is satisfied by allocating a block of size 2^{p+1} where

$$2^p < m \leqslant 2^{p+1}$$

If no block of this size is available then a larger block is subdivided, more than once if necessary, until a block of the required system is generated. When memory is freed it is combined with a free adjacent block (if one exists) to produce a larger block, always preserving the condition that block sizes are exact powers of two.

buffer 1. A temporary memory for data, normally used to accommodate the difference in the rate at which two devices can handle data during a transfer. The buffer may be built into a peripheral device, such as a printer or disk drive, or may be part of the system's main memory. *See* buffering.

2. A means of maintaining a short but varying length of magnetic tape between the reels and the *capstan and head area of a tape transport, in order that the acceleration of the tape at the reels need not be as great as that of the tape at the capstan. There are two principal types of buffer: *tension arm* and *vacuum column*. In the first, the tape passes over a series of rollers, alternate rollers being fixed in position and the rest being attached to a sprung pivoted arm, so that a variable length of tape is taken up in the resulting loops; in the second, the tape is drawn by a difference of pressure into a chamber whose width is just that of the tape. Vacuum column transports are more expensive and noisier but can handle higher tape speeds.

Streaming tape transports and many types of cartridge drives do not use buffers and are therefore limited to lower accelerations of the tape in the area of the head and (if there is one) capstan.

3. Any circuit or device that is put between two others to smooth changes in rate or level or allow asynchronous operation. For example, line *drivers can be used to isolate (or buffer) two sets of data lines.

buffering A programming technique used to compensate for the slow and possibly erratic rate at which a peripheral device produces or consumes data. If the device communicates directly with the program, the program is constrained to run in synchronism with the device; buffering allows program and device to operate independently. Consider a program sending output to a slow device. A memory area (the *buffer) is set aside for communication: the program places data in the buffer at its own rate, while the device takes data from the buffer at its own rate. Although the device may be slow, the program does not have to stop unless the buffer fills up; at the same time the device runs at full speed unless the buffer empties. A similar technique is used for input. *See also* double buffering.

buffer register A storage location or device for the temporary storage of information during the process of writing to or reading from main memory. It generally has a capacity equivalent to one byte or one word.

bug An error in a program or system. The word is usually used to mean a localized implementation error rather than, say, an error introduced at the requirements or system-design stage. *See also* debugging.

bug seeding *See* seeding.

bulk memory *Another name for* backing store.

bulletin board A *teleconferencing system often run on a dedicated computer for use by enthusiasts who can connect their own microcomputers by means of *modems and telephone lines or network connections. The bulletin board allows its users to read messages left by previous users on a variety of topics, make contributions of their own, or *download programs for use on their own systems. This latter activity is one of those blamed for the spread of computer *viruses.

burn *Another term for* blow.

burster A mechanism for separating continuous fan-folded paper used in line printers and some page printers into separate sheets. Frequently it also performs the function of separating out interleaved carbon and sorting the multicopy output into sets. It may also trim the edges to remove the sprocket holes and the ragged edge left by the perforations between sheets. Generally this is done off-line but some versions can be linked directly to the output printer.

burst error (error burst) An error pattern, generally in a binary signal, that consists of known positions where the digit is in error ("first" and "last"), with the intervening positions possibly in error and possibly not. By implication, digits before the first error in the block and after the last error in the block are correct.

burst mode Usually, dedicated use of a multiplexer *channel for a single I/O device, thus permitting that device to operate at high (burst) speed.

bus A signal route to which several items of a computer system may be connected in parallel so that signals can be passed between them. A bus is also called a *trunk* in the US, and a *highway* in the UK. The signals on a bus may be only of a particular kind, as in an *address bus or *data bus, or they may be intermixed. To maximize throughput, the number of lines in the bus should equal the sum of the number of bits in a data word, the maximum address, and the number of control lines. As this is expensive to implement, a *multiplexed bus may be used.

There are a number of widely used proprietory bus systems, such as DEC's *Unibus and Intel's *Multibus. There is also a widely used instrumentation bus standard, referred to as *IEEE 488* or as *GPIB, general-purpose interface bus*; it is defined by ANSI/IEEE 488–1978. It was initially promoted by the Hewlett Packard company as *HP–IB*. For microprocessors there are a number of standardized bus systems, one of the most widely used being the VME bus.

busbar 1. A physical signal carrier that connects several parts of a computer system. The term is frequently contracted to *bus.

2. An electrical conductor that is usually substantial compared to its associated conductors and is common to several electrical loads and/or sources.

bused interface *Another name for* daisychain.

bus terminator An electrical circuit connected at the end of a bus to hold it at a predetermined signal level when it is not active, and also to ensure impedance matching and thus avoid unwanted reflections of signals. It is

often available as a single package for mounting onto a printed circuit board.

It is important to ensure that the electrical impedance of a bus carrying high-frequency signals does not have any abrupt changes. If the ends of the conductors are not terminated, the signals see an almost infinite impedance and are reflected back along the conductor. A fast switching circuit connected to an unterminated bus could detect both the signal and the reflection and so give rise to errors.

bus topology *See* network architecture.

busy signal A signal from a device indicating that it cannot accept any new commands or data for the time being. *Compare* ready signal.

byte A subdivision of a *word in a machine, now almost always comprising eight bits. *Compare* character.

byte machine *See* variable word length computer.

C

C A programming language originally developed for implementation of the *UNIX operating system. C is the preferred language for systems software development in the UNIX environment, and is widely used on microcomputers. It combines the control and data structures of a modern high-level language with the ability to address the machine hardware at a level more usually associated with assembly language. The terse syntax is attractive to professional programmers, and the compilers generate very efficient object code. C is derived from *BCPL, via a short-lived predecessor *B. *See also* Turbo languages.

C++ A programming language derived from *C. C++ is a superset of C that adds type checking, operator overloading, abstract data types, and classes to the original language. It thus combines the power of *object-oriented programming with the efficiency and notational convenience of C.

cache (cache memory) A type of memory that is used in high-performance systems, inserted between the processor and memory proper. The *memory hierarchy on a system contains registers in the processor, which are the highest-speed storage, and, at a slightly lower level of accessibility, the contents of the main memory. The cache is intended to reduce the discrepancy in accessibility between these two types of unit, and functions by holding small regions that map the contents of main memory. The formal behavior of the cache corresponds closely to that of the *working set in a *paging system.

Some magnetic disk *controllers have a cache. The working of the cache is not visible to the main CPU, but again provides a mapping of the current contents of part of the disk units in order to provide improved performance.

Some magnetic tape units have built-in cache memory. In this case the aim is to allow a *streaming tape transport to emulate the behavior of a (more expensive) start-stop unit so that it can be attached to a system designed to support only the latter without substantial software modification. The arrangement was introduced by Cipher in the early 1980s.

CAD *Abbrev. for* computer-aided design.

CADCAM *See* computer-aided design.

caddy A form of *cartridge used specifically for *CD-ROM optical disks. Unlike most cartridges, the operator can readily remove the disk and replace it with another.

CADMAT *See* computer-aided design.

CAFS *Abbrev. for* content-addressable file system. A development by ICL of *associative memory.

CAIS *Acronym for* common *APSE interface set. A US Department of Defense standard for a *PTI. It is now superseded by CAIS-A.

CAL *Abbrev. for* computer-assisted learning.

calculator A device, now usually electronic, by means of which arithmetic operations can be performed on numbers entered from a keyboard. Final solutions and intermediate numbers are generally presented on *LCD or *LED displays. Present-day calculators range from very cheap simple devices capable of performing the basic arithmetic operations to those whose capabilities extend to sophisticated mathematical and statistical manipulation and that may be programmed with large numbers of steps. Add-on memory modules containing sets of specialist programs for particular fields – engineering, navigation, or business for example – may be purchased as accessories to the more expensive calculators, as can small printers.

The dividing line between sophisticated calculators and small microcomputers is becoming less clear-cut; there are significant overlaps in both price and power.

call To transfer control to a *subroutine or *procedure, with provision for return to the instruction following the call at the end of execution of the subroutine/procedure.

call by name *See* parameter passing.

call by reference (call by address) *See* parameter passing.

call by value *See* parameter passing.

calling sequence The code sequence required to effect transfer of control to a subroutine or procedure, including *parameter passing and the recording of the return address. Uniformity of calling sequences is vital if it is required to call procedures written in a different language from the calling program.

call instruction An instruction that saves the contents of the *program counter before branching to a *subroutine or *procedure. *Compare* return instruction.

CAM *Abbrev. for* **1.** computer-aided manufacturing, **2.** content-addressable memory, **3.** cellular automata machine.

CAMAC A standardized multiplexing intermediate interface. It does not usually connect directly to a processor or a peripheral, but provides a standardized interface to which a number of *peripheral interface adapters and a single computer interface controller can be connected.

The peripheral adapters may each have different functions, e.g. digital to analog converter, level changers, parallel to serial converter, and thus have different interfaces facing outward from the CAMAC. Similarly the controller module connects to the CAMAC interface but the outward-facing interface can be chosen to suit the available computer. The name CAMAC was chosen to symbolize this characteristic of looking the same from either direction. The adapters are typically a single printed circuit card that plugs into the internal 86-way connector. The outward-facing connections are usually mounted on a panel attached to the circuit card or may be made via a second connector mounted above the 86-way CAMAC connection. The interface is widely used for connecting instruments and transducers to computers.

CAMAC was proposed as a standard by the UK Atomic Energy Authority and further development and documentation was done by the European Standards of Nuclear Electronics (ESONE) and the Nuclear Instrument Module Committee of USA. The parallel interface is documented in IEC-522 and the modular construction is in IEC-516.

Cambridge Ring A pioneering high-speed *local area network, originally developed at Cambridge University, UK, and now marketed as a commercial product. The Cambridge Ring uses a *minipacket* of 40 bits: 16 bits hold 2 bytes of data, two groups of 8 bits specify the addresses of the source and destination nodes, and the remaining 8 bits are used for control purposes. A master station controls the inter-bit time and the gap between packets, so that the ring circulates an exact number of packets and gaps. Each packet contains a single-bit indicator as to whether it is full (i.e. the packet contains useful data) or empty (i.e. the packet data has been received by the destination node, and the packet has completed a circuit of the ring back to the original source node). The Cambridge Ring is thus an example of an "empty slot" ring. *See also* token ring.

cancellation The loss of significant digits in subtracting two approximately equal numbers. This is a frequent cause of poor accuracy in numerical results but it can usually be avoided by some reorganization of the calculation. Consider, for example, the quadratic equation

$$ax^2 + bx + c = 0$$

The formula for the roots of a quadratic is

$$(-b \pm \sqrt{(b^2 - 4ac)})/2a$$

If b^2 is large compared with $4|ac|$ severe cancellation occurs in one of the roots. This root can be computed from the fact that the product of the roots is c/a.

capability architecture An architecture that extends across both the hardware and the (operating system) software of a computer system. It is intended to provide better protection features to facilitate both multiprocessing and computer security. In this form of architecture there are two types of words in memory: data (including programs) and *capabilities*. Capabilities can only be manipulated by privileged portions of the system. The capability descriptor tells where data is and what sorts of access to that data are permitted.

Examples of systems with capability architecture are the Plessey 250 and the Cambridge CAP. *Object-oriented architecture is an extension of this concept.

capability list The list of permitted operations that a subject can perform on an object. *See* object-oriented architecture, capability architecture.

capacity 1. The amount of information that can be held in a storage device. The amount may be measured in words, bytes, bits, or characters.

2. The maximum range of values that can be held in a register.

3. of a transmission channel. *See* channel coding theorem.

capstan The component of a tape transport that transmits motion (sometimes indirectly) to the magnetic tape and controls the speed of its motion past the head; the motion of the tape reels is usually separately controlled. *Streaming tape transports often have no capstan.

CAR The *LISP function that when applied to a list yields the *head of the list. The word was originally an acronym for contents of address register. *Compare* CDR.

card *See* punched card, magnetic card, chip card, expansion card.

card cage A framework in which *circuit boards can be mounted. It comprises channels into which the boards can be slid and sockets and wiring by means of which they are interconnected.

cardinality A measure of the size of a *set. Two sets S and T have the same cardinality if there is a *bijection from one to the other. S and T are said to be *equipotent*, often written as $S \sim T$. If the set S is finite, then the cardinality of S is the number of elements in the set. For an infinite set S, the idea of "number" of elements no longer suffices. An important fact, discovered by Cantor, is that not all infinite sets have the same cardinality. The two most important "grades" of infinite set can be illustrated as follows.

If S is equipotent to the set of natural numbers
$$\{1,2,3,\dots\}$$
then S is said to have cardinality $\aleph_0$ (a symbol called *aleph null*).

If S is equipotent to the set of real numbers then S is said to have cardinality $\mathbf{C}$, or cardinality of the *continuum*. It can be shown that in some sense
$$\mathbf{C} = 2^{\aleph_0}$$
since the real numbers can be put in bijective correspondence with the set of all subsets of natural numbers.

card punch A machine used to punch a pattern of holes in a card. The pattern has a coded relationship to the data that has been passed to the machine from another data-processing machine or an operator at a keyboard.

card reader A machine that senses the data encoded on a card and translates it into binary code that can be transmitted for further processing (*see also* magnetic card, chip card, punched card).

The *magnetic card reader* can have a power-driven transport that will draw the card into the machine and move it past the read head. In some designs there are cleaning brushes before the read head. The direction of travel is reversed after the card has been read and thus the card is returned to the operator. In designs used with automatic cash dispensers, the direction of travel may not reverse if the card and/or the associated identification number are not valid.

A *slot reader* is a relatively simple device for reading badges or plastic cards. The badge or card is manually moved along a slot that guides it past a sensing station. The data to be read may be encoded magnetically or printed in *bar code or a machine-readable font. Since the rate of movement past the read head is not controlled by the device, the sensing head and electronics are generally designed to work over a range of speeds. Compared to a reader with a powered transport the device is much cheaper and quicker. Some designs for use with bank teller terminals can read the printed encoding on checks and the magnetic encoding on plastic cards.

The *chip card reader* has a guide and a connector that engages contacts on the card. When the machine senses that the card is in place and the related code has been keyed in, the memory device embedded in the card can be read.

See also punched card reader.

carriage-control tape *See* vertical format unit.

carriage return (CR) A control code that is used to affect the format of printed or displayed output. It indicates that the next data character is to appear in the leftmost position on a line. In some serial printers, the CR code may cause a physical movement of the printing carriage to the leftmost print position. In other types of printer the characters will be correctly positioned on the line although they may be printed in some other sequence or even simultaneously.

carrier 1. *See* modulation.

2. of an algebra. *See* signature.

carrier sense multiple access (CSMA), CSMA with collision detection *See* CSMA/CD.

carry lookahead A method that is used in multibit *parallel adders whereby an individual element in the adder can detect when the immediately preceding stage of the adder is about to generate a carry as the result of the addition of the next least significant bits in the addend and augend. The logic required to generate the carry lookahead signal is available in integrated-circuit form.

Carry lookahead affords a considerable improvement in performance over, say, ripple-carry *adders since the carry is generated in parallel at all stages of addition rather than sequentially, as in the ripple adder. Adders using the lookahead technique are thus often called high-speed adders.

Cartesian product of two *sets S and T. The set of all *ordered pairs of the form (s,t) with the property that s is a member of S and t is a member of T; this is usually written as $S \times T$. Formally,

$$S \times T = \{(s,t)|(s \in S) \text{ and } (t \in T)\}$$

If R denotes the set of real numbers, then $R \times R$ is just the set of points in the (Cartesian) plane or it can be regarded as the set of complex numbers, hence the name.

The concept can be extended to deal with the Cartesian product of n sets,

$$S_1, S_2, \ldots, S_n$$

This is the set of ordered n-tuples

$$(s_1, s_2, \ldots, s_n)$$

with the property that each s_i is in S_i. In the case where each S_i is the same set S, it is customary to write S^n for

$$S \times S \times \ldots S \ (n \text{ terms})$$

Cartesian structure Any data structure where the number of elements is fixed and linearly ordered. The term is sometimes used as a synonym for *record.

cartridge A container used to protect and facilitate the use of various computer-related media such as *magnetic tape, *magnetic disk, *optical disk, integrated circuitry, or printer ink *ribbon. It is usually designed so that the medium remains permanently within the cartridge or at least attached to it, and the medium itself is not touched by an operator. *See* magnetic tape cartridge, disk cartridge, ROM cartridge, caddy.

cartridge drive Either a tape transport for handling cartridge tape, or a disk drive for handling disk cartridges.

cartridge tape Tape carried in a *magnetic tape cartridge.

cascadable counter An individual counter element, usually containing a number of *flip-flops in a chain of such elements. Each element has facilities for a count input and is capable of generating an overflow (or carry) output. The counter elements may typically have count lengths of integer powers of 2 (binary counters) or integer powers of 10 (decimal counters). Cascading a counter that has a count length of 4 with one having a count length of 10 will give a counter that has a count length of 40.

Since cascadable counters are available as integrated-circuit blocks or modules, cascadable counters are also called *modular counters. See also* counter.

cascade sort A method of *sorting that is similar to the *polyphase merge sort. Given n ($n > 1$) *key sequences, or files, the sort works as follows. Files 1 to ($n - 1$) are merged onto file n until file ($n - 1$) is exhausted. Then files 1 to ($n - 2$) are merged and the process repeated until there is one unmerged file. The next pass then merges files 2 to n to file 1, and so on.

CASE *Acronym for* computer-assisted software (or system) engineering. A marketing term, generally describing a programming support environment (*PSE) that supports a single method and provides a set of *software tools that supports the method. The term can some-

times be used synonymously with *IPSE (particularly first generation IPSE).

case statement A conditional *control structure that appears in several programming languages, including Pascal and Ada, and allows a selection to be made between several sets of program statements; the choice is dependent on the value of some expression. The case statement is a more general structure than the *if then else statement, which allows a choice between only two sets of statements.

cassette *Nominally another name for* cartridge; in practice the term is normally reserved for the type of cassette originally introduced by Philips for audio purposes under the trademark *Compact Cassette*. Home computers often provide for the use of a consumer-type audio cassette player and use ordinary audio cassettes; for professional use more robust drives and higher precision cassettes are available.

The digital audio tape cartridge (*see* helical scan) is sometimes referred to as a cassette.

cassette drive A tape transport for handling magnetic tape contained in *cassettes. *See* magnetic tape cartridge.

CAT *Abbrev. for* computer-aided testing.

catastrophic code A *convolutional code that is prone to *catastrophic error propagation*, i.e. a situation in which a finite number of *channel errors causes an infinite number of decoder errors. Any given convolutional code is or is not a catastrophic code.

catastrophic error propagation *See* catastrophic code.

category A collection of *objects A*, together with a related set of *morphisms M*. An object is a generalization of a *set and a morphism is a generalization of a *function that maps between sets.

The set M is the *disjoint *union of sets of the form $[A,B]$, where A and B are elements of A; if α is a member of $[A,B]$, A is the *domain* of α, B is the *codomain* of α, and α is said to be a morphism from A to B. For each triple (A,B,C) of elements of A there is a *dyadic operation $\circ$ from the *Cartesian product

$$[B,C] \times [A,B]$$

to $[A,C]$. The image $\beta \circ \alpha$ of the ordered pair (β, α) is the *composition* of β with α; the composition operation is *associative. In addition, when the composition is defined there is an *identity* morphism for each A in A.

Examples of categories include the set of *groups and *homomorphisms on groups, and the set of *rings and homomorphisms on rings. *See* functor.

cathode-ray tube (CRT) An electronic display device in which an electrical signal is used to modulate one or more well-defined and controllable beams of electrons; in a color CRT three electron beams are used. The electron beam or beams are directed onto a target surface, usually a phosphorescent screen, the controlled movement and intensity of the beam(s) producing a visible display, or sometimes a display that must be detected other than by eye. *See also* oscilloscope, storage oscilloscope.

CAV *Abbrev. for* constant angular velocity. Denoting or involving a disk that rotates at a steady speed. This is the mode of operation used for magnetic disks and some optical disks. *Compare* CLV, MCAV, MCLV.

Cayley table (composition table; operation table) A tabular means of describing a finite *group, first used by the 19th-century mathematician Arthur Cayley. To illustrate, the set

$$\{1, -1, i, -i\}$$

forms a group under the *dyadic operation $\circ$ as described by the Cayley table shown in the diagram. The value of -1

	right operand			
$\circ$	1	-1	i	$-i$
1	1	-1	i	$-i$
-1	-1	1	$-i$	i
i	i	$-i$	-1	1
$-i$	$-i$	i	1	-1

Cayley table

$\circ$ i, for example, is $-i$. The name composition table is usually used when the group operation is *composition of functions.

CBL *Abbrev. for* computer-based learning. *See* computer-assisted learning.

CCD, CCD memory *See* charge-coupled device.

CCITT Comité Consultatif Internationale de Télégraphique et Téléphonique (International Telegraph and Telephone Consultative Committee), an agency of the International Telecommunication Union (ITU), itself an agency of the UN. The CCITT provides worldwide coordination for telephone and data communication systems. Its technical recommendations often become internationally recognized standards. *See* V-series, X-series.

The CCITT has the following five classes of members. Class A: national telecommunication administrations such as the *FCC in the US and *PTTs in Europe; class B: recognized private administrations such as AT&T; class C: scientific and industrial organizations; class D: international organizations such as the *ISO; class E: organizations whose primary purpose is in another field, but with some interest in CCITT work. Only the first two classes vote.

CCS *Abbrev. for* calculus of communicating systems. A mathematical treatment of the general theory of *concurrency and *synchronization derived by R. J. Milner.

CCTA Central Computer and Telecommunications Agency, a UK government body that establishes, monitors, and applies standards and acts as a procurement agent on behalf of central government departments in specifying and purchasing computing systems for nonmilitary applications. The agency can provide both legal and technical assistance to its clients.

CDC Control Data Corporation, a long-established manufacturer of mainframe computers with a scientific and engineering bias, and also a force in the *supercomputer field; a subsidiary company produces the ETA 10 range of supercomputers.

CD-I A variant of the *CD-ROM read-only optical disk that supports sound and image as well as data. It is intended primarily for home and educational use, and the standard defines the system on which it is used as well as the disk itself, but it may nevertheless be useful in some computer systems.

CD-PROM A rewritable version of the *CD-ROM optical disk.

CDR The *LISP function that when applied to a list yields the *tail of the list. The word was originally an acronym for contents of decrement register. *Compare* CAR.

CD-ROM The predominant form of *read-only (ROM) optical disk. Both disk and drive are based on the Compact Audio consumer product. The disk is 120 mm in diameter, single-sided, and holds up to 600 megabytes of data. The data is encoded in the form of a spiral of minute bumps impressed into the surface of the disk at the time of manufacture, and cannot subsequently be altered. Many commercial databases are now available on CD-ROM, often as an alternative to an on-line service. *See also* CD-I, CD-PROM, DVI, High Sierra.

Ceefax *Trademark* One of the UK's two *teletext systems. Operated by the British Broadcasting Corporation (BBC), the service also provides for free *downloading of *telesoftware via a suitable adapter to several types of computer.

cell An address, a location in memory, or a register, usually one capable of holding a binary number. It is sometimes a location capable of holding one bit.

cellar *Another name for* stack, rarely used.

cellular automata machine (CAM) A *multiprocessor machine based on an array of *cellular automata*. Each automaton is usually a simple processor capable of simple computational tasks. In a normal architecture, each of these processing nodes can interchange data only with its immediate neighbors and all processing nodes carry out the same computational operation. Although the operations available at each node are quite simple, the aggregated effect of many such nodes can exhibit complex behavior and can rapidly model quite complex dynamic systems.

CEN/CENELEC *Acronyms for* Comité européen normalisation (CEN) and Comité européen normalisation électrotechnique (CENELEC). The official standards bodies of the European Economic Community. CEN/CENELEC adopts existing national or international standards or develops new standards that apply throughout the Community, including those for computing. Through CEN/CENELEC the Commission of the European Communities (CEC) is establishing European Standards. These will eventually replace existing national standards, although many national and international standards are being adopted as European Standards.

central processor (CPU; central processing unit) The principal operating part of a computer. It is usually defined as the *arithmetic and logic unit (ALU) and the *control unit (CU). It must be joined to a *primary memory to form the processor-memory pair of the basic *von Neumann machine.

Centronics interface A de facto standard plug-compatible *parallel interface for printers, first used in printers manufactured by Centronics Corp.

certification 1. A formal demonstration that a system or component complies with its specified requirements and is acceptable for operational use.
2. A written guarantee to this effect.
See also quality management system, conformance testing.

CGA *Abbrev. for* color graphics adapter. A general-purpose *graphics adapter used in IBM-compatible PCs, now largely superseded by more sophisticated units. It can generate a 320 × 200 four-color screen and a 640 × 200 two-color screen. The CGA uses a multibit-per-pixel (mbp) display memory: the four-color system uses two bits per pixel, the two-color system uses one bit per pixel (*see* bit mapping). Only one graphics page is available. *See also* MCGA, EGA, VGA.

CGI *Abbrev. for* computer graphics interface. A device-independent *interface between a graphical input or output device and a graphics utility program. There is an *ISO CGI standard in preparation that should be published by the end of 1990 but some similar interfaces developed by major software companies are already well established in the market.
The initial (*ANSI) name of the interface was *VDI* (*abbrev. for* virtual device interface).

CGM *Abbrev. for* computer graphics metafile. A standardized file format for transmission of pictures. It is widely used as the file format for personal computer drawing programs and is an acceptable form of graphic input to desktop publishing systems.

chad The piece of material that is removed when a hole is punched in a data medium. The preparation of punched cards and tape produces large volumes of chad. The punching of the tractor holes in continuous form paper also produces chad. If the pieces are not cleanly removed they can cause errors. Line printers are often fitted with chad traps to prevent chad from falling between the ribbon and the paper and causing loss of data on the top copy.

chain 1. A *singly linked linear *list.
2. *See* directed set.

chain code 1. A method of describing contours by a succession (chain) of symbols representing a discrete set of directional vectors. It is used in computer graphics and pattern recognition for description of line drawings (including characters).
2. *Another name* (*chiefly UK*) *for* simplex code.

chained file A file that uses *data chaining.

chained list *Another name for* linked list.

chaining An extension of *pipelining in which the results of the operations are used in the operations that follow within the next clock cycle.

chaining search A search in which each item contains the means for locating the next.

chain printer A type of *solid-font *line printer in which the font is etched or engraved on small plates that are linked together to form a chain. The chain is connected around two sprocket wheels so that the straight part of the chain between the wheels runs parallel to the paper and spans the line to be printed. This was one of the first types of computer printer to use the *hit-on-the-fly* principle, developed in the mid-1950s: the chain carrying the type font moves continuously at high speed relative to the paper, and the characters are printed by impacting the paper and an inked ribbon against the moving type font with an electrically operated hammer. The duration of the impact is measured in microseconds and the smear due to the movement of the font is very slight in a well-adjusted machine. The timing of the impact is achieved via detectors that sense index marks on the rotating chain.

Early machines had speeds of 150 lpm, adequate for the input/output rates of the time. IBM was the major promoter of chain printers. By the early 1960s speeds of 600 lpm were achieved when printing alphanumerics, and a speed of over 1200 lpm could be achieved if the repertoire was limited to a numeric and symbols set of 16 characters.

The problems associated with guiding the chain in a horizontal plane, maintaining precise position relative to the timing marks, and achieving very short impact times led to the development of the *train printer, which superseded the chain printer. *See also* band printer.

change dump (differential dump) An output, usually printed, that lists the content of all memory locations that have changed subsequent to a defined event. This is usually the result of a routine that is written and used as an aid to debugging a program.

channel 1. A specialized processor that comprises an information route and associated circuitry to control input and/or output operations. It normally provides for formatting and buffering

and has the necessary control to meet the timing requirements of an I/O device. In an interface that has a number of parallel channels, each is usually separately dedicated to the passing of a single type of information such as data.

Several different I/O devices may be connected to one channel and the control circuitry within the channel directs the data streams to or from the appropriate device. If the I/O devices have a relatively slow data rate, e.g. line printers, displays, document readers, then a *multiplexer channel* is used to connect them to the processor. The transfers to or from the separate devices are multiplexed, i.e. interleaved, character by character, such that several devices can work simultaneously.

When a number of devices with high data rates, e.g. magnetic disk and tape, are to be connected, a *selector channel* is used. This will transfer a complete record to or from a device before reselecting. Usually the selection of a device remains stable for the passage of more than one record. While the selector channel is dealing with one device, the other devices connected to it cannot transfer information but they may still be active, e.g. in a search or rewind mode.

A channel is often a *wired-program processor. As channels have become more elaborate they have tended to become programmed computers (*I/O processors*) in themselves. *See also* peripheral processor.

2. (transmission channel; communication channel) An information route in data transmission. *See also* Shannon's model.

3. A link (physical or virtual) to a *host computer in a communication network.

4. One of the longitudinal rows in which holes may be punched in paper tape. In addition to its use as a data input/output medium, punched tape was widely used in *vertical format units for controlling the format of printer output. Although the paper loop has been replaced by binary information in a memory, the term channel is sometimes still used to refer to the equivalent electronic signal.

channel capacity *See* channel coding theorem.

channel coding The use of *error-detecting or *error-correcting codes in order to achieve reliable communication through a transmission *channel. In channel coding, the particular *code to be used is chosen to match the channel (and especially its *noise characteristics), rather than the source of the information. *See* channel coding theorem, Shannon's model. *Compare* source coding.

channel coding theorem In *communication theory, the statement that any channel, however affected by *noise, possesses a specific *channel capacity* – a rate of conveying *information that can never be exceeded without error, but that can, in principle, always be attained with an arbitrarily small probability of error. The theorem was first expounded and proved by Claude Elwood Shannon in 1948.

Shannon showed that an *error-correcting code always exists that will reduce the probability of error below any predetermined level. He did not, however, show how to construct such a code (this remains the central problem of *coding theory), although he did show that randomly chosen codes are as good as any others, provided they are extremely long.

Among Shannon's results for specific channels, the most celebrated is that for a *power-limited continuous-amplitude channel subject to *white *Gaussian noise. If the signal power is limited to P_S and the noise power is P_N, the capacity of such a channel is

$$C = \tfrac{1}{2}\nu \log_2(1 + P_S/P_N) \text{ bit/s}$$

If it is a discrete-time channel, ν is the number of *epochs per second; if it is a continuous-time channel, ν is the minimum number of samples per second necessary to acquire all the information from the channel. In the latter case, if ν is to be finite, the channel must be *band-limited; if W is its *bandwidth (in Hz), then, by *Nyquist's criterion,

$$C = W \log_2(1 + P_S/P_N) \text{ bit/s}$$

This is sometimes called the *Shannon–Hartley law*, and is often applied, erroneously, in circumstances less restricted than those described. This and other expressions for the capacity of specific channels should not be confused with the channel coding theorem, which states only that there is a finite capacity (which may be zero) and that it can be attained without error.

See also Shannon's model, source coding theorem.

channel controller The control unit for an I/O *channel. *See also* I/O processor.

channel error An error, in a signal arriving at the *decoder in a communication system, whose occurrence is due to *noise in the channel. By contrast, a *decoder error* is an unsuccessful attempt by the decoder (of an *error-correcting code) to correct a channel error.

channel switching 1. A means of communicating on or switching between several different communication channels.
2. *Another name for* circuit switching.

channel time response *See* convolution.

CHAPSE *Acronym for* CHILL/Ada programming support environment. A proposed *PSE that would be applicable to both *CHILL and *Ada program development.

character 1. An element of a given *character set.
2. A subdivision of a *word in a machine, usually comprising six, seven,

or eight bits. This is sometimes called a *byte*.

3. The smallest unit of information in a *record.

character encoding An encoding, normally a *binary encoding, of a given *character set. Examples include ASCII and EBCDIC.

characteristic (biased exponent) *See* floating-point notation.

characteristic function of a *subset S of a *universal set U. A *function that indicates whether or not an element is a member of the subset S. It is the function

$$f : U \to \{0,1\}$$

defined as follows:

$$f(x) = 1 \quad \text{if } x \in S$$
$$f(x) = 0 \quad \text{if } x \notin S$$

The codomain might also be given as {true,false} or {1,2}.

characteristic vector 1. A *vector of bits representing a set in a finite universe. If the universe has n elements $a_1, a_2, \ldots, a_n$ then any set, A, can be represented by a vector of n bits where the ith bit is 1 if and only if $a_i \in A$.

2. *English form of* eigenvector. *See* eigenvalue.

character machine *See* variable word length computer.

character printer A *serial printer, generally a *solid-font printer.

character recognition A process in which a machine senses and encodes printed characters that are also readable by a person. The characters may be printed using a special magnetic ink and/or a special style of character, but modern machines can read good-quality typewritten or equivalent standard of print, in a variety of type fonts. *See* MICR, OCR, ICR.

character representation A representation of a character as a distinctive bit string that is defined by some *character encoding.

special characters	operation characters
space	+ −
, ; : . ? !	* /
( ) [ ] { }	> = <
$ % # & @ ~	
| \ " ' ↑ →	

Character set

character set 1. The set of characters that is handled by a specified machine. The set usually includes the English *alphanumeric characters, special characters, and operation characters (*see* table), all of which are *graphic characters*, and various *control characters*. Graphic characters thus denote a printed mark or a space while control characters produce some particular effect.

Two of the widest used character sets are *ASCII (American standard code for information interchange) and *EBCDIC (extended binary coded decimal interchange code). EBCDIC is used primarily on IBM machines while ASCII, introduced in 1963, is in more general use.

2. The set of characters that is valid within a given programming language.

character string A string of elements from a given *character set.

character type (type character) A *data type whose members can take the values of specified *characters and can be operated on by character operations, such as *concatenation. *See also* ASCII.

charge-coupled device (CCD) A semiconductor device that has the structure of a *MOSFET with an extremely long channel and many gates, perhaps 1000, closely spaced between the source and drain electrodes. A MOS capacitor is formed between each gate and the substrate; since this capacitor is capable of storing a charge, CCDs can be used as memory devices. The CCD essentially acts as a long (high-density) *shift register since, by manipulating the voltages applied to the gates, charge can be transferred from one MOS capacitor to its neighbor, and so on along the channel.

The physical structure of the device and the way in which the gate voltages are manipulated determines the number of gates needed to store one bit of information, typically two or three gates being required. Since the stored charge leaks away, CCDs must be continuously clocked, typically at a frequency of one megahertz.

Charge-coupled memories are particularly suited to applications where memory contents are accessed in a serial manner, as in *refresh memories for CRT terminals. They are slower than comparable RAMs but faster than magnetic backing store.

chassis In general, a mechanical system that is designed to provide a supporting and/or enclosing medium for an item of electronic equipment. The system may be equipped with supporting structures to carry standard-sized *circuit boards in addition to a *mother board or *backplane into which the boards are inserted and connected via sockets. Alternatively the individual components may be hardwired onto tag strips attached to the chassis.

For safety reasons the metal parts of a chassis should be permanently connected to a local zero-voltage reference or ground. In some equipment, however, it is more convenient (but potentially dangerous) to connect the chassis to one side of the a.c. or d.c. line (mains) supply; the equipment is then said to have a *hot chassis*. The chassis may also be left unconnected or floating.

CHDL *Abbrev. for* computer hardware description language. A formal language with a lexicon that enables the nomination of the individual logical or physical elements of a computer. It has a syntax to enable a description of the way such elements are interconnected and the way they behave to provide the structure that is capable of performing a computation. The behavior of these elements is described as the sequence in which they change their state to enable the structure to perform the function. Several CHDLs have been proposed, including *VHDL. *See also* register transfer language, ISP, CONLAN.

Chebyshev approximation, norm *See* approximation theory.

check Some means or process of validating the accuracy of a segment of data, the result of a computation, or completion of a successful message transmission (across a network or to an I/O device). *See also* error detection and correction.

check character A character, or more generally some element of specified size ranging from a single bit to a few bytes, that contains the result of a check computation performed on a segment of data. *See also* error detection and correction.

check digit *Another name for* check character.

checking program A program that examines other programs or data for certain classes of error, usually relatively straightforward ones such as syntax errors in the source text of a program.

checkout All activities concerned with bringing a program to the state where it produces some results (as distinct from, say, failing to compile or terminating abnormally) so that *testing can begin. Such activities might include *desk checking*, i.e. checking by human inspection, and use of a special "checkout" mode of compilation and execution that provides extensive information on erroneous use of the programming language or abnormal program termination.

checkpoint A point in a process or job at which a *dump check is taken (and hence also referred to as a *dump point*), and the point from which a subsequent *restart will be effective.

checksum (modulo-n check, residue check) A simple error detection method that operates on some set of information (usually data or program). If this information is in units that are m bits wide, a sum is taken modulo n, where $n = 2^m$, and appended to the information. At a later time or different location the check may be recomputed and most simple (all single) bit errors will be detected. A *parity check is the simplest version of this check with $m = 1$ and $n = 2$. *See also* error detection and correction, cyclic redundancy check.

chief programmer team A programming team in which responsibility for program design and implementation rests entirely with one highly skilled member, the *chief programmer*. The other team members provide various forms of support. A typical team could consist of the chief programmer, a backup programmer, librarian, administrator, and secretary: the backup programmer assists the chief programmer and is able to take over that role if necessary; the librarian maintains all technical documents on the project, such as design documents, source modules (in all versions), and test histories; the administrator relieves the chief programmer of all administra-

tive duties on the project. Various other services might be obtained from outside the team as needed.

This team organization has been advocated for the production of large programs: a single highly skilled programmer, when properly supported, can produce programs more quickly and more reliably than a team of less talented programmers working as equals. In particular, the problem of communication within the team is minimized.

The approach was pioneered in the early 1970s by the Federal Systems Division of IBM, particularly by Harlan D. Mills. Successful results have been reported from various projects, including some that produced more than 100 000 lines of source code.

child Any node in a *tree, except the root. Every child thus has a *parent.

CHILL A programming language developed by CCITT and adopted as the standard language for the programming of computer-based telecommunication systems and computer-controlled telephone exchanges. CHILL is a *real-time language, bearing a substantial resemblance to *Ada.

Chinese remainder theorem Let
$$m_1, m_2, \ldots, m_r$$
be positive integers that are relatively prime to one another, and let their product be m:
$$m = m_1 m_2 \ldots m_r$$
Let $n, u_1, u_2, \ldots, u_r$ be integers; then there is exactly one integer, u, that satisfies
$$n \leqslant u < (m + n)$$
and
$$u \equiv u_j \text{ (modulo } m_j) \text{ for } 1 \leqslant j \leqslant r$$

chip 1. A small section of a single crystal of *semiconductor, usually silicon, that forms the substrate upon which is fabricated a single semiconductor device or all the individual devices comprising an *integrated circuit.

2. *Informal name for* integrated circuit.

chip card A plastic card similar to a credit card but having some memory and a microprocessor (or specialized logic) embedded within it. It is thought to require a very much higher level of technical competance before fraud or forgery can be achieved. In addition to its use in funds transfer it is also proposed for use in connection with medical treatment. The first cards and associated equipment to be produced commercially were made in Europe by Siemens, Philips, and CII Honeywell Bull; trials were carried out in 1982. The CII Honeywell Bull card contains a variant of the Motorola 6805 microcomputer and up to 8K of *EPROM. *See also* card reader.

chip set A set of integrated circuits that when connected together form a single functional block within an electronic system.

chip socket A device that allows easy replacement of chips (*integrated circuits) on a *printed circuit board. The chip socket is soldered to the circuit board; the chip is pushed into the socket, which has a small hole for each of the chip's legs. With larger chips care is needed to avoid bending the legs of the chip on insertion.

chi-squared distribution An important *probability distribution with many uses in *statistical analysis. Denoted by the Greek symbol χ^2, it is the distribution of the sum of squares of f independent *random variables, each being drawn from the *normal distribution with zero mean and unit variance. The integer f is the number of *degrees of freedom. Critical values of the probability distribution are widely available in tables, but exact calculations involve the incomplete gamma function. The most common applications are

(1) testing for interactions between different classifications of data using *contingency tables;

(2) testing *goodness-of-fit;

(3) forming *confidence intervals for estimates of *variance.

Cholesky decomposition *See* LU decomposition.

Type	Grammar	Automaton
0	arbitrary	Turing machine
1	context-sensitive	linear-bounded
2	context-free	pushdown
3	regular	finite-state

Chomsky hierarchy

Chomsky hierarchy A series of four classes of *formal languages whose definition in 1959 by Noam Chomsky marked the beginning of formal language theory, and that have ever since remained central to the subject. They are called *type 3*, *type 2*, *type 1*, and *type 0*, each one a subclass of the next. Each type can be defined either by a class of *grammars or by a class of *automata, as indicated in the table. Type 0 consists of all *recursively enumerable languages. Type 1 is a subclass of the languages definable by *primitive recursive functions. Types 2 and 3 are significant in providing abstractions of the computational ideas of iteration and recursion respectively.

Chomsky normal form A restricted type of *context-free grammar, namely one in which each production has the form

$$A \to BC \text{ or } A \to d,$$

i.e. each right-hand side consists of either two nonterminals or one terminal. Any context-free language is generated by such a grammar, except that derivation of the empty string, Λ, requires the additional production

$$S \to \Lambda$$

Church–Rosser theorem A theorem, proved jointly by A. Church and J. B. Rosser, concerning Church's *lambda calculus. It states that if a lambda-expression x can be reduced in two ways leading respectively to expressions y_1 and y_2 then there must be an expression z to which both y_1 and y_2 can be reduced. The choice of ways to reduce an expression arises from the possibility of separately reducing different "parts" of the expression. The Church–Rosser theorem shows that either part can be worked on first, without the loss of any possibilities obtainable from working on the other part first. A corresponding theorem exists for combinatory logic. More generally, any language for which there is a notion of reduction is said to have the *Church–Rosser property*, or to be *confluent*, if it admits the Church–Rosser theorem.

Church's thesis A proposition put forward by Alonzo Church in 1935 that, in one version, claims that the only effectively computable functions are those definable using *Turing machines. Rather than being a mathematical assertion, Church's thesis has the nature of a definition: it identifies the informal idea of *effective computability with the formal notion of Turing computability. Hence the thesis is not subject to proof or disproof. However, evidence for its appropriateness has mounted over the years with the failure to discover any intuitively "effective" way of defining functions not already captured by Turing machines. Several formal notions have indeed been shown to be equivalent to that of Turing machines, including *general recursiveness* in the sense of Kleene, *λ-definability*, and *Post generability*. The fact that these notions turn out to be equivalent, despite radical differences in detail, is further evidence of the appropriateness of Church's thesis.

CIM 1. *Abbrev. for* computer-integrated manufacturing.

2. *Abbrev. for* computer input microfilm, i.e. the process, or the input itself; it is not widely used. Input devices that have been produced have relied on optical character recognition (*OCR) to recode alphanumeric data on microfilm or have read special microfilm on which the data was recorded as binary code. *See also* COM.

cipher, ciphertext *See* cryptography.

CIR *Abbrev. for* current instruction register.

circuit 1. The combination of a number of electrical devices and conductors that, when interconnected to form a conducting path, fulfill some desired function. *See also* logic circuit, integrated circuit, printed circuit.
2. A physical (electrical) connection used for communication. *See also* circuit switching.
3. of a graph. *Another name for* cycle.

circuit board A single rigid board of insulating material on which an electrical circuit has been built. It often has an *edge connector at one end for making all the connections to other circuits so that the board may be plugged into a piece of equipment. Circuit boards come in a variety of sizes, some of which are standardized. The term *circuit card* is often used synonymously but is sometimes considered smaller than a circuit board. *See also* printed circuit, backplane.

circuit card *See* circuit board.

circuit switching A method of communications that is used in telephone systems and requires a physical transmission path – a *circuit* – to exist between the two devices wishing to communicate. The end-to-end path must exist before data can be sent. The only delay to which the data is subject is the propagation delay along the transmission medium (6 microseconds per 100 km for copper telephone lines). Since the path is reserved during the entire connection, any unused bandwidth is wasted. *Compare* message switching, packet switching.

circular list A *linked list in which the last item contains a link to the first. This allows access to all of the list from any given point. Circular lists are most useful if the pointer to the list links to the last node, allowing easy access to both ends of the list. *See also* ring.

circular shift (end-around shift) A *shift operation, specified by a *circular shift instruction*, that causes the contents of some register (usually the accumulator) to be shifted circularly to the left or right a prescribed number of positions.

circulating register A *shift register in which quantities (data) shifted out at one end are entered into the other end. This accomplishes a *circular shift and may be performed in either direction.

CISC *Acronym for* complex instruction set computer. A conventional computer in which the *instruction set has evolved to satisfy the needs of system software to enable generation of reliable efficient *object code, often in a time-sharing environment governed by an *operating system. *Compare* RISC.

CIS–COBOL *Acronym for* compact interactive standard COBOL. A version of the programming language *COBOL that runs on many of the popular *personal computers above the hobby level. CIS–COBOL has been implemented for the 8080, 8086, and similar microprocessor chips, making it widely available. A particularly important point is that CIS–COBOL programs are portable between different micros, thus making it a very useful language for the development of program packages on the commercial market.

clamp An electronic circuit that is designed to return the d.c. voltage level at a given point in the circuit to a fixed reference value at fixed points in time, often in response to an externally generated clamp pulse.

class A facility introduced in the programming language *SIMULA. The class provides a form of *abstract data type: it is also the basis of the concept of object that underlies *Smalltalk and other *object-oriented languages.

clear An *instruction or *microinstruction that causes a designated variable, register, or counter to be set to the all-zero state (i.e. cleared).

Clear A language for writing formal *specifications, first described by R.M. Burstall and J.A. Goguen in 1977. The language provides a formalism for expressing a complex specification hierarchically as a combination of simpler ones. This formalism can be given a precise semantics using ideas familiar from *algebra and *category theory.

CLNS *Abbrev. for* connectionless network service.

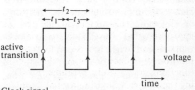

Clock signal

clock An electronic device, generally a stable oscillator, that generates a repetitive series of pulses, known as *clock pulses*, whose repetition rate, or frequency, is accurately controlled.

The *clock rate* is the frequency, expressed in *hertz, at which active transitions of a given clock signal occur.

The active transition may be from a low to a high voltage level, or vice versa, but will always be followed after a fixed time by an opposite inactive transition. The clock signal is thus formed as a series of fixed-width pulses having a fixed repetition rate (*see* diagram). The pulse width, t_1, is often 50% of the pulse repetition period, t_2, i.e. $t_1 = t_3$. The clock rate is $1/t_2$ hertz. A *clock cycle* is considered to be one complete cycle of the clock signal and will always contain one active transition of the clock. For the clock signal illustrated, a clock cycle occurs in t_2 seconds.

Because of its constant rate, the signal from a clock is used to initiate actions within a *sequential logic circuit and to synchronize the activities of a number of such circuits. These circuits are said to be *clocked*. The *primary* clock rate controls the fastest parts of a computer while slower components are timed by numerous submultiples of the basic frequency.

clock cycle *See* clock.

clocked flip-flop *See* flip-flop.

clocking 1. In synchronous communication networks, the use of a single time standard to control all bit transmissions and switching throughout the network. The clocking signal is sent as part of the data or as non-data-carrying clock-transmission signals, depending upon the exact link protocols involved.

2. In modem-terminal interconnection, the use of a timing signal to indicate when data can be properly transferred between the modem and the terminal device. The signal is usually from the modem to the terminal, although in some cases it can be the reverse.

clock pulses *See* clock.

clock rate *See* clock.

clock skew *See* skew.

clone A computer or other system that is claimed by its manufacturer or supplier to behave in exactly the same way as a system from another company, i.e. it will produce identical results from an identical program. A whole industry exists to produce *PC clones*, microcomputers that behave like one of IBM's personal computer range.

CLOS An *object-oriented programming system based on *Common LISP.

closed A term applied to a *set S on whose elements a *dyadic operation ∘ is defined and that possesses the property that, for every (s,t) in S, the quantity $s ∘ t$ is also in S; S is then said to be closed under ∘. A similar definition holds for *monadic operations such as $\sim$. A set S is closed under $\sim$ provided that, when s is in S, the quantity $\sim s$ is also in S.

The set of integers is closed under the usual arithmetic operations of addition, subtraction, and multiplication, but is not closed under division.

closed loop A term used in the early development of programming to describe the repetition construct now known just as a *loop. (Since a loop is necessarily closed, the short term suffices.)

closed semiring A *semiring S with two additional properties:

(a) if $a_1, a_2, \ldots, a_n, \ldots$ is a *countable sequence of elements of S then
$$a_1 + a_2 + \ldots + a_n + \ldots,$$
exists and is unique; the order in which the various elements are added is irrelevant;

(b) the operation · (*see* semiring) distributes over countably infinite sums as well as finite sums.

A special unary operation called *closure* can be defined on closed semirings. Given an element a in S, powers can be defined in the expected manner:
$$a^0 = 1$$

$$a^n = a \cdot a^{n-1} \quad \text{for all } n > 0$$

Then the closure a^* can be defined as follows:

$$a^* = 1 + a + a^2 + \ldots + a^n + \ldots$$

The properties of a semiring imply that

$$a^* = 1 + a \cdot a^*$$

Closed semirings have applications in various branches of computing such as automata theory, the theory of grammars, the theory of recursion and fixed points, sequential machines, aspects of matrix manipulation, and various problems involving graphs, e.g. finding shortest-path algorithms within graphs.

closed shop A method of running a computing facility such that the design, development, writing, testing, and running of programs is carried out by specialist computing staff and not by the originators of the problem. *Closed shop operation* is the operation of a computing system, excluding terminals, by specialist computer operators and not by other computing staff or computer users. *Compare* open shop.

closed subroutine *See* subroutine.

closure *See* closed semiring. *See also* Kleene star.

	closed under complement	closed under intersection
3	yes	yes
2	no	no
1	unknown	yes
0	no	yes

Closure properties for Chomsky hierarchy

closure properties A class of *formal languages L is *closed* under an operation f if the application of f to languages in

L always yields a language in L. For example, if, for any L_1 and L_2 in L,

$$L_1 \cup L_2$$

is also in L, then L is closed under union. Typical operations considered are:

*union, *intersection, *complement, intersection with *regular set;

*concatenation, *Kleene star;

image under *homomorphism, inverse homomorphism, *substitution;

*gsm-mapping, etc.

Most familiar classes of languages are closed under these operations. The detailed picture for the *Chomsky hierarchy is given in the table. Certain classes of languages, e.g. *regular languages, are definable by their closure properties.

cluster 1. A group of similar peripheral devices, usually under the control of one master. As an illustration, a cluster of magnetic tape is a *magnetic tape subsystem consisting of two or more magnetic tape units (MTUs) sharing a single physical interface to the host (processor or network) so that only one MTU can perform a data transfer at a time, although other MTUs may be completing off-line operations such as rewind or tape mark search. The software is not necessarily aware that the MTUs share an interface.

In some cases, particularly on large systems, a cluster may be provided with two interfaces, which gives *dual access* to the cluster and hence resilience in the event of a failure, and also higher throughput.

2. A group of processors used to provide higher processing speed and resilience to failure.

3. A unit of storage, usually on a disk, that comprises a contiguous area made up from a number of basic units of storage.

cluster analysis Any statistical technique for grouping a set of units into clusters of similar units on the basis of observed qualitative and/or quantitative measurements, usually on several variables. Cluster analysis aims to fulfill simultaneously the conditions that units in the same cluster should be similar, and that units in different clusters should be dissimilar. It is not usually possible to satisfy both conditions fully, and no single method can be recommended as best for all sets of data. Among other desirable properties of clusters are that some variables should be constant for all units within a cluster, which makes it possible to provide a simple scheme for identification of units in terms of clusters.

Most cluster analysis methods require a *similarity* or *distance* measure to be defined between each pair of units, so that the units similar to a given unit may be identified. Similarity measures have been proposed for both quantitative (continuous) variables and qualitative (discrete) variables, using a weighted mean of similarity scores over all variables considered. The term distance comes from a geometric representation of data as points in multidimensional space: small distances correspond to large similarities.

Hierarchical cluster analysis methods form clusters in sequence, either by amalgamation of units into clusters and clusters into larger clusters, or by subdivision of clusters into smaller clusters and single units. Whichever direction is chosen, the results can be represented by a *dendrogram* or family tree in which the units at one level are nested within units at all higher levels.

Nonhierarchical cluster analysis methods allocate units to a fixed number of clusters so as to optimize some criterion representing a desired property of clusters. Such methods may be iterative, involving transfer of units between clusters until no further improvement can be achieved. The solution for a given number of clusters need bear little relation to the solution for a larger or smaller number.

Cluster analysis is often used in conjunction with other methods of *multivariate analysis to describe the structure of a complex set of data.

CLV *Abbrev. for* constant linear velocity. Denoting or involving an *optical disk where the rotation rate is varied according to the radius of the track accessed so that a constant data rate corresponds to a constant bit density along the track. This allows an increase in capacity as compared to *CAV, but the access time is also increased. CLV is used in the *CD-ROM disk drive (as in the Compact Audio product on which it is based) and in some other optical disk drives. *See also* MCLV.

CM *Abbrev. for* configuration management.

CMI *Abbrev. for* computer-managed instruction. *See* computer-assisted learning.

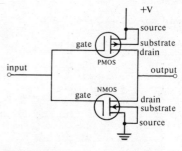

CMOS inverter

CMOS *Acronym for* complementary metal oxide semiconductor. A family of logic circuits that uses pairs of complementary *MOSFETs, i.e. PMOS plus NMOS, to implement the basic logic functions. The complementary transistors are arranged so that there is no direct current flow through each pair of PMOS and NMOS. In the circuit of the

CMOS inverter (*see* diagram), the PMOS conducts when the input is logic 0 and the NMOS conducts (to ground) when the input is logic 1.

By scaling down the dimensions of the MOS devices, higher switching speeds and larger packing densities are possible; these devices are often termed *HMOS.

CMS *See* VM/CMS.

CNF *Abbrev. for* conjunctive normal form. *See* conjunction.

CNF satisfiability *See* P = NP question.

COBOL or **Cobol** *Acronym for* common business-oriented language. A programming language that was developed by *CODASYL and is a de facto standard for commercial data processing. COBOL first came into use in 1960; the current version COBOL 85 replaces the earlier standards COBOL 74 and COBOL 68.

A COBOL program is divided into four divisions, of which the most important are the DATA division and the PROCEDURE division. In the DATA division the programmer defines the working storage and the files to be used by specifying their record structure. The PROCEDURE division is made up of statements, grouped into sentences, paragraphs, and sections. These statements define manipulation of data from the current record(s) of one or more files. The notation is English-like, e.g.

IF X = Y MOVE A TO B;

IF GREATER ADD A TO Z;

OTHERWISE MOVE C TO D.

File input-output is defined in terms of complete records, so the typical program reads a record from its input file, processes it, and writes a record to its output file, repeating this sequence until the whole file is processed. A powerful feature allows the data definition to specify editing that will take place as a side-effect of output, e.g. suppressing non-significant zeros. There are also facilities for handling VDU terminals.

cocktail shaker sort A refinement of the *bubble sort in which alternate passes go in opposite directions.

CoCom Coordinating Committee on Multilateral Export Controls. The export of various technologies, including computing systems, networking, hardware, and software, is restricted where this might enhance the military capability of the other country or place at risk the technology advantage of the exporting country. CoCom is the committee, with representatives from the 15 western nations in the NATO alliance plus Japan, that specifies the technology for which (CoCom) export approval is required.

COCOMO (or **CoCoMo**) *Acronym for* constructive cost model. An algorithmic software *cost estimation model devised by Barry Boehm. The basic model is intended to give an order of magnitude estimate of cost based on three classes of project: *organic mode, semidetached mode, embedded mode.* For each class an estimate for effort and duration can be calculated as a function of thousands of delivered source instructions (kdsi).

Organic mode projects require relatively small teams working in familiar environments on familiar projects. Semidetached mode projects have a mixture of experienced and inexperienced staff, with limited experience of the application type and probably unfamiliar with some of the aspects of the project. Embedded mode projects have tight time constraints, strong coupling between software, hardware, regulations, and operational procedures. Variations in specifications are usually impracticable, and validation is rigorous. Project team members are usually inexperienced in the particular application.

The intermediate COCOMO model applies a series of multipliers to the basic estimates for effort and time. There are 15 modifiers in four groups of attributes: *Product attributes* are required software reliability, database size, product complexity; *computer attributes* are execution time constraints, storage constraints, virtual machine volatility, computer turnaround time; *personnel attributes* are analyst capability, application experience, virtual machine experience, programmer capability, programming language experience; *project attributes* are modern programming practices, software tools, required development schedule.

Each attribute multiplier may be selected from points on a qualitative scale. The modifier value for modern programming practices also varies with the estimated kdsi size of the delivered software. The combined effect of all modifiers leads to a maximum multiplier of 84.6, and a minimum of 0.0076, for the basic estimates for each mode.

The COCOMO models essentially estimate cost to deliver, which may be a small proportion of the total software life-cycle cost. Boehm also provides models to estimate maintenance effort.

CODASYL 1. *Acronym for* Conference on Data Systems Languages. An organization of computing personnel from the computer industry, user organizations, software houses, and other related groups that was founded at a meeting convened at the Pentagon in 1959. Its aims were primarily to develop a standard data-processing programming language. After a number of years it produced the *COBOL standard, which was adopted by the US Department of Defense for all its data-processing installations. CODASYL then extended its activities to all developments that could be useful to COBOL, one of which was the specification of a database system (*see* def. 2).

2. A set of standards for *network database systems, laid down by CODASYL as extensions to *COBOL.

The two most important characteristics are

(a) the extension of the COBOL data division to permit the definition of *sets* of records, which are connected by *links, to allow sequential access to nonsequentially stored records (*see* data chaining);

(b) a two-level architecture, according to which a database is defined in terms of a *schema* and a *subschema* (*see* data description language).

code 1. A rule for transforming a message from one symbolic form (the *source alphabet*) into another (the *target alphabet*), usually without loss of information. The process of transformation is called *encoding* and its converse is called *decoding*. These processes are carried out by an *encoder* and a *decoder* respectively; the encoder and decoder may be implemented in hardware or software, the encoding and decoding processes being algorithmic in nature. The term "an encoding" is sometimes used synonymously with "a code".

From a more formal viewpoint, a code is a one-to-one *homomorphism h from the set of Σ-words, Σ_1^*, to the set Σ_2^*, where Σ_1 and Σ_2 are alphabets (*see* word, formal language). Since h is one to one, $h(w)$ may be "decoded" to obtain w for any w in Σ_1^*.

See also fixed-length code, variable-length code, error-correcting code, error-detecting code, channel coding theorem, source coding theorem, encryption.

2. Any piece of program text written in a programming language (as opposed to a data structure or algorithm illustrated by a diagram or flowchart, or a program specified or sketched out in natural language prose). The term sometimes implies executable code as opposed to declarations or tables, but this is by no means always the case. *See also* coding.

3. The particular language in which some code is written, e.g. *machine code, *source code.

8421 code A *weighted code in which each decimal digit 0 through 9 is represented by a four-bit codeword. The bit positions in each codeword are assigned weights, from left to right, of 8, 4, 2, and 1. *See also* binary-coded decimal, excess-3 code, biquinary code.

codebook *See* cryptography.

codec *Short for* coder-decoder. A device that converts a continuous analog signal into an encoded representation in a digital bit stream, and decodes incoming digital signals back into analog form. Codecs are used in telephone systems to convert analog voice signals into digital signals, which can be transmitted at higher data rates and with lower error rates. Digital signals can be multiplexed to make more efficient use of the transmission medium. Telephone system codecs operate at 8000 samples per second (125 μs/sample), sufficient for the 4 kilohertz bandwidth analog signal. A codec is the inverse of a *modem.

A codec may also be used to convert a digital signal between its original form and one with additional bits containing redundant information. The original digital signal may be recovered with low probability of error, even when it has passed through a noisy communication path such as some satellite transmission systems.

code inspection A *review technique carried out at the end of the coding phase for a module. A specification (and design documentation) for the module is distributed to the inspection team in advance. M. E. Fagan recommends an inspection team of about four people. The module programmer explains the module code to the rest of the team. A moderator records detected faults in the code and ensures there is no discussion of corrections. The code designer and code tester complete the team. Any faults are corrected outside the inspection, and reinspection may take place subject to the quality targets adopted.

code length In an encoder, the number of symbols output when an encoded operation takes place. Usually the number of symbols input to the encoder is fixed; the number output may or may not vary, depending on whether the encoder is designed to give a *variable-length code or a *fixed-length code.

coder-decoder *See* codec.

codeword, codeword length *See* block code.

coding The transformation of a detailed design into an actual program, normally done automatically. Use of the term coding generally implies a straightforward activity – simply expressing an existing design in some formal programming language – and that any decisions made during the activity (such as the choice among arbitrary locations for particular variables) would not be classed as design decisions since they are of a relatively trivial nature. *See also* software life-cycle.

coding bounds A variety of inequalities that apply, generally or specifically, to *error-detecting and *error-correcting codes, setting bounds to their performance as expressed by parameters such as the number of codewords (*see* block code), minimum *Hamming distance, codeword length, and efficiency. Of the many bounds that are known, the most important are the *Hamming bound and the *Gilbert–Varshamov bound.

coding standards *See* programming standards.

coding theorems *See* source coding theorem, channel coding theorem.

coding theory The branch of *communication theory that deals with the mathematical study of *codes with a view to their employment in *communication systems, usually for the purpose of increasing their efficiency and reliability. *See* source coding, channel coding.

codomain *See* function, relation, category.

cohesion A measure of the degree to which parts of a program module are closely functionally related. High cohesion means that each part is directed toward and essential for that module to perform its required function, and that the module performs only that function. Low cohesion might be due to convenience grouping of functions that are unrelated by function, timing, logic, procedure, or by sequence.

Temporal cohesion occurs where a module contains several functions that must be performed at the same time, but are not closely related by function.

Logical cohesion is where several logically related functions are placed in the same module. For example a unit may handle all input to a program irrespective of its source being from disk, communications port, keyboard, etc.

Procedural cohesion is where functions that must be performed in a certain order are grouped together in the same module.

Sequential cohesion occurs when the output from one part of a module is the input to the next part, but if the module is not constructed for functional cohesion it is possible that not all the related parts will occur in the one module.

High functional cohesion might be seen as one characteristic of good design. *See also* coupling.

collating sequence An ordering of the internal character set, used in alphabetic and alphanumeric sorting.

collator A machine associated with card-based data processing that could merge two packs of punched cards: header cards, containing the address and other account information, could automatically be placed in the card file ahead of the related new cards that carried data on current transactions. Some collators could also perform the decollate function.

collision *See* hashing, CSMA/CD.

collocation methods An important approach to the numerical solution of *ordinary differential and *integral equations. Approximations are obtained on the basis that the equation is satisfied exactly at a particular set of points in the given problem range. For example, for

$$y'' = f(x, y, y'), \quad a \leqslant x \leqslant b,$$

an approximation

$$P(x) = \sum_{i=1}^{n} \alpha_i \phi_i(x)$$

can be obtained from a suitable set of orthogonal functions $\phi_i(x)$ by choosing the coefficients α_i for which

$$P''(x_i) = f(x_i, P(x_i), P'(x_i)),$$

for some set of collocation points

$$a \leqslant x_1 < x_2 < \ldots < x_n \leqslant b$$

Initial conditions and boundary conditions may also be incorporated into the process (*see* boundary-value problem).

color display A VDU capable of displaying data in full color.

Colossus An electronic special-purpose digital "computer" that was built in great secrecy by the Post Office Research Station in London and began useful work at the government establishment at Bletchley Park, Buckinghamshire, in late 1943. It contained 1500 vacuum tubes (valves) and could operate at high speed. The strategy or "program" was controlled from patchboards and switches. The faster Mark II machines, operating by mid-1944, contained 2500 tubes. Both versions were used for code-breaking purposes during the war.

coloured book The UK academic networking community was one of the earliest to attempt to devise a complete set of *open systems interconnection (OSI) standards for all aspects of its networking requirements, and to make a concerted effort to apply these to the entire community. A main thrust of the approach was the definition of *protocols for each of the major networking requirements, each protocol being issued in a different colored binder. The important protocols were:

Yellow book – defining a transport service, roughly equivalent to layer 4 of the ISO *seven-layer reference model.
Green book – defining a terminal connection protocol.
Blue book – defining a file transfer protocol.
Grey book – defining an electronic mail service.
Red book – defining a job transfer and submission protocol.
Pink book – defining a transport service to run over an ISO OSI *CSMA/CD service.
Orange book – defining a network service running over a *Cambridge Ring.

column-major order One way of mapping the elements of a two-dimensional *array onto a vector, e.g. for representation in memory. If a two-dimensional array, A, with m rows and n columns is mapped in column-major order onto a vector b with $m \times n$ elements then

$$a_{ij} = b_k$$
where $k = m(j - 1) + i$
See also row-major order.

column-ragged See ragged array.

column vector See matrix.

COM *Short for* computer output on microfilm. Output recorded in miniaturized form on microfilm, either on a reel of film or on card-sized sheets of film known as *microfiche*. The term COM also applies to the techniques used to

produce this form of output. Special optical viewers must be used to enlarge the information on the microfilm for reading purposes. The facility has been available since the early 1960s and currently most COM devices are run off-line. *See also* CIM.

COMAL *Acronym for* common algorithmic language. A programming language developed for use in schools in Denmark. It is defined as a set of extensions to *BASIC, combining modern control structures with the traditional simplicity and familiarity of BASIC. It therefore facilitates the teaching of *structured programming to beginners. Although it enjoyed a brief vogue in the UK, and is still used in some European countries, major use is confined to Denmark. Modern dialects of BASIC (e.g. BBC Basic in the UK) usually include control structures such as

if..then..else and do..while
and are used in preference to COMAL.

combination 1. A *subset of a finite set of elements. The number of combinations of n distinct objects taken k at a time is

$$^nC_k = n!/[k!(n-k)!]$$

2. A method of combining *functions in a parallel manner (*compare* composition). For functions f and g,
$$f : S \to T \text{ and } g : U \to V$$
the combination $f \times g$ is such that
$$f \times g : S \times U \to T \times V$$
where $S \times U$ and $T \times V$ are *Cartesian products, and
$$(f \times g)(s,u) = (f(s),g(u))$$
(*see* ordered pair).

combinational circuit A *logic circuit whose outputs at a specified time are a function only of the inputs at that time. In practice, any physically realizable combinational circuit will have a finite transit time, or delay, between the inputs changing and the outputs changing; the intention of the term combinational is to include algebraic elements

COMBINATIONAL LOGIC

(*AND gates, *OR gates, etc.) and preclude memory elements (*flip-flops, etc.). Analysis and synthesis of combinational circuits is facilitated by *Boolean algebra and *Karnaugh maps. *Compare* sequential circuit.

combinational logic *Digital logic restricted to the description of *combinational circuits. *See also* Boolean expression.

combinator A *lambda expression containing no *free variables. While this is the most general definition, the word is usually understood more specifically to refer to certain combinators of special importance, in particular the following four:

$$I = \lambda x . x$$
$$K = \lambda x . \lambda y . x$$
$$S = \lambda x . \lambda y . \lambda z . x(z)(y(z))$$
$$Y = \lambda f . (\lambda u . f(u(u))) \ (\lambda u . f(u(u)))$$

The combinators I, K, and S were introduced by Schönfinkel and Curry, who showed that any λ-expression can essentially be formed by combining them. More recently combinators have been applied to the design of implementations for *functional languages. In particular Y (also called the *paradoxical combinator*) can be seen as producing *fixed points, since $Y(f)$ reduces to $f(Y(f))$.

combinatorial circuit *Another (UK) name for* combinational circuit.

combinatorics The branch of mathematics concerned with the counting problems and enumeration problems associated with such topics as *combinations, *permutations, number theory, arithmetic, and the theory of *graphs, *groups, and other *discrete structures. *Induction, *recursion, and *recurrence relations tend to play a significant role in much of this work. In computational combinatorics the underlying theory is applied to algorithms of any kind.

combinatory logic A version of *lambda calculus in which all expressions are constructed out of certain basic *combinators.

command 1. *See* job-control language.
   2. *Obsolete name for* instruction or statement, i.e. the elementary unit from which a program is built up.

command control language A programming language designed for the implementation of *command control programs. The earliest such language was *JOVIAL; the latest is *Ada.

command control program A program that controls some piece of equipment, especially in the military context. Such programs are now more usually called embedded systems.

command-driven user interface A widely used method for giving commands to systems or software packages. The user learns the commands by consulting an online *help system or user documentation. Users familiar with the interface may use mnemonic commands to speed access and to reduce the number of keystrokes necessary to perform a given command. *See also* MS-DOS, UNIX, user interface. *Compare* window.

command language *Another name for* job-control language.

comment Part of a program text included for the benefit of the reader and ignored by the compiler. Each language has its own syntax for comments, usually a form of bracketing, e.g.

   {.....} in Pascal,
   /*.....*/ in PL/I

Some languages, including Ada, prefer "end-of-line" comments, which are introduced by a characteristic symbol and are automatically terminated at the end of a line. Older languages such as BASIC and FORTRAN restrict comments to be whole lines and do not allow them to be appended to a line of code.

COMMON area In FORTRAN, an area of storage accessible from more than one program unit (subroutine). Data is local to the subroutine in which it is defined unless it is declared to be in a COMMON area. There is one anonymous COMMON area, called "blank COMMON", and any number of other areas, which are named ("labeled COMMON").

common carrier In the US, a private business or corporation that offers to the public general communication services such as telephone, teletype, or intercomputer communications. Common carriers are regulated by the Federal Communications Commission (FCC), and all services offered must charge according to tariff schedules filed with and approved by the FCC.

common instance *See* unification.

Common LISP A version of *LISP that integrates the facilities of FranzLisp and MACLisp, adopted as an informal standard by the major users and suppliers of LISP systems.

communication channel *See* Shannon's model.

communication network *See* communication system, network.

communication processor A specialized *I/O processor that is used to control a number of communication lines and/or communication devices. These lines/devices operate slowly in comparison to computing speeds so that one communication processor is usually multiplexed across a large number of lines/devices. Communication processors are used for the handling of data (in *blocks, *packets, *messages, *datagrams, etc.) for purposes of protocol, error checking and correction, acknowledgment, buffering,

and also for *encryption and *decryption. They are now (mostly) programmed computers; earlier generations tended to be less general wired-program systems.

Communication processors are sometimes called concentrators, transmission control units, or front-end processors.

communication server *Another name for* gateway. *See also* server.

communication subnetwork (subnet) The dedicated processors and *trunk circuits that are responsible for communication functions in a distributed network. *See* backbone network.

The term is sometimes used to refer to the communication circuits in a computer network, exclusive of any switching equipment.

communication system Any system whereby a source of information is enabled to convey that information, with due regard for efficiency and reliability, to a destination. Such a system may contain more than one source and/or more than one destination, in which case it is called a *communication network*. Communication systems are usually studied with *Shannon's model in mind.

communication theory The study of *communication systems through mathematical models of their operation. It is broadly divided into *information theory (the entropy formulation of sources and channels) and *coding theory (source coding and channel coding).

commutative group (abelian group) *See* group.

commutative law *See* commutative operation.

commutative operation Any *dyadic operation ∘ that satisfies the law

$$x \circ y = y \circ x$$

for all x and y in the domain of ∘. The law is known as the *commutative law*. The usual addition of integers is commutative but subtraction is not.

commutative ring *See* ring.

commutative semiring *See* semiring.

compaction 1. Any of a number of methods to reduce unused or unusable space in primary, secondary, or other memory. *See* memory compaction.
2. Removal of redundant data from a record. Many systems work with fixed-length records as a convenient method of handling files. This has the disadvantage that all records must be capable of holding the longest record, giving uneconomic use of storage. The fixed-length records can be processed (compacted) into a variable-length form. One method involves the removal of trailing spaces; another involves the replacement of long strings of identical characters by a *flag that indicates the occurrence of such a string, together with a count of the number of characters and a single instance of the character. Compaction will require CPU time when the record is stored and again when it is unpacked to fixed-length form, but the consequent saving in storage may justify this.

Compaq Computer Corporation A US manufacturer of microcomputers that emulate IBM's PC series closely (*see* clone). An early and successful entrant into the *portable microcomputer market, Compaq is one of the world's top three microcomputer manufacturers in terms of revenue (1988 figures).

comparator 1. A piece of hardware or software that checks the outputs of a system while that system is operational. For a single channel system (i.e. no redundancy or diversity), the comparator might check across several outputs to see that only valid combinations are produced. The comparator may deal only with binary signals, usually termed *voting logic*, or may compare analog signals.
2. A piece of software that, for example, compares the contents of two text files and highlights any differences between the contents. It is often used in *word processing or editing of program source files and as a *software quality assurance tool in *configuration management.

comparison counting sort A sorting algorithm that stores, for each sortkey, the number of keys less than the given key. If N_j denotes the number of keys less than the jth key then (assuming that keys are unique) the jth record should be in position $N_j + 1$ in a file sorted into ascending order of the keys. This is a simple but inefficient algorithm.

compartmentalization (compartmentation) The process of keeping resources with differing access attributes in separate groupings.

compatibility 1. of hardware. The ability of a subsystem (e.g. memory) or an external device (e.g. terminal) to be substituted for the originally designated equipment. To designate that one manufacturer's hardware can be connected to another manufacturer's hardware, the terms *plug-to-plug compatible*, or *plug-compatible*, are used.
2. of software. The ability of a computer to directly execute program code that was compiled, assembled, or written in machine language for another computer. Generally this occurs for successive computers in a given manufacturer's line. Since later computers are usually more capable (i.e. have a larger instruction set and/or more memory), the ability to run the program of a less capable machine is usually called *upward compatibility*. *See also* portable, emulation.
3. of a new piece of software. The ability to reproduce the behavior of its predecessor, in particular to accept the same input formats.

compilation time The time at which a high-level language program is translated into some other representation, such as machine code, so that the program can subsequently be executed by some computer system. *Compare* run time.

compiler A program that translates high-level language into *absolute code, or sometimes into *assembly language. The input to the compiler (the source code) is a description of an algorithm or program in a problem-oriented language; its output (the object code) is an equivalent description of the algorithm in a machine-oriented language.

compiler-compiler A program that accepts the syntactic and semantic description of a programming language and generates a *compiler for that language. The syntax is expressed in *BNF or a derivative thereof, and must conform to the rules dictated by the parsing technique to be used in the generated compiler. The semantics of the language are usually described by associating a code-generation procedure with each syntactic construct, and arranging to call the procedure whenever the associated construct is recognized by the parser. Thus the user still has to design the run-time structures to be used, and decide how each syntactic construct is to be mapped into machine operations. Then he has to write the code-generating procedures. A compiler-compiler is therefore a useful tool to aid the compiler writer, but nothing more.

Strictly speaking a compiler-compiler includes a parser generator as a component part, but the two terms are often used synonymously.

compiler validation *See* conformance testing.

complement 1. of a *set, S, with respect to some universal set U. The set consisting of elements that are in U but not in S; it is usually denoted by S', $\sim S$, or $\bar{S}$. Formally,
$$S' = \{x \mid (x \in U) \text{ and } (x \notin S)\}$$
The process of taking complements is one of the basic operations that can be performed on sets.

The *set difference (or *relative complement*) of two sets S and T is the set of elements that are in S but not in T; it is usually written as $S - T$. Thus
$$S' = U - S$$
See also operations on sets.

2. *See* Boolean algebra.

3. of a *subgraph G', with vertices V' and edges E', of a *graph G, with vertices V and edges E. The subgraph consisting of the vertices V and the edges in E but not in E'.

4. *See* radix-minus-one complement. *See also* radix complement, complement number system.

complementary logic *See* negative logic.

complemented lattice A *lattice in which there are identity elements 0 and 1 and in which each element a has at least one complement b, i.e.
$$a \wedge b = 0 \quad \text{and} \quad a \vee b = 1$$
It will also be the case that b is a complement of a and that 0 and 1 are the complements of each other.

complement number system An alternative representation of numbers in a fixed-radix *number system. In a complement system each positive integer is represented in its usual form in the given radix system except that it is prefixed by at least one leading zero. Each negative number is then represented by the complement of the corresponding number. For example, in both the ten's complement system and the nine's complement system any number with leading digit 9 represents a negative number. *See also* radix complement, radix-minus-one complement.

complete graph A *graph G in which there is an edge joining every pair of

distinct vertices; every vertex is adjacent to every other vertex. If G contains n vertices then the number of edges is
$$n(n - 1)/2$$

complete lattice A *set D on which there is a *partial ordering and in which every subset of D has both a least *upper bound and a greatest *lower bound in D. By contrast, the weaker notion of *lattice requires only that finite subsets have least upper bounds and greatest lower bounds.

complete tree Any tree constructed from a *full tree of depth k by deleting some of the leaf nodes and the arcs leading to them. In a complete binary tree, the deleted nodes are often constrained to be the rightmost terminal nodes.

The term is also sometimes used as a synonym for full tree.

complex instruction set computer *See* CISC.

complexity The "difficulty" of solving computational problems, measured in terms of some resource consumed during computation. The resource can be an abstract measure or something specific like space or time. The analysis of the complexity of computational problems is a very active area of research at present and has important practical applications. *See also* complexity classes, complexity measure.

complexity classes A way of grouping algorithms or computable functions according to their *complexity. Computable functions with the same *complexity measure are placed in the same complexity class; functions in the same class are equally difficult to compute (with respect to the measure).

The classification is characteristically done for *formal languages that can be recognized by *Turing machine programs. If L is a formal language that can be recognized by a deterministic Turing machine program M, and the time complexity (*see* complexity measure) for M is $T_M(n)$, then L is classified according to the nature of $T_M(n)$. If $T_M(n)$ is bounded (polynomially or exponentially) then there exists a bounding function $S(n)$ such that
$$T_M(n) \leqslant S(n)$$
For a particular function $S(n)$ there is consequently a class of languages for which the above bound holds. This class is denoted by
$$\text{DTIME}(S(n))$$
Thus $\text{DTIME}(S(n))$ is the class of languages recognizable within time $S(n)$.

There is a similar definition of a class of languages
$$\text{DSPACE}(S(n))$$
in terms of the space complexity (*see* complexity measure).

There are various known relations between complexity classes. For example, if for two bounding functions S_1 and S_2
$$\lim_{n \to \infty} S_1(n)/S_2(n) = 0$$
then there is a language in $\text{DSPACE}(S_2(n))$ that is not in $\text{DSPACE}(S_1(n))$. Note that this applies if S_1 is polynomial and S_2 is exponential. There are similar results for time complexity classes.

It can be shown that the class of languages with exponential bounding functions is the union of an infinite set of languages with polynomial bounding functions. If p is any polynomial then *exponential time* and *exponential space* are the union of the complexity classes
$$\text{DTIME}(2^{p(n)})$$
$$\text{DSPACE}(2^{p(n)})$$
respectively, for all nonnegative integers n.

Complexity classes can also be defined for nondeterministic *Turing machine programs. Thus a language L is in
$$\text{NSPACE}(S(n))$$
if there is some nondeterministic Turing machine program that recognizes L and such that on an input string of length n none of the possible computations uses

more than $S(n)$ tape squares. Time complexity classes,

NTIME,

can be similarly defined. It is known for example that

NSPACE$(S(n) \subseteq$ DSPACE$(S(n)^2)$

complexity function (work function) If A is an algorithm for solving a particular class of problems and n is a measure of the size of a particular problem in this class, then $f_A(n)$, the complexity function, is that function of n giving an upper bound on the maximum number of basic operations that algorithm A has to perform to solve any problem of size n. For example, n might be the number of records in a file and $f_A(n)$ the maximum number of comparisons required to sort the file. *See also* complexity measure.

complexity measure A means of measuring the resources used during a computation. During any Turing machine computation various resources will be used, e.g. space and time. These can be defined formally as follows.

Given a Turing machine program M and an input string x, then Time(M,x) is defined as the number of steps in the computation of M on x before M halts. Time is undefined (i.e. equals infinity) if M does not halt on x. The *time complexity* of M is defined to be the integer function T_M where

$$T_M(n) =$$
$$\max(\text{Time}(M,x): |x| = n)$$

for nonnegative integer n.

Space(M,x) is similarly defined as the number of tape squares used by M on x, and the *space complexity* S_M is defined by

$$S_M(n) =$$
$$\max(\text{Space}(M,x): |x| = n)$$

However, in order to distinguish the space required for working as opposed to the space for the input string x, the machine is sometimes considered as having a read-only input tape, and Space

(M,x) is defined as the number of writeable squares used by M on x.

It is also possible to define more general measures of complexity that share many of the common properties of time and space (*see* Blum's axioms).

An algorithm for which the complexity measure $T_M(n)$ or $S_M(n)$ increases with n no more rapidly than a polynomial in n is said to be *polynomially bounded*; one in which it grows exponentially is said to be *exponentially bounded*. Note that both these cases imply that the algorithm terminates.

See also complexity classes.

composition 1. (relative product) A method of combining *functions in a serial manner. The composition of two functions

$$f : X \to Y \text{ and } g : Y \to Z$$

is the function

$$h : X \to Z$$

with the property that

$$h(x) = g(f(x))$$

This is usually written as $g \circ f$. The process of performing composition is an *operation between functions of suitable kinds. It is *associative, and *identity functions fulfill the role of units.

If R denotes the set of real numbers and

$$f : R \to R, f(x) = \sin(x)$$
$$g : R \to R, g(x) = x^2 + 3$$

then $f \circ g$ is the function h:

$$h : R \to R, h(x) = \sin(x^2 + 3)$$

The idea of composition of functions can be extended to functions of several variables.

2. A subdivision of a positive integer n into parts $a_1, a_2, \ldots a_k$ in which the ordering is significant and in which

$$n = a_1 + a_2 + \ldots + a_k$$

where each a_i is a positive integer. It is thus similar to a partition (*see* covering) but in a partition the ordering is not significant. In general the number of compositions of n is 2^{n-1}.

composition table *See* Cayley table.

compression *See* data compression.

compression coding *Another name for* source coding.

computability *See* effective computability.

computable (Turing computable) *See* Turing machine, effective computability.

computable function A *function f, say, for which there exists an algorithm for evaluating $f(x)$ for any element x in the domain of f.

computational psychology A discipline lying across the border of *artificial intelligence and psychology. It is concerned with building computer models of human cognitive processes and is based on an analogy between the human mind and computer programs. The brain and computer are viewed as general-purpose symbol-manipulation systems, capable of supporting software processes, but no analogy is drawn at a hardware level. *Compare* cybernetics.

computer A device or system that is capable of carrying out a sequence of operations in a distinctly and explicitly defined manner. The operations are frequently numerical computations or data manipulations but also include input/output; the operations within the sequence may depend on particular data values. The definition of the sequence is called the program. A computer can have either a *stored program or *wired program. A stored program may exist in an alterable (*read-write or *RAM) memory or in a nonalterable (*ROM) memory. *See also* digital computer, analog computer, von Neumann machine.

computer-aided design (CAD) The application of computer technology to the design of a product, or the design itself. Computer-aided design is used especially in architecture and electronic, electrical, mechanical, and aeronautical engineering. A computer-aided design uses as inputs both the appropriate technical knowledge of individuals who enter design criteria, edit results, and otherwise test and modify the design, and also accumulated information from libraries of standards for components, element sizes, regulations, etc., e.g. standard ICs for a digital design system, standard pipe lengths and fittings for a hydraulic or piping system.

Processing of the data from the inputs takes place in at least two phases:

(a) certain interactive programs are invoked by the technical designer during the design process, these results being generally displayed on a VDU;

(b) programs are applied that may take considerable periods of running time to analyze tolerances, clearances, electrical characteristics, etc., the results of these runs being displayed back to the technical designer.

Output from a computer-aided design system consists of printouts of specifications and other information, and machine-readable files that are passed to *computer-aided manufacturing (CAM) systems and *computer-aided testing (CAT) systems. Examples of output to a CAM system are computer-produced artwork for printed circuit boards, or computer-produced tapes for automatic component insertion and board drilling. The combined process of computer-aided design and manufacture is known as *CADCAM*. The whole procedure – design, manufacture, and testing – is often referred to as *CADMAT*. There is a draft ISO standard (STEP) for the exchange of CAD data.

computer-aided instruction (CAI) *See* computer-assisted learning.

computer-aided manufacturing (CAM) A set of techniques which integrate various subtechniques that can be used in computer control or *process control for various forms of manufacturing. Computer-aided manufacturing implies the integration of all aspects of manufacturing systems within the factory, i.e. the use of computer techniques not only for process control but also for aspects such as automatic ordering of materials, predicting material usage, factory scheduling, inventory control, predicting machine changeover, and projecting manpower requirements. Computer-aided manufacturing is particularly important as it follows naturally from *computer-aided design. *See also* computer-integrated manufacturing, numerical control, computer-aided testing.

computer-aided testing (CAT) The application of computers to control either analog or digital test techniques to evaluate the quality of components and products. Computer-aided testing is used to check that the component parts, subassemblies, and full systems are within specified tolerances and also perform up to specification. Note that performance to specification may require that the unit or system operates under stressful conditions that would not be encountered in normal use. The parameters (test criteria) for computer-aided testing are often derived from *computer-aided design and *computer-aided manufacturing systems.

computer architecture *See* architecture.

computer-assisted learning (CAL) Any use of computers to aid or support the education or training of people. CAL can test attainment at any point, provide faster or slower routes through the material for people of different aptitudes, and can maintain a progress record for the instructor.

Computer-assisted learning is one of several terms used to describe this application of computers. Other terms include *computer-aided* (or *-assisted*) *instruction*, *CAI*, *computer-based learning*, *CBL*, and *computer-managed instruction*, *CMI*.

computer-assisted software engineering *See* CASE.

computer-based learning (CBL) *See* computer-assisted learning.

computer family A group of (digital) computers that are successive generations of a particular computer system. They will tend to have similar but not identical *architectures.

computer fraud Any technique aimed at manipulating information within a computer system for the purpose of personal gain, usually financial.

computer graphics A mode of computer processing and output in which a significant part of the output information is in pictorial form. The information may range from a simple histogram or other plot of information to a complex map or engineering design annotated with alphanumerics and displayed in color. The output may be via a visual display terminal or as a permanent record via a printer/plotter. Suitable input devices include *digitizers, *scanners, and *light pens. The computer can be made to manipulate the information, e.g. straighten lines, move or delete designated areas, expand or contract details, etc. (*see* windowing).

Probably the first successful graphics system was *Sketchpad*, an interactive system devised by Ivan Sutherland at MIT Lincoln Laboratory and published in 1963.

computer hardware description language *See* CHDL.

computer-integrated manufacturing (CIM) The use of computers to control equipment used in manufacturing systems. The term covers systems constructed from machine tools, and *robotics, and includes parts distribution and handling, automated storage of raw materials, work in progress, and finished goods.

computer logic The basic organization, design, and wiring used to realize a particular computer *architecture. Someone involved with computer logic is therefore concerned with the design of building blocks or components, both logical and physical, and with the logic design involved in realizing a particular set of machine-code instructions; this may include the provision of facilities such as *microprogramming whereby the set of basic instructions can be altered.

computer mail *See* electronic mail.

computer-managed instruction (CMI) The use of computers (usually off-line) to produce lesson prescriptions based on student history and test performance. Components comprising each lesson unit are selected in accordance with learners' needs, as indicated by test performance on previous units, academic history, etc.

computer network A *data network with computers at one or more of the *nodes.

computer power A figure-of-merit for a computer system, sometimes defined in terms of performing a specific set of computations. It is described/measured by a number of methods: *add-subtract time, *cycle time, *throughput, and the results of *benchmarks are among the most common ones.

computer science The study of computers, their underlying principles and use. It comprises topics such as: programming; information structures; software engineering; programming languages; compilers and operating systems; hardware design and testing; computer system architecture; computer networks and interfacing; systems analysis and design; theories of information, systems, and computation; applicable mathematics and electronics; computing techniques (e.g. graphics, simulation, artificial intelligence techniques); applications; social, economic, organizational, political, legal, and historical aspects of computing.

It is not a science in the strict sense of being a discipline employing scientific method to explain phenomena in nature or society (though it has connections with physics, psychology, and behavioral science), but rather in the looser sense of being a systematic body of knowledge with a foundation of theory. Since however it is ultimately concerned with practical problems concerning the design and construction of useful systems, within constraints of cost and acceptability, it is as much a branch of engineering as it is a science.

computer word *See* word.

concatenated code The effective compound code (comprising an inner code followed by an outer code) employed in a *concatenated coding system, or a code designed for use in such a system, either as the inner code or as the outer code.

concatenated coding systems *Communication systems in which messages are encoded by means of an *inner code* before being passed through a channel and then being decoded according to the inner code; this entire inner encoder-channel-decoder system is itself regarded as a channel (it is hoped less noisy than the original channel), and therefore has a further encoder and decoder placed before and after it; these implement an *outer code*. Alternatively, such a system may be considered as a channel with a compound encoder before it and a compound decoder after it, the compound encoder and decoder implementing a *factorable code.

To a good approximation, the inner code should be designed to correct any *channel errors arising in the original channel, while the outer code should be designed to cope with decoder errors occurring in the inner decoder. Since these decoder errors tend to occur in bursts, the outer code is usually a burst-error-correcting code: the *Reed–Solomon codes are often used for this purpose. The inner code is often a *convolutional code.

concatenation The operation of joining two *strings to form a longer string. The concatenation of

$$u = a_1, \ldots, a_m \quad \text{and} \quad v = b_1, \ldots, b_n$$

is the following string of length $m + n$:

$$a_1, \ldots, a_m b_1, \ldots, b_n$$

Common notations for referring to it include uv and $u <> v$, but several others have been used.

The term concatenation is also sometimes used in a different though related sense, involving sets of strings (i.e. *formal languages (def. 2)). Let K and L be two sets of strings. Then they can be combined into the following set by concatenating strings from K with strings L in all possible ways:

$$\{uv \mid u \in K, v \in L\}$$

This set is usually written KL. The phrase *language concatenation* is sometimes used to distinguish this from simple concatenation of strings. Both string concatenation and language concatenation gives rise to *monoids, the identity elements being Λ and $\{\Lambda\}$ respectively (where Λ is the *empty string). *See also* free monoid.

concatenation closure *Another name for* Kleene star.

concentrator A communication device that combines input lines whose total *bandwidth is higher than that of the output line; the process is known as *concentrating* or *concentration*. A concentrator is used when the actual traffic of each of the input lines is below its potential traffic. It is possible for the concentrator to become overloaded and to lose data. A common method used by concentrators to combine (multiplex) the input lines is asynchronous *time division multiplexing. *See also* communication processor.

conceptual schema *See* data description language.

concurrency The progressing of two or more activities (processes, programs) in parallel. It is a term that describes the general topic of parallelism in computer systems, specifically *multiprocessing systems. Specification of concurrency, and the consequent problems of *interlock and *synchronization, requires special features in the programming language, and is a feature of the class of *real-time languages.

The usual method of describing parallelism is *Flynn's classification*, which does so in terms of parallelism in the *instruction stream and in the *data stream of a system. Thus there are four categories:

SISD, single instruction, single data;

SIMD, single instruction, multiple data;

MISD, multiple instruction, single data;

MIMD, multiple instruction, multiple data.

The first of these, *SISD*, is the conventional serial processor. The third of these, *MISD*, does not really occur in current systems. The other two are of most interest in multiprocessor systems. The *SIMD* is suited to operating upon data of the sort that exists in vectors and matrices by taking advantage of the inherent parallelism in that data. Thus the *array processor is one such system. Another is represented by the *supercomputer with parallel and different arithmetic units that *overlap arithmetic operations. The *MIMD* system represents a wide range of architectures from the large symmetrical multiprocessor system to the small asymmetrical minicomputer/DMA channel combination.

Shared-memory systems form a distinct group within the MIMD category. They are general-purpose multiprocessor systems that share common memory, and are thus also called *closely coupled* or

CONCURRENT PROGRAMMING

tightly coupled systems. *Distributed systems – *wide area and *local area networks – form another MIMD group, sometimes referred to as *loosely coupled* systems.

concurrent programming A near-synonym for *parallel processing. The term is used both to describe the act of creating a program that contains sections to be executed in parallel as well as its subsequent execution.

condensation *See* connected graph.

P	F	F	T	T
Q	F	T	F	T
$P \rightarrow Q$	T	T	F	T

Truth table for conditional

conditional 1. Taken account of in some but not all circumstances.

2. A logic statement of the form
$$P \rightarrow Q \text{ or } P \supset Q, P \Rightarrow Q$$
that should be read as "if P is true then Q follows", although its meaning in logic only partly resembles its usage in English (*see* table).

conditional jump (conditional branch) A *jump that takes place only if a specified condition holds, e.g. specified register contents zero, nonzero, negative, etc.

condition number A number that gives a measure of how sensitive the solution of a problem is to changes in the data. In practice such numbers are often difficult to compute; even so they can play an important part in comparing algorithms. They have a particularly important role in *numerical linear algebra. As an example, for the *linear algebraic equations
$$Ax = b,$$
if b is changed to $b + \Delta b$ (simulating, for example, errors in the data) then the

corresponding change Δx in the solution satisfies
$$\frac{\|\Delta x\|}{\|x\|} \leqslant \text{cond}(A) \frac{\|\Delta b\|}{\|b\|}$$
where $\text{cond}(A) = \|A\| \|A^{-1}\|$ is the condition number of A with respect to solving linear equations. The expression bounds the relative change in the solution in terms of the relative change in the data b. The actual quantities are measured in terms of a vector norm (*see* approximation theory). Similarly the condition number is expressed in terms of a corresponding matrix norm. It can be shown that $\text{cond}(A) \geqslant 1$. If $\text{cond}(A)$ is large the problem is said to be *ill-conditioned* and it follows that a small relative change in b can lead to a large relative change in the solution x. This means that the accuracy of a computed approximation must be interpreted accordingly, taking into account the size of the possible data errors, machine precision, and errors induced by the particular algorithm.

Similar ideas apply to other problem areas and condition numbers feature in a measure of eigenvalue sensitivity in the matrix *eigenvalue problem.

conferencing *See* teleconferencing.

confidence interval A range of values about a *parameter estimate such that the *probability that the true value of the parameter lies within the range is some fixed value, α, known as the *confidence level*. The upper and lower limits of the range are known as *confidence limits*. Confidence limits are calculated from the theoretical *frequency distribution of the estimating function. The concept may be generalized to several parameters. A *confidence region* at level α contains the true values of the parameters with probability α.

configuration 1. The particular hardware elements and their interconnection in a computer system for a particular period of operation. *See also* reconfiguration.

2. In *configuration management, the functional and physical characteristics of hardware or software as set out in documentation or achieved in a product.

configuration management (CM) Ensuring throughout its lifetime that a product put to some usage is properly constituted for that usage – e.g. that the correct procedures have been followed in creating the product, that the appropriate version of each individual component has been selected, that any required tests have been performed, that the product represents a complete and consistent whole, and that all known problems in any way pertinent to the product have been properly considered. As an illustration, a relatively simple configuration management activity might ensure that the individual components of a software system are the appropriate ones for the particular hardware on which the system is to run. A rather more complex activity might be to assess the impact on all software systems of a newly discovered problem with some version of a compiler, and to initiate any necessary corrective action.

The problems of configuration management can be complex and subtle, and for many projects effective configuration management can be crucial to overall success. Approaches to configuration management fall into two broad classes. One approach attempts to retain control over the product as it evolves, so that configuration management is viewed as a continuous activity that is an integral part of product development. The other approach views configuration management as a separate activity; it is a distinct milestone when the product is first placed under configuration management, and each new revision of the product is subject to the configuration management process, but configuration controls are not imposed during periods of development.

configured-in, -off, -out Terms used to detail the *configuration of a system, or changes (*reconfigurations) therein.

confluent *See* Church–Rosser theorem.

conformance testing Testing carried out to show that a product meets the requirements of a relevant standard. Typically conformance testing is carried out for compilers (thus *compiler validation*), and for products that implement interface specifications such as for *OSI or *EDI. The testing will usually be carried out by a third-party organization approved by the appropriate national body, will use an approved *conformance test suite* and *conformance test procedure*, and will result in the issue of a *conformance certificate* for the product. Usually a certificate will be of limited duration, typically one year, when retesting will be required. If a product is altered in any way retesting will also be required.

congruence relation 1. An equivalence relation defined on the integers in the following manner. Let m be some given but fixed positive integer and let a and b be arbitrary integers. Then a is congruent to b modulo m if and only if $(a - b)$ is divisible by m. It is customary to write this as

$$a \equiv b \ (\text{modulo } m)$$

One of the most important uses of the congruence relation in computing is in generating random integers. A sequence

$$s_0, s_1, s_2, \ldots$$

of integers between 0 and $(m - 1)$ inclusive can be generated by the relation

$$s_{n+1} \equiv as_n + c \ (\text{modulo } m)$$

The values of a, c, and m must be suitably chosen.

2. An *equivalence relation R (defined on a set S on which a *dyadic operation $\circ$ is defined) with the property that whenever

$$x \ R \ u \ \text{and} \ y \ R \ v$$
$$\text{then} \ (x \circ y) \ R \ (u \circ v)$$

This is often referred to as the *substitution property*. Congruence relations can be defined for such *algebraic structures as certain kinds of *algebras, *automata, *groups, *monoids, and for the integers; the latter is the congruence modulo m of def. 1.

conjunction A logical expression of the form

$$a_1 \wedge a_2 \wedge \ldots \wedge a_n$$

where $\wedge$ is the *AND operation. A particular conjunction of interest is the *conjunctive normal form* (*CNF*) of a Boolean expression involving n variables, $x_1, x_2, \ldots, x_n$. Each a_i is of the form

$$(y_1 \vee y_2 \vee \ldots \vee y_n)$$

where $\vee$ is the *OR operation and y_i is equal to x_i or the complement of x_i. Reducing expressions to conjunctive normal form provides a ready method of determining the *equivalence of two Boolean expressions. *See also* propositional calculus. *Compare* disjunction.

conjunctive normal form (CNF) *See* conjunction.

CONLAN *Acronym for* consensus language, a consensus hardware description language. The aim of CONLAN is to provide a common formal syntactic and semantic base for all levels and aspects of hardware and firmware description, in particular for descriptions of system structure and behavior. *See also* CHDL, VHDL.

connected graph A *graph in which there is a *path joining each pair of vertices, the graph being undirected. It is always possible to travel in a connected graph between one vertex and any other; no vertex is isolated. If a graph is not connected it will consist of several components, each of which is connected; such a graph is said to be *disconnected*.

If a graph G has e edges, v vertices, and p components, the *rank* of G, written $\rho(G)$, is defined to be

$$v - p$$

The *nullity* of G, written $\mu(G)$, is

$$e - v + p$$

Thus $\rho(G) + \mu(G) = e$

With reference to a directed *graph, a *weakly connected graph* is one in which the direction of each edge must be removed before the graph can be connected in the manner described above. If however there is a directed path between each pair of vertices u and v and another directed path from v back to u, the directed graph is *strongly connected*.

More formally, let G be a directed graph with vertices V and edges E. The set V can be partitioned into *equivalence classes $V_1, V_2, \ldots$ under the relation that vertices u and v are equivalent iff there is a path from u to v and another from v to u. Let $E_1, E_2, \ldots$ be the sets of edges connecting vertices within $V_1, V_2, \ldots$ Then each of the graphs G_i with vertices V_i and edges E_i is a *strongly connected component* of G. A strongly connected graph has precisely one strongly connected component.

The process of replacing each of the strongly connected components of a directed graph by a single vertex is known as *condensation*.

connectedness A measure of the extent to which a given graph is *connected. An undirected graph is k-connected if for every pair of vertices u and v there are at least k paths between u and v such that no vertex other than u and v themselves appear on more than one path. A *connected graph is 1-connected, a *biconnected graph is 2-connected.

connectionless network service (CLNS) A network in which each *packet of information between a source and destination travels independently of any other packets. In practice, many networks are capable of operating in either a connectionless or a connection-oriented mode, and the choice of which approach is adopted rests as much with the designer of the protocols as with the actual hardware of the network. *See also* connection-oriented network service, datagram.

connection machine A parallel processor in which many processor-memory pairs – small computers – operate simultaneously. Central to the machine is a communication network that permits the small computers to exchange information in a pattern suited to the algorithm being executed. The connection machine described in 1987 consisted of 65 536 small processors giving a total execution rate of several thousand million instructions per second. Particular areas of application include *image processing, *information retrieval, *graphics, *artificial intelligence, and fluid flow.

connection-oriented network service (CONS) A network in which a pair of remote activities that wish to communicate are required to establish some form of circuit before they can exchange data. In a *circuit switching network, the connection will take the form of a physical circuit, while in a *packet switching network it is a *virtual connection. *See also* connectionless network service, datagram.

connective A logical device used for the construction of more complex statements or expressions from simpler statements or expressions. Examples in everyday use are "and", "or", and "not". Connectives also occur in *Boolean algebra, *switching theory, *digital design, *formal logic, and in *programming languages. In all these cases they are used, often as operators, in the formation of more complex logical or Boolean expressions or statements from simpler components. These simpler components inevitably have a value that is either true or false. *Truth tables describe the effect or result of using a

connective, given the truth of the simpler components.

connectivity of a *graph G. The minimum number of vertices (and associated edges) of G whose removal from G results either in a graph that is no longer *connected or in a trivial graph with a single vertex: at least k vertices must be removed from a graph with k-*connectivity*. The higher the connectivity the more edges there are joining vertices.

The quantity described above is sometimes called the *vertex connectivity* to distinguish it from the *edge connectivity*, which by analogy is the minimum number of edges whose removal from G results in a graph that is disconnected or trivial.

connectivity matrix *Another name for* adjacency matrix.

CONS *Acronym for* connection-oriented network service.

consensus In combinational logic, a condition that is said to exist when two terms of a *Boolean function have one shared variable, which in one term is true and in the other complemented. A new term can be generated by the product of the remaining literals in the two terms, with the consensus variable eliminated, without altering the value of the function. For example, if

$$f = ab + a'c$$

then, in addition,

$$f = ab + a'c + bc$$

The term bc is sometimes called an *optional product*. This operation is invaluable in the elimination of circuit static hazards. Its systematic application to a Boolean function provides the basis of a *minimization procedure that is less voluminous than the Quine-McCluskey method, since it does not require the full canonical expansion of the original function.

consistency A term that is usually used in the context of numerical methods for ordinary and partial differential equations. A formula derived from a *discretization is consistent if the local *discretization error has *order at least two with respect to the stepsize, h. Consistency is a necessary condition for convergence of a discretization formula (*see* error analysis).

console The workstation from which the operation of a computer system can be monitored and controlled. In current systems the console is usually a desk-height surface supporting a keyboard and one or more VDUs and reference documents. There may also be a number of other switches and indicators mounted on a panel. In early systems the control unit at the console was often a teleprinter. As systems became larger and more sophisticated the consoles first became more complex and then much simpler as the development of operating systems advanced. Some recent medium-sized systems do not have a console.

constant 1. A quantity or data item whose value does not change.
2. A value that is determined by its denotation, i.e. a *literal.

construct *See* language construct.

constructive function A *function defined (explicitly rather than implicitly) in such a way that there is a rule that describes how the effect of the function can be realized; such functions are utilized by mathematicians who adopt an intuitionist or constructionist view of their subject. For example, it is inadequate to say that cube roots can be derived by solving a cubic equation of the form $x^3 = a$. It is necessary to give guidance on how cube roots can be evaluated.

constructive specification A particular approach to writing *abstract specifications for programs, modules, or data types. Model representations are given for the data items involved, in terms of set-theory constructs such as *sets, *functions, *relations, and *sequences. The effect of the operations involved is then described at this level of abstraction, typically by giving preconditions and postconditions for each operation. An implementation of the specification would involve replacing the set-theory constructs by lower-level ones, while preserving the meaning expressed by the specification. Although expressed at an abstract set-theory level, a constructive specification does give explicit constructions for the data and explicit definitions for the operations; it therefore contrasts with *axiomatic specification, in which the representations are implicit rather than explicit. Widely used constructive specification formalisms are *VDM and the language *Z.

consumable resource Any resource that is, by its nature, usable on only a limited number of occasions. A punched card can only be punched once, although it may be read repeatedly, and must be regarded as consumable. *Compare* reusable resource.

contact bounce *See* debouncing.

content-addressable memory (CAM) *Another name for* associative memory. *See also* associative addressing.

context-free grammar A *grammar in which the left-hand side of each production is a single nonterminal, i.e. productions have the form
$$A \to \alpha$$
where α is a string of terminals and/or nonterminals. For brevity one writes
$$A \to \alpha_1 \mid \alpha_2 \mid .. .. \mid \alpha_n$$
to indicate the separate productions
$$A \to \alpha_1, \ A \to \alpha_2, \ .., \\ .., \ A \to \alpha_n$$
As an example, the following generates a simple class of arithmetic expressions typified by $(a + b) \times c$:
$$E \to T \mid T + E \mid (E)$$

$T \rightarrow E \mid E \times T \mid a \mid b \mid c$

The *BNF notation used in defining the syntax of programming languages is simply a context-free grammar. The term itself was coined to contrast with *context-sensitive grammar.

context-free language (algebraic language) Any formal language generated by a *context-free grammar or, from another viewpoint, any formal language recognized by a *pushdown automaton. It is also the frontier of a regular *tree language.

context-sensitive grammar A *grammar in which each production has the form

$$\alpha A \beta \rightarrow \alpha \gamma \beta$$

where A is a nonterminal and α, β, and γ are arbitrary *words with γ nonempty. If γ was allowed to be empty then any type 0 language of the *Chomsky hierarchy could be generated. To derive the empty word, a production

$$S \rightarrow \Lambda$$

must also be included, with S not occurring in the right-hand side of any production. The term context-sensitive refers to the fact that A can be rewritten to γ only in the "context" $\alpha \ldots \beta$.

In a *length-increasing grammar* each production has a right-hand side at least as long as its left-hand side (apart possibly from $S \rightarrow \Lambda$). Clearly any context-sensitive grammar is length-increasing, but it can also be shown that any length-increasing grammar is equivalent to a context-sensitive one. *Compare* context-free grammar.

context-sensitive language Any formal language generated by a *context-sensitive grammar, or recognized by a *linear-bounded automaton.

context switch A general term covering the situation in which a *process initiates a new type of activity. Any process functions in some form of environment, which defines the currently valid *variables that the process can manipulate, and their actual values, including the "undefined" value in the case where a variable has been created but has as yet had no value assigned to it. These remarks apply equally if the process being considered is one that is being dealt with by a person rather than a machine. A context switch occurs when the environment for the currently active process is replaced by a new environment.

contingency table In statistical analysis, a *frequency distribution of sample data classified by two or more factors, each with two or more classes. A simple example is a medical clinical trial of two treatments in which the number of patients assigned to each treatment is classified according to whether improvement was observed or not. If there is no significant difference between the proportions of patients improving, there is said to be no *interaction* between the two classifications of the table. The statistical analysis of contingency tables depends on certain assumptions (random assignment to classes, absence of other relevant factors) that make the interpretation controversial, and care must be taken in applying the tests correctly. *See also* chi-squared distribution.

continuation 1. A concept in programming language semantics, allowing the meaning of program constructs to be defined in terms of the effect they have on the computation remaining to be done, rather than on the current state of the computation. This is particularly useful in giving the semantics of constructs that effect the flow of control, such as GOTOs and loop exits.

2. An approach to solving a mathematical problem that involves solving a sequence of problems with different parameters; the parameters are selected so that ultimately the original problem is solved. An underlying assumption is that the solution depends continuously on the parameter. This approach is used for example on difficult problems in *nonlinear equations and *differential equations. For example, to solve the nonlinear equations

$$F(x) = 0,$$

let $x^{(0)}$ be a first approximation to the solution. Let α be a parameter $0 \leqslant \alpha \leqslant 1$, then define the equations

$$\hat{F}(x,\alpha) = F(x) + (\alpha-1)F(x^{(0)}) = 0$$

For $\alpha = 0$, $x^{(0)}$ is a solution; for $\alpha = 1$,

$$\hat{F}(x,1) = F(x) = 0,$$

which are the original equations. Hence by solving the sequence of problems with α given by

$$0 = \alpha_0 < \alpha_1 < \ldots < \alpha_N = 1$$

the original problem is solved. As the calculation proceeds each solution can be used as a starting approximation for the next problem.

continuous function A *function from one *partially ordered set to another having the property, roughly speaking, that least *upper bounds are preserved. A function

$$f : S \to T$$

is said to be continuous if, for every *directed subset X of S, f maps the least upper bound of X to the least upper bound of the *image of X under f. Continuous functions are significant in *denotational semantics since they correspond to the requirement that a computational process produces arbitrarily close approximations to the final output, given arbitrarily close approximations to the total input.

continuous signal, system *See* discrete and continuous systems.

continuous stationery *See* stationery.

contradiction *See* tautology.

contrapositive of a conditional, $P \to Q$. The statement

$$\neg Q \to \neg P$$

where $\neg$ denotes negation. The contrapositive of a conditional is therefore equivalent to the original conditional. *See also* converse, inverse.

control bus A *bus that is dedicated to the passing of control signals.

control character A character that when typed at a keyboard or sent to a peripheral device is treated as a signal to control operating functions. *See also* character set, ASCII.

control circuitry Electric circuits within a computer or peripheral that regulate its operation.

Control Data Corporation *See* CDC.

control design The design of a *control unit. Control units were originally designed with *random logic; they are now almost always designed with *microprogramming.

control flow The sequence of execution of statements in a program. *Compare* data flow.

control flow graph A *directed graph representing the sequence of execution in a program unit, in which nodes represent branching points or subprogram calls in a program, and arcs represent linear sequences of code. From the control flow graph an analysis can show
the structure of the program,
starts and ends of program segments,
unreachable code and dynamic halts,
branches from within loops,
entry and exit points for loops,
paths through the program.
See also static analysis.

control key *See* keyboard, control character.

controlled sharing Making used resources available to more than one using resource through an *access control mechanism.

controller A subsystem that governs the functions of attached devices but generally does not change the meaning of the data that may pass through it. The attached devices are usually peripherals or communication channels. One of the functions of the controller may involve processing the data stream in order to format it for transmission or recording.

control line A conductor in a multiwire interface that conveys a control signal.

control memory *Another name for* microprogram store.

control record A record that contains *control totals* derived by summing values from other records in a file. The totals may or may not have some sensible meaning. Their purpose is to check that none of the preceding records has been lost or altered in some way. *See also* hash total.

control stack A stack mechanism that contains an instruction sequence. It is part of the control unit in a computer with stack architecture. *See* stack processing.

control structure A syntactic form in a language to express flow of control. Common control structures are if ... then ... else, while ... do, repeat ... until, and case.

control total *See* control record.

control unit (CU) The portion of a *central processor that contains the necessary *registers, *counters, and other elements to provide the functionality required to control the movement of information between the memory, the *arithmetic and logic unit, and other portions of the machine.

In the simplest form of the classical von Neumann architecture, the control unit contains a *program counter, an *address register, and a register that contains and decodes the *operation code. The latter two registers are some-

times jointly called the *instruction register*. This control unit then operates in a two-step *fetch-execute* cycle. In the fetch step the instruction is obtained (fetched) from memory and the decoder determines the nature of the instruction. If it is a *memory reference instruction the execute step carries out the necessary operation(s) and memory reference(s). In some cases, e.g. a *nonmemory reference instruction, there may be no execute step. When the instruction calls for *indirect addressing, an additional step, usually called "defer", is required to obtain the indirect address from the memory. The last action during the execute step is to increment the program counter or, in some cases – e.g. a *conditional branch instruction – to set the program counter to a value determined by the instruction register, depending on the status of the *accumulator or *qualifier register.

In more complex machines and *non von Neumann architectures, the control unit may contain additional registers such as *index registers, arithmetic units to provide address modifications, registers, *stacks, or *pipelines to contain forthcoming instructions, and other functional units. At present, most control units are microprogrammed (*see* microprogramming). Some exceptions are found in control units that have become powerful and complex; in supercomputers, for example, they may contain specialized hardware that allows for parallel processing of instructions which are issued sequentially.

control word 1. A word whose contents determine actions elsewhere; it may be used to control the use of a resource.

2. A word in a microprogram. *See* microinstruction, microprogramming.

convergence of an algorithm. *See* error analysis.

conversational mode *See* interactive.

converse 1. of a conditional, $P \rightarrow Q$. The statement

$$\neg P \rightarrow \neg Q$$

where $\neg$ denotes negation. *See also* contrapositive, inverse.

2. of a binary relation. *Another name for* inverse.

convolution Mathematically, the operation of combining two functions, w and f, to produce a third function, g, such that

$$g_k = \sum_{i=0}^{\infty} w_i f_{k-i}$$

(or the corresponding continuous operation). This is envisaged as a transformation of an input function f to an output function g, by viewing f through a fixed window w.

In coding theory, f is considered as a *signal and w as the response of a *linear channel; g is then the effect upon that signal (regarded as a sequence of successive elements) brought about by the time response of the linear channel. The *channel time response* is the sequence of successive elements output by the channel in response to a signal that has one element of unit amplitude and all other elements zero. The input signal sequence and the channel time response are said to be *convolved*.

The inverse process is *deconvolution*: the convolved output sequence can be *deconvolved* with the channel time response sequence to restore the original input signal sequence.

It is important, both mathematically and practically, that the convolution of discrete-time signals corresponds to the conventional multiplication of *polynomials.

See also feedback register, feed-forward register.

convolutional code A *linear error-correcting code, characterized by a $k \times n$ generator matrix,

$$G = (g_{ij}[x]),$$

whose elements $g_{ij}[x]$ are *polynomials whose highest degree, m, is called the *memory* of the code. The quantity

$$c = m + 1$$

is called the *constraint length* of the code.

The convolutional encoder operates as follows. The input stream, regarded as the coefficients of a polynomial of arbitrary degree, is cyclically distributed (i.e. demultiplexed) among the inputs of k *shift registers, all of length c: the contents of the ith shift register is serially multiplied by each of the n polynomials $g_{ij}[x]$ (using n serial multipliers in parallel). Then n output streams are formed by summing the outputs of the jth multiplier on each register. These streams are cyclically multiplexed to form the output of the encoder. All this can be carried out to base q, for q prime; such codes are usually implemented in binary form ($q = 2$). In practice, the parameter k is normally equal to 1.

The main decoding algorithms for convolutional codes are *Viterbi's algorithm* and various *sequential algorithms, of which the most important are *Fano's algorithm* and the *stack algorithm*. Viterbi's is a maximum-likelihood algorithm.

Linear *block codes can be regarded as a special case of convolutional codes with $m = 0$ and $c = 1$. Convolutional codes are often specified by the parameters (n, k) or (n, k, c), although the simple phrase (n, k) code usually specifies a block code rather than a convolutional code.

Convolutional codes are of increasing importance as they become better understood theoretically, as better decoding algorithms are found, and as it becomes increasingly economical to provide programmable decoders, the decoding algorithms being best programmed in software owing to their complexity.

coprocessor A microprocessing element designed to supplement the capabilities of the primary processor. For example, several microprocessor manufacturers now offer coprocessors in their product lines that offer expanded mathematical processing abilities, including high-speed floating-point arithmetic and computation of trigonometric functions. The coprocessor extends the set of instructions available to the programmer. When the main processor receives an instruction that it does not support, it can transfer control to a coprocessor that does.

The variety of functions that could be implemented in a coprocessor is unlimited, and more than one coprocessor could be used in a system if the primary processor has been suitably designed. For instance, one coprocessor could provide high-speed math processing and another could provide database management primitives. An example of a coprocessor is the Intel 8087, which is a math chip designed to work with both the 8-bit-bus 8088 and 16-bit-bus 8086 processors.

copy To produce a replica of some stored information in a different part of the store or on a different storage device. This is often done to guard against loss or corruption of important records.

copyright The right to prevent copying. It is a negative right that can be exercised by a copyright holder if he/she chooses. Copyright protects the form in which an idea is expressed but not the idea per se. Computer programs both in *source code and *object code format are protected as literary works under amended copyright laws in all industrial nations. Some developing countries have yet to amend their laws.

Copyright law is now also used to limit the use that is made of computer programs through the granting of *limited licenses* to customers: these restrict customers from legally being entitled to use several copies of individual programs at the same time or use copies on anything except a particular computer.

There are growing conflicts between copyright and competition (antitrust) law arising out of restrictive license terms, copyright in screen layouts, and copyright in interface protocols. The issue of ownership of copyright in works created by computers through an automatic interaction of data, programs, and operator action is not yet decided.

In the USA copyright protection has been expanded by judge-made law into new areas. The 'Look and Feel' of a program has been held to be protectable. Thus a person who writes an entirely different program that appears to the user to be the same or very similar to the original program can be enjoined. It is not thought likely that a "look and feel" argument would succeed in English courts and the US cases are looked on with suspicion even in the USA.

No formalities are required to obtain copyright in computer programs in the UK and other countries in the Berne Union. The USA, however, requires a reservation of copyright to preserve the right. The USA have recently joined the Berne Union and it is anticipated that this requirement will be dropped in the course of the next few years.

CORAL A programming language loosely based on *Algol 60 and developed in the UK for military applications. Although described as a real-time language, CORAL has no built-in facilities for parallel processing, synchronization, interrupt handling, etc. These necessary facilities have to be provided in machine code, and for this purpose CORAL provides a macro facility and a convenient escape to assembler level. The most widely used version of the language is CORAL 66. The use of CORAL is declining as *Ada comes into widespread use.

CORE A method with supporting tools for capturing, structuring, and expressing system and software requirements. It was originally devised by British Aerospace (BAe) in 1979 and later extended by BAe and Systems Designers in the UK. CORE supports the different roles and viewpoints of user, customer, and analyst, and provides techniques to ensure completeness, consistency, and lack of ambiguity by cross-referencing between viewpoints. The informal CORE notation provides a series of diagramming techniques and associated text descriptions.

core store A type of nonvolatile memory in which binary information is stored in an array of toroidal magnetic cores. The cores are made of a *ferrite material that has two stable magnetic states and can be switched from one to the other by imposing a sufficient magnetic flux; the flux is generated by electric currents in conductors threaded through the cores. The principle of the core store was discovered in 1949 by J. W. Forrester of MIT. Although widely used as main storage for processors from the mid-1950s to the late 1970s, core store has been displaced in modern processor design by *semiconductor memory.

coroutine A program component that allows structuring of a program in an unusual way. A coroutine resembles a *subroutine, with one important difference. A subroutine has a subordinate position relative to the main routine: it is *called* and then *returns*. Coroutines, however, have a symmetric relation: each can call the other. Thus a coroutine is *resumed* at a point immediately following its call of another coroutine; it never returns, but terminates its operation by calling (resuming) another coroutine.

Coroutines are not commonly found in high-level languages. They are particularly useful as a means of modeling concurrent activity in a sequential machine.

corrective maintenance *Another name for* remedial maintenance. *See also* software maintenance.

correctness proof *See* program correctness proof.

correlation A measure of a tendency for two or more *random variables to be associated. The formula for r, the sample *correlation coefficient* between two variables x and y, is

$$\frac{\Sigma (x_i - \overline{x})(y_i - \overline{y})}{\sqrt{[\Sigma (x_i - \overline{x})^2 \, \Sigma (y_i - \overline{y})^2]}}$$

which varies between -1 and $+1$. Negative values or r indicate that y tends to decrease as x increases, while positive values indicate that x and y increase or decrease together. If the value of r is zero then x and y are *uncorrelated*.

Rank correlation measures the correlation between the ranks (or order numbers) of the variables, i.e. between the positions when the numbers are arranged in increasing order of magnitude.

Correlation does not imply causation. Variables may be correlated accidentally, or because of joint association with other unmeasured agencies such as a general upward trend with time. If the relationship is not linear the correlation coefficient may be misleading.

coset of a *group G that possesses a *subgroup H. A coset of G modulo H determined by the element x of G is a subset:

$$x \circ H = \{x \circ h \,|\, h \in H\}$$
$$H \circ x = \{h \circ x \,|\, h \in H\}$$

where $\circ$ is the dyadic operation defined on G. A subset of the former kind is called a *left coset* of G modulo H or a left coset of G in H; the latter is a *right coset*. In special cases

$$x \circ H = H \circ x$$

for any x in G. Then H is called a *normal subgroup* of G. Any subgroup of an abelian *group is a normal subgroup.

The cosets of G in H form a partition of the group G, each coset showing the same number of elements as H itself. These can be viewed as the *equivalence classes of a *left coset relation* defined on the elements g_1 and g_2 of G as follows:

$$g_1 \; \rho \; g_2 \text{ iff } g_1 \circ H = g_2 \circ H$$

Similarly a *right coset relation* can be defined. When H is a normal subgroup the coset relation becomes a *congruence relation.

Cosets have important applications in computer science, e.g. in the development of efficient codes needed in the transmission of information and in the design of fast adders.

coset relation *See* coset.

cost estimation model A mathematical model used to predict the overall cost of creating software or hardware. Usually for hardware the model comprises a database of past achieved effort/duration/costs for development and manufacture (sometimes maintenance), and support for the estimator in matching characteristics of the historic data with those of the proposed new systems (or similar parts of the systems). The estimate of cost is then formed from the historic data, from constants and parameters derived from the database, and is modified using engineering judgement and a knowledge of the risk factors and local conditions.

For software the expected size of the software (lines of code) is usually used as the main input to a cost estimation model, with other inputs characterizing the main risk factors in the development. An underlying (software estimation model) database of past projects is built up from experience in a particular company or using one software paradigm. Typical software cost estimation models are *COCOMO (Barry Boehm) and GECOMO (GEC Software, UK),

PRICE S (RCA), PROMPT Estimator (LBMS, UK), and SLIM (Putnam, Norden, Rayleigh model, software from QSM Inc, US). The models make no apportionment of costs to different life-cycle phases, and generally give cost to deliver. Some models (e.g. COCOMO) can be used to estimate maintenance costs.

See also function point analysis.

cost function A scalar measure of a complex situation, used for optimization. *See also* weighted graph.

countable set A *set that, in some sense, is no larger than the set of natural numbers. The elements of the set can be put into order and counted. Such a set is either *finite or *denumerable*; the elements of a denumerable set can be placed in a one-to-one correspondence with the set of natural numbers. The set of rational numbers can be shown to be countable but the set of real numbers is not countable.

counter A clocked digital electronic device whose output takes up one and one only of a number, n, of distinct states upon the application of each clock pulse. The output thus reflects the total number of clock pulses received by the counter up to its maximum capacity, n. All n states are displayed sequentially for n active transitions of the clock, the sequence then repeating. Since n clock pulses are required to drive the output between any two identical states, counters provide a "divide-by-n action" and are thus also known as *dividers*.

A counter whose output is capable of displaying n discrete states before producing an overflow condition can also be called a *mod-n counter* (or *modulo-n counter*), since it may be considered to be counting input pulses to a base of n. The value of n is often an integer power of 2. Counters are generally formed by a cascaded series of clocked *flip-flops (*see* cascadable counter), each of which provides a divide-by-two action. For a counter consisting of m flip-flops, the maximum capacity of the counter will be 2^m since 2^m discrete output states are possible, i.e. n is equal to 2^m. These are known as *binary counters*.

Count lengths of other than integer multiples of two are possible. For example, a *decade counter* (or mod-10 counter) exhibits 10 separate and distinct states. To achieve this digitally requires a counter having at least four individual flip-flop elements, giving 2^4 or 16 possible output states; six of these states are prevented from occurring by a suitable arrangement of logic gates around the individual flip-flops. In *multimode counters* the number, n, of distinct states can be selected by the user.

See also ripple counter, synchronous counter, shift counter.

counting problem 1. The task of finding the number of elements of some set with a particular property. Such counting problems are usually encountered in *combinatorics.

2. The task of counting the number of solutions to a problem. For example, to find the number of *spanning trees of a given graph, there is a formula in terms of the determinant of a certain matrix that is computable in *polynomial time. There are however other problems, like counting the number of *Hamiltonian cycles in a given graph, that are expected to be difficult since determining whether or not a graph has a Hamiltonian cycle is NP-complete (*see* P = NP question). Although it is possible to determine whether or not a graph has a perfect *matching* (a set of edges that do not meet each other but meet every vertex) in polynomial time, computing the number of such matchings can be done in polynomial time only if *P = NP*.

The matching problem referred to is, in the bipartite case, the same as computing the permanent of a 0–1 matrix, for which no good methods are known.

coupled A rather vague term, used to indicate that systems which might operate separately are actually being used in some form of cooperative mode. The term is applied to hardware units, as in *cross coupled*, where a pair of inverting gates are used to form a *latch circuit: the output of each gate serves as an input to the other. It is also applied to complete processors, as in *loosely coupled* and *tightly coupled* processors: there are substantial discrepancies in usage between different users of these terms, especially with respect to the precise overtone associated with the qualifying adverb. *See also* coupling, concurrency.

coupling A measure of the strength of interconnections between modules of a program. A high coupling would indicate strong dependencies between one module and another. Loose coupling allows greater flexibility in the design and better traceability, isolation, and correction of faults. The strength of coupling depends on the number of references of one module by another, the amount of data passed (or shared) between modules, the complexity of the interface between modules, and the amount of control exercised by one module over another. Completely *decoupled* modules have no common data and no control flow interaction. *See also* cohesion.

covariance A measure of the joint variation of two random variables, analogous to variance (*see* measures of variation). If the variables are x and y then the covariance of x and y is

$$\Sigma(x_i - \bar{x})(y_i - \bar{y})$$

The *analysis of covariance* is an extension of the *analysis of variance in which the variables to be tested are adjusted to take account of assumed linear relationships with other variables. *See also* correlation.

covering 1. of a *set S. A finite set of *subsets of S whose *union is just S

itself. The subsets, $A_1, A_2, \ldots, A_m$, are said to cover S. If the elements A_i for $i = 1, 2, \ldots, m$ are mutually *disjoint, then the covering

$$\{A_1, \ldots A_m\}$$

is called a *partition* of S.

2. A relationship between two elements of a partially ordered set S. If x and y are elements of S then y covers x if and only if $x<y$, and whenever $x \leqslant z \leqslant y$ for some element z in S, then either $x = z$ or $z = y$.

covert channel A communication path, usually indirect, by which information can be transmitted in violation of a *security policy. For example, a covert channel may exploit system flags to allow one program to send confidential information to another.

CPL *Abbrev. for* combined programming language. A language developed in the early 1960s at the Universities of Cambridge and London in the UK. Its aim, rather unusual for the time, was to provide a single language for all applications on a new computer, including those areas at that time universally thought to be the province of assembly language. Although it never came into general use, CPL is noteworthy for the fact that it anticipated many of the concepts that are now regarded as characterizing modern "advanced" languages, notably the control structures of *structured programming and the reference concept that forms a major feature of Algol 68. CPL was the direct precursor of *BCPL and thus an ancestor of *C.

CPM *Abbrev. for* criticial path method.

CP/M *Trademark* An operating system intended for use on microprocessor-based systems that support a single user at any one time. The system includes file maintenance, facilities for inspecting and updating the contents of memory, and access to an assembler and compilers.

cps *Abbrev. for* characters per second. A rate of processing, transferring, or printing information.

CPU *Abbrev. for* central processing unit. *See* central processor.

CPU cycle Usually, the time required for the fetching and execution of one simple (e.g. add or subtract) machine instruction. It is one of many figures-of-merit for a computer system. *See also* computer power, add-subtract time, cycle.

CPU time (processor time) The time for which a *process has been receiving service from the processor. *See also* system accounting.

crash A system failure that requires at least operator intervention and often some maintenance before system running can resume. The word is also used as a verb. *See also* recovery.

Cray Research A company formed in 1972 by Seymour Cray at which a series of very high speed *supercomputers have been developed, including the original Cray-1 (launched 1976), and the multiprocessors Cray Y-MP (1988) and Cray-3 (1989). These are suitable for complex numerical applications such as weather forecasting and very sophisticated graphics applications.

CRC *Abbrev. for* cyclic redundancy check, or for cyclic redundancy code.

crisis time The time during which an *interrupt must be serviced, otherwise a fault will occur.

critical path method (CPM) A project planning, management, and scheduling method that divides a project into activities, each with a statement of time and resources required, and their precedence dependencies. These activities are then connected in a graph that expresses the dependencies and the times. The *critical* *path* is defined as the path through the graph that requires the maximum time. Variations of this method allow for statistically distributed time and resources, time/resource tradeoffs, etc. *See also* PERT.

critical region A section of code that may only be executed by one *process at any one time. *See also* critical resource, critical section, mutual exclusion.

critical resource A resource that can only be in use by at most one *process at any one time. A common example is a section of code that deals with the allocation or release of a shared resource, where it is imperative that no more than one process at a time is allowed to alter the data that defines which processes have been allocated parts of the resource.

Where several asynchronous processes are required to coordinate their access to a critical resource, they do so by controlled access to a *semaphore. A process wishing to access the resource issues a P operation that inspects the value of the semaphore; the value indicates whether or not any other process has access to the critical resource. If some other process is using the resource then the process issuing the P operation will be suspended. A process issues a V operation when it has finished using the critical resource. The V operation can never cause suspension of the issuing process but by operating on the value of the semaphore may allow some other cooperating process to commence operation.

critical section Part of a *process that must be executed indivisibly. Originally it was thought that the indivisibility had to be absolute. Now it is considered that it is only necessary for the critical section to be uninterrupted by other critical sections of a particular set of processes, i.e. those among which there is *mutual exclusion.

cross assembler An *assembler that runs on one machine, producing an object program to run on a different machine. It is usually used to generate software for microcomputers that are themselves too small to support an assembler. *See also* cross compiler.

cross compiler A *compiler that runs on one machine, producing an object program to run on a different machine. It is usually used to generate software for microcomputers that are themselves too small to support a compiler. *See also* cross assembler.

cross coupling An interconnection between two *logic gates, permitting them to form a *flip-flop.

cross talk A signal that has leaked or "crossed" from one communication channel to an adjacent channel. This interferes with (causes errors on) the second channel. Cross talk is usually associated with physical communication channels, such as an RS232 connection, or other buses.

CRT *Abbrev. for* cathode-ray tube.

cryogenic memory A type of memory operating at a very low temperature by means of *superconductivity and electron tunneling.

cryptanalysis Processing of an encrypted message to derive the original message by an "attacker" lacking prior knowledge of the secret key. *Compare* decryption.

cryptography The protection of a message so as to render it unintelligible to other than authorized recipients. Many techniques are known for the conversion of the original message, known as *plain text*, into its encrypted form, known as *cipher*, *ciphertext*, or *code*.

In a simple cipher system, for example, the sender and recipient hold identical copies of a secret *key*, and also an algorithm with which they each generate identical *pseudorandom bit sequences. During encryption the sender modifies the plain text string by combining it with the pseudorandom sequence, using mod 2 addition, to produce the ciphertext; the ciphertext is then transmitted. The recipient performs the reverse process by subtracting an identical pseudorandom sequence from the received ciphertext to recover the plain text.

An alternative encryption technique is the use of a *codebook* system where the sender and recipient hold copies of a secret substitution table. This lists the codes to be transmitted as the ciphertext, depending on the value of each byte of the plain text. However, practical codebook schemes normally use substitution codes corresponding to longer blocks of plain text, typically 64 bits. In such schemes the substitution codes must be generated algorithmically by the sender and recipient since the size of the substitution table usually precludes its explicit storage.

cryptology The study of *cryptography.

CSL *Abbrev. for* control and simulation language, one of the earliest *simulation languages. It is now obsolete.

CSMA/CD A *data link control protocol applicable to a broadcast network in which all stations can receive all messages (*see* broadcasting). A station can detect the presence of a transmitted message by sensing the carrier of the transmission. When a station wishes to send a message, it first waits until no other station is transmitting (*carrier sense multiple access, CSMA*). When two or more stations try to send messages concurrently, *collisions* may occur since a station will not see another station's signal until after it has begun its own

transmission. A *collision detection (CD)* mechanism detects the collision, causing the stations to terminate their current transmissions and try again later.

The CSMA protocol was developed by DARPA for use in satellite transmission systems. CSMA/CD now finds its widest application in local area networks, where it is generally referred to as *Ethernet. CSMA and CSMA/CD are forms of asynchronous *time-division multiplexing.

CSP *Abbrev. for* communicating sequential processes, a model for *concurrent computation developed by C. A. R. Hoare. CSP provides the theoretical foundation for the programming language *occam.

CTron *See* Tron.

cumulative distribution function *See* probability distributions.

current address register *Another name for* instruction counter.

current instruction register (CIR) A register, usually in the control unit, that contains the information specifying the instruction that is being (or is about to be) performed. *See also* instruction format.

curried function A *function of one variable that is related to a function of several variables. Let f be a function of two variables, x and y. Then by considering x constant we obtain a function in y; this function depends on the value of x. We write

$$g(x)(y) = f(x,y)$$

where g is called a curried version of f. Note that $g(x)$ denotes a function rather than a plain value. Currying is often used in theoretical work to deal simply with functions of several variables, e.g. in the lambda calculus.

cursor A symbol on a display screen that indicates the active position, e.g.

the position at which the next character to be entered will be displayed. The underline symbol is often used: it is made to blink or flash so that it is easily noticed and can be distinguished from an underline that is part of the text. Other symbols, such as a frame around the character space, are also used.

cut A mechanism used in *Prolog to limit *backtracking. Roughly speaking, the effect of a cut is to fix certain decisions that have already been made, thus preventing the system from undoing those decisions in order to perform further search for solutions to its goals. This is a way of avoiding costly search known in advance to be fruitless, or of excluding alternative solutions that are not wanted. However, writing cuts in a program makes its behavior dependent on the system's search sequence. Such dependency prevents the program from being a pure statement of logical relationships and thus goes against the spirit of *logic programming.

cut-point *See* Floyd method.

cut set of a *connected graph *G*. A set of edges whose removal produces a disconnected graph; no set with fewer elements would produce this effect. *See also* connectivity.

cut sheet feed *See* stationery.

cut vertex (articulation point) of a *connected graph *G*. A vertex of *G* whose removal together with the removal of all edges incident to it results in the remaining graph being disconnected. The term can also be extended and applied to more general graphs. Then the removal of a cut vertex and all arcs incident to it increases the number of connected components of the graph. *See also* connectivity.

cybernetics A discipline concerned with control and communication in animal and machine. Cybernetics attempts to build a general theory of machines independent of the material they are made from, e.g. electronic, organic, clockwork. Cybernetics draws an analogy between brains and electronic circuits. *See also* neural networks.

CYCLADES An early experimental *packet-switching network in France. The first hosts were connected in 1973. CYCLADES was composed of two parts: the *host computers and the *communication subnet CIGALE. CIGALE was a pure *datagram network, delivering individual packets without any sequencing or flow control. The host computers were responsible for providing reliable connections on top of the datagram service. *Compare* RCP.

cycle 1. (cycle time) An interval of time in which one set of events or phenomena is completed. It is usually the time required for one cycle of the memory system – the time between successive accesses – of a computer, and is sometimes considered to be a measure of *computer power.

2. Any set of operations that is repeated regularly and in the same sequence. The operations may be subject to variations on each repetition.

3. (circuit) of a *graph. A path that starts and ends at the same vertex. A cycle is said to be *simple* provided no edge appears more than once, and is *elementary* if no vertex (other than the start) appears more than once. *See also* Euler cycle, Hamiltonian cycle.

4. A *permutation of a set that maps some subset

$$T = \{t_1, t_2, \ldots, t_m\}$$

of *S* in such a way that each t_i is mapped into t_{i+1}

$$(i = 1, 2, \ldots, m-1)$$

and t_m is mapped into t_1; the remaining elements of *S* are left unaltered by the permutation. Two cycles

$$(u_1 \; u_2 \; \ldots) \text{ and } (v_1 \; v_2 \; \ldots)$$

are disjoint provided the sets

$\{u_1, u_2, \ldots\}$ and $\{v_1, v_2, \ldots\}$ are disjoint. Every permutation of a set can be expressed uniquely as the *composition of disjoint cycles.

cycle index polynomial A formal polynomial associated with a *group of *permutations on a set, indicating the decomposition of the permutations into *cycles. Such polynomials occur for example in *switching theory.

cycle stealing (data break) *See* direct memory access.

cycle time *See* cycle.

cyclic access A mode of access to stored information whereby access can only be achieved at certain times in a cycle of events. A magnetic disk is an example of a device with cyclic access.

cyclic code A *linear code in which, given that v is a codeword, then so are all the cyclic shifts of v. For example, if

abcde

is a codeword in a cyclic code, then

bcdea
cdeab
deabc
eabcd

are also codewords.

cyclic redundancy check (cyclic redundancy code; CRC) The most widely used *error-detecting code. Extra digits are appended to each *block in order to provide a means of checking the data for errors that may have occurred, say, during transmission or due to recording and readback processes: the digits are calculated from the contents of the block on input, and recalculated by the receiver or during readback.

A CRC is a type of *polynomial code. In principle, each block, regarded as a polynomial A, is multiplied in the encoder by a generating *polynomial G to form AG. This is affected during transmission or recording by the addition of an error polynomial E, to form

$$AG + E$$

In the decoder this is divided by the same generating polynomial G to give a residue, which is examined to see if it is zero. If it is nonzero, an error is recorded and appropriate action is taken (*see* backward error correction). In practice, the code is made *systematic by encoding A as

$$Ax^r + R$$

where r is the degree of G and R is the residue on dividing Ax^r by G. In either case, the only errors that escape detection are those for which E has G as a factor: the system designer chooses G to make this as unlikely as possible. Usually, in the binary case, G is the product of $(x + 1)$ and a primitive factor of suitable degree.

A binary code for which

$$G = x + 1$$

is known as a *simple parity check* (or *simple parity code*). When applied across each character of, say, a magnetic tape record, this is called a *horizontal check*; when applied along each track of the record, it is called a *vertical check*. Simple checks (horizontal and/or vertical) are much less secure against *burst errors than a nontrivial CRC with G of degree (typically) 16. The term *longitudinal redundancy check (LRC)* usually refers to a nontrivial CRC, but may apply to a simple vertical check.

cylinder *See* disk drive.

cypher *A variant of* cipher. *See* cryptography.

D

DAC *Abbrev. for* digital-to-analog (D/A) converter.

D/A converter (DAC) *Short for* digital-to-analog converter. A device, usually in integrated-circuit form, that can accept a digital signal in the form of an *n*-bit parallel data word and convert it into an equivalent analog representation. Digital output signals from, say, a microprocessor may thus be converted into a form that is suitable for driving analog devices such as motors, meters, or other analog actuators. The *resolution* of a D/A converter is a measure of the change in analog output for a change of one least significant bit in the input. *See also* A/D converter.

daisychain (bused interface) A means of connecting a number of devices to a *controller, or, used as a verb, to connect by this means. A cable is connected from the controller to the nearest of the devices and then a separate cable connects the first unit to the second and the process is repeated as required. This allows a single connector on the controller to serve a variable number of devices. It also reduces cable cost and eases installation when several devices have to be connected. The IEEE 488 interface is suitable for this sort of connection.

Daisychain connection is also used as a means to prioritize I/O interrupts. In this application there is active logic at the points of interconnection to ensure that the priority accorded to a device is directly related to its place in the chain. The device nearest to the controller has highest priority.

daisywheel printer A type of *serial *impact printer in which the font is formed on the end of spring fingers that extend radially from a central hub. The font carrier is rotated by a servosystem until the correct character is opposite the printing position and a single hammer impacts it against the inked ribbon and paper. The carriage on which are mounted the font and hammer – and usually the ribbon – is then moved to the next printing position in the line.

The daisywheel printer was introduced by Diablo Systems Inc. in 1972 and rep-

resented a considerable improvement in speed and reduction in mechanical complexity compared to the *golfball and other typewriters that were used as low-speed printers at that time. The speed was initially 30 characters per second with a repertoire of 96 characters. Developments led to speeds of 65 cps for average text. In 1982 Diablo introduced a machine that can have up to 192 characters on the type wheel; by overprinting it is possible to form a further 250 characters. This development partially overcame the disadvantage – relative to *matrix printers – of the limited character set. Other developments led to lower-cost but slower (12–20 cps) units.

Daisywheel printers have until recently been widely used on word-processor systems for producing letters and documents. The print head and paper position can generally be incremented bidirectionally by control commands. This allows the features associated with typesetting, such as proportional spacing, justification, subscript and superscript characters, etc., to be achieved. By 1989 however, improvements in print quality of *dot matrix printers and the decreasing cost of *page printers had led to diminishing sales of the slower, noisier, and more inflexible daisywheel printer.

DARPA Defense Advanced Research Projects Agency, originally ARPA, Advanced Research Projects Agency. An agency of the US Department of Defense responsible for research and technical development in areas where no single service (Army, Navy, Air Force, Marine Corps) has a clear jurisdiction or interest. It is perhaps most famous for the network technology development that led to the *ARPANET.

DAT *Abbrev. for* digital audio tape. *See* helical scan.

data *Information that has been pre-pared, often in a particular format, for a specific purpose. In computing the word has three particular connotations.

First, data may be distinguished from program instructions. For instance: in source code, data declarations are distinct from executable instructions; at run time, store space is partitioned between data (constants and variables) and instructions; and data files are distinct from program files. (These distinctions depend on context, however, since program files, and source and object code instructions, serve as data to programs such as compilers and link loaders.)

Second, in the context of an individual program or suite of programs, the word data may be used in a more restricted sense to mean the input, as opposed to results (output), as for instance in data preparation or data vetting. (Results from one process are however almost invariably data for a subsequent one.)

Third, and more generally, data is often spoken of as distinct from text, voice, and image – and likewise data processing as distinct from word processing, voice processing, and image processing. This usage focuses on the highly formatted nature of data in traditional data-processing ' applications, as opposed to the much freer structure of natural language text, voice communication, and visual images.

data abstraction The principle of defining a *data type in terms of the operations that apply to objects of the type, with the constraint that the values of such objects can be modified and observed only by use of these operations. This application of the general principle of *abstraction leads to the concept of an *abstract data type.

Data abstraction is of very considerable importance in modern programming, especially for the coarse structuring of programs. Such use yields several bene-fits. The abstract data type provides a natural unit for specification and verification purposes (*see* module specification). It provides some basis for high-level design, and is consistent with the principles of *information hiding. The specification of the data type in terms of available operations provides all the information needed to make use of the data type while leaving maximum freedom of implementation, which indeed can be changed if required without affecting the users. There is also the possibility of developing a "library" of useful data abstractions – stacks, queues, etc.

The typical implementation of an abstract data type within a program is by means of a multiprocedure module. This module has local data that can be used to represent a value of the type, and each procedure implements one of the operations associated with the type. The local data of the module can only be accessed by these procedures, so that the user of the data type can only access the operations and has no direct access to the representation. The implementer is therefore free to choose the representation, which remains "invisible" to the users and can be changed if required. Each instance of the abstract data type employs one instance of the local data of the module to represent its value.

Proper support for such multiprocedure modules demands that the concept be recognized by the programming language, which must, for example, allow for the clustering of modules and data and have scope rules reflecting the desired restrictions on access. The first language to provide such support was SIMULA with its CLASS. Many modern languages now offer a similar facility, e.g. the MODULE of Modula and the PACKAGE of Ada. *See* package.

data acquisition *Another name for* data capture and/or data collection.

databank A system that offers facilities for the deposit and withdrawal of data to a community of users on a particular topic (e.g. biological species, trade statistics, commodity prices). While it need not be an open public facility, the usual implication is that the user community is widespread. Access to a databank may be, for instance, via a *videotex facility, or via any other form of *network, or even via the postal service. The data itself may be organized as a *database or as one or more *files.

database 1. Normally and strictly, a *data file that is defined and accessed using the facilities of a *database management system (DBMS); this implies in particular (a) that it is defined by means of a *schema that is independent of any programs that access the database (*see* data independence), (b) that is uses *direct access storage.

The use of a DBMS offers better control over data (*see* database administrator), and more sophisticated file organization and access methods, than are otherwise normally available. Because of the latter point, databases can be more complex than conventional files, and they often integrate the data previously held in many separate files. Size and complexity, however, are not necessary characteristics of databases: the availability of DBMS software on microcomputers, for instance, leads to many small and simple databases, where the advantage gained by using a DMBS is ease of definition and access.

Database use may be partitioned into three roles: end-users (who supply and/ or receive the data), programmers (who write *applications programs to process the data), and *database administrators. For a large database, each role may be performed by many people; for a small database, one individual may carry out all three roles.

See also database language, database system, data dictionary.

2. Occasionally and loosely, one or more *data files, however defined, accessed, and stored, that hold nontransient data in a computer application.

database administrator (DBA) A person responsible for the specification, design, implementation, efficient operation, and maintenance of a *database. The identification of a distinct role for database administration follows from the concept of *data independence, and from the realization that databases form an important and valuable corporate resource. The DBA works with users in establishing database requirements, as part of the activity of system specification; he uses a *data description language for database definition, as part of the activity of system design; he works with programmers whose programs need to access the database; he is responsible for loading the database with data, as part of the activity of system implementation; he monitors the performance of the database, using available hardware/ software tools, to determine when the data should be reorganized or the database redesigned.

Overall, the DBA should seek to achieve *database integrity, *security, and efficiency. He is particularly concerned with balancing the conflicting requirements (of end-users and programmers) arising from the fact that the database may be shared by a number of different applications. Two distinct roles are emerging: a business-modeling role, and a technical role of making the database management system work.

database integrity The condition of a database in which all data values are correct, in the sense (a) of reflecting the state of the real world – within given constraints of accuracy and timeliness – and (b) of obeying rules of mutual consistency. The maintenance of database integrity involves integrity checking, and recovery from any incorrect state that may be detected; this is the responsibility of a *database administrator, using the facilities of a *database management system.

File integrity can be defined in similar terms. Typically, however, files are subject to less extensive integrity checking than databases.

database language A generic term referring to a class of languages used for defining and accessing *databases. A database language comprises one or more *data description languages and one or more *data manipulation languages; these may be referred to as *data sublanguages*. An important distinction is whether a database language is designed (a) to be used as an extension to an existing programming language (which is referred to as the *host language*), or (b) to be used independently of any programming language (in which case it may be referred to as *free-standing*), or (c) to be used in either way. A particular database language may be associated with a particular *database management system. Bodies concerned with database language standardization include *ANSI/SPARC, *CODASYL, and *ISO.

database management system (DBMS) A software system with facilities for (a) *database language processing, to permit both (b) the handling of run-time calls for database access from application programs and/or end-users and (c) the maintenance of *database integrity. A DBMS thus has features in common both with *compilers and with *operating systems, and may be seen as raising the level of *abstraction that those systems offer to programmers and end-users.

Three classes of DBMS have conventionally been distinguished, supporting *hierarchical, *network, and *relational database systems. The distinctions between these classes are becoming harder to maintain, however, and it seems likely that other classes will emerge; this conventional classification is thus losing its usefulness.

The following are well-known DBMSs: ADABAS, *dBASE IV, DBOMP, DMS-1100, IDMS, IDS, *IMS, *INGRES, MDBS, *NOMAD, QBE, TDMS, and TOTAL.

database recovery The process of restoring *database integrity once a database has been found to be incorrect. *See also* recovery log.

database system 1. A *database together with its *database management system (software) and storage devices (hardware). A database system is a complex form of *associative memory. A data item in a database is typically associated with many other items, some of which may be physically contiguous (i.e. in the same *record) and others not. Data is usually retrieved by giving values of specified items, in order that the system should respond with the values of specified associated items. For example, a system might retrieve employee name and annual salary for a given employee number, or the registration numbers of all cars of a given color, make, and year of registration.

2. *Short for* database management system.

data break (cycle stealing) *See* direct memory access.

data bus (data path) A group of signal lines used to transmit data in parallel from one element of a computer to another. The number of lines in the group is the *width* of the data bus, each line being capable of transferring one bit of information. In a mainframe the width of the data bus is typically equal to the word length, i.e. 32, 48, or 64 bits. The data bus used to interconnect LSI components need not have the same width as is used on the chips themselves. For example, a processor with an internal data bus width of 32 bits could be designed to transmit information over an 16-bit-wide external data bus. Such processors are said to use a multiplexed data bus (*see* multiplexed bus). The wider the data bus, the higher the potential performance of the system, since more information is transmitted in parallel with a wider data bus. Narrower data buses in general degrade performance but are less costly to implement. A multiplexed data bus is often chosen to reduce the number of pins needed on an integrated circuit for the data bus.

data capture A process for achieving the extraction of relevant data while the related transaction or operation is occurring. An example is a supermarket checkout equipped with point-of-sale terminals. The transaction is primarily concerned with the sale to the customer but while the purchased items are being entered onto the bill it is usual for the machine to record, and thus capture, data that will allow calculation of stock movement and other information.

If the equipment for data capture is on-line to a computer system, it is part of a *data collection process and may be referred to as either data capture or data collection equipment.

data cartridge A *magnetic tape cartridge, commonly the 3M-type cartridge.

data chaining Organizing a *data file so that records are linked (*see* link, def. 3). A record may belong to more than one chain. Chaining permits access to records in a number of different sequences. A *network database system is an example of data chaining.

data channel An information route and associated circuitry that is used for the passing of data between systems or parts of systems. In an interface that has a number of parallel channels the channels are usually separately dedicated to the passing of a single type of information, e.g. data or control information.

data cleaning The action of removing format errors and keying errors from data, usually achieved by a *data-vet program.

data collection The process of collecting data from distributed points at which it has been captured or input as a separate operation. Generally the equipment used for the process is connected to a host computer via a communication system; sometimes portable equipment is carried to each site for information to be input into its memory and then the equipment – or a disconnectable module containing the memory – is connected to the host system. *See also* data capture.

data communication equipment *See* DCE.

data communications The collection and redistribution of information (data) through communication channels. Data communications may involve the transmission and reception of data in analog or digital form. *Data sources* originate data while *data destinations* receive it.

data compaction *See* compaction.

data compression Any of many methods in *information theory whereby data can be coded or recoded in order to take advantage of *redundancy in that data. In ordinary alphabetic text the data size can be reduced by a factor of from 2 to nearly 5 by the use of such methods: images of writing and of line drawings can also be compressed effectively, but compression is less effective for photographs. In effect, data compression is synonymous with *source coding. Compression techniques are widely used in image transmission (facsimile) and storage.

data concentrator *See* concentrator.

data contamination The alteration, maliciously or accidentally, of data in a computer system. *See also* data integrity.

data description language (DDL) Part (sublanguage) of a *database language. It is accepted that data needs to be described at several levels of *abstraction, and a different DDL will be appropriate for each level. The description at any level is called a *schema*. Three levels, of data description and of schemas, are most commonly recognized. The first is the conceptual level, which describes relationships between data items arising from relationships in the "real world" of the problem domain; description at this level is part of system specification, and is called a *conceptual schema*. The second is the logical level, which describes how selected relationships will be represented in the record structure of the database. The third is the physical level, which describes how record structures will be represented in terms of the physical characteristics of both primary and secondary storage. Description at the second or third level is part of system design, and is called an *internal schema*.

Orthogonal to these levels of abstraction is the realization that, in addition to describing a database as a whole, it is often necessary to permit different views of a database to be described, where a view may be roughly regarded as a partial and/or redefined description of a database. A view description is often called an *external schema* or a *subschema*. A DDL that permits view description must provide for defining the mapping between the global database description and an individual view, at any level of abstraction.

data dictionary A set of descriptions of the *data components of a computer-based system (which, for purposes of clarity in what follows, will be referred to as the "object system"). A data dictionary has the following features.

(1) It may be held in the form of manual records, or in machine-readable form (as a *file or *database).

(2) In the latter case, the term data dictionary is conventionally extended to include the software that manages and maintains the dictionary entries.

(3) The data components described may be elementary (atomic) or structured. Many will be nontransient (i.e. stored in the files or the database of the object system) but there may also be entries for transient *variables used only within programs.

(4) In many cases, entries are not confined to data components: they may describe complete files, programs, named components of programs (e.g. *modules, *procedures), or even real-world entities in the problem domain of the object system.

For object systems that handle large numbers of *data types, a data dictionary is a vital tool for the central control of naming, and of the semantics and syntax of the system. It is a tool widely used by *database administrators, but also increasingly to assist in the broader task of *system design: many design methodologies are founded on the use of data dictionaries. The terms *data directory* and *system dictionary* may be used synonymously in the case of the more ambitious software-based data dictionary systems.

data directory *See* data dictionary.

data-driven design A design method in which the structure of the software system reflects the structure of the data processed by the system. Examples of data-driven methods are *JSD and *SSADM. *Compare* functional design.

Data Encryption Standard (DES) A particular codebook algorithm used in the USA for the encryption of messages. *See* cryptography.

data entry The process in which an operator uses a keyboard or other device to input data directly into a system. The term is sometimes misapplied to the process of (a) *data capture, where the input of data to the system is not the prime objective of the related activity, and (b) *data preparation, where data is being encoded prior to being entered into the system.

Direct data entry (DDE) is an on-line process in which data is entered into a system and written into its on-line files. The data may be entered by an operator at a keyboard (this is the usual meaning) or by a data capture device. *Compare* key to tape, key to disk.

data file A *file containing data. Data files are normally organized as sets of *records. *Compare* database.

dataflow The relationship between a source of data and the repository or user of that data. An analysis of the dataflow may be used to show

undeclared variables,

uninitialized variables,

unused variables,

use of variables,

mismatch of variables across module interfaces,

frequency/density of variable usage.

See also dataflow graph. *Compare* control flow.

dataflow graph (dataflow diagram) A directed *graph showing processing elements and data repositories with the *dataflow between them. *See also* structured systems analysis, static analysis.

dataflow machine A computer in which the primitive operations are triggered by the availability of operands. In a classical *von Neumann machine, there is the concept of sequential flow of control, and an operation (instruction) is performed as and when flow of control reaches that operation. By contrast, in a dataflow machine there is a flow of data

values from the operations that produce those values to the operations that "consume" those values as operands, and an operation is triggered as soon as all its operands are available. Since the result of one operation can be an operand to many other operations, and hence can potentially trigger many operations simultaneously, there is the possibility of a high degree of parallelism.

Dataflow machines represent one of the major examples of *non von Neumann architecture, and are of considerable research interest. Traditional *imperative programming languages, which prescribe a particular flow of control, are poorly suited to dataflow machines; they are usually programmed in a *single-assignment language or a *declarative language.

datagram 1. A self-contained package of data that carries enough information to be routed from source to destination independently of any previous and subsequent exchanges. A *datagram service* transports datagrams on a "best-effort" basis. There is a nonzero probability that any datagram will be lost or damaged before reaching its destination. The order in which datagrams are submitted by the source is not necessarily preserved upon delivery. In some networks there is the possibility that a datagram may be duplicated and delivered to the destination more than once. It is the responsibility of the application to guard against errors arising from datagram loss or duplication.

2. *See* SADT.

data hierarchy A hierarchical structure of *records, in which (a) a record at level i holds data that is common to a set of records at level $i + 1$ and (b) starting from the higher-level record, it is possible to access the set of lower-level records. Any record may only "own" one set of lower-level records, and may only be a member of one such set. It is possible to store a data hierarchy on either magnetic disk or magnetic tape. A data hierarchy may reflect "real-world" hierarchical relationships, or may be imposed on more complex relationships because of the limitations of a *data management system.

data independence Independence between different levels of data description (*see* data description language). Two forms of data independence are most commonly recognized. Logical data independence, in a shared *database, means that one program's, or one end-user's, view of the database is unaffected by the creation or alteration of other views. Physical data independence, in any database or *data file, means that a program's or end-user's view of the data is unaffected by changes in the way in which it is stored.

data integrity Resistance to alteration by system errors of data stored in a computer. It is a condition that denotes only authorized and proper alteration of data. It is a measure of the reliability of data read from magnetic media, in terms of the absence of undetected errors (*see* error rate). However the undetected error rate perceived by the host system may be worse than that arising at the magnetic tape or disk if undetected errors can arise, e.g. from the effect of noise on connecting cables where the interface concerned has insufficient error detection capability.

From a system point of view the undetected error rate of a peripheral may be inadequate: the system can improve on it by making additional provision for checking in software.

data link A physical connection between two or more devices (called *nodes* or *stations*) by a communication channel that appears "wire-like", i.e. bits arrive in the order sent. Coaxial cables, telephone lines, optical fibers, lasers, and even satellite channels can be data links. Data links are assumed to be susceptible to noise (i.e. have error properties) and have finite data rate and nonzero propagation delay.

data link control protocol A communication *protocol that converts noisy (error-prone) *data links into communication channels free of transmission errors. Data is broken into *frames, each of which is protected by *checksum. Frames are retransmitted as many times as needed to accomplish correct transmission. A data link control protocol must prevent data loss caused by mismatched sending/receiving capacities. A *flow control procedure, usually a simple sliding *window mechanism, provides this function. Data link control protocols must provide *transparent data transfer. *Bit stuffing or byte stuffing strategies are used to mask control patterns that occur in the text being transmitted. Control frames are used to start/stop logical connections over links. *Addressing may be provided to support several *virtual connections on the same physical link.

data link layer of network protocol function. *See* seven-layer reference model.

data logging A procedure that involves recording all data and interactions that pass through a particular point in a system. The point chosen is usually part of a communication loop or a data path to or from a device such as a keyboard and display on which data is transitory. If a system failure or an unexpected result occurs it is possible to reconstruct the situation that existed. Such logs are not generally archived and can be overwritten once the associated job has been completed.

data management A term normally used to refer to systems that offer users an interface that screens them from the majority of the details of the physical handling of the files, leaving them free to concentrate on the logical properties of the data.

data management system A class of software systems that includes *database management systems and *file management systems.

data manipulation language (DML) Part (sublanguage) of a *database language. It provides facilities – more powerful than those conventionally found in programming languages – for storing, retrieving, updating, and deleting data records. It may, for instance, provide for specifying the retrieval of a set of records based on some arbitrarily complex set of conditions that are to be applied to the contents of records in the database. A DML that is available interactively to end-users (i.e. is not embedded in a host language) is often called a *query language*.

data mark *See* address mark.

data matrix A rectangular array of data variables, which may be numerical, classificatory, or alphanumeric. The data matrix forms the input structure upon which statistical procedures for *regression analysis, *analysis of variance, *multivariate analysis, *cluster analysis, or survey analysis will operate.

data medium A material having defined properties, including a physical variable that can be used to represent data. The defined properties ensure that the medium is compatible with devices that can record or read data on the medium. Examples of data media are *magnetic tape, *magnetic disks, and *optical disks, and also paper used for printer output.

data model A term used in a variety of situations in connection with data storage at either a logical or physical level but usually the former. It normally implies a formally defined structure within which the data may be represented.

Data Module The name used by IBM to refer to their removable, hermetically sealed disk pack, incorporating the read/write heads and carriage assembly, that was used with the 3340 *Winchester technology disk drive. The term data module is now used more generally and is interchangeable with disk pack and storage module.

data name A symbolic name chosen by the programmer to identify a data object when using a high-level language. *See also* variable.

data network A communication network that is devoted to carrying computer information, as opposed to voice, video, etc. It consists of a number of nodes (stations) connected by various communication channels (circuits).

Datapac A Canadian *public packet network, operated by the Trans-Canada Telephone System (TCTS). It uses *X.25 to interface to hosts and *X.75 to connect to other public networks. Datapac was one of the world's first operational public packet networks based on the international CCITT standards.

data path *Another name for* data bus, although often used in a wider context to mean any logical or physical connection between a source and destination of digital or analog information.

data preparation The process of converting data into a machine-readable form so that it can be entered into a system via an available input device. The operation of *key-to-tape machines is an example. These machines are not usually connected to the system, but even in the case of machines specifically adapted to allow connection they do not interact with the system in the course of preparation. The process is being superseded by direct *data entry systems and *data capture.

data processing (DP) A term used predominantly in the context of industrial, business, governmental, and other organizations: within that context it refers (a) to a class of computer applications, (b) to a function within the organization.

While it is hard to generalize, data-processing applications may be characterized as those that store and process large quantities of data on a routine basis, in order to be able to produce (regularly or on request) information that is predictably needed by an organization's employees, by its customers or suppliers, by government, or by any other organization. Typical applications within this category include financial accounting, cost and management accounting, market research and sales forecasting, order processing, investment analysis, financial modeling, stock control, production planning and control, transport planning and control, payroll, and personnel records. *COBOL is at present the programming language used for almost all data-processing applications. Data-processing systems are normally long-lived (apart from the need to redesign/rewrite them periodically, they may well last as long as the host organization), and they handle data that is large in volume and complex in structure (which leads to a major concern for the problems and costs of data input and storage).

The data-processing function within an organization is that department responsible for the development and operation of application systems (largely of the types listed above) on behalf of other parts of the organization. Its tasks normally include systems analysis and design, program development and maintenance, database administration, computer operation, data preparation, data control, and network management. The data-processing department may not, however, be responsible for all data-processing applications within an organization (this is a live issue with the current diffusion of microcomputers and small business systems throughout some companies), and conversely it may have responsibility for some applications that are not usually thought of as data processing (e.g. industrial process control).

The term is a rather unfortunate one since all computing could be regarded as the processing of data (in at least one of the senses of that word). It is certainly used in contexts other than the one described above: for instance, scientific data processing means the fairly straightfoward processing of large quantities of experimental results, and personal data processing means an individual's use of a microcomputer to keep personal records.

The term has never seriously been used to refer to any applications other than computer-based ones, but it was recognized that a lot of clerical and unit-record tasks could be described as data processing. In order to exclude this possibility, the terms *automatic data processing (ADP)* or *electronic data processing (EDP)* were coined, and can still occasionally be encountered. The term *integrated data processing (IDP)* had some limited use, mainly in the 1960s, as it became clear that much of an organization's data was common to separately developed systems, and the effort was made to integrate or rationalize them; that effort has mainly been diverted into the growth of *databases and *database management systems.

data-processing manager (DPM) The executive responsible for the *data processing function in an organization, i.e. for organizing, planning, and directing the DP service in accordance with directives laid down by top management, usually in management services, administration, or finance. The DPM will participate in the formulation of DP policy and strategy, and will be responsible for ensuring that the most cost-effective hardware and software is procured, that applications systems appropriate to the organization's needs are developed, and that staff in the department have the necessary levels of technical competence. The reporting level of the DPM to senior management can be a significant determinant of the degree of success of an organization in employing DP.

Data Protection Act 1984 The Act enacted in 1984 by the UK to comply with the Council of Europe Convention. (It is described at the end of the dictionary.)

data protection legislation Legislation that has been or is being introduced all over the world to protect personal data handled in computers. The aim of the legislation is to control the immense potential for misuse of information that arises when personal data is stored in computers. Once the data has been transcribed from paper files into a form that is easily readable and accessible by computers, it is an inexpensive and easy task for the data to be extracted from one record and correlated with personal data concerning the same person from another file. This results in a synergistic combination of information that is considered to be an infringement of *privacy.

To combat the fear of misuse of data, governments have introduced legislation that, among other things, makes the following requirements of organizations that maintain personal records on computers:

to declare and/or register the use for which the data is stored;

to provide the data subject with a right of access to data concerning himself on their computers;

to maintain a prescribed minimum level of electronic and physical *security in their computer installation;

not to transmit personal data to any organization that does not have similar controls over misuse of data.

This last requirement has led to fears that countries without data protection legislation on their statute books are losing contracts for the processing of data, since countries with such legislation can refuse to permit the export of data to countries where data is not adequately protected. For this reason companies that consider that the data protection fears are not borne out by real instances of misuse of data are nonetheless pressing for legislation.

In Europe a convention concerning misuse of data was signed by all member countries of the Council of Europe. The OECD (Organization for Economic Cooperation and Development) has also drafted a convention of similar effect. The USA has a Privacy Act that deals with data stored by government agencies, but it is thought by some in the legal profession that for constitutional reasons the USA could not legislate to prohibit misuse of data along the lines required by the OECD and Council of Europe conventions. The debate is rapidly getting more complicated: third world countries are now finding that data protection legislation may enable them to create a nontariff barrier around indigenous data processing companies, and hence the issues are moving out of civil rights and into economics.

In 1984 the UK enacted the Data Protection Act to comply with the Council of Europe Convention. (The Act is described at the end of the dictionary.)

data reduction The transformation of a large volume of data into a smaller amount. Typically the input data to a particular transformation process will be *raw data obtained from some sensor, and the output data will be produced by sampling or some simple analysis.

data retrieval The process by which data is selected and extracted from a file, a group of files, or a database, following a search of the file(s) for specified keys.

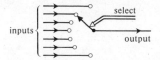

Data selector/multiplexer

data selector/multiplexer A logic circuit that may be considered as a single-pole multiway switch whose output is determined by the position of the switch wiper (*see* diagram). The wiper position is controlled by a select signal, normally digital, that indicates which of the inputs is to be connected to the output. In this way a number of channels of data may be placed sequentially on a time-shared output bus under the control of the select signal, a process known as *time-division multiplexing. Inputs to and outputs from a multiplexer may be in digital or analog form. *See also* decoder/demultiplexer.

data set 1. *Another name for* modem.
2. *Another name for* file.

data sheet A manufacturer's specification of the parameters of a device or integrated circuit, its functions, and its pin connections.

data stream A sequence of data elements, often packed in some manner into a sequence of words having sizes different from the size of the data elements.

data structure (information structure) An aspect of *data type expressing the nature of values that are composite, i.e. not *atoms. The nonatomic values have constituent parts (which need not themselves be atoms), and the data structure expresses how constituents may be combined to form a compound value or selected from a compound value. Thus "date" regarded as a data structure is a set containing a member for every possible day, combined with operations to construct a date from its constituents – year, month, and day – and to select a desired constituent.

An implementation of a data structure involves both choosing a *storage structure and providing a set of procedures/functions that implement the appropriate operations using the chosen storage structure. Formally, a data structure is defined as a distinguished domain in an *abstract data type that specifies the structure. Computer solution of a real-world problem involves designing some ideal data structure, and then mapping this onto available data structures (e.g. *arrays, *records, *lists, *queues, and *trees) for the implementation.

Note that terms for data structures are used to denote both the structure and data having that structure.

See also dynamic data structure, static data structure.

data subject An individual about whom information is stored in a computer-based system. *See* data protection legislation.

data sublanguage *See* database language.

data summarization *See* statistical methods.

data tablet A graphical input device that can generate digital signals (or in some cases analog signals) that represent accurately the positions of a penlike instrument as it is moved over a flat surface. The term was originally a tradename used by Sylvania to describe a product of this type, but it is now used generically.

data terminal equipment *See* DTE.

data transfer rate The rate at which data can be moved between devices. The average rate is determined by the capability of the read or write device but the instantaneous rate is determined by the capability of the interface or transmission path. *Buffer memories are used to achieve the change in rate. For typical magnetic tape operating at 800 bytes per inch and 75 inches per second the rate is about 60 kilobytes per second. Disk storage systems can have transfer rates in excess of 3 megabytes per second. Fast serial interfaces operate up to 50M bps.

data translation The process of converting data from the form used by one system into the form required by another.

data transmission The process of sending data (analog or digital measurements, coded characters, or information in general) from a sender to one or more receivers, i.e. from a source to one or more destinations.

data transparency 1. A property of a communication system (network) such that the output data stream delivered is the exact bit sequence presented to the input of the system without any restriction or exception.

2. A property of a communication system such that the output data stream delivered provides an output bit sequence functionally equivalent to the input bit sequence, from which the exact input bit sequence can be derived.

The second definition implies that the communication system provides protocol translation between input and output devices whereas the first definition implies that there is a compensating translation. The second definition cannot be implemented in all cases since there are functions that are supported by some terminal devices but have no equivalent in others.

data type An abstract set of possible values that an instance of the data type may assume, given either implicitly, e.g. INTEGER, REAL, STRING, or explicitly as, for example, in Pascal:

TYPE color = (red, green, orange)
The data type indicates a class of implementations for those values.

Types may be very complicated and defined in terms of other more primitive types. The concept is not limited to *variables. Some languages consider *procedures to be an example of a data type, and permit their use in the construction of more complex types, such as arrays of procedures.

See also abstract data type.

data validation The process of checking the expected characteristics of specific data. It is usually applied only to data that has recently been input to a system. Checks are made that there are the correct number of characters in each data field and that they are of the right type; for example, in a field defining a quantity they should be numerical characters and should lie within an expected range.

data-vet program A program that checks input data to verify that it conforms to given specifications and satisfies various consistency checks. It is used to prepare input for another program in contexts where the consequences of faulty input would be unacceptable.

data word A word that can only, or is expected only to, contain data.

datum An item of data: the smallest parcel of information that influences the outcome of a computation.

datum-limit register *Another name for* base-bound register.

DBA *Abbrev. for* database administrator.

dBASE IV *Trademark* Ashton Tate's latest version (1988) of their *relational database system for microcomputers. It follows dBASE II, dBASE III, and dBASE III Plus.

DBMS *Abbrev. for* database management system.

DC300, DC600, DC1000 cartridges *See* magnetic tape cartridge.

DCE *Abbrev. for* data communication equipment. The side of an interface that represents the provider of a data communication in a standard such as RS232C or X.25. DCEs are usually analog or digital *modems. *Compare* DTE.

d.c. signaling *See* baseband networking.

DDC *Abbrev. for* direct digital control.

DDCMP *Abbrev. for* digital data communication message protocol. A *data link control protocol developed by Digital Equipment Corporation. It is similar to *SDLC and *HDLC but is character-oriented rather than bit-oriented. It allows a variety of data link characteristics: full duplex or half duplex, asynchronous or synchronous, switched or dedicated, point-to-point or multipoint, and serial or parallel. Data transparency is achieved using a data-length field rather than bit or byte stuffing techniques. Active NAKs are used for error control, in addition to timeouts.

DDE *Abbrev. for* direct data entry. *See* data entry.

DDL 1. *Abbrev. for* data description language.
2. *See* document description language.

deadlock 1. *Another name for* deadly embrace.
2. A specific form of *deadly embrace that arises in a *Petri net, in which some states of the net become forever inaccessible.

deadly embrace (deadlock) A situation that may arise when two (or more) sep-arately active *processes compete for resources. Suppose that process P requires resources X and Y and requests their use in that order, and that at the same time process Q requires resources Y and X and asks for them in that order. If process P has acquired resource X and simultaneously process Q has acquired resource Y, then neither process can proceed, each process requiring a resource that has been allocated to the other process. On larger systems containing more than two processes and more than two resources, it is still possible for deadlock to develop although its detection may be more difficult.

debit/credit benchmark A *benchmark test for measuring the number of office tasks completed on a computer installation per hour. The basic feature of the test is to use a fixed number of terminals on a given computer configuration and to ramp up the number of standardized transactions per second until the system can only complete 95% of requested transactions in under one second.

debouncing A technique to avoid each reverberation of a closing switch or other electrical contact being registered as a separate event. After the detection of the initial closure a short pause is made in order to allow the reverberations of the contact, known as *contact bounce*, to die away. The contact is then sampled again to determine its final state. Debouncing is often used in connection with the reading of keyboards.

de Bruijn diagram (de Bruijn graph) *See* Good–de Bruijn diagram.

debugging The identification and removal of localized implementation errors – or bugs – from a program or system. By contrast, *testing seeks to establish whether bugs exist but does not isolate or remove them. Program debugging is often supported by a *debug* *tool*, a *software tool that allows the internal behavior of the program to be investigated. Such a tool would typically offer trace facilities (*see* trace program), allow the planting of *breakpoints* (i.e. points in the program at which execution is to be suspended so that examination of partial results is possible), and permit examination and perhaps modification of the values of program variables when a breakpoint is reached.

debug tool (debugger) *See* debugging.

DEC Digital Equipment Corporation, a company founded by Kenneth Olsen and Harlan Anderson to build transistorized digital circuit modules. Their first product, the PDP-1, demonstrated the feasibility of building a full-fledged stored-program computer from these modules.

DEC was the first minicomputer manufacturer, and is today the second largest computer manufacturer in the world. The VAX range of computers features the same VMS operating system in desktop workstations as in the 8000 series multiprocessor systems supporting hundreds of simultaneous users. These larger systems are often, confusingly, classed as minicomputers for historical reasons, but compete in the mainframe market. Perhaps DEC's most famous products were the PDP-11 minicomputers that, although built as standalone systems, have been popular with system designers who integrate them into many communication and control systems. The PDP-11 was also the vehicle for the development of the *UNIX operating system and the *C programming language.

decade counter *See* counter.

decay time of a pulse. *See* pulse.

decidable problem *See* decision problem.

decision gate An electronic *logic gate whose output indicates whether a logical relationship is either true or false. The following are examples: an equality *comparator, indicating when two binary numbers are equal; an *odd parity checker, indicating when a binary input has an odd number of ones; a *majority element, indicating when the binary inputs have more 1 entries than 0 entries.

decision problem A computational task that for each possible input requires "true" or "false" to be output, depending on whether the input possesses a certain property. An algorithm that produces the correct decision in each case is called a *decision procedure* for that problem. The problem is then referred to as *solvable*, while an *unsolvable* problem is one for which no decision procedure exists. An example is logical validity, the inputs being logical expressions, with the output "true" for valid expressions and "false" for others. This problem is solvable for *propositional logic (the construction of *truth tables being a decision procedure) but not for *predicate logic. Solvable problems can be further classified according to the efficiency of decision procedures existing for them (*see* $P = NP$ question).

Some unsolvable problems possess a *semidecision procedure*, i.e. an algorithm that correctly outputs "true" but fails to terminate in cases where "false" should be output. This is the same as saying that the inputs requiring the output "true" form a set that is recursively enumerable but not *recursive. Alternatively one can say that the problem corresponds to a predicate that is *semidecidable* but not *decidable*. Yet another formulation is to say that, while the correct mapping from inputs to "true" and "false" is not a *computable function, its restriction to just the "true" inputs gives a computable *partial function.

decision procedure *See* decision problem.

decision support system *See* management information system.

decision table A table that indicates actions to be taken under various condi-

Fig.*a* Parts of a decision table

rain	N N Y – – –
snow	N N N Y – –
fog	N N N N Y Y
temperature	>8 <8 – – >0 <0

take bicycle	×
take automobile	× ×
take train	× ×
stay home	×

Fig.*b* Example of a decision table

tions, the *decision* being the selection between the alternative actions. Conventionally a decision table has four parts that are named and laid out as shown in Fig. *a*. The *condition stub* part lists the individual inputs upon which the decision depends, while the *action stub* part lists the alternative actions that may be taken. The entry parts then show the conditions under which each action is selected. This is done by arranging the *condition entry* part into columns, where each column specifies some condition on each of the input values, and then placing a cross in the same column of the *action entry* part to indicate the particular action to be taken. All the conditions of the column

must be satisfied in order for the column to be selected. Normally the complete table covers all possible combinations of input values in such a way that application of the table always selects precisely one action (*see also* ELSE rule). The example in Fig. *b* shows a table for deciding how to travel to work. A '–' symbol in the condition entry part indicates "don't care".

Decision tables have been used both for program specification and implementation, the latter being achieved by means of systems that can interpret (or generate an executable program from) the decision table format.

decision tree A *binary tree where every *nonterminal node represents a decision. Depending upon the decision taken at such a node, control passes to the left or right subtree of the node. A *leaf node then represents the outcome of taking the sequence of decisions given by the nodes on the path from the root to the leaf. *See also* bifurcation.

deck 1. *Short for* tape deck. *See* magnetic tape.
2. A number of punched cards that form a related collection.

declaration One of the two major kinds of element in a conventional program, the other being a *statement. A declaration introduces an entity for part of the program – its *scope* – giving it a name and establishing its static properties. Examples are declarations of variables, declarations of procedures, declarations of input/output ports or files.

declarative languages (nonprocedural languages) A class of programming languages. With a declarative language a program explicitly states what properties the desired result is required to exhibit but does not state how the desired result is to be obtained; any means of producing a result that displays the required properties is acceptable (*compare* imperative languages).

Since declarative languages are concerned with static rather than dynamic concepts (i.e. what rather than how), they do not depend on any inherent notion of ordering and there is no concept of flow of control and no *assignment statement. Ideally a program in a declarative language would consist solely of an unordered set of equations sufficient to characterize the desired result. However, for reasons of implementation and efficiency, the existing languages fall somewhat short of this, either in semantics or in style of use (or both). Declarative languages are not tied to the von Neumann model of computation and typically there is scope for employing a high degree of parallelism in obtaining the desired result.

See also functional languages, logic programming languages.

decoder 1. The means by which a decoding process is effected (*see* code). It may be implemented in hardware or software, the process being algorithmic in nature.

2. *See* decoder/demultiplexer.

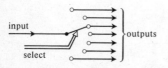

Decoder/demultiplexer

decoder/demultiplexer A logic circuit, usually an integrated circuit, that is capable of setting one of its 2^n output lines active, i.e. at logic 1, in response to an n-bit binary code present at its input. For an n-bit device, 2^n distinct elements of a code can be input.

A decoder/demultiplexer may be considered as a switch that directs data from a time-shared data bus to one of several possible outputs under the control of a select signal, which is normally digital; the select signal indicates which of the outputs is to be connected to the input (*see* diagram). Individual data channels may be recovered from a time-division multiplexed input bus provided that the scanning of the select signal is made synchronous with that of the multiplexer. The input to and outputs from a decoder/demultiplexer may be in digital or analog form. *See also* data selector/multiplexer.

decoder/driver An electronic device that is capable of accepting encoded data at its input and generating unencoded data at its output. The decoding process employed may conform to an agreed standard or be user-defined. The outputs of these devices are capable of directly driving external equipment such as *LCD- or *LED-type displays.

decoder error *See* channel error.

decoding The process of reconverting a coded message to the message from which it was encoded. *See* code.

decollator 1. A machine that can process multicopy printed output into separate stacks of copy and used carbon paper. It is normally done as an off-line activity and may be combined with a *burster that breaks the continuous forms at the perforations to give separate sheets.

2. A machine associated with card-based data processing systems that could separate a punched-card file into its constituent parts, i.e. header cards, which were frequently reused, and detail cards, which, once processed, were kept only for a short time. This facility was sometimes built into the collating machine. *See* collator.

decompiler A program that attempts to do for compiler output what a *disassembler does for assembler output, i.e.

translate back from machine code to something resembling the source language. The task is difficult and not often attempted.

decomposition 1. In switching theory, the realization of an n-variable switching function as a composition of functions, each of which has less than n variables. Like other *minimizations, decomposition is facilitated by *Karnaugh maps.
2. In programming, the analysis of a problem into simpler subproblems. *See* program decomposition, modular programming.

deconvolution *See* convolution.

decryption The processing of an encrypted message by an authorized recipient in order to recover the original message. *See also* cryptography. *Compare* cryptanalysis.

dedicated Committed entirely to a single purpose or device. For example, a computer system may be dedicated to the job of controlling an industrial machine tool. A dedicated device or resource may be idle for significant periods of time.

dedicated mode A *security processing mode where all information in a system is treated as of uniform security classification to which all users of the system can have equal access.

defect skipping A method by which a media defect on a magnetic disk *track is avoided such that no data is written in the vicinity of the defect. When a defect is detected, e.g. after the failure of attempts to write and check-read data at that position, the location of the center of the defect is written in the sector 0 header in terms of the number of bytes from the index point. The area of the defect is also treated such that a preamble pattern is written before, over, and after the defect. A synchronizing pattern is written after the preamble

pattern so that normal data recording can be resumed on a subsequent pass. The defect skipping is invisible to the CPU operating software but it improves the economics of operation.

deferred addressing *Another name for* indirect addressing.

deferred approach to the limit (Richardson extrapolation) *See* extrapolation.

deflation *See* polynomial equation.

degree 1. of a vertex of a *graph. The number of edges incident with the vertex, i.e. that emanate from that vertex. In a directed graph, the *indegree* is the number of edges entering a vertex while the *outdegree* is the number leaving a vertex.
2. of a node in a *tree. The number of children of that node, i.e. the number of subtrees rooted at that node. More correctly, this is the *outdegree* of the node.
3. of a tree. The maximum degree of all the nodes in the tree.
4. of a polynomial. *See* polynomial equation, polynomial.

degree of precision The degree of polynomials that a given rule for *numerical integration integrates exactly. The same concept can be applied in other areas, such as the solution of ordinary differential equations. It is related to the concept of *order of approximation, and provides a measure of the approximating power of a given method.

degrees of freedom In statistical analysis, the number of independent observations associated with an estimate of variance (*see* measures of variation) or of a component of an *analysis of variance. The simplest example is in estimating the variance of a sample of n observations, where the degrees of freedom is $n - 1$, the divisor of the sum of squared deviations from the sample mean. More generally, the degrees of freedom, f, is the difference between the number of *parameters in a given model, and a special case of that model with fewer parameters. The number of degrees of freedom is required when selecting a particular instance of the *chi-squared distribution, *Student's t distribution, or *F distribution.

Dekker's algorithm An algorithm, based on a combination of successive linear *interpolation and binary search, that finds the zero of a function that changes sign in a given interval.

delay differential equations *Ordinary differential equations where the derivatives depend on values of the solution at the current value and several previous values of the independent variable. The simplest form is

$$y'(x) = f(x, y(x), y(x - \tau(x))),$$
$$a \leqslant x \leqslant b$$

where $\tau(x) \geqslant 0$. To determine a solution, $y(x)$ must be specified on an interval $a^* \leqslant x \leqslant a$ where a^* depends on the values taken by $\tau(x)$.

Most of the commonly used step-by-step methods for ordinary differential equations can be adapted to problems of this form, although they have not yet been developed to the same extent. It is necessary to incorporate an *interpolation scheme to approximate

$$y(x - \tau(x))$$

to a value that will not usually coincide with a previously computed approximation.

delayed branch A *conditional branch instruction found in some *RISC architectures that include *pipelining. The effect is to execute the next instruction in sequence before evaluating the condition, thus keeping the pipeline full.

delay line An electronic device that produces a finite accurate time delay between a signal imposed on its input and the appearance of the same signal at its output. These devices may be used

as short-term signal stores or to provide accurate delays in signal-processing circuits. In an *acoustic delay line* electrical signals are converted into a pattern of acoustic (sound) waves that travel through a medium between a transmitter and receiver.

Delay lines were the most common storage devices in *first-generation computers: they were used, for example, in EDSAC, EDVAC, pilot ACE and ACE, UNIVAC 1, and LEO 1. In EDSAC (1949), quartz crystals were used as transducers and the ultrasonic pulses were passed along a tube of mercury about 5 feet (1.5 meters) in length. The delay was approximately 1 millisecond but it enabled nearly 1000 pulses to be stored. Later acoustic memories used magnetostrictive transducers and nickel-iron wire, with the electrical signals converted into stress waves.

delay-power-product A figure of merit that is frequently quoted as characteristic of a particular *logic family. It is the product of the *propagation delay (usually in nanoseconds) and the power dissipation (usually in milliwatts) of a gate typical of the family; it has dimensions of energy, the usual unit being the picojoule, pJ. The smaller the delay-power-product is, the better the logic family is considered to be.

delete One of the basic actions performed on *sets that, when applied in the form

delete(el,S)

removes the element *el* from S; if *el* was not present in S the action has no effect on the membership of S. *See also* operations on sets.

deletion Removal or obliteration of a record or item of data. In a magnetic tape or disk, data is deleted by overwriting with new data or null characters. In paper tape files a character or block can be deleted by punching all holes in the row or block. The character represented by all holes is treated as a null.

delimiter A symbol that serves to mark the beginning or end of some programming construct, e.g. the semicolon that separates statements in Algol-like languages, the period that marks the end of a sentence in COBOL, the ENDIF that marks the end of an IF statement in FORTRAN 77.

delta modulation *Another name for* delta PCM. *See* pulse code modulation.

delta PCM (ΔPCM) *See* pulse code modulation.

demand paging A method of dealing with a situation in which a *process requires access to a *page of memory that has been written to backing store. Some systems attempt to forecast the pattern of demand for pages; other systems rely on demand paging in which no attempt is made to forecast the pattern of behavior, but pages are transferred from backing store into main memory on demand as required by the individual process.

demand reading, writing A process in which data is transferred directly between a processor and a storage device. This is a normal mode of operation for main memory but is sometimes applied to other devices.

demodulator A device that receives analog signals as input and produces digital data as output. Demodulators use the inverse of the methods used by *modulators, which encode data as analog signals. *See also* modulation, modem.

demon In some operating systems, the process that controls a peripheral device. (The word is probably a contraction of *device monitor*.) By an extension of meaning the word is sometimes used for any process within the operating system, even if the process is not actually responsible for a peripheral device.

de Morgan's laws The two laws of a *Boolean algebra that provide a method of expressing the complement of a complex expression in terms of the complements of individual components:
$$(x \lor y)' = x' \land y'$$
$$(x \land y)' = x' \lor y'$$
The pair is self-dual. The term de Morgan's laws is often used to describe instances of these laws as they apply in particular cases, e.g. to sets or to logical expressions. The laws are named for Augustus de Morgan.

demultiplexer 1. In communications, a device that performs the reverse function to a *multiplexer.
2. A *combinational circuit that converts from n inputs to 1 of m outputs, where $m \leqslant 2^n$.
See also decoder/demultiplexer.

dendrogram *See* cluster analysis.

denial of service One of the *threats to computer system security whereby an authorized user is deliberately prevented from processing information, for example because that information has been intentionally corrupted or else because the processing unit is kept busy by spurious tasks.

denotational semantics An approach to the *semantics of programming languages in which the meaning of a program in a particular language is given by a valuation function that associates with each well-formed syntactic construct of the language an abstract value, e.g. a number, truth value, or function. These valuation functions are compositional or recursive in nature: the value of a program is specified as a function of the values denoted by its syntactic subcomponents. A great deal of work in this area is currently directed at the semantics of parallel programs. This approach was initiated and developed by Christopher Strachey and Dana Scott.

density 1. A measure of the amount of information in a given dimension of a storage medium. For magnetic tape it is the amount of information recorded per unit length of tape, usually in bits per inch or bits per millimeter. In general the number of flux reversals per inch (or per mm) is different because of redundancy in the coding. The density is stated for a single track. A tape transport can often read tapes with different densities under program control.

The density of information on a disk is almost always a fixed number of bits per sector, sectors per track, and tracks per disk. The standard density for paper tape is usually 10 holes per inch on a single track.

2. *See* packing density.

denumerable set *See* countable set.

deposit To place a value in a register in a processor, or in a word in memory. On many microprocessor or mini systems this can be achieved by manual operations on the control panel of the system.

depth 1. of a node in a tree. The length of the unique path from the root of the tree to the node. Thus if a node A is the root node then its depth is zero, otherwise its depth is one greater than that of its parent.

In some texts, depth of a node is synonymous with *level of a node.
2. of a tree. The maximum depth of any node in a tree. The depth of a given tree will have the same numerical value as the *height of that tree.

depth-balanced *See* balanced.

depth-first search A search of a directed *graph, and hence of a *tree, conducted as follows. An initial starting vertex u is selected and visited. Then a (directed) edge (u, v) incident upon u is selected

and a visit is made to v. Let x be the most recent vertex visited. Select some unexplored edge (x, y) incident upon x. If y has not been previously visited, visit y and proceed from there. If y has been previously visited select another edge incident upon x. Having completed the search through all paths beginning at y, return to x and continue to explore the edges incident upon x.

Depth-first searches of graphs play an important part in the design of efficient *algorithms on graphs, in game theory, heuristic programming, and in artificial intelligence.

Compare breadth-first search.

deque *Derived from* double-ended queue. A linear *list where all insertions, removals, and accesses are made at the ends. *See also* stack.

derivation sequence In formal language theory, a sequence of *words of the form

$$w_1 \Rightarrow w_2 \Rightarrow \ldots \Rightarrow w_n$$

(for notation *see* semi-Thue system). For a *context-free grammar, such a sequence is *leftmost* (or *rightmost*) if,

for each $1 \leqslant i \leqslant n$,

w_{i+1} is obtained from w_i by rewriting the leftmost (or rightmost) nonterminal in w_i. Such sequences exist for all derivable words.

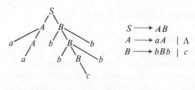

$$S \longrightarrow AB$$
$$A \longrightarrow aA \mid \Lambda$$
$$B \longrightarrow bBb \mid c$$

Derivation tree

derivation tree A way of indicating how a *context-free grammar derives a particular word. The *leaf nodes of the tree are terminals, the other nodes are nonterminals. For example, the tree in the diagram shows a derivation of *aabbcbb* from the grammar that is shown. Many different *derivation sequences can correspond to the same derivation tree.

derivative of a *formal language. The *left-derivative* of a language L, with respect to a word w, is
$$\{w' \mid ww' \in L\}$$
where ww' is the *concatenation of w and w'. Similarly a *right-derivative* is
$$\{w' \mid w'w \in L\}$$

DES *Abbrev. for* Data Encryption Standard.

descendant of a node, A, in a tree. Any node, B, such that A is an *ancestor of B.

descriptor Stored information that describes how other information is stored, e.g. in an array, record, or file. By referring to the descriptor, a program can interpret the other data. *See also* file descriptor, process descriptor.

design database A database concerned with design data, such as that used by *computer-aided design tools. Access to a design database will often be over a long period of time as opposed to the short processing times of *transactions in conventional databases.

design review *See* review.

desktop publishing (DTP) The use of a computer system or *workstation together with a *page printer to perform many of the functions of a print shop. These include page layout and design, the choice of font and typesize, and the inclusion of diagrams and pictures. DTP software normally produces its output in a *page description language that is then interpreted by the page printer to the best of its ability. The DTP program can take its input from, for instance, text files from *word processors or *text editors, pictures from graphics programs, or digitized images from *scanners.

destructive read A read operation that alters the contents of the accessed memory location and must be immediately followed by a rewriting of the contents in order to preserve them. This was the case for example with magnetic core store.

determinant A number associated with a *square matrix of numbers. The determinant of an $n \times n$ matrix A is denoted by $\det(A)$ or $|A|$ and given by
$$\sum_{\sigma} \mathrm{par}(\sigma)\, a_{1\sigma_1} a_{2\sigma_2} \dots a_{n\sigma_n}$$
where the sum is taken over all $n!$ *permutations
$$\sigma = \sigma_1 \sigma_2 \dots \sigma_n$$
of the integers $1, 2, \dots, n$. $\mathrm{par}(\sigma)$, the parity of σ, is either $+1$ or -1 depending on whether σ is an even permutation or an odd permutation.

deterministic Denoting a method, process, etc., the resulting effect of which is entirely determined by the inputs and initial state. *See also* nondeterminism, statistical methods, pseudorandom.

deterministic language Any *context-free language recognized by a deterministic *pushdown automaton. An example of a simple nondeterministic language is the set of all palindromes over an alphabet with two or more letters. A language is deterministic if and only if it is $LR(k)$ for some k (*see* LR parsing).

deterministic Turing machine *See* Turing machine. *See also* nondeterminism.

D flip-flop A clocked *flip-flop having a single D input (*see* diagram). The flip-flop Q output will take on the current state of the D input only when a given transition of the clock signal occurs between its two logic states, i.e. from low to high voltage level (*positive-edge*

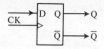

D flip-flop

triggered) or from high to low level (*negative-edge triggered*).

diagnostic routine A routine within a program that is entered as a result of some error condition having been detected, and serves to analyze the cause of that error or to provide information that is subsequently used for such analysis. A typical diagnostic routine might attempt to isolate the cause of the error to a particular hardware or software subsystem, or simply record the values of the major data objects at the time that the error occurred.

diagonalization A proof technique in recursive function theory that is used to prove the unsolvability of, for example, the *halting problem. The proof assumes (for the sake of argument) that there is an effective procedure for testing whether programs terminate. Under this assumption the method of diagonalization allows a contradiction to be derived. From this it is deduced that there is no such effective procedure.

The technique was developed by Cantor to prove that the *cardinality of the real numbers is greater than the cardinality of the integers. In this application the real numbers are enumerated in the form of a grid. A real number is then constructed along the diagonal of the grid that is not part of the original enumeration.

The technique was also used by J. Richard to generate a paradox about the namability of real numbers. This paradox (together with the "liar paradox" of antiquity) is reputed to have prompted Gödel to apply a similar technique of diagonalization in constructing a

number-theory formula not provable in formal arithmetic. *See* Gödel's incompleteness theorems.

diagonal matrix A square matrix A in which $a_{ij} = 0$ if $i \neq j$. The *inverse of a diagonal matrix, if it exists, is particularly easy to calculate and is itself diagonal.

diagrammatic technique A style of analysis or design that relies on the use of diagrams (as opposed to text or databases). The advantage is the direct appeal to users, the disadvantage the limitation to two dimensions. *See* CORE, ERA diagram, JSD, Nassi–Schneidermann chart, SADT, SSADM, Yourdon.

dictionary Any data structure representing a set of elements that can support the insertion and deletion of elements as well as test for membership. *See also* data dictionary.

difference equations Equations that have the same general form as *recurrence relations; however, the term also refers to situations in which the solution is not determined recursively from initial conditions. Difference equations play a large part in numerical computation. The equations are sometimes expressed in terms of differences of function values rather than function values themselves. The standard difference representations are:
forward difference,
$$\Delta f(x) = f(x + h) - f(x)$$
backward difference,
$$\Delta f(x) = f(x) - f(x - h)$$
central difference,
$$\Delta f(x) = f(x + \tfrac{1}{2}h) - f(x - \tfrac{1}{2}h)$$
Difference equations arise in the application of the *finite difference method.

differential dump *Another name for* change dump.

differential equations Equations for one or more unknown functions involving derivatives of those functions. The equations describe changes in a system, usually modeling some physical or other law. Except in simple cases the solution cannot be determined analytically. *See* ordinary differential equations, partial differential equations.

differential PCM (DPCM) *See* pulse code modulation.

digital Operating by, responding to, or otherwise concerned with the use of digits (i.e. discrete units) to represent arithmetic numbers, approximations to numbers from a continuum, or logical expressions/variables. *See also* discrete and continuous systems.

digital audio tape (DAT) *See* helical scan.

digital cassette A particular form of *magnetic tape cartridge.

digital circuit An electronic circuit that responds to *digital signals and produces digital signals as its output.

digital computer A computer that operates on discrete quantities (*compare* analog computer). All computation is done within a finite number system and with limited precision, associated with the number of digits in the discrete numbers. The numerical information is most often represented by the use of two-state electrical phenomena (on/off, high voltage/low voltage, current/no current, etc.) to indicate whether the value of a binary variable is a "zero" or a "one". Usually there is automatic control or sequencing (through a *program) of operations so that they can be carried through to completion without intervention. *See also* discrete and continuous systems.

digital copier A document copier that scans a page (*see* scanner), converts it to a digital image, and then prints it by means of a *page printer. *See also* intelligent copier.

digital data transmission Digital data uses discrete discontinuous signals to represent its meanings. In a DC (direct current) transmission system, different voltage (or current) values are used to represent the values (usually 0 and 1). A digital transmission has a very low error rate and can be sent at very high speeds. Weak signals can be regenerated with low probability of cumulative error. Since all signals are made up of 0s and 1s, signals from many sources can be readily multiplexed using digital techniques. *See* multiplexing.

Digital data can also be transmitted over AC transmission lines. Since DC signals are blocked out by AC transmission lines, a different technique is used. AC lines use analog signals to transmit data; to transform digital data to analog signals a *modulator is used. *See also* modulation.

digital design (logic design) The design of circuits and systems whose inputs and outputs are represented as discrete variables. These variables are commonly binary, i.e. two-state, in nature. Design at the circuit level is usually done with *truth tables and *state tables; design at the system level is done with *block diagrams or *digital design languages.

digital design language A higher-order language, often called a *register transfer language, used to facilitate the description and manipulation of digital systems and their interconnection. *See also* digital design, CHDL.

Digital Equipment Corporation *See* DEC.

digital filtering The employment of *digital signal processing techniques to effect the *filtering of a signal.

digital logic A methodology for dealing with expressions and *state tables containing discrete (usually two-state) variables: in this sense the term is synonymous with *Boolean algebra (*see also* multiple-valued logic). The term is also applied to the hardware – components and circuits – in which such expressions and tables are implemented. *See also* digital design, logic circuit, combinational circuit, sequential circuit, q-ary logic.

digital signal A waveform or signal whose voltage at any particular time will be at any one of a group of discrete levels, generally two; a two-level signal is sometimes called a *binary digital signal* or *binary signal*. In binary logic circuits, in which only two discrete voltage levels are used, one level will correspond to logic 1 (true), usually the high level, and the other will correspond to logic 0 (false).

digital signal processing The branch of *signal processing that uses digital systems to operate on signals. The advantages of digital over analog signal processing are that memory is more easily employed (so that time may be re-run in different speeds and directions) and that a wider range of arithmetic operations and algorithmic complexity is possible; the main advantage, however, is that the possible precision is arbitrarily high. The main disadvantage is that in some instances digital techniques are slower than analog techniques. Many specialized digital devices have been developed that retain the advantages but nevertheless operate at high speed, at the cost of flexibility.

digital sorting *Another name for* radix sorting.

digital system Any system handling digital (discrete) *signals. *See* discrete and continuous systems.

digital-to-analog converter *See* D/A converter.

digitization The process of quantizing a *signal and representing it in digital form. *See also* quantization, discrete and continuous systems, digitizer, A/D converter.

digitizer 1. (digitizing tablet) A flat surface that is used together with a penlike instrument (a *stylus*) for the input of data to a computer graphics system. It allows digital values to be assigned to a set of related points, such as intersections of lines on a drawing or surfaces on a two-dimensional model. The most common version is that used in engineering or architectural drawing offices to translate line drawings into sets of coordinates that can be processed by computer.

The position of the stylus, moved by hand over the surface, can be accurately and rapidly located by any of a variety of methods. In general, the surface carries intersecting magnetic fields and these are used to generate a signal from the stylus and so register its position. A software interface to a *CAD application then passes the signal to a screen display.

2. *Another name for* quantizer, but generally implying that the output is encoded into *binary numbers.

digraph *Short for* directed graph. *See* graph.

Dijkstra's algorithm A method, developed by E. W. Dijkstra in 1959, to find the *shortest path from a specified *vertex in a *weighted graph to all other vertices in the graph.

DIL *Acronym for* dual in-line. *See* DIP, DIL switch.

DIL switch A device similar in form to a *DIP, but instead of an integrated circuit the package contains a row of small switches making or breaking the circuit between opposite pairs of legs. DIL switches are commonly used for setting the default state of printers, terminals, etc.

dimension (dimensionality) of an *array. The number of subscripts needed to locate any element in the array.

diminished radix complement *Another name for* radix-minus-one complement.

diminishing increment sort *Another name for* Shell's method.

diode An electronic device, generally of semiconductor material, that has two terminals and is capable of allowing current flow in one direction only. The terminals are called the *anode* and *cathode*. The diode presents a very low (high) impedance when a *forward bias (*reverse bias) is applied.

diode-transistor logic *See* DTL.

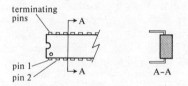

terminating pins

→ A

pin 1
pin 2
→ A

A–A

Dual in-line package

DIP *Short for* dual in-line package. An *integrated circuit encapsulated in a rectangular plastic or ceramic package with a row of metal legs down each of the long sides (*see* diagram). The legs are terminating pins. The number of terminations and hence the package size is a function of the number of external connections to the chip. The legs can either be soldered into holes in a *printed circuit board or inserted into a *chip socket.

direct-access storage device One of a class of storage devices in which physical *records are *addressable and can

therefore be accessed in any order: a sequential search is not required. For all practical purposes direct-access storage is synonymous with disk storage.

direct addressing The "normal" mode of addressing in which the address specified in the instruction is the *absolute address to be used. *See also* addressing schemes.

direct-coupled machines A system in which two (or more) machines are connected by a high-speed link in order to perform the total workload. Typically a small machine, the *master*, deals with file editing, job submission, and all scheduling. Larger jobs that would take too long to process on this small machine are passed to a larger machine, the *slave*, for processing, the results being returned to the user via the small machine. *See also* master-slave machine.

direct data entry (DDE) *See* data entry.

direct digital control (DDC) Control of a process by a digital computer, the information being supplied to the process as (appropriately timed) sequences of digits. *See* numerical control.

directed graph (digraph) *See* graph.

directed set A subset X of a *partially ordered set S, such that every finite subset of X has an *upper bound in X itself. As a special case of this, a *chain* is a countable subset of the form

$$x_0 \subseteq x_1 \subseteq x_2 \subseteq \ldots$$

where $\subseteq$ denotes the partial ordering on S.

directed tree *See* tree.

directive *Another name for* pseudoinstruction.

direct memory access (DMA) A method whereby I/O processes can obtain access to the CPU's memory while a program is running. This is accomplished by permitting the I/O controller or channel that has been previously instructed to move a block of data to or from the memory to temporarily take control of the memory for (usually) one *memory cycle by specifying the memory address, thus allowing a single word (or group of words if the memory is so organized) to be read or written. The method is therefore also referred to as *cycle stealing*. The timing requirement is normally that of the slower external device and is prompted by the ability of that device to receive or provide desired data, hence the alternative synonym *data break*.

directory A means of locating data items, usually files. A directory can be regarded as establishing a set of links between named data items and their locations in a *direct-access storage device. In many systems the directories are highly structured; their organization reflects the relationships between various categories of file. For example, the directory may allow one user to have other subordinate users, and permit controlled access by these subordinate users to their own and others' files. *See also* data dictionary.

direct product (product group) of two *groups G and H with group *operations ρ and τ respectively. The group consisting of the elements in the *Cartesian product of G and H and on which there is a *dyadic operation $\circ$ defined as follows:

$$(g_1,h_1) \circ (g_2,h_2) = (g_1 \, \rho \, g_2, \, h_1 \, \tau \, h_2)$$

The identity of this group is then (e_G,e_H), where e_G and e_H are the identities of groups G and H respectively. The inverse of (g,h) is then (g^{-1},h^{-1}).

These concepts can be generalized to deal with the direct product of any finite number of groups on which there are specified group operations.

disable 1. To make a device inactive.
2. To suppress the action of an interrupt.

disarm To put a device into a state that is still serviceable but requires a preparatory action before it can be used.

disassembler A program that attempts to translate machine code back into assembly language as an aid to debugging. A simple disassembler operates on one instruction at a time, translating the operation code to the appropriate mnemonic, displaying register references and addressing modes in the symbolic form used in the assembly language, and converting addresses into hexadecimal or symbols. More ambitious disassemblers try to show the structure of the program by replacing branch destinations with alphanumeric symbols, and placing the corresponding symbol as a label in the appropriate position in the program.

disc *UK spelling of* disk, sometimes preferred in UK computer literature.

disconnected graph *See* connected graph.

discrete and continuous systems Systems by which *signals are recorded, communicated, or displayed may represent the data in discrete form (e.g. as integers) or in continuous form (as "real" numbers). An important classification results from the choice of discrete or continuous representation of the amplitude, and of discrete or continuous representation of the time at which the amplitude occurred. *Analog computers employ physical quantities that are approximations to continuous representations. Discrete representations of both time and amplitude are required by *digital computers.

The question of whether the signal (or its source) is intrinsically discrete or intrinsically continuous is unresolvable: any experiment to determine this would require infinite *bandwidth (or infinite time) and infinite *signal-to-noise ratio, and so would be impossible in practice. All that is in question is whether a discrete or continuous representation is more convenient, or useful, or appealing.

Signals that appear intuitively to be continuous-time or continuous-amplitude, but for which a discrete-time or discrete-amplitude representation is preferred, are said to have been *time-quantized* or *amplitude-quantized*. Time quantization is either adequate or inadequate according to *Nyquist's criterion. Time-quantized signals are said to be *sampled*, and the systems that handle them are called *sampled-data systems*. Amplitude quantization worsens the signal-to-noise ratio, an effect describable as the introduction of *quantization noise.

Time and amplitude must both be quantized for processing by digital computers (or by other digital devices), which operate at finite speeds on finite amounts of data held to finite precisions. The same physical constraints operate, although in a different way, to limit the extent to which analog computers (or other analog devices) can approximate to the continuous representation of signals.

See also quantization.

discrete channel A communication *channel whose input and output each have an alphabet of distinct letters, or, in the case of a physical channel, whose input and output are *signals that are discrete in time and amplitude (*see* discrete and continuous systems). The size of the alphabet, or the number of amplitude levels, is usually finite.

The *discrete memoryless channel (DMC)* has the property that its treatment of a symbol input at a certain time does not depend on the symbols input, or its treatment of them, at any earlier time.

The *discrete channel with memory (DCM)* has the property that its action depends on its inputs at a number of earlier times.

See also Shannon's model, channel coding theorem.

discrete Fourier transform *See* Fourier transform.

discrete signal *See* discrete and continuous systems.

discrete source A source of information whose output has an alphabet of distinct letters or, in the case of a physical source, whose output is a *signal that is discrete in time and amplitude (*see* discrete and continuous systems). The size of the alphabet, or the number of amplitude levels, is usually finite, although for mathematical analysis it may conveniently be regarded as infinite.

The *discrete memoryless source (DMS)* has the property that its output at a certain time does not depend on its output at any earlier time.

The *discrete source with memory (DSM)* has the property that its output at a certain time may depend on its outputs at a number of earlier times: if this number is finite, the source is said to be of *finite order*, otherwise it is of *infinite order*. DSMs are usually modeled by means of *Markov chains; they are then called *Markov sources*.

An *ergodic source* has the property that its output at any time has the same statistical properties as its output at any other time. Memoryless sources are, trivially, always ergodic; a source with memory is ergodic only if it is modeled by an ergodic Markov chain.

See also information theory, Shannon's model, source coding theorem.

discrete structure A *set of discrete elements on which certain operations are defined. Discrete implies noncontinuous and therefore discrete sets include *finite and *countable sets but not uncountable sets such as the real numbers. The term discrete structure covers many of the concepts of modern algebra, including integer arithmetic, *monoids, *semigroups, *groups, *graphs, *lattices, *semirings, *rings, *fields, and *subsets of these.

discrete system *See* discrete and continuous systems.

discretization The process of replacing a problem defined on a continuum, say an interval [0,1], by an approximating problem on a finite set of points, say nh,

$$n = 0,1,2,\ldots,N,$$

where $h = 1/N$

Examples arise in many branches of numerical analysis, principally ordinary and partial differential equations where the *finite-difference method is the common form of discretization. For the ordinary differential equation

$$y' = f(x,y),$$
$$0 \leq x \leq 1, \ y(0) = y_0,$$

a simple discretization is given by *Euler's method*:

$$(1/h)(y_{n+1} - y_n) = f(x_n,y_n)$$

where

$$x_n = hn, \ n = 0,1,\ldots,N,$$
$$h = 1/N$$

and y_n denotes the approximation to the true solution $y(x)$ at the point x_n. *See also* discretization error.

discretization error (truncation error) The error in a numerical method that has been constructed by a process of *discretization. It results from the discretization of a "continuous" problem, where it is assumed that all arithmetic is done exactly, and is of fundamental importance in methods for differential equations. A distinction is made between global and local errors. For example, in Euler's method (*see* discretization) y_n is the approximation to the solution $y(x)$ at x_n. The *global discretization (or truncation) error* is given by

$$y_n - y(x_n)$$

(Some authors take the maximum of this expression over $n = 0,1,\ldots,N$.) The *local discretization (or truncation) error* is the amount by which the true solution of the differential equation fails to satisfy the discretization formula; for Euler's method it is

$$y(x_{n+1}) - y(x_n) - hf(x_n,y(x_n))$$

This quantity can be regarded as a first measure of the accuracy of the formula. It can be estimated at each step of the integration and provides a means of indirectly controlling the global discretization error. These definitions can be extended to other methods and beyond.

discriminant analysis *See* multivariate analysis.

disjoint A term applied to two sets that have no element in common, i.e. such that the *intersection of the sets results in the *empty set. A number of sets are said to be *mutually disjoint* if each pair is disjoint.

disjunction A logical expression of the form

$$a_1 \lor a_2 \lor \ldots \lor a_n$$

where $\lor$ is the *OR operation. A particular disjunction of interest is the *disjunctive normal form* of a Boolean expression involving n variables, x_1, x_2, $\ldots$, x_n. Each a_i is then of the form

$$(y_1 \land y_2 \land \ldots y_n)$$

where $\land$ is the *AND operation and each y_i is equal to x_i or the complement of x_i. Reducing expressions to disjunctive normal form provides a ready method of determining the *equivalence of two Boolean expressions. *See also* propositional calculus. *Compare* conjunction.

disjunctive normal form *See* disjunction.

disk An item of storage medium in the form of a circular plate. These devices are at present (mid-1989) principally *magnetic disks, in which the information is stored via *magnetic encoding. *See also* optical disk, magneto-optic disk storage.

disk cartridge An *exchangeable disk store in the form of an assembly containing a single rigid *magnetic disk permanently housed within a protective plastic cover. The term has been used to refer to a *disk pack, but conventionally this is no longer the case. The cartridge was introduced by IBM in 1964.

The cartridge, according to its type, may be loaded vertically onto its drive (*top-loading*), or horizontally from the front (*front-loading*). Either way the cartridge hub, to which the disk is clamped, centers onto the drive spindle and is magnetically clamped. The cover contains apertures to allow fixing of the cartridge to the drive, and a door that the drive opens to allow insertion of the magnetic heads. Once loaded, the disk can rotate clear of the covers. On some types the hub has a notch that is sensed by a transducer on the drive and signals the start of each recording track. Additionally, a set of equispaced notches may be present to signal the start of sectors within tracks; their presence and number depend on the requirements of the drive controller. On other types, this information, together with track spacing information, is prerecorded on one of the two surfaces, the *servosurface*.

Disk cartridges have storage capacities up to 50 megabytes, depending on track density, bit density, and disk size. Disk diameters range from 14″ to about 3″ (356–76 mm).

Similar cartridges are used for *optical disks, with capacities from a few hundred megabytes to several gigabytes. In some cases the disk is extracted mechanically from the cartridge for use, rather than rotated within it.

disk drive (disk unit) A peripheral device with *read/write heads and associated electronics that can store and retrieve data from rotating *magnetic disks – either a single disk or *disk cartridge or a *disk pack. The term can also be applied to devices operating with *optical disks.

In a magnetic disk drive the data is recorded on one or both sides of a disk in a set of concentric tracks, which are usually subdivided into *sectors. The read/write heads of the disk drive are mounted on arms that can be moved, by means of an *actuator, to position the heads accurately over the required track. As the disk rotates, the sectors on that track are made accessible. In the case of a drive with a disk pack it is usual for the read/write heads to have a common actuator. The time required to access related records can then be minimized by arranging that the records form a notional *cylinder* by writing them to the same track number on different disk surfaces.

In a *fixed disk drive* the storage medium is permanently attached within the device. In other disk drives an *exchangeable disk store is used: a disk cartridge or disk pack may be removed and replaced by another containing different files. *See also* floppy-disk drive, disk format.

diskette, diskette drive *Other names for* floppy disk, floppy-disk drive.

disk file A set of related records held on a storage disk. The term is sometimes misapplied to refer to a *disk drive together with its *disk or *disk pack and the data it holds.

disk format The *format of information recorded on magnetic (or optical) disk, allowing a system to recognize, control, and verify the data. There are two levels at which formats are defined.

(a) The way in which the data stream is divided into separately addressable portions, called *sectors, with *address marks and data marks to differentiate between the different types of information within the sector, and with a *cyclic redundancy check or *error-correcting code also provided.

(b) The way in which the binary information is encoded as a pattern of magnetic flux reversals.

Since recordings on disks are made as a bit serial stream on a single track at a time, special provision has to be made to allow the reading system to maintain synchronization. This is achieved by the

encoding format, which either includes
*clock pulses or encodes the data in
such a way that there cannot be a case
where there is a succession of eight or
more bit cells without a magnetic flux
transition occurring. The read electronics can maintain synchronization for
short periods without transitions. The
common methods of encoding are as
follows.

Frequency modulation (FM; F2F) is a
form of self-clocking recording. The
beginning of each bit cell is marked by
a clock pulse recorded as a change in
the direction of the magnetic flux. If the
cell is to represent a binary 1 a second
pulse or transition is written at the
center of the cell, otherwise there is no
further change until the start of the next
cell. If the frequency of the clock is F
then a stream of 1s will result in a frequency of $2F$ (hence F2F recording). In
this form of recording the minimum
separation between transitions is half of
one cell and the maximum is one cell.

In *modified frequency modulation
(MFM)* a binary 1 is always represented
by a transition at the center of a bit cell
but there is not always a transition at
the boundary of the cell. A transition is
written at the start of a bit cell only if
it is to represent a binary 0 and does
not follow a binary 1. Thus the minimum separation between transitions is
one cell and the maximum is two cells.
For the same spacing of flux transitions
the MFM method allows twice as many
bits to be encoded in a unit distance; it
is thus sometimes referred to as a *double-density recording.*

*Modified modified frequency modulation
(M²FM)* is a modified form of MFM
that deletes flux transitions between two
0s if they are followed by a 1.

Run-length limited encoding is a form
of *NRZ (nonreturn to zero) recording
in which groups of data are mapped
onto larger groups before recording. A
frequently used method known as *GCR
(group code recording)* breaks the data
stream into groups of four bits and

maps these onto five bit groups. Because
of the resulting redundancy, the five bit
groups can be selected to limit the
number of consecutive 0s and thus control the maximum spacing between flux
transitions. Other similar codes are *EIR
(error indicating recording)*, a form of
four to six mapping that uses only the
groups with odd parity, i.e. three or five
1s, and *3PM (three-phase modulation)*,
which has a minimum sequence of two
0s and a maximum of eleven.

Optical disk formats are broadly similar to those of magnetic disk, except
that the tracks usually take the form of
a continuous spiral and the path of this
is often determined by a groove pressed
into the disk surface during manufacture.

See also formatter.

disk pack One form of *exchangeable
disk store, consisting of an assembly of
identical 14″ diameter rigid *magnetic
disks that are mounted coaxially and
equally spaced. A similar nonrecording
protective disk is fitted above the top
recording disk with another one below
the bottom recording disk. The whole
assembly is rigidly clamped together,
and is designed for dynamic stability at
its intended rotational speed on the
*disk drive, which can be up to 3600
revolutions per minute. Disk packs are
designed to be compatible with disk
drives, mechanically and magnetically,
and most types are the subjects of international standards. The whole pack,
when not mounted on the drive, is contained within sealed plastic covers, in
two parts, which help to ensure that the
pack is protected from damage, dust,
and contamination. The bottom cover is
removed before mounting the pack on
the drive; the top cover can only be
removed when the pack has been
mounted.

The mechanical interface with the
disk drive is via an axial lockshaft in
the pack, having a female thread engaging the male spindle of the drive. On

some types, a notch on the periphery of the bottom protective disk is sensed by a transducer on the drive and signals the start of each recording track. Additionally, a set of equispaced notches may be present to signal the start of *sectors within tracks; their presence and number depend on the requirements of the drive controller. On other types, this information, together with track spacing information, is prerecorded on a surface reserved for this purpose, the *servosurface*.

Storage capacities range from 30 to 300 megabytes, over the range of track densities up to 400 tracks per inch, recording densities up to 6000 bits per inch, and pack sizes of 5 to 12 disks. Disk packs were introduced by IBM in 1963.

disk unit *Another name for* disk drive.

dispatcher *Another name for* low-level scheduler. *See* scheduler.

dispersion *See* measures of variation.

display 1. To make information visible in a temporary form.
2. The device that enables information, either textual or pictorial, to be seen but not permanently recorded.

There are many types of display device but the most widely used is the *cathode-ray tube. Although domestic TV receivers can be used as computer-driven displays, it is usual to have specially designed units if there are to be periods of prolonged use by one operator. Under such conditions it is necessary to optimize the screen characteristics and provide a sharper and more stable image to avoid unnecessary fatigue. *See also* VDU.

The following display technologies are also used in association with computer systems and allow a more compact or *flat screen to be made.

(a) *plasma displays, which for displaying small amounts of information –

up to 240 characters – are an attractive alternative to cathode-ray tubes, although large displays are more expensive;

(b) *LED (light-emitting diode) displays, which are generally only used when up to 40 characters are to be displayed;

(c) *LCDs (liquid crystal displays), which are used in clocks and watches but have also been demonstrated in larger forms suitable for information display, although these are not yet widely adopted;

(d) *electroluminescent displays*, which are beginning to be used in portable computers.

display adapter An adapter that can be fitted to a personal computer to enable it to drive an enhanced display. The enhancement may be for graphics or for an enhanced resolution and/or larger text display.

display processor A specialized *I/O processor used to mediate between a file of information that is to be displayed and a display device. It reformats the information as required and provides the information in accordance with the timing requirements of the display system.

distributed array processor *See* array processor.

distributed database A *database in which the data is contained within a number of separate subsystems, usually in different physical locations. If the constituent subsystems are essentially similar, the system is said to be *homogeneous*, otherwise it is said to be *heterogeneous*. Distributed database systems may vary very considerably. At one extreme is the type where the complete system was conceived, designed, and implemented as a single entity; such systems exist within large commercial organizations and are usually homogeneous. At the other extreme is the case where a number of existing systems, originally planned as isolated systems, continue in their normal operation but in addition are loosely linked to provide a larger distributed system; in this instance the system is often heterogeneous.

Distributed database systems are currently an active topic for database research and development, largely because of the availability of national and international communication facilities.

distributed file system A system in which a number of users, using different processors, have the possibility of shared access to one another's *files. The files may be of any type (e.g. data, programs, text). Versions of *UNIX are available that offer distributed file facilities. *Compare* distributed database.

distributed processing The organization of processing to be carried out on a *distributed system. Each *process is free to process local data and make local decisions. The processes exchange information with each other over a data communication network to process data or to read decisions that affect multiple processes. *See also* open distributed processing.

distributed system Any system in which a number of independent interconnected computers can cooperate. *See* distributed processing.

distribution *See* frequency distribution, probability distributions.

distribution counting sort A sorting algorithm that stores, for each sortkey, the number of records with the given sortkey (thus anticipating that keys might not be unique). With this information it is possible to place the records correctly into a sorted file. The algorithm is useful when the keys fall into a small range and many of them are equal.

distributive lattice A *lattice L, with meet and join operations $\land$ and $\lor$ respectively, in which the two *distributive laws hold for all elements in L. Since these laws are self-duals, the principle of *duality continues to hold for distributive lattices.

distributive laws The two self-dual laws

$$x \land (y \lor z) = (x \land y) \lor (x \land z)$$
$$x \lor (y \land z) = (x \lor y) \land (x \lor z)$$

that are satisfied by all elements x, y, and z in a *Boolean algebra possessing the two operations $\land$ and $\lor$. In the first law the operation $\land$ is said to be distributive over the operation $\lor$, and vice versa for the second law.

diverse programming (n-version programming) The implementation to a common specification of two (or more) different versions of a program, usually using two completely different teams of programmers. The purpose is to create versions of the program that are unlikely to have the same faults. On comparison of the two programs, identification of any differences can point to errors that occurred in interpreting the specification, errors in design, and errors during implementation.

The use of diverse programming inevitably leads to an increase in the development cost of a software system, but this is compensated by an increase in confidence in the quality of the software and often leads to a lower cost in validation, verification, and testing.

divide and conquer sorting A sorting algorithm that is similar to *radix sorting but works from the most significant digit of the sortkey down to the least significant.

divided difference *See* interpolation.

divider *See* counter.

DL/1 The *data manipulation language of *IMS.

DMA *Abbrev. for* direct memory access.

DME *Trademark, acronym for* direct machine environment. A system offered by ICL as a means of using the microcode capabilities of their 2900 range of machines to allow users to run ICL 1900 series software, including the GEORGE operating system. Originally offered as an interim product for users migrating from 1900 to 2900 systems, DME is sufficiently attractive to be used as a main operating environment.

DML *Abbrev. for* data manipulation language.

documentation All material that serves primarily to describe a system and make it more readily understandable, rather than to contribute in some way to the actual operation of the system. Documentation is frequently classified according to purpose; thus for a given system there may be requirements documents, design documents, and so on. In contrast to documentation orientated toward development and maintenance of the system, user documentation describes those aspects of the system that are of interest to the eventual users.

document description language A language for describing the structure and contents of a document, for example Interpress (Xerox) and DDL (Imagen). *See also* SPDL.

document processing The machine processing (reading, sorting, etc.) of documents that are generally readable both by people and machines, e.g. bank checks, vouchers from credit card transactions, and accounts from public utilities. In addition to the printed information for human interpretation, there is also some encoding that is machine-readable and may be in an *OCR or *MICR font.

The documents are frequently referred to as *turnaround documents* since the person receiving them "turns them

around" and returns them to the system to complete a transaction.

document reader A machine for reading documents that are encoded in a way that is readable by person and machine. *See also* document processing.

document scanner A peripheral for a computer system that can input the optical image of a document page. It may be combined with internal or host resident processing of the input to manipulate the image or recognize text and output strings of character codes.

document sorter A device that can read information encoded on documents and place them into separate stacks related to that code. Bank checks are processed in this way. *See also* document processing.

do loop A counting loop in a program, in which a section of code is obeyed repeatedly with a counter taking successive values. Thus in FORTRAN,

```
      DO 10 I = 1,100
         <statements>
10    CONTINUE
```

causes the <statements> to be obeyed 100 times. The current value of the counter variable is often used within the loop, especially to index an array. There are many syntactic variants: in Pascal and Algol-related languages the same basic construct appears as the *for loop*, e.g.

```
   for i := 1 to 100 do
      begin
         <statements>
      end
```

This kind of loop is a constituent of almost all programming languages (except APL, which has array operations defined as operators in the language).

See also do-while loop.

DOL system *See* L-system.

domain 1. *See* function, relation, category. *See also* range.

2. In the *relational model, a set of possible values from which the actual values in any column of a table (relation) must be drawn.

3. In *denotational semantics, a structured set of mathematical entities in which meanings for programming constructs can be found. The idea first arose in the work of Dana Scott, who pioneered the mathematical approach to programming language semantics. Scott required domains to be *complete lattices, but this is no longer considered necessary.

4. *See* protection domain.

domain modeling The modeling of a generic problem domain, usually but not necessarily in the area of business information systems. A domain model is likely to identify entity classes, interentity relationships, and operations on entities, which are likely to be common to most systems in a given problem domain. From such a generic design, individual system designs can be instantiated to take account of specific local requirements more rapidly and correctly than by designing from scratch. Bill of materials and share registration are examples of problem domains. *Compare* enterprise modeling.

dominator A vertex x_i on a graph G is a dominator of vertex x_j, relative to vertex x_k, if every path from x_j to x_k traverses x_i. This is used in flow analysis for code optimization.

do-nothing instruction *Another name for* no-op instruction.

dope vector A vector of data used to assist in accessing the elements in an *array. The dope vector contains

(a) the address of a fixed element in the array – this may be the first element present or the element that has all subscripts equated to zero;

(b) the number of subscripts associated with the array, i.e. its dimensionality;

(c) the *stride* associated with each subscript position, i.e. the number of stored elements that must be skipped over when a subscript's value is changed by 1.

The position in memory of an element is found by taking the inner product of the strides with the differences between the actual subscript values and those that correspond to the fixed element referred to in (a), and adding to this the address of the fixed element.

DOS *Trademark, acronym for* disk operating system. The original DOS written by IBM for the series-700 computers was one of the first major operating systems to be offered by a mainframe manufacturer, and was introduced shortly after the still more primitive system, *OS. DOS gave users the ability to construct files on disks that held images of punched cards and that could serve as the input to programs; similarly output ultimately destined for printers was *spooled into temporary disk files. The user was responsible for much of the management of these files, and had to contend with details of their physical location on disk and with their creation and disposal.

dot matrix printer A printer that creates each character from an array of dots that are usually formed by transferring ink by mechanical impact. It may be a *serial printer, printing a character at a time, or a *line printer.

The serial printer has a print head containing typically 9, 18, or 24 electromagnetically operated styluses. In a *wire printer* the styluses are steel or tungsten wires that are constrained by a guide at the printing tip. The styluses may also be short rods rigidly attached to a pivoting armature or spring fingers. The head is mounted on a carriage that is moved along guides so that it travels parallel to the paper and the position of the line to be printed. The styluses are selectively operated to build up alphanumeric characters and other shapes from a matrix of small dots. Alphanumeric characters of data-processing quality are built up on a matrix of 7 or 9 dots high by 4 or 5 dots wide. These usually have voids and scalloped edges, which can however be removed by making repeated passes of the head along the same line but printing the dots in a slightly different place on each pass: the dots can thus be made to overlap in both horizontal and vertical lines. More recent designs of printers have 18 or 24 styluses and can produce characters that more closely resemble ordinary typewritten quality. The generally available speed range is 100–400 characters per second (cps) for print of data-processing quality, and up to 100 cps for a higher-quality character.

A widely adopted design for dot matrix line printers is to have a row of spring fingers that span the line to be printed. Such printers operate at 200–900 lines per minute.

Enhancements of dot matrix printers include the ability to print in seven colors. Ribbonless printers in which the ink is fed directly to the styluses have been demonstrated.

double buffering A form of *buffering in which two buffers are used. On output the program can be filling one buffer while the device empties the other; the buffers then exchange roles. A similar technique is used for input.

double complement of a *set S. The *complement of the set S', where S' itself is just the complement of S; the double complement of S is thus S itself. In logic double complement implies *double negation* of an element x, say, i.e. x itself.

double-density recording *Another name for* modified frequency modulation. *See* disk format.

double-length arithmetic *See* double precision.

double negation *See* double complement.

double precision The use of double the usual number of bits to represent a number. Arithmetic performed on double-precision numbers is called *double-precision* (or *double-length*) *arithmetic*. For floating-point numbers, most computers use the same number of bits for the exponent in single-length and double-length forms. Consequently, if the length of a single-precision number is l bits, p of which are used for the mantissa, then the mantissa of a double-precision number occupies $(p + l)$ of the $2l$ bits. Occasionally, *multiple precision*, i.e. more than double precision, may be available. Some computers implement double precision in hardware; higher precision, for example quadruple precision, is almost always achieved by software.

doubly linked list (two-way linked list; symmetric list) A *linked list where each item contains links to both its predecessor and its successor. This makes it possible to traverse the list in either direction. The flexibility given by double linking must be offset against the overhead of the storage and the setting and resetting of the extra links involved.

do-while loop A form of programming loop in which the condition for termination (continuation) is computed each time around the loop. There are several variants on this basic idea. For example, Pascal has

```
    while <condition> do
      begin
        <statements>
      end
and also
    repeat
```

<statements>
until <condition>

The first is a *while loop* and the second is a *repeat-until* loop. Apart from the obvious difference that the first specifies a continuation condition while the second specifies a termination condition, there is a more significant difference. The while loop is a *zero-trip* loop, i.e. the body will not be executed at all if the condition is false the first time around. In contrast, the body of a repeat-until loop must be obeyed at least once.

Similar constructs are found in most languages, though there are many syntactic variations. *See also* do loop.

down *Informal* Denoting a system that is unavailable. It is either switched off or is switched on and being repaired.

downline The direction from a central or controlling *node to a remote node in a hierarchical network, or (sometimes) the direction away from the current node without respect to hierarchical ordering.

The word is often used as a verb: to downline or to *downline load*, i.e. to send programs or data from a central or controlling node to a remote node in a network. The remote node may not have the facilities to store the programs or data permanently, in which case the downline load would be necessary each time the remote node is restarted. When the remote node does have permanent storage facilities, downline loading may be used to supply newer versions of programs or data to the remote node. *Compare* upline.

download To send programs or data from a central or controlling computer to a remote terminal. *See also* downline.

down operation *Another name for* P operation. *See* semaphore.

downtime The percentage of time that a computer system is not available for use.

DP *Abbrev. for* data processing.

DPCM *Abbrev. for* differential PCM. *See* pulse code modulation.

dpi *Abbrev. for* dots per inch.

DPM *Abbrev. for* data-processing manager.

DRAM *Abbrev. for* dynamic RAM. *See* dynamic memory, RAM.

DRAW *Abbrev. for* direct read after write. In optical or magnetic data storage, a writing technique in which each bit of data is read a few bit times after it is written. This enables an erroneous sector to be recognized before the next sector starts to be written and errors can be managed accordingly, generally by flagging the defective sector or block and repeating the same data in the next sector. Nearly all magnetic tape drives, and many optical disk drives, use this technique. *See also* DRDW.

The term is sometimes erroneously used simply to imply that written information is immediately ready for reading, without an intermediate processing operation such as would be required for photographic recording.

DRCS *Abbrev. for* dynamically redefinable character set.

DRDW *Abbrev. for* direct read during write. In optical data storage, a writing technique in which each signal element is check-read as it is written, by sensing the light reflected from the medium. It serves the same purpose as *DRAW. In magnetic tape storage, the term is sometimes used to mean the same as DRAW.

driver 1. A routine within an operating system that handles the individual peripheral units on the computer system. Of necessity a driver routine is required to deal with the intimate details of the construction of each unit and of its real-time behavior. Consequently at least some of the driver will often need to be written in a machine-oriented programming language.

2. An electronic circuit, often available in the form of a logic gate, that is capable of providing large currents or voltages to other circuits connected to the driver's output. These devices are often used to place signals onto bus lines, hence the term *bus driver*.

drop-in In magnetic recording technology (disk and tape), the presence among the signals read from the device of one or more bits that had not been deliberately written there. This is the result of a fault condition, often imperfect erasure of data previously on the medium, and will generally be a problem only in interrecord gaps (elsewhere it will be dealt with by the same means provided for *drop-out): magnetic tape and disk systems normally have means of identifying and coping with this problem.

drop-out In magnetic recording technology (disk and tape), the loss of one or a sequence of bits due to a fault condition, most frequently a flaw in the recording medium. Magnetic tape and disk systems employ some form of redundancy to detect and frequently correct the resulting data errors.

drum *See* magnetic drum, drum printer, plotter.

drum plotter *See* plotter.

drum printer A type of *solid-font *line printer in which the font is etched or engraved on the outer surface of a cylinder that extends across the full width of the line to be printed. This font carrier, referred to as a *drum* in the US, is more generally known as a *barrel* in the UK with the printer then referred to as a *barrel printer*. This was the first type of computer output printer to use the "hit-on-the-fly" principle, used on *chain printers and current band and

train printers, and it was a significant change from the mechanically intensive printers that preceded it. The first commercially available machine was introduced by Shepard in about 1955.

dry run Execution of a program in a manner analogous to a *production run, but for purposes of checking that the program behaves correctly rather than for producing useful results. The results of execution are compared with expected results; any discrepancies indicate an error of some sort that must be investigated before the program is put into production usage.

DSL *Abbrev. for* database sublanguage. *See* database language.

DSPACE *See* complexity classes.

DTE *Abbrev. for* data terminal equipment. The side of an interface that represents the user of the data communication services in a standard such as RS232C or X.25. DTEs are usually computers or computer terminals. *Compare* DCE.

DTIME *See* complexity classes.

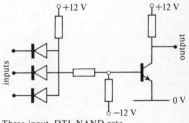
Three-input DTL NAND gate

DTL *Abbrev. for* diode-transistor logic. An early form of *logic family, normally produced in integrated-circuit form, whose principal switching components consist of semiconductor diodes and transistors. The equivalent circuit of a three-input DTL *NAND gate is shown in the diagram. Each input is fed to a diode and the output is taken from the collector of a *bipolar transistor. When all inputs are at logic 1, current can flow to the base of the transistor so driving it into saturation. As a result the collector voltage falls to logic 0.

DTP *Abbrev. for* desktop publishing.

D-type flip-flop *See* D flip-flop.

dual *See* duality.

dual in-line package *See* DIP.

duality The property exhibited by the laws and rules of *set algebra, the *propositional calculus, and *Boolean algebra that each law or rule has a *dual* law or rule, constructed by the simultaneous replacement of each occurrence of 0 by 1, 1 by 0, ∨ by ∧, and ∧ by ∨. Such a pair of laws or rules is then said to be *self-dual*. Thus *de Morgan's laws, for example, are self-dual.

If a law or rule contains the *partial ordering ⩽ inherent in any lattice, then in obtaining duals this should be replaced by ⩾ and vice versa; thus inequalities should be reversed.

dual port memory A memory that is capable of receiving two concurrent access requests. Depending upon the internal memory organization, responses may or may not be simultaneous. Close-coupled *multiprocessor systems use these memories.

dual processor A *multiprocessor system with two central processors. Use of this term sometimes implies a two-processor system in which one processor is redundant so that the total system has a very high level of reliability.

dummy instruction (dummy) An item of data in the form of an *instruction that is inserted in the *instruction stream but is not intended to be executed.

dump 1. In a system handling large numbers of users' files stored on magnetic disks, one of the periodic records of the state of the disks that are made on magnetic tape in order to protect against accidental overwriting or mechanical failure of the disks.

2. A printed version of the contents of system memory taken when a system crash has occurred. In principle it is possible to determine the immediate cause of a system crash by studying the dump and determining the reason for any inconsistencies in its contents. In practice this may be difficult even with the assistance of dump analysis software.

3. To take a dump (defs. 1 or 2).

dump check A copy of the contents of all the workspace associated with a job or *process. If the job or process subsequently fails, it can be restarted at the point at which the dump check was taken. Note that the status of peripheral devices allocated to the job or process must be considered as constituting part of its workspace.

dump point *See* checkpoint.

duplex (full duplex) Involving or denoting a connection between two endpoints, either physical or logical, over which data may travel in both directions simultaneously. *See also* half duplex, simplex, return channel.

duty cycle For pulsed or square-wave signals, the ratio of pulse duration to pulse spacing, often expressed as a percentage. A square wave signal normally has a 50% duty cycle, i.e. pulse duration is equal to the time between pulses.

DVI A variant of the *CD-ROM read-only optical disk format intended for the recording of images, including animated sequences.

DX-2 An X.25-based *public packet network of Japan. It first became operational in 1979.

dyadic Having two operands.

dyadic operation (binary operation) defined on a set S. A function from the domain $S \times S$ into S itself. Many of the everyday arithmetic and algebraic operations are dyadic, e.g. the addition of two integers, the union of two sets, and the conjunction of two Boolean expressions. Although basically functions, dyadic operations are usually represented using an infix notation, as in

$$3 + 4, \ U \cup V, \ P \wedge Q$$

A symbol, such as $\circ$, can be used to represent a generalized dyadic operation.

When the set is finite, *Cayley tables and sometimes *truth tables are used to define the meaning of the operation.

Dyck language A concept used in *formal language theory. Let Σ be the alphabet

$$\{a_1, \ldots, a_n, b_1, \ldots, b_n\}$$

The Dyck language over Σ is the set of all strings that can be reduced to the empty string Λ by "cancellations" of the form

$$a_i b_i \rightarrow \Lambda$$

For example,

$$\Sigma = \{(,)\}$$

gives the Dyck language of all balanced parenthesis strings. An important theorem characterizes the *context-free languages as those representable as the homomorphic image (*see* homomorphism) of the intersection of a Dyck language and a *regular language.

dye-polymer A class of optical recording media in which the sensitive layer consists of dye particles dispersed in a binder. Both *rewritable and *write-once recording are possible, although rewritable media are not yet commercially available. Dye-polymer media are generally cheaper than those using other materials.

dynamic Capable of changing or of being changed. With reference to operating systems, the implication is that the system is capable of changing while it continues to run. As an example, the total amount of memory available may be defined by the contents of a word within the operating system. If this word can be altered without stopping the system and reloading a fresh copy of the operating system, then it is possible to alter dynamically the total amount of memory on the system.

With reference to programming, the adjective is applied to operations that take place while a program is running, as compared with those that take place during the compilation phase. For example, dynamic arrays are allocated space while the program is running.

Compare static.

dynamic allocation An allocation that is made dynamically, i.e. while the system is running, rather than statically at the time of first initiating the system.

dynamically redefinable character set (DRCS) A feature of printer controllers that allows the character set in use to be changed via commands in the data stream. The character sets invoked may be resident in the printer or may be downloaded via the interface.

dynamic data structure A data structure whose organizational characteristics may change during its lifetime. The adaptability afforded by such structures, e.g. linked lists, is often at the expense of decreased efficiency in accessing elements of the structure. Two main features distinguish dynamic structures from *static data structures. Firstly, it is no longer possible to have all structural information in a *header; each data element will have to contain information relating it logically to other elements of the structure. Secondly, using a single block of contiguous storage is often not appropriate, and hence it is necessary to provide some storage management scheme at run-time.

dynamic logic *See* modal logic.

dynamic memory A form of *volatile semiconductor memory in which stored information is degraded with time. The most common example is dynamic *RAM (usually abbreviated to DRAM) where the logic state to be entered in each cell is stored as a voltage on the small capacitance associated with the gate of the MOS output transistor for the cell. The voltage decays away with time because of leakage currents in the cell, and so it must be *refreshed (i.e. recharged) periodically by external circuitry.

dynamic programming The mathematical theory and planning of multistage decision processes; the term was introduced by Richard Bellman in 1957. It may be regarded as a branch of *mathematical programming or *optimization problems formulated as a sequence of decisions. Applications are very varied, including engineering problems and company planning.

dynamic testing *See* testing. *Compare* static analysis.

E

EARN *Acronym for* European Academic and Research Network. Originally established in the mid-1980s, EARN was initially a European copy of the IBM-sponsored *BITNET system and used the same software running only on IBM 370 architecture systems. As with BITNET, the software was subsequently ported onto other hardware, especially onto DEC VAX systems, and the functionality was expanded from the original message switching system that used large-scale systems as the message switches to one using separate front-end systems.

EAROM *Acronym for* electrically alterable read-only memory. A form of semiconductor memory in which it is possible to change the contents of selected memory locations by applying suitable electrical signals. Normally these changes are infrequent.

Easyload *Trademark. See* magnetic tape cartridge.

EBCDIC (extended binary coded decimal interchange code) An 8-bit *character encoding scheme used primarily on IBM machines. *See* character set.

EBNF *Abbrev. for* extended BNF.

echo 1. The reflection of transmitted data back to its source. For example, characters typed on the keyboard of a data terminal (connected to a computer) will not appear on the display of the terminal unless they are echoed. The echoing may be done locally by the terminal itself, by a modem, or by an intervening communication processor. Echoing may also be done by the computer to which the terminal is attached. If the terminal itself echoes the characters, it is often said to be in *half-duplex mode*, although the term *local-echo mode* would be more accurate. In full-duplex character-at-a-time transmission, echoing is generally done at the computer, thus permitting certain application programs, such as editors, to determine whether or not incoming characters should be echoed. Half-duplex and/or line-at-a-time transmission generally implies local echoing.
2. A phenomenon in voice circuits (e.g. telephone circuits) that upsets the operation of *modems. Most modems therefore incorporate *echo suppression*.

echo check A way of establishing the accuracy achieved during the transfer of data over a data link, computer network, etc. When the data is received it is stored and also transmitted back to its point of origin in the transmission loop where it can be compared with the original data.

The term is also applied to other circumstances in which a transmitted signal directly causes a return signal. For example, in some line printers the sharp rise in the current waveform of an electromagnet drive pulse, which occurs when the armature impacts, is sometimes used to verify that the intended event has occurred.

echo suppression *See* echo.

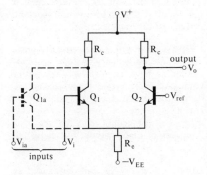

Two-input ECL OR gate

ECL *Abbrev. for* emitter-coupled logic. A high-speed *logic family available in the form of integrated circuits based on *bipolar transistors. The fast switching speeds are achieved by means of a design that avoids driving the transistors into saturation.

The basic circuit element is based on a difference amplifier, as shown in the diagram (ignoring dashed lines). In this symmetrical circuit the combined emitter current flowing through the resistor R_e is substantially constant. If the voltage V_i is equal to V_{ref} then each transistor, Q_1 and Q_2, conducts by the same

amount and the output is at V_{ref}. If V_i is increased above V_{ref} by more than about 0.1 volts, Q_1 will be turned on while Q_2 turns off. As a result V_o increases to V^+. Similarly if V_i is decreased below V_{ref} by more than about 0.1 volts, V_o will decrease to some value largely determined by V_{EE}, R_e, and R_c.

By placing transistors in parallel with Q_1, as shown by the dashed lines, an ECL *OR gate is produced. Additional buffering is required on the gate output to provide the correct voltage swings for subsequent gate inputs.

ECL provides the highest speed of any silicon-based logic family but its power dissipation is high and the output voltage swing is small.

ECMA European Computer Manufacturers' Association, founded in 1961 and based in Geneva. Its aims are "to promote, in the general interest and in collaboration with national and international organizations, all ways and means destined to facilitate and standardize the utilization of data processing systems."

edge A connection between two vertices of a *graph.

edge board A *circuit board that is a modular part of a larger circuit. The term *edge card* is often used synonymously but is sometimes considered smaller than an edge board. Connections between this module and other modules are made through a printed-circuit pattern on the edge of the board that mates with an *edge connector. The edge connector is normally located on a *backplane or *motherboard, which contains wiring that ties all modules together.

edge card *See* edge board.

edge connector Part of a *printed circuit board where a number of the metallic conducting tracks meet the edge of the board, at right angles, to form the male

149

half of a plug and socket. The tracks are broadened, thickened, and usually gold-plated to provide good electrical contact. A single edge connector may have a hundred or more individual connections, half on each side of the board. The female half of the connector is a multiway socket whose sprung metal contacts can mate with the corresponding pads on the PCB. Connections to various points on the circuit board may then be made indirectly via the socket. *See also* backplane.

EDI *Abbrev. for* electronic data interchange.

Edison A programming language for designing reliable real-time programs for multiprocessor systems. Edison is *block-structured and includes modules, concurrent statements, and when statements.

editor *See* link editor, text editor.

Edmonds' algorithm A method of finding the maximum branching of a *weighted directed *graph, due to J. Edmonds (1965).

EDP *Abbrev. for* electronic data processing. *See* data processing.

EDS *Abbrev. for* exchangeable disk store.

EDSAC *Acronym for* Electronic Delay Storage Automatic Calculator. A machine designed in 1946 by M. V. Wilkes of Cambridge University, inspired by the stored-program concept being taught in the US by von Neumann and others. The design was notable for using acoustic *delay lines for memory. EDSAC began operations in May 1949, becoming the first complete operational stored-program computer. *See also* Manchester Mark I.

EDVAC *Acronym for* Electronic Discrete Variable Automatic Computer. An early stored-program electronic digital computer, originally commissioned from the University of Pennsylvania's Moore School by the US Army in 1944 while the *ENIAC was still under construction, but not operational until 1952. In 1945 John von Neumann prepared a proposal for the EDVAC that described the logical design of a computer with a "stored program", where the instructions to the machine would be stored in substantially the same fashion as the data. Although there is some disagreement as to whether von Neumann or the team of Mauchly and Eckert originated the stored-program concept, this was its first written documentation. Regardless of its origin, the stored-program model that formed the basis of the EDVAC design motivated all subsequent machine designs.

EEROM *Acronym for* electrically erasable read-only memory. A form of semiconductor memory in which the entire contents can be erased by subjecting the device to suitable electrical signals. After erasing, the device can be reprogrammed. This procedure may be repeated hundreds of times without damaging the device.

effective address An *absolute address that is either a direct address or has been computed by one of the *addressing schemes such as augmenting, relative addressing, or indexing.

effective computability Let
$$N = \{0, 1, \dots\}$$
$$N^k = N \times \dots \times N$$
(with k factors)
A function
$$f : N^k \to N$$
is effectively computable only in the case when there is an *effective procedure* (i.e. an algorithm) that correctly calculates f. An effective procedure is one that meets the following specifications. Firstly, the procedure must consist of a finite set of "simple" instructions (i.e. a

program) and there must be no ambiguity concerning the order in which the instructions are to be carried out (*see* Turing machine). Secondly, if the procedure is given a *k*-tuple *x* in the domain of *f*, then after a finite number of steps, the calculation must terminate and output *f*(*x*); if the procedure is given a *k*-tuple not in the domain of *f* it must not output a value.

effective enumeration *See* enumeration.

effective procedure *See* effective computability.

EFTS *Abbrev. for* electronic funds transfer system.

EGA *Abbrev. for* enhanced graphics adapter. A color *graphics adapter that provides six graphics modes: a 320 × 200 16-color mode, a 640 × 200 16-color mode, and 640 × 350 16-color and 2-color modes, in addition to the two *CGA modes. The EGA was developed by IBM but is now available on a wide range of other computers. It uses a system of multiplane-per-pixel display memory, using one bit plane to give intensity level and one for each primary color (red, green, and blue). Multiple graphics pages are available so that a range of animation techniques are possible.

egoless programming An approach to software development based on consensus within a small team. The aim is to produce software that is the product of the team rather than of one or a few individuals. The motivation is to avoid personal identification with output, promote group identification, and thus to make it easier for the team to conduct an objective evaluation of the programs produced.

EIA Electronics Industries Association, a US legislation-oriented information, education, and lobbying group made up of manufacturers of electronic equipment.

eigenfunctions *See* eigenvalue problems.

eigenvalue problems Problems that arise frequently in engineering and science and fall into two main classes. The standard (matrix) eigenvalue problem is to determine real or complex numbers,
$$\lambda_1, \lambda_2, \ldots \lambda_n \ (eigenvalues)$$
and corresponding nonzero vectors,
$$x_1, x_2, \ldots, x_n \ (eigenvectors)$$
that satisfy the equation
$$Ax = \lambda x$$
where A is a given real or complex $n \times n$ matrix.

By analogy the continuous eigenvalue problem is to determine similar eigenvalues and corresponding nonzero functions (*eigenfunctions*) that satisfy the equation
$$Hf(x) = \lambda f(x)$$
where H is a given operator on functions f. A simple example arising from a vibrating-string problem is
$$y''(x) = \lambda y(x),$$
$$y(0) = 0, \ y(1) = 0$$
where values of the parameter λ (eigenvalues) are required that yield nontrivial eigenfunctions $y(x)$ (i.e. $y(x) \equiv 0$). *Finite-difference methods applied to such problems generally lead to matrix eigenvalue problems.

eigenvectors *See* eigenvalue problems.

EISA *Abbrev. for* extended industry standard architecture. A *bus structure for microcomputers with Intel 32-bit microprocessors, based on and compatible with that used by IBM in their AT series. EISA was developed by manufacturers other than IBM as an alternative to IBM's *MCA (micro channel architecture), which is not compatible with earlier systems.

elapsed time The actual time between two events, measured by a "clock on the wall". *Compare* CPU time.

electrographic printer A term that embraces *electrostatic, *electrosensitive, and *electrophotographic printers.

electroluminescent display *See* display.

electronic data interchange (EDI) A generic term covering various standards that describe the format, content, and structure of data to be exchanged between computer systems. It is usually used to describe standards at the application level of the OSI *seven layer reference model.

electronic data processing (EDP) *See* data processing.

electronic filing A computer-based system for the storage, cataloguing, and retrieval of documents. It is central to the success of a comprehensive *office automation system in that it provides the basic object management required to create, manipulate, and delete "office objects", which may be letters, complex reports, charts, graphs, or any other information that may be stored in a computer system.

A comprehensive electronic filing system should give a high degree of security for the objects entrusted to it, both against computer failure and against unauthorized access, together with flexible methods of organizing these objects. It should also provide shared access to community items while preserving privacy for confidential items.

Objects in an electronic filing system will generally be stored on magnetic disk or tape; some systems use microfilm techniques for bulk storage of items. Current systems generally allow the cataloguing of "paper objects" that cannot be copied onto the computer system. This allows an easier transition to the computer-based system from an environment that previously relied on paper filing techniques.

electronic funds transfer system (EFTS) Generally, the use of computers in effecting payments between individuals and/or organizations. In some cases it is used to refer to advanced future systems in which debits and credits are made simultaneously with the transactions that give rise to them. In other cases its use covers all computer-based funds transfer systems, including long-established methods for check-clearance by banks.

Full-scale EFTSs cause particular anxiety to those who are concerned about the freedom and privacy of the individual in the information society, since they would enable very accurate profiles to be obtained of people's activities. *See also* SWIFT.

electronic mail (computer mail) Messages sent between users of computer systems, the computer systems being used to hold and transport messages. Sender and receiver(s) need not be on-line at the same time, or even on the same computer, to communicate. Electronic mail is an important component of an office automation system.

The originator of a message creates a specially formatted message file by running a mail-sending program. The message may often be entered and modified using the general-purpose editor of the user's choice. Part of message entry is the acquisition of a list of recipients. When the message is complete, it is posted to a message transport system, which takes responsibility for delivering the message to recipients. This may involve passing the message through a *store-and-forward relay system when the sender and receiver are not connected to the same computer. At some later time the message is delivered into the recipient's incoming "mailbox". The recipient runs a program that retrieves incoming messages, allowing items to be filed, listed, forwarded, replied to, etc. Frequently a single user-interface program is used to send and receive messages both locally and worldwide.

Originally electronic mail was performed by using standard text hardcopy or CRT terminals. Newer systems support the composition and delivery of *multimedia mail*, which can combine text, graphics, voice, facsimile, and other forms of information in a single message. Other functions often performed by an electronic mail system include verification of a user's identity, expansion of named mailing lists into lists of recipients, and the location of a user on the basis of partial information (directory services).

See also X 400 (at X).

electronic office A computer-based system designed for office tasks. It may involve the use of *electronic filing systems, *word processing systems, *databases, *computer graphics systems, *electronic mail, and *teleconferencing systems.

electrophotographic printer A printer in which the required image is written by a beam of light onto a photoconductive drum or band that has a uniform electric charge over its surface. The action of the light beam causes local conductivity and allows the surface to assume the potential of the substrate. The charge pattern on the photoconductor is then developed by applying particles of pigment that carry an appropriate electrostatic charge: the toner particles are attracted to the image but are repelled by the background. The image is then transferred to paper by pressing the paper against the drum or band and applying an electric field. The toner is fixed to the paper by heat and/or pressure or by passing through a solvent vapor bath.

The principle is the same as that used in many office copiers and some recent designs of this type of printer can also function as a copier. In a copier the light image on the photoconductor drum is a projection of the original document via a lens system. In a printer the image is formed by a modulated light beam from a laser, the face of a display tube, an array of light-emitting diodes, or an array of photoelectric shutters.

This type of printer can yield very good print quality, forming its image as a fine matrix of dots. It can thus readily produce graphics and a wide variety of typestyles. There are electrophotographic printers available that can print on both sides of the paper and can print in full color.

electrosensitive printer A type of printer that produces the required image by passing an electric current into the surface of specially prepared paper. The most common form uses paper with one surface coated first with a layer of carbon black and then with a fine coat of aluminum to give it a white appearance. The writing is done by a row of styluses that can be separately energized to pass sufficient electric current into the surface to vaporize the aluminum locally and expose the black undersurface. The styluses may be arranged as a small number (typically 7) that traverse along the line to be printed and print the characters serially, or as many as 400 may be arranged to span a distance of 4″. Such a printer can produce a copy of a display screen showing 25 lines of 80 characters in a few seconds and is compact enough to be built into the case of a VDU. Higher-resolution designs (600 dpi) have been developed for phototypesetting applications.

electrostatic printer A type of printer in which the required image is first written as a pattern of electrostatic charge, and is then made visible by bringing the pattern into contact with particles of pigment that carry a charge of opposite polarity. The pigment is only attracted to the charge pattern and is subsequently fused or bonded to the paper.

In some designs the charge pattern is applied by styluses directly to paper that has been specially treated. An alternative approach is to apply the pattern to a metal drum with a suitable coating such as aluminum oxide. The pattern is made visible by washing the paper or drum with a colloidal suspension of charged particles of pigment. The image on a drum is transferred to plain paper by pressure and the application of an electric field. The particles of pigment are very fine and thus penetrate the fibers of the paper and form a permanent image. A recent development in this technology is to apply the charge to the drum by the controlled projection of ions.

In some literature the term is used to refer to all printers in which an electrostatic image is formed as one of the steps in the process, including *electrophotographic printers.

electrostatic storage device An obsolete storage device in which the data was stored as a charge pattern within a *cathode-ray tube and could be read by a scanning beam of electrons. The data was not usually visible. One of the early designs was the *Williams-tube store*, named for F. C. Williams of the University of Manchester, UK, who led the development work; it was one of the earliest forms of random-access memory. Electrostatic storage was used on a number of first-generation computers (Ferranti Mark I, Whirlwind, IBM 701, IAS). It gave a significant reduction in storage cost compared to the mercury *delay line memory, but the information had to be frequently regenerated (rewritten) and was lost when power was removed. It was displaced in processor designs in the mid-1950s by *core stores. More advanced electrostatic devices have been developed but these did not reach the market.

electrothermal printer A type of *thermal printer in which a thermoplastic ink is transferred from a ribbon to the base medium (usually paper or transparent film) by localized heating. The heating occurs as current is passed from discrete electrical contacts on the print head through a resistive layer in the ribbon to a common return layer. Compared with

*thermal transfer printers, the print quality is less dependent on the surface finish of the receiving medium but the complexity of the ribbon makes the cost of usage higher.

element 1. of a set. *Another name for* member.
2. *See* logic element.

ELSE rule The last (usually rightmost) rule of an incomplete *decision table, i.e. a table that does not include all possible combinations of conditions. The ELSE rule defines the step set for all actions not satisfying the explicit rules of the decision table. A table with an ELSE rule is complete since all possible combinations are taken into consideration.

EMACS A text and program editor, originally developed for the DEC PDP-10 computer, but now available on a wide range of machines. A derivative, Micro EMACS, runs on IBM PCs and compatible machines. EMACS is particularly popular with programmers since its programmable interface allows it to be customized to suit individual preferences.

email (or e-mail) *Short for* electronic mail.

EMAS *Acronym for* Edinburgh multiaccess system. An operating system that was originally developed at the University of Edinburgh and is intended to support large numbers of interactive terminals. It is one of the earliest systems to be implemented almost entirely in a high-level language. A special implementation language, IMP, was devised for this purpose.

embedded computer Any computer used as a component in a device whose prime function is not that of a computer. One example is a weapons-guidance system. Another is a computer-controlled blood analyzer that uses a minicomputer or microcomputer to control various tests that are run on blood in order to produce an integrated printout of all test results. *See also* Ada.

embedded servo *See* actuator.

emitter-coupled logic *See* ECL.

empty list (null list) *See* list.

empty medium A *data medium that does not contain variable data but may have a frame of reference or preformatting. *Compare* virgin medium.

empty set (null set; void set) A *set with no elements. It is usually denoted by φ.

empty string (null string) A string whose *length is zero. It is commonly denoted by ε or Λ. The possibility of strings being empty is a notorious source of bugs in programs.

emulation The exact execution on a given computer of a program written for a different computer, accepting the identical data and producing the identical results. Emulation is thus the imitation of all or part of one computer system by another system. It is formally defined as being achieved primarily by hardware; it is usually accomplished at the microprogram level. A particular emulation could be used as a replacement for all or part of the system being emulated, and furthermore could be an improved version. For example, a new computer may emulate an obsolete one so that programs written for the old one will run without modification. *See also* simulation, compatibility.

emulator Any system, especially a program or microprogram, that permits the process of *emulation to be carried out.

enable To selectively activate a device or function. When a number of devices are connected in parallel, selective operation can be achieved by an enabling action – such as a signal on a discrete line or a pattern of signals on the common line or lines – that will set only the desired device into a state in which it can receive further signals. *Compare* inhibit.

enable pulse A pulse that must be present to allow other signals to be effective in certain electronic logic circuits. Although the term is now used to describe an electronic logic function it was originally used in an analogous way in connection with *core stores, where the coincidence of two pulses is required to change the state of a core: one of the pulses is the write pulse and can be common to a number of cores; an enable pulse is simultaneously applied to a particular core and thus enables the write pulse to change the state of that core.

encapsulation *See* internetworking.

encoder 1. The means by which an encoding process is effected (*see* code). It may be implemented in hardware or software, the process being algorithmic in nature.

2. A logic circuit, usually an integrated circuit, that generates a unique *n*-bit binary word, indicating which of its 2^n input lines is active, i.e. at logic 1. A *keyboard encoder*, for example, may be required to generate a unique binary code indicating which key on the keyboard has been pressed.

If two or more of the device inputs can be active simultaneously then a *priority encoder* is required, which usually encodes only the highest-order data input.

encoding 1. The transformation of a message into an encoded form. *See* code.

2. The representation of symbols in some alphabet by symbols or strings of symbols in some other alphabet. A common example is *binary encoding.

encoding format *See* disk format.

encryption The processing of a message by a sender in order to render it unintelligible to other than authorized recipients. *See also* cryptography.

end-around-carry A type of carry that is required when a *radix-minus-one complement representation of integers is used and two integers so represented are summed. If a carry is generated at the most significant end of the two numbers, then this carry must be added to the digit at the least significant end of the result to give the radix-minus-one complement representation of the sum.

end-around shift *Another name for* circular shift.

endomorphism A *homomorphism from an *algebra to itself.

endorder traversal *Another name for* postorder traversal.

end-to-end encryption The transfer of an encrypted message across a system without intermediate stages of decryption and reencryption. *Compare* link encryption.

energizer A hardware or software mechanism that is used as an aid in testing the behavior of a subsystem. The intention is that the energizer should drive the subsystem in a way that simulates its actual application, and should at the same time analyze the responses from the subsystem in order to detect any erroneous behavior.

ENIAC *Acronym for* Electronic Numerical Integrator and Calculator. The first general-purpose electronic calculator, designed and built by John W. Mauchly and J. Presper Eckert Jr. at the University of Pennsylvania's Moore School during the period 1943–46. Originally designed for the production of ballistic tables for the second world war, the machine was not completed until after the war ended. It was widely used for scientific computation until the early 1950s.

enterprise modeling The modeling of some aspects of a business organization. It offers a better understanding of existing and proposed *information systems, and of their effects within the host company, both to systems analysts and designers and (more generally) to corporate management. Enterprise modeling may address static issues of organizational structure and dynamic issues of corporate processes and flows of information. It should constitute a major early phase in any comprehensive systems methodology. *Compare* domain modeling.

entity In programming, any item, such as a data item or statement, that can be named or denoted in a program.

entity-relationship-attribute diagram, model *See* ERA diagram, ERA model.

entropy A measure of the amount of information that is output by a source, or throughput by a channel, or received by an observer (per symbol or per second). Following Shannon (1948) and later writers, the entropy of a *discrete memoryless source with alphabet $A = \{a_i\}$ of size n, and output X at time t is

$$H(X) = \sum_{i=0}^{n-1} p(x_i) \log_b (1/p(x_i))$$

where

$$p(x_i) = \text{Prob } \{X_t = a_i\}$$

The logarithmic base b is chosen to give a convenient scale factor. Usually,

$b = 2$

$b = e = 2.71828\ldots$

or

$b = 10$

Entropy is then measured in *bits*, in *natural units* or *nats*, or in *Hartleys*, respectively. When the source has memory, account has to be taken of the dependence between successive symbols output by the source.

The term arises by analogy with entropy in thermodynamics, where the defining expression has the same form but with a physical scale factor k (Boltzmann constant) and with the sign changed. The word *negentropy* is therefore sometimes used for the measure of information, as is *uncertainty* or simply "information".

entry 1. An item of data in a list or table.
   2. *Another name for* entry point.

entry point (entry) The instruction to which control is transferred when a subroutine is called.

entry time The time at which a *process is started or restarted by the process scheduler.

enumeration A list of items in order. Thus the items are organized in such a way that they can be counted, and for each nonnegative integer i within an appropriate range there is a unique item associated with it. An enumeration may be finite or infinite; when an infinite set is involved, the infinite set must be *countable. An enumeration is said to be *effective* if there is an *algorithm for producing the enumeration.
   Enumeration is used to define *data types in languages of the Pascal and Jovial families. It also plays a significant role in *combinatorics where one might typically talk of an enumeration of *permutations or *combinations, of *binary trees, of *graphs, of *groups, etc.

enumeration type A *data type comprising values that are explicitly defined by the programmer.

environment *See* IPSE, PSE, software engineering environment.

environment mapping A collection of techniques used to create realistic computer-generated images of objects. For example, consider the generation of an image of an object that has surface characteristics (shiny, polished, curved, etc.) and an orientation (static and dynamic) relative to other objects and sources of light such that it would show reflections of nearby objects. A faithful representation, from the viewpoint of the observer, would require the full-color shaded image with any mirror reflections to be generated by the computer. This requires a knowledge of the spatial disposition and dynamics of objects and the ray tracing of images and reflections of images, hence the term environment mapping.

EOB *Abbrev. for* end of block.

EOD *Abbrev. for* end of data. A code that is written into a serially accessed memory, such as a magnetic tape file, immediately after the last data record. It thus indicates the starting point for new records and is erased when they are added and then rewritten in a new position.

EOF *Abbrev. for* end of file.

EOJ *Abbrev. for* end of job.

EOR *Abbrev. for* end of record.

EOT 1. *Abbrev. for* end of transmission. A character sequence on a data link indicating that the current transmitter has nothing further to send. Active stations on the data link return to their idle state and wait for a new series of messages.
   2. *Abbrev. for* end of tape.

EOT marker *Short for* end of tape marker. A feature of a *magnetic tape by which the tape transport senses on the tape the end of the volume into which data can be or has been recorded. It is complementary to the *BOT marker, and is similarly defined by the standard pertaining to the type of tape.

epimorphism A *homomorphism that, when viewed as a *function, is a *surjection.

EPLD *Abbrev. for* erasable programmable logic device. A *PLD in which the programming is erasable (*see* programmable device).

epoch The time interval between successive elements of a discrete-time signal, or between the discrete-time samples of a continuous-time signal (*see* discrete and continuous systems). Usually, for a given signal, the epochs are of a fixed size.

EPOS **1.** *Acronym for* electronic point of sale, usually used with other words, as in EPOS terminal, EPOS system. *See* point-of-sale system.
   2. A first-generation *IPSE developed in the Federal Republic of Germany and used widely for real-time systems development. EPOS provides an integrated set of tools for requirements expression, data structure and design, code generation, documentation, and project planning and control.

EPPT *Abbrev. for* European printer performance test. A standardized test for establishing the throughput of office printers. The familiar ratings of characters per second, lines per minute, etc., cannot be relied upon to give a true indication of the throughput achievable in a real application. A set of benchmark tests were agreed by a group of European printer manufacturers and a similar proposal was drawn up by a group of representatives of Japanese manufacturers. A draft ECMA standard (Dec. 1988) combined the two preceding proposals, defining standard letter, spreadsheet, and graphic printouts and the way in which the task is timed.

EPROM *Acronym for* erasable programmable read-only memory. A type of *PROM that is capable of being programmed a number of times by the user. The contents of EPROMs are generally erased (i.e. reset to their nonprogrammed state, usually logic 1) by exposure to hard ultraviolet radiation. The EPROM may then be reprogrammed, i.e. selected elements set to logic 0, using a *PROM programmer.

equipotent *See* cardinality.

P	F	F	T	T
Q	F	T	F	T
$P \equiv Q$	T	F	F	T

Truth table for equivalence

equivalence **1.** The logical connective combining two statements or formulas P and Q in such a way that the outcome is true if both P and Q are true or if both are false, as shown in the table. P and Q are said to be *equivalent*. The connective can be read as "if and only if" or "iff", and is usually denoted by one of the symbols
$$\equiv \quad \leftrightarrow \quad <-> \quad <=>$$
See also exclusive-NOR gate, propositional calculus.
   2. A relationship between objects that are operationally or structurally indistinguishable, e.g. in *combinational circuits, *graphs, or *grammars. Equivalence is less strong than identity or equality but much more useful in practice. *See also* machine equivalence.

equivalence class A *subset of a set S (on which an *equivalence relation is defined) that consists of all the elements of S that are equivalent to each other, and to no other elements of S. An equivalence relation provides a partitioning (*see* covering) of a set into a number of mutually *disjoint equivalence classes.
   The relationship "has the same surname as" defined on the set of people produces an equivalence class consisting

of all those with Jones as surname, another consisting of those with Smith as surname, and so on.

equivalence gate *See* exclusive-NOR gate.

equivalence relation A *relation that is *transitive, *symmetric, and *reflexive. The concept is a convenient generalization or abstraction of equality. It covers most notions of equals, equivalence, and similarity as defined between triangles, algorithms, Boolean expressions, algebraic structures, statements, etc. *See also* equivalence class, partial ordering.

equivalent binary digits For a given source alphabet, S, the number of equivalent binary digits is the minimum number of bits that need to be taken in a *block code to give at least as many codewords as there are symbols in S.

equivalent trees *Similar trees with the same data at corresponding nodes.

ERA diagram *Short for* entity-relationship-attribute diagram. A diagrammatic notation for describing and documenting data items and the relationships between data items, using an *ERA model. Entities are shown as boxes in the ERA diagram and have an entity name; usually names are required to be unique. Attributes are generally shown as annotations of the entity boxes. Relationships are shown as lines between entity boxes. Markings on the line indicate the nature of the relationship (one to one, one to many, or many to many). Many *software tools for editing diagrams can handle ERA diagrams.

ERA model *Short for* entity-relationship-attribute model. A model of a set of data relationships in terms of the *entities, relationships, and *attributes involved.

Entities have attributes and have relations with other entities. They have an entity name; usually names are required to be unique. Entities are often implemented as a record comprising a number of fields.

Attributes are usually represented in a *data dictionary and describe the characteristic features of the entity. Each attribute is named; usually names of attributes are required to be unique. Attributes are often implemented as fields with values.

Each relationship is named; usually relationship names are required to be unique. There can be more than one relationship between a pair of entities.

See also ERA diagram.

erasable optical media *See* rewritable.

erasable programmable logic device *See* EPLD.

erasable PROM *See* EPROM. *See also* programmable device.

erase head *See* head.

eraser An item of electronic equipment that can carry out the erasure process for an *EPROM. It often consists of an enclosed source of ultraviolet radiation, close to which the EPROM may be placed, and a timer.

erasure channel A communication *channel in which the effect of *noise is to cause the *decoder sometimes to be presented with an "error" symbol to decode. The decoder may then act in the knowledge that in such symbol positions the symbol actually transmitted is unknown: it is thus in a better position than when presented with an incorrect symbol but not the knowledge that it is incorrect (other than can be deduced by using an *error-detecting or *error-correcting code).

ergodic source *See* discrete source.

error 1. The difference between a computed, observed, or measured value or condition and the true, specified, or theoretically correct value or condition.

2. An incorrect result resulting from some *failure in the hardware of a system.

3. An incorrect step, process, or data definition in for example a program. *See also* semantic error, syntax error.

error analysis A term that when applied to *numerical analysis refers to the mathematical analysis that describes the various aspects of error behavior in numerical methods (or algorithms). *Convergence* of an algorithm is a fundamental requirement. Most algorithms result in the construction of a sequence of approximations. If this sequence tends more and more closely to the true solution of the problem, the algorithm is convergent. How fast the algorithm converges is important for its efficiency; some insight is provided by the *order of the method. Since most algorithms are terminated before convergence is reached, the size of the error after a finite number of steps must be estimated. How big the error is at most can be determined from an *error bound*. This must be reasonably "sharp", i.e. it must not grossly overestimate the error. How big the error is approximately is referred to as an *error estimate* and is usually determined from an asymptotic formula. Such estimates are widely used in step-by-step methods for *ordinary differential equations; here the stepsize, h, must be small enough for the estimate to be accurate.

In *numerical linear algebra *backward error analysis* has proved very successful in analyzing errors. In this approach it is shown that the numerical solution satisfies exactly a perturbed form of the original problem. Bounds for the perturbations are determined and these can be inserted into standard results, thus producing a bound for the error in the numerical solution. The approach can be applied to other areas.

error bound *See* error analysis.

error burst *Another name for* burst error.

error control (error management; error handling) The employment, in a computer system or in a communication system, of *error-detecting and/or *error-correcting codes with the intention of removing the effects of error and/or recording the prevalence of error in the system. The effects of errors may be removed by correcting them in all but a negligible proportion of cases. Error control aims to cope with errors owing to *noise or to equipment malfunction – in which case it overlaps with fault tolerance (*see* fault-tolerant system) – but not ·usually with the effects of errors in the design of hardware or software.

Error control is expensive: the balance between the cost and the benefit (measured by the degree of protection) has to be weighed within the technological and financial context of the system being designed. *See also* error recovery.

error-correcting code A *code that is designed for *channel coding, i.e. for encoding information so that a decoder can correct, with a high probability of success, any errors caused in the signal by an intervening noisy channel.

Error-correcting codes may be *block codes or *convolutional codes, and in either case are employed in a *forward error-correction system. The most common error-correcting block codes are the *Hamming codes, *Bose-Chaudhuri-Hocquenghem (BCH) codes, *Reed-Solomon (RS) codes, *simplex codes, and the *Golay (23, 12) code.

Since errors may be corrected by detecting them and requesting retransmission, the process of error correction is sometimes taken to include *backward error-correction systems and, hence, *error-detecting codes.

See also Shannon's model, coding theory, coding bounds.

error correction *See* error recovery, error-correcting code.

error-detecting code A *code that is designed for *channel coding, i.e. for encoding information so that a decoder can detect, with a high probability of success, whether an intervening channel has caused an error in the signal.

Error-detecting codes are usually *block codes, and are generally employed in a *backward error-correction system. The most common error-detecting codes are the *cyclic redundancy checks, of which the simple parity check is a technologically important case.

See also error-correcting code, Shannon's model, coding theory, coding bounds, Hamming distance.

error detection The detection of errors in data handled by a peripheral device or communication link; it is often associated with *error recovery and error correction. Data to be stored or transmitted can be coded in a way that allows most errors to be detected. The simplest *error-detecting code is the addition of a parity bit to each byte of data, but more powerful codes are often used which operate on larger units such as a sector or block. Some devices also check for marginal conditions, such as low signal amplitude, which are associated with data errors. In storage peripherals, errors may be detected at the time data is written (*see* DRDW and DRAW), as a separate operation after writing (*verification), or during a read operation at some later time. Error detection does not normally involve a bit-by-bit comparison with the original data even if this is still held in a buffer or in host memory. *See also* error control.

error diagnostics Information that is presented following the detection of some error condition and is mainly intended to assist in identifying the cause of the error.

As an example, consider the compilation and subsequent execution of some program. *Syntactic errors* in the program, i.e. failure of the program to conform to the defined *syntax of the programming language, would normally be detected at compilation time, and the compiler would then generally produce error diagnostics to indicate both the location and the kind of error (unrecognized statement, undeclared identifier, etc.). At execution time certain kinds of *semantic errors* may be detected, i.e. improper behavior of a program that conforms to the defined syntax of the language. In this case the error diagnostics may be produced by some run-time system. *See also* error routine.

error estimate *See* error analysis.

error handling *Another term for* error control.

error management *Another name for* error control.

error message *See* error routine.

error propagation A term that refers to the way in which, at a given stage of a calculation, part of the error arises out of the error at a previous stage. This is independent of the further *roundoff errors inevitably introduced between the two stages. Unfavorable error propagation can seriously affect the results of a calculation.

The investigation of error propagation in simple arithmetical operations is used as the basis for the detailed analysis of more extensive calculations. The way in which uncertainties in the data propagate into the final results of a calculation can be assessed in practice by repeating the calculation with slightly perturbed data.

error rate 1. of a communication channel. The frequency with which errors or noise are introduced into the channel. Error rate may be measured in terms of erroneous bits received per bits transmitted. For example, one or two errors per 100 000 bits might be a typical rate for a narrowband point-to-point line. The distribution of errors is usually nonuniform: errors tend to come in bursts (*see* burst error). Thus the error rate of a channel may be specified in terms of percentage of error-free seconds. Frequently an error rate is expressed as a negative power of ten: an error rate of one bit per 100 000 would be expressed as an error rate of 10^{-5}.

Another method of presenting error rate is to consider the errors as the result of adding the data signal to an underlying error signal. The extent of error can then be expressed as the *entropy of the error signal, or, in the case of physical signals, as the ratio of the strengths of the two signals – the *signal-to-noise ratio – expressed in decibels.

2. of a data storage subsystem. A measurement of the proportion of errors occurring in data transfers to or from the storage medium. It is usually expressed in terms of the average number of bytes or bits of data transferred per error, e.g. 1 error per 10^9 bytes, although it can also be useful to express the rate as the average time between errors for typical usage of the subsystem, e.g. 1 undetected error in 6 weeks at 10% duty cycle.

The error rates most frequently specified relate to the following.

A *transient (or recoverable) read error* occurs during reading and can be recovered by the error recovery procedure prescribed for the storage subsystem (*see* error recovery). A typical figure for magnetic tape is 1 in 10^9 bytes. Where the recording format provides sufficient redundancy to allow some error to be recovered *on-the-fly*, i.e. without re-reading the data, it is necessary to define also the *raw error rate*, which is the rate

that would be perceived if on-the-fly error recovery was not applied.

A *permanent (or irrecoverable) read error* cannot be recovered by the prescribed error recovery procedure. A typical figure is 1 in 10^{11} bytes.

A *transient (or recoverable) write error* occurs during writing and can be recovered by the error recovery procedure prescribed. It is desirable, though not easy, to distinguish two components of this error rate: errors attributable firstly to flaws in the media and secondly to failings of the device (one reason for the difficulty is that these tend to interact). A typical figure for magnetic tape, excluding media errors, is 1 in 10^8 bytes.

A *permanent (or irrecoverable) write error* cannot be recovered by the prescribed procedure. Again it is necessary to distinguish between media flaws and device errors: it is now usual not to give a figure for the latter but to regard each occurrence as a fault to be accounted for in the failure rate of the device (*see* hardware reliability).

An *undetected error* is an error that is not detected by the storage subsystem, presumably because of some inadequacy in the error check facilities defined by the format or in their implementation, or because of errors occurring outside the ambit of these facilities (*see* data integrity). A typical figure is 1 in 10^{13} bytes: a higher figure may well be achieved but is difficult to demonstrate.

Note that error rates depend on the *error recovery procedure used; specified figures are therefore valid only in the conditions defined or assumed in the specification.

error recovery 1. The ability of a compiler to resume parsing of a program after encountering a syntax error.

2. Any process whereby it is possible to recover the data from a data unit (such as a sector or block) that has been shown by an *error detection procedure to contain one or more errors.

There are two approaches: *retry* and *error correction*. Retry involves rereading the data unit from the storage medium or retransmitting it over the communication link; this may be repeated more than once. Error correction depends on the data coding being sufficiently redundant to allow errors to be recovered by logical manipulation of the data without rereading it (*see* error-correcting code). In each case, recovery may need intervention by the host software or may be carried out automatically by the device. Where recovery is automatic, the host is able to monitor the number of errors that are recovered.

When the error is detected during writing or verification, the faulty data unit may be corrected or replaced (*see* write error recovery); in a device with powerful error correction, such as an optical disk drive, this is not always necessary.

error routine Any routine within a program that is entered as a result of some error condition having been detected. The actions taken by such a routine will be dependent upon the reliability requirements that the program is expected to meet and upon the strategy for error analysis and recovery. A typical error routine might simply produce an *error message* (i.e. a message that reports the occurrence of an error) or it might attempt to diagnose the cause of the error or attempt to recover so that normal operation can continue.

error seeding *See* seeding.

escape character A control character that changes the meaning of a character or characters immediately following. It is like a temporary *shift character.

escape sequence An *escape character with the associated following characters, used for controlling a peripheral device.

ESPRIT *Acronym for* European strategic program for research and development in *information technology. A major program that has run since 1984, funded by the European Economic Community and the IT industry in the Community and supporting mainly precompetitive collaborative research and development in IT systems, advanced manufacturing technology, and semiconductor technology. Each ESPRIT project is a collaboration between at least two organizations (industry, research institutes, and academia) based in two different countries. Initially only Community members were eligible, but since 1988 other European countries have been permitted to participate using their own funding.

Estelle A formal description technique based on an extended state transition model and published as ISO DIS 9074 in 1987. Estelle is oriented toward formally specifying concurrent information processing systems, and particularly communication protocols and services.

Ethernet Originally, an experimental *local area network, 3 megabits per second on coaxial cable with *CSMA/CD baseband signaling (*see* baseband networking). It was developed (1976) at Xerox PARC for linking personal computers. It was adopted (1980) by DEC, Intel, and Xerox as a standard communication medium, 10 megabits per second on coaxial cable with CSMA/CD baseband signaling. It effectively provides one implementation of the two lower layers of the ISO/OSI *seven-layer reference model.

ETX/ACK A method of terminating a series of transmissions relating to a single complete transaction using *control characters. The sending device transmits an 'ETX' (end-of-transmission) control character when a transaction is completed, and the receiving device acknowledges the satisfactory receipt of the ETX with an 'ACK' (*see* acknowledgment). Termination of transmissions in this way should not be confused with the *flow control necessary to regulate traffic during the transmission process.

Euclidean norm (two-norm) *See* approximation theory.

Euclid's algorithm An algorithm for finding the greatest common divisor of two integers, m and n. If $m > n$ divide m by n and let r be the remainder. If $r = 0$ then n is the answer; otherwise apply the same algorithm to the integers n and r.

Euler cycle (Euler path) A *path in a directed *graph that includes each edge in the graph precisely once; thus it represents a complete traversal of the arcs of the graph. The concept is named for Leonhard Euler who introduced it around 1736 to solve the *Königsberg bridges problem. He showed that for a graph to possess an Euler cycle it should be *connected and each vertex should have the same number of edges entering it as leaving it.

Euler's method *See* discretization.

EUREKA A European program of development in a wide range of technologies including *information technology (IT). The projects are collaborative with at least two different companies from different countries participating in a project. Some funding is provided by the national funding agencies. It is not limited to European Community countries. Significant IT projects include EAST and ESF, which are developing software engineering platforms based on results of national and European (e.g. *ESPRIT) programs in R&D. EUREKA is oriented nearer to market place development that occurs in *ESPRIT.

Euronet A *packet switching network that was sponsored by the Commission of the EEC (European Economic Community) and became operational in 1979. Formally it is known as Euronet-Diane, where Diane stands for direct information access network for Europe. The partners in the project are: the major hosts in the EEC, offering on-line STI (scientific and technological information) interactive retrieval services; the EEC's *PTTs, building specifically for the project the European international data transmission network, which links the EEC countries; and the Commission of the EEC, sponsoring not only the project but common services for the on-line user.

even parity A property that holds when a group of binary values contains an even number of 1s. *See* parity.

event *See* relative frequency.

EVFU *Abbrev. for* electronic vertical format unit. *See* vertical format unit.

exception An error or fault condition that makes further execution of a program inappropriate. Examples include arithmetic overflow, array reference with index out of bounds, fault condition on a peripheral, and external interrupt. Many programming languages respond to an exception by aborting execution, but some (e.g. Ada) allow the programmer to provide a piece of code – called an *exception handler* – that is automatically invoked when the exception occurs. This can take appropriate remedial action, then either resume execution of the program (at the point where the exception occurred or elsewhere) or terminate the program in a controlled manner.

excess-3 code An 8421 *code for which the weighted sum of the four bits in each codeword is three greater than the decimal digit represented by that codeword. For example, 9 is represented by 1100, the weighted sum of which is

$$8 \times 1 + 4 \times 1 + 2 \times 0 + 1 \times 0 = 12$$

excess factor *Another name for* bias. *See* floating-point notation.

excess-n notation (excess notation) *See* floating-point notation.

exchange in a network. *See* node.

exchangeable disk store (EDS) A storage medium that consists of a magnetic *disk pack or *disk cartridge that can be removed from its host system for library storage, and be replaced by another EDS of the same type. The store can be fitted to another host system having the same type of drive and means of recording and reading data.

exchange selection *Another name for* bubble sort.

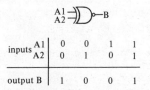

inputs	A1	0	0	1	1
	A2	0	1	0	1
output B		1	0	0	1

Two-input EXNOR gate, circuit symbol and truth table

exclusive-NOR gate An electronic *logic gate whose output is logic 0 (false) only when any one of its inputs is logic 1 (true) and all the others are logic 0, otherwise the output is logic 1. It implements the logical operation of *equivalence and has the same *truth table. It is thus also known as an *equivalence gate*. Like the *exclusive-OR gate it can be used as a simple digital *comparator. The diagram shows the circuit symbol and truth table of a two-input gate.

exclusive-OR gate An electronic *logic gate whose output is logic 1 (true) only when any one of its inputs is logic 1 and all the others are logic 0 (false), otherwise the output is logic 0. It therefore implements the logical *exclusive-OR operation and has the same *truth table; it is thus sometimes known as a

A1
A2 ⟩⟩— B

inputs	A1	0	0	1	1
	A2	0	1	0	1
output B		0	1	1	0

Two-input EXOR gate, circuit symbol and truth table

P	F	F	T	T
Q	F	T	F	T
P XOR Q	F	T	T	F

Truth table for exclusive-OR operation

nonequivalence gate. Like the *exclusive-NOR gate it can be used as a simple digital *comparator. The diagram shows the circuit symbol and truth table for a two-input gate.

exclusive-OR operation The logical *connective combining two statements, truth values, or formulas *P* and *Q* in such a way that the outcome is true if either *P* or *Q* (but not both *P* and *Q*) is true, as shown in the table. Since the outcome is true precisely when the operands are different, it is sometimes referred to as the *nonequivalence operation*. It can be represented in a variety of ways, the more common methods being XOR, xor, and ∨. *See also* OR operation.

execute To carry out an instruction or program. This includes interpreting machine instructions, performing subroutines, and applying functions to sets of parameters.

execute phase The time during a program run in which the target program is actually being executed.

execute step The step in instruction execution that performs the operation(s) of the instruction and the associated memory references. *See* control unit.

execution states The various states in which a computer system may be operating; these states have differing degrees of ability or privilege attached to them. There may be two or more states. In the simplest case there is a *supervisor state* (or *executive state*) and a *user state*. With more than two execution states at different levels, differing degrees of privilege may be granted. These states can represent some of the used resources in an access matrix. *See* access control.

execution time *See* run time.

executive program An early name for a *supervisor. In current terminology an executive is not strictly speaking a program since the latter is usually taken to refer to one or more processes that are collaborating in order to achieve results on behalf of a single user. By contrast an executive is responsible for the supervision of many disjoint processes, which do not cooperate in any way.

executive state (supervisor state) *See* execution states.

exerciser A device or program used to test a subsystem by thoroughly and repetitively performing each of its designed functions and monitoring the results. An example is a floppy-disk exerciser.

existential quantifier *See* quantifier.

exit point (exit) The point at which control leaves a subroutine.

EXNOR gate *Short for* exclusive-NOR gate.

EXOR gate *Short for* exclusive-OR gate.

expansion card (expansion board) A printed circuit board that may be inserted into a computer to give it extra functionality. This may be more memory, a better display capability, more communications interfaces, extra disk or tape controllers, analog to digital converters, in fact anything that the existing hardware can make use of. Expansion cards are often made to be inserted into one or other of the industry standard *buses; consequently a computer built around one of these buses has a very wide choice of expansion cards.

expectation *See* measures of location.

experimental design A system of allocating treatments to experimental units so that the effects of the treatments may be estimated by *statistical methods. The basic principles of experimental design are *replication*, i.e. the application of the same treatment to several units, *randomization*, which ensures that each unit has the same probability of receiving any given treatment, and *blocking*, i.e. grouping of similar units, each one to receive a different treatment. *Factorial designs* are used to allow different types of treatment, or *factors*, to be tested simultaneously. *Analysis of variance is used to assess the significance of the treatment effects. *See also* missing observations.

expert systems Computer programs built for commercial application using the programming techniques of *artificial intelligence, especially those techniques developed for problem solving. *Knowledge engineering* is the subdiscipline of artificial intelligence concerned with building expert systems. Expert systems have been built for medical diagnosis, electronic fault finding, mineral prospecting, computer-system configuration, etc.

explicit address *Another name for* absolute address.

exploratory data analysis (EDA) A term invented by J. W. Tukey to denote techniques for looking at numerical data with a view to discerning pattern.

Exploratory data analysis is open-ended and makes few prior assumptions about the nature of any pattern that may be found. Graphical techniques are freely used. It can be contrasted with model-fitting techniques, which make highly specific prior assumptions. *Statistical methods contain aspects of both these processes.

exponent *See* floating-point notation.

exponentially bounded algorithm *See* complexity measure.

exponential space, time *See* complexity classes.

exponential waveform A nonrepetitive waveform that rises or falls exponentially from some initial value at some initial time, according to the law

$$y(t) = e^{at}$$

For $a>0$ the waveform rises without bound with increasing time t; for $a<0$ the waveform decays to zero. One way in which logic signals can become corrupted as they travel through a system is for their switching edges to become exponentials.

exponentiation The *operation of raising to a power. Repeated multiplication of a quantity x by itself n times is written as x^n. When x is nonzero the value of x^0 is normally assumed to be 1.

Alternatively x^n can be defined inductively (*see* induction) in the following way:

$$x^0 = 1$$
$$x^n = x \times x^{n-1} \text{ for } n > 0$$

The concept of exponentiation can be extended to include exponents that are negative, fractional, or variable or are complex numbers. Exponentiation is an operation that is supplied in some form in most common programming languages (the significant exception being Pascal). It is also a fundamental part of the *floating-point notation for real numbers.

export list In modular languages such as *Modula 2, a list of the names declared inside a module that are accessible to other modules.

expression A component of a programming language that defines the computation of a value, e.g.

$$(-b + \text{sqrt}(b*b - 4*a*c))/(2*a)$$

expression of requirements A statement of the requirements that some envisaged computer system (or program) is expected to meet. In order to define these requirements adequately, it is normally necessary for the expression of requirements to address not just the envisaged system but also the environment in which that system is to operate.

A good expression of requirements should be one of the earliest products of any system-development project, and for a project of significant size it is of crucial importance, not least because errors introduced at the requirements stage tend to be the most expensive to correct. Since it is the first reasonably complete description of any given system, its production presents several significant problems. In particular it may be necessary to obtain information from many individuals, none of whom have a full understanding of all aspects of the envisaged system. There may therefore be a need to resolve several confused, incomplete, and inconsistent views in order to produce a single coherent whole.

The expression of requirements is a primary vehicle for communication between the procurers of a system and its developers, and must therefore be understandable without specialist knowledge of computers or formal languages. A natural language expression of requirements is normally inadequate and more formal notations are usually adopted, often based on a graphical framework within which natural language can be used.

167

extended addressing Any of several methods that permit access to memory with *address space larger than the address space normally accessible in an instruction. *See* addressing schemes.

⟨digit string⟩ ::= ⟨digit⟩ | ⟨digit⟩⟨digit string⟩

⟨sign⟩ ::= + | −

⟨unsigned number⟩ ::= ⟨digit string⟩ | ⟨digit string⟩.

⟨number⟩ ::= ⟨unsigned number⟩ | ⟨sign⟩⟨unsigned number⟩

Fig. 1 BNF notation

digit-string = digit {digit}

unsigned-number = digit-string[.]

number = unsigned-number| ("+" | "−") unsigned-number

Fig. 2 Extended BNF notation

extended BNF (EBNF) A notation for defining the *syntax of a programming language based on *BNF (Backus normal form). EBNF overcomes the main disadvantages of BNF, which are that repetition has to be expressed by a recursive definition and that options and alternatives require auxiliary definitions, by incorporating a notation to specify repetition and alternation. For example, compare the BNF definitions shown in Fig. 1 with the equivalent EBNF definitions in Fig. 2. EBNF uses { ... } to denote repetition, | to denote alternatives, (...) to group constituents, and [...] to denote options. Another significant difference is in the way literals are distinguished from syntactic categories. In BNF, literals are plain and syntactic categories are enclosed in angle brackets; in EBNF, syntactic categories are plain and literals are enclosed in quotation marks. This allows EBNF to define its own syntax.

extended precision *Double precision or more than double precision.

extensibility The capability of a programming language to accept definitions of new constructs.

extensible addressing *See* addressing.

extensible language A programming language having the property of *extensibility.

extension of a source. In coding theory, the process of encoding several symbols at a time, or the results thereof. If the symbols of a *q-ary information source are taken r at a time, and the words of length r are treated (e.g. encoded) as if they were themselves symbols of an alphabet of size q^r, then this compound source is called the rth *extension* of the original source. *See also* source coding theorem.

extension field *See* polynomial.

external device A device that is subsidiary or peripheral to a computer system, usually a terminal or other remote device. In some I/O instructions the designation of an external device is made by specifying a (usually binary) number that distinguishes that device from all others. This number is often called the *external device address* although, strictly speaking, it is not an address in the true sense. *See also* address space.

external fragmentation A form of *fragmentation that arises when memory is allocated in units of arbitrary size. When a large amount of memory is released, part of it may be used to meet a subsequent request, leaving an unused part that is too small to meet any further requests.

external interrupt An interrupt that is initiated by a device that is not part of the processor. Peripherals and communication connections are sources of external interrupts.

external node *Another name for* leaf node.

external path length of a tree. The sum of the lengths of all paths from the root to an external (i.e. a leaf) node.

external schema *See* data description language.

external sorting *See* sorting.

external storage Any type of storage device that is connected to and controlled by a computer but is not integrated within it. Generally the devices are peripheral units such as tape transports or disk drives. An external storage device may be shared by more than one computer.

extrapolation The estimation of the value of a function (given other values of the function) at a point beyond the interval in which the data lies. One possible approach is to use the value of an *interpolation polynomial at this point. An important case arises when the data consists of approximations to the solution of a problem, for different values of a parameter controlling the magnitude of the acceptable error in the method used. A more powerful method can be constructed by extrapolating to the limiting case of the parameter, where the error is zero, using theoretical results giving the dependence of the error on the parameter. This is called *Richardson extrapolation* (or the *deferred approach to the limit*).

extrapolation method A *numerical method for the solution of a problem based on repeated *extrapolation, to produce increasingly more accurate results, from a sequence of basic approximations utilizing different values of a parameter, such as the stepsize (*see* finite-difference method).
Important examples are the *Romberg method for *numerical integration and *Gragg's extrapolation method for the

solution of *ordinary differential equations based on the *midpoint rule. An essential requirement for such methods are theoretical results establishing the existence of an expansion for the error in (usually even) powers of the parameter, for sufficiently smooth problems.

extrinsic semiconductor *See* semiconductor.

F

facsimile Systems that provide electronic transmission of ordinary documents, incuding drawings, photographs, and maps. The original document is scanned at the sending station, converted into an analog or digital representation, and sent over a communication channel to the receiving station, which constructs a duplicate image on paper; this image is referred to as a *facsimile*. Early facsimile systems were exclusively analog, but new systems have been designed that use digital techniques for data encoding and transmission. Commercial facsimile services are known as *fax*.

factorable code An *error-correcting code that can be considered as the result of several coding stages, the output of each being encoded by the next. The constituent codes are the factors of the original compound code. *See* concatenated coding systems.

factor analysis *See* multivariate analysis.

factorial designs *See* experimental design.

Fagan inspection *See* code inspection.

fail-safe Denoting or relating to a computer system that does not make an error in spite of the occurrence of a single fault. *See also* fault-tolerant system.

FAIL-SOFT

fail-soft Denoting or relating to a computer system that can continue to provide a reduced level of service in spite of the occurrence of a single fault. The system is then said to be in a state of *graceful degradation*. *See also* fault-tolerant system.

failure An event or condition in which an entire computer system or some part of it is unable to perform one or more prescribed functions. The failure may be due to a random process causing the hardware to cease to function, in which case hardware *maintenance is required. Failure may also be due to a systematic cause such as an unrevealed or uncorrected *fault* in hardware or software. The fault may be due to an *error*, i.e. a mistake, occurring during (for example) design, specification, or operation. Each fault built into the hardware or software may be later revealed through a variety of processes such as *review, *static analysis, *testing, or failure during operation of the computer. The result of revealing the fault at any time is a failure event for the hardware or software. Whether the failure is significant depends on the consequences and the timing.

There is thus a relationship between failure, fault, and error. Note however that the terms are sometimes used synonymously. *See also* fault-tolerant system.

failure rate The number of *failures of a specified category in a given period, in a given number of computer runs, or in some other given unit of measure. The failure rate of a system or component varies during its lifetime, at first decreasing as problems are detected and repaired and finally increasing due to deterioration. Between these two periods the rate usually remains steady.

failure recovery A procedure that allows for restart of a failed system in a way that either eliminates or minimizes the amount of incorrect system results. This usually requires the program that was running to have used a *checkpoint procedure.

fallback The *restarting of a process at a *checkpoint after correction of a fault. *See also* failure recovery.

false position method (Latin: **regula falsi**) An *iterative method for finding a root of the *nonlinear equation $f(x) = 0$. It employs the same formula as the *secant method, but retains at each stage the two most recent estimates that bracket the root in order to guarantee convergence. Modifications to this general strategy are required to avoid one end-point remaining fixed and slow convergence. The resulting methods are both fast and reliable.

fan-in 1. The number of input lines (normally fixed) to a logic gate or logic device.
2. The number of software modules that call this module.

Fano coding (Shannon–Fano coding) *See* source coding.

Fano decoding The decoding of a *convolutional code by Fano's algorithm.

fan-out 1. The maximum number of devices that can be safely driven by the output from a logic gate or logic device (which have only a limited ability to drive other devices from their output terminals). If the fan-out is exceeded the voltage levels corresponding to a logic 1 and a logic 0 become more similar and errors are more likely.
2. The number of software modules that are called by this module.

farm An arrangement in which several computers cooperate concurrently in the solution of a problem. One of the computers will act as a *scheduler while the remainder act as workers. Each worker has the same copy of the *code and is

170

able to accept a task from the scheduler, carry out the process, then return the result. A farm could comprise a network of *transputers or other similar *RISC machines.

fast Fourier transform (FFT) An algorithm that computes the discrete *Fourier transform accurately and efficiently on digital computers. FFT techniques have wide applicability in linear systems, optics, probability theory, quantum physics, antennas, and signal analysis.

father of a node. *Another name for* parent.

father file *See* file recovery.

fault *See* failure.

fault detection Determination, normally by detection of a failure in a *check, that a fault (error) has occurred in a logic circuit, arithmetic circuit, or an information transfer.

fault diagnosis The task of determining where in a (repairable) computer system a fault has occurred and what the logical nature of that fault is.

fault-tolerant system A computer system that is capable of providing either full functionality (*fail-safe) or reduced functionality (*fail-soft) after a failure has occurred. Fault tolerance is usually provided through a combination of redundant system elements and error detection and correction procedures.

fax The commercial name for *facsimile systems.

FCC Federal Communications Commission, the US regulatory commission for public communications. Its jurisdiction includes land line, cable, radio, and satellite communications. It is a party to international agreements on frequency allocation of the radio spectrum.

FDDI *Abbrev. for* fiber distributed data interface. A high-speed *local area network system that uses a pair of optical fibers to carry digital data between pairs of stations arranged in a *ring topology. The FDDI system itself operates at a nominal 140 Mbps, using a version of a *token ring protocol. The common method of working is to use FDDI as a high-speed *backbone that interconnects *CSMA/CD local networks. It is intended that FDDI will be an ISO OSI standard but the standard has not yet been finalized (Spring 1989), although products are available that operate over the existing definition.

F distribution An important *probability distribution used to test the significance of estimated mean squares in an *analysis of variance and in *regression analysis. Theoretically the F distribution is the distribution of the ratio of two independent random variables S_1/f_1 and S_2/f_2, where S_1 has the *chi-squared distribution on f_2 degrees of freedom. Tables of critical values of the F distribution for ranges of f_1 and f_2 are widely available, but direct computation requires lengthy algorithms to compute the incomplete beta function.

FDM *Abbrev. for* frequency division multiplexing.

feasibility study A study carried out prior to a development project in order to establish that the proposed system is feasible and can serve a useful purpose. Feasibility studies can be purely paper exercises or can involve the construction of experimental or prototype systems. Often a feasibility study will not address the entire scope of the proposed system, but will concentrate on specific areas or decisions where the feasibility is regarded as questionable or the potential risk is greatest.

feed 1. A device for moving media to a position at which the data can be read.

2. To cause data or media to be entered into a system or peripheral.

feedback queue A form of scheduling mechanism often used in multiaccess systems. Individual *processes are allocated a *quantum of time on the processor. A process once started is allowed to run until it has exhausted its quantum, until it initiates a transfer on a peripheral device, or until an interrupt generated by some other process occurs. If the quantum is exhausted, the process is assigned a longer quantum and rejoins the queue. If the process initiates a transfer, its quantum remains unaltered and it rejoins the queue. If an externally generated interrupt occurs, the interrupt is serviced. Servicing the interrupt may free some other process already in the queue, in which case that process may be preferentially restarted.

feedback register (feedback shift register) A *shift register, generally consisting of several cells, in which the first cell has its input supplied by a combinational logic function of the parallel outputs of several cells and of a possible external input. An important case is the *linear feedback register* in which *linear logic is employed for the feedback function.

The linear feedback register has the effect of deconvolving the external serial input with the sequence of combinational coefficients (*see* convolution). If the external input is regarded as a *polynomial in which powers of the indeterminate denote succession in time, and if the combinational coefficients are regarded likewise as a second polynomial, then the linear feedback register has the effect of dividing the former polynomial by the latter. When used in coding or in digital signal processing, feedback shift registers may be binary or *q-ary and may be implemented in hardware or software.

When there is no external serial input, the linear feedback register can be used on its own to generate *m-sequences or,

with parallel loading of the shift register with a source word, as an *encoder for *simplex codes; either of these applications requires that the feedback logic coefficients represent a *polynomial that is primitive. *See also* Good–de Bruijn diagram.

feed-forward (shift) register A *shift register, generally consisting of a number of cells, several parallel outputs of which are combined in a combinational logic function. An important case is the *linear feed-forward register* in which *linear logic is employed for the feed-forward function.

The linear feed-forward register has the effect of convolving the serial input to the register with the sequence of combinational coefficients (*see* convolution). If the input is regarded as a *polynomial in which powers of the indeterminate denote succession in time, and if the combinational coefficients are regarded likewise as a second polynomial, then the linear feed-forward register has the effect of multiplying these polynomials.

When used in coding or in digital signal processing, feed-forward registers may be binary or *q-ary, and may be implemented in hardware or software.

ferrite A sintered ferromagnetic material plus ceramic that combines the high magnetic permeablility of the former with the high electrical resistance of the latter. This means that ferrite can be used for magnetic cores in high-frequency and high-speed switching circuits in which iron losses are a problem. *See also* core store.

FET *Abbrev. for* field-effect transistor.

fetch-execute cycle (instruction cycle) The two steps of obtaining and executing an instruction. *See* control unit.

fetch protect Restriction of the memory reading privilege in a particular memory segment. *See* memory protection.

FFT *Abbrev. for* fast Fourier transform.

fiber optics transmission system A data communication system that uses *optical fibers* – special glass or plastic fibers – instead of copper wire. Information is carried by modulating light. The optical fibers are small, lightweight, and nonconductive. Cables made from optical fibers and other nonconductive materials may be used in military and industrial applications where ordinary conductive cables present a safety risk. Furthermore, since no electromagnetic radiation leaves the cable, and it is difficult to tap into an existing fiber-optic cable, fiber-optic transmissions are relatively secure.

There are three basic types of optical fibers in use: single-mode stepped index, multi-mode stepped index, and multi-mode graded index. They vary in how the optical density of the fiber varies from core to edge, which affects how light propagates down the cable. This leads to differences in transmission efficiency, and in the number of different light signals (wavelengths or polarizations) that may be present simultaneously. *See also* FDDI.

Fibonacci search A searching algorithm that uses Fibonacci numbers in a way that is analogous to the use of powers of 2 in the *binary search. See Fibonacci series.

Fibonacci series A sequence of numbers in which each number is the sum of the two preceding numbers, e.g.

$$0,1,1,2,3,5,8, \ldots$$

The *Fibonacci numbers* F_n are formally defined to be

$$F_0 = 0, \ F_1 = 1,$$
$$F_{n+2} = F_{n+1} + F_n, \ n \geqslant 0$$

Any positive number m can be represented uniquely as a sum of Fibonacci numbers, where the greatest F_n in the expansion does not exceed m and where no two of the F_n are adjacent numbers in the Fibonacci series.

fiche *Short for* microfiche. *See* COM.

field 1. An item of data consisting of a number of characters, bytes, words, or codes that are treated together, e.g. to form a number, a name, or an address. A number of fields make a *record and the fields may be fixed in length or variable. The term came into use with punched card systems and a field size was defined in terms of a number of columns.

2. Normally a way of designating a portion of a word that has a specific significance or function within that word, e.g. an address field in an instruction word or a character field within a data word.

3. In mathematics, a commutative *ring containing more than one element and in which every nonzero element has an *inverse with respect to the multiplication operation. Apart from their obvious relationship to arithmetic involving numbers of various kinds, fields play a very important role in discussion about the analysis of *algorithms. Results in this area mention the number of operations of a particular kind, and these operations are usually related to addition and multiplication of elements of some field.

field-effect transistor (FET) A semiconductor device having three terminals: *source*, *gate*, and *drain*. Current flow in a narrow conduction *channel* between drain and source is controlled by the voltage applied between gate and source, which can deplete the conduction channel of charge carriers. If the source and drain regions are composed of n-type semiconductor the conduction channel is n-type; these devices are known as *n-channel* devices. Devices with p-type source, drain, and channel are called *p-channel* devices. In contrast to *bipolar transistors, FETs are *unipolar devices*; the current flow is electrons (in n-channel devices) or holes (in p-channel devices).

In the *junction FET* the channel is a composite part of the structure. In the *MOSFET the gate is insulated from the source and drain regions and the channel forms when the gate voltage is applied. Unlike the bipolar transistor both types of FET require virtually no input current to the gate except a pulse to charge or discharge the gate capacitance. Junction FETs have relatively slow *switching speeds compared with MOSFETs and bipolar transistors, and are therefore not used in logic circuits.

field-programmable devices *See* programmable devices, PLA.

FIFO or **fifo** *Acronym for* first in first out. *FIFO list* is another name for *queue.

fifth generation The types of computer currently under development in a number of countries, especially Japan, and predicted as becoming available in the 1990s. The features are conjectural at present but point toward "intelligent" machines, which may have massively parallel processing, widespread use of intelligent knowledge-based systems, and natural language interfaces. Progress has not been as fast as originally planned although some significant advances have been made.

file Information held on *backing store (i.e. usually on magnetic disk or magnetic tape) in order (a) to enable it to persist beyond the time of execution of a single job and/or (b) to overcome space limitations in main memory. Files may hold data, programs, text, or any other information. Files with a very brief existence (i.e. in case (b) above, or where they simply carry information between one job and the next in sequence) are called *work files*.

file activity Any storage or retrieval activity performed on a *file. In some systems a record is kept of file activity and the information is used to optimize the use of available *backing store. For example, a file for which the activity has fallen below a certain level may be moved off-line.

file descriptor Information that describes a file, giving details such as it's name, generation number, date of last access, expiry date, and the structure of the records it contains. It is normally stored as a header record at the front of the file, held on magnetic tape or on disk.

file directory *See* directory.

file editing *See* file updating.

file integrity *See* database integrity.

file maintenance Software processes concerned with maintaining *file integrity and file efficiency, usually of *data files. It is concerned with the internal organization of files (unlike *file management, which is not). It is not concerned with changing values within a file (unlike *file updating, which is).

file management Software processes concerned with the overall management of *files, e.g. their allocation to space in *backing store, control over access, writing *backup copies, and maintaining *directories. Basic file management is normally performed by *operating systems, though this may be supplemented by *file management systems. *See also* file maintenance.

file management system A software system that provides facilities for *file management (often specifically of *data files) at a level above that offered by *operating systems (but in the case of data files below that offered by *database management systems).

file mark *See* tape mark.

file organization The structure of a *file (especially a *data file), defined in terms of its components and how they are mapped onto *backing store. Any given file organization supports one or more file *access methods. Organization is thus closely related to but conceptually distinct from access methods. The distinction is similar to that between *data structures and the procedures and functions that operate on them (indeed a file organization is a large-scale data structure), or to that between a database schema (*see* data description language) and the facilities in a *data manipulation language. There is no very useful or commonly accepted taxonomy of methods of file organization: most attempts confuse organization with access methods (which are easier to classify), and in practice a file organization is usually described in terms of the set of access methods that it is designed to support.

file protection The protection of files from the mistaken or unauthorized storage or retrieval of information (or, in the case of program files, from mistaken or unauthorized execution). Protection may be

(a) physical, concerned with the security of the media on which files are held, and implemented by operating procedures, or

(b) logical, concerned with the security of the contents of files, and implemented by software.

file recovery The process of restoring *file integrity once a file has been found to be incorrect. There are two main classes of method. In a *transaction processing system, in which a *master file is updated incrementally, the method is based on *backup copies and *recovery logs. In a *batch processing system, in which a master file is updated by being completely rewritten, the last version of the master file serves as the backup, and the transaction file serves as the recovery log. (The last version of the master file is then referred to as the *father* or *parent*, and the version before that as the *grandfather* or *grandparent*.)

file reel *See* magnetic tape.

file server *See* server.

file transfer Movement of a file from one computer to another in a *network. The data may be moved either by opening a network connection directly to the destination, or by passing the data together with control information to a *message-switching file transfer relay. File transfer *protocols (FTPs) frequently encompass facilities to transform data between host-specific formats and a network standard form. This permits file transfer to take place between otherwise incompatible systems. Unfortunately different networks have developed different standards for file transfer. This has led to the development of internetwork file transfer protocols such as the *NIFTP (network independent file transfer protocol). *See also* FTAM.

file updating Changing a set of values in a *file, especially a *data file, without changing the organization or semantics of the file. File updating may be done in one of two ways. The first, common in *data processing, is when the updating process is carried out separately from the entry of amendments and "invisibly" from any human operator. The second is when a file is displayed on an interactive device, and an operator can then amend it while able to see it: this method is more commonly called file editing.

fill character *Another name for* ignore character.

filter 1. A program that processes a sequential stream of text, carrying out some simple transformation, e.g. condensing multiple spaces to single spaces, counting words, etc. In the *UNIX system powerful effects can be created by connecting a series of filters in a *pipeline*, where each filter takes as its input the output produced by its predecessor.

2. A simple electric circuit or some more complicated device used in the process of *filtering.

filtering 1. The processing of a *signal (by a simple electric circuit or by some more complicated device) in such a way that the behavior of the signal is affected in either the *time domain* or in a *transform domain*.

In time-domain filtering each element of the original signal is replaced by a sequence of elements, proportional in amplitude to the original signal but spaced in time; the sum (assuming linear fitering) of these sequences forms the new signal. In transform-domain filtering the elements of the original signal are not those of its amplitude but rather of its components under, for example, *Fourier analysis or *Walsh analysis; they are then spaced not in time but in *frequency or *sequency respectively. Many other transforms are also used.

Filtering, both in the time domain and in various transform domains, is of great importance in *multiplexing. A simple but very common example of filtering in the frequency (Fourier) domain is the use of resonant circuits to effect *low-pass, *band-pass, *high-pass, and *band-stop functions; these are much used, e.g. in *data transmission lines and *modems.

2. *See* masking.

filtering bridge A *bridge placed between two or more *Ethernets (or other broadcast networks) where it is anticipated that much of the traffic originating on one side of the bridge is to destinations on the same side of the bridge. The filtering bridge receives all packets from each network, and examines the destination address; only if the address is in a different network from the source will the bridge transfer the packet to the network containing the destination. Many filtering bridges are *adaptive* and include some form of learning process that determines which

addresses are in which network, typically by examining the source addresses in each packet as received.

find One of the basic actions performed on *sets that, when applied in the form
$$find(el)$$
produces the set of which *el* is currently a member; if *el* is in no set or in more than one set the effect of the operation is undefined. *See also* operations on sets.

finite automaton *See* finite-state automaton.

finite-difference method A widely applicable *discretization method for the solution of *ordinary and *partial differential equations. In this approach all derivatives are replaced by approximations that involve solution values only, so in general the differential equation is reduced to a system of *nonlinear equations or *linear algebraic equations. For example, in the problem
$$y'' + by' + cy = d \quad 0 \leq x \leq 1,$$
$$y(0) = \alpha, \, y(1) = \beta,$$
where b, c, d, α, and β are given constants, the interval [0,1] is first divided into equal subintervals of length h; h is called the *stepsize* (or *mesh* or *grid size*). This gives the *mesh points* (or *grid points*) x_n,
$$x_n = nh,$$
$$n = 0,1,\ldots,N+1,$$
$$h = 1/(N+1)$$
At interior mesh points the derivatives are now replaced by finite-difference approximations, e.g.
$$y'(x_n) \simeq (\tfrac{1}{2}h)[y(x_{n+1}) - y(x_{n-1})]$$
$$y''(x_n) \simeq (1/h^2)[y(x_{n+1}) - 2y(x_n) + y(x_{n-1})]$$
When combined with the boundary conditions these approximations result in a system of equations for approximations to $y(x_n)$, $n = 1, 2, \ldots, N$. Nonlinear differential equations yield a system of nonlinear equations.

finite-element method A widely applicable approach to solving *ordinary and particularly *partial differential equations and similar problems. The approach embraces several variants, principally *Galerkin's method* and the *Rayleigh–Ritz method*. The basic idea, however, is the same and involves approximating the solution of the problem by a linear combination:

$$u(x) = \sum_{j=1}^{n} c_j \phi_j(x)$$

The functions $\phi_1, \phi_2, \ldots, \phi_n$ are always chosen to be simple and are called *trial functions*. The success of the method is due in part to choosing these functions to be low-degree *splines. This in turn generally leads to a system of equations for the coefficients $c_1, c_2, \ldots, c_n$ that involves the treatment of *sparse matrices, i.e. matrices in which a large proportion of the elements are zero; very efficient software can then be used.

In Galerkin's method the criterion for choosing the coefficients is that the amount by which $u(x)$ fails to satisfy the equation is in a certain sense small. The Rayleigh–Ritz method is a *variational method. The finite-element method can in general be regarded as a process in which a solution in an infinite-dimensional space is replaced by an approximation that lies in a finite-dimensional subspace.

finite field (Galois field) A (mathematical) *field with a finite number of elements. The number of elements must be of the form p^k where p is some prime number and k is a positive integer. Results concerning finite fields are of particular relevance in the areas of error detection and error correction.

finite-length arithmetic (fixed-length arithmetic) The approximation to real arithmetic in a computer. The term arises since the precision to which real numbers can be represented as floating-point numbers in a computer is limited by the length of the mantissa. *See* floating-point notation.

finite sequence (list) *See* sequence.

finite set A *set with a finite number of elements.

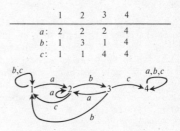

Equivalent transition table and diagram of an FSA

finite-state automaton (FSA; finite-state machine) A simple kind of *automaton. The input string is read once from left to right, looking at each symbol in turn. At any time the FSA has some internal *state*, which changes after each input symbol is read. The new state depends firstly on the symbol just read and secondly on the current state. An FSA is therefore determined by a function f from $I \times Q$ to Q, where I is the set of possible input symbols, Q is the set of states, and $I \times Q$ is the *Cartesian product of I and Q. Q must be finite, hence the name FSA.

The function f is called a *state transition function*. It is commonly represented either by a table or by a directed *graph, known respectively as a *state transition table* and a *state transition diagram*. The figure shows two equivalent representations in which

$$I = \{a,b,c\},$$
$$Q = \{1,2,3,4\}$$

In this example,

$$f(a,1) = 2,$$
$$f(c,4) = 4, \text{ etc.}$$

f extends to strings in the obvious manner: in the example,

$$f(bc,2) = 4,$$
$$f(aaa,3) = 1, \text{ etc.}$$

Let Q be divided into *accepting states* and *rejecting states*, and let q_0 be some member of Q (referred to as the *start state*). The *language recognized* by the FSA is the set of all w such that

$$f(w, q_0)$$

is an accepting state, i.e. the set of all strings that take the start state to an accepting state. For example, in the FSA shown in the figure let q_0 be 1 and let 4 be the only accepting state; the language recognized is then the set of all strings over $\{a, b, c\}$ that somewhere contain *abc* as a substring.

A generalization is to allow more than one state to which the FSA can move, for a given input symbol and current state. This gives a *nondeterministic FSA*. The input string is then accepted if there is some sequence of choices of moves leading to an accepting state. Such a machine can always be converted to a deterministic one recognizing the same language.

See also sequential machine, minimal machine.

FIPS *Acronym for* Federal Information Processing Standard. A publication (FIPS PUB) issued by the US National Bureau of Standards serves as the official source of information in the US federal government regarding standards issued by NBS.

Fire codes A family of *polynomial *block codes designed to correct *burst errors.

firing rule *See* Petri net.

firmware System software that is held in read-only memory (*ROM).

first fit A method of selecting a contiguous area of memory that is to be allocated for a segment. The *free-space list is scanned in order of starting address, and the allocation made from the first free area whose size exceeds that of the request. Despite its apparent simplicity

this algorithm has a number of desirable properties in terms of performance.

first generation of computers. The series of calculating and computing machines whose designs were started between 1940 (approximately) and 1955. These machines are characterized by electronic tube (valve) circuitry, and delay line, rotating, or electrostatic (Williams tube) memory. The majority of them embodied the stored program concept. For the most part, first generation machines used as input/output punched paper tape, punched card, magnetic wire, magnetic tape, and printers. Despite these seeming handicaps, impressive computations in weather forecasting, atomic energy calculations, and similar scientific applications were routinely performed on them.

Important first-generation development machines include the *Manchester Mark I, *EDSAC, *EDVAC, *SEAC, *Whirlwind, *IAS, and *ENIAC while the earliest commercially available computers included the *Ferranti Mark I, *UNIVAC I, and *LEO I.

first in first out *See* FIFO.

first-order logic *Another name for* predicate calculus.

first-order term *See* term.

fixed-base system *Another name for* fixed-radix system. *See* number system.

fixed disk drive A *disk drive in which the storage medium is permanently attached within the device. *Compare* exchangeable disk store.

fixed head of a disk drive. A read/write head that cannot be moved relative to the center of the disk. A large number of these heads are usually incorporated into an assembly so that there is a "head per track", and such drives may be referred to by this expression. The advantage of a fixed head is that the average access time is reduced to the time for half a revolution since there is no track seek time required. Some drives have both fixed and moveable heads.

fixed-length arithmetic *Another name for* finite-length arithmetic.

fixed-length code A *code in which a fixed number of source symbols are encoded into a fixed number of output symbols. It is usually a *block code. (The term fixed-length is used in contrast to *variable-length, whereas block code can be contrasted with *convolutional code.)

fixed point *See* fixed-point theorem.

fixed-point notation A representation of real numbers in which the position of the *radix point is fixed. The position of the point determines the absolute precision of the representation. If the point is fixed at the right-hand end of the number then all of the fixed-point numbers are integers. Due to a number of difficulties, fixed-point arithmetic is rarely used in a modern computer for calculations involving real numbers.

fixed-point theorem A theorem concerning the existence and nature of least fixed points. A *fixed point*, of a *function f, is an element x such that $f(x) = x$. A *least fixed point* is one that, among all the fixed points of f, is lowest in some *partial ordering that has been imposed on the elements. The most often-cited form of the fixed-point theorem (due originally to S. C. Kleene) states that, subject to certain assumptions (notably continuity), f has a least fixed point, which moreover can be characterized as the limit of a sequence of approximations. This abstract fact is of great relevance to the *denotational semantics of programming languages, in particular in specifying the precise meaning of constructs like *iteration, *recursion, and recursive types. Of recent use in semantics, the theorem

originated in *recursive function theory, where it takes a rather different form, although essentially related to the one given here.

fixed-radix system (fixed-base system) *See* number system.

fixed word length computer A computer in which data is constrained to lie within words that are all of the same length. By extension the term is sometimes used to imply that all instructions also fit within one word. *Compare* variable word length computer.

flag A variable whose value indicates the attainment of some designated state or condition by an item of equipment or a program. The flag is subsequently used as a basis for conditional branching and similar decision processes.

flat addressing *See* addressing.

flatbed plotter *See* plotter.

flat screen A type of *display in the form of a thin flat panel. It does not have the protrusion at right angles to the screen that is usually associated with the *cathode-ray tube (CRT) used in many display units.

flexible array An *array whose lower and/or upper bounds are not fixed and may vary according to the values assigned to it. *See also* string.

flexible disk cartridge In international standards, the formal name for a *floppy disk.

flip-flop (bistable) An electronic circuit element that is capable of exhibiting either of two stable states and of switching between these states in a reproducible manner. When used in *logic circuits the two states are made to correspond to logic 1 and logic 0. Flip-flops are therefore one-bit memory elements and are frequently used in digital circuits.

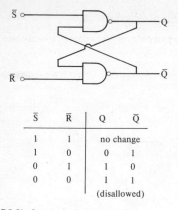

S̄	R̄	Q	Q̄
1	1	no change	
1	0	0	1
0	1	1	0
0	0	1	1
		(disallowed)	

RS flip-flop, logic diagram and truth table

The simplest form is the *RS flip-flop*; an implementation using *NAND gates is shown in the diagram together with the flip-flop's truth table. A logic 1 on one of the two inputs either sets the Q output to logic 1 or resets Q to logic 0. Output Q̄ is the logical complement of Q. When R̄ and S̄ are both logic 1 (which is equivalent to R and S both logic 0), Q does not change state. The situation of both R̄ and S̄ at logic 0 is ambiguous and is avoided in more complex flip-flop implementations (*see* JK flip-flop). The outputs of this (and other) flip-flops are not just functions of the inputs but depend on both inputs and outputs. The device is thus a simple *sequential circuit.

Extra logic gating may be included in the RS device, and in more complex flip-flops, to allow a clock signal to be input to the flip-flop, so producing a *clocked flip-flop* (*see* clock). The Q output will not then change state until an active edge of the clock pulse occurs (*edge-triggered device*) or a complete clock cycle has occurred (*pulse-triggered device*). Provision may also be made to set up a given output regardless of the state of the inputs.

Various forms of flip-flop are available to perform specific functions; these include JK *D, *T, and *master-slave flip-flops. Flip-flops are important as memory devices in digital counters. The RS flip-flop is often considered to be the *universal flip-flop* since it forms the basic building block for more sophisticated implementations. JK, master-slave, and D flip-flops are all available as standard integrated-circuit packages.

float An operator or function that converts a number in *fixed-point notation into an equivalent *floating-point form.

floating-point accelerator (FPA) A device to improve the overall performance of a computer by removing the burden of performing floating-point arithmetic from the central processor.

floating-point notation A representation of real numbers that enables both very small and very large numbers to be conveniently expressed. A floating-point number has the general form
$$\pm m \times R^e$$
where m is called the *mantissa*, R is the *radix (or base) of the number system, and e is the *exponent*.

The following format is typical of the floating-point representation used in computers. The first bit is a *sign bit*, denoting the sign of the mantissa. This is followed by a fixed number of bits representing the exponent, which is in turn followed by another fixed number of bits representing the magnitude of the mantissa. The exponent is often represented using *excess-n notation*, whereby a number, called the *characteristic* (or *biased exponent*), is stored instead of the exponent itself. To derive the characteristic for a floating-point number from its exponent, the *bias* (or *excess factor*) n is added to the exponent. For example, for an 8-bit characteristic, exponents in the range -128 to $+127$ are represented in excess-128 notation by characteristics in the range 0 to 255.

A nonzero floating-point number is *normalized* if the leading digit in its mantissa is nonzero.

floating-point operation The addition, subtraction, multiplication, or division of two floating-point operands to produce a floating-point result. There is an international standard (IEEE standard 754: 1985) that is designed to ensure the reproducibility of floating point operations. *See also* floating-point notation, flops.

flop A unit of computational cost associated with matrix and vector operations. The term is widely used in algorithms for *numerical linear algebra. A flop is approximately the amount of work required to compute, for example in FORTRAN, an expression of the form

$$S = S + A(I,J) * X(J)$$

i.e. a floating point multiplication and a floating point addition, along with the effort involved in subscripting. Thus for example, Gaussian elimination for a system of order n requires $n^3/3$ flops (*see* linear algebraic equations). As computer design and architecture change, this unit of cost may well undergo modification.

floppy disk (diskette) A flexible *magnetic disk consisting of a circular polyester substrate (with a central hole) coated with magnetic oxide and permanently enclosed within a stiff jacket, the inside of which is lined with a cleaning material. The jacket has a radial slot on each side through which the read heads (or head and support pad in the case of a single-sided floppy disk) can contact the disk. As with other magnetic disks, data is recorded in concentric tracks in the magnetic coating; the tracks are divided into *sectors. Developing technology has enabled recording density and track density to be raised, thus increasing total storage capacity. A small *index hole* in the jacket and disk is provided so that a photosensor may be used to generate an index pulse once per revolution. An aperture, the *write protect notch*, on one edge of the jacket can be blocked to prevent the drive from writing to the disk.

The two most common sizes of floppy disk are 3½ inches and 5¼ inches. The jacket of the former is of hard plastic with a metal shutter protecting the read-write slot, while the latter has a flexible jacket and is protected by a paper envelope when not in use. Both kinds of disks come in normal and high-density qualities, and the high-density forms currently (1989) hold 1.44 or 1.2 megabytes respectively.

floppy-disk drive (diskette drive) A device that accepts flexible magnetic disks, i.e. *floppy disks, and reads or writes magnetic patterns that correspond to the data to be retrieved or stored. The data is encoded in one of the appropriate *disk formats. The floppy disk is put into the mechanism through a slot that is normally covered by a hinged flap or door. The mechanism automatically locates and clamps the disk and rotates it – usually at a speed of 360 rpm. The *read/write heads contact the disk through apertures in its cover.

The floppy-disk drive was first introduced by IBM as a diagnostic software load device but it is now used extensively as a data storage device on small computing systems. *See also* disk drive.

flops (or **FLOPS**) *Acronym for* floating-point operations per second. A commonly used measure of *computer power for very powerful computers (*supercomputers, *vector-processing computers) and *array processors. The rating of a computer, which in very powerful machines now exceeds a thousand million flops (i.e. a thousand megaflops of Mflops), must be qualified by a statement of the precision to which the operations are carried out.

flowchart A low-level graphical representation of the structure of a program, with emphasis on control flow and the primitive actions performed by the program rather than on the data structures employed by the program. It consists of a set of *boxes* of various shapes, interconnected by a set of directed *arcs*. The arcs indicate flow of control while the various box shapes indicate different kinds of action or decision. Within the boxes any notation can be employed to describe the action or decision; typical notations are pseudocode and natural language.

Flowcharts have been used extensively for many years but are now rather unpopular. For one reason they tend to obscure the structure of programs that follow the tenets of structured coding (*see* structured programming) and, more important, they ignore the topic of data structuring.

flow control Procedures used to limit the rate at which data is transmitted to the rate at which it can be received. There are two major classes of flow control: *end-to-end* and *hop-by-hop*. End-to-end flow control limits the amount of data according to the capacity of the final destination to absorb it, without regard to the path through the network taken by the data (which may vary from message to message). Hop-by-hop flow control limits the amount of data sent according to the capacity of each individual node and/or link on the path through the network. In this latter case, the path is usually constant for the lifetime of the connection between sender and receiver. *See also* window, acknowledgment.

Floyd method A method for proving the partial correctness of a program (*see* program correctness proof). Certain points in the program are designated as *cut-points*, and to each cut-point is attached an *inductive assertion*. The inductive assertions are chosen so that, whenever a cut-point is reached, the program is in a "correct state", i.e. one that satisfies the inductive assertion attached to that point. To establish this, it is necessary to consider each "minimal path", i.e. each path leading from a cut-point directly to a cut-point, and to show that, provided the program is already in a correct state, it will still be in one after following that path.

fluid logic A means of implementing logic functions, not by the normal use of electronic circuitry but by the flow of incompressible fluids (liquids) or gases through tubing containing intersections and constrictions. The logic gates so formed are useful in situations in which high electromagnetic interference prevents the use of electronic components. If the working medium is a gas, the term *pneumatic logic* is often used.

Flynn's classification *See* concurrency.

FM or **f.m.** *Abbrev. for* frequency modulation. *See* modulation.

FMS 1. *Abbrev. for* flexible manufacturing system. The term *computer-integrated manufacturing (CIM) is now preferred.

2. *Abbrev. for* Fortran Monitor System. An early operating system for use with Fortran, now obsolete.

folding 1. A simple method of *hashing a key, in which the key is subdivided into several parts that are added together to give an address. The *folding ratio* is the ratio of the sizes of the domain of this hashing function to the size of its range.

2. An important method in *program transformation, introduced by Burstall and Darlington. It concerns programs that are expressed as collections of equations forming *recursive function definitions (programs written in a *functional language like *ML are often essentially in that form). The idea is to derive new equations, and in doing so one of the characteristic steps is to replace an instance of a right-hand side of an existing equation by the corresponding instance of the left-hand side (*folding*) or vice versa (*unfolding*). The resulting new equations form a new program equivalent to the original one. Programs derived in this way can often display significantly different algorithms and efficiency conditions from the original programs.

footprint The area of front panel, desk, or floor space occupied by a device: thus if a cartridge tape drive is described as having a 5¼″ floppy footprint it will fit the same shape and size of panel opening as a standard 5¼″ floppy-disk drive.

foreground processing Processing that supports interaction in a system that supports both interactive and batch operations. *See also* background processing.

forest A directed *graph that is a collection of *trees. If the root is removed from a tree together with the arcs emanating from that root, the resulting collection of subtrees forms a forest.

for loop *See* do loop.

form A page of printer media. It may be a single sheet or a multipart set, i.e. a number of sheets interleaved with carbon paper or coated so that a single impact will produce similar marks on all sheets. The sheets are frequently joined to form a continuous web, with sprocket holes at the edges to allow automatic feeding through printers. The paper may be preprinted with headings, fixed information, and lines or boxes. Paper used for general-purpose listing is often preprinted with closely spaced groups of lines – a *stave* – to aid visual alignment.

formal language 1. A language with explicit and precise rules for its syntax and semantics. Examples include programming languages and also logics such as *predicate calculus. Thus formal languages contrast with natural languages such as English whose rules, evolving as they have with use, fall short of being either a complete or a precise definition of the syntax, much less the semantics, of the language.

2. A finite or infinite set of *strings, considered in isolation from any possible meaning the strings or the symbols in them may have. If Σ is any set, a Σ-*language* (or *language over* Σ) is any set of Σ-words (*see* word). Σ is referred to as the *alphabet* of such a language.

formal language theory The study of *formal languages (in the sense of sets of strings). A major branch of formal language theory concerns finite descriptions of infinite languages. Such a representation takes the form of an abstract device for generating or recognizing any string of the language (*see* grammar, L-system, automaton). This branch of the subject has applications to the *syntax of programming languages (as distinct from their *semantics, which require quite different mathematical tools). Thus the set of all legal Pascal programs can be thought of as a formal language over the alphabet of Pascal tokens (*see* lexical analyzer). Grammars provide the basis for describing syntax, while automata underly the design of parsers for it. On the other hand it was the desire to formalize natural languages that led to the initiation of the subject in 1956 by Noam Chomsky.

Automata also provide an abstract model for computation itself, thus linking formal language theory with the study of *computability and *complexity. Other issues in formal language theory include decidability of properties of languages, *closure properties of language classes, and characterizations of language classes (*see* Dyck language). An example of a long-standing open question is the decidability of equivalence for deterministic *push-down automata. Another such question is the closure of the class of *context-sensitive languages under *complement: this question was recently resolved in the affirmative, occasioning considerable suprise about the simplicity of the method used.

The subject has been extended beyond the domain of strings to include *tree-languages, sets of *graphs, and sets of infinite strings.

formal logic The study of the analysis of propositions and of proofs, paying attention only to abstract symbols and form and paying no attention whatsoever to the meaning of the abstractions. *See also* symbolic logic.

formal parameter *See* parameter.

formal specification 1. A *specification written and approved in accordance with established standards.

2. A *specification written in a formal notation, such as *VDM or *Z.

formal system An *interpretation of a *formal language.

format The defined structure of the pattern of information that is to be processed, recorded on magnetic or optical media, displayed on a VDU, or printed on a page. The word is also used as a verb: to put data into a predetermined structure or divide a storage medium, such as a disk into sectors, so that it is ready to receive data. *See* disk format, tape format, printer format, instruction format.

formatter 1. of a storage subsystem. The logic assembly that determines the *format of data recorded on magnetic or optical media, and forms part of a device controller; the term is often misused to identify a storage device controller as a whole, including the logic controlling mechanism movements. The logic assembly is basically hardware but

now often includes firmware executed in a dedicated microprocessor (which may perform all the controller functions and not merely those of the formatter). *See also* disk format, tape format.

2. (text formatter) A program that accepts text with embedded formatting instructions and produces a new version of the document with the specified margins, justification, pagination, etc.

3. A program that checks the surface of a magnetic disk or tape by writing and then reading a set pattern to every point on the medium. Any unusable or damaged portions will be marked as such to avoid their use for data storage; alternative portions may be assigned in their place. New media must be formatted before use; the re-formatting of used media has the effect of totally erasing all the data stored thereon, although specialized recovery techniques can sometimes save information after accidental re-formatting.

form overlay The predetermined patterns of printed lines, logos, and fixed information that may be produced by a computer output printer in addition to the variable information. Many nonimpact printers and some impact matrix printers can print the form overlay concurrently with the variable data.

form stop A sensor on a printer that generates a signal to indicate that there is insufficient paper to allow printing to continue.

FORTH A programming language much in vogue among users of microcomputers. FORTH operands are held on a *stack, and programs take the form of strings in *reverse Polish notation. A vital feature of FORTH is that a symbol (a WORD) can be associated with any program string, and such a user-defined word can then be used in expressions on equal terms with the system words (operators). This makes FORTH a flexible *extensible language in which it is possible to define a customized language for, say, the control of a scientific instrument. The FORTH system is very compact; the interpreter and the dictionary containing the system-defined words can be fitted into 8K bytes.

FORTRAN or **Fortran** *Acronym for* formula translation. A programming language widely used for scientific computation. The first version of FORTRAN, FORTRAN I, was issued by IBM in 1956, to be succeeded by FORTRAN II in 1958. This in turn was succeeded by FORTRAN IV, also known as FORTRAN 66 when it was standardized by ANSI. This became the workhorse of the scientific world until it was replaced by FORTRAN 77. This version retained the flavor of the original FORTRAN but introduced some more modern concepts as a gesture towards *structured programming. Discussion of the next version of FORTRAN has been long and acrimonious: known as FORTRAN 8X its definition is expected to be released by ISO in the very near future.

FORTRAN programs use a notation strongly reminiscent of algebra (hence formula translation), and it is thus fairly easy for the scientist to specify his computation. The only data structure is the *array, which corresponds to the matrix commonly used in scientific calculations. FORTRAN II introduced the important idea of independent compilation of subroutines, making it possible to establish libraries of scientific subroutines. The efficient code produced by the early FORTRAN compilers did much to ensure the acceptance of high-level languages as a normal mode of use of computers.

forward bias The d.c. voltage required to maintain current flow in a *bipolar transistor or *diode or to enhance current flow in a *field-effect transistor. For example, a silicon diode will con-

duct current only if its anode is at a positive voltage compared to its cathode; it is then said to be *forward biased.* This voltage will be approximately 0.6 volts. *Compare* reverse bias.

forward error correction (forward error protection) Error correction that is accomplished by appending redundant data to actual data so that certain kinds of errors can be both detected and corrected. This differs from many error correction methods used in communications in that there is no request to resend the data (e.g. from a memory); there is thus no reverse message, hence the word forward. The nature of the redundancy is a function of the expected type of error. *See also* backward error correction, error-correcting code.

forward error recovery A mechanism that prepares a system for possible future errors by recording information to be used in the event of a detected error.

Fourier analysis The analysis of an arbitrary waveform into its constituent sinusoids (of different frequencies and amplitudes). *See* Fourier transform. *See also* orthonormal basis.

Fourier series The infinite trigonometric series

$$\frac{1}{2}a_0 + \sum_{n=1}^{\infty} (a_n \cos nx + b_n \sin nx)$$

By suitable choice of the coefficients a_i and b_i, the series can be made equal to any function of x defined on the interval $(-\pi, \pi)$. If f is such a function, the *Fourier coefficients* are given by the formulas

$$a_n = (1/\pi) \int_{-\pi}^{\pi} f(x) \cos nx \, dx$$
$$(n = 0,1,2,\dots)$$
$$b_n = (1/\pi) \int_{-\pi}^{\pi} f(x) \sin nx \, dx$$
$$(n = 1,2,\dots)$$

Fourier transform A mathematical operation that analyzes an arbitrary waveform into its constituent sinusoids (of different frequencies and amplitudes). This relationship is stated as

$$S(f) = \int_{-\infty}^{\infty} s(t) \exp(-2\pi i f t) \, dt$$

where $s(t)$ is the waveform to be decomposed into a sum of sinusoids, $S(f)$ is the Fourier transform of $s(t)$, and $i = \sqrt{-1}$. An analogous formula gives $s(t)$ in terms of $S(f)$, but with a normalizing factor, $1/2\pi$. Sometimes, for symmetry, the normalizing factor is split between the two relations.

The Fourier transform pair, $s(t)$ and $S(f)$, has to be modified before it is amenable to computation on a digital computer. This modified pair, called the *discrete Fourier transform* must approximate as closely as possible the continuous Fourier transform. The continuous time function is approximated by N samples at time intervals T:

$$g(kT), \ k = 0, 1, \ldots \ n-1$$

The continuous Fourier transform is also approximated by N samples at frequency intervals $1/NT$:

$$G(n/NT), \ n = 0, 1, \ldots \ N-1$$

Since the N values of time and frequency are related by the continuous Fourier transform, then a discrete relationship can be derived:

$$G(n/NT) = \sum_{k=0}^{N-1} g(kt) \exp(-2\pi i n k / N)$$

four Russians algorithm *Another name for* Kronrod's algorithm.

fourth generation of computers. A designation covering machines that were designed after 1970 (approximately), i.e. the current generation. Conceptually the most important criterion that can be used to separate them from the *third generation is that they have been designed to work efficiently with the current generation of high-level languages and are intended to be easier to program by their end-user. From a hardware point of view they are characterized by being constructed largely from *integrated circuits and have multi-megabyte fast random-access memories fabricated in MOS technology. These volatile memories are intimately connected to high-speed disk units so that on power failure or switch-off data in MOS memory is retained by automatic transfer to the disks. On switch-on commonly the system is started up from a bootstrap ROM, which loads the operating system and resident software back into the MOS memory as required.

fourth generation language (4GL) A term used in the data processing community for a high-level language that is designed to allow users who are not trained programmers to develop applications, in particular for querying databases and generating reports. 4GLs are usually nonprocedural languages in which the user describes what is wanted in terms of application, not the computer. The processor takes the user's description and either interprets directly or generates a program (in a database query language or COBOL) that will perform the desired operation. For this reason the latter are sometimes called *application generators*.

FP A notation for functional programming proposed by J. W. Backus in 1978. Backus propounded a functional style of programming, and developed an *algebra of functional programs. FP has not been implemented as a practical programming language.

FPA *Abbrev. for* floating-point accelerator.

FPLA *Abbrev. for* field-programmable logic array. *See* PLA.

fractional part 1. The part of a number to the right of the radix point.

2. *Another name for* mantissa. *See* floating-point notation.

fragmentation The creation of many small areas of memory, which arises as memory is allocated to and then released by processes. The portions of unallocated memory tend to become so small that they fail to satisfy any request and so remain unused. *See also* external fragmentation, internal fragmentation.

frame 1. A single message or packet on a data link using a *data link control protocol such as HDLC, ADCCP, etc. The frame is the unit of error detection, retransmission, etc. A special pattern of bits – a flag – marks the beginning and ending of the frame. In the HDLC protocol, a flag is the 8-bit sequence

01111110

that when followed by any sequence of bits other than another flag denotes the beginning of a frame of data; the flag is maintained as a unique synchronizing sequence of bits since the rules of the protocol require that a 0 is automatically inserted by the sending equipment whenever it detects the presence of five 1s in the input data stream.

2. In general, a complete or self-identifying message in a data communication system.

3. A section of a recording on magnetic tape that comprises a single bit in each track.

4. *See* frames.

frames A knowledge representation formalism. A frame is a list of named slots. Each slot can hold a fact, a pointer to a slot in another frame, a rule for deriving the value of the slot, or a procedure for calculating the value. Frames can be used to represent all the knowledge about a particular object or event. They are often arranged in hierarchies in which frames representing particular entities inherit their slot values from ancestor frames representing generic entities. *See also* object-oriented programming system.

FranzLisp A dialect of *LISP, now superseded by *Common LISP.

Fredholm integral equation *See* integral equation.

freedom of information A catch phrase that has several meanings:

1. a lack of censorship – a state where there is no restriction on the recording of information or on the use of that information;

2. deregulation of the communications media – the removal of restrictions on the use of broadcasting frequencies and communication cables;

3. fair use of *copyright material – the right to impart news and information in western society;

4. the rights an American citizen has under the Freedom of Information Act to study almost any records concerning a government department;

5. technological transfer to third world countries – the rights of underprivileged people to high-technology information free of charge.

In this last case the difficulties in associating the concept of property to information, and the way in which the imparting of information leads to the creation of yet more information, are supporting arguments in favor of free or low-cost technological transfer.

free list *Another name for* available list.

free monoid A particular kind of *monoid, usually involving *strings. Note first that *concatenation is an *associative operation and also that, if Λ is the *empty string, then

$$\Lambda w = w = w\Lambda$$

for all strings w. Hence, for any alphabet Σ (*see* formal language), the set of all Σ-words forms a monoid under concatenation. Furthermore this monoid has the algebraic property of "freeness", which here means that, given any other monoid M and a function f from Σ to M, there is precisely one way of extending f to a monoid *homomorphism from Σ^* to M. There are other free monoids, but they are all *isomorphic to monoids of strings under concatenation. Hence the latter are representative of the free monoids and the phrase is often taken to refer to them specifically. *See also* initial algebra.

free occurrence *See* free variable.

free semigroup A *free monoid, but without the *identity element. *See also* semigroup.

free-space list A list of unoccupied areas of memory in main or backing store. It is a special case of an *available list.

free text retrieval *Another name for* full text retrieval.

free variable In an expression, a variable whose value must be known in order for the whole expression to be evaluated. The idea depends on distinguishing different ways in which variables can occur in expressions. For example, in the following *lambda expression,

$$\lambda f \cdot g(f(\lambda x \cdot x), x, y),$$

the variable x occurs three times. The first occurrence, since it immediately follows a λ, introduces a new "binding" of x, and is therefore called a *binding occurrence*. The second occurrence of x falls inside the "scope" of this binding and is therefore called a *bound occurrence*. The third x is not within the scope of any such binding and is therefore called a *free occurrence*. Equally, the variable f has a binding occurrence and a bound occurrence, while g and y just have one free occurrence each. Since only x, y, and g have free occurrences, they are referred to as the free variables of the expression. The value of the whole expression then depends on what values are given to these free occurrences.

Note that freeness depends on the expression under consideration; thus, although f does not occur free in the whole expression above, it does so in the subexpression

$$g(f(\lambda x \cdot x), x, y).$$

The idea is not restricted to λ-calculus, but arises in connection with all variable-binding operators, such as the logical *quantifiers. It can also be seen as a formalization of *local and *global variables in programs.

frequency The number of complete cycles of a periodically variable quantity, such as a pulse or wave, that occurs in unit time. It is measured in hertz.

frequency distribution A table of the number of occurrences of each of a set of classified observations. The occurrences might arise from the throw of dice, the measurement of a man's height in a particular range of values, or the number of reported cases of a disease in different groups of people classified by their age, sex, or other category.

It is usual practice to choose a fairly small number of categories so that the *relative frequencies within categories are not too small. If no definite upper or lower limits are known, all values above (or below) a certain value are grouped into a single category known as the *upper (or lower) tail*.

Frequency distributions may be summarized by computing *statistics such as the mean (or other *measures of location) and the standard deviation (or other *measures of variation), and sometimes measures of asymmetry or skewness and of compactness (i.e. the proportion of the sample in the center and in the tails).

The term frequency distribution is applied to observed data in a sample. In contrast, *probability distributions are theoretical formulas for the *probability of observing each event. Fitting probability distributions to observed frequency distributions is a fundamental *statistical method of data analysis.

frequency divider An electronic device that is capable of dividing the frequency of a given digital input pulse train by a fixed integer value, n. It often consists of an n-stage *counter, the output frequency at the nth stage of counting being an nth submultiple of the input frequency.

frequency division multiplexing (FDM) A form of *multiplexing in which the *bandwidth of the transmission medium is divided into logical channels over which multiple messages can be simultaneously transmitted. FDM is commonly used worldwide to combine multiple voice-grade telephone signals: 4000 hertz (Hz) is allocated for each channel, 3000 Hz per signal plus a 500 Hz *guard band* (unused frequency band) on either side of the signal. Each signal starts at DC, but the different signals are raised to different frequencies so that the signals do not overlap. Despite the guard bands, strong signal spikes at the edges of a channel can overlap into the next channel, causing noise interference.

See also broadband networking, time division multiplexing.

frequency function *See* probability distributions.

frequency modulation (FM, f.m.) *See* modulation. *See also* disk format.

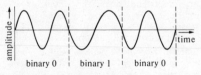

Frequency shift keying, 2 states

frequency shift keying (FSK) A method for representing digital data with analog signals by using a change in the frequency of the carrier to represent information. It is thus a type of *modula-

tion. FSK with two frequencies, corresponding to the digital values 0 and 1 (*see* diagram) is the primary method used by low-speed *modems. *See also* digital data transmission.

front-end processor An *I/O processor that is used to format and/or process input data. The term is sometimes used to refer to a *communication processor. *Compare* back-end processor.

FSA *Abbrev. for* finite-state automaton.

FSK *Abbrev. for* frequency shift keying.

FTAM *Acronym for* File Transfer, Access, and Management. One of the emerging ISO *protocols: it deals with the handling of files in a networked environment. As well as allowing the transfer of files between different operating system environments, the protocol also caters for the situation in which two systems linked via a network wish to allow a *process on one system to access and manipulate parts of a file on the other system. This greater functionality entails a much more complex negotiation phase at the start of the access or manipulation than is needed for the simple transfer of a complete file from one system to the other.

FTP *Abbrev. for* file transfer protocol. *See* file transfer.

Fujitsu A Japanese multiline manufacturing company of interest in the computer field in that, firstly, it was a prime investor in Amdahl Corporation in its formative stages, and, secondly, today manufactures IBM plug-compatible computers, i.e. computers that run IBM systems software. Fujitsu is among the world's top five computing companies in terms of revenues (1988 figures).

full adder *See* adder.

full custom A technique used for the design of *integrated circuits that involves the manipulation of circuit designs at the semiconductor device level. If the device is based on silicon technology for instance, the designer will be concerned with the definition and characterization of silicon structures that will form the elementary components of the IC. The geometric shapes of these components are laid out with a polygon editor on a CAD (*computer-aided design) system. The shapes thus produced may be combined with others from a standard cell library to form the overall geometric design of the IC. Electrical characteristics appropriate for the semiconductor materials that will be used to fabricate the IC are then associated with this geometric definition so that electrical simulation of the behavior of the IC can be carried out. The geometric definition forms the basis of the masks that will be used for fabrication of the device by a process of photolithography. *See also* semicustom.

full duplex *Another name for* duplex.

full subtractor *See* subtractor.

full text retrieval (free text retrieval) A form of information retrieval in which the full text of a document is stored, and retrieval is achieved by searching for occurrences of a given string in the text. This technique can be compared with the alternative of retrieving information by matching one of a set of predetermined keywords.

full tree A tree of *degree m and *level k in which every node at depth less than m has m children and thus, in particular, all leaf nodes are at depth k.

function 1. from one set X to another set Y. A *relation R defined on the *Cartesian product $x \times y$ in which for each element x in X there is precisely one element y in Y with the property that (x,y) is a member of R. It is then customary to talk about a function f, say, and to write

$$f : X \to Y$$

The unique association between elements x and y is denoted by

$$y = f(x) \text{ or } y = fx$$

X is called the *domain* of f, Y the *codomain* of f. Further, y is the *value* of f at the point x or the *image* of x under f. We say that f is a *mapping* or *transformation* between sets X and Y or that f maps X into Y, and that f maps x into y. When the domain X is the Cartesian product of n sets then f is a function of n variables. Otherwise it is a function of one variable.

Examples of functions are readily obtained from the mathematical equivalents of standard functions and operations typically supplied in programming languages. The usual trigonometric functions sin, cos, and tan are functions of one variable. The rule for converting from characters into their integer codes or equivalents is a function.

Functions are often represented pictorially as *graphs.

See also bijection, injection, surjection, operation, homomorphism.

2. A *program unit that given values for input parameters computes a value. Examples include the standard functions such as sin(x), cos(x), exp(x); in addition most languages permit user-defined functions. A function is a "black box" that can be used without any knowledge or understanding of the detail of its internal working. In some languages a function may have *side effects.

functional cohesion *See* cohesion.

functional design A design method in which the system is seen from the functional viewpoint. The design concentrates on isolating high-level functions that can then be decomposed into and synthesized from lower-level functions. Development proceeds as a series of *stepwise refinements of functionality. *Compare* data-driven design.

functional languages (applicative languages) A class of programming languages, and a subclass of the *declarative languages, that is based on *lambda calculus or *recursion equations. Typically a program in a functional language consists of an unordered set of equations that characterize functions and values: functions are characterized by use of recursion, other functions, and values; values are characterized as functions of other values. Ultimately the complete set of equations is sufficient to characterize all functions and values in terms of the primitive functions and values provided by the language. The values that are characterized by the equations include the desired results, and these values are computed by executing the program.

functional partitioning A technique of system or program decomposition in which the primary criterion is that each identified module should contain only elements that all contribute to the achievement of a single goal. Thus each module should perform a single function in the broad sense of an identified job of work (the definition of which is both subjective and dependent upon the level of consideration). The technique is often associated with a general approach, termed *structured design*, that was developed by IBM in the early 1970s.

functional specification *See* module specification.

functional testing *See* performance testing.

functional unit Any major component of a computing system, e.g. CPU, main memory, backing store unit, peripheral device.

function key A key on a *keyboard that initiates an operation or inputs a code that will subsequently initiate an operation.

function point analysis A method derived originally by Albrecht at IBM to estimate the relative complexity and work content of developing a software system. The requirements of a software system are analyzed for five categories: inputs, outputs, files, interfaces, and enquiries. Each of these is then classified into parts that are simple, average, or complex. The results are represented as counts in a matrix with a total of 15 cells; each raw count is weighted by multiplying it by standard factors, and the unadjusted function point count, U, is then obtained by summing each cell-weighted value.

The processing complexity for the software is estimated for each of 14 general characteristics that cover the type of product, and how it is to be used and installed. For each characteristic a value is selected to represent its scale of influence. The 14 values are summed to give the processing complexity adjustment, PC, which will range from 0 to 70. The PC is used to calculate the adjusted function point score from its unadjusted score U. A measure of the work involved in developing the software is then obtained from a formula that allows for further score adjustments where necessary.

functor A *function that maps one *category into another. In computing terms a special functor represents mappings between mathematical concepts, such as *sets and *functions, and their implementation in a programming language; this is often called the *representation functor*. The idea generalizes to include mappings between different *abstract machines.

fusible link (fuse link) A physical link providing electrical continuity across an individual cell in the memory array of a *PROM. With this link intact the cell, when interrogated, will display a known *logic state. During programming this link can be destroyed, forcing the cell to take on the complementary logic state; this process is irreversible.

Fusible links are used in a similar manner in field-programmable logic arrays (*see* PLA).

fuzzy theory A branch of logic designed specifically for representing knowledge and human reasoning in such a way that it is amenable to processing by computer. Thus fuzzy theory is applicable to *expert systems, knowledge engineering, and *artificial intelligence.

The more traditional propositional and predicate logics do not allow for degrees of uncertainty, indicated by words or phrases such as fairly, very, quite possibly. Instead of truth values such as true and false it is possible to introduce a multiple-valued logic consisting of, for example, the values true, not true, very true, not very true, more or less true, not very false, very false, not false, and false. Alternatively an interval such as [0,1] can be introduced and the degree of truth can be represented by some real number in this range. Predicates are then functions that map not into {true, false} but into these more general domains.

Fuzzy theory is concerned with the study of *sets and *predicates of this kind. There emerge such concepts as *fuzzy sets, fuzzy relationships*, and *fuzzy quantifiers*.

G

Galerkin's method *See* finite-element method.

gallium arsenide (GaAs) devices Semiconductor integrated-circuit devices that are implemented using gallium arsenide as the intrinsic *semiconductor material in preference to, say, silicon. Gallium arsenide has certain advantages over other semiconductor materials, in particular in high-speed applications and in the fabrication of optical and optically coupled devices such as light-emitting diodes and optoisolators.

Galois field *Another name for* finite field (named for the French mathematician Évariste Galois).

game theory A mathematical theory of decision-making by participants with conflicting interests in a competitive situation, originated by Emile Borel in 1921 and rigorously established by John von Neumann in 1928. The theory attempts to gain insights into economic situations by isolating these aspects, which occur in their simplest form in games of strategy.

In a two-player game, as defined by the theory, each participant has a choice of plays for which there are several possible outcomes, gains or losses, depending on the opponent's choice. An optimum strategy states the relative frequency with which a player's choices should be used, so as to maximize his average gain (or minimize his average loss). The problem of determining the optimum strategy can be formulated as a problem in *linear programming. Generalizations to *n*-person games are included in the theory.

gap on magnetic tape. Any gap between groups of signals recorded on magnetic tape, but usually the interblock gap (*see* block).

gap theorem A theorem in complexity theory that, like the *speedup theorem, can be expressed in terms of abstract complexity measures (*see* Blum's axioms) but will be more understandable in the context of time:

given any *total *recursive function

$$g(n) \geqslant n$$

there exists a total recursive function $S(n)$ such that

$$\text{DTIME}(S(n)) = \text{DTIME}(g(S(n)))$$

(*see* complexity classes). In other words there is a "gap" between time bounds $S(n)$ and $g(S(n))$ within which the minimal space complexity of no language lies.

This has the following counter-intuitive consequence: given two universal models of computation, say a Turing machine that makes one move per century and the other a very fast random-access machine capable of performing a million arithmetic operations per second, then there is a total recursive function $S(n)$ such that any language recognizable in time $S(n)$ on one machine is also recognizable within time $S(n)$ on the other.

garbage Information in a memory that is no longer valid or wanted. It is usually the result of *memory compaction operations. The removal of this superfluous information from the memory is known as *garbage collection* and is usually associated with memory compaction.

gate *See* logic gate.

gate array A form of *programmable device in which the component *logic gates can be interconnected in an arbitrary manner during manufacture to give a *combinational or *sequential circuit of considerable *height.

gateway A device that interconnects two *networks, and whose presence is usually visible to network users (as distinct from a *bridge, whose presence is generally not visible). A gateway may be required to deal with one or more of the following differences between networks it connects:

(a) change of addressing domain – where the networks have addressing domains managed by separate groups, a gateway may be used to handle address transformations for messages traversing the gateway;

(b) control of charging – where the networks have different approaches to charging (e.g. a local area network that imposes no charges connecting to a wide area network that charges on a per-packet basis) a gateway may be used to handle user authorization and usage accounting;

(c) change of protocol – where the networks use different protocols, a gateway may be used to carry out necessary protocol conversion (if practicable) or to intercept attempts by a user on network to use functions not available on the other and to supply suitable responses.

The terms bridge, gateway, and *relay are among those whose meanings vary between different communities of users at a given time, and within a given community of users at different times.

gather write The function of writing to memory a block of data comprising items of data that have been retrieved directly from scattered memory locations and/or registers.

Gaussian distribution *Another name for* normal distribution.

Gaussian elimination *See* linear algebraic equations.

Gaussian noise *Noise whose distribution of amplitude over time is *Gaussian.

Gaussian quadrature *See* numerical integration.

GBS method The Gragg–Burlisch–Stoer *extrapolation method based on theoretical results obtained by Gragg, implemented by Burlisch and Stoer. *See* Gragg's extrapolation method.

GCD *Abbrev. for* greatest common divisor.

GCR *Abbrev. for* group code recording. *See* disk format, tape format.

generalized linear model (GLM) In regression analysis, one of a wide class of model in which the fitted value is a *transformation of a *linear predictor* and the frequency distribution is not necessarily the *normal distribution. Apart from the standard linear regression model (*see* regression analysis), the most important cases are (1) for integer counts, the logarithmic transformation and the *Poisson distribution, and (2) for proportions, the logistic transformation and the *binomial distribution.

GLMs may be used in regression analysis where inspection of *residuals indicates that the distribution is other than the normal distribution, and may also be used to analyze *contingency tables.

The analysis uses the method of maximum *likelihood, solved by iterative use of *weighted least squares estimation.

generalized sequential machine *See* sequential machine. *See also* gsm mapping.

general-purpose computer (GP computer; GP) A computer that can be used for any function for which it can be conveniently programmed.

general-purpose interface bus (GPIB) *See* bus.

general recursive function *See* recursive function.

generating polynomial *See* polynomial.

generations of computers. An informal system of classifying computer systems as advances have been made in electronic technology and, latterly, in software. Since the design of digital computers has been a continuous process for the past four decades – by a wide variety of people in different countries, faced with different problems – it is difficult and not very profitable to try and establish where 'generations' start and finish. *See* first generation, second generation, third generation, fourth generation, fifth generation.

generator 1. A program that accepts the definition of an operation that is to be accomplished, and automatically constructs a program for the purpose. The earliest example of this kind of program was the *sort generator*, which took a specification of the file format and the sorted order required, and produced a sorting program. This was followed by *report generators*, which constructed programs to print reports from files containing information in a specified format. The best-known program of this kind is *RPG II.

2. An element g of a *group G with the property that the various powers

$$g^0, g^1, g^2, \ldots$$

ultimately include all the elements of G. Such a group is said to be a *cyclic group*; it is also an abelian *group. Generators can also be defined for *monoids in a similar way.

The set of generators S of a group G is a subset of G having the property that every element of G can be expressed as a combination of elements of S. *See also* group graph.

generator matrix *See* linear code, convolutional code.

generic A term used in *Ada to denote a *subprogram or *package that can be parameterized with *parameters that can be types and subprograms as well as values and variables. A generic package or subprogram provides a template from which a particular *instantiation can be produced by providing the appropriate parameters.

geodesic *See* reachability.

giga- (symbol: G) A prefix indicating a multiple of one billion, 10^9, or, when the binary system is used, as in computing, a multiple of 2^{30}, i.e.

$$1\ 073\ 741\ 824$$

GIGO *Acronym for* garbage in garbage out, signifying that a program working on incorrect data produces incorrect results.

Gilbert–Varshamov bound The theorem that the maximum possible number, N, of codewords in a *binary *linear *block code is bounded by

$$N \geqslant \frac{2^n}{\sum\limits_{r=0}^{d-1} \binom{n}{r}}$$

where the *code length is n digits, and the codewords are at a minimum *Hamming distance d. *See also* coding bounds, Hamming bound.

GINO *Acronym for* graphical input output. A package of FORTRAN subroutines for computer graphics. The GINO subroutines define a "language" for the production of elaborate graphics, including three-dimensional objects viewed in various projections. GINO separates the abstract description of the display from the device-dependent features of particular devices, and thus makes graphics programming largely machine-independent. GINO has provided a de facto graphics standard for many years, especially in the UK, but it is now being superseded by *GKS.

GKS *Abbrev. for* graphics kernel system. A set of graphical routines that can be used by application programmers, i.e. an *API. The names and functions are defined in ISO 7942 and ANS X3.124 1985. The language bindings (the way the functions can be invoked from standard programming languages) are defined in ISO/IEC 8651. GKS can be implemented at a level dependent upon the complexity of the task and the available computing resource. The lowest level (0a) is simple support for two-dimensional graphical output. The highest level (2c) handles input requests, simultaneous output to multiple workstations, and input/output to a *CGM (computer graphics metafile). All levels

are within the capability of typical personal computers. A three-dimensional version, *GKS-3D, has been developed and is defined in ISO.

GKS-3D A set of graphical routines for constructing two-dimensional representations of three-dimensional objects. *See also* GKS.

4GL *Abbrev. for* fourth generation language.

glass-box testing (white-box testing) A style of *testing that considers the inputs, the outputs, and the relationships specified between them, together with knowledge of the internal structure or processing, in order to derive test inputs that will demonstrate that the required outputs occur. Usually the term is applied to software. *Compare* black-box testing.

glitch An intermittent transient fault that occurs when two communicating *asynchronous processes fail to complete their hardware interface *protocol. It is usually caused by a *flip-flop in a metastable state.

global A term used to define the scope of an entity: global entities are accessible from all parts of a program. By contrast, *local entities are accessible only in the program module within which they are defined.

global discretization error (global truncation error) *See* discretization error.

global optimization *See* optimization (in programming).

Gödel numbering of a formal system. A one-to-one mapping (i.e. an *injection) of the symbols, formulas, and finite sequences of formulas of the formal system onto some subset of the natural numbers. The mapping must be such that there is an algorithm that, for any symbol, formula, or finite sequence of formulas, identifies the corresponding natural number; this is the *Gödel number* of that object. There must also be an algorithm that, given any natural number, indicates whether it is the Gödel number of the object; if it is, the algorithm must identify the object.

Conferring Gödel numberings has the effect of permitting statements about elements in the nonnumeric system to be transformed into statements about natural numbers. Conversely, since much is known about natural numbers, it becomes possible to prove assertions about aspects of nonnumeric systems. The mapping was first used by the German mathematician Kurt Gödel.

Gödel's incompleteness theorems Two fundamental theorems in mathematical logic, proved by Kurt Gödel in 1931. The first concerns the formalization of basic arithmetic. Gödel showed that, in any logical system powerful enough to express arithmetical operations, there must exist sentences that are neither provable nor refutable. To put it another way, there exist statements about arithmetic that, while true, cannot be proved. The second theorem is similarly negative-sounding: no logical system can be powerful enough to provide a proof of its own consistency. These discoveries marked a turning-pont in our understanding of formal reasoning. In particular they forced the abandonment of "Hilbert's program", i.e. of the search for a provably consistent and complete formal basis for the whole of mathematics itself.

Equally significant are the proof methods that Gödel used. One device was to encode logical formulae as numbers (*see* Gödel numbering), so that manipulations of formulae could be "programmed" as numerical computations. (This early exercise in programming also marked the beginning of *recursive function theory.) The other device was to use this numerical encoding to produce a formula that in effect asserts its own unprovability. The idea is seen in statements such as "this sentence is false", the Cretan liar paradox, and Russell's paradox. Gödel's construction however is fully formal: the reference to "this sentence" is handled by the numerical encoding, without any need for vague English words. A relationship exists with the paradoxical *combinator, while a similar approach can be used to show the undecidability of the *halting problem as well as many results in *complexity theory, where Gödel numbering is applied to *Turing machines rather than logical formulae.

Confusingly perhaps, Gödel is also responsible for a completeness theorem, but this applies to pure *predicate calculus without formalized arithmetic.

Golay codes A family of *perfect *linear *error-correcting *block codes, of which the most important is the binary (23,12) Golay code. There is also a ternary (11,6) Golay code. Golay codes can be arranged to be *cyclic.

golden section search A *binary search algorithm, but instead of taking the middle element of the next section a proportion is taken that speeds up the convergence.

golfball printer A type of *serial *solid-font printer in which the characters of the typeface are molded onto a spherical carrier. The carrier is rotated about two axes to bring the required character opposite the paper, and is then struck against the paper and intervening ink ribbon. The mechanism, first devised as a typewriter, is complex and slow (about 10–12 cps) and is now obsolete.

Good–de Bruijn diagram (Good–de Bruijn graph) A directed *graph illustrating the possible succession of states of a *shift register. Each possible state of the shift register (indicated by its contents) is represented by a node in the graph; from each node a set of arcs lead to all its possible immediate successors. (Succession involves one clocking of the shift register, with some serial input.) If there are n cells in a *q-ary shift register, there will be q^n nodes, each with q arcs leading from it, and thus q^{n+1} arcs altogether.

When the serial input is some function of the current state, the behavior of the shift register is described by a Good–de Bruijn graph with some arcs deleted: such subgraphs are used in the study of *feedback registers.

goodness-of-fit test A statistical *significance test of the hypothesis that a sample *frequency distribution is adequately explained by fitting a particular model. When data are counts of numbers of occurrences, the test uses the *chi-squared distribution. Testing goodness of fit of continuous observations is less easy, requiring understanding of *analysis of variance, and is only possible when some observations are replicated.

Goppa codes A family of *linear *error-correcting *block codes. The most important classes of Goppa codes are the *Reed–Solomon codes and the binary *Golay (23,12) code. Goppa codes are not in general *cyclic.

GOSIP *Acronym for* government open systems interconnection profile. A set of functional standards based predominantly on ISO OSI standards and intended to form the basis for the procurement of computer systems to be purchased by the UK government.

GOTO statement A program statement that causes a *jump; it is thus a jump instruction in a high-level language. It causes the normal flow of control to be broken by designating an explicit successor statement, usually identified by a label, e.g.

```
        GOTO 99
        <statements>
99:  ...
```

Modern programming practice deprecates the use of GOTO since its use makes programs more difficult to follow, the flow of control being less visibly explicit. GOTO is, however, sometimes unavoidable, particularly in error situations where it is necessary to abort execution of a number of nested loops or procedures, when the language does not provide for exceptions.

GP *Short for* general purpose, general-purpose computer.

GPIB *Abbrev. for* general-purpose interface bus. *See* bus.

graceful degradation *See* fail-soft.

Gragg's extrapolation method (GBS method) An *extrapolation method for the solution of *ordinary differential equations based on the *midpoint rule. For stiff problems a similar scheme can be based on the implicit midpoint rule:

$$y_{n+1} = y_n + h f(x_n + \tfrac{1}{2}h, (y_n + y_{n+1})/2)$$

where h is the stepsize.

grammar One of the principal ways of specifying an infinite *formal language by finite means. Like a *semi-Thue system, a grammar consists of a set of rules (called *productions*) that may be used to derive one string from another by substring replacement. The strings of the specified language are obtained by repeated application of these rules, starting from some initial string. A grammar however has the additional feature that the alphabet is divided into a set T of *terminal symbols* and a set N of *nonterminal symbols*. While productions may be composed arbitrarily of terminals and nonterminals, the specified language contains strings of terminals only.

A grammar G can therefore be defined as comprising two sets of symbols T and N, a semi-Thue system over the union $T \cup N$, and a distinguished member S of N. The *language generated by G* is the set of all strings over T that can be derived from S by a sequence of substring replacements (*see* semi-Thue system); S is known as the *start symbol* or *sentence symbol*. As an example, let T be $\{b,c\}$, N be $\{S,A\}$ and let the productions be

(1) $S \rightarrow SA$

(2) $S \rightarrow A$

(3) $A \rightarrow bc$

Then, for instance, starting from S we can derive *bcbcbc* via the following sequence (among others):

SA	–	by production 1
SAA	–	by production 1
AAA	–	by production 2
$bcAA$	–	by production 3
$bcbcA$	–	by production 3
$bcbcbc$	–	by production 3

The language generated is

$$\{bc, bcbc, bcbcbc, \ldots, \text{etc.}\}$$

These are the only strings of *b*s and *c*s derivable from S. A string such as *SAbcA*, which is derivable from S but still contains nonterminals, is referred to as a *sentential form*.

This is the most general form of grammar. Typically however some restriction is placed on the form that productions may take (*see* regular grammar, context-free grammar, context-sensitive grammar). The syntax of programming languages is usually specified by context-free grammars; the example given above is context-free, although the language specified is regular.

A slightly different way of generating a language is by means of an *L-system. A different approach altogether is to define a machine that tests any string for membership of the language, i.e. an *automaton.

grandfather file (grandparent file) *See* file recovery.

granularity A measure of the size of the *segments into which memory is divided for purposes of either *memory protection or *virtual-memory management.

graph 1. A nonempty but finite set of *vertices* (or *nodes*) together with a set of *edges* that join pairs of distinct vertices. If an edge e joins vertices v_1 and v_2, then v_1 and v_2 are said to be *incident* with e and the vertices are said to be *adjacent*; e is the unordered pair (v_1,v_2).

A graph is usually depicted in a pictorial form in which the vertices appear as dots or other shapes, perhaps labeled for identification purposes, and the edges are shown as lines joining the appropriate points. If direction is added to each edge of a graph, a *directed graph* or *digraph* is obtained. The edges then form a finite set of *ordered pairs of distinct vertices, and are often called *arcs*. In the pictorial representation, arrows can be placed on each edge. With no direction specified, the graph is said to be *undirected*.

Although helpful visually these representations are not suitable for manipulation by computer. More useful representations use an *incidence matrix or an *adjacency matrix.

Graphs are used in a wide variety of ways in computing: the vertices will usually represent objects of some kind and the edges will represent connections of a physical or logical nature between the vertices. So graphs can be used to model in a mathematical fashion such diverse items as a computer and all its attached peripherals, a network of computers, *parse trees, logical dependencies between *subroutines or nonterminals in a *grammar, *VLSI diagrams, and related items in *databases. *Trees and *lists are special kinds of graphs.

Certain variations exist in the definition of a graph. There is some dispute about whether one edge can join a vertex to itself, whether empty sets are involved, whether an infinite number of vertices and edges are permitted, and so on.

See also connected graph, network, weighted graph.

2. of a function f. The set of all *ordered pairs (x,y) with the property that $y = f(x)$. Often such a graph is represented by a curve.

graphic characters See character set.

graphics See computer graphics.

graphics adapter (or **adaptor**) A printed circuit board that can be added to a personal computer to enable it to drive a VDU capable of displaying computer graphics, or allowing higher resolution or color. It therefore determines the maximum graphics capability of the system. The most widely used graphics adapters are for IBM and IBM-compatible systems and include the *VGA, *EGA, *MCGA, and *CGA.

graph plotter See plotter.

gray book A publication by the National Computer Security Center (*NCSC) that deals with the security aspects of subsystems intended to form secure parts of an overall secure system.

Gray code A binary (n, n) *block code having the following properties:
(a) there are 2^n codewords, each of length n bits;
(b) successive codewords differ by the complementation of a single bit, i.e. the *Hamming distance between them is unity.
A Gray code can be conveniently represented by its *transition sequence*, i.e. the ordered list of bit positions that change when moving from one codeword to the next. The *Good-de Bruijn graph of a Gray code forms a *Hamiltonian cycle. Gray codes are used in encoding the positions of shafts, wheels, etc., in order to avoid the problems that would arise when several digits were supposed to change at the same time.

gray-level array An array of numbers, each of which represents the level of brightness in the corresponding area of a visual scene. The gray-level array

might represent the output of a television camera or similar device.

gray scale A scale that assigns values to the range of gray tones that exist between black and white. The term is also used to refer to gradations between other extremes − in particular, levels of brilliance on a cathode-ray tube display. The information content and apparent resolution of a picture on a graphics display can be improved if the relative brilliance of each dot can be specified.

greatest common divisor (GCD) of two integers m and n. The largest integer, d, that exactly divides both m and n. If $d = 1$ then m and n are said to be *relatively prime*. For example, the GCD of 18 and 24 is 6; 21 and 25 are relatively prime.

greedy method An algorithm that, with a certain goal in mind, will attempt at every stage to do whatever it can, whenever it can, to get nearer to that goal immediately. In other words the method surrenders a possible longer-term advantage in favor of an immediate move toward the objective.

green book The *coloured book defining the virtual terminal protocol used within the UK academic community.

Greibach normal form A restricted type of *context-free grammar, namely one in which all productions have the form
$$A \to bC_1 \dots C_n$$
i.e. each right-hand side consists of a terminal followed by (zero or more) nonterminals. Any context-free language is generated by such a grammar, except that derivation of the empty string, Λ, requires the additional production
$$S \to \Lambda$$
One significance of this form is that it makes clear the existence of an equivalent *pushdown automaton: on reading b the PDA can pop A from the stack and push $C_1 \dots C_n$.

grey book The *coloured book defining the electronic mail protocol used within the UK academic community. *See also* gray book.

Grosch's law The best known of many attempts to provide a measure of computer performance in terms of price, originally formulated by H. R. J. Grosch in 1953 as:

performance = constant × price²

Reliance on this law, which was approximately true at the time, led to the concept of "economy of scale", i.e. that large computers were less expensive per operation than small computers. Since that time other values of the exponent have been suggested: a good case can be made for the value 1 rather than 2. Current (LSI) technology has almost completely invalidated Grosch's law.

group A *set G on which there is defined a *dyadic operation ∘ (mapping $G \times G$ into G) that satisfies the following properties:

(a) ∘ is *associative;

(b) ∘ has an identity, i.e. there is a unique element e in G with the property that

$$x \circ e = e \circ x = x$$

for all x in G; e is called the *identity* of the group;

(c) *inverses* exist in G, i.e. for each x in G there is an inverse, denoted by x^{-1}, with the property that

$$x \circ x^{-1} = x^{-1} \circ x = e$$

These are the *group axioms*.

Certain kinds of groups are of particular interest. If the dyadic operation ∘ is *commutative, the group is said to be a *commutative group* or an *abelian group* (named for the Norwegian mathematician Niels Abel).

If there is only a finite number of elements n in the group, the group is said to be *finite*; n is then the *order* of the group. Finite groups can be represented or depicted by means of a *Cayley table.

If the group has a *generator then it is said to be *cyclic*; a cyclic group must be abelian.

The group is a very important *algebraic structure that underlies many other algebraic structures such as *rings and *fields. There are direct applications of groups in the study of symmetry, in the study of transformations and in particular *permutations, and also in error detecting and error correcting as well as in the design of fast adders.

Groups were originally introduced for solving an algebraic problem. By group theory it can be shown that algorithmic methods of a particular kind cannot exist for finding the roots of a general polynomial of degree greater than four. *See also* semigroup.

group code *Another name for* linear code.

group code recording (GCR) *See* disk format, tape format.

group graph A directed *graph that represents a finite *group; the vertices of the graph represent elements of the group and the edges represent *generators of the group. If edge E (representing generator g) joins vertices V and V' (representing group elements v and v' respectively) then

$$v \circ g = v'$$

where ∘ is the group operation. Each vertex of the group graph will have outdegree (*see* degree) equal to the number of generators of the group.

group mark A notation within a record that indicates the start or finish of a group of related fields. In the case of repeated fields, the group mark often indicates the number of repetitions of such fields.

Grzegorczyk hierarchy *See* hierarchy of functions.

gsm mapping *Short for* generalized sequential machine mapping. A function that is the response function of a generalized *sequential machine, and therefore generalizes the notion of *sequential function. Without constraining the machine to have a finite state-set, generalized sequentiality is equivalent to the following property of *initial subwords preservation*:

for all u,v in I^*, $f(uv)$ has the form $f(u)w$ for some w in O^*, where I^* and O^* are the sets of all input and output strings.

guard band *See* frequency division multiplexing.

gulp *Rare* Several, usually two, *bytes.

H

hacker 1. A person who attempts to breach the *security of a computer system by access from a remote point, especially by guessing or otherwise obtaining a *password. The motive may be merely personal satisfaction, for example by endeavoring to access a system in another country, but it may occasionally have a sinister intent.
2. Originally, a person who develops software by trial and error.

Hadamard codes *See* Hadamard matrices.

Hadamard matrices A family of matrices, a Hadamard matrix H of order m being an $m \times m$ matrix, all of whose elements are either $+1$ or -1, and such that

$$H H^T = \lambda I$$

where H^T is the *transpose of H, I is the *identity matrix, and λ is a scalar quantity. They are usually written in "normalized" form, i.e. the rows and columns have been signed so that the top row and left column consist of $+1$ elements only. Hadamard matrices exist

only for order $m = 1$, 2, or $4r$ for some r. It is known that they exist for all orders $m = 2^s$. It is conjectured, but not known that they exist for all orders $m = 4r$.

The rows of any Hadamard matrix form an *orthonormal basis, from which property follows many of their applications in the theory of *codes, *digital signal processing, and statistical *sampling. When the order $m = 2^s$, they are called *Sylvester matrices*.

A Sylvester matrix has an equivalent matrix whose rows form a set of m-point *Walsh functions or, in a different arrangement, Paley functions. Various *linear *Hadamard codes* can be derived from a normalized Sylvester matrix in which $+1$ has been replaced by 0, and -1 by 1.

half adder *See* adder.

half duplex Involving or denoting a connection between two endpoints, either physical or logical, over which data may travel in both directions, but not both simultaneously. An important parameter of a half-duplex connection is the *turnaround time*, i.e. the time it takes to reverse the roles of sender and receiver. *See also* duplex, simplex.

half subtractor *See* subtractor.

half word A unit of storage comprising half the number of bits in a computer's *word.

halt or **HALT** A program instruction that stops execution of the program. Originally a halt instruction actually halted the processor (hence the name), but now it more often causes a *trap into the operating system so that the operating system can take over control and, for example, start another program.

halting problem A *decision problem that was investigated by Alan Turing. Suppose M is a *Turing machine and let x be an input to M. If we start the machine running two things might happen: after a finite number of steps the machine might stop, or it might run on forever. Is there any way to test which of these two situations will occur? This is the halting problem. In fact there is no effective procedure that, given any Turing machine and its input, will decide whether or not the calculation ever terminates.

The halting problem is said to be unsolvable or undecidable. It is one example of many unsolvable problems in mathematics and computer science. It has profound practical implications: if it were solvable it would be possible to write a "program tester" that, given (say) any Pascal program and its input, would print "yes" if the program terminated after a finite number of steps and "no" if it did not.

Hamiltonian cycle (Hamilton cycle) A *cycle of a *graph in the course of which each vertex of the graph is visited once and once only.

Hamming bound (sphere-packing bound) The theorem that the number, N, of codewords in a *binary *linear code is bounded by

$$N \leqslant \frac{2^n}{\sum\limits_{r=0}^{e} \binom{n}{r}}$$

where the *code length is n digits, and the code is capable of correcting e errors. *See also* coding bounds, Gilbert–Varshamov bound.

Hamming codes A family of *binary *linear *perfect *error-correcting *block codes. They are capable of correcting any single error occurring in the block. Considered as (n, k) block codes, Hamming codes have

$$n = 2^m - 1, \quad k = n - m$$

where m characterizes the particular code. Where multiple-error-correcting abilities are required, Hamming codes

may be generalized into *Bose-Chaudhuri-Hocquenghem (BCH) codes. The code was discovered by R. W. Hamming in 1950.

Hamming distance (Hamming metric) In the theory of *block codes intended for error-detection or error-correction, the Hamming distance $d(u, v)$ between two words u and v, of the same length, is equal to the number of symbol places in which the words differ from one another. If u and v are of finite length n then their Hamming distance is finite since

$$d(u, v) \leqslant n$$

It can be called a distance since it is nonnegative, nil-reflexive, symmetric, and triangular:

$$0 \leqslant d(u, v)$$
$$d(u, v) = 0 \text{ iff } u = v$$
$$d(u, v) = d(v, u)$$
$$d(u, w) \leqslant d(u, v) + d(v, w)$$

The Hamming distance is important in the theory of *error-correcting codes and *error-detecting codes: if, in a block code, the codewords are at a *minimum Hamming distance* d from one another, then

(a) if d is even, the code can detect $d - 1$ symbols in error and correct $\frac{1}{2}d - 1$ symbols in error;

(b) if d is odd, the code can detect $d - 1$ symbols in error and correct $\frac{1}{2}(d - 1)$ symbols in error.

See also Hamming space, perfect codes, coding theory, coding bounds, Hamming bound.

Hamming metric *Another name for* Hamming distance.

Hamming radius *See* Hamming space.

Hamming space In coding theory, a mathematical space in which words of some given length may be situated, the separation of points in the space being measured by the *Hamming distance. The dimensionality of the space is equal to the number of digits in the words;

the coordinate in each dimension is given by each successive digit in the words.

The *Hamming sphere* is the set of all words in Hamming space whose Hamming distance from some given word (the "center") does not exceed some given value (the *Hamming radius*).

Hamming sphere *See* Hamming space.

Hamming weight In coding theory, the number of nonzero digits in a word. It is numerically identical with the *Hamming distance between the word in question and the *zero word.

handle *See* bottom-up parsing.

handshake An exchange of signals that establishes communications between two or more devices. The handshake synchronizes the devices and allows data to be transferred successfully. The signals have various meanings, including
"I am waiting to transmit."
"I am ready to receive."
"I am not ready to receive."
"I am switched on."
"The data is available."
"Data has been read successfully."

hands off *See* hands on.

hands on A mode of operation of a system in which an operator is in control. The operator literally has hands on a keyboard and other switches to control the processes to be carried out by the system. The dependence on the capability of the operator to run a medium-size or large computer has been reduced by the introduction of supervisor programs or operating systems.

When no operator intervention is required the mode of operation can be described as *hands off*.

hang-up 1. A state in which a program has come to an unexpected halt, e.g. because it is trying to read data from a device that is not connected to the processor.

2. In the context of time-sharing systems, the signal received by the program when a remote terminal breaks its connection ("hangs up the telephone").

hard copy A printed or otherwise permanent copy of data from a processing system.

hard disk (metallic disk) A magnetic recording medium consisting of an aluminum substrate coated or plated – usually on both sides – with a magnetic material. Hard disk is used as a generic term and includes the *magnetic disks used in *Winchester technology, *disk cartridges, and *disk packs. *Compare* floppy disk, optical disk.

hard-sectored disk *See* sector.

hardware The physical portion of a computer system, including the electrical/electronic components (e.g. devices and circuits), electromechanical components (e.g. a disk drive), and mechanical (e.g. cabinet) components. *Compare* software.

hardware character generation A technique whereby a display device such as a VDU, printer, or plotter will, on receipt of certain codes, display characters of a style and size determined by the device's internal circuitry. The computer driving the peripheral specifies only which character is to be displayed; it has no control over the individual *pixels that make up the character. *Compare* bit mapping.

hardware circuitry *See* logic circuit.

hardware description An unambiguous method of describing the interconnection and behavior of the electrical and electronic subset of the computer hardware. There are a number of computer hardware description languages (*see* CHDL).

hardware maintenance *See* maintenance.

hardware reliability A statement of the ability of hardware to perform its functions for some period of time. It is usually expressed as MTBF (mean time between failures).

hardware security The use of hardware, e.g. *bounds registers or *locks and keys, to assist in providing computer security.

hardwired Denoting circuits that are permanently interconnected to perform a specific function, as distinct from circuits addressed by software in a program and therefore capable of performing a variety of functions.

Harvard Mark I The name given at Harvard University to the Automatic Sequence Controlled Calculator (ASCC), an electromechanical computer based on the ideas of Harvard's Howard H. Aiken. This machine, which followed a sequence of instructions on paper tape, was started in 1938; it was developed and built in collaboration with IBM engineers at their laboratories, and became operational at Harvard in 1944. It was donated by IBM to Harvard later that year. The Mark I was used by the US navy for ballistics and ship design.

hash function *See* hashing algorithm, hashing.

hashing A technique that is used for organizing tables to permit rapid *searching or *table look-up, and is particularly useful for tables to which items are added in an unpredictable manner, e.g. the symbol table of a compiler. Each item to be placed in the table has a unique *key*. To place it in the *hash table* a *hash function* is used, which maps the keys onto a set of integers (the *hash values*) that range over the table size. The function is chosen to distribute the keys fairly evenly over the table (*see* hashing algorithm); since it is not a unique mapping, two different keys may map onto the same integer.

In the simplest version of the technique, the hash value identifies a primary position in the table; if this is already occupied, successive positions are examined until a free one is found (treating the table as circular). The item with its key is inserted in the table at this position. To locate an item in the table a similar algorithm is used. The hash value of the key is computed and the table entry at this position is examined. If the key matches the required key, the item has been located; if not, successive table positions are examined until either an entry with a matching key is found or an empty position is found. In the latter case it can be concluded that the key does not exist in the table, since the insertion procedure would have placed it in this empty position. For the technique to work, there must be rather more table positions than there are entries to be accommodated. Provided that the table is not more than 60% full, an item can on average be located in a hash table by examining at most two table positions.

More sophisticated techniques can be used to deal with the problem of *collisions*, which occur when the position indicated by the hash value is already occupied; this improves even further the performance of the table look-up. Table look-up and insertion of new items can be interleaved, but if items are deleted from the table the space they occupied cannot normally be reused.

hashing algorithm An algorithm that, for a given key k, yields a function $f(k)$; this in turn yields the starting point for a *hash search* for the key k. The function f is called the *hash function*. A typical hash function is the remainder modulo p, where p is a prime,

$$f(k) \equiv k \pmod{p}$$

where k is interpreted as an integer. Another hash function uses a constant A and defines $f(k)$ as the leading bits of the least significant half of the product *Ak*. *See also* hashing.

hash P complete *See* counting problem.

hash search *See* hashing algorithm.

hash table *See* hashing.

hash total A number produced by adding together (or otherwise combining) corresponding fields over all the records of a file, when such a total does not have any external meaning but is used solely to verify the records in the file. The hash total is amended whenever a change occurs to the relevant field; the file is verified by recomputing the hash total, and any corruption to the values in the field will be shown by a discrepancy between the stored total and the recomputed total. *See also* control record.

hash value *See* hashing.

hazard A potential or actual malfunction of a *logic circuit during change(s) of state of input variables. Hazards result from the nonideal behavior of actual switching elements, e.g. noninstantaneous operation, turn-on time different from turn-off time.

In the UK the word hazard is sometimes used as the equivalent of *race condition.

HCI *Abbrev. for* human-computer interface (or interaction).

HDLC *Abbrev. for* high-level data link control. A *data link control protocol developed by ISO in response to IBM's *SDLC protocol, which is a subset of HDLC. CCITT defined a different subset of HDLC (*see* LAP) as the second (data link) layer of the *X.25 protocol.

head 1. The part of a peripheral mechanism that is in contact with the medium or very close to it and that is directly responsible for writing data or patterns onto the medium or for reading or erasing them. The word is most frequently used of a *magnetic head* in a *disk drive or tape transport (*see* magnetic tape), an *optical head* in an optical storage device, or a *print head* in a *serial printer. *See also* read/write head.

2. The first item in a *list. *See also* list head.

head crash The accidental and disastrous contact of a *read/write head with the surface of a hard disk as it rotates in a *disk drive. Normally the head flies just above the surface. The disk has to be thrown away after a head crash since the contact destroys the track so affected – and any data stored in that track. A head crash is often caused by the head passing over a dust grain on the surface. Particles of surface material produced by the contact cause other tracks to be destroyed.

The possibility of a head crash is reduced by keeping the disk clean and at a constant temperature and humidity. Disks are copied at regular intervals so that in the event of a crash a duplicate is available.

headend *See* broadband coaxial system.

header Some coded information that precedes a more general collection of data and gives details about it, e.g. its length. The header of a data-structure representation is logically distinct from the data elements themselves and may serve several purposes:

(a) to hold global information about the whole structure, e.g. list length, array index bounds;

(b) to represent an empty structure;

(c) to provide links into the structure, e.g. pointers to first and last nodes in a list;

(d) to represent the entire structure in any other data structures of which it may be a part.

heap 1. An area of storage used for the allocation of data structures where the

DAT 1

order of releasing the allocated data structure is random. *Compare* stack.

2. A *complete binary tree in which the value at each node is at least as large as the values at its children (if they exist).

heapsort A sorting algorithm developed by Williams and Floyd in 1964 and employing the ideas of *tree selection. It is more efficient for larger numbers of records but on average is inferior to *quicksort. However, the worst possible distribution of keys does not cause the efficiency of heapsort to deteriorate too much. The worst case for quicksort can then be worse. Some of the ideas of heapsort are relevant to *priority queue applications.

height 1. of a node in a tree. The length of a longest path from the node to a *leaf node.

2. of a tree. The maximum height of any node in a tree. The height of a given tree will have the same numerical value as the *depth of that tree.

height-balanced *See* balanced, AVL tree.

DAT

helical scan A method of using magnetic tape, derived from video recording, in which the tape is wrapped in a helical path around a rotating drum so that one or more heads embedded in the drum record diagonal tracks on the tape. The tape is moved slowly so that a separate track is recorded at each pass of a head.

Helical scan allows data to be recorded at a very high density and hence at very low storage cost. When first introduced (using standard video cartridges) the error rates were too high for general use. More recently powerful error-correcting codes have been introduced, and in this form the method is suitable for backing up hard disks and for short-term archiving (long-term stability has yet to be proved). The *digital audio tape (DAT)* cartridge is popular for this purpose.

help system The part of an interactive system responsible for providing the user with information about the workings of the program on request. Help can be obtained in a number of ways: by typing the word "help", by pressing a particular *function key on the keyboard, or by using a mouse or other pointing device to select a "help" item from a menu. Help can be hierarchical, where each topic has subtopics that can be explored down to an arbitrary number of levels, or context-sensitive, where the information provided is appropriate to the part of the program currently being used. Some help systems can be browsed through like a manual. A particular system may combine any or all of these methods. A good help system is a crucial feature of any non-trivial program.

Hercules A monochrome *graphics adapter of 640 × 350 *resolution.

Hermite interpolation *See* interpolation.

hertz (symbol: Hz) The SI unit of *frequency. A periodic phenomenon has a frequency of one hertz if each cycle of the phenomenon repeats itself in a period of one second. A *megahertz* (MHz) is one million (10^6) hertz.

heuristic Employing a self-learning approach to the solution of a problem. The construction of a nonheuristic system directly reflects existing knowledge of some algorithm that can yield a solution to some problem. By contrast, a heuristic system has to be constructed so that it can acquire the knowledge needed to produce the required solution.

For example, in the absence of good known algorithms for the problem, heuristic methods have been used to control traffic routing in communications networks: feedback from the actual performance of the network is used to influence subsequent routing decisions, thereby maintaining satisfactory routing behavior despite changes in load or failures of network components.

Heuristic techniques are also employed in *artificial intelligence. Certain procedures are learned through experience of problem solving in a particular domain. These may involve knowledge of when best to use a particular strategy or problem-solving method, and are frequently encoded as *production rules in *expert systems.

Hewlett-Packard A California-based electronic instrument, calculator, test equipment, and minicomputer manufacturer. HP is noted as the first manufacturer of a hand-held scientific calculator.

hex *Short for* hexadecimal.

hexadecimal notation The representation of numbers in the positional number system with base 16. The sixteen hexadecimal digits are usually represented by 0–9, A–F.

hex pad A *keypad with 16 keys that are labeled 0–9, A–F so that they correspond to *hedadecimal notation.

hidden-line algorithm An algorithm used in graph-plotting, etc., to determine which lines should not be visible when a three-dimensional surface is plotted.

hierarchical addressing *See* addressing.

hierarchical cluster analysis *See* cluster analysis.

hierarchical communication system 1. A physical organization of communications facilities, each higher level covering a wider or more general area of operation than the next lower level. As an example, a large bank might have a *local area network within each branch, connecting the teller stations. Several branches might be linked to a data *concentrator, connected to regional concentrators, which in turn link to the bank's main data processing center.

2. A logical organization of communication facilities, in which the lowest levels deal with the physical network while higher levels deal with the communication between specific applications. *See also* protocol.

hierarchical database system A *database system in which the DBMS only supports a *data hierarchy. The best-known hierarchical DBMS is *IMS.

hierarchical memory structure *See* memory hierarchy.

hierarchy A set of entities that are partially ordered; the word is frequently misused. *See* partial ordering.

hierarchy of functions A sequence of sets of functions F_0, F_1, F_2,... with the property that
$$F_0 \subseteq F_1 \subseteq F_2 \subseteq \ldots$$
(*see* subset). Typically the functions in F_0 will include certain initial functions; the sets of functions F_1, F_2,... are normally defined by combining initial functions in some way.

Hierarchies of *primitive recursive functions can be defined by letting F_i represent those functions that can be computed by programs containing at most i loops nested one within the other. Then
$$F_i \subseteq F_{i+1}$$
for all integers $i > 0$. The *union of all these sets includes all the primitive recursive functions and only those functions. Consequently the hierarchy is often called a *subrecursive hierarchy*. This same hierarchy can be expressed in a slightly different form, so resulting in the *Grzegorczyk hierarchy*.

In an attempt to circumvent problems caused by *recursion, Bertrand Russell invented a *theory of types*, which essentially imposed a hierarchy on the set of functions; functions at one level could be defined only in terms of functions at lower levels.

The study of hierarchies of functions dates from work of David Hilbert around 1926 on the foundations of mathematics. More recent interest stems from their applicability to computational *complexity.

higher-order term *See* term.

high-level design (architectural design) *See* program decomposition, program design, system design.

high-level language A variety of programming language in which the *control and *data structures reflect the requirements of the problem rather than the facilities actually provided by the hardware. A high-level language is translated into *machine code by a *compiler.

high-level scheduler *See* scheduler.

high-order language *Another name for* high-level language, used only by the US Department of Defense.

high-pass filter A *filtering device that permits only those components in the *Fourier transform domain whose frequencies lie above some critical value to pass through with little attenuation, all other components being highly attenuated.

High Sierra Widely used informal name for ISO 9660, the *CD-ROM file structure standard now followed by most databases on these disks.

highway *Another (UK) name for* bus.

hi res *Short for* high resolution. *See* resolution.

histogram A chart showing the *relative frequencies with which a measurable quantity takes values in a set of contiguous intervals. The chart consists of rectangles whose areas are proportional to the relative frequencies and whose widths are proportional to the class intervals. It can be used to picture a *frequency distribution.

hit rate 1. The fraction of references to one level of the *memory hierarchy that must otherwise be fulfilled in the less accessible levels within the hierarchy. Thus for a *cache memory the hit rate is the fraction of references that do not result in access to main memory. For a *page the hit rate is the fraction of references that do not result in a page turn.

2. The proportion of records or blocks on a file that are retrieved or updated in a batch run or in a given period of time.

HMI *Abbrev.* for human-machine interface. *See* human-computer interface.

HMOS A name applied by Intel Corp. to high-speed MOS technology, usually NMOS although it will be used in CMOS. HMOS implies both a short channel between source and drain, and also design (layout) rules that deal with minimum feature size of less than two micrometers.

Hoare logic A formalism for partial correctness proofs (*see* program correctness proof). Sentences have the form A{P}B, where A and B are assertions and P is a program. The meaning of such a sentence is that, starting from a state in which A is true, if P terminates it will result in a state in which B is true. A Hoare logic for a particular programming language comprises a system of rules for deducing such sentences from other simpler ones. By repeated use of these rules it is possible ultimately to derive facts about an entire program, starting from facts about its smallest constituents. Like the *Floyd method however, the approach requires judicious choice of loop *invariants. As another application, Hoare logics can be taken as *axiomatic semantics for programming languages.

HOL A system for specifying, designing, and verifying the design of digital systems; it was devised at Cambridge University, UK. The HOL system includes a theorem prover, an editor, and consistency checkers. The HOL specification language has basic types that handle n-bit digital numbers, the natural numbers, and the Boolean values true/false. More complex types can be built by binding together the basic types. A library of functions and list operators is used to perform transformations on variables.

hold time The length of time for which a signal must be held constant on a *bus, following the instant when all devices using the signal have nominally responded to its presence.

Hollerith code A code for relating alphanumeric characters to holes in a punched card. It was devised by Herman Hollerith in 1888 and enabled the letters of the alphabet and the digits 0–9 to be encoded by a combination of punchings in 12 rows of a card.

holographic memory A storage device that records binary information in the form of holograms, which are produced (as interference patterns) on photographic or photochromic media by means of laser beams, and are read by means of low-power laser beams. The advantage of a hologram is the way in which the image is dispersed over the recording surface so that dust or scratches do not totally obscure data though they may reduce the contrast. Development of a mass store using this technology was done by RCA and Plessey Co. Ltd. in 1972 but it did not result in a commercially available product. In 1977 Holofile Industries announced a device developed from work done by TRW's Defence and Space Systems Group. It could store 200 million bits on a $4'' \times 6''$ fiche, but it was a read-only device and did not achieve widespread application.

holographic scanner A type of *scanner in which a beam of light (usually from a laser) is deflected by a rotating hologram so that it scans a plane in a multitude of directions. Some of the light reflected from an object on or close to the plane is returned via the hologram and brought to focus on a sensor. The most widely known use is for reading *bar codes at retail checkouts.

homomorphic image of a formal language. *See* homomorphism.

homomorphism A structure-preserving mapping between *algebras. The idea is that it "represents" the structure of one algebra within another, possibly in a contracted form. Let A and B be algebras and h a function from A to B. Suppose that A contains an n-ary function f_A, while B contains a corresponding function f_B. If h is a homomorphism it must satisfy

$$h(f_A(a_1, \ldots, a_k)) = f_B(h(a_1), \ldots, h(a_k))$$

for all elements $a_1, \ldots, a_k$ of A. The idea that f_A and f_B are "corresponding" operations is made precise by saying that A and B are algebras over the same *signature Σ, while f is a symbol in Σ with which A and B associate the functions f_A and f_B respectively. A homomorphism from A to B is any function h from A to B that satisfies the condition given above for each f in Σ. As applications of this idea, the semantic functions involved in *denotational semantics can be viewed as homomorphisms, as can any *primitive recursive function definition.

Special cases of this general definition occur when A and B belong to one of the familiar classes of algebraic structures. For example, let A and B be *monoids, with *binary operations $\circ_A$

and $\circ_B$ and *identity elements e_A and e_B. Then a homomorphism from A to B satisfies

$$h(x \circ_A y) = h(x) \circ_B h(y)$$
$$h(e_A) = e_B$$

A further specialization from *formal language theory arises with monoids of *words, where the binary operation is *concatenation and the nullary operation is the empty word. Let S and T be alphabets, and let h be a function from S to T^*, i.e. a function that gives a T-word for each symbol in S. Then h can be extended to S-words, by concatenating its values on individual symbols:

$$h(s_1, \ldots, s_n) = h(s_1), \ldots, h(s_n)$$

This extension of h gives a monoid homomorphism from S^* to T^*. Such an h is said to be Λ-*free* if it gives a nonempty T-word for each symbol in S.

h can be further extended to a mapping on languages, giving, for any subset L of S^*, its *homomorphic image h (L)*:

$$h(L) = \{h(w) \mid w \in L\}$$

Similarly the *inverse homomorphic image* of $L \subseteq T^*$ is

$$h^{-1}(L) = \{w \mid h(w) \in L\}$$

These language-mappings are also homomorphisms, between the monoids of languages over S and over T, the binary operation being concatenation of languages.

HOOD *Acronym for* hierarchical object-oriented design. One version of *object-oriented design.

hop *See* store-and-forward. *See also* flow control.

HOPE A *functional language, one of the first such languages to be widely used.

horizontal check *See* cyclic redundancy check.

horizontal microinstruction *See* micro-programming.

horizontal recording *See* magnetic encoding.

Horn clause In the clausal form of logic, an expression of the form

   A if B_1 and B_2 and ... and B_n

This should be contrasted with the general form of clause

   A_1 or A_2 or ... or A_m
   if
   B_1 and B_2 and ... and B_n

where $A_1 \ldots A_m$ are the alternative conclusions and $B_1 \ldots B_n$ are the joint conditions. A Horn clause is a special case of this general form in that it contains at most one conclusion.

Horn clauses were first investigated by the logician Alfred Horn. The majority of formalisms employed in computer programming bear greater resemblance to Horn clauses than to the more general form. The logic programming language *PROLOG is based upon the Horn clause subset of logic.

Horner's method An algorithm for evaluating a *polynomial by adding brackets in such a way that no powers greater than one need be evaluated. This reduces the number of evaluations. The polynomial, in effect, ends up in the following form:

$$p(x) =$$
$$[\ldots((anx + a(n-1))x + a(n-2))x \ldots$$
$$a1]x + a0$$

host computer (host) 1. A computer that is attached to a *network and provides services other than simply acting as a *store-and-forward processor or communication switch. Host computers range in size from small microcomputers to large time-sharing or batch mainframes. Many networks have a hierarchical structure, with a *communication sub-network providing *packet-switching services for host computers to support time-sharing, remote job entry, etc. A host computer at one level of a hierarchy may function as a packet or message switch at another. Sometimes host computers are divided into two classes: *servers*, which provide resources, and *users*, which access them.

2. A computer used to develop software for execution on another computer, known as the *target computer*.

3. A computer used to emulate another computer, known as the *target computer. See also* emulation.

host language *See* database language.

hot-key 1. A key or combination of keys on a computer keyboard that has been programmed to cause an immediate change in the operating environment, such as the execution of a *pop-up program.

2. To use such a key.

housekeeping Actions performed within a program or system in order to maintain internal orderliness rather than to address the externally imposed requirements. For example, the housekeeping of a program often includes *memory management.

HPF *Abbrev. for* highest priority first. Where several *processes are free to proceed, the *scheduler will initiate the process that has been assigned the highest priority.

HP–IB *See* bus.

HSI *Abbrev. for* human-system interface. *See* human-computer interface.

hub polling *See* polling.

Huffman encoding A (usually) *binary encoding of the elements of a finite set, A,
$$A = \{a_1, a_2, \ldots, a_n\}$$
where each element a_i in A has an assumed probability, p_i, of occurring in a message. The binary encoding satisfies the *prefix property and is such that messages will have a minimum expected length. Thus an element a_i with a high probability of occurring in a message is encoded as a short binary string while an element with a low probability of occurring is encoded with a longer string. *See also* source coding.

human-computer interface (HCI) The means of communication between a human user and a computer system, referring in particular to the use of input/output devices with supporting software. Devices of increasing sophistication are becoming available to mediate the human-computer interaction. These include graphics devices, *touch-sensitive devices, and *voice-input devices. They have to be configured in a way that will facilitate an efficient and desirable interaction between a person and the computer. *Artificial intelligence techniques of knowledge representation may be used to model the user of a computer system, and so offer the opportunity to give personalized advice on its use. The design of the machine interface may incorporate *expert-system techniques to offer powerful *knowledge-based computing to the user.

The terms *human-system interface* (HSI), *human-machine interface* (HMI), and *man-machine interface* (MMI) are all used as synonyms.

hybrid computer A computer (system) that contains both a digital and an analog computer. The digital computer usually serves as the controller and provides logical operations; the analog computer normally serves as a solver of differential equations.

hybrid integrated circuit A complete electronic circuit that is fabricated on an insulating substrate using a variety of device technologies. The substrate acts as a carrier for the circuit and also has the interconnecting tracks between devices printed on it by multilayer techniques (*see* multilayer device). Individual devices, which comprise chip diodes, transistors, integrated circuits, and thick-film resistors and capacitors and which form the circuit function, are attached to the substrate and are connected together using the previously defined interconnecting tracks.

hypercard A software package for the Apple Macintosh computer in the *object-oriented design paradigm. It is a programming system that uses the *wimp interface to switch between, select from, and structure objects on screen and in the underlying database, and to pass messages between objects. New data can be entered into objects, for example a diary. A new application can be constructed by manipulating objects on screen: there is no need to program in the conventional sense, although a programming language, *HyperTalk*, is provided. Hypercard has been used to implement *hypertext-style systems.

hypercube In its simplest form, a four-dimensional cube, which can be considered as two three-dimensional cubes connected at equivalent corners. Connecting the corners of four-dimensional cubes gives a five-dimensional hypercube. In general, an $(n+1)$-dimensional hypercube can be generated by connecting the corners of n-dimensional hypercubes, and has twice as many corners as the n-dimensional hypercube.

Several *multiprocessing systems have an architecture based on the hypercube, where processors replace corners and communication links replace edges. In an n-dimensional hypercube network, no processor is more than n links from any other processor; doubling the number of processors by using an $(n+1)$-dimensional network means information has to travel over only one additional connection. However, as the number of processors increases, the number of connections each one must make has also to be increased.

hypertext A generic term covering a number of techniques used to create and view multidimensional documents, which may be entered at many points and which may be browsed in any order by interactively choosing words or key phrases as search parameters for the next text image to be viewed. Generally a *wimp style interface is used and tools are provided to help structure the text, create indexes of the text of a document, and to cross-reference between documents. The technique is related to full-text database systems.

The concept can be explained by example. A novel can be considered to be a document in a single dimension, normally read from start to finish sequentially. An encyclopedia is an example of a multidimensional document that is read in small parts only, and the part to be read is selected from and the encyclopedia entered via an index. For the encyclopedia the order of reading is often controlled by an association of ideas by the reader. Taking the dimensionality a further stage, the pictorial information in the encyclopedia could also be linked to maps and to descriptions of the symbolism used in the maps.

A typical reference chain following an association of ideas might begin by the reader looking at an index to locate the correct "map", getting and opening the map, then looking at the "map symbol table" to interpret something seen on the map; the reader may then perhaps look up the dictionary meaning of the word "tumulus" as seen on the map and perhaps divert to look up in another reference book the meaning of a town name or the history of a battle fought at some location on the map. Using books and other documents, this browsing chain involves identifying the correct book, locating its position on the shelves, looking up contents lists and indexes to find the correct page, reading the contents, and if the place needs to be saved inserting a paper marker.

Hypertext systems provide facilities for windowing viewed text, selecting next view by mouse/keyboard marking of text fragments, searching the text database or indexes, and displaying the new text.

I

IA5 *Abbrev. for* International Alphabet, Number 5. An internationally agreed alphabet, specified by *CCITT. It consists of a subset of *ISO-7 in which characters that are "for national use" are either specified or not used at all.

IAL *Acronym for* international algorithmic language, the original name for the language later called Algol 58 and now obsolete. *See* Algol. *See also* JOVIAL.

IAS *Abbrev. for* immediate access store.

IAS computer The model for a class of computing machines designed by John von Neumann. The IAS (Institute for Advanced Study) machine was started at Princeton in 1946 and was completed in 1951. This machine used *electrostatic storage devices – cathode-ray tubes – as the main memory. Such tubes, called Williams tubes, could each store 1024 bits. Other computers modeled after the IAS computer included ORACLE, JOHNNIAC, ILLIAC I, MANIAC, and IBM 701.

IBG *Abbrev. for* interblock gap. *See* block.

IBM International Business Machines Corporation, the world's largest computer manufacturer. It was incorporated in 1911 as the Computing Tabulating Recording Company as a result of a merger of three companies, one of which had been Hermann Hollerith's Tabulating Machine Company, formed 1896. It adopted its present name in 1924.

IBM produce a diverse range of computers, peripherals, software, and associated equipment, from the PS/2 personal computers to the 3090 series mainframes. IBM's size and breadth make it a dominating influence in computing strategy worldwide.

IBM system 360 IBM's famous *third generation computer family that used essentially the same architecture to span a wide range of performance and price objectives. The common architecture permitted upward mobility of users to larger versions of the same machine when their workload grew. Programs written for a smaller version of the 360 would run unchanged on the larger machines. Many of the principles embodied in the 360 operating systems are still to be found in contemporary IBM mainframes.

IC *Abbrev. for* integrated circuit.

ICL International Computers Ltd., a wholly British company and one of the leading computer system manufacturers in Europe. In 1984 ICL became a wholly owned subsidiary of the UK company Standard Telephones and Cables (STC). ICL markets or distributes a range of computing equipment from minicomputers to mainframes.

icon (or **ikon**) A pictorial symbol used in a *menu to avoid dependence on natural language. *See also* wimp.

ICON A programming language developed as a successor to *SNOBOL. ICON is a general-purpose programming language in the style of Pascal, but includes many features for processing strings of characters and other nonnumerical data. ICON's main use is in research in humanities computing, and in teaching computing to students of the humanities.

ICR *Abbrev. for* intelligent character recognition. A system of *OCR (optical character recognition) in which the meaning is assigned after reference to things other than merely the printed shape. Basic OCR systems rely on matching the scanned shape with a set of templates held within a store or on processing the image to extract features, such as lines and loops, and then searching for a match. Both approaches need good-quality printing to achieve usable recognition rates. In desktop publishing applications it is possible to use context to assist the recognition process. The resident dictionary or spelling checker can be used and provision may also be made for the unrecognized shape to be displayed so that the operator can assign a meaning that is then stored for future reference.

idempotent law The law satisfied by any *dyadic operation ∘ for which
$$x \circ x = x$$
for all elements x in the domain of ∘. *Union and *intersection of sets satisfy these laws. In a *Boolean algebra both of the dyadic operations are idempotent.

identification 1. The process of determining the identity of a user or a using process; it is necessary for *access control. Identification is usually accomplished by *authentication.
2. The process of determining how a control parameter influences a system.

identifier A string of characters used to identify (or *name) some element of a program. The kind of element that may be named depends on the programming language; it may be a variable, a data structure, a procedure, a statement, a higher-level unit, or the program itself.

identity burst See tape format.

identity element of a *set S on which some *dyadic operation ∘ is defined. An element e with the property that
$$a \circ e = e \circ a = a$$
for all elements a in S. It can be shown that e is unique. In normal arithmetic, 0

and 1 are the identity elements associated with addition and multiplication respectively. In a *Boolean algebra, 0 and 1 are the identities associated with the OR and the AND operations respectively.

identity function A *function
$$I : S \rightarrow S$$
with the property that
$$I(s) = s \text{ for all } s \text{ in } S$$
Such a function leaves every element in its domain unaltered. Identity functions are needed for such purposes as the definition of *inverses of functions.

identity matrix (unit matrix) A *diagonal matrix, symbol I, with each diagonal element equal to one.

idle time See available time.

IDP Abbrev. for integrated data processing. See data processing.

IED Abbrev. for Information Engineering Directorate, the UK government department responsible for the program of IT research and development that follows the *Alvey Programme. The programme itself is also called IED.

IEE Institution of Electrical Engineers, a UK organization founded in 1871. It is a qualifying body for professional engineers, a learned society, and a provider of scientific and engineering information services.

IEEE Institute of Electrical and Electronics Engineers, a US organization formed in 1963 by the merger of the IRE (Institute of Radio Engineers) and the AIEE (American Institute of Electrical Engineers).

if and only if statement A well-formed formula of the form
$$A \equiv B$$
where A and B are also appropriate well-formed formulas. See biconditional, propositional calculus.

IFE *Abbrev. for* intelligent front end.

iff *Short for* if and only if.

IFIP International Federation for Information Processing, founded in 1959 and coming into official existence in 1960 as the International Federation of Information Processing Societies. Its secretariat is in Geneva. It aims to "promote information science and technology, advance international cooperation in the field of information processing, stimulate research, development, and application of information processing, further dissemination and exchange of information in information processing, and encourage education in information processing."

if then else statement The most basic conditional construct in a programming language, allowing selection between two alternatives, dependent on the truth or falsity of a given condition. Most languages also provide an *if ... then* construct to allow conditional execution of a single statement or group of statements. Primitive languages such as BASIC restrict the facility to a conditional transfer of control, e.g.

"IF A = 0 THEN 330"

which is reminiscent of the conditional jump provided in the order code of every CPU. *See also* conditional.

ignore character (fill character) A character used in transmission to fill an otherwise empty position and whose value is thus ignored.

IH *Abbrev. for* interrupt handler.

IKBS *Abbrev. for* intelligent knowledge-based system. Applied *artificial intelligence. See also* knowledge base, machine intelligence, expert systems.

ikon *See* icon.

ill-conditioned *See* condition number.

illegal character Any character not in the *character set of a given machine or of a given programming language.

illegal instruction An instruction that has an invalid *operation code. It is sometimes deliberately inserted in an instruction stream when debugging in order to have a program halt at a particular point.

ILLIAC IV An *array processor that was designed by Daniel Slotnick and used a 16-by-16 array of processing units (PUs), each interconnected to its four nearest neighbors. The array of PUs was regulated by a single processor that controlled the flow of instructions to the PUs. The ILLIAC IV was sponsored by ARPA and built by Burroughs Corporation. It became operable at the Ames Research Center of NASA in the early 1970s, and was finally dismantled in 1981.

image 1. A copy in memory of data that exists elsewhere.

    2. Another name for picture. *See* picture processing.

    3. See function.

image processing *Another name for* picture processing.

immediate access store (IAS) A memory device in which the access time for any location is independent of the previous access and is usually of the same order as the cycle time of the processor. Such devices are normally only used for main memory.

immediate addressing A method used to refer to data (often small constants or similar) that is located in an address field of an instruction. Strictly this is not a method of generating an address at all; it does provide a reference to the desired data in a way that is both compact and requires less memory reference time.

IMP *Acronym for* interface message processor. One of the switching computers that together form(ed) the *backbone network for the *ARPANET. The primary function of the IMPs is to forward packets between the ARPANET hosts using 56 Kbps leased lines. Specially configured IMPs have, however, performed other functions in the ARPANET. The most important of these are the *TIPs* (terminal interface (message) processors). TIPs are IMPs with additional hardware and software to provide network access for asynchronous terminals at speeds up to 1200 baud. The TIP thus functions as a small host computer in addition to its packet-switching responsibilities as an IMP.

Other special IMP configurations include satellite IMPs with extra memory buffers for high-delay satellite links, IMPs with message encryption hardware for secure communication, and IMPs that run special control programs for high-bandwidth packet speech and video traffic.

impact printer Any device that makes use of mechanical impact to print characters onto paper. Typewriters come within this definition but the term is not usually applied to machines that are only operated through a keyboard. A character may be formed by impacting an inked ribbon against the paper with an engraved type character, or it may be built up from a number of dots printed by the impacts of separate styluses. *See* solid-font printer, dot-matrix printer.

imperative languages A class of programming languages. With an imperative language a program explicitly states how the desired result is to be produced but does not explicitly define what properties the result is expected to exhibit – the result is defined only implicitly as whatever is obtained by following the specified procedure (*compare* declarative languages).

The procedure for producing the desired result takes the form of a sequence of operations, and thus with imperative languages the notions of flow of control and ordering of statements are inherent. Such a language is typically characterized by the presence of the *assignment statement, which, being destructive (the assigned value replaces the previous value of the variable), also depends on the notion of ordering. Imperative languages are closely associated with the von Neumann model of computation, and the majority of widely used languages – including COBOL, FORTRAN, Algol, and Pascal – are imperative.

implementation The activity of proceeding from a given design of a system to a working version (known also as an *implementation*) of that system, or the specific way in which some part of a system is made to fulfill its function. For example, a control unit may be implemented by random logic or by microprogramming; a multiplier may be implemented by successive additions and shifts or by a table look-up. Another example occurs in computer families, where different implementations may differ in the type of circuit elements used or in the actual parallelism (as opposed to logical parallelism) of the ALU.

With software, use of the term normally implies that all major design decisions have been made so that the implementation activity could be relatively straightforward. For many systems a number of important characteristics may not become bound until the implementation activity; examples include the programming language in which the system is written, the type of computer employed, the actual hardware configuration, or the operating system used. With such systems there may be a number of distinct implementation activities in order to provide several versions of the system, e.g. written in different languages or operating on different hardware.

implicant A *product term that covers at least one of the *standard sum of product terms in a *Boolean function, but will introduce no new (unwanted) standard sum of product terms.

A *prime implicant* is an implicant that includes a *standard product of a function that is not otherwise included.

implied addressing (inherent addressing) A type of *addressing scheme, the term referring to the fact that in many instruction formats the location of one or more operands is implied in the instruction name and is specified in the instruction description. An implied address is usually that of one of the machine registers.

import list In modular languages such as *Modula-2, a list of the names used inside a module that are declared in other modules.

impulse noise *Noise of large amplitude and some statistical irregularity, affecting an analog channel severely but (relatively) infrequently. In contrast, *white noise affects it (relatively) unseverely but continuously. Impulse noise affecting an analog channel carrying a binary signal usually causes *burst errors.

IMS *Trademark* A well-established *database management system provided by IBM. It was originally a *hierarchical system but has gained additional nonhierarchical features as a result of practical needs.

inactive Not running (pertaining to the state of a process).

incidence matrix A representation of a *graph G employing a *matrix in which there is a row for each vertex v of G. The entries on this row are just the vertices that are joined by an edge to v.

inclusive-OR gate *Another name for* OR gate.

inclusive-OR operation *Another name for* OR operation, making explicit the difference between this and the *exclusive-OR operation.

incompleteness theorems *See* Gödel's incompleteness theorems.

incremental compiler A compiler that can compile partial programs, and can compile additional statements for a program without recompiling the whole program. Incremental compilers were at one time in vogue for interactive programming, but interactive language systems nowadays are almost always implemented in an interpretive manner.

incremental plotter A device that can draw graphs and other line images when fed with digital data. The plotter forms the image by moving a pen or the paper or both in a succession of increments. The increments are typically 200 per inch for drum plotters and can be 500 per inch for flatbed plotters. *See also* plotter.

indegree *See* degree.

indeterminate system A logic system whose *logic states are unpredictable.

index 1. A set of *links that can be used to locate records in a *data file. In a *single-level index*, and at the lowest level of a *multilevel index*, an entry points directly to an individual record or to a group of records. At the higher levels of a multilevel index an entry points to a group of entries at the next lower level; a multilevel index is used where the size of a file would give rise to excessive search time using a single-level index. The B+ tree (*see* B-tree) is an efficient form of multilevel index. *See also* indexed file.

2. The value held in an *index register.

3. (subscript) An integer value selecting a particular element of an *array. In some high-level languages, arrays can be indexed by ordered sets of discrete values that are not integers, such as the names of the days of the week or the names of the chemical elements.

indexed addressing (indexing) A method of generating an *effective address that modifies the specified address given in the instruction by the contents of a specified *index register. The modification is usually that of addition of the contents of the index register to the specified address. The automatic modification of index-register contents results in an orderly progression of effective addresses being generated on successive executions of the instruction containing the reference to the index register. This progression is terminated when the index register reaches a value that has been specified in an index-register handling instruction.

indexed file A *data file in which *records can be accessed by means of an *index. If the same field is used both in the index and for sequencing the records in the file, the index is called a *primary index* (and the file is called an *indexed sequential file*). Otherwise the index is called a *secondary index* (*see* inverted file).

indexed sequential file A file combining properties of *random-access files and *sequential files. *See* indexed file, ISAM.

indexing *See* indexed addressing.

index register A register that can be specified by instructions that use *indexed addressing. An index register is usually controlled by one or more instructions with the ability to increment or decrement the register by a fixed amount, to test the register for equality with a specified value (often zero), and to jump to a specified location when

equality is achieved. It is part of the *processor status word.

indicator 1. A bit or bit configuration that may be inspected to determine a status or condition. Examples are an *overflow bit, a device status, any portion of the *program status word. *See also* qualifier register.

2. A visual, sometimes aural, indication of the occurrence of a specific status or condition, e.g. system running (halted), undefined instruction.

indirect addressing A method of addressing in which the contents of the address specified in the instruction (which may itself be an *effective address) are themselves an address to be used to provide the desired memory reference. Two memory references are thus needed to obtain the data.

One use of indirect addressing is to supply a way of circumventing short address field limitations since the first memory reference provides a full word of address size. Another use is as a pointer to a table. Since an operand is not available at the usual time in the fetch-execute cycle, completion of that cycle must be deferred until the operand is finally available. Indirect addressing is thus sometimes referred to as *deferred addressing*.

induction A process for proving mathematical statements involving members of an ordered set (possibly infinite). There are various formulations of the principle of induction. For example, by the *principle of finite induction*, to prove a statement $P(i)$ is true for all integers $i \geqslant i_0$, it suffices to prove that

(a) $P(i_0)$ is true;

(b) for all $k \geqslant i_0$, the assumption that $P(k)$ is true (the *induction hypothesis*) implies the truth of $P(k+1)$.

(a) is called the *basis* of the proof, (b) is the *induction step*.

Generalizations are possible. Other forms of induction permit the induction step to assume the truth of $P(k)$ and also that of

$$P(k-1), P(k-2), \ldots, P(k-i)$$

for suitable i. Statements of several variables can also be considered. *See also* structural induction.

inequality A *binary relation that typically expresses the relative magnitude of two quantities, usually numbers though more generally elements of a partially ordered set (*see* partial ordering).

The inequalities defined on the integers usually include

$<$ (less than)
$\leq$ (less than or equal to)
$>$ (greater than)
$\geq$ (greater than or equal to)
$\neq$ (not equal to)

A similar set of inequalities is usually defined on the real numbers; such inequalities can produce errors when used in programming languages because of the inherent inaccuracies in the way real numbers are usually represented (*see* floating-point notation).

The term inequality is often applied to any comparison involving algebraic expressions and using the above symbols. A special case is the *triangle inequality*:

$$|a + b| \leq |a| + |b|$$

where $| \ |$ denotes the absolute value function.

inference The formal method of reasoning that underlies logical deduction. Rules of inference provide the means whereby a logician or a theorem-prover program (*see* theorem proving) may use previous results, theorems, or axioms to derive new results. *See also* propositional calculus, predicate calculus.

inference engine Within the context of *expert systems, the part of the expert system program that operates on the *knowledge base and produces inferences. If the knowledge base is regarded as a program then the inference engine is the interpreter. The expressions in the knowledge representation language are its inputs, and its outputs constitute an interpretation of this input with respect to stored knowledge. The interpreter may be logic-based in that it operates within a certain logic formalism, for instance first-order *predicate calculus.

inference rules *See* program correctness proof, propositional calculus.

infix notation A form of notation in which operators appear between their operands, as in

$$(a + b) * c$$

Infix notation requires the use of brackets to specify order of evaluation, unlike prefix and postfix notation, i.e. *Polish notation and *reverse Polish notation respectively.

influence In *regression analysis, the effect on estimates of *parameters of varying the value of a particular observation. Observations that have greatest influence are also called *leverage* points. Influence functions help to warn of possible over-reliance on too few data values, and also provide a method of allocating new data observations most effectively.

information Formally, collections of symbols. This is the sense in terms such as *information processing, *information technology, or *information theory. Symbols in turn may be defined as patterns that carry meaning, which therefore serves as an alternative definition of information.

A piece of information may be regarded from three main viewpoints.

(a) From the human behavioral viewpoint, some purpose underlies the creation of a piece of information, and some effect (observed action or inferred state of mind) may follow from its receipt.

(b) From the analytical, linguistic viewpoint, a piece of information may be described in terms of what it refers to, its meaning, and its structure.

(c) From the physical, engineering viewpoint, a piece of information may be described in terms of its physical manifestation – the medium that carries it, the resolution and accuracy with which it is inscribed, the amount that is output, conveyed, or received, etc.

The following operations may be performed on information: create, transmit, store, retrieve, receive, copy (in the same or a different form), process, destroy.

The patterns that constitute information may be created in a great diversity of forms including: light, sound, or radio waves; electric current or voltage; magnetic fields; marks on paper. In principle any conceivable material structure or energy flow could be used to carry information.

The scale of our use of information is one of the most important distinctions between the human species and all others, and the importance of information as an economic commodity is one of the most important characteristics of the "post-industrial" civilization, which we are often said now to be entering.

information destination *See* Shannon's model.

information engineering The engineering approach applied to *information systems. The term shows considerable variation in scope. At its broadest, as in the Information Engineering Directorate (*IED) it refers to the engineering discipline covering a spectrum from *software engineering and *systems engineering to device-level electronics. At its most limited (but perhaps best known), it is the name of a specific proprietary method for the development of organizational information systems, primarily associated with James Martin; this method begins with *enterprise modeling and carries through to the generation of program code, and at least three major software toolsets are available for its support.

Information Engineering Directorate *See* IED.

information hiding A principle, used when developing an overall *program structure, that each component of a program should encapsulate or hide a single design decision. The principle was first expounded by David Parnas, who advocated an approach to program development in which a list is prepared of design decisions that are particularly difficult or likely to change; individual components or modules are then defined so that each encapsulates one such decision. The interface to each module is defined in such a way as to reveal as little as possible about its inner workings.

This approach leads to modules that are readily understood and can be developed independently. More important, it also leads to programs that are easy to change, with many desired changes requiring modification of only the inner workings of a single module.

information management system A term not yet in common use, and that may best be understood by contrast with *data management system. A data management system is one that, because it operates on data, has relatively well defined syntax, semantics, and operations. The contents of an information management system include other forms of information (e.g. text); its syntax and semantics are accordingly less capable of precise definition, and its effective use is much more dependent on interaction with users.

information processing The derivation of "information objects" from other "information objects" by the execution of algorithms. Processing is one of the fundamental operations that can be performed on *information. It is the principal operation by which the amount and variety of information is increased.

The term has related meanings outside the computing field. It is used in psychology, for instance, and may also be used to refer to clerical operations.

information retrieval *See* information storage and retrieval.

information source *See* Shannon's model.

information storage and retrieval Information storage is the activity of recording information for subsequent use, usually on backing store, e.g. magnetic disk or tape. Storage is one of the fundamental operations that can be performed on *information. It is the principal operation by which information is retained over a period of time.

Information retrieval is the activity of retrieving stored information, and is another of the fundamental operations that can be performed on information. The term information retrieval has a related but distinct meaning in the field of librarianship, where it refers to techniques (such as keywords and indexes) for locating text and/or references on a specified topic. In this sense the information store is usually (though not invariably) held on a machine-readable medium and accessed by computer.

The term *information storage and retrieval (ISR)* refers not only to the activities of information storage and information retrieval, but also to the techniques involved – of which there are many. Storage and retrieval are intimately linked. Information is only stored in order that it may be subsequently retrieved; it may only be retrieved in ways that have been allowed for at storage time. ISR embraces all methods for labeling stored information in order to enable it to be accessed later, whether these are in the context of data-processing files/databases, textual files, graphic databases, etc.

information structure *Another name for* data structure.

information system A computer-based system with the defining characteristic that it provides information to users in one or more organizations. Information systems are thus distinguished from, for example, real-time control systems, message-switching systems, software engineering environments, or personal computing systems.

The term could have a very much wider meaning than that suggested, considering the range of meaning of the words *information and *system. It could, for instance, be broadened to include all computer-based systems, or further broadened to include many non-computer-based systems. Thus, within the domain of computer-based systems, the more specific term *organizational information system* is sometimes used.

Information systems include *data processing applications, *office automation applications, and many *expert system applications. When their primary purpose is to supply information to management, they are commonly called *management information systems.

The following are among the more important characteristics of information systems, and make their design and construction particularly difficult.

(a) Their environment is complex, not fully definable, and not easily modeled.

(b) They have a complex interface with their environment, comprising multiple inputs and outputs.

(c) The functional relationships between inputs and outputs are structurally, if not algorithmically, complex.

(d) They usually include large and complex databases (or, in future, knowledge bases).

(e) Their "host" organizations are usually highly dependent on their continuing availability over very long periods, often with great urgency attending their initial provision or subsequent modification.

information technology (IT) Any form of technology, i.e. any equipment or technique, used by people to handle *information. Mankind has handled information for thousands of years; early technologies included the abacus and printing. The last three decades or so have seen an amazingly rapid development of information technology, spearheaded by the computer; more recently, cheap microelectronics have permitted the diffusion of this technology into almost all aspects of daily life and an almost inextricable cross-fertilizing and intermingling of its various branches. The term information technology was coined, probably in the late 1970s, to refer to this nexus of modern technology, electronic-based, for handling information. It incorporates the whole of computing and telecommunication technology, together with major parts of consumer electronics and broadcasting. Its applications are industrial, commercial, administrative, educational, medical, scientific, professional, and domestic.

The advanced nations have all realized that developing competence in information technology is important, expensive, and difficult; large-scale information technology systems are now economically feasible and there are national programs of research and education to stimulate development. The fundamental capabilities that are usually recognized to be essential comprise VLSI circuit design and production facilities, and a common infrastructure for the storage and transmission of digital information (including digitized voice and image as well as conventional data and text). Major research problems include improved systems and software technology, advanced programming techniques (especially in *knowledge-based systems), and improved *human-computer interfaces.

information theory The study of information by mathematical methods. Informally, information can be considered as the extent to which a message conveys what was previously unknown, and so is new or surprising. Mathematically, the rate at which information is conveyed from a source is identified with the *entropy of the source (per second or per symbol). Although information theory is sometimes restricted to the entropy formulation of sources and channels, it sometimes includes coding theory, in which case the term is used synonymously with *communication theory.

INGRES *Trademark* A *relational database system originally developed by M. Stonebraker at Berkeley, California, and now marketed commercially.

inherent addressing *Another name for* implied addressing.

inherently ambiguous language A context-free language that has no nonambiguous grammar (*see* ambiguous grammar). An example is the set
$$\{a^i b^j c^k \mid i = j \text{ or } j = k\}$$

inheritance In a hierarchy of *objects an object generally has a parent object (superclass) at the next higher level in the hierarchy and one or more child objects (subclass) at the next lower level. Each object can have various *attributes associated with it. The attributes can be local to that object, or can be inherited from the parent object. Attributes can be further inherited by child objects (often without limit on the number of inheritances). In addition an object can be an instance of a more general object (not a parent object) with which it shares variables and also inherits its attributes.

Inheritance is thus a means by which characteristics of objects can be replicated and instantiated in other objects. Inheritance is both static by *abstract data type and dynamic by *instantiation and value. *Inheritance rules* define what can be inherited and *inheritance links* define the parent and child of inheritance attributes.

See also object-oriented programming system.

inhibit To prevent the occurrence of an event, e.g. to use a logic gate to inhibit another signal. *Compare* enable.

initial algebra An *algebra A, from some class of algebras C, such that for every algebra B in C there is a unique *homomorphism from A to B. Such an algebra is said to be initial in the class C or, more precisely, initial in the *category that has all the algebras in C as its objects and all the homomorphisms between them as its *morphisms. Depending on the choice of C, there may or may not exist initial algebras; however if any do exist they will all be isomorphic to each other. Initial algebras have importance for the *semantics of programming languages, *abstract data types, and *algebraic specifications. Of particular significance is the fact that, in the class of all Σ-algebras for a given *signature Σ, an initial algebra is given by the *terms or *trees over Σ; this is often called the *word algebra* for Σ.

initialization The act of assigning initial values to variables before the start of a computation. Some programming languages provide a facility for specifying initial values when a variable is first declared.

initial-value problem *See* ordinary differential equations, partial differential equations.

injection (one-to-one function) A *function with the property that distinct elements in its domain are mapped onto distinct elements in the codomain. Formally,

$$f : X \to Y$$

is an injection if

$$f(x_1) = f(x_2) \text{ implies } x_1 = x_2$$

A common use of injections is to map or include elements of some smaller set, such as the set of integers, into a larger set, such as the set of real numbers.

ink jet printer A printer that forms the required image by projecting droplets of ink onto the paper. The technique has been used for a number of years in the printing and labeling industry. Although there have been devices for use in the data-processing environment since the late 1960s, the IBM 6640 (1976) was the first ink jet machine to achieve widespread use.

The *pulsed jet printer* has one or more columns of nozzles mounted in a head that can traverse along the line to be printed. Each nozzle ejects a single drop of ink onto the paper. The line of characters is printed as a matrix array of the drops of ink. With a single column of jets, speeds up to 400 characters per second have been achieved. Printers with larger numbers of nozzles offer higher resolution or multicolor capability.

One design of the *continuous stream printer* has a print head with a single nozzle that emits a jet of ink. The ink jet is made to break up into a constant-velocity stream of droplets of uniform size. Just prior to its separation from the jet each droplet receives an electric charge. In the ballistic flight toward the paper the droplets pass between electrode plates and each droplet is therefore deflected. The deflection is generally used to position the dot along the vertical axis of the printed character and the head is moved to give horizontal placement. Print speeds of 100 cps are achieved.

in-line program A program that has been written sequentially, without loops. When *control units were simpler, such a program required more memory but executed in less time since there were no counters to increment and test. As these functions became part of the control unit in the form of *index registers and associated instructions, these time savings lost importance. The procedure is still valuable in simpler computers, specifically low end microcomputers.

inner code *See* concatenated coding system.

inorder traversal *Another name for* symmetric order traversal.

input 1. The process of entering data into a processing system or a peripheral device, or the data that is entered.
2. A signal that is applied to an electrical circuit, such as a logic circuit.
3. To enter data or apply a signal.

input area The area of main memory that is currently allocated to hold incoming data. The processing system will usually retrieve data from the input area and transfer it to a working area or register before it is processed. The result of the processing may be written to an *output area. Subroutines are usually organized so as to replenish the input area from a source such as an input peripheral or communication line and clear the output area by transfer to backing store.

input device Any device that transfers data, programs, or signals into a processor system. Such devices provide the human-computer interface, the keyboard being the most common example. Early computers also used punched paper tape and cards but these are largely obsolete. Current devices include *digitizers, *data collection terminals, *speech recognition units, magnetic *card readers, and *document scanners.

input-limited process A process whose speed of execution is limited by the rate at which input data is available or obtained.

input/output (I/O) The part of a computer system or the activity that is primarily dedicated to the passing of information into or out of the central processing unit. An important function of most I/O equipment is the translation between the host processor's signals and the sounds, actions, or symbols that are understood or generated by people. In some cases it may be translation between two types of machine-readable signals, as when a *bar code scanner reads the data-encoded package and translates it into an ASCII code. *See also* I/O.

input-process-output *See* IPO.

inquiry station A terminal from which information can be retrieved from a *database. Generally the terminal has a display and a keyboard, but there may also be ancillary devices such as a *badge reader. The user makes the inquiry via the keyboard either in the form of a question in plain text or by indicating a selection from a menu on the display. The display will show a series of possible selections that successively narrow the field of search. An inquiry station may also update information as the result of an action arising from an inquiry. An airline booking terminal is an example of an inquiry station. *See also* interrogation.

inscribe To encode a document by printing information that is readable by both a person and a machine.

insert 1. One of the basic actions performed on *sets that, when applied in the form

insert(el, S)

adds the element *el* to the set *S*. If *el* is already in *S* the operation has no effect on the membership of *S*. *See also* operations on sets.
2. One of the basic actions performed on *lists, that places a new element into a list, not necessarily at one end or the other.

instance *See* unification. *See also* object-oriented programming.

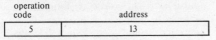

operation code	address
5	13

Simple one-address instruction

indexregister increment
indirect addressing

operation code	select partial word	destination register	index register			address
6	4	4	4	1	1	16

Complex one-address instruction

operation code	register containing one operand	index register	base address register	address (as modified by index and base) of second operand
8	4	4	4	12

Complex two-address instruction using registers and memory

Instruction formats

instantaneously decodable *See* prefix codes.

instantiation A more defined version of some partially defined object.

instruction The description of an operation that is to be performed by a computer. It consists of a statement of an operation to be performed and some method of specifying the operands (or their locations) and the disposition of the result of the operation. Instructions are often divided into classes such as *arithmetic instructions, *program control instructions, *logic instructions, and *I/O instructions. They may or may not be of fixed length. The set of operations available in a particular computer is known as its *operation code or order code. *See also* instruction format.

instruction counter (current address reg- **ister; program counter)** A counting *register that normally increments one memory address at a time and is used to obtain the program sequence (i.e. the sequence of instructions) from sequential memory locations. This counter will have its contents changed by branch instructions. It is part of the *processor status word.

instruction cycle *Another name for* fetch-execute cycle. *See* control unit.

instruction format An instruction is normally made up of a combination of an *operation code and some way of specifying an *operand, most commonly by its location or *address in memory though *nonmemory reference instructions can exist. Some operation codes deal with more than one operand; the locations of these operands may be specified using any of the many *addressing schemes.

Classically, the number of address references has been used to specify something about the architecture of a particular computer. In some instruction formats and machine architectures, the number of operand references may be fixed; in others the number is variable. In the former case descriptions of formats include *one-address*, *two-address*, *three-address*, and (now rarely) *four-address*. An example (symbolically) of a one-address instruction is

add x   i.e.

add contents of address x
to contents of accumulator;
sum remains in accumulator.

An example of a three-address instruction is

add x,y,z   i.e.

add contents of address x
to contents of address y;
sum is placed in location z.

In some cases the last address is the address of the next instruction to be executed. The ability to specify this address was important when rotating (drum) main memories were prominent. Thus a two-address instruction such as

add x,y   i.e.

add contents of address x
to contents of address y;
sum is placed at address y,

may become

add x,y,z   i.e.

add contents of address x
to contents of address y;
sum is placed at address y;
next instruction is taken
from address z.

The latter may be called either a three-address instruction or a *two-plus-one-address* instruction. In a similar way the term *one-plus-one address* instruction represents a one-address instruction together with the address where the next instruction is to be found. In these two cases the instructions do not come from sequential addresses; an instruction counter, if present, is bypassed.

The figure shows three examples of possible/typical instruction formats.

In early computers instruction formats were forced into a fixed word size, that of the computer. An instruction format consisted of two fields: one containing the operation code and the other containing the address(es). As additional features of address modification became available, it was necessary to add special bit positions in the instruction word to specify functions such as *indirect addressing, use of *index registers, use of base registers in *relative addressing, etc. Still other bits were sometimes used to allow for reference to parts of a data word; this was usually as fractions of the word, as character positions, more recently as byte positions.

As registers became common, distinct operation codes were used to refer to register locations; these locations could be specified in many fewer bits than normal addresses, and variable-length instruction formats were developed. *See also* stack processing.

instruction register *See* control unit.

instruction repertoire *Another name for* instruction set.

instruction sequencing The order in which the instructions in a program are carried out. Normally the sequence proceeds in a linear fashion through the program, and the address of the instructions is obtained from the program counter in the *control unit. This sequence is interrupted when a *branch instruction is executed; at such a time the address of the branch instruction is inserted into the program counter and the process continues.

instruction set (instruction repertoire) The totality of *instructions that a computer is capable of performing. The list of all the *operation codes and the permitted *addressing schemes pertinent to each.

instruction stream The sequence of *instructions from memory to the control unit.

instrument To add code to software, or devices to hardware, in order to monitor (and sometimes control) operation of a system or component while under test or analysis. The code or devices so used are called *instrumentation*. Instrumenting code may, for example, write to a report file the before and after values of a variable together with a source reference to the code each time the variable is referenced. Some software environments provide tools to automatically add (and remove) the instrumentation and to analyze report files or screen-directed output.

integer programming *See* mathematical programming.

integer type (type integer) A *data type comprising only integer (whole number) values, lying between specified maximum and minimum values; legal operations include integer arithmetic operations such as addition, subtraction, and multiplication.

integral domain *See* ring.

integral equation Any equation for an unknown function $f(x)$, $a \leqslant x \leqslant b$, involving integrals of the function. An equation of the form

$$f(x) = \int_a^x K(x,y) f(y) \, \mathrm{d}y + g(x)$$

is a *Volterra equation* of the second kind. The analogous equation with constant limits

$$f(x) = \int_a^b K(x,y) f(y) \, \mathrm{d}y + g(x)$$

is a *Fredholm equation* of the second kind. If the required function only appears under the integral sign it is a Volterra or Fredholm equation of the first kind; these are more difficult to treat both theoretically and numerically. The Volterra equation can be regarded as a particular case of the Fredholm equation where

$$K(x,y) = 0 \text{ for } y > x$$

Fredholm equations of the second kind occur commonly in boundary-value problems in mathematical physics. Numerical techniques proceed by replacing the integral with a rule for *numerical integration, leading to a set of *linear algebraic equations determining approximations to $f(x)$ at a set of points in $a \leqslant x \leqslant b$.

integrated circuit (IC) An implementation of a particular electronic-circuit function in which all the individual devices required to realize the function are fabricated on a single *chip of semiconductor, usually silicon. The individual devices normally consist of semiconductor diodes and transistors.

In *MOS integrated circuits* the active devices are *MOSFETs, which operate at low currents and high frequencies. A very large number of MOSFETs can be packed together on one silicon chip, i.e. MOS circuits have a high packing density. They also consume very little power. The development of MOS technology has allowed extremely complex functions to be performed on a single chip.

In *bipolar integrated circuits* the components are *bipolar transistors and other devices that are fabricated using the p-n junction properties of semiconductors. Compared with MOS circuits, bipolar circuits have higher operating speeds but have the disadvantages of high power consumption and low packing density. They are also less simple to fabricate than MOS circuits.

The improvement in the fabrication technology of integrated circuits has made possible the construction of a huge number of components on a single chip. These may be combined on the chip to make a wide variety of digital and analog circuits. The complexity of a digital circuit produced on a single chip is usually described in terms of the number of *transistors involved, or sometimes of the number of *logic gates. This leads to the following differentiation:

VLSI, very large-scale integration;
LSI, large-scale integration;
MSI, medium-scale integration;
SSI, small-scale integration.

Digital integrated circuits are often represented by their logic function rather than their electronic function in order to ease their understanding. *See also* hybrid integrated circuit.

integrated data processing (IDP) *See* data processing.

integrated office system (IOS) A program for use on personal computers or small multiuser business computers that combines some of the functions previously performed by a series of single-purpose programs such as *wordprocessors, *spreadsheets, *database management systems or programs to create graphs and charts. A typical mix of functions in an integrated office system might be spreadsheet, wordprocessor, and graphics. The results of the various sections can usually be merged to form a final document containing pictorial, tabular, and textual material.

integrated project support environment *See* IPSE, PSE (def. 2).

integrated services digital network *See* ISDN.

integrated systems factory *See* ISF.

integration testing *See* testing.

integrity Resistance to alteration by system errors. A user who files data expects that the contents of his files will not be changed by system errors in either hardware or software. Since such errors inevitably will occur from time to time, the prudent system manager maintains a system of protective *dumps, organized in such a way that there

always exists a valid copy of a recent version of every file on the system. For this to be possible, the manager must run system utilities that operate at such a level of privilege that they bypass the normal checks present to maintain the *privacy and *security of users' files. The dump utilities must be able to read the users' files in order to make copies, and must have write access to the users' files in order to reinstate a recent version of a file lost or corrupted by system error. Thus the system for maintaining the integrity of a user's files automatically constitutes a security *vulnerability and represents a weakening of the system for maintaining privacy.

integro-differential equation Any equation for an unknown function involving integrals and derivatives of the function. Many different types can arise and there is no straightforward classification. The initial-value problem (*see* ordinary differential equations) given by

$$f'(x) = F\left(x, f(x), \int_a^x K(x,y) f(y) \, dy\right)$$
$$f(a) = f_0$$

also contains features common to Volterra integral equations (*see* integral equation). Boundary-value problems and equations involving partial derivatives also occur in practice.

Intel A US manufacturer of semiconductors, notable for being one of the first suppliers of 1K dynamic RAM chips. It is reputed to be the first manufacturer of *microprocessors, i.e. the 4004 and the 8008. The IBM PC and its successors and clones all use Intel 8088, 8086, 80286, or 80386 processors, or copies of them.

intelligent character recognition *See* ICR.

intelligent copier A *digital copier in which image manipulation, scaling, merging, reversing, etc., can be performed before printing.

intelligent front end (IFE) A program designed to improve the accessibility of an existing program or computer system. IFEs are useful where complex and highly sophisticated software already exists. The expertise to use this software may take considerable time to acquire; the purpose of an IFE is to alleviate this. The IFE may contain knowledge about the domain of the software (e.g. mathematics or finite element modeling) and also expert knowledge about how best to use the software to solve problems in that domain. IFEs have been built for a wide range of programs (e.g. statistics, finite element modeling, and ecology) and are potentially important in widening the availability of existing software.

intelligent knowledge-based system *See* IKBS.

intelligent terminal A device with some processing capability, by means of which information may be transferred to and from a larger processing system. The device is often a combination of a display and keyboard with at least one built-in microprocessor to provide facilities such as editing and prompts for the operator. Modern application terminals for banking, retail, and industrial data collection are other examples of intelligent terminals.

interactive A word used to describe a system or a mode of working in which there is a response to operator instructions as they are input. The instructions may be presented via an input device such as a keyboard or light pen, and the effect is observable sufficiently rapidly that the operator can work almost continuously. This mode of working is thus sometimes referred to as *conversational mode*. An interactive system for multiple users will achieve the effect by time sharing. *See also* multiaccess system.

interactive graphics A property of a system that enables it to produce and amend pictorial information in response to inputs from an operator at a terminal. Although interactive graphics systems are not yet widely used by comparison with interactive alphanumeric systems, they are growing rapidly in importance as an aid to understanding data. A number of packages are becoming available that allow numerical data to be presented in a variety of forms, e.g. pie charts, histograms, and cartesian or polar graphs. *See also* computer graphics.

interblock gap (IBG) *See* block.

interface 1. A common boundary between two systems, devices, or programs.
2. The signal connection and associated control circuits that are used to connect devices. *See also* standard interface.
3. Specification of the communication between two program units. For example, if a procedure does not refer to nonlocal variables, its interface is defined by the parameter list. Careful definition of interfaces makes it possible to use a program unit without knowledge of its internal working, and is vital to the design of a system that is to be implemented by a team of programmers. The concept is an important feature of *Ada; in Ada a *package is defined in two parts, the interface and the body. The interface specifies exactly what identifiers are visible outside the package, and is sufficient to permit separate compilation of program units that use the package. Similar facilities are found in *Modula 2 and *Turbo Pascal.
4. To provide an interface.
5. To interact.

interior node *Another name for* nonterminal node.

interior path length of a tree. The sum of the lengths of all paths from the root to an interior (i.e. a nonterminal) node.

interleaving A technique for achieving *multiprogramming in a relatively simple system without a supervisor program. Each of the programs that are to be run concurrently are broken down into segments that are then linked up into a single program. The function of each segment and the order of linking is arranged so that maximum use is made of processor time. A segment that initiates a transfer to a peripheral, i.e. a relatively slow task not requiring processor activity, is linked to a segment of some other program for which processor activity is required. A multiplexer channel interface will interleave transfers from several slow peripherals.

interlock A hardware or software method of coordinating and/or synchronizing multiple processes in a computer. Such a method can be used, for example, in the situation in which a certain process should not begin until another process is completed. A common interlock method uses *flags to do this. Another typical situation is one in which requests for some service, e.g. memory access, arrive simultaneously. A hardware interlock procedure will force the requests to become sequential, usually according to a predefined rule.

intermediate storage Any part or type of storage that is used for holding information between steps in its processing.

internal fragmentation A form of *fragmentation that arises when allocations are made only in multiples of a subunit. A request of arbitrary size must be met by rounding up to the next highest multiple of the subunit, leaving a small amount of memory that is allocated but not in use. Internal fragmentation is reduced by reducing the size of the subunit; such a reduction increases *external fragmentation.

internal schema *See* data description language.

internal sorting *See* sorting.

internet protocol (IP) 1. The *DARPA internet protocol, which links defense-research centers in the US and Europe using underlying networks such as the *ARPANET, satellite networks, and many different *local area networks. Host addresses use a 32-bit field, which is broken into one, two, or three octets of network numbers, with the remainder of the 32-bits being used for addressing within networks. The IP protocol provides a uniform *datagram network service on top of a heterogeneous underlying network.

2. The Xerox internet protocol, which provides *datagram network service on top of heterogeneous underlying networks, using a 32-bit network address and a 48-bit host address that is independent of the network.

See also internetworking.

internetworking Connecting several computer *networks together to form a single higher-level network. There are two basic approaches: *encapsulation* and *translation*. The junctions between networks are called *gateways, and their functions depend on which internetworking approach is taken.

When encapsulation is used, a new protocol layer (or layers) is defined; this provides uniform semantics for services such as *datagram packet switching, *electronic mail, etc. When a message is entered into the internetwork, it is wrapped (encapsulated) in a network-specific protocol (local network datagram headers, or virtual circuits). The encapsulated packet is sent over the network to a gateway, which removes the old network-specific encapsulation, adds a new set of network headers, and sends the packet out on another network. Eventually the message reaches its destination, where it is consumed.

When protocol translation is used, messages are sent on a local network using the protocols and conventions of that network. A gateway receives the message and transforms it into the appropriate message on another network; this may involve interpreting the message at multiple protocol levels.

The encapsulation approach provides a uniform set of semantics across all networks, while the translation approach results in unanticipated problems due to subtle differences between protocols. The encapsulation approach generally requires that new software be written for all hosts on all networks, while the translation approach requires new software only in the gateways.

interoperability The ability of systems to exchange and make use of information in a straightforward and useful way; this is enhanced by the use of standards in communication and data format.

interpolation A simple means of approximating a function $f(x)$ in which the approximation, say $p(x)$, is constructed by requiring that

$$p(x_i) = f(x_i), i = 0,1,2,\ldots,n$$

Here $f(x_i)$ are given values $p(x_i)$ that fit exactly at the distinct points x_i (*compare* smoothing). The value of f can be approximated by $p(x)$ for $x \neq x_i$. In practice p is often a polynomial, linear and quadratic polynomials providing the simplest examples. In addition the idea can be extended to include matching of $p'(x_i)$ with $f'(x_i)$; this is *Hermite interpolation*. The process is also widely used in the construction of many numerical methods, for example in *numerical integration and *ordinary differential equations. The interpolating polynomial can be represented in many equivalent forms. For example, when the x_i are equally spaced, the forward and backward difference forms (*see* difference

equation) are convenient. More commonly, nonequally spaced x_i give rise to the *divided difference* form, which incorporates successive differences

$$(f(x_{i+1}) - f(x_i))/(x_{i+1} - x_i),$$
$$i = 0,1,2,\ldots,n - 1$$

These are the first divided differences; second divided differences are obtained by a similar differencing process and so on for higher order differences.

interpretation The process of attaching meanings to the expressions of a *formal language, or the meanings so attached. Without interpretation, expressions are purely formal entities, neutral with respect to meaning; this neutrality allows one to separate syntactic from semantic concerns, and to consider different interpretations for one formal language. Examples: *propositional logic interpretations attach *Boolean values to primitive symbols; *predicate logic interpretations involve *relations or *functions over some underlying *set; *algebras similarly attach functions to the symbols of a *signature; interpretations are also central to the *denotational semantics of programming languages. Interpretations can give completely arbitrary meanings to primitive symbols, as long as they respect *data types; by contrast, *models* must also satisfy certain logical sentences. With primitive symbols interpreted, meanings for all expressions in the language then follow by systematic extension; the phrase "semantics of a language" refers sometimes to the rules of extension but at other times to the choice of a particular interpretation.

interpreter A language processor that analyzes a line of code and then carries out the specified actions, rather than producing a machine-code translation to be executed later.

interpretive language A programming language that is designed for or suited to interpretive implementation. In extreme cases, it is a language that can only be implemented by means of an *interpreter. Some languages are more conveniently interpreted but most can be compiled. BASIC is often interpreted on small computers, but the language does not make this essential. Thus the decision whether to compile or interpret is usually a property of the implementation rather than the language.

interquartile range *See* measures of variation.

interrogation The sending of a signal that will initiate a response. A system may interrogate a peripheral to see if it requires a data transfer. The response is normally a status byte. When a number of devices are interrogated in a sequence the process is called *polling. Interrogation terminals are more generally called *inquiry stations.

interrupt A signal to a processor indicating that an *asynchronous event has occurred. The current sequence of instructions is temporarily suspended (interrupted), and a sequence appropriate to the interruption is started in its place. Interrupts can be broadly classified as being associated with one of the following.

(a) Events occurring on peripheral devices. A processor having initiated a transfer on a peripheral device on behalf of one process may start some other process. When the transfer terminates, the peripheral device will cause an interrupt. *See also* interrupt I/O.

(b) Voluntary events within processes. A process wishing to use the services of the operating system may use a specific type of interrupt, a *supervisor call* (SVC), as a means of notifying the *supervisor.

(c) Involuntary events within processes. A process that attempts an undefined or prohibited action will cause an interrupt that will notify the supervisor.

(d) Action by operators. An operator wishing to communicate with the supervisor may cause an interrupt.

(e) Timer interrupts. Many systems incorporate a timer that causes interrupts at fixed intervals of time as a means of guaranteeing that the supervisor will be entered periodically.

See also interrupt handler.

interrupt handler (IH) A section of code to which control is transferred when a processor is interrupted. The interrupt handler then decides on what action should be taken. For instance, a *first level interrupt handler (FLIH)* is the part of an operating system that provides the initial communication between a program or a device and the operating system. When an interrupt occurs, the current state of the system is stored and the appropriate FLIH is executed: it leaves a message for the operating system and then returns, restoring the system to its original state and allowing the original task to continue as though nothing had happened. The operating system will periodically check for new messages and perform the appropriate actions.

interrupt I/O A way of controlling input/output activity in which a peripheral or terminal that needs to make or receive a data transfer sends a signal that causes a program interrupt to be set. At a time appropriate to the priority level of the I/O interrupt, relative to the total interrupt system, the processor enters an interrupt service routine. The function of the routine will depend upon the system of interrupt levels and priorities that is implemented in the processor.

In a single-level single-priority system there is only a single I/O interrupt – the logical OR of all the connected I/O devices. The associated interrupt service routine polls the peripherals to find the one with the interrupt status set.

In a multilevel single-priority system there is a single interrupt signal line and a number of device identification lines. When a peripheral raises the common interrupt line it also sets its unique code on the identification lines. This system is more expensive to implement but speeds the response.

In a single-level multiple-priority system the interrupt lines of the devices are logically connected to a single processor interrupt in such a way that an interrupt from a high-priority device masks that of lower-priority devices. The processor polls the devices, in priority order, to identify the interrupting device. A multilevel multiple-priority system has both the property of masking interrupts according to priority and of immediate identification via identification lines.

interrupt mask A means of selectively suppressing interrupts when they occur so that they can be acted upon at a later time. *See also* masking.

interrupt priority An allocated order of importance to program interrupts. Generally a system can only respond to one interrupt at a time but the rate of occurrence can be higher than the rate of servicing. The system control may arrange *interrupt masks to suppress some types of interrupt if a more important interrupt has just occurred.

interrupt vector *See* vectored interrupts.

intersection 1. of sets. The set that results from combining elements common to two sets S and T, say, usually expressed as

$$S \cap T$$

$\cap$ is regarded as an *operation on sets, the *intersection operation*, which is *commutative and *associative. Symbolically

$$S \cap T =$$
$$\{x \mid x \in S \text{ and } x \in T\}$$

When two sets S and T intersect in the empty set, the sets are *disjoint. Since the intersection operation is associative, it can be extended to deal with the intersection of several sets.

2. of two graphs, G_1 and G_2. The graph that has as vertices those vertices common to G_1 and G_2 and as edges those edges common to G_1 and G_2.

intersegment linking The links between the *segments of a (large) program. Where segments are separately compiled it is necessary to provide a mechanism for transferring control out of one segment and into another, usually by introducing a specific type of labeled statement that identifies the point at which a segment can be entered, and whose value can be made accessible to other segments when the program is link-edited.

interval timer A digital circuit that is used to determine the time interval between an initial trigger pulse and subsequent *logic states that appear after a predetermined delay.

intrinsic semiconductor (i-type semiconductor) *See* semiconductor.

invariant A property that remains TRUE across some transformation or mapping. In the context of *program correctness proofs, an invariant is an assertion that is associated with some program element and remains TRUE despite execution of some part of that element. For example, a *loop invariant* is an assertion that is attached at some point inside a program loop, and is TRUE whenever the attachment point is reached on each iteration around the loop. Similarly a *module invariant* is associated with a given module, and each operation provided by the module assumes that the invariant is TRUE whenever the operation is invoked and leaves the invariant TRUE upon completion.

Note that invariants cannot accurately be described as TRUE AT ALL TIMES since individual operations may destroy and subsequently restore the invariant condition. However the invariant is always TRUE between such operations, and therefore provides a static characterization by which the element can be analyzed and understood.

inventory *See* pattern.

inverse 1. (converse) of a binary *relation R. A derived relation R^{-1} such that
$$\text{whenever } x \; R \; y$$
$$\text{then } y \; R^{-1} \; x$$
where x and y are arbitrary elements of the set to which R applies. The inverse of "greater than" defined on integers is "less than".

The inverse of a function
$$f: X \rightarrow Y$$
(if it exists) is another function, f^{-1}, such that
$$f^{-1}: Y \rightarrow X$$
and
$$f(x) = y \text{ implies } f^{-1}(y) = x$$
It is not necessary that a function has an inverse function.

Since for each monadic function f a relation R can be introduced such that
$$R = \{(x,y) \,|\, f(x) = y\}$$
then the inverse relation can be defined as
$$R^{-1} = \{(y,x) \,|\, f(x) = y\}$$
and this always exists. When f^{-1} exists (i.e. R^{-1} is itself a function) f is said to be *invertible* and f^{-1} is the *inverse* (or *converse*) *function*. Then, for all x,
$$f^{-1}(f(x)) = x$$
To illustrate, if f is a function that maps each wife to her husband and g maps each husband to his wife, then f and g are inverses of one another.

2. *See* group.

3. of a *conditional $P \rightarrow Q$. The statement $Q \rightarrow P$.

inverse homomorphic image *See* homomorphism.

inverse matrix For a given $n \times n$ matrix of numbers, A, if there is an $n \times n$ matrix B for which

$$AB = BA = I$$
where I denotes the *identity matrix, then B is the inverse matrix of A and A is said to be *invertible* with B. If it exists, B is unique and is denoted by A^{-1}.

inverse power method An *iterative method used to calculate *eigenvalues other than the dominant (largest in value) eigenvalue. *See also* power method.

inverted file A *data file in which one or more secondary indexes are used (*see* indexed file). For each indexed field, the file is said to be inverted with respect to that field. If secondary indexes exist to all possible fields, the file is said to be *fully inverted*.

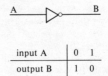

input A	0	1
output B	1	0

Inverter circuit symbol and truth table

inverter (negator) An electronic *logic gate that inverts the signal it receives so that a logic 1 (true) is converted to logic 0 (false) and vice versa. It therefore implements the logical *NOT operation. The diagram shows the circuit symbol and *truth table.

invertible matrix *See* inverse matrix.

involution operation Any *monadic operation f that satisfies the law
$$f(f(a)) = a$$
for all a in the domain of f. The law is known as the *involution law*. It is satisfied by the elements of a *Boolean algebra where the monadic function is the process of taking a complement.

Taking complements of sets and negation in its different forms also satisfy the law, as does the principle of *duality as it applies in Boolean algebras.

I/O *Abbrev. for* input/output.

I/O buffering The process of temporarily storing data that is passing between a processor and a peripheral. The usual purpose is to smooth out the difference in rates at which the two devices can handle data.

I/O bus A *bus, or signal route, to which a number of input and output devices can be connected in parallel.

I/O channel *See* channel.

I/O control Either the hardware that controls the transfer of data between main memory and peripheral devices, or the part of the system software that in turn controls that hardware.

I/O device Any unit of a system that is the entry and/or exit point for information. Such devices, which are a type of peripheral unit, are the link between the system and its environment. *See also* input device, output device.

I/O file A file used to hold information immediately after input from or immediately before output to an *I/O device.

I/O instruction One of a class of *instructions that describes the operations concerned with input and output.

I/O-limited Denoting a process that is either *input-limited, *output-limited, or both.

I/O mapping A technique used primarily in microprocessing whereby peripheral devices are interfaced to a processor whose architecture supports input and output instructions. An I/O mapped device is assigned one or more of the processor's I/O port addresses, and data and status information are transferred between the processor and the peripheral device using the processor's input and output instructions. *Compare* memory mapping.

ionographic printer A type of *electrostatic printer in which the required electrostatically charged image is formed by the controlled projection of ions.

IOP *Abbrev. for* I/O processor.

I/O port *See* port.

I/O processor (IOP) A specialized computer that permits autonomous handling of data between I/O devices and a central computer or the central memory of the computer. It can be a programmable computer in its own right; in earlier forms, as a *wired-program computer, it was called a *channel controller*. *See also* direct memory access.

I/O register A *register, perhaps one of several, used during the process of exchanging data between I/O devices and the main computer. An I/O register often has the ability to compose smaller units, such as bytes or characters, into units of machine-word size, or to perform the reverse decomposition.

I/O supervisor A more specific term than *I/O control, referring almost invariably to the appropriate software within the operating system.

I/O switching A means of selecting one out of several alternative hardware routes to a particular peripheral device, with consequent benefits either in system throughput or reliability.

IP *Abbrev. for* internet protocol.

IPL 1. *Abbrev. for* initial program load. The action of loading the operating software into a "cold" machine.
2. *Abbrev. for* information processing language. In the early days of research into artificial intelligence the need for special-purpose languages capable of

manipulating *dynamic data structures was recognized. IPL-I to IPL-V were a series of *list-processing languages developed to meet this need. They have long been obsolete.

IPO *Abbrev. for* input-process-output. A method for representing system designs in terms of system functions and relations between system functions. The method provides a simple diagram notation. Each IPO diagram has a name describing the function to be performed, usually some reference number, and a substructure of three rectangular boxes, one each for the input, process, and output for the named function. Relationships between IPO diagrams are shown as a functional hierarchy with unnamed links between boxes named and/or referenced.

IPSE *Acronym for* integrated *project support environment. Within the *Alvey Programme of IT research and development in the UK, three generations of IPSE were described.

First-generation IPSEs were characterized as comprising a set of *tools to support programming activities throughout the *software life-cycle and a set of management tools to support project, configuration, and quality management activities across all life-cycle activities. These tools stored all project information as files within a filestore. However there was a low degree of integration, interaction, and exchange of information between the various tools. There was also limited flexibility in the choice of tools and methods available within the IPSE.

Second-generation IPSEs are characterized as having an *object management system (OMS) usually based on a *relational database. Through the OMS the tools could exchange information and cooperate in providing coverage of the various activities taking place within and across life-cycle phases. Second-generation IPSEs also had a common user

interface to the tools, but not necessarily a portable tool interface (*PTI).

Third-generation IPSEs are characterized by in-built support from *knowledge bases and *expert systems to guide the user in the choice of tools and methodology for software development and management.

Further concepts included an *IPSE framework* that provided the basic user support of an OMS, a user interface, and the ability to add user-selected methods and tools. IPSE frameworks would be configurable to create the specific environment required by a user for the user's application domain. To enable tool integration, IPSE frameworks used a PTI that specified the interfaces to the OMSs and the user interface. Two examples of PTIs that have been publicly announced are *PCTE (also PCTE+) and *CAIS-A.

irrecoverable error of peripheral storage. *See* error rate.

irreducible polynomial *See* polynomial.

irreflexive relation A *relation R defined on a set S and having the property that $x R x$ does not hold for any x in the set S. Examples are "is son of", defined on the set of people, and "less than", defined on the integers. *Compare* reflexive relation.

irreversible encryption A cryptographic process that transforms data deterministically to a form from which the original data cannot be recovered, even by those who have full knowledge of the method of encryption. The process may be used to protect stored *passwords in a system where the password offered is first encrypted before it is matched against the stored encrypted password. Illegal access to the stored password therefore does not permit access to the system.

ISAM *Acronym for* indexed sequential access method. An *access method for *data files, supporting both *sequential access and indexed access (*see* indexed file). *COBOL contains facilities for defining files to be accessed in this way, and the access method is implemented by an ISAM utility package. *See also* VSAM.

ISDN *Abbrev. for* Integrated Services Digital Network. A concept that the *PTTs have been developing as a vehicle for the provision of a single service that supports all forms of signal traffic on a single platform. The intention of the ISDN is that it will offer standardized interfaces that will support speech, low-speed and high-speed data, and video traffic; all these will be carried on a digital signaling system. This is clearly an ambitious approach, especially in view of the wide range of data rates to be supported and the differing requirements for activities such as call set-up and response to errors. These services will be offered in "circuit" modes at rates of 64 kbps, 384 kbps, 1536 kbps (North America), and 1920 kbps (Europe). There will also be "packet" modes offering both connection-oriented and connectionless bearer services.

At present (Spring 1989) no PTTs are offering a full ISDN service although a number of countries (USA, Canada, West Germany, UK, France) are offering services that are closely aligned on ISDN in functionality and overall performance.

The "basic rate" access offers digital interfaces at 64 kbps, usually referred to as a *B-channel*, carrying digitized speech or digital data. A second type of channel, a *D-channel*, operates at 16 kbps and is intended solely for digital data. Two B-channels and a D-channel, together with timing and control signals, can be supported on a single 192 kbps local loop. The "primary rate" access offers digital interfaces at nominal rates of 1.536 Mbps (North America) or 1.920 Mbps (Europe). These are presented as either (23B + D) or (30B + D) and again there are requirements for some

bandwidth to be used for timing and control.

There are active discussions on *broadband ISDN* services, offering cutomer access at about 32 Mbps, 44 Mbps, and 132 Mbps, and what might best be classed as informed speculation on services at 150 Mbps and 600 Mbps. *See also* red book, blue book.

ISF *Abbrev. for* integrated systems factory. A third-generation *IPSE.

ISO International Organization for Standardization, the body by which international standards are established for everything from data-processing equipment to machine screw sizes. It was founded in 1946 and its members comprise national standards bodies in over 70 countries. It is of interest in the area of information processing in that it establishes the standard link protocols, coding standards, machine-readable media-interchange standards, etc., that are required to make it possible for data to be communicated electronically between equipment of various manufacturers and from various countries.

ISO-7 An internationally agreed character code (ISO 646-1973), using 7 bits for each character. The code includes certain positions designated for national use, to allow different countries to include special characters for letters with diacritical marks, or currency symbols, etc. The US version is *ASCII, which is normally used in computing.

isolation Any technique aimed at separation of the parts of a system or its database in order to enhance computer security.

isomorphism A *homomorphism that, when viewed as a function, is a *bijection. If

$$\phi : G \to H$$

is an isomorphism then the algebraic structures G and H are said to be *isomorphic* and so exhibit the same algebraic properties. *Isomorphic trees* are *trees that are isomorphic as directed graphs.

ISO/OSI reference model A general architecture proposed by the International Standards Organization for communication systems, allowing open systems interconnection. *See* seven-layer reference model.

ISP *Abbrev. for* instruction set processor. A programming language for the algorithmic description of instruction sets and architectures. It was developed in conjunction with *PMS and is an effective *register transfer language to describe computer architectures and thus to enable their *simulation.

ISR *Abbrev. for* information storage and retrieval.

IT *Abbrev. for* information technology.

iteration 1. The repetition of a numerical or nonnumerical process where the results from one or more stages are used to form the input to the next. Generally the recycling of the process continues until some preset bound is achieved, or the process result is constantly repeated. This is one of the key ideas used in the design of *numerical methods (*see also* iterative methods).

An iterative process is *m-stage* if the new value is derived from *m* previous values; it is *m-stage, sequential* if the new value depends upon the last *m* values, i.e.

$$x^{k+1} = G_k(x^k, x^{k-1}, \ldots, x^{k-m+1})$$

The iteration is *stationary* if the function G_k is independent of k, i.e. the new value is calculated from the old values using the same formula. For example,

$$x^{k+1} = \frac{1}{2}(x^k + a/x^k)$$

is a stationary, one-stage iteration (used for evaluating the square root of a); this is a particular application of *Newton's method. The *secant method is a stationary two-stage sequential iteration.

*False position is an example of a nonsequential iteration.

2. of a formal language. *See* Kleene star.

iterative improvement A technique that approaches a solution by progressive approximation, using the kth approximate solution to find the $(k+1)$th approximate solution (*see also* iteration). Examples of methods that rely on iterative improvement are the Jacobi method and Gauss–Seidel method, used in *numerical analysis.

iterative methods *Numerical methods that are based on or utilize the idea of *iteration. Such methods are widely used in the solution of many different types of problem, ranging from linear and nonlinear *optimization to discretized systems of *partial differential equations. Starting from an initial estimate x_0 of the solution x^*, the methods generate a sequence of approximations $x_0, x_1, x_2, \ldots$. The main objectives are to design methods that will converge from poor initial estimates and also converge rapidly in the vicinity of x^*. Different ideas may be employed in these two phases. *Newton's method, together with its variants, is of fundamental importance for all types of *nonlinear equations.

For the linear system $Ax = b$ where A is large and perhaps sparse (*see* sparse matrix), or has some other special structure, an important class of iterative methods is obtained by "splitting" A into the form $A = M - N$. The splitting is such that systems of the form $Mz = d$ are "easy" to solve, e.g. M could be lower triangular. The iteration then takes the form

$$Mx_{k+1} = Nx_k + d, \ k = 0,1,2,\ldots,$$

where x_0 is an approximation to the solution. Convergence for any x_0 is guaranteed if all the eigenvalues (*see* eigenvalue problems) of $M^{-1}N$ have modulus less than one. The objective is to choose splittings for which each step is efficient and the convergence is rapid.

In *partial differential equations, linear systems arise for which the method of *successive over-relaxation* is particularly suitable. This is given by

$$(D + \omega L)x_{k+1} = \{(1 - \omega)D - \omega U\}x_k + \omega b,$$

where $A = D + L + U$, D consists of the diagonal elements of A, and L, U are respectively the strictly lower and upper triangular parts. The scalar ω is a free parameter and is chosen to try to maximize the rate of convergence. For special problems in partial differential equations, optimal values of ω can be computed. More recently the sucessive over-relaxation method is an important technique in the *multigrid method.

ITron *See* Tron.

J	K	Q	$\bar{Q}$
0	0	Q_n	$\bar{Q}_n$
0	1	0	1
1	0	1	0
1	1	$\bar{Q}_n$	Q_n

JK flip-flop, truth table and symbol

of the Q output prior to the current active transition of the clock. The ambiguous condition of J and K both being true, logic 1, causes the device to "toggle", i.e. change to the complementary logic state, on active transitions of the clock signal. The JK flip-flop (together with the D flip-flop) is the most useful type of flip-flop and is available as a standard integrated-circuit package. *See also* flip-flop.

job A set of programs and the data to be manipulated by these programs. The word also means the execution of the set of programs. In its simplest form a job may consist of loading a binary program and then executing this program using supplied data. In more complex forms whole series of steps may be taken, certain of which may be contingent on the outcome of earlier steps. The complete description of a job is written in a *job-control language.

job-control language (JCL; command language) A language used to write the sequence of commands that will control the running of a job. In a normal programming language the objects manipulated and the operations applicable to these objects correspond to variables within the original problem. In a JCL the objects manipulated are such things as complete programs, or the input and output streams for these programs. Most JCLs incorporate features to control the sequence in which actions will be per-

J

Jackson method *See* JSD, JSP.

JANET *Acronym for* Joint Academic Network. The name was probably first used for the *X-25 based network operating within the UK academic community; there are now several JANETs in existence.

Jarrot's method A method that minimizes a function in one variable using successive parabolic interpolation. The method may diverge or converge to a maximum unless used in conjunction with a safe method such as *golden section search.

JCL *Abbrev. for* job-control language.

JK flip-flop A clocked flip-flop that has two inputs, J and K, and two outputs Q and $\bar{Q}$. The truth table for this device is shown in the diagram, along with the circuit symbol. Q_n represents the state

formed, including some form of conditional statement.

job file A file containing in some suitable intermediate form one or more jobs awaiting execution. The jobs are commonly presented as JCL statements that may be preprocessed so as to eliminate the more blatant errors of syntax or other detectable errors before being appended to the job file.

job mix The set of jobs actually being executed within a multiprogramming system at any one time. *See* scheduler.

job monitoring The control of the jobs running within a system. The term is almost synonymous with *job scheduling.

job scheduling Selecting jobs for execution. *See* scheduler.

job step A single identifiable execution of a program on its data within a job. A typical job step will load a program module and execute it with appropriate data from files, producing output in files suitable for passing on to the next job step. Each job step will also produce an indication as to whether or not its outcome was successful.

job stream A sequence of jobs awaiting processing.

join operator *See* lattice. *See also* relational model.

Josephson junction A junction between two metals that exhibits controllable electron tunneling properties at cryogenic temperatures. First reported by Brian Josephson in 1962, it is a superconducting device that can act as an extremely fast electronic switch with very low power dissipation. *See* Josephson technology.

Josephson (junction) technology A computing technology based on *superconductivity and electron tunneling between metals. These effects occur at extremely low temperatures, obtained by immersing the whole system in liquid helium or (with the most recent superdconducting materials) in liquid nitrogen. Logic circuits and nonvolatile memories can be made out of the technology, which has the potential for ultrafast switching speeds and very low power dissipation (*see* Josephson junction). This combination of properties offers the potential of extremely fast computers that can be realized within minimum linear dimensions and that do not have the heat-transfer problems of VLSI silicon devices. As switching speeds become measured in picoseconds, system linear dimensions must be reduced accordingly. (One nanosecond is the order of 10 cm on a transmission line.)

journal tape The record produced in an *audit trail. It was once usually a magnetic tape.

JOVIAL *Acronym for* Jules' own version of international algorithmic language. A programming language designed by Jules Schwarz of System Development Corporation for military command-and-control systems. It was based on the international algorithmic language (IAL), otherwise known as *Algol 58, suitably extended for its purpose. JOVIAL was implemented on a number of military computers, and is still in use for military projects in the US.

joystick A device for generating signals that can cause the cursor or some other symbol to be moved rapidly about on a display screen. It is a shaft, a few inches in height, that is vertically mounted in a base and can be pulled or pushed by the fingers in any arbitrary direction. The normal mode of operation is to tilt the joystick from its upright position to produce the corresponding direction of cursor motion; in some cases it may respond to finger pressure in the desired direction of cursor motion.

JSD *Abbrev. for* Jackson system development. A proprietary structured method for the analysis and design of data processing and real-time systems, originally devised by Michael Jackson in 1983. JSD is fully integrated with *JSP (Jackson structured programming). The JSD notation covers entity structures (similar to *SSADM entity life histories), and network diagrams connecting entity and process structures. Rules assist the designer to structure and sequence the design process iteratively and to transform and trace requirements into the software design.

JSP *Abbrev. for* Jackson structured programming. A proprietary brand of *structured programming, developed by the British consultant Michael Jackson specifically for use in *data processing. He observed that the inputs and outputs of programs could be defined in terms of particular data structures, which are mostly static and easier to define than programs. He then proposed that programs should be constructed by a systematic method based on data structure diagrams.

Two main problems arise. First, it may not be possible to combine the separate data structure diagrams involved in a program because of what are called *structure clashes*; this is solved by a form of program decomposition called *inversion*. Second, error handling is not accommodated by the simple method, and gives rise to a technique called *backtracking*, which is programmed by using *assertions and the notation posit/quit/admit.

JSP is used in conjunction with Cobol and PL/I. Translators exist to convert from textual equivalents of Jackson data-structure diagrams into the required target language. It is claimed that the same code will always be produced from a given data specification.

JTMP *Acronym for* Job Transfer and Manipulation Protocol. *See* red book.

jukebox *Colloquial name for* optical disk library.

jump 1. A departure from the normal sequential execution of program instructions. The departure is achieved during execution by means of a *jump instruction*. (Jump instruction is usually regarded as synonomous with *branch instruction.) A jump may be *conditional or *unconditional. *See also* GOTO statement.

2. (transfer) To undergo such a departure.

jump instruction (branch instruction) *See* jump.

junction The area of contact between two *semiconductor materials having different electrical properties, or between a semiconductor and a metal. Junctions play a fundamental role in semiconductor devices. The most frequently used is the *p-n junction*, which is formed between n-type and p-type *semiconductors. A p-n junction has rectifying properties as a result of the potential barrier built up across the junction by the diffusion of electrons from the n-type to the p-type material.

justify To move the bit pattern stored in a register so that either the least or most significant bit is at the appropriate end of the register. This is analogous to the similarly named process used in typesetting and word-processing systems to achieve uniform vertical edges to pages or columns of print. Some serial printers used with word-processing systems have a built-in justify facility. The space between words and/or letters is increased until the printed line fills the distance between the margins.

K

k (or **K**) *Symbols for* kilo-.

KAPSE *Acronym for* kernel Ada programming support environment. The underlying tools and facilities of *APSE, i.e. the Ada programming support environment.

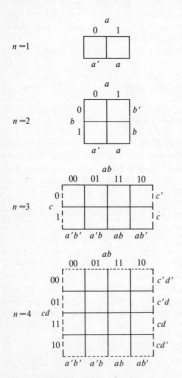

$n = 1$

$n = 2$

$n = 3$

$n = 4$

Karnaugh maps

Karnaugh map (Veitch diagram) A graphical means for representing *Boolean expressions so that the manner in which they can be simplified or minimized is made apparent. It may be regarded as a pictorial representation of a *truth table or as an extension of the *Venn diagram. The method was proposed by E. W. Veitch and modified slightly by M. Karnaugh. The Karnaugh maps for expressions involving one, two, three, and four variables are shown in the diagram. When $n = 2$, for instance, the 00 square represents the term $a'b'$ (where ' denotes negation), the 11 square represents ab, and so on.

Terms that differ in precisely one variable can be combined. Such terms will appear as adjacent squares on a Karnaugh map and so can readily be identified. For example, the terms abc and abc' can be combined since

$$abc \lor abc' = ab$$

These two terms should each occupy one square on the $n = 3$ map and appear side by side, i.e. share a common edge. However, so too should the $a'b'c$ and the $ab'c$ squares. This complication can be overcome by stipulating that the two edges marked with dashes should be identified or joined together, i.e. the Karnaugh map for $n = 3$ should be drawn on one side of a ring of paper. When $n = 4$ the situation is even more complex: the two edges marked with dashes are identified, as are the dotted edges. The map can then be viewed as drawn on the outside of a torus.

Karnaugh maps are useful for expressions of perhaps up to six variables. When $n > 6$, the maps become unwieldy and too complex. Alternative methods of simplification, such as the Quine–McCluskey algorithm, are then preferable.

k-connectivity *See* connectivity, connectedness.

kernel The lowest layer into which a large operating system is subdivided, each layer dealing with some aspect of the system hardware. The kernel is responsible for allocating hardware resources to the processes that make up the operating system and to the programs running under the operating system. Formal verification of the kernel is usually necessary for systems professing high *integrity or *security. *See* security kernel.

Nucleus is a near-synonym for kernel and tends to be used where the effects are achieved by a mixture of normal programming and microcoding. The microprogram is written in such a way as to complement the functions achieved by the normal code, with a gain in running speed.

kernel field *Another name for* base field. *See* polynomial.

key 1. A value used to identify a member of a set. Usually the elements of the set are records (*n*-tuples), in which one of the fields holds the key. Variations allow multiple key fields or any field to be used as a key.

2. A value used to establish authority to access particular information. *See* locks and keys.

3. A value used as a basis for encryption. *See* cryptography.

4. *See* keyboard.

keyboard An array of keys that may be captioned buttons or marked areas on a plane, each of which can cause a discrete signal or action when pressed with a finger. In current systems the operation of the key is detected and turned into a coded electrical signal; in the past mechanical coupling was used to allow depression of keys to directly punch a pattern of holes in a punch card or paper tape, or to print a character.

Computer keyboards consist of the standard typewriter layout – the QWERTY keyboard – plus some additional keys. These can include a *control key*, *function keys*, *cursor keys*, and a *numeric keypad*. The control key operates in the same way as a shift key but allows noncharacter information to be sent to the computer; the function keys send not one but a whole sequence of characters to the computer at a time,

and can often be programmed by the user to send commonly used sequences; the cursor keys are used to move the screen *cursor to a new position; the numeric *keypad duplicates the normal typewriter number keys and speeds up the entry of numerical data.

keyboard encoder *See* encoder.

keypad A limited but compact form of keyboard, sometimes hand-held, with a small number, often 12 or 16, of captioned buttons or pressure-sensitive areas on a plane. It is used in conjunction with data collection equipment or as a means of entering limited information such as a personal identification number (PIN).

keypunch A *card punch that is controlled from a keyboard.

key sorting A form of *address table sorting in which the sortkey is placed with the addresses.

key to disk A data entry system in which the data entered by a number of keyboard operators is accumulated on a magnetic disk. The data is often verified by comparing it with data entered by a second operator working from the same original document. The small computer that routes the data from the operator to the correct file on the disk can also be used to carry out *data validation and produce statistics on operator productivity.

key to tape A data entry system in which the data entered by each keyboard operator is written to a magnetic tape. The data is verified by having a second operator read and enter data from the same source document on a machine that has been set to compare the keyboard input with the data already on the tape.

keyword A symbol in a programming language that has a special meaning for the *compiler or *interpreter. For example, keywords in BASIC include LET, IF, THEN, PRINT. The keywords guide the analysis of the language, and in a simple language each keyword causes activation of a specific routine in the language processor. *See also* keyword parameter, reserved word.

keyword parameter A parameter of a subroutine, procedure, or macro that is identified by name rather than by its position in the parameter list, e.g.

SORT(INPUT = FILE A,
OUTPUT = SYSPRINT)

kilo- (symbol: k) A prefix indicating a multiple of 1000 (10^3), as in kilometer or kilowatt. When the binary system is used, as in computing, it indicates a multiple of 2^{10} (1024), as in kilobit or kilobyte. The use in computing of the symbol K (rather than k) for kilo- should be discouraged, as should its use to symbolize kilobyte and kilobit.

Kimball tag *See* punched tag.

Kleene closure *Another name for* Kleene star.

Kleene-plus *See* Kleene star.

Kleene star (star closure; Kleene closure; iteration) An operation on *formal languages that gives for any language L the language L^*, defined by

$$\{\Lambda\} \cup L \cup LL \cup LLL \cup \ldots$$

where Λ is the empty word. Thus a *word w is in L^* if and only if it has the form

$$w_1 w_2 \ldots w_n$$

with each w_i in L, i.e. is a *concatenation of words in L.

L^+, the *Kleene-plus* of L, is defined by

$$L \cup LL \cup LLL \cup \ldots$$

Thus L^+ comprises the nonempty strings of L^*.

Kleene's theorem on fixed points. *See* fixed-point theorem.

Kleene's theorem on *regular expressions. A theorem in *formal language

theory proposed by S. C. Kleene and stating that a language is definable by a regular expression if and only if it is recognized by a *finite-state automaton. A regular expression equivalent to a finite-state automaton can be found by solving a set of simultaneous linear equations (*see* linear grammar, Arden's rule).

k lookahead *See* LR parsing, LL parsing.

kludge *Informal* An inelegant but effective mechanism (software and/or hardware).

KMP algorithm *Short for* Knuth–Morris–Pratt algorithm.

knapsack problem A common example of an integer programming problem: a knapsack has volume V and there are an unlimited number of each of N different items. For $i = 1, \ldots, N$ one unit of item i has known volume V_i and known value m_i. Integer numbers of the various items may be put into the knapsack and the objective is to pack as much value as possible into the knapsack without exceeding the total volume V.

knot 1. An intersection of arcs in a *graph that is not a *planar graph. Where the arcs represent linear code sequences in a program, and the nodes represent branch points in the program, then the presence and frequency of knots is a measure of the *complexity of the program (*see* control flow graph).
   2. *See* spline.

knowledge base A collection of knowledge in a particular domain that has been formalized in the appropriate representation with which to perform reasoning. It is most frequently encountered within the context of *expert systems, where the knowledge base might represent the rules and experience of an expert practitioner in that domain (e.g. medicine or electronics). Typically the knowledge will be expressed in *production rule format and will represent the *heuristic approach that a practitioner has developed through applying formal knowledge in the course of problem solving. Other knowledge representation formalisms are *logical formulae, *semantic nets, and *frames. Within expert systems there are two important classes of knowledge base, *static* and *dynamic*. A static knowledge base consists of the domain knowledge necessary to perform problem solving and remains unchanged during the course of a problem-solving session. The dynamic knowledge base is used to store information relevant to solving a particular problem (e.g. the results of laboratory tests) and varies from one problem-solving session to the next.

knowledge engineering *See* expert systems.

Knuth–Bendix algorithm An algorithm for turning a set of equations into an equivalent set of rewrite-rules. This process is relevant to the implementation of specification languages, such as OBJ, that allow equational specifications to be written and executed.

Knuth–Morris–Pratt algorithm (KMP algorithm) A method of finding patterns, developed by D. E. Knuth, J. H. Morris and V. R. Pratt. It can be used for example to find a certain pattern within a list of letters: the first letter in the list is stored in an array and subsequent letters added until the pattern is no longer followed or is completed; on failure the next letter is chosen and so on.

Königsberg bridges problem A problem solved by Euler in about 1736 for the inhabitants of Königsberg (now Kaliningrad). Two islands in a river are connected to each other by one bridge and to the banks by six other bridges; one island has two bridges from the left bank and two from the right bank while the other island has one bridge from the left bank and one from the right bank. The problem is whether or not it is possible to follow a circular walk starting and finishing at the same river bank and crossing each bridge precisely once. *See* Euler cycle.

Kraft's inequality When an instantaneously decodable code is to be formed from an alphabet of q letters, with the ith codeword being λ_i letters in length, Kraft's inequality

$$\sum_{i=1}^{n} q^{-\lambda_i} \leqslant 1$$

is a necessary and sufficient condition for such a code to be constructable with n codewords. In a code with no codewords remaining for allocation, the equality sign operates. *See also* prefix codes.

Kronrod's algorithm (four Russians algorithm) A method of Boolean matrix multiplication developed by M. A. Kronrod. It saves computational time and storage space by doing computations in a strict order.

Kruskal's algorithm A method of finding the minimum-cost *spanning tree of a weighted undirected *graph, proposed by J. B. Kruskal Jnr (1956).

L

label 1. (tape label; volume label) A record at the very start of a magnetic tape, holding the identity and other characteristic information about the tape. Labels are written by the utility program, and checked at run time by the operating system to ensure that the specified tape is the one that has been loaded. A tape label only holds information about the physical tape, which remains constant irrespective of the file(s) held on the tape. Labels are thus distinct from file *headers, which precede every file on a tape.

Magnetic disks normally have similar labels, though there is no commonly accepted term for them.

2. (statement label) A numeric or alphanumeric identifier associated with a line or statement in a program and used in other parts of the program to refer to that statement.

lambda calculus (λ-calculus) A formalism for representing functions and ways of combining functions, invented around 1930 by the logician Alonzo Church. Examples:

$\lambda x.x$ denotes the *identity function*, which simply returns its argument;

$\lambda x.c$ denotes the *constant function*, which always returns c regardless of what argument it is applied to;

$\lambda x.f(f(x))$ denotes the composition of the function f with itself, i.e. the function that, for any argument x, returns $f(f(x))$.

Much of the power of the notation derives from the ability to represent higher-order functions. For example,
$$\lambda f.\lambda x.f(f(x))$$
denotes the (higher-order) function that, when applied to a function f, returns the function obtained by composing f with itself.

As well as a notation, the λ-calculus comprises rules for *reducing* λ-expressions to equivalent ones. The most important is the rule of *β-reduction*, by which an expression of the form
$$(\lambda x.e_1)(e_2)$$
reduces to e_1 with all *free occurrences of x replaced by e_2. For example,
$$(\lambda x.f(\lambda x.x,x))(a)$$
reduces to
$$f(\lambda x.x,a)$$
As a second example, involving a functional variable, the expression
$$(\lambda f.f(a))(\lambda x.g)(x,b))$$

reduces to
$$(\lambda x.g(x,b))(a)$$
and hence to
$$g(a,b)$$

In theoretical terms, the formalism of λ-calculus can be shown to be equivalent in expressive power to that of *Turing machines. More significantly one can point to its influence on the design of languages such as LISP and ML, to Landin's reduction of Algol 60 to λ-calculus, and to Scott's achievement in constructing a set-theory meaning for the full unrestricted λ-calculus – a construction that ushered in the theory of *domains in the *denotational semantics of programming languages.

lambda expression (λ-expression) An expression in the *lambda calculus.

LAN *Abbrev. for* local area network.

language *See* programming language, formal language.

language construct A syntactic structure or set of structures in a language to express a particular class of operations. The term is often used as a synonym for *control structure.

LAP *Acronym for* link access protocol. The second-layer (data link layer) protocol that is a subset of *HDLC and is used in *X.25-based networks in setting up channels between *DTE and *DCE. An alternative protocol, *LAPB*, developed after LAP, allows the DTE/DCE interface to operate in "balanced mode".

laptop computer A microcomputer that can be simply carried around by one person and used in transit from internal battery power. Laptops typically have all the features of a desktop model but have a flat display screen, either a *plasma display or an *LCD display, that folds over the keyboard when not in use. They are also rather more expensive than their desktop equivalents. *See also* portable.

large-scale integration *See* LSI, integrated circuit.

laser A light source with special properties (principally spectral purity and narrow output beam) that make it particularly useful in optical storage devices and some kinds of printer, and also in optical fiber communication systems.

laser printer An *electrophotographic printer in which a laser is used as the light source. The term is also often used to refer to *page printers of this type that use *LEDs or *LCDs as the active element.

last in first out *See* LIFO.

latch An electronic device that can store temporarily a single bit of data. It can be considered as an extension of a simple *flip-flop. The storage is controlled by a *clock signal, a given transition of which fixes the contents of the latch at the current value of its input. The contents will remain fixed until the next transition of the clock.

latency The time taken for the start of a given sector of data on a storage disk to reach the read/write head. The time is measured from the instant that the head settles at the track within which the sector lies. The average latency is the time for half a revolution of the disk. *See also* seek time.

L^AT_EX A macro package built on top of *T_EX. L^AT_EX implements a form of descriptive markup system, in which the user specifies the function of each piece of text (heading, paragraph, footnote, etc.) but not its printed appearance. The actual layout is defined in a collection of style files, thus ensuring uniformity of appearance and conformity to house style. L^AT_EX hides much of the complication of T_EX from the user, and is widely used in the academic community as a way of producing typeset research papers and reports.

lattice An *algebraic structure, such as a *Boolean algebra, in which there are two *dyadic operations that are both *commutative and *associative and satisfy the *absorption and *idempotent laws. The two dyadic operators, denoted by $\wedge$ and $\vee$, are called the *meet* and the *join* respectively.

An alternative but equivalent view of a lattice is as a set L on which there is a *partial ordering defined. Further, every pair of elements has both a greatest *lower bound and a least *upper bound. The least upper bound of $\{x,y\}$ can be denoted by $x \vee y$ and is referred to as the *join* of x and y. The greatest lower bound can be denoted by $x \wedge y$ and is called the *meet* of x and y. It can then be shown that these operations satisfy the properties mentioned in the earlier definition, since a partial ordering $\leqslant$ can be introduced by defining

$$a \leqslant b \text{ iff } a \vee b = a$$

Lattices in the form of Boolean algebras play a very important role in much of the theory and mathematical ideas underlying computer science. Lattices are also basic to much of the approximation theory underlying the ideas of *denotational semantics.

lazy evaluation An execution mechanism in which an object is evaluated only at the time when, and to the extent that, it is needed. This allows programs to manipulate objects, such as lengthy or infinite lists, whose evaluation would otherwise be needlessly time-consuming or indeed fail to terminate at all. An illustration is the problem of comparing two *trees, t_1 and t_2, to test whether the *leaves of t_1, read from left to right, form the same list as the leaves of t_2. The simplest solution is first to construct the two leaf-lists and then to compare them element by element. Lazy evaluation allows this program to interleave the construction of the two leaf-lists and then test for equality. The program can then terminate as soon as the lists are found to differ, without having unnecessarily constructed both lists in toto. *See also* strictness.

LBA *Abbrev. for* linear-bounded automaton.

LCA *Abbrev. for* logic cell array. A form of *PAL in which the programming information is held in a *SIPO *shift register, so that the mode of operation of the device can be read into it when the system of which it is a part is started up. The contents of the register, and therefore the mode of operation of the LCA, remain unchanged while the system is running.

LCC *Abbrev. for* leadless chip carrier.

LCD *Abbrev. for* liquid-crystal display. A device incorporated into many digital watches, calculators, some small computers, instruments, etc., in order to display numerical, alphabetical, and sometimes other characters. The display comprises groups of segments from which individual characters can be formed. Each segment consists of a normally transparent anisotropic liquid sandwiched between two transparent electrodes. Application of an electric field across the electrodes causes the reflectivity of the liquid to change and the segment becomes opaque. Individual segments can therefore be selectively darkened to form a character. The digits and some letters are typically produced from groups of seven segments. Unlike *LED displays, LCDs do not generate their own light and thus require external illumination; they do however have a lower current drain than other forms of *display.

LCM *Abbrev. for* least common multiple.

LCSAJ *Abbrev. for* linear code sequence and jump. A section of program code that will always be executed in sequence and followed by a particular sequence. *See also* control flow graph.

LDU decomposition *See* LU decomposition.

leader A blank section of a tape, preceding recorded information, that is needed for threading the tape into a reading device.

leadless chip carrier (LCC) A form of *integrated circuit packaging where connections to the device are not made by means of pins extending beneath the device (as for instance in *DIPs), but instead by means of studs arranged around the package's periphery. This means that the device can be inserted into a socket mounted on a PCB.

leaf *Short for* leaf node.

leaf node (terminal node; tip node; external node) Any node of a tree with no descendants and hence of *degree zero.

least common multiple (LCM) of two integers m and n. The smallest integer p such that m divides p exactly and n divides p exactly. For example, the LCM of 9 and 6 is 18.

least fixed point *See* fixed-point theorem.

least significant character In a *string where the position of a character determines its significance, the character at the end of least significance. Such a string is normally written with the least significant position on the right. For example, the *least significant digit (LSD)* and the *least significant bit (LSB)* contribute the smallest quantity to the value of a digital or binary number.

least squares, method of A method of estimating *parameters in a model by minimizing the sum of squares of differences between observed and theoretical values of a variable. If
$$y_i, \ i = 1, \ldots, n,$$

is a sample of n observations, and μ_i is a set of theoretical values corresponding to a set of unknown parameters, θ, and a set of known associated observations, x_i, then the criterion to be minimized with respect to variations in θ is the sum of squares,

$$\Sigma(y_i - \mu_i)^2$$

The values of θ at which the minimum occurs are known as *least squares estimates*.

The method of *weighted least squares* is used when each observation is associated with a weight, w_i (*see* measures of location), and the criterion to be minimized is

$$\Sigma w_i(y_i - \mu_i)^2$$

See also likelihood, regression analysis.

least squares approximation *See* approximation theory.

LED display A device used in some calculators, digital watches, etc., to display numerical and alphabetical characters. It consists of an array of *light-emitting diodes*, LEDs, which are semiconductor diodes that emit light when a *forward bias is applied; the color of the light is usually red. LEDs are small, cheap, and have relatively low current and voltage requirements and long life. Their power requirements are, however, significantly higher than those of *LCDs. In an LED display these diodes are arranged in such a way that by selectively illuminating individual ones in the array, simple characters are formed on the display. Seven diodes suffice to display the digits and some letters. *See also* display.

Lee distance (Lee metric) In the theory of *block codes intended for error detection or error correction, a distance measure analogous to the *Hamming distance but modeling more accurately a *linear *q-ary channel, such as the phase-modulated carrier used in *modems. When $q = 2$ or $q = 3$, the Lee and Hamming distances are the same.

left-linear grammar *See* linear grammar.

left shift *See* shift.

left subtree *See* binary tree.

left-to-right precedence A simple form of *precedence hierarchy, used in APL, in which operators are taken in the order in which they appear in the expression. Each operator takes everything to the right as its right operand, thus

$$a * b + c$$

evaluates as

$$a * (b + c)$$

Note that, paradoxically, left-to-right precedence actually causes operators to be applied in right-to-left sequence.

length 1. of a sequence. The cardinality of the domain of the sequence. Thus the sequence

$$a_1, a_2, \ldots, a_n$$

has length n.
  2. of a string. The upper bound of the string, hence the number of elements in the string.
  3. of a vector. The number of elements in the vector.

length-increasing grammar *See* context-sensitive grammar.

LEO A line of computers, and a company, of historic importance in the British computing industry. J. Lyons & Co (a large firm in the catering industry) initiated in 1947 a project to build a computer to mechanize clerical functions in their own offices. (This decision was almost simultaneous with a similar decision in the US by Eckert and Mauchly, which led to UNIVAC 1.) The project was led by T. R. Thompson, a mathematician, and J. Pinkerton, an electrical engineer. The machine they built, LEO (Lyons Electronic Office), was fully operational at the end of 1953.

In 1954, LEO Computers Limited was founded. The company traded until 1963, when it was merged with the computing division of English Electric. During that time it marketed the LEO III, an extremely advanced commercial machine for its time.

letter (in formal language theory) *See* word.

letter distribution *See* Parikh's theorem.

letter-equivalent languages *See* Parikh's theorem.

level of a node in a tree. A numerical value equal to one greater than the *depth of the same node. The level of the root node is thus one; the level of any other node is one greater than that of its parent. In some texts, the term level is used as a synonym for depth.

leverage *See* influence.

LEX A lexical analyzer generator for the *UNIX system. LEX automatically generates a *lexical analyzer, given the syntactic rules describing the *tokens of a language. It is usually used in conjunction with the compiler generator *YACC.

lexical analyzer (scanner) The part of a *compiler that breaks up the input into meaningful units, e.g. names, constants, reserved words, operators. The lexical analyzer will also remove redundant characters, e.g. spaces, and may deal with character-set mappings, e.g. replacing upper-case letters by the equivalent lower-case letters. The units recognized by the lexical analyzer are called *tokens*, and are output in some conveniently coded form for subsequent processing by the compiler.

lexicographic order The order of words in a dictionary, given the order of letters in the alphabet. In general, let a set S be *well-ordered by relation $<$, and for $n > 0$ let T be a set of n-tuples

$$(x_1, x_2, \ldots, x_n)$$

of elements x_j in S. Then the ordering relation $<$ over such n-tuples can be defined so that

$$(x_1, \ldots, x_n) < (y_1, \ldots, y_n)$$

iff $x_1 < y_1$ or there is some k, $1 \leq k \leq n$, for which

$$x_i = y_i \text{ for } 1 \leq i < k$$
$$x_k < y_k$$

The set T is in lexicographic order if the n-tuples are sorted with respect to this relation. The concept can be extended to strings whose lengths may be different. The order would then be that in which words are placed in a dictionary.

lexicographic sort Any sorting algorithm for putting n-tuples into *lexicographic order.

library, library program *See* program library.

life-cycle *See* software life-cycle, system life-cycle.

LIFO or **lifo** *Acronym for* last in first out. *LIFO list* is another name for *stack. A stack implemented in hardware is sometimes referred to as a *lifo*.

light-emitting diode (LED) *See* LED display.

light pen A penlike input device that is used with a cathode-ray tube display. It can be used to point to areas of the screen and thus indicate a selection from a displayed list, or it can be used to draw shapes. The light pen has· a photosensor at the tip that responds to the peak illumination that occurs when the CRT scanning spot passes its point of focus. The display system correlates the timing of the pulse from the photosensor with the timing of the display scan to determine the position of the light pen.

When the light pen is used to draw shapes, the difficulties of parallax – due to thickness of the screen – and the lack of a fine point at the tip of the pen are overcome by use of a tracking cross. The display system generates a fine-line tracking cross and positions it so that its intersection is central in the field of view of the light pen. As the light pen is moved across the screen the tracking cross follows it closely and the path of the intersection point is stored in the display file. A switch – usually on the pen – is used to indicate the intended start and finish points of a stroke.

likelihood The *probability that an observation belongs to a *probability distribution with *parameters θ, considered as a function of the parameters rather than of the observation.

The method of *maximum likelihood*, originated by R. A. Fisher, estimates *parameters in statistical models by maximizing the likelihood of observing the data with respect to the parameters of the model. The values taken by the parameters at the maximum are known as *maximum likelihood estimates*. This method is computationally equivalent to the method of *least squares when the distribution of the observations about their theoretical means is the *normal distribution.

limited license *See* copyright.

Lindenmeyer system *See* L-system.

linear algebraic equations (simultaneous equations) A problem in *numerical linear algebra that requires the solution of n equations in the unknowns $x_1, x_2, \ldots, x_n$ of the form
$$Ax = b$$
where A is a square $n \times n$ matrix. The solution obtained by computing the inverse matrix and forming $A^{-1}b$ is less accurate and requires more arithmetical operations than elimination methods. In *Gaussian elimination* multiples of successive equations are added to all succeeding ones to eliminate the unknowns $x_1, x_2, \ldots, x_{n-1}$ in turn. Properly used, with row interchanges to avoid large

multiples, this leads to a solution that satisfies exactly a system close to the one given, relative to the machine precision. The accuracy of the solution, which can be cheaply estimated, depends on the *condition number of the problem.

Many other methods are used to deal with matrices of special form. Very large systems where the matrix A has predominantly zero entries occur in the solution of *partial differential equations. Elimination methods tend to fill in the zeros causing storage problems and *iterative methods are often preferred for such problems.

linear array *Another name for* one-dimensional array, i.e. for a *vector. *See also* array.

linear-bounded automaton (LBA) A *Turing machine M such that the number of tape cells visited by M is bounded by some linear function of the length of the input string. Of equivalent power is the smaller class of Turing machines that visit only the cells bearing the input string. The *context-sensitive languages are precisely those recognized by such Turing machines.

For arbitrary Turing machines, a nondeterministic one always has an equivalent deterministic one. It is still unknown whether this is the case for linear-bounded automata.

linear channel A transmission channel in which the information *signal and the *noise signal combine additively to form the output signal. In a *q-ary linear channel, with a finite number, q, of amplitudes, the signals add modulo-q; in the binary case ($q = 2$), this has the same effect as an *exclusive-OR operation between the signals.

linear codes In coding theory, codes whose encoding and decoding operations may be expressed in terms of linear operations. The term is usually applied to certain *error-correcting codes in which the encoding operation involves a *generator matrix* and the decoding operation involves a *parity-check matrix*. Linear codes are, therefore, also called *parity-check codes*. A particular linear code forms a commutative *group that has the zero codeword as its identity.

In the case of linear (n, k) *block codes, the generator matrix is $k \times n$ and the parity-check matrix is $(n - k) \times n$; the elements of both matrices are elements of the base field (this being $\{0, 1\}$ for *binary codes). *See also* convolutional code.

linear grammar A *grammar in which each production contains at most one nonterminal in its right-hand side. Such a grammar is *right-linear* if a nonterminal can only occur as the rightmost symbol, i.e. if each production has one of the forms

$$A \rightarrow w$$
$$A \rightarrow wB$$

where A and B are nonterminals and w is a string of terminals. A *left-linear grammar* can be similarly defined:

$$A \rightarrow w$$
$$A \rightarrow Bw$$

The right- and left-linear grammars generate precisely the *regular languages.

The word linear relates to an analogy with ordinary algebra. For example, a right-linear grammar such as

$$S \rightarrow aS|abT|abcT|abcd$$
$$T \rightarrow S|cS|bcT|abc|abcd$$

corresponds to the simultaneous linear equations

$$X = \{a\}X \cup \{ab,abc\}Y \cup \{abcd\}$$
$$Y = \{\Lambda,c\}X \cup \{bc\}Y \cup \{abc,abcd\}$$

where X and Y are sets of strings and Λ is the empty string. *Union and *concatenation play roles analogous to addition and multiplication. The smallest solution to the equations gives the language generated by the grammar. *See* Arden's rule.

linear independence A fundamental concept in mathematics. Let

$$x_1, x_2, \ldots, x_n$$

be m-component vectors. These vectors are linearly independent if for some scalars $\alpha_1, \alpha_2, \ldots, \alpha_n$,

$$\sum_{i=1}^{n} \alpha_i x_i = 0$$

implies

$$\alpha_1 = \alpha_2 = \ldots = \alpha_n = 0$$

Otherwise the vectors are said to be *linearly dependent*, i.e. at least one of the vectors can be written as a linear combination of the others. The importance of a linearly independent set of vectors is that, providing there are enough of them, any arbitrary vector can be represented uniquely in terms of them.

A similar concept applies to functions $f_1(x), f_2(x), \ldots, f_n(x)$ defined on an interval $[a,b]$, which are linearly independent if for some scalars $\alpha_1, \alpha_2, \ldots, \alpha_n$, the condition,

$$\sum_{i=1}^{n} \alpha_i f_i(x) = 0$$

$$\text{for all } x \text{ in } [a,b],$$

implies

$$\alpha_1 = \alpha_2 = \ldots = \alpha_n = 0$$

linear list *See* list.

linear logic A system of *combinational and possibly *sequential circuits in which the combinational component comprises *exclusive-OR gates only. This is sometimes referred to as *strongly linear logic* in order to distinguish it from *weakly linear logic* in which *inverters are permitted.

In nonbinary (q-valued) systems, the EXOR gates are generalized to modulo-q adders and subtractors.

linearly dependent *See* linear independence.

linear multistep methods An important class of methods for the numerical solution of *ordinary differential equations. For the initial-value problem

$$y' = f(x,y), \, y(x_0) = y_0$$

the general form of the k-step method is

$$\sum_{i=0}^{k} a_i \, y_{n+i} = h \sum_{i=0}^{k} \beta_i \, f_{n+i}$$

where $f_r = f(x_r, y_r)$ and h is the stepsize, $h = x_r - x_{r-1}$. The formula is said to be *explicit* if $\beta_k = 0$ and *implicit* otherwise.

The most important and widely used formulae of this type are the *Adams formulae* and the *backward differentiation formulae (BDF)*. These formulae are derived from *interpolation polynomials to previously computed values of $f(x,y)$ or $y(x)$ respectively. They form the basis for some of the best modern software, in which the stepsize and the step number k are chosen automatically. The BDF codes, intended for stiff equations (*see* ordinary differential equations), have been particularly successful in relation to other methods used for the same class of problems.

Linear multistep methods are more efficient than *Runge-Kutta methods when evaluations of $f(x,y)$ are sufficiently expensive. The ease with which the step number k can be varied automatically permits the design of codes that can be efficient over a wide range of requested accuracies.

linear predictor *See* generalized linear model.

linear programming A technique in *optimization, pioneered by George B. Dantzig, that is widely used in economic, military, and business-management decisions. It deals with the problem of finding nonnegative values of the variables $x_1, x_2, \ldots, x_n$ that satisfy the constraints

$$a_{i1}x_1 + a_{i2}x_2 + \ldots + a_{in}x_n = b_i,$$
$$i = 1, 2, \ldots, m$$

and minimize the linear form

$$c_1x_1 + c_2x_2 + \ldots + c_nx_n$$

Maximizing problems and problems with inequality constraints or unrestricted variables can be converted to this form. An optimum solution (if any exist) is known to be a *basic fea-*

sible solution, which is one that satisfies the constraints and has at most m positive x_i values.

Computationally such problems are solved by the *simplex method*, which starts at a basic feasible solution and searches the set of such solutions in such a manner that the value of the linear form is nonincreasing. Very large problems occur in practice involving *sparse matrices. Recent work has suggested that improvements on the simplex method may soon be available.

linear recurrence A relationship that defines the next term in a sequence in the form of sums and differences of multiples of earlier terms in the sequence. For example,

$$a_{r+1} = 2a_r + 1$$
$$b_{r+1} + 2b_r - b_{r-1} = 0$$

See also recurrence.

linear regression model *See* regression analysis.

linear structure (totally ordered structure) A collection of items ordered by a single property so that each item, except possibly for the first or last, has a unique "predecessor" and a unique "successor". It is the most commonly used structure and appears under a variety of names depending on storage representation and its intended use. Linked representations are normally called *lists while sequential representations are called *arrays.

line feed (LF) A format command for printers, signaling the requirement that the data that follows should be printed one line pitch below the preceeding data. In impact printers it invokes the physical movement required to move the paper at right angles to the print line by a distance equal to the previously specified pitch between printed lines. In nonimpact page printers it invokes an analogous action in the stored image that is subsequently transferred to the paper in a continuous movement.

line finder Any computer program that detects lines in a *gray-level array. The line finder might look for the boundaries of regions of similar gray-level, or for a bar of similar gray-levels, etc.

line printer A computer output device that produces a line of print per cycle of its operation. The number of character positions in a line generally ranges from 80 to 160, and lines are printed at rates from 150 to 3000 lines per minute. A complete line of information has to be assembled in a buffer memory within the machine before it can start printing. When a line of print has been completed a paper-feed system moves the paper so that the position for the next line of print is opposite the printing mechanism.

The paper to be printed is usually supplied as a continuous web of up to 2000 forms divided by perforations. To ensure positive control of the forms, the margins are punched with holes that engage on the tractors of the printer's paper-feed system.

line protocol A formally specified set of possible bit sequences that will guarantee that two ends of a communication link will be able to pass information between them in an understandable way. A number of standards have been devised for the implementation of such protocols, including *SDLC and *BISYNC protocols (originally developed by IBM) and *HDLC and *ADCCP (developed by standards organizations as an outgrowth of the efforts of a number of manufacturers).

line switching The most common form of concentration (*see* concentrator), used to connect *n* transmitting devices to *m* receiving devices, where *n* is much greater than *m*. Buffering of data is done by the input devices of the line-

switching system if the transmission medium is busy.

link 1. To join together two or more separately compiled program modules, usually with additional library modules, to form an executable program. *See also* link editor.

2. (linkage) A part of a program, possibly a single instruction or address, that passes control and *parameters between separate portions of the program. The instruction, address, etc., *links* the separate portions.

3. (pointer) A character or group of characters that indicates the storage of an item of data. Thus when a field of an item A in a data structure contains the address of another item B, i.e. of its first word in memory, it contains a link to B. Two items are *linked* when one has a link to the other. An important case is the link left pointing into the calling code by the *call of a subroutine, i.e. the value of the *program counter at the point of call. *See also* linked list.

4. (line) A path for communication that may be physical (as in a circuit) or either physical or logical (as in a channel).

linkage *Another name for* link (def. 2).

linkage editor *Another name for* link editor.

link editor (linkage editor, linker) A utility program that combines several separately compiled modules into one, resolving internal references between them. When a program is assembled or compiled, an intermediate form is produced into which it is necessary to incorporate library material containing the implementation of standard routines and procedures, and to add any other modules that may have been supplied by the user, possibly in other high-level languages. The final stages of *binding references within the original program to storable address forms appropriate to the hardware is performed by the link editor. *See also* link loader, loader.

linked list (chained list) A *list representation in which items are not necessarily sequential in storage. Access is made possible by the use in every item of a *link that contains the address of the next item in the list. The last item in the list has a special *null link* to indicate that there are no more items in the list.

link encryption The transfer of an encrypted message across a system where the message is decrypted and reencrypted after each stage of its journey. Typically, link encryption is used in a switched communication network where the message is decrypted at each switching node to read the routing information prior to reencryption and onward transmission via the appropriate switch˙ outlet. *Compare* end-to-end encryption.

linker *Another name for* link editor.

link layer of network protocol function. *See* seven-layer reference model.

link loader A utility program that combines all the separately compiled modules of a program into a form suitable for execution. *See also* link editor, loader.

link testing Testing of a group of modules to ensure that the modules operate correctly in combination. It is normally performed after the individual modules have been tested in isolation and prior to the integration testing that is performed for the complete system.

liquid-crystal display *See* LCD.

LISP *Acronym for* list processing. A programming language designed for the manipulation of nonnumeric data. The basic data structure is a *list whose elements are either atomic symbols or lists.

An unusual feature of LISP is that programs are also expressed as lists, i.e. the programs and the data they manipulate have an identical structure. Pure LISP is a *functional language, having no assignment operator. The original LISP 1.5 developed into two distinct dialects, *FranzLisp* and *MACLisp*, but these have recently been combined to form *Common LISP. LISP is the language used for much *artificial intelligence research.

list A finite ordered *sequence of items $(x_1, x_2, \ldots x_n)$, where $n \geqslant 0$. If $n = 0$, the list has no elements and is called the *null list* (or *empty list*). Unless stated otherwise, the items in a list can be arbitrary in nature. In particular it is possible for an item to be another list, in which case it is known as a *sublist*. For example, let L be the list

(A,B,(C,D),E)

then the third item of L is the list (C,D), which is a sublist of L. If a list has one or more sublists it is called a *list structure*. If it has no sublists it is a *linear list*. Certain items of a list are often of particular interest, in particular the first item, or *head* of the list. The two basic representation forms for lists are sequentially allocated lists and *linked lists, the latter being of greater flexibility.

list head In many list representations, special header cells that are added to a list and possibly any sublists to aid management and traversal algorithms.

listing *Short for* program listing.

list insertion sort *See* list sorting.

list processing A programming technique for dealing with data structures that consist of similar items linked by pointers (*see* linked list).

list sorting A form of sorting that utilizes a *link field in each record. The links are manipulated so that each link points to the following record in the sorted file to form a straight linear *list. An insertion sort that utilizes link fields is a *list insertion sort*.

list structure *See* list.

literal A word or symbol in a program that stands for itself rather than as a name for something else, i.e. an object whose value is determined by its denotation. Numbers are literals; if other symbols are used as literals it is necessary to use some form of quoting mechanism to distinguish them from variables.

literate programming A style of programming introduced by D. E. Knuth in which the code is split up into fragments, each accompanied by a paragraph or paragraphs of explanatory text. The fragments are presented in the order most appropriate for explanation, rather than the order dictated by the rules of the programming language. A utility called *tangle* is used to rearrange the code fragments into the right order for compilation. Knuth's system, called *WEB*, was developed for Pascal programs, but versions for C have also been produced.

liveness A property of a system that it will eventually do something good. Possible causes of loss of liveness include *deadly embrace and *starvation. *Compare* safety.

LL parsing The most powerful *top-down parsing technique that proceeds without backtracking, LL standing for *Left*-to-right *Leftmost* derivation sequence. In general an LL parser uses a k-symbol lookahead, where k is an integer $\geqslant 1$, to effect parsing decisions. For most practical purposes, however, k is taken to be 1.

An LL parser may be implemented as a *pushdown automaton or by the method of recursive descent (*see* top-down parsing). In the former method a stack is used to store that portion of a leftmost *derivation sequence that has not been matched against the input string. Initially the start symbol of the grammar is pushed onto an empty stack. Subsequently, if the top element of the stack is a terminal symbol it is matched against the next symbol in the input string. If they are the same then the stack symbol is popped and the input marker advanced, otherwise there is an error in the input string. If the top stack symbol is a nonterminal A, say, it is removed from the stack and replaced by the right-hand side symbols of a production with left-hand side A. The right-hand side symbols are pushed onto the stack in right-to-left order. Thus if the production is

$$A \rightarrow XYZ$$

the first symbol to be stacked is Z, then Y, and finally X. The choice of a production is made by consulting a parsing table that contains an entry for each combination of nonterminal symbol and k-symbol lookahead. Parsing is successfully completed when the input is exhausted and the stack is empty.

A grammar that can be parsed using this technique is said to be an *LL(k) grammar*. Not all grammars are LL(k); in particular any grammar that uses left recursion is not LL(k) for any value of k.

load and go A method of operation, now obsolete, in which program loading together with a possible compiling or assembling is followed immediately by the program's execution phase.

load and store A method of operation, now obsolete, in which program loading together with a possible compiling or assembling is concluded by storage of the object code.

loader A utility program that sets up an executable program in main memory ready for execution. This is the final stage of the compiling/assembly process. *See also* link editor, link loader.

local A term applied to entities that are accessible only in a restricted part of a program, typically in a procedure or function body. By contrast, *nonlocal* entities are accessible in a wider scope and *global* entities are accessible throughout a program. The use of local entities can help to resolve naming conflicts, and may lead to a more efficient use of memory.

local area network (LAN) A communication network linking a number of *nodes in the same "local" area, variously defined as the same building, a radius of one kilometer, or a single plant. Local area networks generally provide high-speed (100K bps to 100M bps) data communication services to directly connected computers. *Gateways are used to connect local networks to each other, or to longer-distance communication networks. Due to limited distance, controlled environments, and (usually) homogeneous implementation, local networks have very low error rates and can utilize simplified data communication protocols. *See also* wide area network.

local discretization error (local truncation error) *See* discretization error.

local-echo mode *See* echo.

local error A measure of the accuracy over one step of a method for the numerical solution of *ordinary differential equations. This is a useful concept in the practical implementation of numerical methods. If the step is described by the general formula

$$y_{n+1} = y_n + h\phi(x_n, y_{n-1}, \ldots, y_{n-k}; h)$$
$$x_{n+1} = x_n + h$$

then the local error is defined to be

$$y_{n+1} - z(x_{n+1})$$

where $z(x)$ is the exact solution of the differential equation through the previous computed point, i.e. it satisfies $z(x_n) = y_n$.

An estimate of the local error is normally obtained by using two different formulae on each step (*see* predictor-corrector methods). This estimate is kept below a user-specified tolerance, if necessary by rejecting steps and repeating with a reduced stepsize h. With further modifications this leads to efficient and reliable variable stepsize programs.

The local error is the same *order in h as the local truncation error (*see* discretization error), which is defined in terms of the exact solution of the original problem rather than the current computed values used here.

local optimization (peephole optimization) *See* optimization (in programming).

location *Another name for* address.

location operator An operator in a programming language that yields the address of its operand.

lock (lock primitive) An indivisible operation that allows a *process to ensure that it alone has access to a particular resource. On a single-processor system the indivisible nature of the operation can be guaranteed by turning off interrupts during the action, ensuring that no process switch can occur. On a multiprocessing system it is essential to have available a *test-and-set instruction that, in a single uninterruptible sequence, can test whether a register's contents are zero, and if they are will make the contents nonzero. The same effect can be achieved by an exchange instruction. *See also* unlock, semaphore.

lockout A mechanism for arranging controlled access to a shared resource. *See* lock, semaphore.

locks and keys A system of *memory protection in which segments of memory are assigned identification numbers (the locks) and authorized users are provided the numbers (the keys) by the operating system. This provision is done by a privileged process in some location, such as a *program status word, not accessible to the user.

logarithmic search algorithm *Another name for* binary search algorithm.

logic 1. A knowledge representation and reasoning formalism originally developed by mathematicians to formalize mathematical reasoning. In mathematical logic the investigation involves mathematical methods taken from algebra or the theory of algorithms. The two most common systems are *propositional calculus and *predicate calculus. *See also* resolution.

Logic has been widely adopted within artificial intelligence, for example as an alternative to *production rules in expert systems and for representing the meaning of natural language statements (*see* natural language understanding). Many alternative logics have been developed in artificial intelligence to represent the vagueness and uncertainty of common sense (as opposed to mathematical knowledge) and to represent the tentative nature of common sense reasoning; these include *nonmonotonic reasoning and uncertain reasoning (*see* uncertainty).

2. *See* digital logic.

logical 1. Involving or used in logic.

2. Conceptual or virtual, or involving conceptual entities, as opposed to physical or actual.

logical cohesion *See* cohesion.

logical connective *See* connective.

logical encoding The representation of symbols in a source alphabet by strings of logical values. It is hence equivalent to binary encoding.

logical expression *Another name for* Boolean expression.

logical formulae A representation of meaning or knowledge. *See* logic, resolution.

logical operator, logical operation *See* logic operation.

logical shift *See* shift.

logical type 1. (Boolean type) A *data type comprising the logical values *true* and *false*, with legal operations restricted to *logic operations.

2. Loosely, an *abstract data type.

logical value (Boolean value) Either of the two values *true* and *false* that indicate a truth value. Although a single bit is the most obvious computer storage structure that can be applied to logical data, larger units of store, such as a byte, are frequently used in practice since they can be addressed distinctly.

logic analyzer An electronic instrument that monitors the *logic states of digital systems and stores the results for subsequent display. The storage of data is initiated in the analyzer by the recognition of preset "trigger states" as these arise in the system under test. *Synchronous* analyzers sample data at intervals determined entirely by the external system. *Asynchronous* analyzers sample at intervals determined internally by the analyzer. The essence of a logic analyzer is that it copes with many (often 8, 16, or 32) channels in parallel, and that the data recorded can be read back from memory at will, either in binary or after *decoding in some way, often by means of a *disassembler. *Compare* storage oscillator.

logic card A printed circuit board that is of a standard size and carries a number of digital logic devices in a circuit arrangement capable of fulfilling a specific function. The board will, in general, also carry a standard connector by means of which power and ground connections are provided and control and data signals may be transferred to and from a standard *bus.

logic cell array *See* LCA.

logic circuit An electrical circuit concerned with logical systems. The term *logic device* is often used synonymously. A logic circuit is required to produce specified binary outputs as a result of specified binary inputs. This may be accomplished by using *logic gates, producing what is called *hardware circuitry*. Alternatively the inputs may be associated with the address lines of a *ROM and the outputs with the data lines of a ROM; this is called *firmware circuitry*.

Hardware circuitry constructed from integrated-circuit packages on circuit boards requires two types of wiring. The first type carries the logical information between gates. The second type provides the power for the individual chips. The process of locating the power paths so that they do not interfere with the logic paths is called *power routing*.

Logic circuitry may be mathematically analyzed using *Boolean (or switching) algebra. In this representation the binary 1 is associated with the *identity element and the logic 0 is associated with the null element, i.e. zero.

See also combinational circuit, sequential circuit, digital logic, multiple-valued logic.

logic design *Another name for* digital design.

logic device *See* logic circuit.

logic diagram A diagram that displays graphically, by interconnection of *logic symbols, the digital design of a *logic circuit or system.

logic element A small part of a digital *logic circuit, typically a *logic gate. Logic elements can be represented by *operators in symbolic logic.

logic family A range of electronic devices that is made by the same manufacturing technique and provides a number of logic functions. The range includes *logic gates, *flip-flops, and *counters. Families in common use are *ECL and *TTL, which are based on *bipolar transistors, and the *NMOS and *CMOS families, which are based on *MOSFETs.

Logic families vary as regards *switching speed, *propagation delay, and power dissipation, although developments in the fabrication technology of the different families often improve these characteristics. A member of a logic family whose output changes state typically within a few nanoseconds (10^{-9} seconds) is considered a high-speed logic device. These devices are also characterized by short propagation delays, also in the order of a few nanoseconds. A particular family is characterized by its *delay-power-product, a figure of merit that is frequently quoted in catalogues. *See also* logic circuit.

logic function *Another name for* Boolean function.

logic gate A device, usually but not exclusively electronic, that implements an elementary logic function; examples include *AND, *OR, *NAND, and *NOR gates, and *inverters. There are typically between two and eight inputs and one or two outputs. In order to represent the two *logic states, true and false, in electronic logic gates, the input and output signals are held at either of two different voltage levels; a high voltage level usually represents true (logic 1) and a low level false (logic 0).

Each type of logic gate has a *logic symbol that conveys its logic function but does not indicate the electronic circuitry involved. The use of these symbols in circuit diagrams simplifies the understanding of a complex logic circuit and means that technological advances in electronics need not be taken into account.

Logic gates based on *fluid logic have been successfully used and optical logic gates, triggered by light, have recently been demonstrated. *See also* logic circuit, digital logic, multiple-valued logic.

logic instruction An instruction that performs one of the class of *logic operations on one or more specified operands. These operations may apply to a single variable, as in complementation, or more generally are defined on two variables. *See also* Boolean algebra.

logic level 1. In a *combinational circuit, the maximum number of logic gates between any input and any output. The logic level represents a measure of delay time through such a circuit.
2. Either of the two voltage levels used in a binary *logic gate. *See also* multiple-valued logic.

logic operation An operation on *logical values, producing a Boolean result (*see also* Boolean algebra). The operations may be *monadic or *dyadic, and are denoted by symbols known as *operators*. In general there are 16 logic operations over one or two operands; they include *AND, *OR, *NOT, *NAND, *NOR, *exclusive-OR, and *equivalence.

Logic operations involving more than two operands can always be expressed in terms of operations involving one or two operands. Those involving two operands can be expressed in terms of other operations involving one or two operands.

*Logic circuits are fabricated for the implementation of logic operations on their input signals. The inputs may be words (or bytes), and the logic operation is applied to each bit in accordance with Boolean algebra.

logic operator *See* logic operation.

logic probe An item of electronic test equipment that is capable of displaying the logic state – true (logic 1), false (logic 0), or undefined – of a digital signal applied to its input probe. It is generally used to check the operation of individual devices within a digital logic circuit.

logic programming languages (logic languages) A class of programming languages, and a subclass of the *declarative languages, that is based on the use of logical formulae. The interpreter is usually some version of *resolution, or another logical inference process. The ideal is that the programmer has only to make a series of true assertions about the problem and the interpreter will find a way to run these as a program to solve the problem. In practice, it is still necessary for the programmer to give regard to the procedural interpretation of these logical assertions. The most widely used realization of these ideals is the *Prolog programming language.

Logic programming languages are important because of their declarative nature, their potential power and flexibility, and their suitability for execution on highly parallel architectures.

logic state The logical sense, true or false, of a given binary signal. A binary signal is a *digital signal that has only two valid values. In physical terms the logical sense of a binary signal is determined by the voltage level or current value of the signal, and this in turn is determined by the device technology. In *TTL circuits, for example, a true state is represented by a logic 1, approximately equal to +5 volts on a signal line; logic 0 is approximately 0 volts. Voltage levels between 0 and +5 volts are considered undefined.

Since only two logic states, logic 1 and logic 0, are possible, the techniques of *Boolean algebra may be used to analyze digital circuits involving binary signals. The term positive logic is applied to circuits where logic 1 is assigned to the highest voltage level; in

Combinational logic symbols
AND function

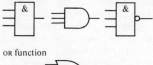

OR function

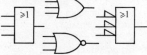

exclusive-OR function

Commonly used logic symbols

Indicator symbols
negation indicator

polarity indicator

Flip-flops

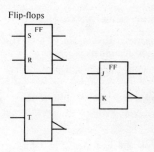

negative logic circuits a logic 1 is indicated by the lower voltage level. *See also* multiple-valued logic.

logic symbols A set of graphical symbols that express the function of individual *logic gates in a *logic diagram. The most common symbols are those for the simple Boolean functions and for flip-flops, as shown in the diagram.

login (logon) The process by which a user identifies himself to a system. The terms are also used as verbs: log in, log on, or *sign on*. A system with many registered users will require each user to log in, and to produce some form of *authentication (such as a password) before allowing the user access to system resources. The login activity will also open an *accounting file for the session.

logistic function A ratio of sums of

exponentials widely used in statistical analysis. The logistic function lies in the range $(0,1)$, and its inverse, known as the *logit* of a proportion, is the logarithm of the odds-ratio (*see* odds).

logit *See* logistic function.

LOGO A programming language developed for use in teaching young children. LOGO is a simple but powerful language: it incorporates the concept of *procedures, and helps children to think algorithmically. The original version of LOGO incorporated *turtle graphics.

logoff (logout) The process by which a user terminates his session. The terms are also used as verbs: log off, log out, or *sign off*. By logging off, the user ensures that all the system resources that have been used during the session are accounted for, and any temporary files created during the session are deleted.

logon 1. (or **log on**) *See* login.

2. A unit of information, equal to the product of one unit of *bandwidth by one unit of time, in Denis Gabor's physical theory of communication. (In contrast, Shannon's mathematical theory of communication uses the concept of *entropy.

logout or **log out** *See* logoff.

longitudinal redundancy check (LRC) *See* cyclic redundancy check.

lookahead *Short for* carry lookahead.

lookahead unit A unit forming part of an instruction unit pipeline in computers such as *Stretch.

Look and Feel *See* copyright.

look-up table *See* table look-up.

loop 1. A sequence of instructions that is repeated until a prescribed condition, such as agreement with a data element or completion of a count, is satisfied. *See also* do loop.

2. A configuration of a *local area network that consists of nodes connected serially in a ring topology. *See* ring network.

3. (local loop) The (twisted pair) connection from a switching exchange to the subscriber terminal.

loop invariant *See* invariant.

Lotus 1-2-3 *Trademark* A *spreadsheet program for microcomputers. It also provides simple statistical and database facilities and graph drawing of pie charts, bar charts, and line graphs.

lower bound of a set S on which the *partial ordering $<$ is defined. An element l with the property that $l < s$ for all s in S. Also l is a *greatest lower bound* if, for any other lower bound h, $h < l$.

Since numerical computing demands the truncation of infinite arithmetic to finite arithmetic, the computation of greatest lower bounds of real numbers, indeed of any limit, can only be achieved to a machine tolerance, usually defined to be machine precision: the smallest epsilon eps, such that

$$1.0 - eps < 1.0$$

See also array, upper bound.

low-level language A variety of programming language in which the control and data structures directly reflect the underlying machine architecture.

low-level scheduler (dispatcher) *See* scheduler.

low-pass filter A *filtering device that permits only those components in the *Fourier transform domain whose frequencies lie below some critical value to pass through with little attenuation, all other components being highly attenuated.

lpm *Abbrev. for* lines per minute, one of the terms used to describe the rate of output of line printers.

LQ *Abbrev. for* letter quality. Printed output indistinguishable from that produced by a good electric typewriter. *See also* NLQ.

LR parsing A *bottom-up parsing technique, LR standing for *L*eft-to-right *R*ightmost derivation sequence. Originally developed by D. E. Knuth, it is the most powerful left-to-right, no backtracking parsing method for *context-free grammars.

An LR parser consists of a pushdown stack, a parsing table, and a driving routine. The driving routine is the same for all grammars. The stack is manipulated by the driving routine using the information contained in the top stack element and the next k symbols in the input stream (called the *k lookahead*); *k* is an integer $\geqslant 0$, but for most practical purposes $k = 1$. The stack consists of a string

$$s_0 X_0 s_1 X_1 \ldots s_n X_n s_{n+1}$$

where each X_i is a symbol of the input grammar and each s_i is called a *state*.

The parsing table is indexed by pairs (s,a) where s is a state and a is the lookahead. Each entry in the table has two parts: (a) an action, which may be shift, reduce p (for some production p), accept, or error, and (b) a state, called the *goto state*. When the action is shift, the next input symbol and goto state are pushed onto the stack (in that order). When the action is reduce p the top $2l$ elements of the stack will spell the right-hand side of p but with goto states interspersed, where l is the length of this right-hand side. These $2l$ elements are popped from the stack and replaced by the left-hand side of p and the new goto state. This operation corresponds to adding a new node to the *parse tree for the input string. The accept action is only encountered when the start symbol S is the only symbol on the stack (i.e. the stack contains $s_0 S s_1$ for some states s_0 and s_1) and the lookahead is the end-of-input symbol. It signifies that parsing has been successfully completed. On the other hand an error entry in the parse table indicates an error in the input string.

A grammar that can be parsed by an LR parser using *k*-symbol lookahead is called an *LR(k) grammar*. The power of the LR parsing method comes from the fact that the LR(1) grammars properly include other grammar types like precedence grammars and LL(1) grammars (*see* LL parsing). This and its efficiency make it a popular choice of parsing method in *compiler-compilers. If a grammar is not LR(1) this will be evidenced as multiply defined entries in the parsing tables called *shift-reduce conflicts* or *reduce-reduce conflicts*.

Many different parsing tables may be constructed for one grammar, each dif-

fering in the number of states it defines. The so-called *canonical LR table* tends to be too long for practical purposes and it is commonly replaced by an *SLR* (simple LR) or *LALR* (lookahead LR) table. A grammar that is LR(1) may not however be SLR(1) or LALR(1).

LSD, LSB *Abbrevs. for* least significant digit, least significant bit.

LSI *Abbrev. for* large-scale integration, i.e. integrated-circuit fabrication technology that allows a very large number of components (at least 10 000 transistors) to be integrated on a single chip. *See* integrated circuit, VLSI.

L-system (Lindenmeyer system) A way of generating infinite sets of strings. L-systems are similar to *grammars with the crucial difference that, whereas for grammars each step of derivation rewrites a single occurrence of a nonterminal, in an L-system all nonterminals are rewritten simultaneously. An L-system is therefore also known as a *parallel rewriting system*. L-systems were first defined in 1968 by Lindenmeyer as a way of formalizing ways in which biological systems develop. They now form an important part of *formal language theory.

The subject has given rise to a large number of different classes of L-systems. The simplest are the *DOL systems*, in which all symbols are nonterminals and each has a single production. For example, with productions

$$A \to AB$$
$$B \to A$$

one derives starting from A the sequence

A AB ABA ABAAB ABAABABA ...

This is called the *sequence* of the DOL-system, while the set of strings in the sequence is called the *language*. The *growth-function* gives the length of the ith string in the sequence; in the example this is the Fibonacci function.

Note that the productions form a *homomorphism – in this example from $\{A,B\}^*$ to itself. A DOL-system consists therefore of an alphabet Σ, a homomorphism h on Σ^*, and an initial Σ-word w. The sequence is then

$$w \; h(w) \; h(h(w)) \; \ldots$$

The letter D in DOL stands for deterministic, i.e. each symbol has just one production. An *OL-system* can have many productions for each symbol, and is thus a *substitution rather than a homomorphism. Other classes are similarly indicated by the presence of various letters in the name: T means many homomorphisms (or many substitutions); E means that some symbols are terminals; P means that no symbol can be rewritten to the empty string; an integer n in place of O means context-sensitivity – the rewriting of each symbol is dependent on the n symbols immediately to the left of it in the string.

LU decomposition A method used in *numerical linear algebra in order to solve a set of linear equations,

$$Ax = b$$

where A is a square matrix and b is a column vector. In this method, a lower *triangular matrix L and an upper *triangular matrix U are sought such that

$$LU = A$$

For definiteness, the diagonal elements of L may be taken to be 1. The elements of successive rows of U and L may easily be calculated from the defining equations.

Once L and U have been determined, so that

$$LUx = b,$$

the equation

$$Ly = b$$

is found by *forward substitution*. Thereafter the equation

$$Ux = y$$

is found by *backward substitution*. x is then the solution to the original problem.

A variant of the method, the method of *LDU decomposition*, seeks lower and upper triangular matrices with unit diagonal and a diagonal matrix D, such that

$$A = LDU$$

If the matrix A is *symmetric and positive definite, there is an advantage in finding a lower triangular matrix L such that

$$A = L \, L^{\mathrm{T}}$$

This method is known as *Cholesky decomposition*; the diagonal elements of L are not, in general, unity.

M

M *Symbol for* mega-.

MAC A project at Massachusetts Institute of Technology to introduce the first practical *multiaccess system. The name is an acronym derived from machine-aided cognition (expressing the broad project objective) and multiple-access computer (describing its major tool). The system incorporated not only a new approach to operating systems, but also introduced novel forms of highly interactive compilers and of terminals. *See also* MULTICS.

machine Usually, a real – or imagined – computer (*see also* virtual machine, abstract machine, Turing machine), which may or may not be sequential and deterministic. In formal language theory it may imply a *sequential machine.

machine address *Another name for* absolute address, now deprecated.

machine code The *operation code of a particular machine, and hence, by association, code specific to a particular machine.

machine equivalence The property describing two usually abstract machines that can simulate one another. Machines M_1 and M_2 are said to be equivalent if M_1 can simulate M_2 and M_2 can simulate M_1. *See* machine simulation.

machine-independent A term applied to software that is not dependent on the properties of a particular machine, and can therefore be used on any machine. Such software is also described as *portable*.

machine intelligence *Another name for* artificial intelligence, but sometimes used to indicate only the technologically oriented aspects.

machine language Strictly, the written representation of machine code. The term is also used as a synonym for machine code.

machine-oriented language *See* MOHLL.

machine simulation The process whereby one machine M_1 can be made to behave like a second machine M_2. Formally, let there be *functions g and h that perform encoding and decoding roles respectively:

$$g : M_1 \rightarrow M_2, \quad h : M_2 \rightarrow M_1$$

g encodes information for machine M_1 and produces corresponding information for machine M_2; h is the *inverse function. Machine M_2 is said to *simulate* machine M_1 if it is possible to specify an *algorithm such that, when given a program P_1 for M_1, it produces a corresponding program P_2 for M_2; further the effect of P_1 on M_1 should be equivalent to the effect of

applying function g
then executing P_2 on M_2
then applying function h

Machine simulation of this kind is generally discussed in relation to idealized abstract machines, such as *Turing machines, which are free from physical limitations. *See also* machine equivalence.

machine word *See* word.

Macintosh *See* Apple.

MACLisp A dialect of *LISP, now superseded by *Common LISP.

macro *Short for* macro-instruction. An instruction in a programming language (almost always but not necessarily *assembly language) that is replaced by a sequence of instructions prior to assembly or compiling. A *macro-assembler* permits the user to define macros, specifying the macro-instruction form, its arguments, and a replacement text (otherwise called the *body* of the macro), and then allows macro-instructions to be interspersed among the assembly code. On encountering a macro-instruction the assembler replaces it by the macro body, substituting the parameters provided in the places marked in the macro body. The macro thus provides a mechanism for inserting a particular body of text at various places in a program (and is thus the same thing as an open *subroutine, though this nomenclature is obsolete).

A *macro-processor* provides similar facilities, though not in combination with an assembler. It accepts macro definitions and then reads arbitrary text in which *macro calls* (i.e. instances of a macro name) can occur. Text is copied to the output until a macro name is encountered: when this happens the arguments (parameters) are found and the macro call is replaced by the macro body in the output stream, with appropriate substitution of the parameters.

macro-assembler *See* macro.

macro-generator *Another name for* macro-processor. *See* macro.

macro-instruction *See* macro.

macro-processor (macro-generator) *See* macro.

magnetic bubble memory A type of digital memory in which data is represented by magnetic bubbles that are made to move through a stationary planar medium by applying suitable magnetic fields; the bubbles are tiny circular areas (stable magnetic domains) in which the medium is magnetized in the reverse direction to the rest of the medium. Bubble memory thus differs from magnetic tape and disk stores, in which the medium moves and the data bits are stationary with respect to it.

There is usually only one input point and one output point per device so that data flow is serial. However, within the device it is usual to divide the data path into a series of parallel loops, with means of distributing the data stream between them, so that the access time to a particular item of data is only a fraction of the time taken to fill the whole device with data. Typically the data rate is 100 kilobits per second and the access time 30 milliseconds. A number of such devices can be used together to provide a greater total storage capacity, and if required these can be arranged so that several are accessed in parallel to give a higher data rate.

Bubble memory consumes little power, has a large functional *packing density, is normally nonvolatile, and is resistant to cosmic rays and similar particles. Having no moving parts it is more rugged than disk memory. Bubble memory has found limited application where these properties are of value. However the initial promise of the technology (pioneered by Bell Telephone Laboratories) has not been realized in full since manufacturing costs have proved higher than expected.

magnetic card A data medium consisting of a card that is partly or completely coated on one side with ferromagnetic film on which data can be encoded and read (*see* card reader). The credit card is one example, the encoding being restricted to a single *magnetic stripe* that can contain three tracks. Other sizes of card have been used as interchangeable media in data-processing and word-processing applications, one example being the IBM magnetic card. In the late 1960s a number of mass storage devices were designed in which large magnetic cards were filed and retrieved automatically. These were superseded by *automated tape libraries and *magnetic disk stores.

magnetic cell A *memory element in which two different states of its magnetic flux pattern are used to represent binary values. The element may be a ferromagnetic core, part of a perforated ferromagnetic plane, or the intersection of two coated wires, and it can store a single bit of information.

magnetic disk A rotatable storage medium in the form of a circular plate coated on one or both sides with a magnetic film. Data is recorded in concentric tracks in the film. The disk substrate may be rigid, in which case it is usually made of an aluminum alloy, or it may be flexible, in which case it is usually a polyester. The coating may be a compound of ferric oxide in a binder or a thin metallic plating of an alloy such as cobalt/nickel or cobalt/chrome. Metallic coatings have advantages in being homogeneous, having a better hysteresis loop shape, and allowing storage densities 10 times that achievable with conventional ferric oxide coatings. Flexible disks (i.e. *floppy disks) with oxide coating provide low-cost lightweight media that can be handled in a normal office environment.

Data is stored on and retrieved from magnetic disks by means of a *disk drive. The disks used in these peripheral devices range in diameter from 3″ to 36″ (76–914 mm). *See also* disk pack, disk cartridge, magnetic encoding, disk format, Winchester technology, memory hierarchy.

magnetic drum The earliest form of rotating magnetic storage device, used in some of the first computers at a time when random-access store was volatile, bulky, and expensive. The drum therefore formed the main memory of some of these machines, the random-access stores being used only as registers. Although random-access store developed rapidly it was still relatively expensive and the drum was retained as a local backing store on some computers. Magnetic disk, when introduced, took over a large part of the backing store function. Drums remained in use however on certain systems that required faster access than was generally provided by disk, but today they are obsolete apart from a few special applications.

A magnetic drum consists of a cylinder whose curved surface is coated with a suitable recording medium, either metal or iron oxide. On the *head-per-track drum* the drum rotates past a number of fixed read/write heads, one for each track of recorded information. On the *moving-head drum* the drum rotates past a single head or small group of heads that can be moved axially to access any track. The latter was rapidly superseded by disk stores but the head-per-track drum survived: track selection requires only electronic switching between heads rather than movement of the head so that such drums have much shorter access times than disk stores.

magnetic encoding The method by which binary data is recorded on magnetic media. In *horizontal recording* on magnetic disks, tapes, and cards, magnetic domains in the media are aligned along the direction of the applied magnetic field with either north or south pole leading: each domain is a tiny bounded region in which the magnetic moments of the component atoms are aligned, and it therefore behaves like a magnet. The domains are arranged end to end along a track, which may be either a

concentric ring on a disk or run the length of a tape or card. There may not be a one-to-one relationship between the binary information of the data and the orientation of the magnetic domains. *See* disk format, tape format.

In 1975 Shun-ichi Iwasaki published his work on *vertical recording* methods. The magnetic domains are oriented through the thickness of the magnetic film and have either a north or a south pole at the exposed surface. The magnetic material is usually a vacuum-deposited film of metal such as an alloy or combination of cobalt and chromium over a layer of permalloy. Linear densities as high as 200,000 bits per inch have been demonstrated. Vertical recording can thus yield an increase of at least 25 times and possibly 100 times the bit density achievable by current horizontal recording techniques.

magnetic head *See* head.

magnetic-ink character recognition *See* MICR.

magnetic media The various types of media on which data recording is effected by writing a magnetic pattern onto the magnetizable surface of the medium. The term distinguishes these types of media from others that use different recording techniques, e.g. optical disks and paper tape. *See* magnetic tape, magnetic tape cartridge, magnetic disk, disk cartridge, disk pack, floppy disk, Winchester technology.

magnetic stripe *See* magnetic card.

magnetic tape 1. An information storage medium consisting of a magnetic coating on a flexible backing in tape form. The coating usually consists of fine particles of iron oxide suspended in an inert binder, and the backing is usually polyester. Data is recorded by *magnetic encoding of tracks on the coating according to a particular *tape format.

MAGNETIC TAPE CARTRIDGE

Magnetic tape is wound on *reels* (or *spools*), usually contained within a *cartridge or *cassette. To use magnetic tape, the reel containing the tape – the *file reel* – is placed on a peripheral device known as a *tape transport*. (This device is also called a *magnetic tape unit*, *tape drive*, *tape deck*, and *tape mechanism*.) The tape transport is capable of moving the tape from the file reel, past one or more magnetic heads, and winding it onto a *take-up reel*; the latter may be associated, detachably or not, with the transport or alternatively be contained in a cartridge or cassette.

An electrical signal is applied to the *write head* to record information as a magnetic pattern on the tape (*see also* write ring); in most cases the tape passes first over an *erase head* to erase any signal previously written on the tape. As the tape passes over the *read head* the magnetic pattern induces an electrical signal that can be processed electronically to recreate the signal that was recorded. Sometimes a single *read/write head* is provided, with its connections switched so that it can be used for either reading or writing; more often two separate heads – or two gaps and windings in the same head – are used, and this permits a *read-while-write check* to be made by reading and checking information as soon as it has been recorded (*see* error management).

The most common dimensions for an individual magnetic tape – a *volume* – are ½ inch wide and 2400 feet long, wound on a 10½ inch diameter reel; 1200 and 600 ft lengths of ½" tape, on 8½" or 7" reels, are less frequently used, and occasionally a thinner plastic backing is used to allow 3600 ft to be wound on the standard 10½" reel. Various other widths and lengths of tape are used, generally in some form of cartridge.

The most important uses of magnetic tape in computer systems are as follows.

(a) Data interchange. There are international standards for the format of data recorded on magnetic tape (*see* tape format); it is the most widely used medium for the interchange of data between separate computer systems, including those of different makes, and also between systems and off-line peripherals such as printers.

(b) Backup of magnetic disk memory, particularly fixed disks (*see* memory hierarchy).

(c) Software distribution.

(d) Input, when the tape is written by a key-to-tape system. Tape is now rarely used in this way.

(e) Serial processing. Although this function was once very important, the use of magnetic disk memories has made it obsolescent.

Magnetic tape was introduced for computer use in the 1950s, when it was already widely used for audio and instrumentation purposes. It largely superseded punched tape and punched cards although these remained in use for limited applications. The demise of magnetic tape as a computer medium has often been predicted but its use is likely to continue at least through the 1980s, at least in cartridge form: IBM announced a completely new high-performance cartridge tape system in 1984.

2. A term sometimes used by software and systems people to mean *magnetic tape subsystem.

magnetic tape cartridge (tape cartridge) A casing containing one or more reels carrying a length of *magnetic tape, so arranged that it can be loaded on a suitable tape transport for access without the tape being handled by the operator. There are many forms of tape cartridge, some containing both the file reel and the take-up reel (*see* magnetic tape) and some the file reel only. The term is also used to describe a file reel without a separate casing but with some other provision, such as a special leader to protect the tape and avoid the need for the operator to touch it.

The best-known forms of tape cartridge are as follows.

(a) The *autoload* or *Easyload cartridge*, introduced by IBM and consisting essentially of a collar clamped around the periphery of a standard 10½″ reel of ½″ wide magnetic tape. Its purpose is to facilitate *autothreading of tape on suitably equipped tape transports. The reel can be removed from the cartridge for use on other transports.

(b) The *DC300 cartridge*, introduced by 3M and consisting of a metal and plastic casing containing two small reels of ¼″ wide magnetic tape, driven by a flexible band that forms part of the cartridge. The cartridge is used in a transport whose heads protrude through a window in the cartridge to make contact with the tape as it passes from one reel to the other. Variants of this cartridge carry 300, 450, or 600 feet of tape in similar housings; the latter two are the *DC450* and *DC600 cartridges*. It is usual for the drive to record several tracks of data on the tape, one at a time (i.e. serially); a number of different *tape formats are used. The capacity has been extended (mid-1989) to about 300 megabytes and further development to 1000 megabytes is expected within two years. *DC1000* and *DC2000 cartridges* are similar but smaller. These cartridges are used mainly on small computers in an office environment.

(c) The *digital cassette*, based on the standard audio cassette developed by Philips and made to similar dimensions though with more precision. The plastic casing contains two small reels of tape 0.15″ wide, in various lengths, and is used in a transport whose heads protrude through a window in the cartridge to make contact with the tape. The tape is moved by direct contact with a capstan against which it is pressed by a pinch roller, both being part of the transport; the transport also connects mechanically to the hubs of both reels to control the winding and unwinding of the tape. Cassette tape is now used mainly on hobbyist computers and these often use standard audio cassettes and decks rather than the higher-quality digital variety.

(d) Various designs of cartridge containing a relatively short length of wide tape on a single reel, used in *automated tape libraries.

(e) Cartridges consisting of a few hundred feet of ½″ wide tape on a single reel permanently mounted in an outer casing, with a coupling attached to the outer end of the tape to allow the end to be drawn out and mechanically loaded into the tape path of a suitable cartridge tape drive. The most widely used design is the *3480 cartridge*, introduced by IBM in 1984 for its 3480 cartridge tape drive and since adopted by other manufacturers.

(f) Cartridges consisting of small (typically 3″ or 4″ diameter) reels of ½″ tape without an outer casing, but with a tough protective leader slightly wider than the tape so that it gives full protection when wound onto the reel.

magnetic tape subsystem A subsystem provided in order to enable a host system to obtain access to data on magnetic tape. The subsystem consists of one or more tape transports (*see* magnetic tape) and a device controller that incorporates a *formatter. The device controller has an interface by which it is connected to the host. Some manufacturers specify their own proprietary interface, but there are several standard interfaces that are widely used.

magnetic tape unit (MTU) *Another name for* tape transport. *See* magnetic tape.

magnetographic printer A type of printer in which the required image is first written on a band or drum of magnetic recording material as a pattern of closely spaced magnetic poles. The image is then developed by brushing it with a pigment that is also ferromagnetic and thermoplastic. The image is transferred and bonded to paper by applying pressure and/or heat.

magneto-optic storage A storage method, used in rewritable optical disk drives, that combines magnetic and optical recording techniques. The disk is coated with film that initially is uniformly magnetized. A laser beam is used to demagnetize a small spot on the film by heating it above a critical temperature (the Curie point or compensation point), and a local magnetic field determines the direction in which the spot is magnetized when it cools. To read the information the disk is scanned by polarized light from a low-power laser. The plane of polarization of the light reflected from a magnetized surface is rotated according to the direction of the magnetic field – the Kerr effect. This rotation can be detected and the original binary signal can be reproduced.

The technique achieves recording densities similar to those of other optical stores and much higher than has been achieved by magnetic recording.

mag tape *Short for* magnetic tape.

mainframe 1. Generally, the combination of central processor and primary memory of a computer system. The term excludes the I/O, backing store, etc., and is sometimes used synonymously with central processor.
2. Any large computer system.

main memory (main store; main storage; primary memory) The storage that is closely associated with the processor of a computer system and from which the program instruction and data can be directly retrieved and to which the resulting data is written prior to transfer to *backing store or *output device. In modern machines this is *semiconductor memory but in somewhat earlier machines *core stores were used. The majority of storage activity takes place in the main memory but the backing store has usually the larger capacity. *See also* memory hierarchy.

main program The section of a program that is entered first and from which program units and procedures are called. It is the outermost block of a block-structured program.

main store, main storage *Other names for* main memory.

maintenance 1. (hardware maintenance) The performance of *preventive or *remedial maintenance on hardware in order to anticipate the onset of incipient faults or to correct a *failure due to a hardware fault.
2. *See* software maintenance.

majority element (majority gate) A logic element with an odd number of inputs, and whose output agrees with the majority of the inputs. *See also* threshold element.

malfunction The occurrence of a fault, usually a hardware fault.

management information system (MIS) An *information system whose prime purpose is to supply information to management. The early concept of an MIS, commonplace in the 1960s and early 1970s, was that systems analysts would determine the information requirements of individual managers in an organization, and would design systems to supply that information routinely and/or on demand.

Decision support systems form a new class of MIS, giving managers much greater independence in their use of computer-based information. They depend on the union of office information systems (including personal computing facilities for managers, operated by themselves) with more conventional database and data-processing systems. They assume that managers will be able to build and access their own personal databases, as well as accessing the corporate databases, and that they will be able to formulate their own access enquiries without depending on specialist intermediaries.

Manchester coded *Another term for* phase encoded. *See* tape format.

Manchester Mark I The world's first operational stored-program computer, running its first program in June 1948. It was designed by T. Kilburn and F. C. Williams at the University of Manchester, UK, commencing in 1946. Several improvements were added and the first realistic problem to be solved by the machine was achieved in April 1949, shortly before *EDSAC began operations. It became the world's first commercially available computer when marketed by Ferranti Ltd in 1951 as the Ferranti Mark I. The effectiveness of the machine was due to its use of *electrostatic (Williams tube) storage.

man-machine interface (MMI) The means of communicating between a human user and a computer system, referring in particular to the use of input/output devices with supporting software. Devices of increasing sophistication are becoming available to mediate the human-computer interaction. These include graphics devices, *touch-sensitive devices, and *voice input devices. They have to be configured in a way that will facilitate an efficient and desirable interaction between a person and the computer. *Artificial intelligence techniques of knowledge representation may be used to model the user of a computer system, and so offer the opportunity to give personalized advice on its use. The design of the machine interface may incorporate *expert system techniques to offer powerful *knowledge-based computing to the user.

The terms *human-computer interface* (HCI), *human-machine interface* (HMI),

and *human-system interface* (HSI) are all used as synonyms.

Mann Whitney U-test *See* nonparametric techniques.

mantissa (fractional part) *See* floating-point notation.

many-sorted signature *See* signature.

map 1. (mapping) *See* function.
  2. *See* memory map.
  3. *See* Karnaugh map.

MAP *Acronym for* Manufacturing Automation Protocol. A set of *protocols originally devised by a group of US manufacturers of mechanical engineering products. This original group has been expanded to include other parties, and the protocols are likely to become ISO OSI (*open systems interconnection) standards. The protocols are intended to facilitate the exchange of data relevant to mechanical-engineering design and manufacture. They cover not only the problems of process control and assembly within a single manufacturing plant, but also the exchange of design and manufacturing data between a main contractor and his subcontractors. *See also* TOP.

map method A procedure for minimizing Boolean functions using a *Karnaugh map.

mapping 1. (map) *See* function.
  2. *See* memory mapping, I/O mapping, bit mapping.

MAPSE *Acronym for* minimal Ada programming support environment. The minimum *APSE to be provided by all Ada implementations.

marginal check (marginal test) *See* preventive maintenance.

mark 1. One of the binary signaling states on terminal and teleprinter serial communication lines; the other state is called *space*. Mark often corresponds to a negative voltage, space to a positive voltage.

2. A line drawn on specially formatted cards or forms that are used with *mark sensing or *mark reading equipment.

3. *See* tape mark.

marker on a magnetic tape. *See* BOT marker, EOT marker.

Markov chain A sequence of discrete random variables such that each member of the sequence is probabilistically dependent only on its predecessor. An *ergodic* Markov chain has the property that its value at any time has the same statistical properties as its value at any other time.

Markov source A *Markov chain, whose random variables are regarded as *internal states*, together with a mapping from these internal states to the symbols of some *external alphabet*. The mapping need not be a *bijection. A Markov source is ergodic if and only if its underlying Markov chain is ergodic. *See also* discrete source.

mark reading (mark scanning) *See* OMR.

mark sensing A method for data input in which electrically conductive marks, usually made with a soft graphite pencil on a preformatted card or form, are electrically sensed. This method has been displaced by the more reliable method of *OMR (i.e. optical mark reading) in which the marks are detected photoelectrically.

mark-space ratio *See* pulse train.

marriage problem In a certain community every boy knows exactly *k* girls and every girl knows exactly *k* boys. The problem is to show that every boy can marry a girl he knows and vice versa. This problem is a case of showing that any *bipartite graph whose *vertices all have the same nonzero number of edges incident to it has a *perfect matching.

MASCOT *Acronym for* modular approach to software construction operation and test. A method for designing and building software, aimed at realtime embedded systems and originally devised at the Royal Signals and Research Establishment, UK.

MASCOT comprises a design method, a diagrammatic and textual notation, and a model environment supporting the building, testing, and execution of systems. It may be applied to both single processor and distributed multiprocessor systems.

The design method is based upon identifying the dataflow through the system, and the data accumulation within the system. The design consists of concurrent active components (*activities*) and passive components (*intercommunication data areas*, of which *pools* and *channels* are special cases), possibly hierarchically.

The notation provides for describing software components and the interfaces between them, together with a set of rules for assembling and testing them. It shows the network of intercommunicating processes, possibly in a hierarchy. In general, there is equivalence between the components of the design and the modules of the implementation.

MASCOT was devised to be language-independent. The original tools to support MASCOT were for use with *CORAL; tools are now available for use with *Pascal and *Ada. MASCOT is compatible with the *CORE requirements method.

masking 1. (filtering) A logical operation carried out on a byte, word, or field of data in order to modify or identify a part of it. A bit pattern – the same length as the item to be masked – is generated and stored in a register as a *mask*. By use of the appropriate operation, e.g. subtract, logical AND, logical

OR, the mask can be used to suppress bits in the data, or set them to zero, etc. The process is used for purposes such as identifying the presence of high-priority bits in a status byte or resetting interrupts.

2. The use of a chemical shield, the *mask*, to determine the pattern of interconnects in an integrated circuit. Read-only memories (*ROMs) and programmable logic arrays (*PLAs) are customized for their particular applications by the masking process, unless they are field-programmable. *See* programmable devices.

mask-programmable device *See* programmable devices, ROM.

mass storage An on-line backing store system capable of storing larger quantities of data (sometimes an order of magnitude more) than conventional backing store. The quoted capacity of mass storage has increased with advances in technology: in the early 1960s a megabyte of storage came in this category; the term currently applies to devices that can store several hundred gigabytes of data.

master file A *data file subject to frequent *file updating and *query processing. A master file is thus distinct, for instance, from a *transaction file, an *I/O file, a *work file, a *reference file, or an *archived file.

mastering of a CD-ROM disk. *See* master tape.

master record A record on a *master file.

master-slave flip-flop A type of clocked *flip-flop consisting of master and slave elements that are clocked on complementary transitions of the clock signal. Data is only transferred from the master to the slave, and hence to the output, after the master-device outputs have stabilized. This eliminates the possibility of

ambiguous outputs, which can occur in single-element flip-flops as a result of *propagation delays of the individual logic gates driving the flip-flops.

master-slave system A system that has more than one processor and in which one of the processors is designated as being the *master* and all other processors are *slaves*. The master processor is capable of actions that the slaves cannot perform, usually in connection with resource scheduling and the initiation of peripheral transfers. This approach means that the problems of *synchronization are greatly reduced, since only the master processor can be active in what might otherwise be *critical regions. It has the drawbacks of introducing an artificial asymmetry between processors, and of causing delays when processes that might be able to proceed are in fact delayed since the only available processors do not have the necessary privileges.

master tape 1. In data processing, a magnetic tape volume that is used without any change to its contents. It is usually protected by a *write ring, or some equivalent mechanical device, by which the operator can protect the tape from being erased or over-written even though this is commanded by the host.

The term master tape was also used in connection with paper tape.

2. A tape used in the preparation of a *CD-ROM disk. It contains all the information to be placed on the disk, in a format defined by the disk manufacturer. A *master disk* is prepared from this tape (by *mastering*), and many final disks can then be copied by a pressing process.

matching of a graph. *See* perfect matching.

mathematical programming A wide field of study that deals with the theory, applications, and computational methods for *optimization problems. An abstract formulation of such problems is to maximize a function f (known as an *objective function*) over a constraint set S, i.e.

maximize $f(x)$, $x \in S \subseteq R^n$,

where R^n denotes the space of real n-component vectors x,

$$x = (x_1, x_2, \ldots, x_n)^T$$

and f is a real-valued function defined on S. If S consists only of vectors whose elements are integers, then the problem is one of *integer programming*. *Linear programming treats the case of f as a linear function with S defined by linear equations and/or constraints. Nonlinear objective functions with or without constraints (defined by systems of *nonlinear equations) give rise to problems generally referred to as optimization problems.

Mathematical-programming problems arise in engineering, business, and the physical and social sciences.

matrix A two-dimensional *array. In computing, matrices are usually considered to be special cases of n-dimensional arrays, expressed as arrays with two indices. The notation for arrays is determined by the programming language. The two dimensions of a matrix are known as its *rows* and *columns*; a matrix with m rows and n columns is said to be an $m \times n$ matrix.

In mathematics (and in this dictionary), the conventional notation is to use a capital letter to denote a matrix in its entirety, and the corresponding lower-case letter, indexed by a pair of subscripts, to denote an element in the matrix. Thus the i,jth element of a matrix A is denoted by a_{ij}, where i is the row number and j the column number.

A deficient two-dimensional array, in which one of the dimensions has only one index value (and is consequently elided), is a special kind of matrix known either as a *row vector* (with the column elided) or *column vector* (with the row elided). The distinction between row and column shows that the two dimensions are still significant.

matrix inversion A numerical method by which the *inverse matrix of a given matrix is produced.

matrix multiplication The multiplication of two matrices A and B according to the rule

$$c_{ij} = \sum_{k=1}^{n} a_{ik} b_{kj}$$

matrix norm *See* approximation theory.

matrix printer A printer that forms the character or shape to be printed from an array of dots. The dots can be formed on paper by a stylus impacting an inked ribbon, by separate drops of ink ejected from a nozzle, or by one of the other nonimpact technologies in which dots are formed by changing the color of the media by heating (thermal printer), etching or burning (electrosensitive printer) or by ink adhering to an electric charge or magnetic pole pattern (electrographic and magnetographic printers).

A significant advantage of matrix printers over *solid-font printers is the ability to accommodate a very large repertoire of character shapes and styles and also to print the ideograms of oriental languages and script characters of Arabic. Diagrams and pictures can also be reproduced. When the term is used in reference to a single type of printer it generally means an *impact printer or *dot matrix printer.

matrix-updating methods *See* optimization.

maximum-length sequence *See* m-sequence.

maximum likelihood, method of *See* likelihood.

maximum-likelihood decoding A strategy for decoding an *error-correcting code: it chooses the *codeword conditional upon whose occurrence the probability of the word actually received is greatest. *Compare* minimum-error decoding.

max sort A *sorting algorithm in which the largest key in the unsorted section of the file is successively placed at the end of the file, which becomes the sorted section of the file.

maxterm (standard sum term) A sum (OR) of n Boolean variables, uncomplemented or complemented but not repeated, in a Boolean function of n variables. With n variables, 2^n different maxterms are possible. The complement of any maxterm is a *minterm. *See also* standard product of sums.

MCA *Trademark; abbrev. for* micro channel architecture. A *bus structure for microcomputers that was introduced in 1987 with the IBM PS/2, models 50 and above, and is the successor to the structures used in the IBM PCs. It was made necessary by the requirements of 32-bit microprocessors. *See also* EISA.

MCAV *Abbrev. for* modified constant angular velocity. A modification of *CAV in which the rotation rate of the disk is constant but the clock rate and data rate are varied in proportion to the radius of the track being accessed, thus obtaining the high data density of *CLV without the long access time that usually goes with it. In practice the tracks are usually grouped into 4 to 8 bands; clock and data rates vary between bands but not within a band.

MCGA *Abbrev. for* multicolor graphics array. A color *graphics adapter that is available for some low-end models of the IBM PS/2 series. It is an extension of the *CGA: in addition to the standard 320 × 200 four-color mode and the 640 × 200 two-color mode, the MCGA provides a 640 × 480 two-color

mode and a 320 × 200 256-color mode. Unlike the CGA, the MCGA is analog in composition: each of the three colors that constitute the image can take on a range of intensities between zero and a maximum value.

MCLV *Abbrev. for* modified constant linear velocity. A modification of *CLV in which the data tracks on an optical disk are grouped in a number of bands; the same angular velocity is used while accessing all the tracks within a band, but a different velocity is used for each band. It is thus a compromise between CLV and *CAV.

MDA *Abbrev. for* monochrome display adapter. *See* display adapter, graphics adapter.

MDR *Abbrev. for* memory data register.

Mealy machine *See* sequential machine.

mean *See* measures of location.

mean deviation *See* measures of variation.

means/ends analysis A technique used in *artificial intelligence for forming plans to achieve goals. A plan consists of a sequence of actions. The sequence is put together by comparing the goals that each action achieves (the means) with the goals and action preconditions that must be achieved (the ends).

measure 1. A quantity ascertained or ascertainable by measurement.
   2. A number assigned to a property of an entity according to well-defined rules, so as to describe or represent that property objectively.
   3. A number or other *symbol assigned to a specific property by means of observation.

measures of location Quantities that represent the average or typical value of a *random variable (*compare* measures of variation). They are either properties of

MEASURES OF VARIATION

a *probability distribution or computed *statistics of a sample. Three important measures are the *mean*, *median*, and *mode*.

The *mean* of a sample of n observations, denoted by $\bar{x}$, is

$$\sum_i x_i / n$$

The mean of a probability distribution, denoted by μ, is

$$\sum x.p(x)$$

for a discrete distribution and

$$\int x.f(x) \, dx$$

for a continuous distribution; it is also called the *expectation* of x, denoted by $E(x)$.

A *weighted mean* is used when members of a sample are known with different reliability. To each observation x_i corresponds a *weight* w_i, and now $\bar{x}$ is

$$\sum (w_i . x_i) / \sum w_i$$

If each observation is the mean of w observations, the formulas for the weighted and unweighted means agree.

The *median* is the value of x exceeded by exactly half the sample or distribution. The median of a distribution is the value for which the cumulative distribution function, $F(x)$, equals 0.5 (*see* probability distributions).

The *mode* is the most commonly occurring value. For distributions in which the frequency function, $f(x)$, has one or more local maxima, each maximum is called a mode.

These measures may be illustrated on the following sample of eight values of x:

$$1,1,1,2,3,3,5,7$$

The mean is 2.875, the median is 2.5, and the mode is 1.

measures of variation Quantities that express the amount of variation in a *random variable (*compare* measures of location). Variation is sometimes described as *spread* or *dispersion* to distinguish it from systematic trends or differences. Measures of variation are either properties of a *probability distribution or sample estimates of them.

The *range* of a sample is the difference between the largest and smallest value. The *interquartile range* is potentially more useful. If the sample is ranked in ascending order of magnitude two values of x may be found, the first of which is exceeded by 75% of the sample, the second by 25%; their difference is the interquartile range. An analogous definition applies to a probability distribution.

The *variance* is the expectation (or mean) of the square of the difference between a *random variable and its mean; it is of fundamental importance in statistical analysis. The variance of a continuous distribution with mean μ is

$$\int (x-\mu)^2 f(x) \, dx$$

and is denoted by σ^2. The variance of a discrete distribution is

$$\sum (x-\mu)^2 . p(x)$$

and is also denoted by σ^2. The sample variance of a sample of n observations with mean $\bar{x}$ is

$$\sum (x_i - \bar{x})^2 / (n-1)$$

and is denoted by s^2. The value $(n-1)$ corrects for *bias.

The *standard deviation* is the square root of the variance, denoted by σ (for a distribution) or s (for a sample). The standard deviation has the same units of measurement as the mean, and for a *normal distribution about 5% of the distribution lies beyond about two standard deviations each side of the mean. The standard deviation of the distribution of an estimated quantity is termed the *standard error*.

The *mean deviation* is the mean of the absolute deviations of the random variable from the mean.

mechanical verifier A system that provides automated assistance to the production of a *program correctness proof. Typically such a system consists of two distinct parts: a *verification condition generator* and a *theorem prover*. The former is responsible for generating the theorems that must be proven in order to demonstrate that *preconditions and *postconditions are consistent with the semantics of the statements to which they relate. The theorem prover is then responsible for proving these verification conditions.

Different mechanical verifiers vary considerably in their capabilities. A relatively simple system might require that assertions giving all relevant information are attached between every pair of successive statements (simple or compound), and would present any nontrivial verification conditions to the user for manual proof; this system is sometimes called an *assertion checker*. A more sophisticated mechanical verifier requires only major assertions to be attached prior to verification (perhaps only the input assertion and output assertion) and is able to generate its own intermediate assertions as necessary. Further, the theorem prover is capable of proving complex verification conditions, perhaps presenting only the occasional lemma to the user for confirmation.

median *See* measures of location.

medium *See* data medium. The plural form is *media*, although this is often used as a singular form.

meet operator *See* lattice.

mega- (symbol: M) A prefix indicating a multiple of one million (10^6), as in megawatt. When the binary system is used, as in computing, it indicates a multiple of 2^{20}, i.e. 1 048 576, as in megabyte.

member (element) of a *set S. An object x that is in S, usually denoted by $x \in S$. One of the basic actions that can be performed on sets is asking whether or not an object is in a set. *See also* operations on sets.

memory A device or medium that can retain information for subsequent retrieval. The term is synonymous with *storage* and *store*, although it is most frequently used for referring to the internal storage of a computer that can be directly addressed by operating instructions. *See* main memory, cache memory, semiconductor memory, memory hierarchy, memory management.

memory compaction (block compaction) Any of several methods used to relocate information blocks in main memory in order to maximize the available free space in the memory. *See also* storage allocation.

memory cycle 1. The complete sequence of events for a unit of memory to go from a quiescent state through a read and/or write phase and back to a quiescent state.
2. The minimum length of time that is required between successive accesses (read or write) to a memory. *See also* cycle.

memory data register (MDR) A *register used for holding information (either program words or data words) that is in the process of being transferred from the memory to the central processor, or vice versa.

memory dump A representation, which can be read by a person, of the contents at some time of some part of the main memory of a computer system. A variety of representation formats might be employed, but typically these would all be relatively low-level – e.g. purely numeric or assembler-code format. A memory dump is normally taken for *postmortem purposes.

memory element A device that stores one item of information: if it has q stable states it is said to be *q-ary, and if $q = 2$ it is said to be binary. It is usually implemented electronically, sometimes with the assistance of the magnetic, optical, or acoustic properties of a storage medium. In practice, most memory elements are binary. In fast computer circuitry, the *flip-flop is the most common type of memory element.

Memory elements are employed specifically in computer memories and generally in *sequential circuits. A memory element is any smallest part of such a system that possesses more than one stable state. For example, a binary *shift register contains four flip-flops and has 16 states, but each of its four memory elements has only two states; a similar ternary shift register would have 81 states, but would still consist of four memory elements, each having three states.

memory fill An aid to program debugging in which every location in the memory is filled with a predetermined character before being overwritten by the incoming program.

memory guard A form of hardware *interlock used in some systems to control access to memory that is currently involved in a peripheral transfer. At the time of initiating the transfer the channel sets an indication that the buffer area is associated with the transfer; this indication is cleared by the channel on completion of the transfer. Any attempt to access the buffer area (other than by the channel) will suspend the process attempting to access the buffer until the transfer has been completed.

memory hierarchy Physically different kinds of memory have significant differences in the time to access the contents of a particular location in memory, the total volume of information that can be stored, and the unit cost of storing a

given amount of information. In order to optimize system performance while achieving the lowest overall system cost, memory is organized in a number of levels arranged in a hierarchy as follows.

1. Register – A single word held in a *register within the processor; typically each word contains say 4 bytes, and a processor may have say 8 registers. (This is sometimes not considered as part of the memory hierarchy.)

2. Cache – Groups of words within the *cache; the size of the cache varies very much as between systems, but where present it will consist of a number of subunits each holding say 8 words (i.e. 32 bytes) and the entire cache will hold 1024 such subunits, a total of 32 K bytes.

3. Main memory – Individual words within *main memory; groups of words are transferred between main memory and the cache. On a high performance system this group of words will correspond to a single unit in the cache, and this requires a correspondingly wide data path between cache and memory. The algorithm that controls this movement is implemented entirely in hardware. On a system without a cache at all, data passes directly between memory and registers within the processor. Main memory sizes are highly variable, from 1 M bytes on a small system up to as much as 512 M bytes on a large system.

4. On-line backing store – Blocks of words held on permanently on-line *backing store. There are two functionally distinct sublevels:

(a) **swapping devices** – *pages of memory held on a *swapping device – complete pages, typically of say 4 K bytes, are transferred between their backing store home and a page frame in memory in accordance with the software algorithm implemented by the operating system;

(b) **backing store devices** – complete files, or clearly identifiable subsections of files, are moved between the backing store device and main memory in

unit		realized as	access time	cost, $	capacity	cost/ bit
register						
	L	row of ECL flip-flops	0.1 ns	100	32 bits	300 c
	M	row of TTL flip-flops	1 ns	2	32 bits	6 c
	W	row of MOS flip-flops	5 ns	0.5	32 bits	1.5 c
	P	row of MOS inverters	20 ns	0.05	16 bits	0.3 c
cache						
	L	bipolar RAM	10 ns	50K	32K bytes	20 c
	M	bipolar RAM	50 ns	5K	4K bytes	15 c
	W	not present				
	P	not present				
main memory						
	L	MOS DRAM	100 ns	1M	128M bytes	0.1 c
	M	MOS DRAM	100 ns	125K	32M bytes	0.05 c
	W	MOS DRAM	200 ns	8K	8M bytes	0.01 c
	P	MOS DRAM	500 ns	500	1M bytes	0.005 c
swapping						
	L	bulk RAM	1 ms	50K	64M bytes	10 mc
	L	Winchester	25 ms	5K	300M bytes	0.2 mc
	M	Winchester	25 ms	5K	300M bytes	0.2 mc
	W	Winchester	25 ms	1K	60M bytes	0.2 mc
	P	Winchester	40 ms	500	20M bytes	0.3 mc
file store						
	L	Winchester	25 ms	30K	7.5G bytes	0.05 mc
	M	Winchester	25 ms	10K	1.0G bytes	0.12 mc
	W	Winchester	40 ms	1K	100M bytes	0.12 mc
	P	floppy disk	100 ms	200	1M bytes	2.5 mc
back-up						
	L,M,W reel to reel					
		mounted	100 s	10K	100M bytes	1.2 mc
		unmounted	1000 s	10	100M bytes	1.2 μc
	L,M,W cassette					
		mounted	100 s	10K	100M bytes	1.2 mc
		unmounted	1000 s	10	100M bytes	1.2 μc
	L,M,W video cassette					
		mounted	1000 s	5K	2.5G bytes	25 μc
		unmounted	2000 s	10	2.5G bytes	50 nc
	P audio cassette					
		mounted	100 s	100	1M bytes	1.2 mc
		unmounted	1000 s	1	1M bytes	12 μc

Memory hierarchy

response to explicit actions by the programmer, usually via a supervisor call into the operating system.

5. Demountable storage – Complete files backed up onto demountable media, usually some form of demountable magnetic disk or magnetic tape. The creation of back-up copies and the reinstatement of a backed-up file may be automatic or may require explicit action by the user, or may be a combination of these. For larger systems the back-up medium may be reel-to-reel tape, a cassette tape of roughly equivalent performance and capacity, or one of the high-capacity tapes based on a modified video cassette system. Smaller systems may use one of the two types of cassette, or on a very small system back-up may be onto floppy disk.

The table indicates typical access times and unit costs for memory in each of the major classifications as at Spring 1989. Four categories of systems are considered:

L – large systems
M – midi- or mini-systems
W – workstations
P – personal computers

This division is quite arbitrary; there are no clear boundaries between systems and there are many anomalies in the systems actually available in the market place, especially in the workstation and personal computer systems. However, the overall picture is reasonably coherent.

memory management Control of the *memory hierarchy of a system as a whole, or control of allocation at a fixed level within the memory hierarchy. In the former case information stored within the system is shuttled between one realization of memory and another, the objective being to maintain maximum *hit rate in each form of memory. This movement may be controlled by

(a) voluntary user action, e.g. copying a file from disk to memory in order to edit it;

(b) system software, e.g. transfer of a page between swapping device and memory when a page fault occurs;

(c) system hardware, e.g. movement of a set of words from memory to cache when a word within the set is accessed.

At a given level of the hierarchy the operating system will control what fraction of that level is to be allocated to each process. This can clearly only occur where control is by system software, and refers most particularly to the allocation of memory to a process, or to the allocation of space on the swapping device. Movement between disk and magnetic tape is often separately treated as archiving. *See also* storage protection.

memory map A schematic presentation of the use to which memory is being put, often presented as a byproduct during the compilation of a program. The memory map may be useful in the diagnosis of faults in the compiled program.

memory mapping A technique for managing peripheral devices, used on many microprocessor systems and on some smaller miniprocessor systems. The control registers of the peripheral device appear to the processor as words in memory whose contents can be written and read using the normal store and fetch operations.

memory protection Any of many methods for controlling access to or use of memory. This control may be to prevent inadvertent user interference, to provide for system security, or both.

A mechanism for controlling the types of access permitted to an area of memory is known as a *memory protect*. In virtual memory systems it may be possible to assign certain areas as being capable of designated modes of access; for example, an area that is known to contain only the code of shared subroutines may be designated as having "execute only" access, and can only be read during the instruction-fetch phase of executing an instruction. The permitted mode of access may differ for different processes. Definition of memory areas may use *bounds registers; fixed memory areas may be controlled by *locks and keys; individual words may be controlled by *tags.

A violation of the memory protection system usually leads via an interrupt to a forced process termination.

memory reference instruction An *instruction that has one or more of its operand addresses referring to a location in memory, as opposed to one of the CPU registers or some other way of specifying an operand location.

memory-to-memory instruction An instruction that transfers information from a memory and returns it to a memory. The information may be modified during the transfer (e.g. incremented); the information may or may not be returned to the same location. The term is also used to refer to an instruction that transfers information between levels of a *memory hierarchy. Transfers may be word by word or block transfers.

menu A list displayed either horizontally or vertically on a screen from which one or more items may be selected. There are a number of ways in which the selection may be made. If a mouse or other *pointing device is available, then the *cursor may be moved to the desired item and a selection made by clicking a mouse button or its equivalent. Otherwise the cursor may be moved by means of the arrow keys on the keyboard. Each item on the list may have a unique number of letter to identify it, or the first or some other character unique to the item may be emphasized in some way. In this case the selection may be made by pressing the appropriate key on the keyboard. If no pointing device is available then this method becomes the only possibility.

See also pull-down menu, tear-off menu, menu-driven program.

menu bypass A technique whereby expert users of a *menu-driven program may avoid the rather slow and cumbersome process of stepping through a number of menus. This usually involves preempting the menus by typing in the selections before they appear.

menu-driven program A program that obtains input from a user by displaying a list of options – the *menu – from which the user indicates his/her choice. Systems running menu-driven programs are commonplace, ranging from microprocessor controlled washing machines to bank cash dispensers. In the case of the cash dispenser, single keys are pressed to indicate the type of transaction (whether a receipt is wanted with cash or a statement of the bank balance is required) and with many, a single key is pressed to indicate the amount of money required.

Menu-driven systems are advantageous in two ways: firstly, because input is via single key strokes, the system is less prone to user error; secondly, because only a limited range of characters are "allowed", the way in which the input is to be entered is unambiguous. This contributes toward making the system more user-friendly.

mergeable heap Any data structure representing a set of ordered elements that can support the insertion and deletion of elements as well as the set operation of union and the calculation of the minimum elements in a set. *See also* operations on sets.

merge exchange sort *Another name for* Batcher's parallel method.

merging Combining multiple sets of data to produce only one set, usually in an ordered sequence. This approach is usually employed in external *sorting, where the data is kept on backing store.

The *polyphase merge sort is an example of a merging method.

message 1. The unit of information transferred by a *message switching system. Messages may be of any length, from a few bits to a complete file, and no part of a message is released to its final recipient until all of the message has been received at the network node adjacent to the destination.

2. *Another name (deprecated) for* packet. The distinction between packet and message is valuable, since it refers to whether or not a partial transmission of a complete document can occur; a *packet switching system may allow this whereas a *message switching system may not.

3. *See* Shannon's model (of a communication system).

4. A specially formatted document sent in an *electronic mail system.

5. *See* object-oriented language.

message queueing The process of storing a message in a node of a *message switching network until sufficient resources are available for the message to be forwarded to the next node along the path to its destination.

message store One of three major entities defined by the X 400 electronic mail *protocol. Its function is to act as a buffer between the stream of incoming mail messages and the machine that a human recipient will use to run his *user agent, when this machine is unable or unwilling to receive incoming mail from the *MTA (message transfer agent). The message store was added to the protocol in order to prevent the situation in which a user whose user agent runs on a personal computer or other system that has been powered off, or disconnected from the network, finds that on powering on or reconnecting, he is deluged with messages.

message switching A data-switching strategy that requires no physical path to exist between sender and receiver before communication can take place. Message switching passes *messages via relays, called *switching offices*, in a *store-and-forward network. Each switching office receives a message, checks it for errors, and retransmits it to the next switching office on the route to the destination. Because of the large buffers and variable delays of message switching, most computer networks use *packet switching or *circuit switching techniques for their underlying network components, and add message switching functions (such as *electronic mail and *file transfer protocol) at higher levels.

meta-assembler A program that accepts the syntactic and semantic description of an assembly language, and generates an *assembler for that language.

METAFONT A system for designing digital typefaces, designed to complement the *TEX typesetting system. The designer specifies character shapes in terms of curves called *splines*, and the system then generates bit-map images for use in printing.

metalanguage A language used to specify some or all aspects of a programming language. *BNF is an example.

metallic disk *Another name for* hard disk.

methodology In general, a coherent set of methods used in carrying out some complex activity. The word is most frequently used in terms such as *programming methodology* or *(system) design methodology*.

metric 1. A specific type of *mapping in which the codomain is a number, and the triangle inequality applies.

2. *Informal name for* measure.

3. A number representing the degree to which software, or an entity related to software, possesses some notional property, as observed or perceived by an individual or group.

MFM *Abbrev. for* modified frequency modulation. *See* disk format.

M²FM *Abbrev. for* modified modified frequency modulation. *See* disk format.

MHS *Abbrev. for* message handling system. A form of *electronic mail service.

MICR *Abbrev. for* magnetic ink character recognition. A process in which data, printed in ink containing ferromagnetic particles, is read by magnetic read heads. The shape of the characters resembles those of normal typescript but each generates a unique signal as it is scanned by the read head. The most common application is for encoding numbers on bank checks.

There are two standardized fonts: the E13B and CMC7. The E13B font is very rectangular in appearance and some parts of the vertical limbs may be thickened to accentuate the difference in the generated wave form. This font is widely used in the US and the UK. The CMC7 font has the character shape sliced into seven vertical strips with the six intervening spaces either wide or narrow. Each of the numerical symbols and the four special symbols is coded with a combination of two wide and four narrow spaces.

micro 1. (symbol: μ) A prefix to a unit, indicating a submultiple of one millionth, 10^{-6}, of that unit, as in microsecond.
2. *Short for* microcomputer.

microcircuit An *integrated circuit, generally one performing a very complex function. An example is a *microprocessor comprised of arithmetic logic unit, control circuits, registers, program counter, and some memory, all within a single integrated circuit.

microcode A sequence of *microinstructions, i.e. the program code in a microprogrammed *control unit. *See* microprogramming.

microcomputer 1. A single LSI chip containing all the logic elements needed for a complete computer system, in contrast to a *microprocessor, which requires additional support chips.
2. A computer system that utilizes a *microprocessor as its central control and arithmetic element. The power and price of a microcomputer is determined partly by the speed and power of the processor and partly by the characteristics of other components of the system, i.e. the memory, the disk units, the display, the keyboard, the flexibility of the hardware, and the operating system and other software.

Memory sizes range from half a megabyte or so up to tens of megabytes and the access speed can also vary considerably. The capacity of floppy disk drives varies over a much smaller range, starting at less than 0.5 Mbyte but usually not extending as far as 2 Mbyte. Hard disk capacities lie in the range tens to hundreds of Mbytes, while *optical disks extend this considerably. Microcomputer displays range from domestic TV receivers to high-definition color monitors based on a technology in advance of current TV standards. Other kinds of display include flat LCD and plasma screens used on *laptop and portable models. There are many keyboard designs, and the number and arrangement of keys is not a guide to quality, rather the physical construction and action. The flexibility of the hardware can be measured by the number and type of enhancements available. These might include extra memory, more disk drives, *coprocessors, *pointing devices, communications interfaces, and the ability to participate in networks. The *operating system can be characterized by its use of memory, how much can be accessed and how well it is done, how many tasks can be run concurrently, and how it appears to the user.

microcontroller 1. An LSI microprocessor designed specifically for use in device control, communication control, or process-control applications. A typical microcontroller chip might have a relatively short word length, a rich set of bit-manipulation instructions, and lack certain arithmetic and string operations found on general-purpose microprocessors.

2. A microprocessor-based device or system designed for control applications.

Microdata A US manufacturer of minicomputers. The Microdata computers are notable in that they were some of the earliest machines that were microprogrammable and could (in theory) be modified by the user.

microfiche, microfilm *See* COM.

microinstruction One instruction in a microprogram that specifies some of the detailed control steps needed to perform an *instruction. *See* microprogramming.

microprocessor A semiconductor chip, or chip set, that implements the *central processor of a computer. Microprocessors consist of, at a minimum, an *arithmetic and logic unit and a *control unit. They are characterized by speed, word length (internal and external), *architecture, and *instruction set, which may be either fixed or microprogrammed. It is the combination of these characteristics and not just the cycle time that determines the performance of a microprocessor.

Most microprocessors have a fixed instruction set. Microprogrammed processors have a control store containing the microcode or firmware that defines the processor's instruction set; such processors may either be implemented on a single chip or constructed from *bit-slice elements.

The processor's architecture determines what register, stack, addressing, and I/O facilities are available, as well as defining the processor's primitive data types. The data types, which are the fundamental entities that can be manipulated by the instruction set, typically include bit, nibble (4 bits), byte (8 bits), word (16 bits), and double words (32 bits). Note that a word is usually defined as the number of bits in the processor's internal data bus rather than always being 16 bits. Instructions generally include arithmetic, logical, flow-of-control, and data movement (between stacks, registers, memory, and I/O ports). With some microprocessors, *coprocessors can be added to the system in order to extend the range of data types and instructions supported, e.g. floating-point numbers and the set of arithmetic operations defined on them.

The first microprocessor, the four-chip set Intel 4004, appeared in 1971 accompanied by considerable debate about its utility and marketability. It was the outcome of an idea proposed by Ted Hoff of Intel Corp. for a calculator that could implement a simple set of instructions in hardware but permitted complex sequences of them to be stored in a read-only memory (ROM). The result of his proposal was a design for a four-chip set consisting of a CPU, *ROM, *RAM, and a *shift-register chip, the chip design proceeding in 1970 under the direction of Federico Faggin, later the founder of Zilog, Inc. The Intel 4004 had a 4-bit data bus, could address 4.5K bytes of memory, and had 45 instructions. Its 8-bit counterpart, the Intel 8008, was introduced in 1974 and its improved derivative, the Zilog Z80, in 1976. By this time there were over 50 microprocessors on the market.

The next generation of microprocessors included the Zilog Z8000, Motorola 68000, Intel 8086, National 16000, as well as the older Texas Instruments 9900 and Digital Equipment Corporation LSI-11. All of these chips use a 16-

bit-wide external data bus. Still higher performance microprocessors using 32-bit external data buses are now available. Examples include the Intel 80386 and 80486, the Motorola 68030, Bell Lab's Bellmac-32, and Digital Equipment's VAX 78032 and 78132 (processor and FPA). *See also* RISC.

microprogramming A method of accomplishing the *control unit function by describing the steps in that function as a sequence of operations that are much more elementary than *instructions. In this method of designing and building a control unit, an additional memory, commonly called a *microprogram store*, contains a sequence of *microinstructions*. A number of microinstructions will be required to carry out an ordinary machine instruction, thus the microprogram store should be faster − have a shorter *cycle time − than the normal fast memory.

Microinstructions are usually classified as either *horizontal* or *vertical*. In a horizontal microinstruction most of the bit positions have a one-to-one correspondence with specific control functions. Horizontal microinstructions provide explicit control of functions at particular points within the CPU. For example, a particular bit in the microinstruction would call for a specific register to be cleared at a specific clock time. A vertical microinstruction generally contains highly coded fields describing elementary operations to be performed by certain elements of the control unit and *arithmetic and logic unit, and the sources and destinations of information passing between these units. In such a microinstruction, a field, say of three bits, might be decoded to indicate which of eight registers is to be one source of an operation to be performed in an ALU. Other fields would define the operation and any other necessary sources. Horizontal microinstructions will in general contain more bits, or be wider, hence the word horizontal. Vertical microinstructions, although containing fewer bits, require more decoding.

Some microprogrammed control units go through two levels of microprogramming. The first level consists of addresses of horizontal microinstructions. The second level is the used or useful subset of all horizontal microinstructions. This provides for more efficient use of a horizontal microprogram memory at the expense of two memory references per microinstruction execution. In this form of microprogramming the first memory has been called the microprogram store and the second memory has been called the *nanostore*.

Almost all control units are now microprogrammed. This permits a more orderly and flexible approach to control unit design and permits changes in a control unit by changing the memory contents. Most microprogram stores are made with *ROM. These memories are generally faster and are potentially less prone to errors. Other microprogram stores, usually called *writeable control stores (WCS)*, are made with *RAM. These provide greater ease of change of control unit function; in some cases users are permitted or encouraged to "build" specialized instructions. Some microprogrammed control units have a mixture of ROM and RAM microprogram stores. These permit special microprograms to be loaded for maintenance and diagnostic purposes.

The only control units that are not now microprogrammed are those in some of the *supercomputers where it is found that hardwired control can provide faster operation than several microinstruction executions.

microprogram sequencer The part of a microprogrammed control unit that provides the equivalent of a *program counter at the microprogram level. *See* microprogramming.

microprogram store (control memory) The memory that contains a microprogram. It may be fixed (ROM) or alterable (writeable control store). *See* microprogramming.

microrelief A technique used in optical recording. The surface of the medium is impressed with a very fine pattern that scatters light. When a spot on the surface is heated by a laser beam, the material flows to leave a smooth reflective surface. The technique is sometimes called *moth-eye* recording because the pattern resembles that of the cornea of a moth's eye.

microsequence A sequence of *microinstructions, i.e. a microprogram or a portion thereof. *See* microprogramming.

middleware Products that in some sense occupy a position between hardware and software. In particular where microcoded systems are used, the actual microcode is sometimes spoken of as middleware.

midpoint rule The explicit rule
$$y_{n+2} = y_n + 2hf(x_{n+1}, y_{n+1})$$
for the solution of ordinary differential equations (h is the stepsize). It is an example of a *linear multistep method, important for its use as the basis of *Gragg's extrapolation method.

milli- (symbol: m) A prefix to a unit, indicating a submultiple of one thousandth, 10^{-3}, of that unit, as in millisecond.

MIMD processor *Short for* multiple instruction (stream), multiple data (stream) processor. *See* concurrency.

min *Abbrev. for* minimum. **1.** A *monadic operation applied to a language L and defined in such a way that $min(L)$ is the set of strings in L that have no proper *prefixes that are also in L.
2. One of the basic actions performed on a set on whose elements a *total ordering $\leq$ is defined; when applied in

the form $min(S)$ it produces the smallest element of the set S with respect to $\leq$.

minicomputer (mini) Originally, a computer that physically went within a single equipment cabinet, i.e. on the order of a few cubic feet. Compared with larger computers, minicomputers were and still are cheaper and slower, with smaller memory and usually shorter word length. The word minicomputer is no longer used very specifically. It predates the term *microcomputer and the boundary between these two classes of device is unclear.

minimal machine A machine possessing no redundant states. To any *finite-state automaton or *sequential machine there corresponds a unique (up to isomorphism) minimal machine that recognizes the same language (in the case of finite automata) or has the same response function (in the case of sequential machines). This is true for infinite as well as finite state-sets.

There are two ways in which a state q may be "redundant": it is either "inaccessible" in that there is no input string that takes the start-state to q, or else it is equivalent to another state q' in that the subsequent behavior of the machine is the same whether it is in state q or q'. In a minimal machine all inaccessible states have been dropped and all equivalent states have been merged. There is a simple algorithm that will give the minimized version of any machine. *See also* Myhill equivalence, Nerode equivalence.

minimax A basic algorithm in *artificial intelligence, in particular when constructing programs to play games such as chess. A *tree of possible moves, alternating with possible opponent's moves, is constructed to some depth. Evaluation of the positions at the leaves is then passed back up the tree, choosing always the minimum evaluation for the opponent and the maximum for the program itself.

minimax procedure A procedure usually used in *approximation theory in order to find an approximating function, often a polynomial, that has the smallest maximum error on a given interval.

minimization 1. The process of manipulating a logical expression and thereby transforming it into a simpler but equivalent expression with the same truth table. In practice this commonly means reducing the number of *logic gates, number of gate inputs, or number of *logic levels in a *combinational circuit that realizes the logical expression. Minimization methods include use of *Karnaugh maps and algebraic manipulation (often computer-aided).

2. The process of converting a *finite-state machine to an equivalent *minimal machine.

3. In the study of *effective computability, the process of defining a function using the *minimization operator* or *μ-operator*. The functions involved are usually over the *natural numbers. Let g be a function of $n+1$ variables. Then, for any given values of $x_1, \ldots, x_n$, the expression

$$\mu y . g(x_1, \ldots, x_n, y)$$

is evaluated by searching for the smallest value of y for which

$$g(x_1, \ldots, x_n, y) = 0$$

This can be done by letting y run through all natural numbers, in increasing order, until a suitable y is found, whereupon that value of y is returned as the value of the $μ$-expression. If no suitable y exists the $μ$-expression is undefined. Also it may happen that before a suitable y is found a value of y is encountered for which

$$g(x_1, \ldots, x_n, y)$$

is itself undefined; in this case again the $μ$-expression is undefined.

This construct can be used to define a function f of n variables:

$$f(x_1, \ldots, x_n) = \mu y . g(x_1, \ldots, x_n, y)$$

Because of the possibility of the $μ$-expression being undefined, f is a *partial function. The use of minimization is an essential factor that allows the formalism of *recursive functions to define all the *computable functions.

4. *See* optimization.

minimization operator (μ-operator) *See* minimization.

minimum-access code A form of programming for early computers with magnetic-drum storage. It was also known as *optimum programming*. In programs for this kind of machine, each instruction specifies the address of its successor, and it is desirable to place instructions in addresses so chosen that they are available under the reading heads when required. Since the execution time of instructions varies, it was necessary to work out how far the drum would rotate during execution of an instruction: this then determined the optimum position of its successor. Since this address might already be occupied, obtaining an optimal (or nearly optimal) distribution of instructions on the drum was extremely difficult.

The most widely used machine of this kind was the IBM 650; the success of the machine was largely due to the SOAP assembler, which produced near-optimal code positioning without any special effort on the part of the programmer.

minimum-cost spanning tree *See* spanning tree.

minimum-error decoding A strategy for decoding an *error-correcting code: it chooses the *codeword most likely to have been transmitted, given the word actually received. This is by contrast with *maximum-likelihood decoding, but the two strategies become identical when all the codewords are equally probable.

minterm (standard product term) A product (AND) of n Boolean variables, uncomplemented or complemented but not repeated, in a Boolean function of n variables. With n variables, 2^n different minterms are possible. The complement of any minterm is a *maxterm. *See also* standard sum of products.

mips *Abbrev. for* million instructions per second. A measure of processing speed.

MIRANDA A functional programming language, similar to *ML.

MIS *Abbrev. for* management information system.

MISD processor *Short for* multiple instruction (stream), single data (stream) processor. *See* concurrency.

missing observations Values unavoidably absent from a set of structured data, as in an *experimental design. Algorithms exist to estimate values to be substituted for those that are missing, to allow the analysis to be completed.

mixed-base system *See* number system.

mixed logic A *digital design that includes both *positive and *negative logic.

mixed-radix system *See* number system.

ML A functional programming language. ML provides the full range of facilities of a functional language and a list processing language, and includes a powerful module system with separate compilation. It is available on about 30 different computer systems.

MMI *Abbrev. for* man-machine interface.

mnemonic code A simple form of *assembly language: the name arises from the use of mnemonic abbreviations for operation codes, e.g. LDA for "load accumulator".

MOB *Acronym for* movable object block. *Another term for* sprite.

modal logic Any logical system that allows the use of *modal operators*. For a modal operator α, the value of a formula αF in an *interpretation I depends on the values of F in a whole class of interpretations related to I, rather than on the value of F in just I itself as is the case in a nonmodal logic. The two most common operators are "necessity" and "possibility", usually written as $\square$ and $\diamondsuit$. $\square F$ is true in an interpretation (or *world*) w if F is true in all worlds w' related to (or *accessible from*) w, while $\diamondsuit F$ is true in w if F is true in at least one such w'. In discussing the semantics of modal logic, therefore, one considers *frames* of the form (W,R), where W is a set of worlds and R is an *accessibility relation* on W. Each world attaches a value to all the primitive symbols in the language.

In *dynamic logic* the modal operators correspond to programs, and the worlds correspond to states of execution. Then the formula αF is true in a particular state s if F is true in all states reachable from s by running the program α. Dynamic logic is similar to *Hoare logic in the fact that its formulae involve both programming and logical constructs.

In *temporal logics the modal operators deal with interpretations that might depend on the time. Other modal operators express notions of belief, desirability, and obligation. All these ideas are of great relevance in reasoning about programs and systems, hence recent years have seen extensive use of modal logics in *program verification and *formal specification.

mode 1. A term used in many contexts concerning the operation and use of a computer system. For example: conversational mode refers to interactive computer use; interpretive mode refers to a way of executing a language; there are addressing modes in instruction descriptions.

2. *See* measures of location.

modem *Short for* modulator and demodulator. A device that can convert a digital bit stream into an analog signal suitable for transmission over some analog communication channel (*modulation), and can convert incoming analog signals back into digital signals (*demodulation). Modems are used to connect digital devices across analog transmission lines. Most modems are designed to match specific national or international standards so that data communication equipment from one manufacturer can talk to that of another.

modifier bits Usually a small subset of bits (i.e. bit locations) in an instruction, used to provide some additional specification of the way in which the operation code and/or operand addresses are to be used or interpreted. *See* instruction format.

mod-n counter (modulo-n counter) *See* counter.

Modula A programming language developed from *Pascal as a research exercise to demonstrate that operating systems can be written entirely in a high-level language. It is now superseded by *Modula 2.

Modula 2 A high-level programming language designed by Wirth (the designer of Pascal) as the programming language for the Lilith personal computer system. Modula 2 is a derivative of *Pascal. Its name derives from the fact that a program is made up of *modules* – collections of procedures and data objects that exist independently of other modules and have a controlled interface with other modules (*compare* package (as used in Ada)). Modula 2 also provides facilities for describing parallel computations together with their interaction and synchronization. It is now available on most popular microcomputers.

modular arithmetic (residue arithmetic) Arithmetic based on the concept of the *congruence relation defined on the integers and used in computing to circumvent the problem of performing arithmetic on very large numbers.

Let $m_1, m_2, \ldots, m_k$ be integers, no two of which have a common factor greater than one. Given a large positive integer n it is possible to compute the remainders or residues $r_1, r_2, \ldots, r_k$ such that

$$n \equiv r_1 \ (\text{mod } m_1)$$
$$n \equiv r_2 \ (\text{mod } m_2)$$
$$\ldots$$
$$n \equiv r_k \ (\text{mod } m_k)$$

Provided n is less than

$$m_1 \times m_2 \times \ldots \times m_k$$

n can be represented by

$$(r_1, r_2, \ldots, r_k)$$

This can be regarded as an internal representation of n. Addition, subtraction, and multiplication of two large numbers then involves the addition, subtraction, and multiplication of corresponding pairs, e.g.

$$(r_1, \ldots, r_k) + (s_1, \ldots, s_k) =$$
$$(r_1 + s_1, \ldots, r_k + s_k)$$

Determining the sign of an integer or comparing relative magnitudes are less straightforward.

modular counter *See* cascadable counter.

modular programming A style of programming in which the complete program is decomposed into a set of components, termed *modules*, each of which is of manageable size, has a well-defined purpose, and has a well-defined interface to the outside world. Since the only alternative – that of completely monolithic programs – is untenable, the point is not whether programs should be modular but rather what criteria should be employed for their decomposition into modules. This was raised by David Parnas, who proposed that one major criterion should be that of *information hiding. Prior to this, decomposition had typically been performed on an ad-hoc basis, or sometimes on the basis of "stages" of the overall processing to be carried out by the program, and only minor benefits had been gained. More recently there has been great emphasis on decomposition based on the use of *abstract data types; such a decomposition can remain consistent with the principles of information hiding.

modulation The process of varying one signal, called the *carrier*, according to the pattern provided by another signal. The carrier is usually an analog signal selected to match the characteristics of a particular transmission system. Modulation signals and techniques may be combined to produce composite signals carrying many independent channels of information (*see* multiplexing).

The primary types of modulation are as follows:

(a) *Amplitude modulation (AM)* – the strength or amplitude of the carrier signal is varied. This form of modulation is not often directly used in computer communication.

(b) *Frequency modulation (FM)* – the frequency of the carrier is varied. This technique is often used by *modems. See also* frequency shift keying.

(c) *Phase modulation (PM)* – the phase of the carrier wave is varied. This technique is often used together with amplitude modulation in high-speed modems. *See also* phase shift keying.

(d) *Pulse code modulation (PCM)* – an analog signal is encoded as a series of pulses in a digital data stream. This technique is used by *codecs.

(e) *Spread-spectrum modulation (SSM)* – the carrier wave is frequency modulated by the analog or digital data signal in conjunction with a third or code signal. This technique is used by *packet radio networks for military applications.

The term shift keying, as in frequency shift keying, denotes specialized modulation techniques in which the modulating signal is digital rather than analog.

modulator A device that translates a digital signal into an analog signal: the modulator uses the digital signal as a pattern that determines the wave shape that the analog signal will have. A *demodulator performs the reverse transformation to recover the original digital signal. *See also* modulation, modem.

module 1. A program unit in Modula 2 and other languages, equivalent to the *package in Ada. *See also* modular programming, module specification.
2. A component of a hardware system that can be subdivided.

module coding review *See* review, code inspection.

module design review *See* review.

module invariant *See* invariant.

module specification A precise statement of the effects that a software module is required to achieve. It can be employed both by the implementer of the module, since it gives a definitive statement of the requirements that are imposed on the module, and by users of the module, since it gives a precise statement of what the module provides. A good module specification makes no commitment as to how the module's effects are achieved.

A variety of techniques have been developed for module specification. A *functional specification* identifies the operations that the module makes available and provides an individual specification for each operation, typically in the form of an input-output specification describing the mapping that the operation provides from a set of input values to a set of output values. In the typical case where a module has local data, a simple functional specification will need to refer to this local data when specifying each individual operation. This tends to obscure the specification, and also violates the principle that a specification should state what a module does but not how this is done.

The state machine model technique developed by Parnas treats the module as a *finite-state machine and distinguishes operations that can observe the state of the machine from those that can alter the state of the machine. The specification is given by indicating the effect of each operation that can change the state on the result of each operation than can observe the state. This technique therefore avoids the need to refer to the module's local data.

The same applies to the technique of *algebraic specification*, largely due to Guttag and Horning. With this technique, which is tailored to the specification of *abstract data type modules, the specification is given in two parts – a syntactic specification and a set of equations. The syntactic specification states the names, domains, and ranges of the operations provided by the module. Each equation specifies the net effect of some sequence of operations (or perhaps a single operation), and the complete set of equations must be sufficient to specify the effects of all operations under all conditions.

Because of the need for precision, module specifications are best given in some formal *specification language*. A variety of such languages have been developed, many drawing heavily on first-order *predicate calculus. Specific examples include the SPECIAL language of the HDM system, which adopts the finite-state machine approach, and the language used by the AFFIRM system, which employs algebraic specification techniques.

module testing (unit testing) *See* testing.

modulo-*n* check *Another name for* checksum.

modulo operation An arithmetic operation in which the result is the remainder after one integer is divided by another. Hence

$$i \bmod j \text{ or } i \bmod j$$

is the remainder of the division of integer i by integer j. The exact definition of the operation, when the integers may be negative, is not defined. *See also* modular arithmetic.

MOHLL *Acronym for* machine-oriented high-level language. A programming language with the control structures of the typical high-level language (if-then, while-do, etc.), whose data types and structures map onto the underlying machine architecture. Thus such a language will allow variables of type bit, byte, word, etc. These languages, also known simply as *machine-oriented languages*, provide an alternative to assembly language for systems programming at the hardware-interface level. Well-known examples are *Babbage and *PL/360. MOHLLs are now largely replaced by the language *C. *Compare* POL.

monadic Having one operand.

monadic operation (unary operation) defined on a set S. A *function from the domain S into S itself. The *identity function is a monadic operation. Other examples are the operations of *negation in arithmetic or logic and of taking *complements in set theory or in *Boolean algebra. Although basically functions, monadic operations are frequently represented using a special notation, e.g. $\neg A$ or A' or $\bar{A}$. When the set S is finite, a *truth table can be used to define the meaning of the operation.

monic polynomial *See* polynomial.

monitor 1. A device that is used for checking the progress and operation of a system. A visual display and keyboard may be used in the roles of both a control console and a monitor. Visual display screens without keyboards may be used as remote monitors to allow the status of the system to be observed from remote locations.

2. *Another name for* supervisor, or even a complete operating system.

3. A programming construct devised by Hoare to allow controlled sharing of resources by otherwise asynchronous processes, and involving the provision of controlled passing of variables between the processes.

monoid A *semigroup that possesses an *identity element, *e*. If *S* is a semigroup on which there is defined a *dyadic operation ∘, then

$$x \circ e = e \circ x = x$$

for all elements *x* in *S*. Monoids play an important role in various areas of computing, especially in the study of *formal languages and *parsing.

monomorphism A *homomorphism that, when viewed as a function, is an *injection.

monostable (one-shot) A digital circuit that has only one stable output state. It is constructed in such a way that it may be triggered by an externally generated signal to produce a single pulse. The time duration of the pulse is specified by the choice of external components, usually a capacitor.

Monte Carlo methods Numerical methods in which randomly generated numbers play a part in the calculations. A probabilistic model is constructed, corresponding to the mathematical or physical problem, and random samples are taken within the model. By taking more samples, a more accurate estimate of the result is obtained. Such methods are used for example on problems in particle physics, evaluation of multiple integrals, traffic problems, and large-scale operational problems generally. *See also* stochastic process.

Moore machine *See* sequential machine.

morphism *See* category.

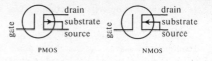

MOSFET circuit symbols

MOSFET (MOS transistor) *Acronym for* metal oxide semiconductor field-effect transistor. A type of *field-effect transistor that has an insulating layer of oxide, usually silicon dioxide, separating the gate from the drain-source conduction channel in the semiconductor. In an *NMOS* the channel is formed between n-type source and drain by negative charge carriers (i.e. electrons). In a *PMOS* the channel is formed between p-type source and drain by positive charge carriers (i.e. holes). The circuit symbols are shown in the diagram.

MOSFETs require no gate input current, other than a pulse to charge or discharge their input capacitance. They can operate at higher switching speeds and lower currents than *bipolar transistors. However, *integrated circuits fabricated in MOS technology often operate at slower speeds than their bipolar counterparts because of the space allocated to each transistor.

MOS integrated circuit *See* integrated circuit.

most general common instance *See* unification.

MOS transistor *Another name for* MOS-FET.

most significant character The character in the most significant position in a number, word, signal, etc. Common examples are the *most significant digit (MSD)* and the *most significant bit*

(MSB), which contribute the greatest quantity to the value of a digital or binary number.

mother *Another name for* parent, rarely used.

mother board A *printed circuit board into which other boards can be plugged. In some microcomputer systems the mother board carries all the major functional elements, e.g. the processor and some of the memory; the function can be enhanced by additional boards that perform specific activities such as memory extension or disk control and that communicate to the mother board via sockets onto a standard bus. *See also* backplane.

moth-eye *See* microrelief.

Motorola A US communications firm primarily devoted to automobile and other forms of mobile wireless communications and entertainment radios. Motorola entered the semiconductor field in the late 1950s and is now a major US manufacturer of VLSI design chips. The Motorola 6800 was an also-ran behind the Intel 8080. The Motorola 68000 series of high-performance 16-bit processors is widely used in microcomputers and workstations.

mouse A *pointing device that is moved by hand around a flat surface: the movements on the surface are communicated to a computer and cause corresponding movements of the cursor on the display. The mouse has one or more buttons to indicate to the computer that the cursor has reached a desired position. It is normally connected by cable to the computer; a "tail-less" mouse communicates by means of infrared rather than electrical signals.

movement file *Another name for* transaction file.

moving-average methods *See* time series.

MPU *Abbrev. for* microprocessor unit, the primary control and arithmetic element of a microcomputer system. *See* microprocessor.

MSD, MSB *Abbrevs. for* most significant digit, most significant bit.

MS-DOS An operating system developed by Microsoft Corp. for computers using the Intel 16- and 32-bit family of microprocessors. It provides a set of software services for programs running in a single-user environment and a simple command line interpreter as its user interface. A major facility is a set of services for managing files and I/O devices. It is the system most often run on the IBM PC and similar machines, although its inability to address more than 640 kilobytes of memory means that it will be gradually eclipsed by newer systems such as *OS/2.

m-sequence A periodic sequence of symbols generated by a linear *feedback shift register whose feedback coefficients form a primitive *polynomial. A *q-ary register (with q prime) whose generating polynomial is of degree n will have period $q^n - 1$, provided that the initial state is nonzero, and its contents will proceed through all the nonzero q-ary n-tuples. The termwise modulo-q sum of two m-sequences is another m-sequence: the m-sequences (of a given generating polynomial), together with the zero sequence, form a *group.

The term is short for maximum-length sequence. It is so called because the generating shift register only has q^n states, and so such a register (with arbitrary feedback logic) cannot generate a sequence whose period exceeds q^n. But with linear logic the zero state must stand in a loop of its own (*see* Good–de Bruijn diagram) and so the period of a linear feedback register cannot exceed $q^n - 1$. This period, which can be achieved when and only when the polynomial is primitive, is therefore the maximum that can be achieved.

m-sequences have many useful properties. They are employed as *pseudorandom sequences, *error-correcting codes (as they stand, or shortened, or extended), and in determining the time response of linear channels (*see* convolution). *See also* simplex codes.

MSI *Abbrev. for* medium-scale integration, i.e. integration in the range of 100 to 10 000 transistors on a single chip. *See* integrated circuit.

MS-WINDOWS A *window manager software system developed by Microsoft Corp. for the Intel 8086 family of microprocessors.

MTA *Abbrev. for* message transfer agent. One of three major entities defined by the X 400 electronic mail *protocol, the others being the *user agent and *message store. The function of the MTA is to take a message created by the sender's user agent, and to deliver this to the receiver's user agent. If delivery is not possible because the receiver's user agent is not active (for example because it runs on a personal computer that is currently disconnected from the network or is not powered on), the message will be placed in the message store to await collection by the receiver's user agent when it becomes active.

MTBF *Abbrev. for* mean time between failures. A figure of merit for system reliability.

MTBI *Abbrev. for* mean time between incidents. A measure of reliability similar to *MTBF but sometimes distinguished from it by the exclusion of failures that can be rectified without engineer attention.

MTS *Acronym for* Michigan terminal system. An operating system that was developed at the University of Michigan in the late 1960s, and is specifically

intended to offer interactive computing to large numbers of users, each carrying out relatively straightforward tasks.

MTTR *Abbrev. for* mean time to repair. *See* repair time.

MTU *Abbrev. for* magnetic tape unit. *See* magnetic tape.

mu-law (μ-law) encoding *See* pulse code modulation.

multiaccess system A system allowing several users to make apparently simultaneous use of the computer. Each user has a terminal, typically a keyboard plus VDU display, and is connected via a multiplexer or front-end processor to the main system. As individual users type their commands, the system will multiprogram among the several users of the system, each command being processed as it is received. *See also* time sharing.

multiaddress *Short for* multiple-address.

Multibus *Trademark* A flexible bus structure designed by Intel Corp. and now used in many commercial microprocessor systems. It is capable of supporting both 8- and 16-bit processors and 20-bit addresses, allowing up to one megabyte of physical address space. The bus supports master-slave and multi-master configurations, with *handshaking to permit devices of different speeds to communicate. Up to 16 masters can share Multibus resources. Multibus boards are approximately 12″ wide by 6.75″ high (about 30 by 17 cm). Electrical interfacing is via two adjacent card edge connectors, one of 43/86 pins and the other a 30/60 pin connector.

multicasting *See* broadcasting.

MULTICS *Trademark* A *multiaccess operating system designed in project *MAC to provide a MULTiplexed Information and Computing Service.

The MULTICS system makes extensive use of "rings" of hardware protection of access to memory in order to achieve management of a very large virtual memory. Users operating on files move their entire file into memory in order to operate on it. The MULTICS system was implemented on specially commissioned hardware constructed by GEC and the entire project was later taken over by Honeywell Computer Systems.

multidimensional array An *array of dimension greater than one.

multidrop line A single communication line that connects multiple stations – terminals or computers. Typically, one station will use *polling to coordinate access to the line and prevent collisions (multiple stations transmitting at once). A control protocol such as *SDLC is used. *See also* multipoint connection. *Compare* point-to-point line.

multigrid methods A broad class of methods for the numerical solution of certain classes of *partial differential equations. In its simplest form, after a suitable *finite-difference replacement of the problem, a system of *linear algebraic equations is obtained, perhaps involving thousands of unknowns. These equations are solved iteratively by a process that involves the solution of smaller linear systems arising from a sequence of coarser meshes (*see* finite-difference method). The method of successive over-relaxation has an important role in the solution of these subsystems. *See* iterative methods.

multilayer device An electronic device that is fabricated by a technique that involves the deposition of a number of layers of conductive track onto an insulating substrate, the individual layers being separated by a layer of insulating material. Interconnections are made to the various conductive layers by means of holes in the insulating material. The technique is used, for example, to produce compact multilayer circuit boards for hybrid integrated circuits and to fabricate multilayer CMOS integrated circuits.

multilevel memory A memory system containing at least two memory subsystems with different capacity and access-time attributes. *See* memory hierarchy.

multilevel security A *security processing mode where users with differing security clearances have correspondingly limited access to a database holding objects of different classifications. Output material carries *trusted *security labels.

multilinked Having a *link to several distinct data structures. For example, a *sparse matrix is frequently held so that each element belongs to two separate linear lists corresponding to a row list and a column list. A multilinked structure is sometimes called a *multiple chain*.

multimedia mail *See* electronic mail.

multimode counter *See* counter.

multipart stationery *See* stationery.

multiple-address machine A computer whose *instruction format specifies (for at least some instructions) more than one operand address.

multiple assignment A form of *assignment statement in which the same value is given to two or more variables. For example, in Algol,

$$a := b := c := 0$$

sets a, b, c to zero.

multiple chain *See* multilinked.

multiple precision (multiprecision) *See* double precision.

multiple-range tests *Significance tests for differences between means of several samples. The significance levels are adjusted to take account of the fact that more than one comparison is being made.

multiple regression model *See* regression analysis.

multiple-valued logic (multivalued logic; nonbinary logic) Digital logic for use in *logic circuits that are designed to handle more than two levels (voltages, etc.). In q-valued logic there are q levels and each *memory element (flip-flops, etc.) can exist in q different states. The classification of logic circuits into *combinational and *sequential circuits applies to multiple-valued logic exactly as it does to binary logic.

There is much interest currently in *ternary logic* $(q = 3)$ and, to a somewhat lesser extent, in *quaternary logic* $(q = 4)$. Such logics promise reduced numbers of logic gates, memory elements, and – perhaps most significantly – interconnections. Ternary logic is simple to implement in *CMOS technology, and is likely to become important in the design of *VLSI circuits. Its increased logical richness is shown by the fact that there are 16 possible two-input binary gates, but 19 683 such ternary gates (ignoring degeneracies in both cases).

multiplexed bus A type of bus structure in which the number of signal lines comprising the bus is less than the number of bits of data, address, or control information being transferred between elements of the system. For example, a multiplexed address bus might use 8 signal lines to transmit 16 bits of address information. The information is transferred sequentially, i.e. time-domain multiplexed, with additional control lines being used for sequencing the transfer.

multiplexer 1. A device that merges information from multiple input channels to a single output channel. *See* multiplexing.

2. A *combinational circuit that converts from 1 of m inputs to n outputs, where $m \leqslant 2^n$. *See also* data selector/ multiplexer.

multiplexer channel *See* channel.

multiplexing The process of combining multiple messages simultaneously on the same physical or logical transmission medium. There are two main types: *time division multiplexing (TDM) and *frequency division multiplexing (FDM). In TDM a device is allocated specific time slots in which to use the transmission medium. FDM divides the transmission medium into channels of smaller *bandwidth to which the user has exclusive rights. FDM and TDM can be combined to provide devices with time slots of logical channels.

multiplier A specific part of an *arithmetic and logic unit that is used to perform the operation of multiplication. It is not always explicitly present in an ALU; for example, a multiplication can be accomplished by a sequence of additions and shifts under the direction of the *control unit.

multiply connected Denoting a node in a communication network that has links, circuits, or channels to more than one of its neighbors. If one link fails, the node may still communicate using the remaining links.

multipoint connection A connection of a number of terminals in parallel, analogous to a *multidrop connection. Sometimes the terms are used synonymously, although multidrop strictly implies that the connections are all served from a common connection point (node), whereas multipoint implies that connections are made through a series of (analog) bridging connections where some or all of the terminals are served by different common carrier offices interconnected by communication trunks.

multipoint line A data communication link that connects more than two *nodes. Individual nodes are identified by unique addresses. A *data link control protocol is used to determine which node has the right to transmit on the line, and which node(s) should be receiving.

multiport memory A memory that provides more than one access *port to separate processors. The mechanism may be a *bus. It is used as a method of interconnecting computers. *See also* shared memory, central processor.

multiprecision (multiple precision) *See* double precision.

multiprocessing system (multiprocessor; multiunit processor) A system in which more than one processor may be active at any one time. While the processors are actively executing separate processes they run completely asynchronously. However it is essential to provide synchronization between the processors when they access critical system resources or critical regions of system code. A multiprocessing system is also a *multiprogramming system. *See also* concurrency.

multiprocessor *Another name for* multiprocessing system.

multiprogramming system A system in which several individual programs may be active. Each active program implies a running *process, so there may be several processes, but only one process runs at any one time on any particular processor. It is perfectly feasible to run a multiprogramming system containing only one processor; a *multiprocessing system, containing several processors, will also be a multiprogramming system.

multiset *Another name for* bag.

multitape Turing machine A *Turing machine that has a finite number of tapes, each tape having a tape head that can move independently. Such machines have the same computational power as single-tape Turing machines. Consider a multitape Turing machine T. If for no input word of length n does T scan more than L(n) cells on any tape then T is said to be an *L(n) tape-bounded Turing machine*. If for no input word of length n does T make more than T(n) moves before halting then T is said to be a *T(n) time-bounded Turing machine*.

multitasking The concurrent execution of a number of tasks, i.e. of a number of jobs or processes. *See* parallel processing.

multithreading A form of code that uses more than one *process or processor, possibly of different types, and that may on occasions have more than one process or processor active at the same time. *See also* single threading, threading.

multiunit processor *Another name for* multiprocessing system.

multiuser system A system that is (apparently) serving more than one user simultaneously, i.e. a *multiprogramming or *multiprocessing system.

multivalued logic *See* multiple-valued logic.

multivariate analysis The study of multiple measurements on a sample. It embraces many techniques related to a range of different problems.

*Cluster analysis seeks to define homogeneous classes within the sample on the basis of the measured variables. *Discriminant analysis* is a technique for deciding whether an individual should be assigned to a particular predefined class on the basis of the measured variables. *Principle component analysis* and *factor analysis* aim to reduce the number of variables in the study to a few (say two or three) that express most of the variation within a sample.

Multivariate *probability distributions define probabilities for sets of random variables.

multivibrator An electronic oscillator that consists of two resistor-capacitor amplifier stages that interact in such a way that the amplifier's outputs are complementary and exhibit two stable mutually exclusive states, i.e. fully on and fully off. The circuit can be made to oscillate continuously, producing a square wave (astable mode), produce single pulses (monostable mode), or change state on application of an external trigger (bistable mode). *See also* flip-flop.

multiway search tree of degree n. A generalization of a *binary search tree to a tree of degree n where each node in the ordered tree has $m \leqslant n$ children and contains $(m-1)$ ordered key values, called subkeys. For some given search key, if the key is less than the first subkey then the first subtree (if it exists) is searched for the key; if the key lies between the ith and $(i + 1)$th subkey, where

$$i = 1, 2, \ldots, m-2$$

then the $(i + 1)$th subtree (if it exists) is searched; if the key is greater than the last subkey then the mth subtree (if it exists) is searched. *See also* B-tree.

mu operator (**μ-operator, minimization operator**) *See* minimization.

mutual exclusion A relationship between processes such that each has some part (the *critical section) that must not be executed while the critical section of another is being executed. There is thus exclusion of one process by another. In certain regions of an operating system, for example those dealing with the allo-cation of nonsharable resources, it is imperative to ensure that only one process is executing the relevant code at any one time. This can be guaranteed by the use of *semaphores: at entry to the critical region of code a semaphore is set; this inhibits entry to the code by any other process until the semaphore is reset as the last action by the process that first entered the critical region.

MUX *Short for* multiplexer.

MVS *Trademark, acronym for* multiprogramming with a variable number of processes. An operating system commonly used on large IBM or IBM-compatible processors.

Myhill equivalence An *equivalence relation arising in *formal language theory. If L is a language over Σ (*see* word) then its Myhill equivalence is the relation $=_M$ on Σ^* defined as follows:

$$u =_M u'$$

if, for all w_1, w_2 in Σ^*,

$$w_1 u w_2 \in L \text{ iff } w_1 u' w_2 \in L$$

Similarly (and more generally), if f is a function from Σ^* to any set, its Myhill equivalence is defined by:

$$u =_M u'$$

if, for all w_1, w_2 in Σ^*,

$$f(w_1 u w_2) = f(w_1 u' w_2)$$

See also Nerode equivalence.

An important fact is that L is *regular iff $=_M$ is of finite index (i.e. there are finitely many *equivalence classes). Indeed, L is regular iff it is a union of classes of any equivalence relation of finite index. In addition $=_M$ is a *congruence on Σ^*, i.e.

$$u =_M u' \text{ and } v =_M v' \text{ implies}$$
$$uv =_M u'v'$$

The equivalence classes therefore can be *concatenated consistently and form a *semigroup. This is in fact the semigroup of the *minimal machine for L (or f).

N

NAK *Short for* negative acknowledgment. *See* acknowledgment.

name A notation for indicating an entity in a program or system. (The word can also be used as a verb.) The kinds of entity that can be named depend on the context, and include variables, data objects, functions, types, and procedures (in programming languages), nodes, stations, and processes (in a data communication network), etc. The name denotes the entity, independently of its physical location or address. Names are used for long-term stability (e.g. when specifying a node in a computer program) or for their ease of use by humans (who recognize the name more readily than an address). Names are converted to addresses by a process of *name look-up*.

In many languages and systems, a name must be a simple identifier, usually a textual string. In more advanced languages, a name may be composed from several elementary components according to the rules of the language.

name look-up *See* name.

NAND gate An electronic *logic gate whose output is logic 0 (false) only when all (two or more) inputs are logic 1 (true), otherwise it is logic 1. It thus implements the logical *NAND operation and has the same *truth table. The diagram shows the usual circuit symbol of a two-input gate (which implies by the small circle that it is equivalent to an *AND gate whose output has been inverted) and the associated truth table.

NAND operation The logical *connective combining two statements, truth values, or formulas P and Q in such a way that the outcome is true only if either P or Q or both is false (*see* table). The NAND operation may be

A1 ⎤
A2 ⎦ ⟩o— B

inputs	A1	0	0	1	1
	A2	0	1	0	1
output B		1	1	1	0

Two-input NAND gate, circuit symbol and truth table

P	F	F	T	T
Q	F	T	F	T
$P\,\vert\,Q$	T	T	T	F

Truth table for NAND operation

represented by the *Sheffer stroke*, $\vert$, or by Δ. $P\,\vert\,Q$ is just the negation of $P \wedge Q$, hence the name (*see* AND operation).

The NAND operation is of particular significance to computer designers since any Boolean expression can be realized by an expression using only the NAND operation. In practical terms, circuits can be built using only *NAND gates.

nano- (symbol: n) A prefix to a unit, indicating a submultiple of one billionth, 10^{-9}, of that unit, as in nanosecond.

nanostore *See* microprogramming.

narrowband *See* bandwidth.

Nassi–Schneidermann chart (NS chart) A kind of diagram (devised 1973–74) for representing the sequence of execution in a program. The diagram takes the form of a rectangle divided mainly into smaller rectangles with the sequence of execution going from top to bottom of the diagram. There are various standard constructs, including NS sequence structures, NS repetition structures, and NS selection structures.

natural binary-coded decimal (NBCD) *See* binary-coded decimal.

natural language understanding The processing of utterances in human language (natural language as opposed to programming language) in order to extract meaning and respond appropriately. The main natural language studied has been written English, although there has also been work on other languages and on speech. The processing requires both syntactic knowledge about the language concerned and semantic knowledge of the relationship between the utterance and what it means, usually in a *knowledge base containing an internal representation of the world. Grammatical and semantic rules are used to analyze the utterance into *logical formulae or *semantic nets, where the meaning representation can be used by a reasoning system.

natural number A nonnegative integer, i.e. a member of the set $\{0,1,2,\dots\}$. Some authors exclude 0.

NBCD *Abbrev. for* natural binary-coded decimal. *See* binary-coded decimal.

NCP *Abbrev. for* network control protocol. A transport layer protocol that was designed for the *ARPANET. The DARPA internetworking project developed the *TCP protocol to replace NCP.

NCSC National Computer Security Center, a US agency active in formulating bases for the classification and evaluation of secure systems. For an establishment working in such a topic the Center has a remarkably open approach to the publication of material.

NEC Corporation A Japanese electronics company that produces a wide range of computer products and is one of the world's top five computer companies in terms of revenue (1988 figures).

negation 1. In arithmetic, the operation of changing the sign of a nonzero arithmetic quantity; the negation of zero is zero. Negation is usually denoted by the minus sign.
   2. In logic, the application of the *NOT operation on a statement, truth value, or formula.

negative acknowledgment (NAK) *See* acknowledgment. *See also* backward error correction.

negative logic 1. A logic system in which the normal meanings of the binary signal levels are interchanged, e.g. high voltage equals logic 0, low voltage equals logic 1.
   2. (complementary logic) A logic system in which all the Boolean variables and Boolean functions behave as though they were complements.
   Compare positive logic.

negator *Another name for* inverter.

negentropy *See* entropy.

Nerode equivalence An *equivalence relation, $=_N$, arising in *formal language theory. It is defined analogously to the *Myhill equivalence by the weaker properties:
for a language L over Σ,
$$u =_N u'$$
if, for all w in Σ^*,
$$uw \in L \text{ iff } u'w \in L$$
for a function f,
$$u =_N u'$$
if, for all w in Σ^*,
$$f(uw) = f(u'w)$$
Although coarser than the Myhill equivalence, it is finite only if the latter is. Unlike the latter, it gives only a right congruence:
$$u =_N u' \text{ implies } uv =_N u'v$$
and thus does not give rise to a *semigroup. The number of *equiva-

lence classes is the number of states in the *minimal machine for *L*.

nested blocks, nested scopes *See* block-structured languages.

nesting A feature of language design in which constructs can be embedded within instances of themselves, e.g. nested loops:

> **while** b1 **do**
> **begin**
>> **while** b2 **do**
>> **begin**
>>> . . .
>> **end**;
> **end**;

Nesting of blocks in *block-structured languages provides an elegant, though not entirely practicable, control over the scope of *identifiers, since identifiers are local to the innermost level of nesting at which they are declared.

nesting store *Another name for* stack, implemented in hardware.

network 1. In communications, a rather loosely defined term applied to a system that consists of terminals, *nodes, and interconnection media that can include lines or trunks, satellites, microwave, medium- and long-wave radio, etc. In general, a network is a collection of resources used to establish and switch communication paths between its terminals. *See also* local area network, wide area network, network architecture, packet switching, message switching, network delay.

2. In electronic circuitry, an interconnection of various electrical elements. A *passive network* contains no active (amplifying or switching) elements such as transistors; a *linear network* is a passive network that contains no nonlinear elements such as diodes.

3. (net) In mathematics, a *connected directed *graph that contains no cycles. Interconnections involving objects such as telephones, logic gates, or computers could be represented using a connected but not necessarily directed graph.

network architecture The design and implementation of a communication network with respect to its communication disciplines and its interconnection topology. Network architecture deals explicitly with the encoding of information, its transmission, *error detection and correction and *flow control, techniques for *addressing subscribers on the network, analysis of network performance under abnormal or degraded conditions (such as missing communication lines or improperly functioning switching nodes), etc. Examples of generalized network architectures are OSI (*open systems interconnection, an architecture propounded by the ISO) and SNA (systems network architecture, proposed and supported by IBM).

Interconnection topology is also considered a part of network architecture. There are three generic forms of topology: *star*, *ring*, and *bus*. Star topology consists of a single hub node with various terminal nodes connected to the hub; terminal nodes do not interconnect directly. By treating one terminal node as the hub of another star, a *tree-like* topology is obtained. In ring topology all nodes are on a ring and communication is generally in one direction around the ring; some ring architectures use two rings, with communication in opposite directions. Various techniques (including time division multiplexing, token passing, and ring stretching) are used to control who is allowed to transmit onto the ring. Bus topology is noncyclic, with all nodes connected; traffic consequently travels in both directions, and some kind of arbitration is needed to determine which terminal can use the bus at any one time. *Ethernet is an example. Hybrids that mix star and ring topologies have been employed.

A special area of network architecture is involved with the necessary disciplines required of some of the newer network architectures (*see* ring network, token ring, CSMA/CD).

network database system A *database system in which the DBMS supports a network organization: any record (called an *owner record*) can hold data that is common to a set of other records (called *member records*), and it is possible to access all records in the set starting from the owner. Access to a set of records is implemented by means of pointers. A *hierarchical database system is a special and limited case of a network database system. Examples of network DBMSs include DBOMP, DMS-1100, IDMS, IDS, and TOTAL. *See also* CODASYL.

network delay Broadly speaking, the time needed for a signal to traverse a network. In a *circuit switching network the only contribution to network delay arises from the finite speed with which signals propagate along the transmission medium. Since for electrical signals this speed is in the same order as the speed of light, network delay is typically a few microseconds per kilometer.

In a *packet switching network the situation is more complex. The time needed to traverse the network is normally measured as the period between the sender indicating that transmission is to start, and the delivery of the last bit of the packet to the destination. This is the sum of the times needed to traverse each sector of the network, firstly between the data source and the *PAD that connects it to the network, then between each pair of *nodes, and finally into the destination. Each sector has contributions from

(a) the transit time along the medium connecting the two nodes;

(b) the time needed to disassemble the packet into its component bits at the transmitting node (necessarily identical to the time needed to reassemble the packet at the receiving node);

(c) the time needed by a switching node to determine the route the packet is to follow, and to carry out the switching.

The first of these is essentially similar to the transit time in a circuit switched network, and has a similar value of a few microseconds per kilometer. The second is essentially equal to the packet size times the interbit time on the transmission line. The third is a function of the organization of the switching nodes and of their processing speed.

A further complication arises from the fact that in a heavily loaded network there will be queues (lines) of packets in each node. The queues will arise as outgoing packets, which have been routed onto a line, wait to be transmitted behind other packets queued for that line (which has the effect of apparently slowing down the packet disassembly activity) or as incoming packets wait to be rerouted by the node behind other packets queued for service by the processor (which has the effect of slowing down the switching time).

In a network using only terrestrial links, the total network delay is usually dominated by packet assembly times – (b) above. This is not true of networks that use satellite links, especially where geostationary satellites are involved.

Network File Service (NFS) A set of protocols that run over a *CSMA/CD network and offer support for *file transfer and access, and for *paging. The system was originally developed by *Sun to allow the use of workstations without disks: it provides the ability for one workstation, without disks, to use another workstation, with disks, to supply both a file store and paging support. The system is now offered by other suppliers and has become a de facto standard for work of this kind.

network front end An auxiliary processor or system attached to another, usually larger, computer specifically to connect that computer to a network. The goals of a network front end are to improve overall performance by doing network-related tasks that would be expensive on the main computer, and to convert the standard interfaces and protocols used by the external network into a form better suited to the local system's internal operation (and vice versa). A network front end may also be used to multiplex a single network interface among several computers, in which case the network front end may be considered a *gateway or *bridge.

network interconnection *See* internetworking.

network layer of protocol function. *See* seven-layer reference model.

network management system As networks become more complex, and contain larger numbers of independently operating units often from a number of different suppliers, the problem of managing the network has become increasingly severe. There have been a number of proposals for network management systems, which allow those responsible for the maintenance and repair of the network to locate and isolate faulty components. To date, none of these proposals has met with universal support, not least because many suppliers of network components have invested heavily in their own proprietary approaches and these cannot generally interwork. There are now moves toward the definition of nonproprietary standards for the movement of network management data across the network, but it is unlikely that usable and stable standards will emerge for some years yet.

network topology *See* network architecture.

network virtual terminal (NVT) *See* TELNET. *See also* virtual terminal.

neural net (or network) A form of computation inspired by the structure and

function of the brain. One version of this is as follows. The topology is a *weighted directed graph. Nodes can be on or off. Time is discrete. At each time instant all the on nodes send an impulse along their outgoing arcs to their neighbor nodes. All nodes sum their incoming impulses, weighted according to the arc. All the nodes at which this sum exceeds a threshold turn on at the next time instant; all the others turn off. Computation proceeds by setting some input nodes, waiting for the network to reach a steady state, and then reading some output nodes. Nodes can be trained, using examples, to recognize certain patterns, for instance to classify objects by features.

neuron A node in a *neural net.

Newton–Cotes rules *See* numerical integration.

Newton's method An iterative technique for solving one or more *nonlinear equations. For the single equation
$$f(x) = 0$$
the iteration is
$$x_{n+1} = x_n - f(x_n)/f'(x_n),$$
$$n = 0,1,2,\ldots$$
where x_0 is an approximation to the solution. For the system
$$f(x) = 0,$$
$$f = (f_1, f_2, \ldots f_n)^T,$$
$$x = (x_1, x_2, \ldots, x_n)^T,$$
the iteration takes the mathematical form
$$x_{n+1} = x_n - J(x_n)^{-1} f(x_n),$$
$$n = 0,1,2,\ldots$$
where $J(x)$ is the $n \times n$ matrix whose i,jth element is
$$\partial f_i(x)/\partial x_j$$
In practice each iteration is carried out by solving a system of linear equations. Subject to appropriate conditions the iteration converges quadratically (ultimately an approximate squaring of the error occurs). The disadvantage of the method is that a constant recalculation of J may be too time-consuming and so

the method is most often used in a modified form, e.g. with approximate derivatives. Since Newton's method is derived by a linearization of $f(x)$, it is capable of generalization to other kinds of nonlinear problems, e.g. boundary-value problems (*see* ordinary differential equations).

NFS *See* Network File Service.

nibble *Rare* Half a byte, i.e. generally four bits.

NIFTP *Abbrev. for* network independent file transfer protocol. The file transfer *protocol defined by the *blue book and used within the UK academic community. *See* file transfer.

nine's complement *See* radix-minus-one complement.

(n, k) code *See* block code.

NLQ *Abbrev. for* near letter quality. Printed output somewhat inferior to that produced by a good electric typewriter but acceptable for most purposes. *See also* LQ.

NMOS A type of *MOSFET.

no-address instruction An instruction that does not require the designation of an operand address, e.g. "complement the accumulator". *See* implied addressing.

node 1. A substructure of a hierarchical data structure that cannot be further decomposed, e.g. a vertex in a *graph or *tree.

2. A point in a computer *network where communication lines, such as telephone lines, electric cables, or optical fibers, are interconnected. The device used to make the connection(s) may be a simple electric *interface – as used in a *local area network. In more complex longer-distance networks a computer is required.

Node computers vary in their functional capabilities but their basic use is to switch incoming information to the necessary output line so that the information ultimately reaches its specified destination. The information may be transmitted as a whole or may be split into segments (*see* packet switching, message switching). When the information reaches its final destination, the node computer at this point will send it through to the recipient(s).

Nodes can also be called *stations*, and in many X.25 networks the switching nodes are known as *exchanges*.

noise Any signal that occurs in an electronic or communication system and is considered extraneous to the desired signal being propagated. Noise can be introduced, for example, by external disturbances and may be deleterious in a given system since it can produce spurious signals, i.e. errors.

The *noise immunity* is a measure of the magnitude of external disturbances that a digital circuit can tolerate without producing errors. Logic values are represented electronically by two different voltage levels. Any noise introduced into logic circuitry by external disturbances is added (or subtracted) from the real digital logic signal. The *noise margin* is the maximum noise voltage that can be added or subtracted from the logic signal before a threshold voltage for a logic state is passed. *See also* impulse noise, white noise, Gaussian noise.

noise immunity *See* noise.

noiseless coding In communication theory, the use of a code to improve the efficiency of a *communication system in which *noise is absent or negligible. Noiseless coding is thus generally the same as *source coding. Note that the process of coding is itself usually noiseless: there is no need for encoders or decoders to introduce noise, so the term noiseless coding is not used to imply the absence of such noise.

noise margin *See* noise.

noise sequence *See* pseudonoise sequence.

noise source *See* Shannon's model.

noisy mode A method of operation that is sometimes used when normalizing a floating-point number. If the mantissa is shifted m bits to the left during normalization, then in noisy mode the digits generated to fill the m rightmost bits in the normalized mantissa are not necessarily zeros.

NOMAD A commercial *database management system that supports both hierarchies and relations.

nonbinary logic *Another name for* multiple-valued logic.

nondestructive read The process of reading a memory device in such a manner that the contents of the memory are not altered. The reading of most integrated-circuit devices is nondestructive.

nondeterminism A mode of computation in which, at certain points, there is a choice of ways to proceed: the computation may be thought of as choosing arbitrarily between them, or as splitting into separate copies and pursuing all choices simultaneously. The precise form of nondeterminism depends on the particular computational formalism.

For example, a nondeterministic *Turing machine will have a choice of moves to make for a given internal state and tape symbol being read. After a choice has been made, other choice-points will be encountered. There is therefore a *tree of possible different overall computations, with the *nonterminal nodes representing choice-points. If, for example, the algorithm performs some kind of "search", then the search succeeds if at least one sequence of choices (path through the tree) is successful. Many algorithms are expressed most conveniently in this way; nondeterminism also arises naturally in connection with *concurrency.

Nondeterminism is important in the field of *complexity: it is believed that a nondeterministic Turing machine is capable of performing in "reasonable time" computations that could not be so performed by any deterministic Turing machine.

nonequivalence gate *Another name for* exclusive-OR gate.

nonequivalence operation *Another name for* exclusive-OR operation.

nonerasable programmable device *See* programmable device.

nonhierarchical cluster analysis *See* cluster analysis.

nonimpact printer A printer in which the image is formed without use of mechanical impact. *Ink jet, *thermal, and *electrographic printers are examples of this type.

nonlinear equations In general, a problem that requires the determination of values of the unknowns $x_1, x_2, \ldots, x_n$ for which

$$f_i(x_1, x_2, \ldots, x_n) = 0,$$
$$i = 1, 2, \ldots, n$$

where $f_1, f_2, \ldots, f_n$ are given algebraic functions of n variables, i.e. they do not involve derivatives or integrals. This in both theory and practice is a very difficult problem. Such systems of equations arise in many areas, e.g. in numerical methods for nonlinear *ordinary and *partial differential equations. When $n = 1$ the single equation can be solved by a variety of effective techniques (all involving *iteration); the case of *polynomial equations can give rise to complex solutions. For systems of equations, *Newton's method and principally its many variants are widely used. For cases of extreme difficulty where, for example, only poor starting approximations are available, methods based on the idea of *continuation can be of value.

nonlinear regression model *See* regression analysis.

nonlocal entity *See* local.

nonmemory reference instruction An instruction that can be carried out without having to obtain an operand from, or return a result to, memory. Immediate instructions and some branch instructions are examples. *See also* zero-address instruction.

nonmonotonic reasoning A form of reasoning in which the acquisition of new knowledge can cause earlier conclusions to be withdrawn, so that the body of inferred knowledge does not grow monotonically (i.e. does not increase consistently) with the body of received knowledge. Various systems of nonmonotonic reasoning have been developed, among which are nonmonotonic logic, circumscription, default reasoning, autoepistemic logic, and negation as failure.

nonparametric techniques *Statistical methods that make no assumptions about the precise form of the *frequency distribution from which the data are sampled. They are mainly of use for hypothesis testing using the information in the rank order within each sample. For example, the *Mann Whitney U-test* may be used to test whether two samples are drawn from the same distribution, and the *rank correlation coefficient* may be used to test whether two variables are independent.

These methods can be contrasted with *parametric techniques*, which require specific models with *parameters to be estimated.

nonpreemptive allocation An allocation that does not preempt a resource from a process to which it is already allocated. *Compare* preemptive allocation.

nonprocedural language *Another name for* declarative language.

nonreturn to zero *See* NRZ, tape format.

nonsingular matrix A square matrix, A, of numbers whose *determinant is nonzero. A is nonsingular if and only if it is invertible (*see* inverse matrix).

nonstop processing The use of multiple computers in a redundant configuration to provide high *availability of computing service and tolerance to failures of service in a single computer.

nonterminal (nonterminal symbol) *See* grammar.

nonterminal node (interior node) of a tree. Any node that is not a terminal node (i.e. a leaf node) and hence has one or more children.

nonvolatile memory A type of memory whose contents are not lost when power to the memory is removed. *ROM and *PROM are examples. *Compare* volatile memory.

non von Neumann architecture Any computer architecture in which the underlying model of computation is radically different from the classical von Neumann model (*see* von Neumann machine). A non von Neumann machine may thus be without the concept of sequential flow of control (i.e. without any register corresponding to a "program counter" that indicates the current point that has been reached in execution of a program) and/or without the concept of a variable (i.e. without "named" storage locations in which a value may be stored and subsequently referenced or changed).

Examples of non von Neumann machines are the *dataflow machines and the *reduction machines. In both of these cases there is a high degree of parallelism, and instead of variables there are immutable bindings between names and constant values.

Note that the term non von Neumann is usually reserved for machines that represent a radical departure from the von Neumann model, and is therefore not normally applied to multiprocessor or multicomputer architectures, which effectively offer a set of cooperating von Neumann machines.

no-op instruction (pass instruction; do-nothing instruction) An instruction that causes no action to take place in the computer except for consumption of time and instruction storage space. There are several uses for this instruction including time adjustment of a program, filling out program space in a system where instruction boundaries do not always coincide with word boundaries, and replacement of unwanted instructions without having to recompute all other program addresses.

NOR gate An electronic *logic gate whose output is logic 1 (true) only when all (two or more) inputs are logic 0 (false), otherwise it is logic 0. It thus implements the logical *NOR operation and has the same truth table. The diagram shows the usual circuit symbol of a two-input gate (which implies by the small circle that it is an inclusive *OR gate whose output has been inverted) and the associated truth table. *See also* exclusive-NOR gate.

norm *See* approximation theory.

normal distribution (Gaussian distribution) An important *probability distribution for data in the form of continuous measurements. The frequency function is given by

$$(2\pi\sigma^2)^{-\frac{1}{2}} \exp[-\frac{1}{2}(x - \mu)^2/\sigma^2]$$

inputs A1	0	0	1	1
A2	0	1	0	1
output B	1	0	0	0

Two-input NOR gate, circuit symbol and truth table

P	F	F	T	T
Q	F	T	F	T
$P \downarrow Q$	T	F	F	F

Truth table for NOR operation

The distribution is symmetric about the mean μ, and its variance is σ^2. The range of x is infinite $(-\infty, \infty)$. Many sampling distributions tend to the normal form as the sample size tends to infinity.

normal form A term applied to relations in a *relational database. A relation is said to be in normal form, or *normalized*, if it satisfies certain defined constraints. Codd's original exposition of the relational model of data defined three normal forms, but two further normal forms have since been defined. The constraint that is common to all normal forms is that relations must not be nested, i.e. a relation may not be defined as a member of another relation. The purpose of any normal form is to avoid inefficiencies that would otherwise occur during updating – so-called *update anomalies*.

normalize *See* floating-point notation. *See also* normal form, orthonormal basis, orthogonal functions.

normal subgroup *See* coset.

307

NOR operation The logical *connective combining two statements, truth values, or formulas P and Q in such a way that the result is true only if both P and Q are false (*see* table). The NOR operation is the dual of the *NAND operation (*see* duality). It may be represented by the *Pierce arrow*, $\downarrow$, or by ∇. $P{\downarrow}Q$ is just the negation of $P \vee Q$, hence the name (*see* OR operation).

The NOR operation is of particular significance to computer designers since any Boolean expression can be expressed using the NOR operation alone. In practical terms, circuits can be built using only *NOR gates.

notch filter *See* band-stop filter.

not-equivalence gate *Another name for* exclusive-OR gate.

NOT gate *Another name for* inverter.

NOT operation A logical *connective with just one operand. When applied to a statement, truth value, or formula P, the outcome is false if P is true, and vice versa, i.e. it produces a negation. It can be denoted in a variety of ways, e.g.

$$\text{not } P,\ \neg P,\ \sim P,\ P',\ \bar{P}$$

NP, NP-complete, NP-hard *See* P=NP question.

NRZ *Abbrev. for* nonreturn to zero. A way of encoding binary signals that aims to achieve the highest possible data transfer rate for a given signal frequency. The name is derived from the principle of operation, i.e. the signal line does not return to zero – make any transition – between a succession of 1 bits. The method was first used for communications signaling in which there was always a 1 bit at the start of a character and thus there was a predictable and acceptable short interval over which the sending and receiving devices had to maintain synchronism independently.

Many variants of the basic principle have been derived to overcome synchronization problems that occur at high speeds and long bit streams, one of which is *NRZI, nonreturn to zero inverted.* (This should not be confused with NRZ1, nonreturn to zero one (or mark) – *see* tape format.) NRZI is a form of encoding used for magnetic recording in which a 1 bit is always indicated by a magnetic flux transition, regardless of direction. Zeros do not give rise to transitions and thus a long sequence of zeros could exceed the capability to maintain synchronism. For this reason it cannot be used in single bit stream recording such as that used on a disk, but can be used in multitrack systems such as magnetic tape provided that choice of parity ensures that there is at least one transition per character and the skew between tracks is small compared to the pitch of transitions. *See also* disk format, tape format.

NRZI 1. (more correctly **NRZ1**) *Abbrev. for* nonreturn to zero one, or mark. *See* tape format.
   2. *Abbrev. for* nonreturn to zero inverted. *See* NRZ.

NS chart *See* Nassi–Schneidermann chart.

NSPACE, NTIME *See* complexity classes.

***n*-tuple** *See* ordered pair, Cartesian product.

n-type semiconductor *See* semiconductor.

nucleus *See* kernel.

nullary operation *See* operation.

null character A special character in a *character set, denoting nothing, and usually (as in ASCII and EBCDIC) represented by zero.

nullity of a, graph. *See* connected graph.

null link *See* linked list.

null list (empty list) *See* list.

null matrix (zero matrix) A square matrix, all the elements of which are zeros.

null set *Another name for* empty set.

null string *Another name for* empty string.

number cruncher *Informal name for* supercomputer.

number system Although early number systems were not positional, all of the number systems most commonly used today are *positional systems*: the value of a number in such a system is determined not just by the digits in the number but also by the position in the number of each of the digits. If a positional system has a *fixed radix* (or *fixed base*) R then each digit a_i in any number

$$a_n a_{n-1} \ldots a_0$$

is an integer in the range 0 to $(R - 1)$ and the number is interpreted as

$$a_n R^n + a_{n-1} R^{n-1} + \ldots + a_1 R^1 + a_0 R^0$$

Since this is a polynomial in R, such numbers are sometimes called *polynomial numbers*. The decimal and binary systems are both fixed-radix systems, with a radix of 10 and 2, respectively.

Fractional values can also be represented in a fixed-radix system. Thus,

$$\cdot a_1 a_2 \ldots a_n$$

is interpreted as

$$a_1 R^{-1} + a_2 R^{-2} + \ldots + a_n R^{-n}$$

In a *mixed-radix* (or *mixed-base*) system, the digit a_i in any number

$$a_n a_{n-1} \ldots a_0$$

lies in the range 0 to R_i, where R_i is not the same for every i. The number is then interpreted as

$$(\ldots ((a_n R_{n-1}) + a_{n-1}) R_{n-2} + \ldots + a_1) R_0 + a_0$$

For example, 122 days 17 hours 35 minutes 22 seconds is equal to

$$(((((1 \times 10) + 2)10 + 2)24 + 17)60 + 35)60 + 22 \text{ seconds}$$

numerical analysis A branch of mathematics dealing with the numerical solution of problems formulated and studied in other branches of mathematics. Numerical analysis now plays an important part in engineering and in the quantitative parts of pure and applied science.

The tasks of numerical analysis include the development of appropriate *numerical methods together with the provision of a suitable *error analysis. On the practical side it involves the writing of efficient and reliable computer subroutines for a wide variety of problems.

numerical code A code whose target alphabet contains only digits and/or strings of digits, e.g. a binary code.

numerical control The application of digital computer techniques to the control of a manufacturing process. The concept has been applied primarily to various kinds of machine tools such as milling machines, metal-cutting lathes, welding machines, and some specialized machines. The machines are controlled by numerical specification of parameters such as position, where the numbers are usually calculated beforehand by a computer and recorded on a medium such as punched paper tape. In the computer field, standard numerically controlled machines are used for drilling holes in printed circuit boards and for inserting components into a printed circuit board. *See also* computer-aided manufacturing, computer-integrated manufacturing.

numerical differentiation The problem of approximating the derivative of a function using values of the function. An obvious approach is to use the derivative of an *interpolation polynomial. Such estimates involve differences of function values, and loss of potential accuracy occurs, due to *cancellation, if the data values are at points too close together.

numerical integration (quadrature) The problem of finding the numerical value for a definite integral. The underlying approximation behind most methods is the replacement of a function $f(x)$ by an *interpolation polynomial, based on a set of points $x_1, x_2, \ldots, x_n$. This leads to integration rules of the form

$$\int_b^a w(x)f(x)\mathrm{d}x \simeq w_1 f(x) + w_2 f(x_2) + \ldots + w_n f(x_n)$$

in which the w_i are called *weights*.

The standard problem has a,b finite and $w(x) \equiv 1$. For this case the rules with equally spaced points x_i are called *Newton–Cotes rules*. Well-known examples are the *trapezium rule and *Simpson's rule. Most program libraries implement the more powerful *Gaussian rules* in which the points x_i are chosen to maximize the *degree of precision. This is achieved by choosing the x_i as the zeros of the Legendre polynomials that are *orthogonal polynomials with respect to $w(x) \equiv 1$ on the interval $[-1, 1]$. Another important idea is the *extrapolation method due to Romberg, based on the trapezium rule.

For infinite range problems Gaussian rules can also be defined in terms of suitable orthogonal polynomials. A useful case is where

$$w(x) = e^{-x},\ a = 0,\ b = \infty$$

where the appropriate orthogonal polynomials determining the x_i are the Laguerre polynomials.

In practice the interval of integration is subdivided and the chosen rule applied to each subinterval, together with a companion rule to provide an error estimate (*see* error analysis). By then subdividing the interval where the error is largest, a greater concentration of effort is placed where the integrand is most difficult. This is known as *adaptive quadrature*. Such nonuniform distribution of effort, adapted to the particular problem, is essential for the efficient solution of all practical problems.

Multiple integrals over a large number of dimensions may be treated by *Monte Carlo methods, involving the use of randomly generated evaluation points.

numerical linear algebra A fundamentally important subject that deals with the theory and practice of processes in linear algebra. Principally these involve the central problems of the solution of *linear algebraic equations

$$Ax = b$$

and the *eigenvalue problem in which eigenvalues λ_k and the eigenvectors x_k are sought where

$$Ax_k = \lambda_k x_k$$

Numerical linear algebra forms the basis of much scientific computing. Both of these problems have many variants, determined by the properties of the matrix A. For example, a related problem is the solution of overdetermined systems where A has more rows than columns. Here there are good reasons for computing x to minimize the norm

$$\|Ax - b\|_2$$

(*see* approximation theory).

A major activity is the computing of certain linear transformations in the form of matrices, which brings about some simplification of the given problem. Most widely used are orthogonal matrices Q, for which

$$Q^\mathrm{T} Q = I$$

(*see* identity matrix, transpose). An important feature of large-scale scientific computing is where the associated matrices are sparse, i.e. where a high proportion of the elements are zero (*see* sparse matrix). This is exploited in the algorithms for their solution.

There is now available high-quality software for an enormous variety of linear algebra processes.

numerical methods Methods designed for the constructive solution of mathematical problems requiring particular numerical results, usually on a computer. A numerical method is a complete and unambiguous set of procedures for the solution of a problem, together with computable error estimates (*see* error analysis). The study and implementation of such methods is the province of *numerical analysis.

numerical stability *See* stability.

n-version programming *Another name for* diverse programming.

Nyquist interval The time interval between successive samples of a continuous-time band-limited signal that is being sampled at the Nyquist rate. *See* Nyquist's criterion.

Nyquist rate *See* Nyquist's criterion.

Nyquist sampling The process of *sampling a continuous-time band-limited channel at, or possibly more frequently than, the Nyquist rate. *See* Nyquist's criterion.

Nyquist's criterion The statement that when a continuous-time *band-limited channel is to be sampled, the *sampling process may or may not cause information to be lost according to whether the sampling rate, v, is less than, greater than, or equal to twice the *bandwidth, W.

If $v = 2W$, sampling is said to occur at the *Nyquist rate*.

If $v < 2W$, *sub-Nyquist sampling* is said to take place, and some information will be lost; this may be quite acceptable in certain cases.

If $v > 2W$, *super-Nyquist sampling* occurs; it cannot cause any more information to be extracted than sampling at the Nyquist rate.

Super-Nyquist sampling (at somewhat over the Nyquist rate) is, however, commonly employed to allow a margin of safety since there may be some doubt about the actual value of the bandwidth. There is no harm in it, if it is convenient, but the samples taken at a super-

Nyquist rate will not be independent of one another.

See also discrete and continuous systems.

Nyström methods A class of *Runge–Kutta methods directly applicable to second-order equations of the form

$$y'' = f(x,y,y'), \ a \leqslant x \leqslant b,$$
$$y(a) = y_0, \ y'(a) = y_0'$$

without requiring a reduction to first-order systems (*see* ordinary differential equations). *Extrapolation methods and *linear multistep methods of this direct type have also been developed. Such methods can be particularly advantageous for equations of the type $y'' = f(x,y)$, where y' does not appear explicitly.

O

OBERON A programming language developed as a successor to *Modula 2.

OBJ An executable specification language.

object *See* object-oriented programming system, object-oriented language, object-oriented architecture.

object code The output of a *compiler.

object language The language in which the output of a *compiler or *assembler is expressed.

object management system (OMS) That part of an *IPSE which is concerned with maintaining information about the system under development. The OMS may be based on a relational database management system, and includes relationships between elements such as derivation and configurations.

object-oriented architecture An architecture in which everything (processes, files, I/O operations, etc.) is represented as an *object*. Objects are *data structures in memory that may be manipulated by the total system (hardware and software); they provide a high-level description that allows for a high-level user interface. Objects have descriptors that are referred to variously as *names, pointers*, and *labels*. These descriptors also provide information as to the type of object and a description of capabilities that apply to the particular object. Object-oriented architecture systems can thus be considered as an extension or generalization of *capability architecture systems, and have the same ability to provide a basis for protection and computer security.

Examples of object-oriented architecture systems are the IBM System 38, the Carnegie-Mellon experimental C.mmp/Hydra, and the Intel iAPX 432.

object-oriented design (OOD) A software development technique in which the system is seen as a collection of *objects* that communicate with other objects by passing *messages* (*see* object-oriented programming system). Design is targeted toward defining the kinds of objects, the methods (i.e. procedures of objects), and the messages passed. OOD is based on the principle of *information hiding.

object-oriented language (OOL) A programming language for an *object-oriented programming system. In such a system the concept of procedure and data, which is embodied in conventional programming systems, is replaced by the concepts of *objects* and *messages*: an object is a package of information and a description of its manipulation, and a message is a specification of one of an object's manipulations. Unlike a procedure, which describes how manipulations should be carried out, a message merely specifies what the sender wants done, and the receiver determines exactly what will happen. *See also* Smalltalk, C++.

object-oriented programming system A programming system that combines *data abstraction, *inheritance, and dynamic type binding. The central feature is the *object*, which comprises a data structure definition and its defined procedures in a single structure. Objects are instances of a *class, each instance having its own private instance variables. The class definition defines the properties of the objects in that class: hierarchical class structures are possible in which objects in a class inherit the properties of the parent class in addition to properties explicitly defined for the class. This facilitates sharing of code, since users can inherit objects from system collections of code.

The procedures of an object (often called *methods*) are activated by *messages* sent to the object by another object. Thus in an object-oriented programming system the basic control structure is message passing. The programmer identifies the real-world objects of the problem and the processing requirements of those objects, encapsulating these in class definitions, and the communications between objects. The program is then essentially a simulation of the real world in which objects pass messages to other objects to initiate actions.

The most complete realization of an object-oriented programming system is *Smalltalk; the concepts also appear in combination with conventional languages, for example *C++ and *CLOS.

object program Like object code, the output of a *compiler. The object program is the translation into *object language of the *source program.

occam *Trademark* A programming language devised specifically for use with *transputer based systems. occam facilitates the writing of parallel programs for execution on one or more transputers, and is intended to be the normal way of programming transputers. The current version is occam 2.

occam programs are built up from *processes*, which may be executed sequentially or in parallel: the simplest process is a sequence of actions (assignment, input, or output). Input and output take place through *channels* that link processes, and *synchronization of parallel processes is achieved by causing a process that requests input to halt until some other process generates an output on the specified channel.

It is straightforward to write complex parallel programs in occam: the user does not need to be aware of the number of transputers actually executing his program, since processes are distributed over available transputers in a transparent manner by the underlying system.

OCR *Abbrev. for* optical character recognition. A process in which a machine scans, recognizes, and encodes information printed or typed in alphanumeric characters. The first devices, marketed around 1955, could only recognize a limited repertoire of characters that had to be produced in a font that was optimized for machine recognition but was still recognizable by people. By the mid-1970s OCR A font and OCR B font were the dominant fonts and were close to a normal letter-press appearance. Modern OCR equipment can read most typed or printed documents and high recognition rates are achieved (*see* ICR). OCR A and B fonts are still used for applications requiring high accuracy and in cases when context cannot aid recognition. In some instances printed information intended for *MICR (magnetic ink character recognition) is read by optical recognition techniques, as with some check readers associated with bank teller terminals.

octal notation The representation of numbers in the positional number system with radix 8. The octal digits are denoted by 0–7. Any octal number may be simply converted into its binary equivalent, and any binary number into its shorter octal equivalent.

octet Eight contiguous bits; an eight bit byte. The term is used instead of byte to prevent confusion in cases where the term has preexisting hardware associations, as in machines with 7 bit bytes, 9 bit bytes, 12 bit bytes.

ODA *Abbrev. for* open document architecture. Originally called office document architecture, it was renamed when it was taken up by ISO (ISO 8613) as part of the set of standards aimed at enabling easy interchange of information between computer systems. *See also* SPDL.

odd-even check *Another name for* parity check.

odd-even transposition sort A refinement of the *bubble sort in which adjacent pairs, starting with an odd position, are sorted then adjacent pairs, starting with an even position, are sorted. The two phases alternate until sorting is completed.

odd parity A property that holds when a group of binary values contains an odd number of 1s. *See* parity.

odds The ratio of the *probability that an event occurs to the probability that it does not occur. The ratio of two odds, known as the *odds-ratio*, is used especially in the comparison and modeling of conditional probabilities.

ODP *Abbrev. for* open distributed processing.

OEM *Abbrev. for* original equipment manufacturer. Usually, the purchaser of large volumes of equipment to be integrated within a system. In some instances the term is used to refer to the supplier of the large volumes of equipment – possibly as a contraction of OEM supplier.

office automation The application of computers to office tasks. This may involve the use of *electronic filing systems, *word processing systems, *computer graphics systems, *electronic mail, *desktop publishing, *decision support systems, *database management systems, and *teleconferencing systems.

off-line Of peripheral devices or files: not connected to the system or not usable. A device may be physically connected but off-line if the system has been instructed not to use it.

OMR *Abbrev. for* optical mark reading. A method for data input in which marks made on preformatted documents are sensed by photoelectric means. The marks are interpreted as either characters or values according to their position on the form. This provides an efficient type of data input in applications in which there are relatively few answers to a limited number of questions. No further data preparation activity or machines are required since the reader can be connected directly to the system. Special readers are available to handle large documents. OMR documents are printed on paper, and information to the user as to where the marks should be put and what significance they will have is usually printed in a color that will not be detected by the photoelectric sensors. Machine-readable timing marks are preprinted along the edge of the document.

OMS *Abbrev. for* object management system.

one-address instruction *See* instruction format.

one-level store The original term used for what is now called *virtual memory. The term arose from the fact that although the memory in use was found

on units at different levels within the *memory hierarchy, the user saw all his memory at a single level of accessibility.

one-pass program A program that requires only one linear forward scan of its input data.

one-plus-one address instruction *See* instruction format.

one's complement *See* radix-minus-one complement.

one-shot *Another name for* monostable.

one-to-one function *Another name for* injection.

one-to-one onto function *Another name for* bijection.

one-way filter A type of access controller that restricts the flow of information in a distributed system having parts of differing security clearance. The filter allows a part with high clearance to read from a part of lower clearance but prevents the converse operation.

one-way linked list *Another name for* singly linked list.

on-line 1. Connected to the system and usable. *See also* off-line.
2. In automaton theory, describing an automaton that, having read the first k symbols of the input string, has already produced the first k symbols of the output string. The concept of being on-line is analogous to the initial subwords-preserving property of *gsm-mappings.

O notation, o notation *See* order.

on-the-fly error recovery *See* error rate.

onto function *Another name for* surjection.

OOD *Abbrev. for* object-oriented design.

OOL *Abbrev. for* object-oriented language.

op-amp *Short for* operational amplifier.

op code *Short for* operation code.

open-collector device A particular implementation of an electronic logic device

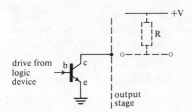

Open-collector device

in which the output of the device is formed by the open-circuit collector termination of the output transistor (*see* diagram). The device's output is thus active-low and a *pull-up resistor is required to establish the active-high state. These devices are used to drive loads with high supply voltages or to implement *wired-logic buses.

open distributed processing (ODP) An *open system of *distributed processing. In a distributed processing system the various cooperating *processes that jointly make up the total activity may run on separate processing systems linked only by communications channels. In an open distributed system the components are physically separated and are linked by communications channels that use *open systems standards for their interfaces and protocols, and the intercommunication between the processes is again in accordance with a (different) set of open systems standards. It is clear that there is still a long way to go before open distributed processing will be a commercial reality.

open shop A method of running a computing facility such that the design, development, writing, and testing of computer programs is carried out by the problem originator and not by specialist computing staff. *Open shop operation* is the operation of a computing system by the writer or user of a program and not by specialist computer operators. *Compare* closed shop.

open subroutine *Obsolete name for* in-line *subroutine, usually provided by a *macro.

open system Any system in which the components conform to nonproprietary standards rather than to the standards of a specific supplier of hardware or software.

open systems interconnection (OSI) A concept whereby communication-oriented computer equipment with different *protocols can be interconnected by means of a data network. The principal methods being developed are those of the major computer vendors (especially IBM) and of the International Standards Organization (ISO). The term open systems interconnection is specifically related to the efforts of the ISO and its *seven-layer reference model.

operand 1. A quantity upon which a mathematical or logical operation is performed.
2. The parts of a machine instruction that specify the objects upon which the operation is to be performed. For instance, in the instruction
ADD A,B
A and B are the operands and could be *registers in the central processor, or actual values, or *addresses of values, or even addresses of addresses of values.

operating system (OS) The set of software products that jointly controls the system resources and the processes using these resources on a computer system.

operation A *function from S^m (*see* Cartesian product) into S itself, where S is some set specific to the function. Such a function is usually referred to as an *m*-ary or *m*-adic operation over S, m being some *natural number, sometimes referred to as the *arity* of the operation. The most common operations are the *dyadic (or binary) operations that map $S \times S$ into S and the *monadic (or unary) operations that map S into S. The case where the arity is zero gives the so-called *nullary* operations, which correspond simply to elements of S. There is also a more general kind of operation that involves more than one set. For example, in a *finite-state automaton the next state depends on the current input symbol and the current state, and is thus given by a dyadic operation from $I \times Q$ into Q, where I is the set of input symbols and Q the set of states. *See also* logic operation, arithmetic operation, operations on sets.

operational amplifier (op-amp) A very high gain voltage amplifier having a differential input, i.e. its output voltage is proportional to (and very much greater than) the voltage difference between its two inputs. Operational amplifiers usually have feedback circuits of resistors and/or capacitors connected between their output and inputs. These circuits make op-amps operate as voltage amplifiers with a gain precisely defined by the values of the resistors, or else enable them to perform mathematical operations, such as integration, or signal-conditioning functions, such as filtering.

operational research *See* operations research.

operational semantics An approach to the *semantics of programming languages that uses the concept of an "abstract machine" that has a state and some primitive instructions. The machine is defined by specifying how the components of the state are changed by each of the instructions. The abstract machine is not meant to be a model of any realistic machine; it is meant to be simple enough so that the language can be unambiguously defined. No misunderstanding should arise with respect to its set of primitive instructions, or order code (elsewhere called *operation code). The semantic description of the programming language specifies a translation into this code. Unlike *denotational semantics there is no guarantee that the meaning of a whole program will be a function of the meanings of its parts. Examples of this approach include the Vienna Definition Language used to define PL/I.

operation code (op code; order code) 1. The portion of the *instruction that specifies the operation to be performed by the instruction. *See also* instruction format.

2. The set of such portions available for a particular computer, and defining the repertoire of operations it can perform.

operation register The part of the *control-unit instruction register that contains the *operation code.

operations on sets The simple *operations that can be performed on sets are those of *union, *intersection, and *complement, and possibly *set difference. Using these it is possible to create new sets from existing sets. Certain other actions that have to be performed on sets are sometimes considered as operations, although they do not conform to the strict definition of the word. These include the actions *find, *insert, *delete, *split, and *min.

operations research (operational research; OR) The study of some human operation or set of operations by quantitative means. It is usually conducted with the aid of computer modeling; models may be hypothesized and fitted to experimental data, or experimental data may be analyzed to derive a model. Once a model is available, the effects of changes in the operations under study can be developed and predicted in a quantitative way.

operation table *Another name for* Cayley table.

operator 1. A person responsible for the immediate supervision of the hardware of a computer system.

2. An entity that can be applied to one or more operands so as to yield a result. It is (usually) a symbol representing an operation to be carried out, as opposed to a *variable, which represents a data value. *See also* arithmetic operator, logic operation, relational operator, precedence.

optical card A form of *optical storage in which the medium is in credit-card form, intended for uses similar to those of a magnetic-stripe card but with much higher capacity (several megabytes).

optical character recognition *See* OCR.

optical disk A type of *optical storage in which the medium is in the form of a disk that is rotated to give one dimension of access while the light beam is scanned radially to give the second dimension. In nearly all cases the disk is exchangeable: this is easily arranged because there is a substantial clearance, typically 1 mm, between the outer surface of the disk and the nearest component of the optical system. The optical system is heavy and expensive compared to the corresponding components of a magnetic disk drive, so all current (1989) drives have been designed to access a single recording surface: if the disk has recording surfaces on both sides it is removed from the drive and reversed to give access to the second surface. Multiple disk packs are not used.

Rewritable (erasable), write-once, and read-only media have been developed for optical disk drives: *multifunction*

drives can read two or all three of these media types. Disk sizes range from 350 mm downward with 300 mm and 130 or 120 mm apparently the most widely accepted. In the 120 mm size a read-only format standard known as *CD-ROM and derived from that of the consumer 'compact audio' disk has been published by Philips and Sony.

The first optical disk drives suitable for data storage (with a read error rate after correction better than 1 in 10^{12} bits) appeared on the market at the end of 1984: these all use write-once media on large diameter disks (350 mm to 200 mm). Drives for smaller disks and for read-only media are now on the market.

Optical disk drives suitable for storing images of written text, where a higher error rate (typically 1 in 10^5 bits) is acceptable and so error correction is unnecessary, appeared on the market in 1983: they are particularly successful in Japan where the use of Kanji characters makes it convenient to store written material in image rather than coded form.

optical disk library (jukebox (*colloquial*)) A peripheral device in which many optical disks (usually in cartridges) are stored in slots in a storage rack. The device contains one or more *optical disk drives; any disk can be taken from its slot and loaded into a drive by a *picker mechanism*, at the command of the host computer. The picker can also return a disk to its slot, turn a disk over (since most drives can only read one side), and move a disk to or from a *drawer* where it can be reached by the operator. Standard disks and cartridges are used.

optical font A printing font or style of character specially designed to be accurately read by reading machines and by people. The most widely used are OCR A and OCR B and they are defined in internationally recognized standards.

Although reading machines are available that can process a wide variety of fonts, provided that they are clearly printed, lower cost machines and lower error rates can be achieved if the specialized optical fonts are used. *See also* OCR.

optical mark reading *See* OMR.

optical media *See* optical storage.

optical storage The storage or retrieval, or both, of data or images by optical means. Numerous methods have been explored, including holography, but current techniques depend on the use of a semiconductor laser and optical system to generate a very small spot of light (typically one micrometer in diameter) focused on a thin layer of a suitable medium to access each information bit in turn.

When writing data or images the beam power is sufficient (typically 10 milliwatts) to heat the illuminated area of the medium so as to change its optical characteristics, reversibly or irreversibly. (In the case of *magneto-optic recording, a magnetic field is also applied to control the state taken by the medium as it cools.) When reading, the beam power is reduced to the point where it does not produce any change in the state of the medium, and the light reflected (or in some cases transmitted) by the medium is detected and its intensity or polarization is observed to decide whether each storage location stores a 1 or 0 bit.

Optical storage is capable of higher areal storage densities than have been achieved by magnetic media, and does not require the close medium-to-head spacing of magnetic storage; the medium is rugged, since the sensitive layer is beneath a clear protective layer and the light beam is out of focus at the outer surface of this and thus reasonably insensitive to dust or scratches. There is thus the potential of low-cost storage on rugged readily interchangeable volumes. On the other hand the optical components are relatively expensive and bulky, and the flaw density in the medium is higher than in magnetic storage thus requiring elaborate error correction techniques for most applications.

Three classes of media can conveniently be distinguished: *rewritable*, where recorded data can be erased and rewritten as in magnetic storage; *write once* (or *WORM*), where information once written cannot be erased; *read-only*, where the information is impressed on the medium during manufacture and cannot subsequently be changed. Some technologies allow two of these classes to be combined on the same media volume.

Write-once media offer permanent storage once recorded (manufacturers guarantee 10–30 years) and are an alternative to magnetic tape for archival storage. Read-only media have potential as a very cheap means of distributing large databases in machine-readable form. Rewritable media compete directly with magnetic storage and the relative advantages of the two have yet to be resolved (1989).

The principal configurations used are *optical disk, *optical card, and *optical tape.

optical switch A device whose optical transmission properties (e.g. refractive index and polarizing properties) can be varied by an externally applied field or by some other external influence. Electrical, magnetic, and surface acoustic wave techniques are all used for this purpose. By these means, light may be deflected away from a detector, thus switching the beam. LCD shutters are also used. The light that is processed in this way often originates in a laser source.

optical tape An optical medium in tape form. It is handled by a mechanism similar to a *magnetic tape drive, but written and read by similar methods to those used in *optical disk drives. Not (in 1989) widely used.

optimal binary search tree A *binary search tree constructed to be of maximum expected efficiency for a given *probability distribution of search data.

optimization The process of finding the best solution to some problem, where "best" accords to prestated criteria. The word is used in a number of contexts.

1. In mathematics the word is generally used to describe the theory and practice of maximizing, or minimizing, a function (known as an *objective function*) of several variables that may be subject to a set of constraints. The special case of a linear objective function is the subject of *linear programming. The case of nonlinear objective functions, with or without constraints, is treated in a quite well-developed field. The unconstrained optimization problem (usually expressed as *minimization*) is:

$$\text{minimize } f(x)$$

where $f(x)$ is the given objective function of n real variables,

$$x = (x_1, x_2, \ldots, x_n)^T$$

A necessary condition for a minimum is that

$$\partial f / \partial x_i = 0, \ i = 1, 2, \ldots, n$$

which is a system of *nonlinear equations. *Newton's method can be applied, but in practice this technique has been extensively modified to improve computational efficiency. *Matrix-updating methods* are a broad class of methods that involve a sophisticated means of computing approximations to the matrices required in Newton's method.

For constrained problems, x must also satisfy a system (possibly nonlinear) of equations or inequalities. Some of the ideas and methods for unconstrained problems can be suitably modified to handle the constraints.

Optimization problems are widespread in control theory, chemical engineering, and many other fields.

2. In programming the word is usually applied to part of the code-generation phase of a *compiler, denoting production of object code that is in some sense optimal, i.e. making best use of the resources provided by the target machine, or at least using these resources in a manner that is not blatantly wasteful. Programs can be space-efficient in the sense of occupying minimal storage, or time-efficient in the sense of executing in the minimum time.

Compiler optimization is usually directed toward generating time-efficient programs, and takes three forms. *Global optimization* seeks to reorder the sequencing of a program so as to eliminate redundant computations (moving invariant operations outside loop bodies, coalescing loops, etc.). *Register optimization* adjusts the allocation of machine registers to variables and intermediate quantities in such a way as to minimize the number of occasions on which a register has to be stored and later reloaded. *Local (peephole) optimization* seeks to adapt the code to exploit particular features of the machine architecture and to remove local mishandling such as loading a register with a value that it already contains.

optimum programming *Another name for* minimum-access code.

optional product *See* concensus.

optoelectronics An increasingly important technology concerned with the generation, processing, and detection of optical signals that represent electrical quantities. Major areas for application of this technology include communications, where electrical signals may be transmitted along fiber-optic cables (*see* fiber optics transmission system) and where two unconnected electrical circuits may exchange signals by means of an optical link yet remain electrically isolated; these latter devices are called *optoisolators*. The technology is also being used to implement logical gating functions employing lasers and liquid crystals (*see* LCD), the advantages being high speeds of operation.

Optical signals may be generated from electrical signals using *LEDs. Detection of optical signals is often achieved using *phototransistors*, i.e. *bipolar transistors whose base drive is made dependent on incident light. *See also* optical storage.

optoisolator *See* optoelectronics.

Oracle 1. One of the UK's two *teletext systems, operated by the Independent Television network.

2. *Trademark* A commercial *relational database system and *CASE toolset.

orange book 1. The *coloured book that defines a network service running over a *Cambridge Ring.

2. A publication by the National Computer Security Center (*NCSC) that sets out a formal basis for the classification of *trusted computer systems.

order 1. A means of indicating the way a function varies in magnitude as its argument tends to some limits, usually zero or infinity. More precisely if there is some constant K such that

$$|f(x)| \leqslant K \phi(x)$$

for all $x \geqslant x_1$, then we say that $f(x)$ is order $\phi(x)$ as x tends to infinity, and we write

$$f(x) = O(\phi(x))$$

For example,

$$100x^2 + 100x + 2 = O(x^2)$$
$$\text{as } x \to \infty$$

If

$$\lim_{x \to a} f(x)/g(x) = 0$$

then we write

$$f(x) = o(g(x))$$

For example,

$$x = o(x^2) \quad \text{as } x \to \infty$$

Both these notations are statements about maximum magnitude and do not

exclude f from being of smaller magnitude. For example,

$$x = O(x^2)$$

is perfectly valid, but equally

$$x = O(x)$$

If

$$\lim_{x \to a} f(x)/g(x) = \text{const. } k \neq 0$$

then we write

$$f(x) \simeq k\, g(x) \quad \text{as } x \to a$$

For example,

$$10x^2 + x + 1 \simeq 10x^2$$
$$\text{as } x \to \infty$$

The term order and the O notation is used in numerical analysis, particularly in *discretization methods. In *ordinary differential equations, if h denotes the step size, then a method (or formula) has order p (a positive integer) if the global *discretization error is $O(h^p)$. This means that as the step size h is decreased, the error goes to zero at least as rapidly as h^p. Similar considerations apply to *partial differential equations. High-accuracy formulas (order up to 12 or 13) are sometimes used in methods for ordinary differential equations. For reasons of computational cost and stability, low-order formulas tend to be used in methods for partial differential equations.

2. *Another name for* operation code.

3. of a matrix. *See* square matrix.

4. of a finite group. *See* group.

order code *Another name for* operation code.

ordered pair A pair of objects in a given fixed order, usually represented by

$$(x,y) \text{ or } \langle x,y \rangle$$

for objects x and y. Two ordered pairs are said to be equal if and only if the first elements of each pair are equal and the second elements are equal. Typical situations in which ordered pairs are used include discussion of points in the Cartesian plane or complex numbers.

The idea can be extended to cover ordered triples, such as

$$(x_1, x_2, x_3)$$
and indeed ordered n-tuples, such as
$$(x_1, x_2, \ldots x_n)$$

ordered tree *See* tree.

ordering relation A relation that is *reflexive, *antisymmetric, and *transitive. The relation "less than or equal to" on integers is an ordering relation. *See also* partial ordering. *Compare* equivalence relation.

order of precedence *See* precedence.

order register *Another name for* instruction register. *See* control unit.

order statistics A branch of statistics that uses not the numerical value of an observation but its ranking relative to other observations. The rth *order statistic* of a sample of n observations is simply the rth smallest variate value in the sample. Examples of statistical tests for ordering include: the median test, the sign test, Cochran's test, the Wald-Wolfowitz "runs test", the Mann-Whitney test, the Wilcoxen test, the Kruskal-Wallis test, and the Friedman test.

ordinary differential equations *Differential equations that involve one independent variable, which in practice may be a space or time variable. Except in simple cases the solution cannot be determined analytically and approximation methods are used.

Numerical methods are mainly developed for equations involving first derivatives only, written in the form
$$y' = f(x, y), \quad a \leqslant x \leqslant b,$$
where y and f are s-component vectors with component functions
$$y_i(x),$$
$$f_i(x, y_1(x), y_2(x), \ldots, y_s(x))$$
Equations involving higher derivatives can be equivalently written in this form by introducing intermediate functions for the higher derivatives. Alternatively

direct methods may be derived for such problems (*see* Nyström methods).

In general, s conditions must be imposed to determine a particular solution. If the values $y(a) = y_0$ are specified, it is an *initial-value problem*. These problems can be solved directly using step-by-step methods, such as *Runge-Kutta methods, *linear multistep methods, or *extrapolation methods, which determine approximations at a set of points in $[a, b]$. The problem is a *boundary-value problem* if the s conditions are given in terms of the component functions at a and b. In general, such problems require iterative methods, such as the *shooting method. However, if f is linear in y, *finite-difference methods can be advantageous. Excellent software has been developed for both types of problem.

An area of particular interest in many applications is the solution of *stiff equations*. A stiff system possesses solutions that decay very rapidly over an interval that is short relative to the range of integration, and the solution required varies slowly over most of the range. To allow large steps in the slowly varying phases, it is necessary to use special methods, such as the implicit *trapezoidal rule*:
$$x_{n+1} = x_n + h$$
$$y_{n+1} = y_n + \tfrac{1}{2}h(f(x_{n+1}, y_{n+1}) + f(x_n, y_n))$$
At each step a system of equations has to be solved for y_{n+1}, using very often a modification of *Newton's method. More straightforward explicit methods rapidly lead to catastrophic error growth unless the stepsize h is prohibitively small. These problems are still the subject of very active research interest.

organizational information system *See* information system.

OR gate An electronic *logic gate whose output is logic 0 (false) only when all (two or more) inputs are logic 0, otherwise it is logic 1 (true). It therefore

inputs	A1	0	0	1	1
	A2	0	1	0	1
output	B	0	1	1	1

Two-input OR gate, circuit symbol and truth table

P	F	F	T	T
Q	F	T	F	T
$P \vee Q$	F	T	T	T

Truth table for OR operation

implements the logical *OR operation and has the same *truth table. The diagram shows the usual circuit symbol and the truth table for a two-input gate. The device is more correctly called an *inclusive-OR gate* since the condition of both inputs true generates a true output. *See also* exclusive-OR gate.

OROM *Abbrev. for* optical read-only memory. *See* ROM optical disk.

OR operation (inclusive-OR operation) The logical *connective combining two statements, truth values, or formulas P and Q in such a way that the outcome is true if either P or Q or if both P and Q is true (*see* table). The latter outcome distinguishes the OR from the *exclusive-OR operation. The OR operation is usually denoted by $\vee$ and occasionally by $+$. It is one of the dyadic operations of *Boolean algebra and is both *commutative and *associative.

One way of implementing the OR operation (e.g. in LISP) is to test P first, and then evaluate Q only if P is false. The resulting operation is noncommuta-tive; in some languages there is a distinct notation for this.

When it is implemented as a basic *machine code instruction, OR usually operates on pairs of bytes or pairs of words. In these cases the OR operation defined above is normally applied to pairs of corresponding bits.

orthogonal analysis *See* orthonormal basis.

orthogonal basis *See* orthonormal basis.

orthogonal functions Let
$$f_1(x), f_2(x), \ldots, f_n(x)$$
be a set of functions defined on the interval (a,b); also let $w(x)$ be a given positive function (a *weight function*) on (a,b). The functions $f_i(x)$,
$$i = 1,2,\ldots,n$$
are said to be orthogonal with respect to the interval (a,b) and weight function $w(x)$, if
$$\int_a^b w(x)\, f_i(x)\, f_j(x)\, \mathrm{d}x = 0,$$
$$i \neq j, \quad i,j = 1,2,\ldots,n$$
If, for $i = j$,
$$\int_b^a w(x)\, f_i^2(x)\, \mathrm{d}x = 1,$$
$$i = 1,2,\ldots,n$$
then the functions are said to be *orthonormal*.

A similar property is defined when (a,b) is replaced by the set of points
$$x_1, x_2, \ldots, x_N$$
and the integral is replaced by a sum,
$$\sum_{k=1}^N w(\quad (x_k)\, f_j(x_k) = 0,$$
$$i \neq j$$
Orthogonal functions play an important part in the approximation of functions and data.

orthogonal list A two-dimensional orthogonal list has list cells that are linked symmetrically to both left and right horizontal neighbors and up and down to vertical neighbors. This idea can be generalized to higher dimensions and suggests an efficient representation for *sparse matrices.

orthogonal memory *See* associative memory.

orthonormal analysis *See* orthonormal basis.

orthonormal basis The set of orthonormal functions employed in calculating the terms of a transform of the kind exemplified by the *Fourier transform and the Walsh transform (*see* Walsh analysis): the orthonormal basis of the Fourier transform consists of the imaginary exponential functions, and that of the Walsh transform consists of the *Walsh functions.

In order to calculate the terms of a transform effectively, the basis functions must be *orthogonal but need not also be normal (orthonormal). Such a nonnormalized basis is called an *orthogonal basis*. The calculation of the transform terms is correspondingly called *orthonormal analysis* or *orthogonal analysis*. Such analysis is only possible if there are sufficient functions in the set to form a basis: such a set is called a *complete set of functions*.

orthonormal functions *See* orthogonal functions.

OS *Abbrev. for* operating system. The abbreviation was used as the name for a specific operating system (OS/360) introduced by IBM, but is now used generically.

OS/2 An operating system produced by IBM and Microsoft for microcomputers with Intel 80286 and 80386 processors, specifically the IBM PS/2 range. OS/2 is intended to be the successor to *MS-DOS and allows *multitasking and programs larger than the MS-DOS 640 kilobyte limit. It has a *wimp user interface called *Presentation Manager*. *OS/2 extended edition* includes *Database Manager* and *Communications Manager*,

which allow their eponymous functions to be carried out from within the operating system.

oscillation sort A method of *sorting in which *sortkeys are alternately distributed onto tapes and merged so that much of the sorting takes place before the input has been completely examined. The tapes are read both forward and backward.

oscilloscope An item of electronic test equipment that can display a wide variety of waveforms of electrical signals. It does this effectively by "plotting" the amplitude variations of the signal with time on a display device, normally a *cathode-ray tube. The electron beam of the CRT is deflected horizontally so that the display is scanned linearly in a preset time period. Vertical beam deflections, derived from the input signal, are then superimposed on the display, the horizontal and vertical deflections being synchronized by means of trigger circuits. *See also* storage oscilloscope.

OSF Open Software Foundation, an IT industry organization founded in 1988 to promote public standards for *UNIX. Founder members included IBM, DEC, Hewlett-Packard, Microsoft, and Nixdorf.

OSF/Motif A graphics user interface available under license from *OSF, based on Microsoft Presentation Manager, Hewlett-Packard New Wave, and the DEC Windowing Toolkit implementation of *X windows.

OSI *Abbrev. for* open systems interconnection.

outdegree *See* degree.

outer code *See* concatenated coding system.

outlier *See* residual.

output 1. The result of data processing activity when it is presented external to the system, or the process of presenting the data externally. The output from a computer can be in a form for use by people, e.g. printed or displayed, or it may be ready for input to another system or process, when it may be encoded magnetically on a tape or disk.
2. A signal that is obtained from an electrical circuit, such as a logic circuit.
3. To produce a result or signal.

output area The area of main memory that is allocated for storage of data prior to transfer to an output device. *See also* input area.

output device Any device that converts the electrical signals representing information within a computer into a form that can exist or be sensed outside the computer. Printers and visual displays are the most common type of output device for interfacing to people, but voice is becoming increasingly available. Devices such as magnetic tape transports are really types of intermediate or backing store but are sometimes referred to as output devices.

output-limited process A process whose speed of execution is limited by the rate at which output data can be accepted.

overflow The condition that arises when the result of an arithmetic operation exceeds the size of the location allotted for receipt of that result, or the amount by which the result exceeds the allotted number.

overlap A form of parallelism in which events that are not mutually dependent take place concurrently in order to increase computer performance, e.g. fetching a second instruction while a first instuction is being executed. When there is overlap between portions of arithmetic operations (i.e. when the portions are *overlapped*), the process is usually called *pipelining.

overlay A section of code that is loaded into memory during the execution of a program, overwriting what was previously there. The loading of an overlay is under the explicit control of the programmer, and should not be confused with *paging. In general several overlays are loaded into the same area of memory, "overlaying" the code already residing in that part of memory. Overlays can be thought of as a form of voluntary memory management.

overwrite To destroy information in a memory location by writing in new information.

P

P *See* P=NP question.

pack 1. To store compactly in order to reduce the amount of memory required to hold the same data. There are several ways of doing this, for example by storing several bytes in one word or by replacing multiple occurrences of a character or word by a triplet consisting of
(a) a special code indicating the start of a triplet;
(b) a single instance of the replicated character or word;
(c) a count of the number of times the character or word occurs.
2. *Short for* disk pack.

package 1. *See* application package.
2. In *Ada, a self-contained collection of entities (data objects and procedures) that are available for other parts of a program to use. A package consists of two parts that can be separately compiled: its *specification* and its *body*. The specification provides the public information about the entities that the package makes available, in the form of declarations of constants, variables, and data types, and procedure headers. It

may also contain a private part giving further information about types and constants that is needed by the compiler but not by a programmer using the package. The package body contains the procedure bodies for the procedures that form part of the package, together with local variables and types that these procedures may need. The separation of specification and body means that the implementation of the procedures is hidden from the users, thus a package is a realization of an *abstract data type.

Similar features are found in other languages, particularly Modula 2: here the term *module* is used in preference to package. In Modula 2 a module comprises a *definition part* and an *implementation part*, corresponding to the specification and body of the Ada package. The main difference is that the definition part of a module contains declarations of all the objects required by the module, together with an *export list* specifying which objects are visible outside the module.

packed decimal An economical method of storing decimal digits represented as binary-coded decimals (BCD), using only four bits per digit. Thus two decimal digits may be stored in one *byte. This is only slightly less compact than storing a number in binary, and avoids decimal-to-binary conversion. *See also* character encoding.

packet A group of bits of fixed maximum size and well-defined format that is switched and transmitted as a composite whole through a *packet switching network. Any message that exceeds the maximum size is partitioned and carried as several packets.

packet assembler/disassembler *See* PAD.

packet radio A transmission method that makes use of radio broadcast signals carrying *packets of data. There is no assurance that only a single transmitter

is active at a time, so it is necessary to have a convention for the action to be taken when packets "collide". Logically, packet radio is essentially equivalent to bus architecture networks that are used in some local network architectures. *See* CSMA/CD.

packet switched data service A data communication service offered to the public by some *PTTs and *common carriers. *See* public packet network.

packet switching A technique by which communication resources are allocated dynamically to multiple communicating entities. Messages between entities are partitioned into segments with a fixed maximum size. The segments, or *packets*, are passed through a *store-and-forward switching network until they reach their destination (or are discovered to be undeliverable). The packets are reassembled, if necessary, into complete messages when they reach their destination. Packet switching, as it applies to electronic communication, was first proven feasible by the development of the *ARPANET in 1969.

A *packet switching network* may provide a variety of levels of service, depending upon the sophistication of the underlying communication technology and the requirements of the network's customers. The simplest packet switching networks provide only *datagram service, which is unordered unreliable delivery of packets. Other networks may provide only reliable individually flow-controlled *virtual connections. The decision between datagrams, virtual connections, or other modes of operation can be made independently for the internal operation of a packet switching network, and the interface that it presents to its customers.

packing density 1. functional packing density A measure of the number of electronic devices per unit area contained on one *integrated circuit.

2. A measure of the amount of information in a given dimension of a storage medium.

PAD *Acronym for* packet assembler/disassembler. A translating computer that provides access for asynchronous character-at-a-time terminals to a synchronous *packet switching network.

padding A filler used to extend a string or record to some prescribed length. *See also* block.

page The unit of interchange between memory and swapping device involved in a *paging system. The number of words or bytes in a page is usually fixed for a given system and is almost invariably an exact power of 2. The term *page frame* is used as an alternative name for page, but is more particularly used to apply to the copy of a page that is held on the swapping device.

page description language (PDL) A language for describing the composition of a printed page. PDLs such as *PostScript and *L^A^T~E~X have been developed, but each has its own structure and command set and thus inhibits information interchange. *See also* SPDL.

page frame *See* page.

page printer A type of printer that prints a complete page of output in one cycle. It is generally a *nonimpact printer, such as a *laser printer, in which the printing process requires continuous movement of the paper. The information for one page of output is usually accumulated within a buffer in the printer before the printing process is started. *Compare* line printer, serial printer.

page table A table within a computer that contains a mapping between logical page addresses and physical page addresses. In many systems the table is

supported in a fast-acting memory area. *See* paging.

paging A method of managing *virtual memory. The logical address is subdivided into two fields: the low-order bits indicate a word or byte within a *page and the high-order bits indicate a particular page. Active pages are held in main memory and a page that is not active may be transferred out to the *swapping device. An associative memory indicates the physical location within memory of those pages that are present. For pages that are not in memory the associative memory will contain a pointer to the backing-store home for that particular page. When reference occurs to a page, an interrupt is generated if the page is not in main memory and the operating system will transfer the relevant page from the swapping device into main memory.

paging drum One form of *swapping device used to hold the images of *pages no longer held in main memory in a *paging virtual management system. Paging drums typically are designed to have a relatively small capacity, low latency, and very high transfer rate.

PAL *Abbrev. for* programmable array logic. A form of *PLA in whose *sum of products the products (*AND operations) are programmable, but the sums (*OR operations) are either fixed, or programmable only to a limited extent. In the latter case, any product terms that can take part in a programmable sum are called *shareable P terms*.

paper slew (*UK name*: **paper throw**) A rapid and continuous movement of the paper in a line or serial printer such that the space of several line pitches occurs without printing. In high-performance line printers the slew rate may be 75 inches per second (190 cm/s).

paper tape A near-obsolete but once widely used data medium in the form of a continuous tape of paper with uniform width and thickness and specified physical attributes; other materials of greater durability or strength are also found, e.g. laminates of paper and polyester. All these forms can be referred to as *punched tape* or *punch tape*.

Data is encoded by punching patterns of holes on the tape. Generally a data character is punched as a coded set of holes across the tape at standard pitch. One-inch wide tape will accommodate characters of up to 8 bits. A longitudinal set of holes or hole positions at a fixed distance from the reference edge of the tape is known as a *track*: 1″ tape can therefore be 8-track while narrower tapes can be 5-track or 7-track.

In addition to the data tracks, a full track of smaller-diameter sprocket or feed holes is always punched and is now an essential feature for synchronization. In most tapes the center line of a feed hole is in line with that of data holes. The data and feed holes are now sensed optically, thus the optical characteristics of the material are now part of the specification. The tape is normally in the form of a *reel* wound onto a core of standardized dimensions.

Punched tape was in use for data communication purposes (telex) prior to its use for computer input/output. Initially the 5 bit International Telegraph Alphabet encoded in 5 tracks on 11/16″ wide tape was used, but as I/O usage began to generate a significant market, 6, 7, and 8 bit codes were introduced and the tape width was increased to 1″.

Punched tapes have been largely superseded by other forms of media for data storage, interchange, and program loading in data processing. They are still in use for programmed control of industrial equipment, and on some computer printers the preprogrammed control of the continuous paper through the printer is by tape loops (*see* vertical format unit).

paper tape I/O A near-obsolete but once widely used means of entering data into and extracting it out of a processor system using punched *paper tape as the medium. Paper tape I/O was adopted for many of the early computers: *tape punches* and *tape readers* were already in use for telex and were lower in cost than punched card equipment.

Early tape readers operated at about 10 characters per second (cps) by moving the tape in discrete steps, and sensed the holes by pressing a row of pins against the tape. The next generation of machines moved the tape continuously and sensed the holes via star-shaped wheels that rotated only when the points engaged a punched hole. Photoelectric sensing allowed speeds of up to 1500 cps to be achieved by 1975. There have been higher-speed readers but they were not able to stop within a character pitch. Tape punches as fast as 300 cps have been available but 110 cps was the more usual speed for volume output.

paper throw *UK name for* paper slew.

PAR *Acronym for* positive acknowledgment and retransmission. *See* backward error correction.

paradigm A model or example of the environment and methodology in which systems and software are developed and operated. For one operational paradigm there could be several alternative development paradigms. Examples are functional programming, logic programming, semantic data modeling, algebraic computing, numerical computing, object-oriented design, prototytping, and natural language dialogue.

paradoxical combinator *See* combinator.

parallel Involving the simultaneous transfer or processing of the individual parts of a whole, such as the bits of a character. *Compare* serial.

parallel access Access to a storage device in which a number of bits are transferred simultaneously rather than sequentially. For example, access to semiconductor memory almost invariably yields a number of bytes in parallel; by contrast access to the contents of a disk is usually serial in nature.

parallel adder A binary adder that is capable of forming sum and carry outputs for addend and augend words of greater than one bit in length by operating on corresponding pairs of addend and augend in parallel, i.e. at the same time. Parallel adders require a short settling time to allow carries to be propagated between subsequent stages of addition. *See also* adder, serial adder.

parallel algorithm An algorithm designed to run "efficiently" on a *parallel computer such as the Cray-3 or the ICL DAP (distributed array processor). A parallel algorithm may involve a greater number of arithmetic operations than a serial counterpart. It is designed, however, so that many arithmetic operations are independent and can be performed in parallel, i.e. simultaneously.

parallel arithmetic Operation upon more than one bit or digit of a number at the same time.

parallel computer A computer that is capable of *parallel processing.

parallel in parallel out (PIPO) A term used to describe a *shift register that can be loaded in parallel and also read in parallel, in addition to which (by implication) data can enter and leave the device serially.

parallel input/output (PIO) A method of data transfer between devices, typically a computer and its peripherals, in which all the bits associated with a character or byte are presented to the interface simultaneously on separate conductors. There are usually other parallel conduc-

tors to carry the control signals. PIO is frequently used since it is compatible with the format used within the processor and enables high rates of data transfer to be achieved. When connection over any significant distance has to be made, the cost of the conductors and the associated drive circuits becomes significant and it is then preferable to convert to a *serial input/output.

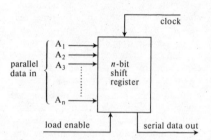

Parallel in serial out

parallel in serial out (PISO) A term used to describe a class of digital device that can accept parallel n-bit data words and convert them into serial sequential n-bit data streams. These devices often consist of an n-bit *shift register that is parallel loaded with the data word (*see* diagram). This data is then clocked out of the register in serial form. *Compare* serial in parallel out.

parallel interface A connection point that comprises a set of individual electrical connections, each having a specified function, usually either data or control. The transfer of data across the interface is achieved by one connection per bit of a data word or byte; for example for 8 bits there would be 8 connections in parallel. The control signals are also carried on individual electrical connections in parallel with the data connections. *Compare* serial interface, serial-parallel.

parallel processing A term applied rather loosely to a number of rather similar concepts but with important detailed differences. The essence of parallel processing is that more than one particular *process is active at any given instant; however the term is often applied to a situation in which a large number of processes are potentially active but at any one instant only one is active. Strictly speaking the term parallel processing should only be applied where more than one processor is active among a group of processes at any one instant. In practice it is seldom used with this accurate connotation. *See also* concurrent programming.

parallel rewriting system *See* L-system.

parallel running *Another term for* parallel processing.

parallel shooting method *See* shooting method.

parallel transfer To transmit multiple units of information concurrently. For example, if two computers connected by eight wires wish to communicate an 8 bit unit of information, the sending computer would present all eight bits at the same time, one bit per wire. The receiving computer would accept the bit from the wires, and recreate the 8 bit unit. Thus an 8 bit parallel transfer would have occurred. *Compare* serial transfer.

parameter 1. Information passed to a subroutine, procedure, or function. The definition of the procedure is written using *formal parameters* to denote data items that will be provided when the subroutine is called, and the call of the procedure includes corresponding *actual parameters*. *See also* parameter passing.
2. A quantity in a function or mathematical model whose value is selected or estimated according to the circumstances. Parameters should be distinguished from *constants*, which are fixed for all uses of the function or model, and *variables*, which are the actual recorded measurements involved in the function or model.

Many properties of functions and mathematical models can be deduced from their structural characteristics without reference to particular values; such properties include continuity, differentiality, and linear independence. A function or model for a specific purpose may be formulated by first establishing the appropriate structure (e.g. polynomial, differential equation of a certain form) in which particular values are not yet determined; such values are parameters of the function or model. Various techniques can then be used to find the most suitable value or range of values for the parameters when considering the observed set of data.

For simple models, such as elementary *probability distributions, parameters may be estimated from the *statistics of the sample, such as the mean and the variance. General principles of estimation, in which the criterion is the agreement between model and data, lead to procedures that may require iterative computing to obtain estimates; important examples are the method of *least squares and its generalization, the method of maximum *likelihood.

The *probability distribution of a parameter estimate is often required, and it is usual to compute its standard deviation, known as its standard error (*see* measures of variation), its *correlation with other parameter estimates, and its confidence limits where appropriate (*see* confidence interval).

parameter passing The mechanism used to pass. *parameters to a procedure (subroutine) or function. The most common methods are to pass the value of the actual parameter (*call by value*), or to pass the address of the memory location where the actual parameter is stored (*call by reference*). The latter method allows the procedure to change the value of the parameter, whereas the former method guarantees that the procedure will not change the value of the parameter. Other more complicated parameter-passing methods have been devised, notably *call by name* in Algol 60, where the actual parameter is re-evaluated each time it is required during execution of the procedure.

parametric techniques *See* nonparametric techniques.

parent (father) A node A is the parent of node B in a *tree if B is the root of one of the subtrees of the tree rooted at A.

parent file (father file) *See* file recovery.

parenthesis-free notation *See* Polish notation, reverse Polish notation.

Parikh's theorem A theorem in formal language theory that concerns the nature of *context-free languages when order of letters is disregarded.

Let the alphabet Σ be the set $\{a_1, \ldots, a_n\}$. The *letter distribution*, $\phi(w)$, of a Σ-word w is the n-tuple
$$<N_1, \ldots, N_n>$$
with N_i the number of occurrences of a_i in w. The *Parikh image*, $\phi(L)$, of a Σ-language L is
$$\{\phi(w) \mid w \in L\}$$
i.e. the set of all letter-distributions of words in L. L_1 and L_2 are *letter-equivalent* if
$$\phi(L_1) = \phi(L_2)$$
Letter distributions may be added component-wise as vectors. This leads to the following: a set S of letter distributions is *linear* if, for some distributions d and $d_1, \ldots, d_k$, S is the set of all sums formed from d and multiples of d_is. S is *semilinear* if it is a finite union of linear sets.

Parikh's theorem now states that if L is context-free $\phi(L)$ is semilinear. It can also be shown that $\phi(L)$ is semilinear if and only if L is letter-equivalent to a *regular language. Hence any context-

free language is letter-equivalent to a regular language – although not all such languages are context-free.

parity A function that is computed to provide a check on a group of binary values (e.g. a word, byte, or character) by forming the modulo-2 sum of the bits in the group. The generated sum, a redundant value, is called the *parity bit*. The parity bit is 0 if the number of 1s in the original group was even. The parity bit is 1 if the number of 1s in the original group was odd.

The parity computation just defined will cause the augmented group of binary values (the original group plus the parity bit) to have an even number of 1s; this is called *even parity*. In some cases, hardware considerations make it desirable to have an odd number of 1s in the augmented group, and the parity bit is selected to cause the total number of 1s to be odd; this is called *odd parity*. *See also* parity check.

parity bit *See* parity.

parity check (odd-even check) The computation, or recomputation for verification, of a parity bit to determine if a prescribed parity condition is present. *See* parity. *See also* checksum.

parity-check code, parity-check matrix *See* linear code.

PARLOG A parallel version of *PROLOG.

parser (syntax analyzer) *See* parsing.

parser generator A program that accepts the syntactic description of a programming language and generates a *parser for that language. *See also* compiler-compiler.

parse tree (syntax tree) A tree defining the syntactic structure of a sentence in a *context-free language. The interior nodes are labeled by nonterminals of

Parse tree

is a valid arithmetic expression with structure specified by the statement that its subexpressions are

1,2,3 and 1−2

(Note that 2−3 is not a subexpression.)

The input to a parser is a string of tokens supplied by a *lexical analyzer. Its output may be in the form of a *parse tree or a *derivation sequence. *See also* bottom-up parsing, top-down parsing, precedence parsing.

partial correctness, proof of. *See* program correctness proof.

partial differential equations Differential equations that involve two or more independent variables, which in practice are often space and time variables. Because more than one independent variable is present, the "derivatives" that occur are partial derivatives. Such equations are widespread in science and model physical phenomena; they also arise frequently in the form of systems of equations. Simple examples in space and time are given by the heat conduction (or diffusion) equation,

$$\partial u / \partial t = \alpha \partial^2 u / \partial x^2$$

and the wave equation,

$$\partial^2 u / \partial t^2 = \beta \partial^2 u / \partial x^2$$

where α and β are physical constants. Steady-state phenomena in two space variables are typified by Laplace's equation,

$$\partial^2 u / \partial x^2 + \partial^2 u / \partial y^2 = 0$$

Appropriate initial and boundary conditions must be specified for these equations. The majority of partial differential equations that arise in practice require numerical techniques for their solution, the most successful and widely used being *finite-difference and *finite-element methods.

the context-free *grammar; the descendants of a node labeled by A, say, spell from left to right the right-hand side of some production having left-hand side A. The leaf nodes of a parse tree may be terminals or nonterminals. If all the leaves are terminals then they spell from left to right a sentence of the language.

An example of a parse tree is shown in the diagram. It is assumed that the grammar in question has productions

$$A \to BC, \; B \to b, \; C \to cc$$

Note that it is conventional for the top of the tree to be its root and the bottom to be its leaves.

An early stage in compiling a program usually consists of generating a parse tree in which the constructs that make up the program are expressed in terms of the *syntax of the programming language.

parsing (syntax analysis) The process of deciding whether a string of input symbols is a sentence of a given language and if so determining the syntactic structure of the string as defined by a *grammar (usually *context-free) for the language. This is achieved by means of a program known as a *parser* or *syntax analyzer*. For example, a syntax analyzer of arithmetic expressions should report an error in the string

1− +2

since the juxtaposition of the minus and plus operators is invalid. On the other hand the string

1−2−3

partial evaluation An *optimization technique. Parts of a program that have just enough data are evaluated, other parts are kept unchanged. For *logic programming languages, *unification and *resolution automatically support mechanisms for partial evaluation such as: unfolding of procedure calls with their bodies, forward and backward propagation of data structures, and evaluation of built-in functions wherever possible. Special techniques, for example *lazy evaluation, are necessary for partial evaluation of *functional languages.

partial function Roughly, a *function

$$f : S \rightarrow T$$

that holds for only a proper *subset of S. Strictly, if the subset over which it holds is R, then

$$f : R \rightarrow T$$

is a function. However it may be more convenient to work with S rather than with R. The set U,

$$U = S - R,$$

is nonempty, and f has no value (or rather has the *undefined value*) at points in U; f is then said to be *undefined* on U and *defined* for all elements in the subset R of S, i.e. in S but not in U.

Partial functions arise naturally in computing. When recursive definitions of functions are given, the definition can sometimes loop for certain parameters. Definitions of functions can also give rise to overflow or *exception situations. In these cases it is convenient to talk about partial functions. *Compare* total function.

partially ordered set *See* partial ordering.

partial ordering (partial order) A *relation defined between elements of some *set and satisfying certain properties, discussed below. It is basically a convenient generalization of the usual comparison operators, such as $>$ or $<$, that are typically defined on the integers or the real numbers. The generalization also captures the essential properties of the set operations such as "is a subset of", the alphabetical ordering of strings, and so on. In *denotational semantics, partial orderings are used to express some *approximation relation* between partially defined computational objects.

Two different but equivalent definitions of a partial ordering are possible. The first, denoted by $\preccurlyeq$, is a generalization of the usual $\leq$ operation in which $\preccurlyeq$ must be a *transitive, *antisymmetric, and *reflexive relation defined on the set S. The second definition, denoted by $\prec$ is a generalization of the usual $<$ operation in which $\prec$ must be a transitive, *asymmetric, and *irreflexive relation defined on S. A set with a partial ordering defined on it is called a *partially ordered set* or sometimes a *poset*.

partial recursive function A *function that can be obtained from certain initial functions by a finite number of applications of *composition, *recursion, and *minimization. In general it may not be defined for certain values of its parameters and so is a *partial function. The initial functions used are normally the *zero function, *successor function, and *projection functions. *See also* primitive recursive function.

partition 1. The term used in some operating systems to refer to a static area of memory for use by jobs, and also applied by association to the jobs executed in that area.

2. of a set. *See* covering.

partition-exchange sort *Another name for* quicksort.

Pascal A programming language in very common use. Pascal was designed as a tool to assist the teaching of programming as a systematic discipline. To that end it incorporates the *control structures of *structured programming – sequence, selection, and repetition – and *data structures – arrays, records, files, sets, and user-defined types. It is an austere language, with a minimum of facilities, but what is provided is so well suited to its task that the language is in practice more powerful than its more elaborate competitors.

Pascal was relatively easy to implement on a variety of machines since the Pascal compiler was written in Pascal. Used first as an educational tool, Pascal became a more-or-less standard language for the teaching of computer science. It spread into microcomputing in the form of the UCSD p-System: this is now little used, the dominant version in the micro world now being *Turbo Pascal. In 1982 ISO Standard Pascal was defined, but modern compilers, particularly Turbo Pascal, implement an extended and nonstandard version of the language.

Pascal-Plus A derivative of *Pascal, providing facilities for *concurrent programming.

pass A single scan through a body of data, e.g. a compiler reading the program text or a statistical package reading its data.

passband A range of frequencies with a lower limit and an upper limit, such that all frequencies between these limits (but not necessarily excluding other frequencies) are passed, with little attenuation, by a filter or a channel. *See also* bandwidth, band-pass filter, filtering.

pass instruction *Another name for* no-op instruction.

passive star A network topology in which the outer *nodes connect to a single central node. The central node does not process the message in any way but simply connects the transmission paths between the outer nodes. The central node is unlikely to fail due to its passive operation. It is thus unlikely that the entire network will be disabled during normal operation. *See also* active star, star network, network architecture.

password An *authentication process in which each user holds a unique character string, a copy of which is stored within the system, e.g. in an *access controller. During *login, the password entered by the intending user must correspond with the stored value before the user is accepted by the system. Passwords may be allocated by the system or chosen by the user. *See also* irreversible encryption.

patch 1. *Informal* A change to a program – usually to correct some error – that is introduced in a manner that emphasizes convenience and speed of change rather than security, and is intended to effect only a temporary repair. Even where a program is written in some high-level language, the patching might be carried out in machine-code terms on the compiled version of the program. Often during testing a series of minor errors will be corrected by patching in order to permit testing to continue without the delay of recompilation. Subsequently the corresponding changes will all be incorporated into the program source text at a single compilation.

2. *See* patchboard.

patchboard (plugboard) A matrix of sockets that can be interconnected manually by means of *patchcords*, i.e. cables with plugs attached to each end. Thus one socket can be *patched* to another. Patchcords are used to make temporary connections between devices, to program *analog computers, and to connect different peripheral devices to computer lines.

patchcord *See* patchboard.

patent A government grant to an inventor assuring him/her the exclusive right to exploit or sell the invention for a limited period (usually 20 years). Under the 1985 Guidelines for Examination in the European Patent Office, patent protection is available to inventive computer programs in Europe if the invention is expressed in terms of a programmed machine. Programs can be patented in the USA if they comply with the originality and other requirements of the US Patent Act. Inventive hardware is patentable in Europe and this leads to a serious flaw in the law; the same task can be performed by both software and hardware but the former is expressly excluded from protection by a clause in the European Patent Convention. The question of whether a program that performs the same task as a piece of patented hardware infringes the patent in the hardware has not yet been decided in Europe, nor has it been decided whether a PROM is a piece of software or hardware. Many of these inventions are now given a special type of copyright protection under new laws protecting chip masks. *See also* trade secrets.

path 1. A route between two vertices of a *graph, passing along edges and, in the case of a directed *graph, with attention paid to the direction along the edges. More formally there is a path between vertices V_0 and V_k if each pair (V_i, V_{i+1}), $i = 0,1 \ldots ,k-1$ is an edge of the graph and, in the case of a directed graph, is suitably directed.

In typical applications, the existence of paths between vertices indicates physical connections between them or perhaps logical connections or dependencies. *See also* cycle.

2. A sequence of instructions that may be performed in the execution of a program. A path through a program is equivalent to a traversal of the *control flow diagram for that program from the start node or vertex to the end node of the graph.

path testing A test strategy equivalent to finding all possible *paths through the *control flow diagram of a program. Testing each path at least once is a typical test strategy, but for much real software complete path *test coverage would require an impracticably large test run/time. Path testing almost always requires more test runs than

either *branch testing or *statement testing.

pattern An *equivalence class associated with a special kind of *relation defined on functions. Let
$$F = \{f \,|\, D \to A\}$$
be a set of functions mapping elements from some domain D into some set A, which can be regarded as an alphabet. With each function f in F is associated a *weight* $w(f)$, defined as the formal multiplication of all the images $f(x)$ under f. In effect $w(f)$ describes the number of occurrences of the different images in A.

An equivalence relation can then be defined between two functions of F in such a way that equivalent functions have equivalent weights, though the reverse is not in general true. The patterns of F are the equivalence classes that emerge from this equivalence relation.

The weight of a pattern is just the weight of any member of that pattern; the weight of the equivalence class $[f]$ containing f is just $w(f)$. The formal sum of the weights $w(f)$ taken over all the equivalence classes in F gives the *pattern inventory* of the set F. An important theorem due mainly to George Pólya indicates the close link between pattern inventory and *cycle index polynomial.

These ideas are often applied in *combinatorics and *switching theory. For example, a pattern inventory can indicate the number of essentially different wiring diagrams or logic circuits needed to realize the different possible logic functions.

pattern inventory *See* pattern.

pattern matching The technique of comparing two patterns in order to say how similar they are, or of comparing one pattern with a set of patterns in order to say to which member of the set it is most similar. This usually implies that a numerical value can be computed, as a *function of two patterns, by means of a pattern matching algorithm. The patterns concerned may be purely logical (i.e. *data structures) or physical (e.g. one-, two-, or three-dimensional images, represented as arrays). The term is commonly used where the patterns are *expressions represented either abstractly or as *strings. When the patterns are physical images, the term *pattern recognition is more common.

pattern recognition The process of detecting the presence of a specified pattern in a *signal, or assigning a probability to its possible presence. For example, visual pattern recognition involves the identification of two-dimensional patterns in a *gray-level array. The specification of one of more patterns is done either analytically, or, more usually, by the provision of *templates*, which are model patterns for comparison. Pattern recognition employs the techniques of *digital signal processing, *picture processing, and *artificial intelligence.

PC *Abbrev. for* personal computer, printed circuit.

PCB or **pcb** *Abbrev. for* printed circuit board. *See* printed circuit.

PC clone *See* clone.

PCM *Abbrev. for* pulse code modulation.

p-code An intermediate language designed as the target language for *UCSD Pascal and other languages in the *p-system software.

PCTE *Abbrev. for* portable common tool environment. A European specification for a *PTI developed within an *ESPRIT project. PCTE offers bindings to various aspects of tool support facilities, including the *user interface and *object management system, in *Ada and *C. A number of implementations are available on *UNIX and *VMS operating systems and on platforms supporting these operating systems. *Abstract specifications are being prepared, using *VDM. Standardization of PCTE is being undertaken within *ECMA through *CEN/CENELEC.

PCTE+ is a European NATO specification based on PCTE with enhancements particularly in the security features, which will be the basis for the ECMA standard.

PDA *Abbrev. for* pushdown automaton.

PDL *Abbrev. for* **1.** program design language. **2.** page description language.

PDP series A family of machines manufactured by *DEC.

PE *Abbrev. for* phase-encoded. *See* tape format.

peek To examine the contents of an absolute memory location from a high-level language, usually by means of a function of this name whose argument is the address in question. *Compare* poke.

peephole optimization *See* optimization (in programming).

penetration A technique of *security evaluation.

perfect codes *Error-correcting codes in which the Hamming spheres surrounding the codewords entirely fill the *Hamming space without overlap. These spheres all have radius e, where the code can correct e errors, and their centers (codewords) are separated from each other by a distance of $(2e + 1)$; thus the spheres have no points (words) in common where they touch, but their surfaces are separated by unit distance with no points between them. Perfect codes attain the *Hamming bound exactly.

The only *binary *linear perfect codes are the *repetition codes, the *Hamming codes, and the (23,12) *Golay code.

perfective maintenance *See* software maintenance.

perfect matching A term used in *graph theory. A matching of a *graph is any subset of its edges such that no two members of the subset are adjacent. A perfect matching is a matching in which every *vertex of the graph is an endpoint of some element of the matching.

performance monitoring Measurement, by direct observation or by programmed processes, of activity at various points in a computer system to find out where bottlenecks and delays are taking place. Results are used for system *reconfiguration in order to improve overall performance.

performance testing The specification for a system will usually have some requirements for how well the system should perform certain functions, additional to a statement of required functions. Thus while *functional testing* will, for example, demonstrate that the sum and average of a set of numbers will be calculated, *performance testing* will concentrate on how well the calculation is done (speed, accuracy, range, etc.). Typically, performance testing will consist of one of more of the following.

Stress and timing tests, for example measuring and demonstrating the ability to meet peak service demand measured by number of users, transaction rate, volume of data, and the maximum number of devices all operating simultaneously.

Configuration, compatibility, and recovery tests, for example using a combination of the slowest processor, the minimal memory, the smallest disk, and the last version of the operating system, and checking that other valid combinations of processor, memory, disk, communications, and operating systems will interoperate and recover from faults.

Regression tests, showing that the new system will perform all the required

application functions of the system it replaces.

periodogram In *time series analysis, a diagram showing the most important cyclical regularity in the data. Peaks in the diagram correspond to periods of cycles that most closely correlate with the data. Interpretation of periodograms is by spectral analysis.

peripheral Any device, including I/O devices and backing store, that is connected to a computer.

peripheral interface adapter (PIA) A set of electronic circuits fitted to a processor or a peripheral to achieve compatibility between the interfaces. The interface offered by the vendor of a peripheral may not be appropriate for direct connection to a given system for several reasons: the system manufacturers may have designed a unique interface to prevent the connection of unauthorized peripherals, or the interface fitted may have been optimized for low cost and short cable length, e.g. parallel input/output, and thus be incompatible with a peripheral interface optimized for long lines or network connection. Many vendors of peripheral equipment provide space and power within their equipment to accommodate a PIA, which may be available as an option or may be designed and manufactured by the system supplier or user. In microprocessors the interface to peripherals is often provided via a PIA integrated into a single package. The device may provide control of bidirectional data flow, handling of interrupts, etc. The function may be altered by appropriate signals on its control inputs.

peripheral processor The name used in CDC systems for a special-purpose processor used to control peripheral units. (These processors go by a variety of names: on IBM systems they are referred to as *channels, and have a much more restricted order code than a

CDC peripheral processor.) In all cases the essence of the peripheral processor is that its order code is specifically tailored to the requirements of transferring information between main memory and the peripheral device or devices controlled by the peripheral processor.

permanent error of peripheral storage. *See* error rate.

permutation of a *set *S*. A *bijection of *S* onto itself. When *S* is finite, a permutation can be portrayed as a rearrangement of the elements of *S*. The number of permutations of a set of *n* elements is *n*!

A permutation of the elements of {1,2,3} can be written

1 2 3
2 1 3

indicating that 1 is mapped into 2, 2 into 1, and 3 into 3. Alternatively the above can be written, using a *cycle notation, as (1 2); this implies that the element 3 is unaltered but that 1 is mapped into 2 and 2 into 1.

For collections of elements in which repeated occurrences of items may exist, a permutation can be described as a rearrangement of elements in which each element appears with the same frequency as before.

permutation group A *subgroup of the group that is formed from the set, S_n, of all *permutations of *n* distinct elements and on which is defined the dyadic operation of *composition of functions. The full group S_n is usually called the *symmetric group* and possesses *n*! elements. Every finite group is isomorphic to some permutation group.

permutation matrix A square matrix in which each column contains precisely one nonzero element, which is equal to unity. If *P* is an $n \times n$ permutation matrix and *x* is a vector of *n* elements, the vector *Px* will be a *permutation of the elements of *x*.

personal computer A general-purpose single-user microcomputer designed to be operated by one person at a time. Personal computers range from cheap domestic or hobby machines with limited memory, program storage on cassette tape, and an ordinary TV as the display device, to extremely sophisticated machines with powerful processors, large-capacity disk storage, high-resolution color-graphics systems, and many other options. In scientific, engineering, and business environments the personal computer is a real alternative to a terminal connected to a time-sharing system, especially since communication ports and network connections allow transfers of data between the personal computer and other computers. The development of the personal computer is a consequence of the ratio of computing power to cost increasing to a point where it is no longer necessary for a computer to work continuously to be cost-effective.

PERT *Abbrev. for* performance evaluation and review techniques. Management techniques for planning, scheduling, and controlling projects. Dependencies are drawn as directed *graphs to show the logical sequence of activities that must occur before a project can be completed. *See also* critical path method.

PERT chart A method of expressing the dependence of distinct activities for project management (*see* PERT). The chart is drawn as a *weighted directed *graph where each edge represents a specific activity and its weight is the time required to complete that activity. The activity can only be started when those edges (activities) incident to it have been completed. The chart has one start point and one termination point.

The critical path for time to project completion is calculated together with the float, earliest start, and latest start times on individual activities. Some PERT tools allow different types of resource to be allocated to an activity, with limits on total resource of each type, and for "hammocks" (dummy activities) to be used to monitor project milestones and resource usage. *See also* activity network, critical path method.

PES *Acronym for* programmable electronic system. A term used in certain official guidelines and standards to describe a complete computer-based system. For example in an industrial process-control application, the input sensors, the computer hardware and software, and the output actuators would comprise the PES.

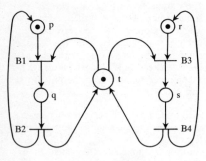

Example of a Petri net

Petri net A model of a concurrent system that is expressed in a specific graphical notation and can be used to explore certain properties of the system. A Petri net consists of a set of *places*, a set of *transition bars*, and a set of directed edges. Each transition bar has an associated set of input places and an associated set of output places. A transition bar is linked to each of its input places by a directed edge from the place to the bar, and to each of its output places by a directed edge from the bar to the place.

States of the concurrent system are represented by the presence of *tokens* at places, with a specific state being repre-

sented by a specific allocation of tokens to places. Such an allocation is called a *marking*.

The example net shown in the diagram employs the conventional graphical notation. Places are represented by the circles labeled p ... t, transition bars are represented by the lines labeled B1 ... B4, and the initial marking is shown by the use of dots to represent tokens.

Transition bars represent possible changes of state in the concurrent system. A transition bar can only *fire* (i.e. the change of state occur) when each of its input places holds at least one token. When a bar fires it removes one token from each of its input places and deposits one token at each of its output places. Thus the combination of the input and output places for a transition bar represents both the conditions under which the change of state can occur and the effects of that state change.

The firing of a transition bar is an indivisible event and simultaneous firing of two or more bars is therefore not possible. When the state is such that two or more bars are candidates to fire, each candidate must be considered individually.

By starting from an initial marking that represents an initial state of the system and applying a straightforward procedure that generates other markings that can be reached from this initial marking, it is possible to explore the possible states of the system and the ways in which these states can be reached. For example, both deadlock states and unproductive looping can be readily detected, and in general it is possible to check that the behavior of the system is as expected. However, while the procedure for generating reachable markings is straightforward, attempts at full analysis are often frustrated by the sheer number of such markings, and indeed this number can be infinite. Thus the general problem of determining whether a given marking is reachable from a given initial state is undecidable.

With the initial marking shown in the example net, both B1 and B3 are able to fire. Suppose that B1 fires. This removes the tokens from places p and t, and deposits a single token at place q. Now only B2 is able to fire. (B3 is no longer able to fire because there is no longer a token at place t.) When B2 fires, the token is removed from place q and new tokens are deposited at places p and t, thus restoring the initial marking. Should B3 now fire, a single token is deposited at place s, and B4 then fires, again restoring the initial marking. (This net may be viewed as modeling a system in which two processes compete for a shared resource. Availability of the resource is represented by the presence of a token at place t. Relevant states of one process, holding the resource or not holding the resource, are represented by tokens at places p and q respectively. Similarly tokens at places r and s represent relevant states of the other process.)

Petri nets were devised in Germany in the early 1960s by C. A. Petri.

PGA 1. *Abbrev. for* programmable gate array. A form of *PLA that has products (*AND operations), but no *sums of products (*OR operations).

2. *Abbrev. for* pin grid array.

phase of a regularly recurring (periodic) quantity. The stage or state of development of the quantity. It can be expressed, in the form of an angle, as the fraction of a cycle of the periodic quantity that has been completed, with respect to a fixed datum point. Two sinusoidally varying quantities of the same frequency can be *in phase* (reaching corresponding phases at the same time) or *out of phase*. In the latter case the difference in phase – the *phase difference* – is usually expressed as an angle.

phase change An optical recording technology where the process of writing changes the area of the medium that is to represent a 1 bit from one physical state to another, e.g. from crystalline to amorphous, rather than producing a change in its external configuration or state of magnetization. This technology can be used either reversibly or nonreversibly, in some cases in the same medium by adjustment of the power of the laser beam. However, it is not yet (1989) used in commercial rewritable storage devices because it suffers from a fatigue effect if repeatedly erased and rewritten.

phase-encoded (PE) *See* tape format.

phase modulation (PM) *See* modulation.

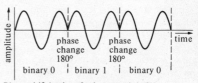

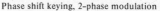

Phase shift keying, 2–phase modulation

phase shift keying (PSK) A method for representing digital data with analog signals by changing the phase of the analog carrier to represent the digital information (*see* diagram). It is a type of *modulation.

There are two ways of detecting the phase information in a signal. *Fixed-reference PSK* assigns a meaning to each phase position. The *demodulator uses a signal source of the same frequency to compare with the incoming signal and detect its phase. *Differential PSK* assigns meaning to phase changes, e.g. a phase change of 180° could be taken to mean a 1, while no phase change means a 0. No comparison with another wave is needed in the demodulator.

The amount of information associated with a phase or phase change depends on the number of discrete phases that the carrier may assume. If the carrier may assume two phases then each phase or phase change represents a single bit. If four phases are used then each phase or phase change represents a different combination of two bits. The greater the number of discrete phases, the more difficult it is to generate, transmit, and detect the analog signal, thus the cost is higher; for this reason, *modems that require eight or more discrete signals usually combine the phase changes with changes in amplitude in order to make the signals more distinct.

See also digital data transmission.

PHIGS *Abbrev. for* programmers hierarchical interactive graphics standard. An *API for interactive graphics work. Although the names and definitions of some of the output primitives are common with *GKS, this graphics interface offers much greater functionality and consequently is much more demanding on processor and storage resource. It is not currently (1988) published as a standard.

phototransistor *See* optoelectronics.

physical Actual, or involving actual entities, as opposed to logical or conceptual.

physical layer of network protocol function. *See* seven-layer reference model.

PIA *Abbrev. for* peripheral interface adapter.

pi benchmark A program that uses integer arithmetic to calculate π to some arbitrary accuracy. It is used as a *benchmark to measure the time to complete calculation to a stated accuracy or to measure the number of digits accuracy achieved per second of execution.

pico- (symbol: p) A prefix to a unit, indicating a submultiple of a millionth of a millionth, 10^{-12}, of that unit, as in picosecond.

picture 1. The principal means of defining *data types in *COBOL. The syntax of an elementary data item is defined by means of a character string. Simple examples are "A(20)" defining a string of 20 alphabetic characters, or "9(4)" defining a string of 4 digits. Particularly in the case of numeric items that are to be printed or displayed, the PICTURE clause provides considerable power: it is possible, for instance, to specify the position of the decimal point (explicit or implicit); the presence and position of the sign (+ or −) or of currency symbols; filling out digit strings with zeros or blanks (leading, embedded, or trailing); insertion of commas into long numbers. The MOVE verb, which is used to assign the value of one variable to another, automatically carries out format conversion according to the picture of the receiving item.

2. (image) *See* picture processing.

picture processing (image processing) The analysis, generally by *digital signal processing techniques, of the information contained in *pictures* (or *images*). The original picture may be a drawing, photograph, scene, etc., which is digitized in such a way that it can be regarded as a two-dimensional array of data, i.e. as a two-dimensional spatial *signal whose amplitude represents the brightness at the position in the *space domain. Sometimes the amplitude is taken to include the color (hue and saturation). The process of spatial sampling of a scene is usually carried out by a TV camera or, for example, by a scanning electron microscope.

Each element of the two-dimensional array is called a *pixel* (picture element). The *definition* is the fineness of spatial sampling; it is expressed in terms of pixels, e.g. high definition is usually considered to be 1024 by 768 pixels. The amplitude is generally encoded by between three and eight bits for *gray scale (monochrome) or up to 16 bits for color.

Typical processing operations include contrast distortion, expansion of a specified range of brightness, bright outlining of objects, correction of over- or underexposure of portions of the picture, recognition (and perhaps counting) of predefined objects, and comparison of one picture with another. The last two of these operations are examples of *pattern recognition. Some of the more advanced operations make use of the concepts of *artificial intelligence. The development of picture processing has been prompted by applications such as satellite and unmanned spaceprobe observations, undersea exploration, medical physics, and industrial robotics.

Pierce arrow *See* NOR operation.

piggyback acknowledgment *See* acknowledgment.

PILOT *Acronym for* programmed inquiry, learning, or teaching. A special-purpose language for developing *computer-assisted learning (CAL) software.

pin or **PIN** *Abbrev. for* personal identification number. A number issued to a holder of a *magnetic card, for example a credit card or bank card, that the card holder is required to keep secret. Together with the magnetic card the pin acts as an identifier and password to access computer-based services such as *ATMs, *EPOSs, or *EFTS.

pin grid array (PGA) A form of *integrated circuit packaging, capable of providing up to several hundred connections to one chip. Connections to the device are made by means of an array of pins around the package periphery. The array may be formed as several parallel rows of pins at two opposite

sides of the package or around all four sides, depending on the size and complexity of the IC.

pin header A device similar in form to a *DIP but containing no circuitry. Instead each leg is extended vertically through the package allowing pins to be connected together in any configuration by soldering small pieces of wire across the relevant pins. A pin header is more flexible but clumsier than a *DIL switch.

pink book The *coloured book that defines a network service operating over a *CSMA/CD bearer network.

PIO *Abbrev. for* parallel input/output.

pipeline processing A form of processing in which the time required to pass through some functional unit (e.g. a floating point ALU) of a computer system is longer than the intervals at which data may enter that functional unit, i.e. the functional unit performs its process in several steps. When the first step is completed, the results are passed to a second step that uses separate hardware; the first-step hardware is thus free to begin processing new data. This provides fast throughput for sequential processes, but at the expense of complicating the control unit, which must keep account of operations that are simultaneously in progress. The technique is commonly used in supercomputers, which require maximum performance, and in vector and array processors, which provide long orderly sequences of data as input to pipeline processors.

pipelining *Pipeline processing itself, or the use of pipeline processing.

PIPO *Abbrev. for* parallel in, parallel out. *See also* shift register.

PISO *Abbrev. for* parallel in, serial out. *See also* shift register.

pixel *Derived from* picture element. One of the elements in a large *array that is holding pictorial information. It contains data representing the brightness and possibly color of a small region of the image. *See also* picture processing.

pixelization (space quantization) *See* quantization. *See also* picture processing, discrete and continuous systems.

PL/1 *See* PL/I.

PL/360 The first machine-oriented high-level language (or *MOHLL), developed by Wirth as an implementation tool for Algol-W on the IBM System/360.

PLA *Abbrev. for* programmed logic array, or programmable logic array. A read-only device that is a generalized *combinational circuit and may include a *sequential circuit. By means of connections on a semiconductor device, the PLA usually provides a "programmable" *sum of products function that feeds an output register, and sometimes an internal register. When the internal register is used to provide part of the input variables, the PLA is a sequential circuit; otherwise it is a combinational circuit.

The product terms in the function can be thought of as representing values that are to be acted upon when they occur; thus the PLA is a form of fixed *associative memory or a specialized *table look-up device adapted to the situation when the truth table has sparse entries.

Since the PLA is made specific only by the interconnections, it represents a general-purpose building block that requires changes in only one or two steps of the production process to provide different functionality. PLAs can be programmed at the time of manufacture; alternatively they may be programmed by the user, and are then called *field-programmable*. *See also* programmable device.

plain text *See* cryptography.

planar graph A *graph that can be drawn on paper (with points representing vertices and lines joining vertices representing edges) in such a way that edges intersect only at vertices.

plasma display A form of *display used in association with computer systems in which a red or orange light is provided by an electrical discharge through a gas. A matrix of cells in which discharge can be arranged is fabricated by bonding a sheet of perforated material between layers – one of which is transparent – on which there are electrodes and connecting tracks. They are frequently configured as rows of character-sized (5 × 7 or 7 × 9) groups of cells, but panels that have a continuous matrix over the whole area, and thus can display graphics, are available. For displaying small amounts of information – up to 240 characters – they are an attractive alternative to display devices incorporating a cathode-ray tube; large displays however are more expensive.

platter The metallic substrate of a rigid magnetic disk.

PL/C, PL/CT *See* PL/I.

PLD *Abbrev. for* programmable logic device. A form of *PAL in which the outputs emerge through output cells, an output cell being a *logic circuit that is programmable for a number of characteristics. These characteristics include the choice of *positive or *negative logic, whether the output can be used as an input, whether it is to be fed back into the circuit, whether it is to emerge via a *latch, and whether it is to be *tri-state.

plex A *multilinked structure consisting of a collection of cells of various sizes linked together by pointers into essentially a connected directed *graph, possibly containing cycles. *See also* list processing.

PL/I A programming language designed initially by the IBM users' group SHARE, and adopted by IBM as a major product. PL/I was intended to replace all pre-existing programming languages, incorporating the best features of COBOL, FORTRAN, and Algol 60. The resulting language is large and complex: it was not taken up by manufacturers other than IBM, and has had only limited acceptance among IBM users.

PL/I was adopted as a teaching language by a number of universities, notably Cornell, who produced their own versions, PL/C and PL/CT. It was also used as a basis for the microcomputer language *PL/M.

PL/M A systems programming language for microcomputers in the Intel family. It is based on and bears a strong resemblance to *PL/I.

plotter An output device for translating information from a computer into pictorial or graphical form on paper or a similar medium. There are a wide variety of plotters to match the differing requirements for size, accuracy, speed, and other attributes such as color.

One of the simplest implementations is a *flat-bed plotter*. One or more pens are mounted on a carriage that can be moved to precise positions on a bar that spans the width of the medium, i.e. the *x*-axis. The bar is mounted so that it can be moved precisely on tracks that lie parallel to the lengthwise edge of the medium, i.e. the *y*-axis. It is thus possible to move the pen to any point that lies within the available range of *x* and *y* coordinates. The pen can either touch the surface as it moves, thus producing a line, or it can be lifted off the surface as it moves. When drawing a diagonal line the computer generally has to provide only the coordinates of the start and finish points.

Although large flatbed plotters are produced it is often preferable to use the *drum plotter* configuration for large drawings, or for a sequence of drawings. The drum plotter has an arrangement similar to the flatbed plotter for moving the pen across the width of the medium, but the bar is fixed parallel to the axis of a drum. The medium is wrapped around part of the drum surface and is often wound onto take-up spools on either side of the drum axis. The medium has holes punched at its edges that engage with pintles on the drum and thus maintain registration with the rotation of the drum as it translates longitudinal axis coordinates.

plugboard *Another name for* patchboard.

plug compatible (plug-to-plug compatible) *See* compatibility.

PL/Z The family name for the systems programming languages provided by Zilog for the Z8000 microcomputer. PL/Z–SYS is a variant of *Pascal, while PL/Z–ASM is an assembly language.

PMOS A type of *MOSFET.

PMS *Abbrev. for* processor-memory-switch. A notation consisting of a number of structural primitives, such as memory, M, switch, S, processor, P, etc., connected to form a network that describes the *architecture of a computer system. It allows complex computer systems to be specified at many levels. At the lowest, register transfer, level it is used in conjunction with *ISP.

pneumatic logic *Fluid logic in which the working medium is a gas.

p-n junction *See* junction.

P = NP question One of the major open questions in theoretical computer science at present.

P is the class of formal languages that are recognizable in *polynomial time. More precisely a language *L* is in *P* if there exists a *Turing machine program *M* and a polynomial $p(n)$ such that *M* recognizes *L* and

$$T_M(n) \leqslant p(n)$$

for all nonnegative integers *n*, where T_M is the time complexity of *M* (*see* complexity measure). It is generally accepted that if a language is not in *P* then there is no algorithm that recognizes it and is guaranteed to be always "fast".

NP is the class of languages that are recognizable in polynomial time on a nondeterministic *Turing machine.

Clearly

$$P \subseteq NP$$

but the question of whether

$$P = NP$$

has not been solved despite a great amount of research.

A language is said to be *NP-hard* if any language in *NP* can be polynomially reduced to it, even if the language itself is not in *NP*.

Contained in *NP* is a set of languages *NPC*, said to be *NP-complete*. A language L_1 is in *NPC* if every language L_2 in *NP* can be polynomially reduced to L_1, i.e. there is some function *f* such that

(a) $x \in L_1$ iff $f(x) \in L_2$
(b) $f(x)$ is computable in time bounded by a polynomial in the length of *x*.

It can be shown that if any NP-complete language is also in *P* then *P = NP*.

A wide variety of problems occurring in computer science, mathematics, and operations research are now known to be NP-complete. As an example the problem of determining whether a Boolean expression in conjunctive normal form (*see* conjunction) can be satisfied by a truth assignment was the first problem found to be NP-complete; this is generally referred to as the *satisfiability* (or *CNF satisfiability*) *problem*. Despite considerable effort none of these NP-complete problems have been shown to be polynomially solvable. Thus it is widely conjectured that no NP-complete problem is polynomially solvable.

PN sequence *Short for* pseudonoise sequence.

pocket sorting *Another name for* radix sorting.

pointer 1. (link) A character or group of characters that indicates the storage location of an item of data. Thus when a field of an item A in a data structure contains the address of another item B, i.e. of its first word in memory, it contains a pointer to B; it is said to *point* to B.

2. *Another name for* pointing device.

pointing device (pointer) Any means of passing two-dimensional spatial information to a computer system. The computer is usually programmed to display the current position by means of crosshairs or a cursor on the screen. *See* bitpad, digitizer, joystick, light pen, mouse, touch-sensitive device, trackerball.

point-of-sale system (POS system) A system in which *point-of-sale terminals* are used as input to a digital computer. A point-of-sale terminal is a specialized cash register, credit-card recording system, or ticket dispenser that causes all information on the transaction to be relayed to a central computer. Some point-of-sale systems include credit validation. Better stock, cash, and credit control are maintained by having the data entered into a computer as soon as it is available at the point of sale. Point-of-sale systems are also useful in monitoring petty theft of cash and merchandise.

point-to-point line A dedicated communication link that joins only two nodes in a network. *Compare* multidrop line.

Poisson distribution The basic discrete *probability distribution for data in the form of counts of random events. If each event occurs with the same probability and the mean frequency of events is μ, the probability that exactly r events will occur is

$$e^{-\mu}\mu^r/r!$$

The Poisson distribution is discrete, taking the values $r = 0, 1, 2, \ldots$ and it can be obtained as a limiting case of the *binomial distribution as n tends to infinity while np is held fixed. The mean and variance of the Poisson distribution are both equal to μ.

poke To modify the contents of an absolute memory location from a high-level language, usually by means of a procedure of this name whose two arguments are the address in question and the value to be deposited there. *Compare* peek.

POL *Acronym for* problem-oriented language. A programming language whose control structures and (in particular) data structures reflect in some measure the characteristics of a class of problems, e.g. commercial data processing or scientific computation. By contrast, the structures of a machine-oriented language reflect the internal structure of the underlying machine.

Polish notation (prefix notation) A form of notation, invented by the Polish mathematician Jan Lukasiewicz, in which each operator precedes its operands, e.g.

$$a + b \text{ is expressed as } +ab$$

If all operators take exactly two operands, or if each operator has a specific number of operands, then no brackets are required since the order of evaluation is always uniquely defined; the notation can then be described as *parenthesis-free*. *See also* reverse Polish notation.

polling The process by which one station on a *multidrop line (the primary station) addresses another station (a secondary station), giving the secondary station access to the communication channel. The secondary station is then able to send status information and/or data to the primary. The primary station resumes control of the line and may send data of its own or poll another station.

Polling is a form of *time division multiplexing. The precise polling strategy used depends upon the application. In *roll-call polling* the primary station addresses each secondary station in turn. Some stations may be addressed more often than others if their response-time requirements or traffic loads are heavier. *Hub polling* is used to minimize line turnaround delays on *half duplex multidrop lines. The primary station polls the station at the opposite end of the line, which transmits any data it has and polls the next closest station. This process is repeated until control reaches the primary station again. Since data is flowing in one direction only, from the outermost nodes toward the primary station, the only turnaround delays occur when the primary station wishes to transmit.

Polling is not suitable for situations where the response delay time is fairly large, as is the case in satellite transmission systems.

polyadic operation An *operation that may apply to different numbers of operands on different occasions.

polymorphic Denoting programming languages in which variables and routines can hold, take, and return differently typed values at different times. *See* polymorphism.

polymorphism A feature of some modern high-level programming languages that allows arguments to procedures and functions to vary systematically over a whole class of *data types, rather than being restricted to a single type. A simple example would be a function to find the length of a list. The code for such a function should be the same for lists of integers, lists of Booleans, or lists of anything. In a language like Pascal, however, the argument to such a function must have a single type; hence to handle both lists of integers and lists of Booleans, two functions would have to be defined. This can be avoided in languages (such as *ML) that support *polymorphic types* like "list of alpha", where alpha is a *type variable* standing for an arbitrary type. A *polymorphic function* is one that takes one or more arguments of polymorphic types.

polynomial A formal power series, i.e. a sum of multiples of powers of an independent variable known as the *indeterminate* (often written as x, s, or t), e.g.

$$3x^4 + 7x^2 + 2x + 5$$

or, in general,

$$p(x) = \sum_{i=0}^{\infty} a_i x_i$$

The coefficients (a_i) are elements of some algebraic system, S, having appropriate addition and multiplication operations; the expression is then described as a polynomial over S. For example, if the coefficients are all integers, the polynomial is said to be over the integers. If $a_r \neq 0$ but $a_i = 0$ for all $i > r$, then r is called the *degree* of the polynomial, usually written

$$r = \deg(p)$$

If $a_r = 1$, the polynomial is *monic*.

Arithmetic on polynomials consists primarily of addition, subtraction, and multiplication of polynomials; in some cases division, factoring, and taking the greatest common divisor are also important operations.

Addition and subtraction are done by adding or subtracting the coefficients of like powers of x.

Multiplication is done by the rule

$$(a_r x^r + \ldots a_1 x + a_0)(b_s x^s + \ldots b_1 x + b_0)$$
$$= (c_{r+s} x^{r+s} + \ldots c_1 x + c_0)$$

where

$$c_k = a_0 b_k + a_1 b_{k-1} + \ldots a_{k-1} b_1 + a_k b_0$$
$$a_i, b_j = 0 \quad \text{for } i > r, j > s$$

In coding theory, much use is made of polynomials over the *ring of integers modulo q, for some integer $q > 1$. Such polynomials themselves form a commutative *ring with an identity. More particularly, coding theory employs polynomials over the *field of integers modulo p, for some suitable prime number p. (For binary systems, $p = 2$.) These polynomials can be multiplied and divided; in general, they may be factorized. A polynomial (over a field) that can be factorized is said to be *reducible*; otherwise it is *irreducible*. When divided by another, a polynomial over a field gives a unique quotient and remainder. Every such polynomial can be uniquely factorized into irreducible factors.

The set of polynomials (over a field), modulo a given monic irreducible polynomial (over the same field), itself forms a field; this is called an *extension field* of the original *base field* of coefficients (which were integers modulo p). Extension fields of this kind are fundamental to much of coding theory.

The extension field of polynomials modulo G, over the integers modulo p, contains p^g elements, where g is the degree of G. G is called the *generating polynomial* of the extension field. A polynomial that is an element of this field is said to be *primitive* if and only if it does not exactly divide the polynomial $x^c - 1$ (over the field of integers modulo p) for any c less than $p^g - 1$.

A practical problem of some importance is to find all the values of x that satisfy the equation

$$p_n(x) = 0$$

where $p_n(x)$ is a *polynomial equation* of degree n. Such equations have n solutions, called *roots*, which in general are complex. If the given coefficients a_i are real the complex roots occur in conjugate pairs. It is quite common for some of the roots to be very sensitive to small changes in the coefficients, i.e. to have a large *condition number.

A single root α may be found by an iteration such as *Newton's method or the *secant method. The polynomial

$$p_{n-1}(x) = p_n(x)/(x - \alpha)$$

has the same roots as p_n except for α; it may be used to determine the other roots. The process of calculating p_{n-1} is known as *deflation*, and is used after each root is found; thus the polynomials used are of progressively lower degree. Deflation depends on the roots being accurate. If an approximate root is used, the deflated polynomial will have inaccurate coefficients, and possibly very inaccurate roots. To minimize deterioration of the successive polynomials used, it is important to determine each root to the greatest possible precision and, where feasible, to determine the roots in increasing order of magnitude.

polynomial codes A family of *linear *error-correcting or *error-detecting codes whose encoding and decoding algorithms may be conveniently expressed in terms of *polynomials over a base field (and therefore easily implemented in terms of *shift registers with *linear combinational logic).

polynomial equation *See* polynomial.

polynomial interpolation *See* interpolation.

polynomially bounded algorithm *See* complexity measure.

polynomial number A number in a fixed-radix system. *See* number system.

polynomial space A way of characterizing the *complexity of an algorithm. If the space complexity (*see* complexity measure) is polynomially bounded, the algorithm is said to be executable in polynomial space. Many problems for which no *polynomial time algorithms have been found, nevertheless can easily be solved in an amount of space bounded by a polynomial in the length of the input.

Formally **PSPACE** is defined as the class of formal languages that are recognizable in polynomial space. Defining **P** and **NP** as the classes of languages recognizable in polynomial time and recognizable in polynomial time on a nondeterministic Turing machine, respectively (*see* P = NP question), it can be shown that **P** is a subset of **PSPACE** and that **NP** is also a subset of **PSPACE**. It is not known, however, whether

$$NP = PSPACE$$

although it is conjectured that they are different, i.e. that there exist languages in **PSPACE** that are not in **NP**.

Many problems associated with recognizing whether a player of a certain game (like GO) has a forced win from a given position are **PSPACE**-*complete*. In a similar manner to NP-completeness (*see* P = NP question) this means that such languages can be recognized in polynomial time only if

$$PSPACE = P$$

Such problems can thus be considered to be even harder than NP-complete problems.

polynomial time A way of characterizing the *complexity of an algorithm. If the number of elementary operations required to apply the algorithm to data of length n increases with n no more rapidly than a polynomial in n, the algorithm is said to be executable in polynomial time. *See also* complexity measure, P = NP question.

polyphase merge sort A method of *merging in which the *keys are kept on more than one backing store or file. Items are merged from the source files onto another file. Whenever one of the source files is exhausted, it immediately becomes the destination of the merge operations from the nonexhausted and previous-destination files. When there is only one file left the process stops. The repeated merging is referred to as *polyphase merging*.

pooling block An area of memory used to contain many short records that are to be transferred to or from a device for which the access time is long compared with the actual transfer time. *See also* buffer.

pop *See* stack.

POP-2 A programming language developed by the University of Edinburgh (UK) for research in *artificial intelligence. POP-2 provided the facility to manipulate the linked data structures characteristic of *LISP, but retained a more familiar procedural structure, and was thus more accessible to programmers raised in the Algol environment of the time. *POP-11 is a modern version of POP-2.

POP-11 A programming language for artificial intelligence that claims to combine *LISP and *POP-2.

P operation (down operation) *See* semaphore.

POPLOG A programming environment combining *POP-11 and *PROLOG.

population *See* sampling.

pop-up program A program that is permanently resident in memory and "pops up" onto the screen at the touch of a key. *See also* TSR.

port 1. (I/O port) A connection point with associated control circuitry that allows I/O devices to be connected to the internal bus of a microprocessor. Generally the port can be switched to input or output and is often associated with a *peripheral interface adapter. The PIA has connections compatible with

the I/O port on one side and one or more interfaces to suit various peripherals on the other. It also allows longer connection cables to be used.

2. A point through which data can enter or leave a *network, either on the network or the *DTE (computer) interface.

3. To move software from one type of computer system to another, making any necessary changes en route. In a simple case little more than recompilation may be required, while in extreme cases the software might have to be entirely rewritten.

portable 1. *Another word for* machine-independent.

2. A word applied to software that can readily be transferred to other machines, although not actually *machine independent.

3. A microcomputer that can be simply carried from one place to another by one person. These computers fold up into a suitcase or attache case format. They typically have all the features of a desktop model but are rather more expensive. They cannot necessarily be used in transit. *See also* laptop computer.

POS *Abbrev. for* point of sale. *See* point-of-sale system.

poset *Short for* partially ordered set. *See* partial ordering.

POS expression *Short for* product of sums expression.

positional system *See* number system.

position-independent code Program code that can be placed anywhere in memory, since all memory references are made relative to the *program counter. Position-independent code can be moved at any time, unlike *relocatable code, which can be loaded anywhere but once loaded must stay in the same position.

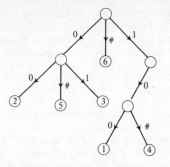

Position tree for 10010 #

position tree Let $\alpha = a_1a_2 \ldots a_n$ denote a string, or *word, in the set of all Σ-words, Σ^*, and let # be in the alphabet Σ. Then the position tree, $T(\alpha)$, for $\alpha\#$ is a tree whose edges are labeled with elements of
$$\Sigma \cup \{\#\}$$
and is constructed according to the following rules:

(a) $T(\alpha)$ has $(n + 1)$ leaves labeled
$$1, 2, \ldots, n + 1$$
(*see* diagram);

(b) the sequence of labels on the edges of the path from the root to the leaf labeled i is the *substring identifier for position i in $\alpha\#$.

positive acknowledgment *See* acknowledgment. *See also* backward error correction.

positive logic A logic system in which all the Boolean variables and Boolean functions behave as described. *Compare* negative logic.

POSIX An IEEE trial-use standard that defines the behavior of a set of *supervisor calls, basing these closely on those found in *UNIX. However, POSIX is not itself an operating system so much as a formal description of one form of operating system of which UNIX is a specific instance. The intention is that a program written in such a way as to use only those functions defined by the POSIX specifications will be readily *portable between different operating systems, provided that these are all conformant to the POSIX definitions.

Postal, Telegraph, and Telephone administration *See* PTT.

postcondition of a statement S in some program. An *assertion that characterizes the state of the program immediately after execution of S. The postcondition is expressed in terms of properties of certain program variables and relationships between them. Where a program text is annotated by attaching assertions, a postcondition is attached immediately after the statement to which it relates. *See also* precondition, program correctness proof.

postedit *See* postprocessor.

postfix notation *Another name for* reverse Polish notation.

postmortem Analysis of the cause of some undesired system behavior, based upon information recorded at the time that the undesired behavior was detected. For example, *abnormal termination of a program might result in a record of the state of the program at the time of termination, and this record might subsequently be used for postmortem analysis of the reason for termination.

postorder traversal (endorder traversal) A tour of the nodes of a binary tree obtained by using the following recursive algorithm: visit in postorder the left subtree of the root (if it exists); visit in postorder the right subtree of the root (if it exists); visit the root of the tree. *Compare* preorder traversal, symmetric order traversal.

postprocessor A program that performs some operations on the output of another program, typically formatting the output for some device or filtering out unwanted items. This operation is sometimes called a *postedit*.

Post-production system An approach to *effective computability on strings of symbols, formulated by E. L. Post. A *Post-production* is a string rewriting rule. A set of strings is said to be *Post-generable* if there exists a finite set of axioms (strings) and a finite set of Post-productions Σ such that each string in the set can be obtained from the axiom set by some finite derivation, where each step in the derivation is sanctioned by an application of some production in Σ. It turns out that the class of Post-generable sets is exactly the class of *recursively enumerable sets (on some fixed alphabet).

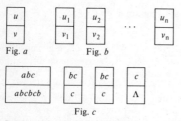

Fig. *a* Fig. *b*

Fig. *c*

Post's correspondence problem

Post's (correspondence) problem A well-known algorithmically unsolvable problem. Given a finite set of "dominoes" of the form shown in Fig. *a*, with *u* and *v* being *strings, the question is whether or not one can form a sequence, as shown in Fig. *b*, such that reading all the *u*s in order gives the same string as reading all the *v*s. Fig. *c* shows such a sequence, where Λ is the empty string. Even though there are only finitely many different dominoes given, there is an infinite supply of duplicates for each one; the same domino can thus be used

more than once in the sequence. Dominoes cannot be inverted.

Depending on the dominoes given, it is sometimes obvious that the answer to the question is "no". However there is no algorithm that can discover this in all cases.

PostScript *Trademark* A *page description language developed by Adobe Systems Inc. It is used in word processors and desktop publishing packages to construct a description of pages to be printed. Pages may contain mixtures of text and graphics. In the printer a Post-Script interpreter converts the page description into a bit image for output.

Powell's algorithm An algorithm that minimizes a function of several variables without calculating derivatives. The method searches to find a direction in which the function decreases and then moves to a new point in that direction. It then searches from this new point. The process continues until no direction can be found that will decrease the function.

power-fail recovery A method of dealing with the effects of a loss of the incoming power supply. The system is equipped with a power line monitor, which detects any long-term deviation in the supply-line voltage from acceptable limits, and causes a *power-fail interrupt* when deviations occur. The service routine for this interrupt stores the *process descriptors for all processes in *nonvolatile memory and then halts all activity. When the supply-line voltage is restored, the system restarts and can reinstate all processes from the previously stored process descriptors.

power-limited channel A physical transmission channel whose rate of throughput of energy is limited to some value. *See* signal-to-noise ratio, channel coding theorem.

power method A method of finding the eigenvalues of a matrix (*see* eigenvalue problems) by successively multiplying a starting vector by the matrix. Convergence depends on the properties of the matrix and in the case of complex eigenvalues further work is needed to find them after convergence.

power routing *See* logic circuit.

power set of a *set S. The set of all *subsets of S, typically denoted by 2^S. It can be described as

$$\{A \mid A \subseteq S\}$$

The number of elements in the power set of S is 2^N, where N is the number of elements in S.

pragma 1. A statement in a programming language that is intended to convey information to a particular implementation, and can be ignored in other implementations of the language.

2. A statement in a programming language that provides information that may assist the compiler in translating the program, but can be ignored without affecting the correct working of the program.

precedence The rules determining the order in which operations are carried out, if this is not defined unambiguously by brackets. For example, in most languages the expression

$$a * b + c$$

will be evaluated by doing the multiplication first, and brackets would be used to enforce the alternative order thus:

$$a * (b + c)$$

There is no consensus about precedence of operations in language, particularly when new operators may be introduced. A simple order used in *Pascal is as follows:

unary NOT
multiplying operators
adding operators
relational operators

Other languages may have further operators such as exponentiation and further categories such as logic operators, whose position in the order would be defined. Operators of the same precedence are usually applied in order from left to right, but in some languages the order is undefined.

precedence parsing A *bottom-up parsing technique that exploits precedence relations on the symbols of the grammar to decide when a string of symbols may be replaced, i.e. form a handle. Two precedence parsing techniques, *operator precedence* and *simple precedence*, are in common use.

In simple precedence three relations, $<\cdot$ $\cdot>$ and $\doteq$, are defined on the symbols (terminal and nonterminal) of the *grammar. If

$$X <\cdot Y, \; X \doteq Y, \text{ or } X \cdot> Y$$

then, respectively, X is said to yield precedence to Y, have the same precedence as Y, or take precedence over Y. Note that these relations are not symmetric. By inserting the precedence relations between symbols in a sentential form and then regarding the $<\cdot$ and $\cdot>$ symbols as matching brackets, a handle is determined as the leftmost string delimited by $<\cdot$ at its left end and $\cdot>$ at its right end.

Operator precedence differs from simple precedence in that the three precedence relations are defined on just the terminal symbols of the grammar. Furthermore the grammar must satisfy the property that nonterminals on the right-hand side of a production must always be separated by at least one terminal.

Arithmetic expressions provided the original motivation for operator precedence since conventionally multiplication takes precedence over addition. Simple precedence is a generalization of operator precedence. Both methods are limited in the scope of their application to grammars for which at most one precedence relation exists between any ordered pair of symbols. In addition the right-hand side of productions must be unique.

precision The number of digits to which numbers are represented. For example, if p bits are allocated to the mantissa in the representation of floating-point numbers used in a particular computer, then in that computer floating-point numbers have p bits of precision. In general, the precision of floating-point numbers is proportional to their value (i.e. relative) whereas the precision of fixed-point numbers is absolute (independent of the value).

It is important not to confuse the term precision with *accuracy*. For example, the number

3.142 8571

has eight-decimal digit precision, irrespective of what it represents. If this number represents 22/7 then it is also accurate to eight decimal digits but if it represents the irrational number π then it is accurate only to three decimal digits.

precondition of a statement S in some program. An *assertion that characterizes the state of the program immediately prior to execution of S. The precondition is expressed in terms of properties of certain program variables and relationships between them. Where a program text is annotated by attaching assertions, a precondition is attached immediately before the statement to which it relates. For a consistent annotation the precondition of S must be implied by the *postcondition of any statement whose execution can immediately precede execution of S. *See also* program correctness proof, weakest precondition.

predicate A *function from some domain to a truth value. If the domain comprises n variables

where $n = 0,1,2, \ldots$

the function is called an n-place predicate. In the special case where $n = 0$,

the predicate is a *statement*. Predicates are the fundamental building blocks of the *predicate calculus.

predicate calculus (predicate logic, first-order logic) A fundamental notation for representing and reasoning with logical statements. It extends *propositional calculus by introducing the *quantifiers, and by allowing *predicates and *functions of any number of arguments. The syntax involves *terms, *atoms*, and *formulae*. An atom (or *atomic formula*) has the form $P(t_1, \ldots, t_k)$, where P is a *predicate symbol* and $t_1, \ldots, t_k$ are terms. Formulae may be built from these atoms in the following ways:

(i) any atom is a formula;

(ii) formulae can be combined by the usual propositional connectives (*negation, *conjunction, *disjunction, etc.);

(iii) if F is a formula, then $\forall v.F$ and $\exists v.F$ are also formulae (*see* quantifier).

A *sentence* is a formula with no *free variables. An example of a sentence is

$$\forall x . G(x,c) \leftrightarrow \forall y . G(f(x,y),y)$$

where $\leftrightarrow$ signifies the *biconditional and G is a predicate symbol, f is a function symbol, x and y are variables, and c is a constant symbol. The overall meaning of a sentence (true or false) depends on the *interpretation given to the symbols occurring in it. For example, let G be interpreted as the predicate "greater than", f as the operation of multiplication, and c as the number 1. Then the above sentence says that a number x is greater than 1 if and only if it has the property that, for all y, xy is greater than y. This is true if the *domain of interpretation* is the *natural numbers, but not if it is the integers (because of the possibility of negative y).

Predicate calculus can claim to be the underlying language of formal discourse since all the more complicated logics can, in some sense, be reduced to it. One possible extension is *second-order logic*, which allows predicate and function variables, such as P in the following:

$$\forall P . [P(a) \wedge \forall k . P(k) \Rightarrow P(s(k))]$$
$$\Rightarrow \forall n . P(n)$$

($\wedge$ and $\Rightarrow$ signify *conjunction and *conditional.) This example, given the appropriate interpretation of a and s, expresses a principle of *induction: if P is true for zero, and true for $k+1$ whenever it is true for k, then it is true for all n. Again this holds for natural numbers but not integers.

Applications of predicate calculus in computer science include formal *specification and *logic programming. *See also* modal logic.

predicate transformer A function that maps predicates to predicates. Specifically, the predicate transformer for some statement S is a function that maps some predicate R into the *weakest precondition of S with respect to R. The term was introduced by Dijkstra in 1975 in conjunction with a calculus for the derivation of programs; this provides for development of a program to be guided by the simultaneous development of a total correctness proof for the program. *See* program correctness proof.

predictive PCM *See* pulse code modulation.

predictor-corrector methods The standard approach in the implementation of *linear multistep methods for the solution of *ordinary differential equations. Two such formulae are used on each step, one of which is implicit (*see* linear multistep methods). An example of such a formula pair are Euler's method (*see* discretization) and the trapezoidal rule (*see* ordinary differential equations). A predictor-corrector method based on these formulae has the form

$$y^p_{n+1} = y_n + hf(x_n, y_n) \text{ (prediction)}$$
$$y_{n+1} = y_n + \tfrac{1}{2}h(f(x_n, y_n) +$$
$$f(x_n, y^p_{n+1})) \text{ (correction)}$$

This permits the more accurate implicit formula to be used effectively, without solving an equation for y_{n+1}, and provides an estimate for the *local error,

namely $y^p_{n+1} - y_{n+1}$. Such estimates are used to control accuracy and *stability.

preemptive allocation An allocation that removes a resource from one *process and transfers it to another. When a process requests use of a resource, the appropriate resource controller will at some stage assign the resource to the process. A resource such as a processor is used for a period of time, during which no other process can use the resource. If during this period of use a second process becomes available to run, the processor scheduler may preempt the processor and transfer it to the second higher-priority process.

A more important type of preemptive allocation arises when a nonsharable resource, such as a tape transport, has been allocated to a process but not yet used by it. If a second process requests a tape transport then use of the transport may be denied the first process, and the transport preempted for use by the second process.

prefix of a string α. Any string β where α is the *concatenation $\beta\gamma$ for some string γ. Thus in coding theory, a word is said to be a prefix of another word if the former word matches the first symbols of the latter. *See also* prefix codes.

prefix codes Codes in which no codeword is a *prefix of any other codeword. The idea is usually applied to *variable-length codes. A prefix code has the property that, as soon as all the symbols of a codeword have been received, the codeword is recognized as such. Prefix codes are therefore said to be *instantaneously decodable*. (They are of necessity *uniquely decodable.)

prefix notation *Another name for* Polish notation.

prefix property The property that no codeword is the *prefix of any other codeword. *See* prefix codes.

preorder traversal A tour of the nodes of a binary tree obtained by using the following recursive algorithm: visit the root of the tree; visit in preorder the left subtree of the root (if it exists); visit in preorder the right subtree of the root (if it exists). *Compare* postorder traversal, symmetric order traversal.

preprocessor A program that performs modifications to data in order to make it suitable for input to another program, especially a *compiler. The modifications may be simple changes of format, or may include *macro expansions.

presentation graphics A field of computer graphics that is limited to the production of the line graphs, bar charts, and pie charts used as visual aids in the presentation of quantitative information on trends and statistics.

presentation layer of network protocol function. *See* seven-layer reference model.

Prestel *Trademark* The public *videotex system run by British Telecom. A number of value-added services are provided, including electronic mail, stockmarket information, banking, and telesoftware.

prestore To store, in advance, data needed by a program, or storage of such data.

pretty printer A program that takes a text file and produces a listing or copy of that file in a format that conforms to some set of conventions for textual layout. Pretty printers are most commonly employed to format the source text of high-level language programs; by performing syntax analysis the pretty printer can produce a layout in which indentation is used to give a simple visual indication of program structure.

preventive maintenance Maintenance performed on a regular basis, and intended to prevent failures or to detect incipient failures. An example of the former is routine lubrication and cleaning of devices that have moving magnetic media. An example of the latter is a *marginal check* in which electrical parameters may be varied to induce failures in marginally performing circuits. *Compare* remedial maintenance.

primary index *See* indexed file.

primary memory *Another name for* main memory, specifically the form used as the medium for storing instructions and data that are currently undergoing processing by a CPU.

prime implicant *See* implicant.

primitive Not capable of being broken down into simpler form. The term is used for example with reference to actions requested by a process via supervisor calls, especially the use of P and V operations (*see* semaphore).

primitive element An element α of a *finite field F whose various powers,
$$\alpha^0 \ (= 1), \ \alpha, \ \alpha^2, \ \alpha^3, \ldots$$
will ultimately include all the nonzero elements of F. Every finite field contains such an element.

primitive polynomial *See* polynomial.

primitive recursion *See* recursion.

primitive recursive function A *function that can be obtained from certain initial functions by a finite number of applications of *composition and *recursion. The initial functions are normally the *zero function, *successor function, and *projection (or generalized identity) functions, where all functions are defined on the nonnegative integers.

The arithmetic functions of addition and multiplication are examples of primitive recursive functions. Indeed many of the functions that can be evaluated by a computer are primitive recursive.

The idea is not restricted to numerical functions: for example, a primitive recursive function on lists satisfies a definition analogous to the one given above, with the successor function adding an element to the front of a list. There is also a notion of *primitive recursive set*, namely one whose *characteristic function is primitive recursive. *See also* recursive function.

primitive type A *data type, such as integer, real, logical, and character, that is made available to the user by the basic hardware. More complex data structures are built up from the primitives, usually by software.

Prim's algorithm A method of finding the minimum-cost *spanning tree of a weighted undirected *graph, developed by R. C. Prim (1957).

principal component analysis *See* multivariate analysis.

printed circuit A physical realization of an electronic circuit design in which the connections between the terminals of individual components are formed from copper conductors laminated onto a flat supporting sheet of an insulating material such as fiber glass. The conductor pattern is normally printed and etched onto the sheet and components are then attached to the copper "lands" by hand or dip soldering. The supporting sheet plus circuit is known as a *printed circuit board (PCB)*.

Double-sided PCBs are commonly produced. These consist of an insulating sheet with a circuit on each side, with interconnections possible between the two circuits. Multilayer printed circuits are also fabricated (*see* multilayer device).

A PCB connects via an appropriate socket to the internal wiring of, say, a computer system. Smaller modular PCBs may be connected to a PCB to enhance its function. *See also* expansion card, edge connector, mother board.

printer An output device that converts the coded information from the processor into a readable form on paper. There are many types, varying in method, speed, and quality of printing: there are *serial printers, *line printers, and *page printers, and these may be *solid-font or *matrix printers. The technology involved may or may not use mechanical impact to transfer ink (*see* impact printer, nonimpact printer).

printer format The *format for printed output, defining the character and line spacing and the areas of the page where printing will occur. In some *line and *serial printers the pitch of characters and lines is selected by switches or is not variable. The format aspect that is often different for each job involves the lines on which printing is not required; this is controlled by a *vertical format unit. Recent designs of serial and *page printers allow the host system to control all aspects of the format by the use of control codes.

printout The output of a printer. Usually it is a stack of fanfolded paper prior to any bursting or trimming operations. Increasingly, desktop printers have the ability to print onto single sheets of paper. *See also* stationery.

print quality The characteristics of the printed characters on a *printout that make them acceptable for their application. These characteristics include degree of conformity with the intended shapes of the characters, uniformity of limb width, uniformity of print density, contrast with the paper, amount of smudging, accuracy of location of the characters compared with their intended positions on the paper, and amount of extraneous ink (or toner in an *electrophotographic printer). The print quality depends on the type of *printer, its age, cleanliness, and condition, the type and amount of previous use of the *ribbon (on impact printers), and the characteristics of the *stationery.

The basic print quality requirement is that all characters must be legible out of context. In the most demanding application, the printed page must have all characters accurately and completely printed with uniform density and high contrast, and no visible flaws. Print quality close to this is known as *correspondence quality*; it is intended to match the quality attainable with a good typewriter. In general, slower impact printers produce higher quality print (*see* daisywheel printer).

Some printouts are intended for data capture via *OCR equipment; examples are debit and payment slips and cheques. These must conform to the standards specifying font shape (e.g. OCR B) and with the minimum print quality standards specified for OCR. These are international standards.

print server *See* server.

prioritize To put into an order according to the relative urgency or importance. In a multiprogramming environment the programs should be prioritized so that urgent jobs are not delayed by background processing tasks. Program interrupts should be similarly treated. *See also* interrupt priority.

priority Relative importance or urgency. Priority is the quality of having precedence, i.e. requiring early attention, and can be quantified by numerical value, used to determine the order in which several requests for a resource are satisfied. In the situation where several otherwise identical processes are free to run, the one with the highest priority will be run next, hence the term *priority processing*. A *priority interrupt* in a system will be dealt with ahead of stan-

dard interrupts that may be awaiting a response. In data transmission a field is allocated to the holding of a code that indicates the relative urgency of the associated message. *See also* interrupt priority.

priority encoder *See* encoder.

priority queue A linear *list where each insertion specifies a priority number as well as the element to be inserted, and each removal or access takes the earliest of the elements with highest priority.

privacy Roughly speaking, the right to be left alone. The law on privacy is vague and judge-made in both the USA and the UK. It is complicated by cases on *trade secrets and has been overtaken by the computer-related version of privacy, data protection. *See* data protection legislation.

With regard to protection against unauthorized reading of computer data, i.e. to the privacy of data, there are two concepts.

1. Protection of data about an individual or corporate entity. Where data can be determined to refer to a specific person, or in some cases to a specific organization, there may exist a legal right to limit access to that data and, in many cases, associated rights to guarantee accuracy and completeness. This form of privacy exists only for data about an identifiable individual, and exists to protect the rights of the individual to whom the data refers. *See* data protection legislation.

2. Protection of data owned by an individual or corporate entity. Where data is deemed to be in some sense the property of someone (or some group) there may exist a right to limit access to that data. This form of privacy exists for data belonging to someone, and exists to protect the rights of the owner of the data. *See* trade secrets. *See also* integrity, security.

privileged instructions Instructions that can only be issued when a computing system is operating in one of the high, or the highest, *execution states.

probability A number between 0 and 1 associated with an event (*see* relative frequency) that is one of a set of possible events: an event that is certain to occur has probability 1. The probability of an event is the limiting value approached by the relative frequency of the event as the number of observations is increased indefinitely. Alternatively it is the degree of belief that the event will occur.

The concept of probability is applied to a wide range of events in different contexts. Originally interest was in the study of games of chance, where correct knowledge of probability values allowed profitable wagers to be made. Later the subject was studied by insurance companies anxious to predict probable future claims on the basis of previously observed relative frequencies. Today probability theory is the basis of statistical analysis (*see* statistical methods).

The *probability calculus* is the set of rules for combining probabilities for combinations of events, using the methods of symbolic logic applied to sets.

See also probability distributions.

probability calculus *See* probability.

probability distributions Theoretical formulas for the *probability that an observation has a particular value, or lies within a given range of values.

Discrete probability distributions apply to observations that can take only certain distinct values, such as the integers 0, 1, 2, ... or the six named faces of a die. A probability, $p(r)$, is assigned to each event such that the total is unity. Important discrete distributions are the *binomial distribution and the *Poisson distribution.

Continuous probability distributions apply to observations, such as physical measurements, where no two observations are likely to be exactly the same. Since the probability of observing exactly a given value is about zero, a mathematical function, the *cumulative distribution function*, $F(x)$, is used instead. This is defined as the probability that the observation does not exceed x. $F(x)$ increases monotonically with x from 0 to 1, and the probability of observing any value between two limits, x_1 and x_2, is

$$F(x_2) - F(x_1)$$

This definition leads, by differential calculus, to the *frequency function*, $f(x)$, which is the limiting ratio of

$$F(x + h) - F(x) \text{ to } h$$

as h becomes small, so that the probability of an observation between x and $(x + h)$ is $h.f(x)$. The most important continuous distribution is the *normal (or Gaussian) distribution.

Probability distributions are defined in terms of *parameters, whose values determine the numerical values of the probabilities.

problem definition A precise statement of some problem to be solved, with the emphasis on providing a complete and unambiguous definition of the problem rather than an easy introduction to it. *Compare* problem description.

problem description A self-contained overview of some problem to be solved, perhaps with accompanying information on constraints that the solution must respect, possible approaches to the solution, etc. *Compare* problem definition.

problem-oriented language *See* POL.

procedural abstraction The principle that any operation that achieves a well-defined effect can be treated by its users as a single entity, despite the fact that the operation may actually be achieved by some sequence of lower-level operations (*see also* abstraction). Procedural abstraction has been extensively employed since the early days of computing, and virtually all programming languages provide support for the concept (e.g. the SUBROUTINE of Fortran, the **procedure** of Algol, Pascal, Ada, etc.).

procedural cohesion *See* cohesion.

procedural language An *imperative *procedure-oriented language.

procedure A section of a program that carries out some well-defined operation on data specified by *parameters. It can be *called from anywhere in a program, and different parameters can be provided for each call.

The term procedure is generally used in the context of high-level languages; in assembly language the word *subroutine is more commonly employed.

procedure-oriented language A programming language that enables a program to be specified by defining a collection of *procedures. These procedures may call each other, and are called by the main program (which can itself be regarded as a procedure).

process 1. (task) A stream of activity. A process is defined by its code, i.e. the ordered set of machine instructions defining the actions that the process is to take, the contents of its *workspace, i.e. the set of data values that it can read, write, and manipulate, and its *process descriptor, which defines the current status of any resources that are allocated to the process.

2. To carry out the actions defined by the sequence of instructions that make up the code of a program.

process control Use of a dedicated computer (known as a *process controller*) to control a specific industrial or manufacturing process. Information (sensed) from that process is used as a source of data; computations made upon that data determine control signals to be sent to the process.

In general there are two forms of process control: *continuous* and *discrete*. Continuous process control is involved with the manufacturing of some form of continuous product, primarily chemicals, e.g. the automatic control of a catalytic cracker for petroleum distillation. Although chemicals may be manufactured in batches, this is still considered a continuous process since the variables that control the process can be varied continuously. Discrete control is concerned with the manufacturing of individual (discrete) items, e.g. the welding of two parts to form a larger assembly. Discrete process control is very closely allied to what is now referred to as *applied robotics*. *See also* numerical control, computer-aided manufacturing, computer-integrated manufacturing.

process descriptor A set of information that defines the status of resources allocated to a *process. When a system contains a number of processes, any of which may be active at any one time, there will be for each process a descriptor defining the status of that process. Within the descriptor the *ready* indicator shows whether the particular process is able to proceed, or whether it must await the completion of some other activity before it can be executed by the CPU. For processes that are unable to run, the process descriptor will indicate the reason for which that process is *suspended* and will contain pointers to relevant queues and semaphores. The process descriptor will also contain a copy of the contents of the processor registers that are to be reinstated when the process is restarted. When a process is running, the process descriptor will contain information (the *resource descriptor*) on the resources allocated to the process and on the permissible operations on these resources.

processor A computer, usually/often the *central processor. *See also* microprocessor, I/O processor, communication processor.

processor allocation The measure of the amount of processor resource that is available to a *process. Normally the allocation will be expressed as a time, or as a number of instructions to be executed.

processor status word (PSW) A word that describes fully the condition of a processor at each instant. It indicates which classes of operations are allowed and which are forbidden, and the status of all interrupts associated with the processor. It will also contain the address of the instruction currently being executed and in many cases contains the address of the word that holds the next instruction to be executed. The PSW is held in a *register known as the *processor status register. See also* program status word.

processor time (CPU time) The time for which a *process has been receiving service from the processor. *See also* system accounting.

product group *Another name for* direct product.

production *See* semi-Thue system, grammar.

production rule system A programming language in which the programs consist of *condition* ⇒ *action* rules. The programs are interpreted by a repetition of the following operations: all rules whose conditions are satisfied are found, one of them is selected, and its action is called. Such systems have been extensively used in *computational psychology and *expert systems. Production rule systems are a kind of *inference engine.

production run Execution of a program in the normal way to produce useful results. *Compare* dry run.

productive time *See* available time.

product of sums expression (POS expression) A *Boolean function expressed as a product of sum terms, i.e. as an AND of OR terms containing uncomplemented or complemented variables. An example is
$$f = (x \lor y) \land (x' \lor z')$$
The function is also realizable as the NOR of a group of NOR terms. *See also* standard product of sums, sum of products expression.

product term A product (AND) of Boolean variables, uncomplemented or complemented. *See also* sum of products expression.

profiling Production of a histogram (or equivalent) concerning some aspect of a system. For example, an *execution profile* for a program might show the proportion of time spent in each individual procedure during a run of the program, while a *statement profile* might show the distribution of the statements in a program between the different kinds of statement provided by the language.

program A set of statements that can be submitted as a unit to some computer system and used to direct the behavior of that system. A *procedural program* gives a precise definition of the procedure to be followed by the computer system in order to obtain the required results. By contrast, a *nonprocedural program* specifies constraints that must be satisfied by the results that are produced but does not specify the procedure by which these results should be obtained; such a procedure must be determined by the computer system itself.

program analysis *See* static analysis.

program compatibility A measure of the degree to which programs can effectively be used together in a common environment. Factors affecting program compatibility include machine and operating system dependencies, and the structure of the data that are read and written by the programs.

program control Control of a computer's functioning by a sequence of instructions that comes from a memory and is called the program.

program correctness proof A formal mathematical demonstration that the *semantics of a program are consistent with some specification for that program (*see* program specification). There are two prerequisites to the provision of such a proof: there must be a formal specification for the program, and there must be some formal definition of the semantics of the programming language. Such a definition may take the form of a set of axioms to cover the semantics of any simple statement in the language, and a set of *inference rules* that show how the semantics of any compound statement, including a complete program, can be inferred from the semantics of its individual component statements (simple or compound).

For a typical sequential program written in some *imperative (procedural) language, the program specification can conveniently be given in the form of two *assertions: an *input assertion* and an *output assertion*. These are expressed in terms of properties of certain program variables and relationships between them. The proof then consists of a formal demonstration that the semantics of the program are consistent with the input and output assertions; this demonstration is of course based upon the formal definition of the semantics of the programming language. Interpreted operationally, the assertions characterize program states and the proof shows that if execution of the program is initiated in a state for which the input assertion is "true" then the program will eventually terminate in a state for which the output assertion is "true".

This kind of proof is known as a *proof of total correctness*. Historically, however, such a proof has often been resolved into two parts: first, a *proof of partial correctness*, which shows that if the program terminates then it does so in a state for which the output assertion is "true", and second, a *proof of termination*, which shows that the program will indeed terminate (normally rather than abnormally).

A common approach to the proof of partial correctness begins by attaching the input and output assertions to the program text at the very beginning and very end respectively. Further assertions, called *intermediate assertions*, are attached to the program text both before and after every statement (simple or compound). The assertion attached immediately before and immediately after a statement are known respectively as the *precondition and *postcondition of that statement.

The proof of partial correctness consists of a formal demonstration that the semantics of each statement in the program, whether simple or compound, are consistent with its precondition and postcondition. This demonstration can begin at the level of the simple statements and then proceed through the various levels of compound statement until eventually it is demonstrated that the semantics of the complete program are consistent with its precondition and postcondition, i.e. with the input assertion and the output assertion. The semantics of an individual statement are shown to be consistent with its precondition and postcondition by applying to the precondition and postcondition the appropriate axiom or inference rule for that statement. This yields a theorem, called a *verification condition*, that must be proved using conventional mathematics in order to demonstrate the required consistency.

Note particularly that the overall proof of correctness is achieved not by consideration of execution histories, but rather by treating the program as a static mathematical object to which certain axioms and inference rules apply.

The central problem with such a proof is the devising of the intermediate assertions. This requires a full appreciation of the design of the program and of the semantics of the programming language. Often the key lies in finding appropriate intermediate assertions to attach inside the various loops in the program, i.e. loop *invariants. Devising intermediate assertions for some arbitrary program is often extremely difficult and a constructive approach, in which program and proof are developed together, is definitely preferable.

In order to present a proof of termination it is necessary to demonstrate first that the program does not suffer from abortive termination and second that the program does not endlessly repeat some loop. A demonstration of the former may become very complex, e.g. it may be necessary to demonstrate that arithmetic overflow will not occur. A demonstration that the program will eventually exit from some loop can be based on a *well-ordered set. For example, suppose that for some loop an expression E can be found such that the loop can be shown to terminate immediately if the value of E is negative. Further suppose that the value of E can be shown to decrease on each iteration around the loop. It then follows that the loop must terminate.

Proofs of correctness do not offer a complete solution to the problems of software reliability in practical systems. The sheer size and complexity of proofs presents many difficulties that are only partly alleviated by *mechanical verifier systems. Issues such as the limitations of computer arithmetic, indeterminacy, and parallelism all present additional prob-

lems. It may be very difficult to develop a specification against which to verify a program, and impossible to demonstrate that this specification is itself "correct" in that it properly reflects the intentions of the developers.

Work on proofs of correctness has made a major contribution to software engineering in that many advances in the understanding of programming languages, principles, and methods have their origins in this work. In addition the scope for practical applications of program proofs is growing and the formal approach to program correctness is of increasing significance.

program counter (instruction counter; current address register) A counting *register that normally increments one memory address at a time and is used to obtain the program sequence (i.e. the sequence of instructions) from sequential memory locations. This counter will have its contents changed by branch instructions.

program decomposition The breaking down of a complete program into a set of component parts, normally called modules. The decomposition is guided by a set of design principles or criteria that the identified modules should reflect. Since the decomposition determines the coarse structure of the program, the activity is also referred to as *high-level* or *architectural design*. *See also* modular programming, program design.

program design The activity of progressing from a specification of some required program to a description of the program itself. Most phase models of the *software life-cycle recognize program design as one of the phases. The input to this phase is a specification of what the program is required to do. During the phase the design decisions are made as to how the program will meet these requirements, and the output of the phase is a description of the program in some form that provides a suitable basis for subsequent implementation.

Frequently the design phase is divided into two subphases, one of coarse *architectural design* and one of *detailed design*. The architectural design produces a description of the program at a gross level; it is normally given in terms of the major components of the program and their interrelationships, the main algorithms that these components employ, and the major data structures. The detailed design then refines the architectural design to the stage where actual implementation can begin. *See also* program design language.

program design language (PDL) A language, used for expressing *program designs, that is similar to a conventional high-level programming language but emphasizes structure and intention rather than the ability to execute programs expressed in the language. PDLs are often employed in conjunction with *structured programming. When not executable they are termed *pseudolanguages.

Typically the formal syntax of a PDL would cover data definition and overall program structure. Facilities in the latter area would include the basic control-flow constructs – sequential, conditional, and iterative – plus those for the definition and invocation of subroutines. These facilities would be used to define the overall framework of the program, but individual actions within the framework would be expressed using pseudolanguage – natural English or a more formal semantically rich language. Correspondingly, the PDL facilities for data definition may be expected to be richer than those of a typical programming language, encompassing a broader range of basic types and a more extensive set of data-structuring facilities. A wide variety of PDLs have been defined; normal practice is to select one that is well-matched to the target programming language.

program development system A computer system that provides support to the program development phase of a software project. A typical program development system employs a simple database (or perhaps just a basic filing system) as a repository for information, and offers *software tools for editing of program source texts, compiling, link loading, and debugging. Usually some form of command-language interpreter is also available; this may have been produced specifically for the program development system, or may have been inherited from the underlying operating system. *Compare* software engineering environment.

program file A *file containing one or more programs, or program fragments, in *source code or *object code form.

program library (software library) A collection of programs and packages that are made available for common use within some environment; individual items need not be related. A typical library might contain compilers, utility programs, packages for mathematical operations, etc. Usually it is only necessary to reference the library program to cause it to be automatically incorporated in a user's program.

program listing (source listing; listing) An output produced by a *compiler or *assembler, consisting of the source program neatly laid out and accompanied by diagnostic information and error messages. In the case of an assembler, the listing may also include a readable version of the object code.

programmable array logic *See* PAL.

programmable devices 1. Devices under the control of a *stored program obeyed by a *fetch-execute cycle. *See* computer, central processor.

2. Integrated circuits whose action is determined by the user either until reprogrammed (*erasable programmable devices*) or for the life of the device (*nonerasable programmable devices*). Erasable devices are usually implemented by the storage of static electric charges, whereas nonerasable devices either employ *fusible links or have their structure determined at the final masking stage of manufacture.

Static charge or fusible-link devices are called *field-programmable*, since they may be programmed by the user "in the field", i.e. on the customer's premises; masked devices are called *mask-programmable*, implying programmability only at the time of manufacture. This terminology is common for *programmed logic. In the case of read-only memory the same distinction often appears as "programmable" (*PROM) and, by implication, as "nonprogrammable" (*ROM).

programmable gate array *See* PGA.

programmable logic array *See* PLA.

programmable logic device *See* PLD.

programmable ROM *See* PROM.

program maintenance *See* software maintenance.

programmed I/O A way of controlling input/output activity in which the processor is programmed to interrogate a peripheral or a number of peripherals to see if they are ready for a data transfer. When a number of peripherals are involved the interrogation process is called *polling. *Compare* interrupt I/O.

programmed logic In general, *programmable devices that are more complicated (logical) than read-only memories, thus including programmed logic arrays (*see* PLA), programmed gate arrays (PGAs), programmed-array logic (PAL), and uncommitted logic arrays (ULAs).

programmed logic array *See* PLA.

programmer 1. A person responsible for writing computer programs. *See* applications programmer, systems programmer.

2. *See* PROM programmer.

programmer unit *Another name for* PROM programmer, and also applied to equipment for programming other field-programmable devices (*see* programmable devices).

programming In the broadest sense, all technical activities involved in the production of a *program, including analysis of requirements and all stages of design and implementation. In a much narrower sense it is the coding and testing of a program from some given design. This narrower usage is most common in the context of commercial programming, where a distinction is often drawn between systems analysts, who are responsible for analysis of requirements and design, and programmers, who are responsible for implementaton and testing.

programming language A notation for the precise description of computer programs or algorithms. Programming languages are *artificial* languages, in which the *syntax and *semantics are strictly defined. Thus while they serve their purpose they do not permit the freedom of expression that is characteristic of a natural language.

programming standards A set of rules or conventions that constrain the form of the programs that are produced within an organization. Such rules may range in scope from those that address the high-level design and decomposition of the program to *coding standards*, which govern the use of individual constructs provided by the programming language.

programming support environment *See* PSE (def. 1).

programming theory A general term for a number of interrelated and rapidly developing subjects concerned broadly with the application of formal mathematical methods to the study of programming concepts. Principle areas are: *semantics of programming languages, *program correctness proof; *program transformation, *program specification, and programming methodology.

program proving *See* program correctness proof.

program specification A precise statement of the effects that an individual program is required to achieve. It should clearly state what the program is to do without making any commitment as to how this is to be done. For a program that is intended to terminate, the program specification can take the form of an input-output specification that describes the desired mapping from the set of input values to the set of output values. For cyclic programs, which are not designed to terminate, it is not possible to give a simple input-output specification; normal practice is to focus attention on the individual functions performed by the program during its cyclic operations.

For both terminating and cyclic programs a variety of notations have been employed for program specifications, ranging from natural language with embedded equations and tables to formal notations such as those based upon first-order *predicate calculus. *See also* software specification, module specification.

program status word (PSW) A collection of information that permits an interrupted process to resume operation after the interrupt has been handled. The information is held in the *program status register*, and usually contains the value of the program counter and bits indicating the status of various conditions in the ALU such as overflow and carry,

along with the information on supervisor privileged status. *See also* processor status word.

program structure The overall form of a program, with particular emphasis on the individual components of the program and the interrelationships between these components. Programs are frequently referred to as either *well structured* or *poorly structured*. With a well-structured program the division into components follows some recognized principle such as *information hiding, and the interfaces between components are explicit and simple. By contrast, with a poorly structured program the division into components is largely arbitrary (or even nonexistent), and interfaces are implicit and complex. At a finer level, a well-structured program employs appropriate data structures and program units with a single entry point and a single exit point (*see* structured programming, def. 2), while a poorly structured program has arbitrary data structures and flow of control.

program testing Checking by means of actual execution whether a program behaves in the desired manner. The program is executed and supplied with test data, and the way in which the program responds to this test data is analyzed. *Compare* program correctness proof.

program transformation The study of systematic ways of transforming a program into another program that has some desirable property and is equivalent to the original program (or, if not equivalent, has a meaning bearing a simple relation to that of the original).

Often the aim of such transformation is to produce a more efficient program. It is widely felt that much of the complexity of programming results from the need to produce efficient programs, and that it is therefore desirable to begin with a simple (yet inefficient) program and then transform it to an efficient (but complicated) one. Such transformations may be carried out by hand, by machine, or by a mixture of the two.

Other aims of transformation include expressing certain *language constructs in terms of others (*transformational semantics*). Also, developing algorithms by transformation can serve to verify their correctness, to elucidate their structure, and to provide a classification of the space of possible algorithms. *See also* refinement.

program unit A constituent part of a large program, and in some sense self-contained.

program verification Any method that will ensure that a program will do exactly what it is supposed to do. *See also* program correctness proof.

projection function The function U_i^n that extracts the ith coordinate from an ordered n-tuple (*see* ordered pair). More formally

$$U_i^n(x_1, x_2, \ldots x_n) = x_i$$

See also primitive recursive function.

project support environment *See* PSE (def. 2).

PROLOG (or **Prolog**) A *logic programming language, widely used in artificial intelligence. The basic element of PROLOG programs is the *atom*, which expresses a simple relationship among individuals, the latter being named (in the simplest sense) either by constants or by variables. (Note that this is not the usual meaning of "atom" in programming.) Examples of atoms are "Mary is the sister of Jane", where Mary and Jane are both constants; "Adam is an ancestor of x", where Adam is a constant and x is a variable.

A program in PROLOG consists of a collection of (*Horn clause) sentences, where each sentence is either a simple assertion or an implication. The former consists of a single atom, while the latter takes the form

"A if B1 and B2 and ... and Bn" where the conclusion A and the conditions B1 ... Bn are all atoms. An example of an implication is

"x is a grandfather of y if x is the father of z and z is a parent of y"

A PROLOG program is invoked by presenting a *query* in the form of a collection of atomic conditions

"A1 and A2 and ... and An"

Execution of the program then determines a set of values for the variables of the query such that the truth of the query then follows from the assertions and implications of the program (assuming that such a set of values exist).

PROLOG has been selected as the basis for the Japanese *fifth generation computers. *See also* Turbo languages.

PROM *Acronym for* programmable read-only memory. A form of semiconductor read-only memory, *ROM, whose contents are added by a separate process after the device has been manufactured. This process of programming the PROM is accomplished by means of a device known as a *PROM programmer. In general the programming process involves the destruction of *fusible links within the PROM and is irreversible, i.e. the contents of the memory cannot be altered. Certain PROMs, including *EPROMs, can however be reprogrammed numerous times.

PROM programmer (programmer unit) An item of equipment that establishes the correct conditions for the programming of a *PROM device and thus allows the user to program the PROM. The programming process often requires the physical destruction of fusible links within the PROM using relatively high voltage pulses, hence the jargon terms PROM zapping, blowing, blasting, and burning. Such equipment may be capable of programming a number of different types of PROM and/or *EPROM devices.

$$\langle wff \rangle ::= \langle atf \rangle \mid (\sim \langle wff \rangle) \mid (\langle wff \rangle \vee \langle wff \rangle) \mid$$
$$(\langle wff \rangle \wedge \langle wff \rangle) \mid (\langle wff \rangle \supset \langle wff \rangle) \mid$$
$$(\langle wff \rangle \equiv \langle wff \rangle) \mid$$
$$(\text{IF } \langle wff \rangle \text{ THEN } \langle wff \rangle \text{ ELSE } \langle wff \rangle)$$

Fig. 1 Class of wffs in BNF notation, used in propositional calculus

$$\frac{\Gamma \rightarrow A \text{ and } \Gamma \rightarrow B}{\Gamma \rightarrow A \wedge B}$$

$$\frac{\Gamma \rightarrow A \wedge B}{\Gamma \rightarrow A} \qquad \frac{\Gamma \rightarrow A \wedge B}{\Gamma \rightarrow B}$$

Fig. 2 Rule of inference for $\wedge$

prompt A short message, sent from a *process to a user, indicating that the process expects the user to present fresh data. The prompt frequently has some mnemonic content indicating the type of data expected.

PROM zapping *Jargon* The process of programming a *PROM using a *PROM programmer.

propagation delay The time required for a change in the input to a *logic gate or *logic circuit to produce a change in the output. It is usually very brief. It is inherent in any gate or circuit, being caused by unavoidable delays in transistor switching and propagation of electrical signals through passive components.

proper ancestor *See* ancestor.

proper subset, subgroup, subgraph *See* subset, subgroup, subgraph respectively.

propositional calculus A system of *symbolic logic, the study of which is known as *propositional logic*. There are many alternative but equivalent definitions, one of the more useful for the computer scientist being given below.

The only admissible terms of the propositional calculus are the two symbols *T* and *F* together with logical propositions that are denoted by small letters; these symbols are basic and indivisible and are thus called *atomic formulas*.

The propositional calculus is based on the study of *well-formed formulas* or wffs for short. Common wffs of the form

$(\sim A)$, $(A \vee B)$, $(A \wedge B)$,
$(A \supset B)$, $(A \equiv B)$,
(IF *A* THEN *B* ELSE *C*)

are formed from appropriate wffs *A*, *B*, and *C* using logical *connectives; they are called respectively *negation, disjunction, conjunction, implication, equivalence,* and *conditional*. If $<atf>$ denotes the class of atomic formulas, then the class of wffs, $<wff>$, can be described in *BNF notation (*see* Fig. 1).

Proofs and theorems within the propositional calculus should be conducted in a formal and rigorous manner: certain basic axioms can be assumed and certain *rules of inference* must be followed. In particular these rules must provide some formal method of dealing with the various connectives.

The rules of inference are stated using a form such as

$$\frac{\alpha}{\beta}$$

The rule should be interpreted to mean that on the assumption that α is true, it can be deduced that β is then true. (This notation is used in computing circles though logicians often use a notation such as $\alpha\vdash\beta$.) In writing the rules it is convenient to employ a notation such as

$$\Gamma, A \Rightarrow B$$

Γ is some set of wffs whose truth has been established; A and B are some other wffs highlighted for the purposes of the rule; $\Rightarrow$ denotes implication (to avoid confusion with the symbol $\supset$). For example, the rules for the introduction and elimination respectively of the $\wedge$ connective are shown in Fig. 2.

protected location A memory location that can only be accessed by an authorized user or process. *See also* memory protection.

protection domain A set of access privileges to protected resources. Where many *processes coexist, each process having differing access permission to a number of protected resources via some form of key, it may be convenient to group together a set of such keys in order to provide a single process with access to the resources that it requires. Access control can then be manipulated independent of the processes concerned. The protection domain is either the set of keys, or equivalently, the set of resources to which the keys give access.

protocol An agreement that governs the procedures used to exchange information between cooperating entities. More specifically, a protocol is such an agreement operating between entities that have no direct means of exchanging information, but that do so by passing information across a local interface to so-called *lower-level* protocols, until the lowest, physical, level is reached. The information is transferred to the remote location using the lowest-level protocol, and then passes upward via the interfaces until it reaches the corresponding level at the destination. In general, a protocol will govern the format of messages, the generation of checking information, and the flow control, as well as actions to be taken in the event of errors.

A set of protocols, governing the exchange of information between (physically remote) communicating entities at a given level, and the set of interfaces governing the exchange between (physically adjacent) protocol levels, are collectively referred to as *protocol hierarchy* or a *protocol stack*.

See also seven-layer reference model.

protocol hierarchy *See* protocol.

protocol stack *See* protocol.

protocol translation *See* internetworking.

prototype *See* software prototyping.

PSE 1. *Abbrev. for* programming support environment. A computer system that provides support for the programming aspects (only) of the *expression of requirements, and in development, repair, and enhancement of programs. A typical system contains a central database and a set of *software tools. The central database acts as a repository for all the information related to the programming activities.

PSEs vary in the general nature of their databases and in the coverage provided by, and the degree of cooperative interaction of, the set of tools and the programming languages supported (*see* APSE). In particular some encourage (even enforce) one specific *software engineering methodology, while others provide only general support and thereafter allow any of a variety of methodologies to be adapted.

A programming support environment might be considered as a technology level intermediate between a *program development system and computer-assisted software engineering (*CASE); the term is sometimes used synonymously with both.

2. *Abbrev. for* project support environment. A computer system that provides support for the programming aspects AND the project control and management aspects of a software-intensive project. The project support environment will have all the features of a programming support environment (see above) plus a set of *software tools associated with the management and control of the project. *See also* IPSE.

pseudocode *Another name for* pseudo-language.

pseudoinstruction **(pseudo-operation; directive)** An element in an assembly language that is similar to an instruction but provides control information to the assembler as opposed to generating a particular instruction. Examples are:

generate absolute code/generate relative addresses;

start a new segment;

allocate space for constants or variables.

pseudolanguage (pseudocode) A notation resembling a programming language, used for program design. Pseudolanguage is an effective substitute for the *flowchart: unlike a programming language it is not necessary to have a compiler to convert it into executable code. A pseudolanguage usually incorporates the control-flow primitives of a programming language, but combines these with a narrative prose description of the computation to be carried out, e.g.

while not end-of-file

deal with the next character

pseudonoise sequence (PN sequence) A sequence of symbols with *pseudoran-dom properties intended to simulate *noise. Most commonly *m-sequences are used.

pseudo-operation *Another name for* pseudoinstruction.

pseudorandom Mimicking randomness. A *deterministic process, which cannot in principle be random, may nevertheless exhibit any number of the properties of randomness to any desired degree (by appropriate design), and so may serve as a surrogate random process; it is then called pseudorandom.

pseudorandom numbers *See* random numbers.

PSK *Abbrev. for* phase shift keying.

PSL/PSA *Abbrev. for* problem statement language/problem statement analyzer. A computerized system that can be used for the development and analysis of an *expression of requirements and to provide assistance during system design. The expression of requirements is maintained in a computer database: PSL is the input language to this database while PSA is the management system and report generator for the database.

The basic database model consists of objects that may have properties and may be interconnected by means of relationships. The types of object and relationship are predefined within PSL, there being more than 20 kinds of object and more than 50 kinds of relationship. The objects and relationships are concerned with various aspects of the system for which requirements are being expressed: system input/output flow, system structure, data structure, data derivation, system size and volume, system dynamics, system properties, and project management. PSA permits the analysis of the database and the production of various kinds of report, e.g. on database modifications, database content, and on unused data objects or breaks in information flow.

PSL/PSA was developed by Daniel Teichroew on the ISDOS project at the University of Michigan. The system has been implemented on a wide range of computers and has been used extensively by many organizations.

PSPACE, PSPACE-complete *See* polynomial space.

PSS *Abbrev. for* packet switch stream. The *public packet network of British Telecom; it offers a national packet switched data service and has been available since 1981. It uses the *X.25 interface protocol, providing full duplex working at a range of speeds up to and including 48 000 bps; it can also provide intercommunication between data terminal equipment operating at different speeds. Connections to other public packet networks can be made.

PSW *Abbrev. for* processor status word, program status word.

p-system A software system for microcomputers developed from *UCSD Pascal. The system provides a number of languages in a uniform manner, using p-code as a common intermediate language.

PTI *Abbrev. for* public tool interface. A concept made necessary as *PSEs – project and programming support environments – increase the degree of and demand for information exchange and interaction between various *software tools, especially tools from different suppliers. A common specification is required for the interface between the tools and the *object management system. Similarly as an increasing number of tools are used within a single development, it becomes desirable to have a common *user interface for the tools (assisting the user to learn the interface and get the best out of the tools). Both these interfaces are included within a PTI. Examples of PTI standards include

*PCTE, PCTE+ and *CAIS-A. *See also* IPSE.

PTIME *See* polynomial time.

PTO *Abbrev. for* Public Telecommunications Operator. A UK agency licensed to provide data transmission services between widely separated points. Until the reorganization of the UK telecommunications market in the mid-1980s, British Telecom (BT) held a virtual monopoly in the provision of data transmission services in the UK. At the time of the BT privatization, legislation was enacted that meant PTOs could act as providers of such services. There are at present only three PTOs: BT, Mercury (a privately owned company), and for purely historical reasons Hull City Corporation.

PTT Postal, Telegraph, and Telephone Administration, the national governmental agency that provides communication services in many countries, and that frequently also acts as the regulatory agency for these services. In many cases the PTT has a monopoly on communication services; even where there is not a monopoly the PTT will be the agency that represents the country on the *CCITT, and will be responsible for the provision of international services. The image of PTTs has been as suppliers of limited data communications facilities, based on lower-speed services such as 300 bps lines for the telex system, or voice-grade medium-speed lines requiring the use of modems and operating at speeds up to 9600 bps, using *V.24 or *RS232C standards.

However, in response to external competition and to internal pressure from within each country, PTTs have become much more aggressive: they offer services using inherently digital interfaces such as X.21 or V.35 at speeds of 48 or 64 kbps, or in some countries even higher speeds of 2.048 Mbps (1.536 Mbps in the USA and Canada), as well as both national and international packet switching services based on *X.25 protocols. *See also* common carrier.

p-type semiconductor *See* semiconductor.

public key system A system of *cryptography in which the enciphering and deciphering processes use different keys, thereby allowing the encryption key to be made public. In a typical system, each user has a unique secret decryption key for which there is a corresponding public encryption key issued to any intending message originator. The originator encrypts the message using the public key but only the recipient is able to decipher the message.

public packet network (public data network) A network providing *packet switching services to public customers. In most countries the public packet networks are offered by the national *PTT, a governmental organization; public packet networks in the US are offered by *common carriers licensed by the FCC. Most public packet networks are based on the *X.25 interface protocol and related CCITT standards. Examples of public networks are *Telenet, *Tymnet, *PSS, *Transpac, and *Datapac.

public tool interface *See* PTI.

pull-down menu A *menu that appears on a computer screen when its title, often one of a row of such titles across the top of the screen, is selected by means of a *mouse or other *pointing device or a sequence of keystrokes. One or more of the menu options may then be selected in the same way, after which the menu will normally vanish.

pull-up resistor A resistor that is connected between the power-supply line and a logic line and ensures that the line is normally pulled up to the supply potential. *Open-collector logic devices may be connected to the logic line and each device is then capable of pulling the line low, i.e. to ground.

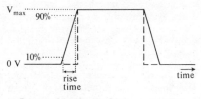

Rectangular voltage pulse

pulse A transient change in voltage, current, or some other normally constant physical parameter. This transient consists of a fixed-amplitude geometrically defined transition, followed, after a fixed time, by an opposite and often equal amplitude transition.

For rectangular pulses the transitions should in theory be stepwise, i.e. instantaneous. In reality however they require a finite time in which to occur. For transitions from low to high voltage, current, etc., a convenient measure of this time is the *rise time*, defined as the time required for the pulse amplitude to rise from 10% to 90% of its maximum value (*see* diagram). The *decay time* is an analogous measure for high to low transitions and is defined as the time required for the pulse amplitude to decay from 90% to 10% of its maximum value.

The time interval between the rising and falling edge of a rectangular pulse is called the *pulse width*. The *pulse height* is the amplitude of a pulse, usually its maximum to minimum voltage, current, etc., ignoring any short-duration spikes or low-amplitude ripple superimposed on the main pulse. *See also* ringing.

pulse code modulation (PCM) A technique used by *codecs to convert an analog signal into a digital bit stream.

The amplitude (usually) of the analog signal is sampled (8000 samples per second for voice-quality telephone lines with 4000 Hz bandwidth), and a digital code is selected to represent the sampled value. The digital code is transmitted to the receiving end, which uses it to generate an analog output signal. Encoding techniques may be used to reduce the amount of data that is transmitted between the sender and the receiver, based on known characteristics of the analog signal. For example, *mu-law (μ-law) encoding* converts the analog signal to a digital code based on the logarithm of its value, rather than on a linear transformation.

Differential PCM (DPCM) transmits the difference between the current sample and the previous sample. DPCM assumes that the difference requires fewer bits than the signal amplitude.

Delta (Δ) PCM is a version of DPCM in which a single bit is used for each sample, representing a signal change of plus or minus one unit. A constant signal is represented as a series of plus or minus transitions.

Predictive PCM extrapolates from the previous few samples what the next sample should be, and transmits the difference between the actual value and the predicted value.

See also modulation.

pulse generator A circuit or instrument that generates a sequence of *pulses, usually (but not necessarily) of uniform height, width, and repetition rate or frequency.

pulse height *See* pulse.

pulse repetition rate (pulse repetition frequency) of a *pulse train. The average number of pulses that occur per second, expressed in hertz.

pulse shaping Alteration of the shape of a *pulse. Usually pulse-shaping circuits receive pulses that are distorted and convert them into rectangular pulses; sometimes they incorporate a *monostable circuit to set the output pulse width.

pulse stretcher An electronic device that is often included in logic circuitry in order to extend the duration of very short input pulses. This ensures that the pulses are of adequate length, i.e. they are of the minimum duration required for reliable processing by the circuitry. A *monostable is often used for this purpose.

pulse train A repetitive series of *pulses, separated in time by a fixed and often constant interval. The duration of each pulse and its amplitude are also often made constant. This type of waveform may be defined by its *mark-space ratio*, i.e. the ratio of pulse duration, t_1, to pulse separation, t_2, and by its *pulse repetition rate, which is given by

$$1/(t_1 + t_2)$$

pulse-triggered flip-flop *See* flip-flop.

pulse width *See* pulse.

pumping lemmas Two theorems in formal language theory that express necessary conditions for languages to be *regular or *context-free:

If language L is regular, there exists an integer n such that, for any *word z in L, $|z| > n$, there exist u,v,w with

$z = uvw$, v nonempty, $|vw| \leqslant n$,

such that:

$$uv^k w \in L, \text{ for all } k \geqslant 0$$

If language L is context-free, there exist integers p and q such that, for any z in L, with $|z| > p$, there exist u,v,w,x,y with

$z = uvwxy$, v and x nonempty,

$$|vwx| \leqslant q,$$

such that:

$$uv^k wx^k y \in L, \text{ for all } k \geqslant 0$$

punch card *Another name for* punched card, sometimes used to refer to a card that has not yet been punched.

punched card (punch card) A rectangular paper card, typically 0.007″ (0.178 mm) thick, into which data has been – or can be – encoded by punching holes that are sensed by a *punched card reader. Punched cards were used extensively for input, output, and file storage of data on early computer systems but are now obsolete.

The cards are of a uniform size and are notionally divided into a number of *columns* that are parallel to the short edge and a number of *rows* – usually 12 – parallel to the long edge. The 80 column card, 7.375″ by 3.25″ (18.73 by 8.25 cm) in size, was the most common type; each column is divided into 12 positions at which holes can be punched, a particular combination of holes in a column representing a specific character. Other types of card have also been devised with as few as 21 columns and as many as 160. The last type of punched card to be widely used was the 96 column IBM card.

Prior to the development of computers a variety of machines were available that enabled the various activities of data processing, e.g. sorting, collating, and listing or tabulating, to be carried out using data files composed of punched cards. Stout cards with holes punched in them were used by Jacquard to control the weaving of patterns on a loom in about 1800. Charles Babbage saw the possibility of using punched cards to control his *Analytical Engine, conceived in the 1830s.

In the 1880s Herman Hollerith, a statistician at the US Census Bureau, developed a machine that electrically sensed holes punched in cards and could sort and accumulate totals; the machines were used in the 1890 census. In 1896 Hollerith formed his own company, which was later to become IBM.

punched card reader An obsolete but once widely used machine that could sense data encoded on a card as a pattern of punched holes and convert it into a series of binary codes. In many later designs a stack of punched cards was placed in the input hopper and the machine would pick the cards singly and in sequence and enter them into a track. The card was driven at a constant speed between a light source and 12 photocells, which sensed the light passing through the punchings; the card was then deposited in a stacker.

The electronics associated with the reader mechanism converted the signals from the 12 photocells into appropriate 6 or 8 bit binary codes and either transmitted them via an interface or put them into an internal buffer for subsequent transmission. In a *serial card reader* cards were read column by column (i.e. one character at a time), generally at speeds between 150 and 2000 cards per minute. In a *parallel card reader* cards were read row by row, so reducing the time to read a card.

punched tag A small card that is encoded with a pattern of holes and attached to a product in a shop or factory. When the product is sold or moves to a different part of the factory the tag – or part of it – is removed and fed into a machine that senses the holes. The data thus captured is a valuable aid to stock and production control. The most prominent punched tag system in retail applications is the *Kimball tag*.

punched tape *See* paper tape.

punch tape *See* paper tape.

pure BCD *Another name for* natural BCD. *See* binary-coded decimal.

push *See* stack (def. 1).

pushdown automaton (PDA) A *finite-state automaton augmented by a *stack of symbols that are distinct from the symbols in the input string. Like the finite-state automaton, the PDA reads its input string once from left to right, with acceptance or rejection determined by the final state. After reading a symbol, however, the PDA performs the following actions: change state, remove top of stack, and push zero or more symbols onto stack. The precise choice of actions depends on the input symbol just read, the current state, and the current top of stack. Since the stack can grow unboundedly, a PDA can have infinitely many different configurations – unlike a finite-state automaton.

A *nondeterministic PDA* is one that has a choice of actions for some conditions. The languages recognized by nondeterministic PDAs are precisely the *context-free languages. However not every context-free language is recognized by a deterministic PDA.

pushdown stack, pushdown list *Other names for* stack (def. 1).

pushup stack, pushup list *Other names for* queue. *See also* stack (def. 2).

PXBLT (or **pxblt**) *Abbrev. for* pixel block transfer. A graphics function that can move a block of pixels from one position on a display to another.

Q

QA *Abbrev. for* quality assurance.

q-ary (q-valued) Having q values, where q is a positive integer not less than 2. In *logic circuits, the treatment of q values is called *multiple-valued logic, or binary logic for $q = 2$. In coding theory, some codes are restricted to the binary case; others can operate with arbitrary q or with q a prime number. Throughout switching and coding theory, the binary

case is by far the most important. *See also* polynomial.

q-ary logic *Digital logic employing q states. The term is sometimes used to mean digital logic in general, but more usually has the implication that there are more than two states, in which case the term is synonymous with *multiple-valued logic.

QC *Abbrev. for* quality control.

QL *Abbrev. for* query language.

QR factorization A method used in *numerical linear algebra in order to solve a set of linear equations, $Ax = b$, where A is a real square matrix and b is a column vector. In this method, the matrix A is decomposed into the form
$$A = QR \quad (1)$$
where Q is *orthogonal and R is upper (or right) *triangular. If equation (1) is transposed as
$$A' = RQ \quad (2)$$
then, since Q is orthogonal, (1) gives
$$R = Q^{T}A \quad (3)$$
Replacing (3) with (2) gives
$$A' = Q^{T}AQ \quad (4)$$
which is solved for the eigenvalues of A.

quadrature *Another name for* numerical integration.

qualifier register A set of *indicators that record the status or condition of the last result output from the *arithmetic and logic unit. It forms part of the *processor status word.

quality assurance *See* software quality assurance.

quality control (QC) The use of sampling, inspection, and testing methods at all levels of system production to produce defect-free hardware and software.

quality management system *See* software quality assurance.

quantifier One of the two symbols ∀ or ∃ used in *predicate calculus. ∀ is the *universal quantifier* and is read "for all". ∃ is the *existential quantifier* and is read "there exists" or "for some". In either case the reference is to possible values of the variable v that the quantifier introduces. $\forall v . F$ means that the formula F is true for all values of v, while $\exists v . F$ means that F is true for at least one value of v. As an example, suppose that $P(x,y)$ is the predicate "x is less than or equal to y". Then the following expression

$$\exists x . \forall y . P(x,y)$$

says that there exists an x that is less than or equal to all y. This statement is true if values range over the *natural numbers, since x can be taken to be 0. It becomes false however if values are allowed to range over negative integers as well. Note also that it would be false even for natural numbers if the predicate were "x is less than y". Other notations such as $(\forall v)F$ in place of $\forall v . F$ are also found.

quantization The process of constructing a discrete representation of a quantity that is usually regarded as continuous (*see* discrete and continuous systems). For example, the measurement of the amplitude of a *signal at discrete intervals of time, when the signal occurs over continuous time, is called *time quantization*, or *sampling*; the measurement of the brightness of picture elements (*pixels) in a space-continuous picture is called *space quantization*, or *pixelization*.

The term quantization without the predication of time or space usually refers to the quantization of amplitude; the same applies to *digitization, which is nearly synonymous with quantization.

quantization noise The effective continuous noise power, the addition of which to a continuous signal has the same effect as the amplitude *quantization to which the signal is subjected (*see* dis-

crete and continuous systems). The effect of time *quantization may also be described by the addition of noise, but in a more complex way. *See also* Nyquist's criterion.

quantizer An electronic device that can convert an *analog signal into a signal having values that are identical to the analog signal only at discrete instants of time. The action is analogous to observing, i.e. *sampling, the analog signal, approximating it by the nearest preferred value and holding this value until the next observation time. The output signal thus consists of a number of steps between specified levels. *See also* digitizer.

quantum The amount of time allocated to an individual *process in a *time-slicing process-management system. *See also* scheduling algorithm.

quasi- Seemingly; mimicking. It is a combining form used sometimes in computing in place of pseudo-, as in quasi-random numbers or quasi-instruction.

quaternary logic *See* multiple-valued logic.

Qube A US *videotex system.

query by example A screen-based form-filling *user interface to *databases, usually oriented toward less experienced users. The software derives the searches to be made from the examples given by the user, who marks fields or fills in values for fields on the form.

query language (QL) A *data manipulation language that is available interactively to end-users. *See also* query processing, SQL.

query processing 1. The retrieval of a set of values from a *file or a *database according to a set of retrieval criteria, leaving the contents of the file or database unchanged. In the case of a database, the retrieval criteria may be expressed in a query language (*see* data manipulation language).

2. In the specific context of a query language (see def. 1), the translation of the retrieval criteria into a set of primitive commands for transmission to the operating system.

queue (FIFO list; pushup stack; pushup list) A linear *list where all insertions are made at one end of the list and all removals and accesses at the other. Like a pushdown *stack, a queue can be implemented in hardware as a specialized form of addressless memory, and is most commonly used for speed buffering between a real-time data input/output stream and a form of memory that requires start/stop time.

queue management A queue is characterized by the way in which customers (i.e. processes) join it in order to wait for service, and by the way in which customers already in the queue are selected for servicing. Both of these activities are controlled by the *queue manager*.

queuing theory The study of systems in which customers, arriving at random and requiring varying periods of service, may have to wait in order to be served. From the number of service points and the *probability distributions of arrival times and service times, the distribution of the length of queue and the waiting time before service may be predicted.

Queuing theory has important applications in any system liable to congestion, where the costs of improved service may be balanced against the costs of congestion.

quibinary code *Another name for* biquinary code.

quickersort An algorithm published in 1965 by R. S. Scowen using a method similar to *quicksort. It repeatedly splits the array to be sorted into parts such that all elements of one part are less

than all elements of the other, with a third part in the middle consisting of a single element.

quicksort (partition-exchange sort) A form of sorting by exchanging due to C. A. R. Hoare. By comparing sortkeys from the two extremes of the file, and alternately working up the file from the bottom until an exchange is necessary and then working down the file from the top, the original problem can be reduced to two smaller problems. The same process is then applied to each part, and is further repeated until the problems are trivially small. *See also* heapsort.

quiesce To render a device or system inactive by, for example, rejecting new requests for work.

q-valued *See* q-ary.

R

RACE *Acronym for* research and development in advanced communication technologies for Europe. A cooperative venture of some 350 organizations, coordinated and part-funded by the European Community.

race condition (race) A condition in *sequential circuits in which two or more variables change at one time. In practice, i.e. with nonideal circuits, there is a possibility of incorrect operation under such a condition. *See also* hazard.

racking *See* scroll.

radix (base) The number of distinct digits in a fixed-radix *number system. These digits represent the integers in the range zero to one less than the radix. The radix of a number can be indicated by means of a subscript, as in 24_8 or

101_2. *See also* binary system, hexadecimal notation, octal notation.

radix complement (true complement) For an integer represented in a fixed-radix *number system, a number formed by adding one to the *radix-minus-one complement of the given integer. For example, in the decimal system the *ten's complement* of 0372 is 9628 (i.e. 9627 + 1); in the binary system the *two's complement* of 1100 is 0100 (i.e. 0011 + 1). *See also* complement number system.

radix exchange A form of *sorting by exchanging. Instead of comparing two sortkeys, individual bits are compared, starting with the most significant bit. The file is then split into two subfiles, one with keys having 0 as first bit, the other with 1 as first bit. The process continues on the first subfile, comparing the second bits, and similarly on the second subfile, and so on until the file is sorted.

radix-minus-one complement (diminished radix complement) For an integer represented in a fixed-radix *number system, a number formed by replacing each digit d in the integer by its *complement*, i.e. by

$$(R - 1 - d)$$

where R denotes the radix of the system. For example, in the decimal system the *nine's complement* of 0372 is 9627; in the binary system the *one's complement* of 1100 is 0011. *See also* complement number system, radix complement.

radix notation *See* radix point.

radix point A symbol, usually a dot, used to separate the integral part from the fractional part of a number expressed in a *radix notation*, i.e. in the notation used in a positional *number system.

radix sorting (digital sorting; pocket sorting) A sorting algorithm in which the file is first sorted on the least significant digit of the sortkey, then the next least significant until in the final pass a sort is made on the most significant digit. The algorithm is best implemented using *linked lists. *See also* divide and conquer sorting.

ragged array A two-dimensional array where the numbers of elements in each row (or column) are not equal: such arrays are described as *row-ragged* (or *column-ragged*). A ragged array is usually represented using an *access vector or a vector of pointers, each pointer referring to a row (or column) of the ragged array.

RAM *Acronym for* random-access memory. A semiconductor *read-write memory device in which the basic element consists of a single cell that is capable of storing one bit of information. Large-capacity memories are formed as two-dimensional arrays of these cells. An individual cell is identified uniquely by row and column addresses, which are derived by decoding a user-supplied address word. A typical organization is shown in the diagram. Each cell in a RAM is thus independent of all other cells in the array and can be accessed in any order and in the same amount of time, hence the term *random access. Since RAM devices are read-write memories, data can be both read from and written to the cells in the array. RAM is usually *volatile memory and is used for temporary storage of data or programs.

RAM devices can be classified as *static* or *dynamic*. Static RAMs are fabricated from either bipolar or MOS components (*see* bipolar transistor, MOSFET); each cell is formed by an electronic *latch whose contents remain fixed until written to or until the power is removed. Dynamic RAM (DRAM) cells, which comprise MOS devices, utilize the charge stored on a capacitance as a temporary store (*see* bucket); due to leakage currents, the cell contents must be *refreshed at regular intervals,

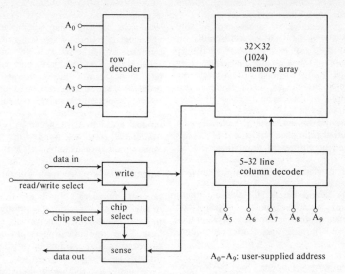

Typical organization of a RAM

typically every millisecond. Static and dynamic RAMs are both well suited to fabrication in integrated-circuit form. Compared with static RAMs, dynamic RAMs have larger cell densities, lower power consumption, but slower access times. *Compare* ROM.

Ramp-C benchmark A *benchmark that measures the limiting capacity of a computer system by a combination of an increasing number of transactions from a standardized mix and an increasing number of terminals, until no more transactions or terminals can be added. This is represented for a number of configurations of the computer until the highest capacity is reached. A percentage (typically 70%) of the highest capacity is then taken as the benchmark result.

random access 1. A type of memory access in which storage locations are *addressable and can therefore be accessed in any order.

The term is applied to two classes of memory. The first is random-access main memory. Until the late 1960s such memory was fabricated from ferrite-core stores but this type has been replaced by semiconductor memory, either *RAM or *ROM. Any word, or byte, in random-access main memory is accessible in a fixed time, i.e. the access time to any item of information is independent of the address of that item and of the address of any previous item referred to; the access time is typically on the order of 0.02–0.5 microsecond.

The term random-access memory is also used to describe memory implemented using magnetic disk, for which the access time contains two components: a seek time necessary to locate the appropriate track and a latency necessary to allow the information in that track to become available under the read/write heads. Typical seek times are in the range 10–30 milliseconds. The latency is usually quoted as one half the time for a complete revolution of the device, say 8 milliseconds.

2. A method of access to a *file (especially a data file) or a *database: a file or database is said to be randomly accessed if the sequence of transactions submitted to it does not match any sequence in which records may be organized.

random-access device A peripheral such as a magnetic disk on which data can be read in a different order from that in which it was written. *See* random access. *See also* von Neumann machine.

random-access file A *file that is organized to support *random access. The two most common random-access methods are *hashing and *indexed sequential.

random-access memory *See* RAM. *See also* random access.

random-access stored-program machine A general-purpose computer in which the program and data are contained in (usually the same) read-write random-access memory. *See also* von Neumann machine.

random algorithms Algorithms that are fast but instead of always giving the correct answer give the correct answer with high probability. They have been devised because of the difficulty (impossibility?) of finding *polynomial time algorithms for some problems (*see* P = NP question).

An example is that of trying to test whether or not a number is prime. Given an integer n there is a test that uses a "guess" i, chosen at random between 1 and n, that takes $O(\log_2 n)$ time to perform. If the test is successful n is known to have factors; on the other hand if n has factors then the test will be successful for at least half of the integers in the range 1 to n. Thus if the test fails k times it can be said that n is prime

with probability $1 - 2^{-k}$

Several other examples of problems amenable to a similar approach have now been found. However, all such examples are either already known to be solvable in polynomial time anyway (although the random algorithms are an order of magnitude faster) or like prime-testing, under suspicion of so being.

random logic A term generally used to describe a relatively nonuniform digital logic circuit. For example, a control unit will contain random logic; an ALU, having a regular structure, will not.

random numbers Numbers that are drawn using a random *sampling technique from a set of permissible numbers. True random numbers are difficult to obtain, and programs using them are difficult to debug.

Attempts to produce random numbers using the arithmetic properties of a computer result in *pseudorandom numbers*, since in principle the numbers generated depend on their predecessors. However, their *frequency distribution may be assumed to correspond to a given theoretical form, and they may be assumed to be independent of each other. Basic pseudorandom numbers are uniformly distributed in the range (0,1), and may be transformed to provide other distributions.

Many methods for their generation have been proposed over the years, one of the earliest being the *middle square method* proposed by von Neumann: the previous random number is squared and the middle digits extracted from the result to form the next number in the sequence. More successful methods are based upon the linear congruential method in which a sequence of numbers is generated using the formula

$$X_{n+1} = aX_n + c \pmod{m}$$

for particular choices of a, c and m.

Pseudorandom numbers are used in a number of applications: in *Monte Carlo methods of numerical integration, to sample a large set and so gain insight into the set, and to simulate natural phenomena such as the collision of nuclear particles.

random sampling *See* sampling.

random variable A quantity that may take any of a prescribed set of values with *relative frequency determined by its *probability distribution.

range 1. of a binary *relation R, a subset of $S_1 \times S_2$, say. The *subset of S_2 consisting of all elements to which some element of S_1 is related. If R is the relation "is the wife of" defined from men to women, the range of R is the set of married women.

Since a *function is a special kind of relation, the range of
$$f : X \to Y$$
can be written as
$$\{y \mid y \in Y \text{ and } y = f(x)$$
$$\text{for some } x \text{ in } X\}$$
2. *See* measures of variation.

rank 1. The number of linearly independent rows or columns of a matrix of numbers.
2. of a graph. *See* connected graph.

rank correlation *See* correlation.

rank correlation coefficient *See* nonparametric techniques.

RARE Réseaux Associés pour la Recherche Européenne. A loose association of private or semiprivate packet networks operated by a number of European countries for the use of their academic and research communities. *JANET is one such network. RARE was formed to foster cooperation on matters of common interest. It is not intended that RARE shall operate a network itself.

raster-mode graphic display (raster graphics) A widely used method of presenting graphical or pictorial images in which

the desired shape is built up by means of a succession of parallel movements of the pen of a plotter or the spot on a VDU, in a similar manner to a television picture, i.e. without each line being traced as a continuous movement of the pen or spot. *Compare* vector-mode graphic display.

raster scan A mode of exploration or reproduction of an image in which an electron beam is made to trace a succession of adjacent parallel lines. This pattern of lines is called the *scanning raster* or *raster*. The most common example of a raster scan is the way in which a television picture is written on the screen.

rate 1. of a code. For any (n, k) *block code or *convolutional code, the value defined as
$$R = k/n$$
It is a measure of "efficiency" in the sense that the more *redundancy there is in the code, the lower the rate. On the other hand, high redundancy may bring about greater efficiency in detecting or correcting errors. Thus the rate measures only one aspect of the overall efficiency.
2. *See* data transfer rate.

rational language *Another name for* regular language.

raw data Data in the form in which it reaches a computer system from the outside world: data that has not been vetted for correctness, nor sorted into any sequence, nor processed in any other way.

raw error rate of peripheral storage. *See* error rate.

Rayleigh–Ritz method *See* finite-element method.

RCP *Abbrev. for* Rescau à Commutation par Paquets. An experimental network that was run by the French PTT, beginning in 1974, and served as a testbed for the public packet network *Transpac. RCP pioneered individually flow-controlled virtual connections over the interface between the backbone network and the network hosts. This prevents any one connection from consuming an unfair portion of network or host's communication resources, and was an important contribution to the development of the *X.25 interface protocol. *Compare* CYCLADES.

RDAT *Abbrev. for* rotating-head digital audio tape. *Another name for* DAT. *See* helical scan.

reachability A concept from graph theory concerned with whether there is a *path between two vertices in a directed *graph. Vertex *V* is said to be *reachable* from vertex *U* provided that there is a path from *U* to *V*. There may be several different paths from one vertex to another, the shortest being called a *geodesic*. The set of points that can be reached from a given vertex *V* is called the *reachable set* of *V*.

A directed graph is *unilaterally connected* when, for any pair of vertices, at least one vertex is reachable from the other.

reachability matrix *Another name for* adjacency matrix.

read To sense and retrieve (or interpret) data from a form of storage or input medium. The word is often used to qualify the meaning of a noun, as in read head.

reader A device for holding or moving a data medium and sensing the data encoded on it. *See* card reader, document reader.

read error *See* error rate.

read head *See* head.

read instruction A program step that causes data to be retrieved from a

defined storage location and written into a register or buffer.

read-mostly media *See* write-once.

read-only memory *See* ROM.

read-only optical media Optical storage media that cannot be written by the user but that carry data imprinted during manufacture, usually by pressing from a master disk. *See* optical storage.

read out To copy words or fields from a specified location in an internal memory of a computer into an external storage or display device. Both the operation and the copy are referred to as *read-out*.

read time The period between the availability of the first and last bits of data concerned in a single read instruction. It does not include any latency or waiting time or any regenerative action that may be associated with a destructive read operation.

read-while-write check *See* magnetic tape.

read/write head A component of a *disk drive that records and retrieves data from magnetic disks. Read/write heads are also used sometimes to record and retrieve data from *magnetic tapes. In the case of disk drives the assembly consists of a head, sometimes known as a *slider*, and a mounting arm, known as a *flexure*. There are two categories of head: those used in floppy drives in which the slider is in contact with the media, and those used in "rigid drives" in which the head flies above the surface of the media. The flying height of the latter depends upon the slider geometry, the flexure loading force, and the rotational speed of the disk.

Early drives (e.g. the IBM 3330–11) employed a flexure with a high load force, typically 350 grams, and the heads were withdrawn from the disk surface before rotation stopped. The

3340 Winchester drive first delivered by IBM in 1973 employed a radically new head design. Heads of this type are now known as *Winchester heads*, and have the following characteristics:

the read/write head is supported by a trimaran structure, with two outriggers supporting a narrow inner "hull", i.e. the slider;

before drive operation, and when it ceases, the heads rest on the disk surface, which is lubricated;

the loading force was reduced to 10 grams;

the flying height was reduced to 0.25 micrometers compared to 0.8 μm in the 3330.

With the introduction of the IBM 3370 (Whitney drive) in 1979 the head design was again changed. The size of the slider was made smaller and was fabricated using "thin film" technology; also the flexure was made much simpler. The result of this was a much more stable head that can be loaded, although not in the 3370, toward the media while it is rotating. Winchester heads cannot be so loaded. The term *Whitney* is now used to describe the type of head and flexure outlined above even if it is not manufactured by thin film techniques, in which case it is sometimes called a *mini-composite head*.

read/write memory A type of memory that, in normal operation, allows the user to access (read from) or alter (write to) individual storage locations within the device. The choice of read or write operation is normally determined by a read/write signal applied to the device. *RAM devices are typical read/write memories. *Compare* ROM.

ready signal A signal from a device indicating that it can accept new commands or data. *Compare* busy signal.

real-time clock A clock that runs regardless of whether *processes that refer to the clock are running or not. The clock

may take two forms, either as a peripheral device that can be read by a process when the process chooses, or as a source of interrupts that occur at precisely determined intervals. A real-time clock measures *elapsed time. *See also* relative-time clock.

real-time language A programming language designed for programming systems in which the response time of the computer to stimuli is time critical. For instance, if a computer is controlling an elevator, then the computer must be able to respond quickly to the movements of the cage. *Ada, *Modula, *CORAL 66, and RTL-2 are real-time languages.

real-time system Any system in which the time at which output is produced is significant. This is usually because the input corresponds to some movement in the physical world, and the output has to relate to that same movement. The lag from input time to output time must be sufficiently small for acceptable timeliness. Timeliness is a function of the total system: missile guidance requires output within a few milliseconds of input whereas scheduling of steamships requires responses measured in days. Real-time systems are usually considered to be those in which the response time is of order milliseconds; interactive systems are those with response times of order seconds and batch systems are those with response times of hours or days. Examples of real-time systems include process control, embedded computer systems, point-of-sale systems, and computer-aided testing.

real type (type real) A *data type comprising values that are real numbers (i.e. have a fractional part) and can be operated on by real-number arithmetic operations such as addition, subtraction, multiplication, division, and square root. Usually the representations do not include transcendental real numbers but are limited to a subset of rational numbers. *See also* floating point notation.

recognize (accept) *See* automaton.

reconfiguration The process of redefining and in some cases reconnecting the units of a multiple-unit computer system. This procedure may be accomplished automatically, manually, or by a combination of both. The purpose may be to provide different system functionality or continued operation after the failure of one unit. If done automatically the latter case would represent a *fail-soft situation. *See also* configuration.

reconstitute To rebuild, generally used to denote the recovery process necessary to restore a system to an operational state after some error. It usually involves resorting to a backup state and running appropriate programs.

record 1. A collection of data handled together in transfers to and from peripheral devices. Files held on backing store are frequently treated as sequences of records. The collection of data transferred as a unit is called a *physical record*. In contrast, the collection of data relating to one subject is then called a *logical record*. The number of logical records in a physical record is the *blocking factor*.

2. A *data structure in which there are a number of named components, called *fields, not necessarily of the same type. It may have variants in which some of the components, known as *variant fields*, are absent; the particular variant for a given value would be distinguished by a discriminant or *tag field. The record is widely recognized as one of the fundamental ways of aggregating data (another being the *array) and many programming languages offer direct support for data objects that take the form of records. Such languages permit operations upon an entire record

object as well as upon its individual components.

3. *Another term for* write, used particularly when writing the value of data that may change or disappear.

recoverable error of peripheral storage. *See* error rate.

recovery The process of restoring normal operation after the occurrence of a *failure. *See* failure recovery, power-fail recovery, database recovery, error recovery.

recovery data Data saved during execution of a system to enable *error recovery. The data includes *recovery points, and information allowing all data to be restored to the values that existed prior to the recovery point. Thus for data changed by operations following the recovery point, the value of the data prior to this change must be saved as recovery data at the time that the change is being made.

recovery log A file created to permit *database recovery (or *file recovery). The log contains information about all changes made to a database or file since it was last established as being correct and a *backup copy was last taken. The form in which changes may be recorded in a recovery log may vary considerably, depending on the recovery algorithms to be used. In general, a recovery log may be used in one of two ways:
(a) to redo all changes since the last backup (if the database or file has been corrupted);
(b) to undo all incorrect changes (if the source of error is in the changes).

recovery point Points in a computation for which the (then) current state can be restored. *See* recovery data, backward error recovery, forward error recovery, atomic action.

recurrence A statement describing some quantity such as $f(n)$ (where f is some *function and n is a positive integer) in terms of values of $f(m)$, where m is a nonnegative integer smaller than n; initial values such as $f(0)$ or $f(1)$ can be assumed to be defined. The concept can be extended to include functions of several variables. A recurrence will then involve defining $f(m,n)$, say, in terms of $f(m',n')$ where in some sense (m',n') is smaller than (m,n); again initial values can be assumed. The numbers in the *Fibonacci series can be defined by a recurrence.

In general, a recurrence can be considered as an equation connecting the values of the function at a number of related points. It has the form

$$g(n, f(n), f(n-1), \ldots, f(n-k)) = 0$$
$$n = k, k + 1, \ldots, N$$

Assuming initial values for $f(0)$, $f(1)$, $\ldots$, $f(k-1)$, values for other points n can be calculated.

Equations of this type arise naturally in the *discretization of continuous problems, and in a slightly different form, known as a *difference equation, appear repeatedly in *combinatorics.

recursion 1. The process of defining or expressing a function, procedure, language construct, or the solution to a problem in terms of itself, so producing a *recursive function, a *recursive subroutine, etc.

2. (primitive recursion) In the study of *effective computability, a particular way of defining a new function in terms of other simpler ones. The functions involved are usually taken to be functions over the nonnegative integers. Recursion is then the process of defining a function f of $(n + 1)$ variables in the following manner:

$$f(x_1, x_2, \ldots, x_n, 0) = g(x_1, x_2, \ldots, x_n)$$
$$f(x_1, x_2, \ldots, x_n, y + 1) =$$
$$h(x_1, x_2, \ldots, x_n, y, f(x_1, \ldots, x_n, y))$$

where g and h are functions of n and $(n + 2)$ variables respectively. *See also* primitive recursive function.

recursion theorem A variant of the *fixed-point theorem of recursive function theory.

recursive descent parsing *See* top-down parsing, LL parsing.

recursive doubling A method in which a total computation is repeatedly divided into two separate computations of equal complexity that can be executed in parallel. Recursive doubling is used in *parallel computers (e.g. Cray X-MP) and works best when the operation on pairs of operands is *associative.

recursive function 1. In mathematics, a *function whose usual or natural definition is in terms of itself.

2. In a program, a result-delivering *procedure that calls itself.

3. (general recursive function, total recursive function) In the study of *effective computability, a *partial recursive function that happens to be *total. For some authors the terms recursive and general recursive are synonymous with partial recursive. It is useful here to summarize the various terms used in this area:

A *partial recursive function can involve both *recursion and the μ-operator (*see* minimization). Not all such functions are *total functions since the use of the μ-operator allows the possibility of nontermination.

A *primitive recursive function, however, cannot involve the μ-operator and is hence guaranteed to be total. The *Ackermann function is the standard example of a total recursive function that is not primitive recursive.

recursive list (self-referent list) A *list that contains itself as a sublist element or is a sublist element of one of its sublists.

recursively decidable problem *Another term for* decidable problem. *See* decision problem.

recursively enumerable set A subset A of a set B is said to be recursively enumerable, relative to B, if there is an effective procedure that, given an element b in B, will output "yes" if and only if b is an element of A. If b is not in A then, in general, the procedure will never terminate. This is a weaker notion than that of a *recursive set. A set can be recursively enumerable without being recursive. The set of *Ada programs that terminates (for a given input) is recursively enumerable (with respect to the class of all Ada programs) but it is not recursive.

recursively solvable problem *Another term for* solvable problem. *See* decision problem.

recursively undecidable, unsolvable *Other terms for* undecidable, unsolvable. *See* decision problem.

recursive relation A *relation whose *characteristic function is recursive.

recursive set A *set whose membership is defined by a general *recursive function. In principle, it is a subset of a larger set over which a *characteristic function is defined, that function being generally recursive. For example, the set of programs in a particular language is recursive in the larger set consisting of all strings that can be made up from the basic alphabet of symbols defined for that language. Thus it can be decided whether or not a given string of the symbols is actually such a program by use of a general recursive function. This must be so since one task of a compiler is to determine whether or not such a string of symbols constitutes a syntactically well-formed program. *See also* recursively enumerable set.

recursive subroutine A *subroutine that calls itself. Such a self-referential call must occur as one branch of a conditional statement, otherwise there would be an infinite series of calls. As an example, a recursive subroutine to calculate factorial (n) would call itself to calculate factorial $(n-1)$, unless $n = 1$ when the value 1 will be returned.

red book 1. The *coloured book defining the job submission protocol used within the UK academic community. It is sometimes referred to as *JTMP, Job Transfer and Manipulation Protocol*.

2. Part of the defining documentation for the *ISDN standard, covering the protocol reference model for the ISDN together with numbering and addressing and the functional descriptions of connection types.

3. A National Computer Security Center (*NCSC) publication that discusses the security aspects of *trusted computer systems, with especial emphasis on the networking implications.

reduced instruction set computer *See* RISC.

reducible polynomial *See* polynomial.

reduction machine A machine that evaluates expressions by successively reducing all component subexpressions until only simple data values remain. Evaluation is achieved by expression substitution. For each expression that is not a simple data value, a set of rules define what should be substituted when that expression appears. The machine operates by matching each subexpression of the expression currently being evaluated with its appropriate rule, and substituting as specified by that rule. This process of expression substitution continues until only simple data values remain, representing the value of the original expression.

All subexpressions can be matched and substituted concurrently, and thus there is the potential for a high degree of parallelism. A major objective of reduction machines is to exploit this parallelism.

Reduction machines represent one of the major examples of *non von Neumann architecture, and are of considerable research interest. Traditional *imperative programming languages are wholly unsuited to reduction machines, so *declarative languages are employed.

redundancy The provision of additional components in a system, over and above the minimum set of components to perform the functions of the system, for purposes of *reliability or *robustness. For example, with *triple modular redundancy* three components are deployed in parallel, all performing the same function. Their outputs are compared, and when one component produces a different result from the other two, this item is assumed to be faulty and is ignored. Redundancy covers not only the incorporation of duplicate or triplicate hardware for backup in case of *failure, but also the inclusion of excess symbols in messages sent through communication systems in order to combat the effects of noise (*see* error-correcting code, error-detecting code).

redundancy check A check made with redundant hardware or information that can provide an indication that certain errors have occurred. *See* redundancy, cyclic redundancy check.

Reed-Muller codes (RM codes) A family of *binary *cyclic $(2^m, k)$ *error-correcting *block codes.

Reed-Solomon codes (RS codes) An important and practical family of *linear *error-correcting *block codes, especially suited to the correction of *burst errors. They can be regarded as a generalization of *Bose–Chaudhuri–Hocquenghem (BCH) codes, and as a special case of *Goppa codes. RS codes can be arranged to be *cyclic.

reel *See* magnetic tape, paper tape.

re-entrant program A program whose instructions are invariant, hence it can be used again without being reloaded. Re-entrant programs consist of logically separate code and data segments, and two instances of such a program can share the same code.

reference file A file that contains reference information and thus changes infrequently.

referential integrity Internal consistency of data, and data relationships, within a database system.

referential opacity The opposite of *referential transparency.

referential transparency A property of a function signifying that evaluation of the function with a particular set of arguments always returns the same value, whatever the context in which evaluation takes place. In programming terms this means that the function must not exhibit any side effects, i.e. it must not reference or change variables defined outside the function, except for the variables passed as parameters.

refinement The process in programming whereby higher-level ideas are progressively reexpressed in terms of lower-level ones. This can involve both the implementation of procedures in terms of lower-level ones, and also the representation of abstract data items in terms of more concrete ones. Both kinds of refinement can involve *specifications, with each step of refinement being shown to preserve the specified behavior of the procedure or data type being refined. Although both terms are rather fluid in meaning, there is a possible distinction to be made between refinement and *program transformation, with the latter involving the replacement of one program fragment by an equivalent one at the same level of abstraction rather than its representation in terms of a lower level of abstraction.

Refinement and transformation are two of the main ideas in the increasingly important study of the systematic derivation of correct programs from specifications.

reflexive closure *See* transitive closure.

reflexive relation A *relation R defined on a set S and having the property that
$$x \, R \, x$$
for all elements x in S
The relation "is the same age as" defined on the set of people is reflexive. *Compare* irreflexive relation.

refresh (regenerate) 1. To replenish the charge on the storage capacitors used in *dynamic memory cells and other similar devices. Some devices are provided with internal circuitry that automatically refreshes dynamic cells whenever these cells are read. The word refresh is also used as a noun.
2. To repeat at regular intervals the display of digital information on a cathode-ray tube or television monitor in order that the display can appear continuous. A refreshed display is also necessary for applications involving simulated motion, and can provide dynamic viewing capabilities for a three-dimensional computer model of a complicated object.

regenerate *Another term for* refresh.

regenerative memory A type of memory, not widely used in modern computing systems, in which the content has to be regularly rewritten to avoid depreciation. Such devices frequently store information as a train of pulses circulating in a loop that includes a read and a write transducer. For continued storage the output of the read transducer is connected to the write transducer, and thus the depreciation of the signal that occurs during its passage around the loop is corrected at the start of each pass. Some types of semiconductor memory are regenerative in that they

need a *refresh cycle to prevent loss of data.

register A group of (usually) *bistable devices that are used to store information within a computer system for high-speed access. A register of n bistables can store a word of length n bits, which can represent any n bits of information. Different interpretations can be given to the bit configuration stored in the register, e.g. the configuration could represent an instruction, a binary number, an alphanumeric character, etc. A register is often the same size as the computer word; it may also be byte- or character-size or some other size as required. Some registers can behave as *counters as well, or they may behave as *shift registers. *See also* memory hierarchy.

register optimization *See* optimization.

register transfer language (RTL) Any of several programming languages that allow the declaration of *register configurations within a structure to perform a computation. The timing of transfers between registers, to describe the behavior, is specified by the order in which such transfers are interpreted during the execution of the program. *See also* CHDL.

regression analysis A statistical technique that is concerned with fitting relationships between a dependent variable, y, and one or more independent variables, $x_1, x_2, \ldots$, usually by the method of *least squares.

A *linear regression model* is one in which the theoretical mean value, μ_i, of the observation y_i is a linear combination of independent variables,
$$\mu = \beta_0 + \beta_1 x_1 + \ldots + \beta_k x_k$$
when k x-variables are included in the model. The multiples $\beta_0, \beta_1, \ldots \beta_k$ are parameters of the model and are the quantities to be estimated; they are known as *regression coefficients*, β_0 being the *intercept* or *constant term*. A model

with more than one x-variable is known as a *multiple regression model*.

Nonlinear regression models express μ as a general function of the independent variables. The general functions include curves such as exponentials and ratios of polynomials, in which there are parameters to be estimated.

Various procedures have been devised to detect variables that make a significant contribution to the regression equation, and to find the combination of variables that best fits the data using as few variables as possible. *Analysis of variance is used to assess the significance of the regression model. See also generalized linear model, influence.

regression testing Following maintenance to a system, tests performed to demonstrate that the system still performs all the functions required prior to the maintenance. Regression testing is additional to tests made to ensure that the modifications work satisfactorily. *See also* performance testing.

regula falsi *Another name (Latin) for* false position method.

regular event *Another name for* regular language.

regular expression An expression built from finite *formal languages (i.e. finite sets of strings) using the operations of *union, *concatenation, and *Kleene star. For example, the following two regular expressions each denote the set of all strings of alternating *a*s and *b*s:

$$\{a,\Lambda\} \{ba\}^* \{\Lambda,b\}$$
$$\{ba\}^* \cup \{a\}\{ba\}^* \cup \{ba\}^*\{b\} \cup$$
$$\{a\}\{ba\}^*\{b\}$$

where Λ is the empty string. A language is *regular if and only if it is representable by a regular expression. Thus the class of regular languages is the smallest one that contains all finite languages and is closed under concatenation, union, and star – the so-called *regular operations*. These three operations correspond to "sequence", "choice", and "iteration" in structured iterative programs.

regular grammar A *grammar in which each production has one of the forms

$$A \to b$$
$$A \to bC$$

where b is a terminal and A,C are nonterminals. Like the right-linear and left-linear grammars (*see* linear grammar) regular grammars generate precisely the *regular languages.

regular language (regular set; rational language) A language recognized by a *finite-state automaton. Of the language classes commonly studied, the class of regular languages is the smallest and mathematically the simplest. Its importance is shown by the existence of several alternative definitions; for some of them *see* regular grammar, linear grammar, regular expression, Myhill equivalence, Nerode equivalence, tree grammar.

regular operations *See* regular expression.

regular representation A representation of a *group as a particular set of transformations.

regular set *Another name for* regular language, since in formal language theory a language is simply a set of strings.

relation (defined on sets S_1, S_2, ... S_n) A *subset R of the *Cartesian product

$$S_1 \times S_2 \times \ldots \times S_n$$

of the n sets S_1, ..., S_n. This is called an *n*-ary relation. When a relation R is defined on a single set S the implication is that R is a subset of

$$S \times S \times \ldots \times S \ (n \text{ terms})$$

The most common situation occurs when $n = 2$, i.e. R is a subset of $S_1 \times S_2$. Then R is called a *binary relation* on S_1 to S_2 or between S_1 and S_2. S_1 is the *domain* of R and S_2 the *codomain* of R. If the *ordered pair

(s_1,s_2) belongs to the subset R, a notation such as

$$s_1 \; R \; s_2 \quad \text{or} \quad s_1 \; \rho \; s_2$$

is usually adopted and it is then possible to talk about the relation R or ρ and to say that s_1 and s_2 are related.

An example of a binary relation is the usual "is less than" relation defined on integers, where the subset R consists of ordered pairs such as (4,5); it is however more natural to write $4 < 5$. Other examples include: "is equal to" defined on strings, say; "is the square root of" defined on the nonnegative reals; "is defined in terms of" defined on the set of subroutines within a particular program; "is before in the queue" defined on the set of jobs awaiting execution at a particular time.

The *function is a special kind of relation. *Graphs are often used to provide a convenient pictorial representation of a relation.

Relations play an important part in theoretical aspects of many areas of computing, including the mathematical foundations of the subject, databases, compiling techniques, and operating systems. *See also* equivalence relation, partial ordering.

relational algebra *See* relational model.

relational calculus *See* relational model.

relational database system A *database system in which the DBMS supports the *relational model of data. Examples of relational DBMSs are *dBase IV, *INGRES, *Oracle, QBE, and *SQL/DS.

relational model A model that permits the definition of (a) data structures, (b) storage and retrieval operations on them, (c) integrity constraints that are to be maintained on them. The model is based on the mathematical concept of the *relation, but the concept has been enhanced by a considerable body of special terminology and theory. The

model was first proposed by E. F. Codd in 1970 and has proved of immense influence and value. It is used exclusively in the context of *database management systems. It is often, though not necessarily, expressed in terms of a set of *normal forms.

The common data structure (the relation) may be thought of as a table, in which each row of values (tuple) corresponds to a logical record, and the column headings are the names of the fields (items) in the records. Using the conventions of normalization, each tuple contains data representing the properties either of a "real-world" entity or of the relationship between two or more entities. In itself, a set of relations leaves the relationships between relations implicit; these can be made explicit in, for instance, an entity-relationship diagram (*see* era diagram).

The storage and retrieval operations fall into two classes: the set *operations (union, intersection, difference, product) and the relational operations (select, project, join, divide). Any *data manipulation language providing all these operations is said to be *relationally complete*. Any such language is said to be either a *relational algebra* or a *relational calculus*, depending on the way in which expressions are formed in the language.

The area of integrity constraints (which may be regarded as a class of *invariants) is the least well-developed part of the theory.

Relational database management systems may compromise with some of the constraints of the strict relational model, in order to achieve operational efficiency.

relational operator 1. An operator representing a comparison between two operands that returns a truth value. The common comparisons are shown in the table, together with the relational operators normally used in computing; "not equal to" has many denotations.

2. *See* relational model.

comparison	operator
less than	<
less than or equal to	<=
equal to	=
greater than or equal to	>=
greater than	>
not equal to	<>¬=!= #

Relational operators

relative addressing Usually either of two ways to expand a short specified address. The first is *self-relative addressing* where the specified address is added to the address of the instruction (generally the current contents of the program counter) that contains the self-relative reference to produce a direct address. The second is *base addressing* in which the specified address is added to the contents of a *base register* containing a base address to produce a direct address. *See also* addressing schemes.

relative complement *Another name for* set difference.

relative frequency The number of occurrences of a particular event, E, divided by the total number of observed events. An *event* is a particular instance of a class of observations, such as the result of the throw of dice, the recording of a man's height, or the survival of a patient given a particular treatment. Relative frequency should be distinguished from *probability. For example, the probability that a fair coin when tossed lands heads up is 0.5, whereas the relative frequency in a particular run of 100 tosses might be 47/100 or 0.47.

The set of relative frequencies for all the events that are possible is called a *frequency distribution. It may be displayed graphically as a *histogram.

relatively prime *See* greatest common divisor.

relative product *Another name for* composition.

relative-time clock A free-running clock that raises an interrupt at regular intervals, often associated with the period of the incoming supply of electricity. These interrupts allow the supervisory system to track the passage of real time, and also guarantee that if a process does not call the supervisor explicitly, the supervisor will nevertheless be entered.

relay In networking, a device that offers a means of passing information between two or more networks, each offering a similar network function but each using a different *protocol. In general a relay differs from a *gateway or *bridge in offering a *store-and-forward service rather than a real-time service. As an example, a *mail relay* may be used to pass mail messages between networks using different mail protocols.

The term relay is used in some communities as synonymous with bridge or gateway. These three terms have meanings that vary between different communities at the same time, and within a given community at different times.

release Transfer of a system from the development stages into wider usage, e.g. into operational use. *See also* software life-cycle.

reliability 1. The ability of a computer system to perform its required functions for a given period of time. It is often quoted in terms of percentage of *uptime, but may be more usefully expressed as MTBF (mean time between failures). *See also* hardware reliability, repair time.

2. of software. *See* software reliability.

relocatable code Program code that can be loaded anywhere in memory. Typically the code is divided into *control sec-

tions and all memory addresses are expressed relative to the start of a control section. The compiler/assembler produces a table of all such memory references, and the *loader converts them into absolute addresses as part of the loading process. *See also* position-independent code.

remedial maintenance (corrective maintenance) Maintenance that is performed after a fault, in hardware or software, has been found, in order to correct that fault. *Compare* preventive maintenance.

remote A term used to describe a process or system that uses a communication link, as in remote job entry, remote sensing, and remote procedure call.

remote job entry (RJE) A system by which a communications link is used to submit work from an input device and to receive results on a printer or other output medium. Strictly RJE refers only to the entry of jobs, but the term is commonly applied to cover both input and output. Early computer systems had all their input/output devices in the same room or at best in a room adjacent to the computer mainframe. In the early 1960s the introduction of long-distance telecommunications made it possible to site card readers and line printers at a distance from the computer center. It was this that led to the concept of remote job entry.

remote procedure call A procedure call in which the actual execution of the body of the *procedure takes place on a physically distinct processor from that on which the procedure call takes place. In general the system invoking the procedure call is separate from the one executing it. Further the two systems and the communication channel linking them are all liable to fail in the period between the start of the procedure call and the final completion of execution and return of any results from the processor executing the procedure body to that executing the procedure call.

These factors have given rise to a number of different proposals for the course of action to be followed in the event of one or other of the systems failing; essentially to have the procedure body executed either at least once (by *retry) or at most once. These proposals tend to reflect the different priorities attached to the effect on the total system in the event of part of it failing.

remote sensing The technique whereby sensors located remotely from a computer are used to produce inputs for a digital system. These inputs are then transmitted either by wire or radio techniques to the computer. An example is the use of digital thermometers and humidity detectors in large buildings: the sensors transmit their readings to a central computer that optimizes energy use by regulating heat and air conditioning.

repair time The (sometimes average) time required to diagnose and repair a computer failure, either hardware or software. In combination with MTBF (mean time between failures) the MTTR (mean time to repair) provides a figure-of-merit for system *reliability and/or *uptime.

repeat-until loop *See* do-while loop.

repertoire *Short for* instruction repertoire. *See* instruction set.

repetition codes A trivial family of *cyclic *perfect *error-correcting *block codes, in which the codewords are formed merely by repeating the message words r times. Considered as (n, k) codes (*see* block code), these codes have $n = rk$ for some k.

report generator *See* generator, RPG.

requirements analysis The analysis that is necessary for the production of an *expression of requirements.

requirements description *See* expression of requirements.

requirements specification *See* specification, expression of requirements, review.

rerun To run a program again, usually due to a machine malfunction. (The word is also used as a noun.) Some languages allow the programmer to specify restart points: at such points a memory image is preserved so that in the event of a rerun the program does not need to be restarted from scratch.

rescue dump A copy of the workspace associated with a *process, taken with a view to allowing the process to be restarted following a system failure. *See* dump.

reserved word A word that has a specific role in the context in which it occurs, and therefore cannot be used for other purposes. For example, in many programming languages the words 'IF' 'THEN' 'ELSE' are used to organize the presentation of the written form of statements (between 'THEN' and 'ELSE' and following 'ELSE') whose execution is governed by the value of the Boolean expression between 'IF' and 'THEN'. The use of if, then, else as *identifiers is thus not permitted in these languages since they are reserved words. *See also* keyword.

reset To set a variable, register, or counter back to a prescribed state.

resident Permanently present in main memory, as opposed to transient material that is loaded from disk when required.

residual The difference between a data observation and its corresponding fitted value obtained by *regression analysis.

The *residual mean square* is the sum of squared residuals divided by the appropriate *degrees of freedom, and is an estimate of *variance of random variation about the fitted model. Plots of residuals against data variables may suggest important modifications to the model. Plots of ranked residuals against percentage points of the *normal distribution provide a check on the assumptions used in *significance tests in regression analysis. Large residuals identify observations as *outliers*, whose exclusion from the analysis will make a large difference to the conclusions.

residual mean square *See* residual.

residue arithmetic *Another name for* modular arithmetic.

residue check *Another name for* checksum.

resistor-transistor logic *See* RTL.

resolution 1. The amount of graphical information that can be shown on a visual display. The resolution of a display device is usually denoted by the number of lines that can be distinguished visually. The resolution of a computer-graphics system is also defined by the number of displayable lines, or alternatively, by the number of points or pixels (picture elements) that can be displayed in the vertical and horizontal directions. Computer graphics systems are now capable of over 7000 lines of resolution. This is generally described as a *high resolution*, or *hi res*. Many microcomputer manufacturers however have adopted the term high resolution to describe the highest resolution their particular system can achieve. This ranges (1988) from 320 × 200 (i.e. 320 pixels across the screen by 200 pixels down) to 640 × 480. *See also* graphics adapter.
2. *See* A/D converter, D/A converter.
3. A rule of inference in mathematical *logic, used to deduce a new logical formula from two old ones. It has been

used extensively in the automatic derivation of mathematical theorems since it is an efficient alternative to traditional rules of inference. *See also* unification.

resource Any of the component parts of a computer system and the facilities that it offers. All computer systems must include one or more processors, which actually manipulate the stored information, some form of memory in which to store both instructions for the processors and data awaiting manipulation, and input/output devices capable of reading information from the outside world and writing results to the outside world.

resource allocation Either the act of making a resource available to a *process, or the amount of a particular resource that has been allocated. The context almost invariably makes clear which meaning is intended. The amount allocated in the second form of usage may either be a period of time if the entire resource is allocated, as with a processor, or it may be a number of subunits in the case of a resource, such as memory, that is made up of a large number of essentially identical subunits, of which some are allocated to the process.

resource descriptor *See* process descriptor.

response function *See* sequential machine.

response time Usually the elapsed time between an action by a computer-system user and the receipt of some form of response or feedback from the system.

restart To set running again after a temporary halt. The term (also used as a noun) applies particularly to the situation in which a transient hardware error has caused the entire operating system (and all the *processes running under its control) to halt. In such cases it is often found that only processes that were

actively running at the time of the error have suffered damage. The damaged processes must be *aborted, but all other processes can be restarted since the resources allocated to them are unaltered, and their *process descriptors are still an accurate reflection of their behavior up to the time of the system error.

restore To reset to an earlier value. For example, when a *process is about to be *restarted on a processor, the contents of the working registers of the processor must be restored to the values they last held when the process was previously running.

restriction of a *relation R or *function f. A relation or function obtained by restricting the domain of R or f. If "is the son of" is a relation defined on all the males in a certain country, a restriction would be this same relation defined on the males of a particular city.

retry *See* error recovery.

return channel In a *duplex transmission channel, it is sometimes the case that the main channel operates only in one direction (i.e. *simplex), but that a channel of much lower capacity (and much lower cost) operates in the opposite direction: this is the return channel. It is chiefly used for monitoring the main channel, and for notifying the transmitter of errors detected by the receiver on the main channel. *See also* backward error correction.

return instruction An instruction used to effect the return to the regular program from a *subroutine or an *interrupt. A return instruction must restore the *program counter to the correct value; in the case of a return from interrupt, certain status bits must also be restored. *Compare* call instruction.

reusable resource A resource, such as a CPU or tape transport, that is not rendered useless by being used. A magnetic tape or disk can be used often indefinitely and are to be regarded as reusable resources. *Compare* consumable resource.

reversal function The *function $r : L \rightarrow L$, where L denotes strings of characters from some *alphabet, defined in such a way that r reverses the order of the elements in its parameter. If & denotes *concatenation of strings, then

$$r(s) = s$$

if s is null or a single character and

$$r(s \,\&\, t) = r(t) \,\&\, r(s)$$

The idea can be extended to include reversing of items in a *list, of items in some *sequence, or of items in an arbitrary one-dimensional *array. Reversal is an *involution operation.

reverse authentication *See* authentication.

reverse bias The applied d.c. voltage that prevents or greatly reduces current flow in a diode, transistor, etc. For example, a negligible current will flow through a diode when its cathode is made more positive than its anode; the diode is then said to be *reverse biased. Compare* forward bias.

reverse Polish notation (RPN; postfix notation; suffix notation) A form of notation, invented by the Polish mathematician Jan Lukasiewicz, in which each operator follows its operands. Thus, for example,

$$a + b \text{ is written } ab+$$
$$a + b * c \text{ is written } abc* +$$

If each operator has a specific number of operands (e.g. if all operators take exactly two operands), then no brackets are required since the order of evaluation is always uniquely defined; the notation can then be described as *parenthesis-free.*

The importance of RPN is that an expression in this form can be readily evaluated on a *stack. Thus translation to RPN, followed by stack evaluation, is a simple but effective strategy for dealing with arithmetic expressions in a programming language. *See also* Polish notation.

reverse video *See* VDU.

reversible execution *See* recovery point, backward error recovery.

review An important and effective method for verifying the output from a particular *software life-cycle phase, known as a task. The output from a task is scrutinized by a team of reviewers against the documentation (specification) available at the start of that task. The purpose is to evaluate the emerging software in order to discover faults as early as possible.

Reviews can be conducted at most life-cycle phases and at different levels of detail, hence for example:

software requirements specification review
system design review
module design review
module coding review (or code inspection)
module test procedure review
integration test plan review
acceptance test review

Informal reviews are usually conducted on the documented output of an individual by fellow (technical) members of the project team. For example, in a module design review the module author will guide the reviewers through the design, and differences between the module specification and the design will be recorded for later analysis and reworking of the design. Project verification and validation plans, together with the quality plan, will give guidance on procedure, and acceptance levels for unresolved differences.

Formal technical reviews may be conducted by project staff, by independent reviewers from other projects, or by independent third parties. They are usually planned as milestones in verification and validation activities.

Management reviews are usually more concerned with progress monitoring, *risk assessment, plans, and scheduling.

rewritable (erasable) Denoting storage media on which the user can write data, and can also erase or overwrite so that new data replaces the old. *See* optical storage.

rewriting system *See* L-system.

ribbon The means by which an *impact printer forms the printed characters on the top copy of printer *stationery, ink being transferred from ribbon to paper. The characteristics of a ribbon depend mainly on the printer for which it is intended. There may however be two or three varieties of ribbon available for one printer type, depending for example on whether maximum utilization of the ribbon (and thus minimum ribbon cost) is important at the expense of *print quality, or vice versa.

Ribbon materials are normally nylon fabric, in various thicknesses and thread types, or polyester film. Fabric is soaked with ink, film is coated with ink-bearing wax. In the past fabrics of silk and cotton were used. A typical nylon thickness is 0.005 inches. Thinner fabrics give better print quality, usually at the expense of ribbon life.

Nylon ribbons can be continually reused until print quality has deteriorated, through ink depletion, to the limit of acceptability. The printer recycles such a ribbon continuously, either by use of a continuous loop or by reversing it at each end. With film ribbons a much greater proportion of the ink is transferred at each strike, leading to shorter ribbon life. They can however provide much better print quality than fabric ribbons.

Ink formulation for a particular ribbon will depend on whether maximum contrast at the expense of life is impor-

tant, or the converse. Color variety is available. Degree of inking in a ribbon is a carefully controlled parameter.

Ribbon dimensions depend on the printer type. Wide ("towel") ribbons may be up to 17″ wide, and travel vertically through the printer. Narrow ribbons, 0.5–2″ wide, traverse across the printing area. Narrow fabric ribbons may be on open spools or contained in purpose-designed cartridges to facilitate ribbon handling. Modern small character printers are designed for cartridge ribbons, and all narrow film ribbons are in cartridges. Fabric ribbons in cartridges are often "stuffed" (packed in concertina fashion) in continuous loops rather than being on spools.

*Thermal transfer printers also require a ribbon, in this case a film ribbon coated with a thermoplastic or wax-based ink.

Richardson extrapolation (deferred approach to the limit) *See* extrapolation.

right-linear grammar *See* linear grammar.

right shift *See* shift.

right subtree *See* binary tree.

ring 1. An *algebraic structure R on which there are defined two *dyadic operations, normally denoted by + (addition) and · or juxtaposition (multiplication). With respect to addition, R is an abelian *group,

$$<R, +>$$

i.e. + is *commutative and *associative. With respect to multiplication, R is a *semigroup,

$$<R, ·>$$

i.e. · is associative. Further, multiplication is *distributive over addition.

Certain kinds of rings are of particular interest:

(a) if multiplication is commutative the ring is called a *commutative ring*;

(b) if $<R, ·>$ is a *monoid, the ring is called a *ring with an identity*;

(c) a commutative ring with an identity, and having no nonzero elements x and y with the property that $x \cdot y = 0$, is said to be an *integral domain*;

(d) a commutative ring with more than one element, and in which every nonzero element has an inverse with respect to multiplication, is called a *field.

The different identity elements and inverses, when these exist, can be distinguished by talking in terms of additive identities (or zeros), multiplicative identities (or ones), additive inverses, and multiplicative inverses.

The concept of a ring provides an algebraic structure into which can be fitted such diverse items as the integers, polynomials with integer coefficients, and matrices; on all these items it is customary to define two dyadic operations.

2. *Another name for* circular list, but more generally applied to any list structure where all sublists as well as the list itself are circularly linked.

ring counter *See* shift counter.

ringing A damped oscillation that occurs in many electrical circuits when signals change rapidly, and is due often to unwanted capacitance and inductance in devices and connecting wires.

ring network A network constructed as a *loop of unidirectional links between network stations (*nodes). It generally uses a bit-serial medium such as twisted pairs or coaxial cable. A master clock may be used to tell each station when to read and write bits, or the timing information may be encoded into the data as long as certain restrictions are met to prevent the ring from overflowing.

Each station receives messages on its incoming link. Address and control information is present at the beginning of the message. Based on this information and the control procedure being

used on the ring, the station must make two decisions: whether or not to make a copy of the message in its local memory, and whether to pass the message on via its outgoing link or delete the message from the ring. If a station determines that no message is being received on its incoming link, then it may have the option of inserting a message on its outgoing link.

Several different control structures have been used on ring networks:

(a) *daisychain* – dedicated wires pass control information from station to station;

(b) *control token* – a special bit pattern identifies control information: a station, upon receiving the control token, may insert a message into the ring and reissue the token;

(c) *message slots* – a series of "slots" are continuously transmitted around the ring: a station detecting an unused slot may mark it "in use" and fill it with a message;

(d) *register insertion* – a station loads a message into a shift register, then inserts the register into the ring when the ring is idle or at the end of any message; the register contents are shifted onto the ring. When the message returns to the register, the register may be removed from the ring.

ripple-carry adder (ripple adder) *See* adder.

ripple counter An *n*-stage *counter that is formed from n cascaded *flip-flops. The clock input to each of the individual flip-flops, with the exception of the first, is taken from the output of the preceding one (*see* diagram). The count thus ripples along the counter's length due to the *propagation delay associated with each stage of counting. *See also* cascadable counter, synchronous counter.

RISC *Acronym for* reduced instruction set computer. A computer based on a

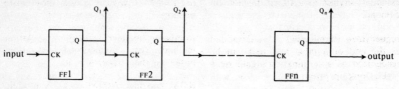

Ripple counter

processor or processors designed to execute a small number of simple instructions extremely fast, preferably one instruction for every cycle of the system clock. RISC processors employ *pipelining and on-chip instruction and data *cache memory among other techniques. Well-known manufacturers who have produced RISC chips include Acorn, Hewlett-Packard, IBM, Intel, and Sun.

rise time of a pulse. *See* pulse.

risk assessment 1. An assessment in quantitative or qualitative terms of the damage that would be sustained if a computer system were exposed to postulated *threats. A quantitative risk analysis may ascribe a probable financial loss if each specified threat successfully exploited each possible *vulnerability of the system. In this sense it is often assumed that the risk would occur during the operation (life-cycle phase) of a computing system (*assessment of operational risk*).

2. (project risk assessment) A quantitative or qualitative analysis of a range of threats and vulnerabilities that may affect a project being completed on time, on budget, and meeting the requirements specification. In this sense it is often assumed that the risk would occur up to system delivery/acceptance.

3. (investment risk assessment) A quantitative or qualitative analysis of a range of threats and vulnerabilities that may affect the achievement of investment targets (usually adversely) from the first commitment of money and resources to a project through to the

retirement of that system from operation.

RJE *Abbrev. for* remote job entry.

RM code *Short for* Reed-Muller code.

robotics A discipline lying across the border between *artificial intelligence and mechanical engineering. It is concerned with building *robots*: programmable devices consisting of mechanical manipulator(s) and sensory organ(s), which are linked to a computer. Most robots in current industrial use have no sensory capability and follow a fixed but reprogrammable sequence of instructions. The main goal of robotics research in artificial intelligence is to provide the robot with an artificial eye, typically a television camera, and to use visual perception to guide a mechanical arm in a flexible manner. *See also* process control.

robustness A measure of the ability of a system to recover from error conditions, whether generated externally or internally, e.g. a robust system would be tolerant to errors in input data or to failures of internal components. Although there may be a relationship between robustness and reliability, the two are distinct measures: a system never called upon to recover from error conditions may be reliable without being robust; a highly robust system that recovers and continues to operate despite numerous error conditions may still be regarded as unreliable in that it fails to provide essential services in a timely fashion on demand.

rogue value (terminator) A value added at the end of a table and that can be recognized as a termination signal by a *table look-up program.

roll back To restart at a *checkpoint.

roll-call polling *See* polling.

roll-in roll-out A method of handling memory in a system dealing with a number of simultaneously active *processes. When a process becomes active, all its associated workspace and code is brought into main memory. As soon as the process is unable to continue for any reason, typically because the user associated with the process is providing input, the entire workspace and code of the process is copied out onto backing store, retaining only a small buffer capable of receiving input from the user. When the user ceases his input and the process is able to continue running, the workspace and code are rolled back into main memory. When the process requires to output results to the user or is awaiting further input from the user, it is rolled out onto backing store. *See also* swapping.

roll stationery *See* stationery.

ROM *Acronym for* read-only memory. A *nonvolatile semiconductor memory device used for the storage of data that will never require modification: the memory contents are permanently built into the device during its manufacture according to a specially created pattern or mask. It is thus sometimes called *mask ROM* to distinguish it from programmable ROM, i.e. *PROM. Although it is possible only to read data from the memory locations of a ROM, the locations can be accessed in any order with equal speed. Hence there is *random access to any of the locations in ROM. *Compare* RAM, read-write memory.

Romberg method An *extrapolation method for *numerical integration, based on the *trapezium rule.

ROM cartridge (ROM pack) A module containing software that is permanently stored as *ROM. The module can easily be plugged into and later removed from a microcomputer or other equipment without the integrated circuitry being handled. ROM cartridges are used for example to provide extra programs to a home computer or extra fonts to a printer.

ROM optical disk (ROM OD, OROM) An *optical disk carrying information that is inserted at the time of manufacture and cannot subsequently be altered. Manufacture is usually by pressing copies from a master; copies are therefore cheap although the master is expensive. The predominant format is *CD-ROM.

romware Software (machine instructions) stored more-or-less permanently in a *ROM, *PROM, *EPROM, etc.

root 1. of a tree. The unique node in the tree with no parent. *See* tree.

   2. of a polynomial equation. *See* polynomial.

rooted tree *See* tree.

rotation position sensor A feature of some disk drives that allows the central processor to be made aware that a required sector is about to come under the read head of the drive.

roundoff error The error caused by truncating numbers in a calculation, usually necessitated because registers in a computer can only hold numbers of a fixed length, say t binary digits. Arithmetical operations on such numbers often give results requiring more than t digits for their representation, which must then be reduced to t digits for further calculation. The nearest t-digit approximation may be used (rounding) or digits after the tth may be dropped (chopping or truncation). The repeated reduction to t digits can cause systematic buildup of error in certain types of calculation.

round robin A method of allocating CPU time in a multiuser environment. Each user is allocated a small amount or quantum of processor time. Once a user has exhausted his quantum, control passes to the next user. The round robin scheduler bears many resemblances to the *feedback queue, which can be thought of as a refinement of the simple round robin scheduler.

route The path used to move information from one place to another. In a packet switching network it is the list of nodes that a particular packet or class of packets is to follow or has followed.

routine *Another name for* subroutine, used usually in combinations, as in input routine.

routing The procedure used to determine the *route taken by a packet in a packet switching computer network. Routing may be *fixed* (computed once at system starting or session initiation) or *dynamic* (recomputed periodically or on a packet-by-packet basis). Routing may be centralized or *distributed* (computed by different nodes independently).

row-major order One way of mapping the elements of a two-dimensional array onto a vector. If a two-dimensional array, A, with m rows and n columns is mapped in row-major order onto a vector b with mn elements then
$$a_{ij} = b_k$$
where $k = n(i - 1) + j$
See also column-major order.

row-ragged *See* ragged array.

row vector *See* matrix.

RPG *Acronym for* report program generator. A programming language used in commercial data processing for extracting information from files. The input to an RPG consists of a description of the file structure, a specification of the information required, and of its layout on the page. From this information, the RPG constructs a program to read the file, extract the desired information, and format it in the required manner. The best-known example is RPG II.

RPN *Abbrev. for* reverse Polish notation.

RSA encryption A method of *encryption (devised by Rivest, Shamir, and Adleman) in which the key that is used for decryption is not the same as that required for encryption; the method may thus be used for *public key encryption.

A message is encrypted by mapping it onto an integer, M say, raising M to a (publicly known) power e and forming the remainder on division by a (publicly known) divisor, n, to give the encrypted message S. Decryption is achieved by similarly raising S to a (secret) power d, and again forming the remainder on division by n; the result will be the value of M. The method relies on the choice of n as the product of two large secret prime numbers, p and q. The values of e and d are chosen such that
$$e * d \equiv 1 \bmod ((p-1) * (q-1))$$
Security is achieved largely by the difficulty of finding the prime factors of n.

RS232C interface A widely used standard interface that covers the electrical connection between data communication equipment, such as a *modem, and data terminal equipment, such as a microcomputer or computer terminal. The RS232C interface standard was developed by the EIA (Electronic Industries Association) and is essentially equivalent to the CCITT's *V.24 interface.

In 1975 the EIA introduced two new specifications in order to upgrade system capabilities; these are the RS423 interface, which closely resembles RS232C, and the RS422 interface, both of which allow higher transmission rates.

RS code *Short for* Reed-Solomon code.

RS flip-flop (SR flip-flop) *See* flip-flop.

RSL A specification language for time-critical real-time systems. Statements in RSL are machine processed to produce an abstract system semantic model. RSL has four language primitives: elements, relationships, attributes, and structures. Users may define new elements, relationships, and attributes to the set predefined in RSL.

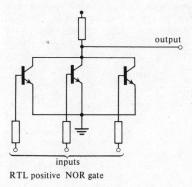

RTL positive NOR gate

RTL 1. *Abbrev. for* resistor-transistor logic. An early *logic family, usually produced in integrated-circuit form, whose principal component parts consist of integrated resistors and *bipolar transistors.

The diagram shows the equivalent circuit of an RTL positive *NOR gate. The output is at a high voltage (logic 1) only if all the inputs are low (logic 0). If any input is high, the associated transistor will be driven into saturation and

the output voltage will be low (*see* bipolar transistor).

Despite its low power dissipation, RTL is now little used since it has a relatively slow switching speed and small *fan-out.

2. *Abbrev. for* register transfer language.

rule of inference *See* propositional calculus, inference.

Runge–Kutta methods A widely used class of methods for the numerical solution of *ordinary differential equations. For the initial-value problem
$$y' = f(x,y), \; y(x_0) = y_0,$$
the general form of the m-stage method is
$$k_i = f\left(x_n + c_i h, \; y_n + h \sum_{j=1}^{m} a_{ij} k_j\right)$$
$$i = 1, 2, \ldots, m$$
$$y_{n+1} = y_n + h \sum_{i=1}^{m} b_i k_i$$
$$x_{n+1} = x_n + h$$
The derivation of suitable parameters a_{ij}, b_i, and c_i requires extremely lengthy algebraic manipulations, except for small values of m.

Some early examples were developed by Runge and a systematic treatment was initiated by Kutta about 1900. Recently, significant advances have been made in the development of a general theory and in the derivation and implementation of efficient methods incorporating error estimation and control.

Except for stiff equations (*see* ordinary differential equations), explicit methods
$$\text{with } a_{ij} = 0, \; j \geq i$$
are used. These are relatively easy to program and are efficient compared with other methods unless evaluations of $f(x,y)$ are expensive.

running (active) Currently being executed, usually on a CPU. The *process descriptor for a process that is running will contain an indication that this is the case. Clearly, once the process becomes suspended for any reason, the "running" bit in the process descriptor will be reset.

run time The time at which a program begins to execute, in contrast to the time at which it may have been submitted, loaded, compiled, or assembled. The amount of time – elapsed time or processor time – used in executing a program is called the *execution time* or sometimes the *run time*.

run-time system A collection of procedures that support a high-level language at run time, providing functions such as storage allocation, input/output, etc.

Russell's paradox A contradiction originally formulated by Bertrand Russell and phrased in terms of *set theory. Let T be the set of all sets that are not members of themselves, i.e.

$$T = \{S \mid S \notin S\}$$

Then it can be shown that T is a member of T if and only if T is not a member of T.

The paradox results from certain kinds of recursive definitions. It arises for example in the following situation: the barber in a certain town shaves everyone who does not shave himself; who shaves the barber?

S

SAA *Acronym for* systems application architecture. A set of IBM standards for *application packages.

SADT *Trademark, abbrev. for* structured analysis and design technique. A method for modeling complex problems and systems, developed by Douglas Ross in the mid-1970s. Although SADT is a general-purpose modeling tool, it is particularly effective for requirements definition for arbitrary systems problems and is widely used for this purpose in the software engineering field. SADT can be viewed as having three main parts: a set of methods that can assist an analyst in gaining an understanding of a complex system, a graphical language that can be used to record and communicate that understanding, and administrative guidelines that contribute to the orderly progress of the analysis and early detection of problems.

The methods of SADT are based upon several concepts. Top-down decomposition allows information to be dealt with at progressive levels of detail. Model-building both assists understanding and permits communication of that understanding. Adoption of a variety of complementary viewpoints allows all relevant aspects of a system to be considered while limiting consideration at any time to one well-defined topic. The dual "things" and "happenings" aspects of any subject are used to reinforce understanding and promote consistency. Review and iteration procedures ensure the quality of the model that is developed.

The graphical language of SADT consists basically of boxes and arrows that are used to construct SADT diagrams. The language is concerned only with the structured decomposition of the subject matter, and any other language (e.g. natural language) can be used within the boxes and to label the arrows. A single SADT diagram may model either processes or data. A diagram that models processes, called an *actigram*, uses boxes to show the individual processes and uses arrows to show data flows between processes, any constraints that apply, and the mechanisms for carrying out the processes. The arrows entering and leaving a box serve to bound the context of the process, and this can then be decomposed on further actigrams through successive levels of detail to any level required. Similarly the corresponding data decomposition is presented in *datagrams* and consideration proceeds from highly abstract data objects through successive levels of decomposition and definition.

The administrative guidelines of SADT provide among other things for independent review of the diagrams as they are produced and for configuration control of the emerging model.

safety A property of a system that it will never do anything bad. The definition of what is "bad" is application-dependent: the safety requirements for a system controlling an aircraft would obviously be more stringent than those for, say, a stock control system. *Compare* liveness.

sampled-data system *See* discrete and continuous systems. *See also* sampling.

sampling 1. (time quantization) A process by which the value of an analog, or continuous, signal is "examined" at discrete fixed intervals of time. The resulting *sampled value* will normally be held constant until the next sampling instant, and may be converted into a digital form using an *A/D converter for subsequent processing by a computer.

The *rate* at which a given analog signal is sampled must be a certain minimum value, dependent upon the bandwidth of the analog signal; this ensures that none of the information in the analog signal is lost. The sampling rate may also affect the stability of an analog system if the system is to be controlled by a computer. *See also* Nyquist's criterion.

2. The act of selecting items for study in such a way that the measurements made on the items in the sample will provide information about similar items not in the sample. Items can be people, machines, periods of time, fields of corn, games of chance, or whatever is being studied. *Sample size* is the number of items included in the sample. If the variance of the measurement (*see* meas-

ures of variation) is approximately known, the variance of its mean in a sample is the population variance divided by the sample size. This formula can then be used to indicate an appropriate sample size.

A *population* is a complete set of items about which information is required. It must be defined before selecting the sample or results may be ill-defined. The sample is the basis for inference about *probability distributions of measurements on the population. Problems of sampling include avoidance of *bias and selection of enough samples to ensure adequate precision.

Random sampling is the process that results in each item having the same probability of inclusion in the sample. Items may be selected with the aid of tables of random numbers or with mechanical devices such as cards or coins.

Systematic sampling selects items in some regular manner. It is valid when the order in which items are encountered is irrelevant to the question under study, but can be an unintentional source of bias.

sanitization The erasure of sensitive material from a system, especially its storage media, e.g. by overwriting or degaussing magnetically.

satellite computer A computer that forms part of a computing system but is generally much less capable than the mainframe. It is located at a distance from the main system and serves auxiliary functions such as remote data entry or printing. It is now often nearly synonymous with *terminal.

satisfiability The property exhibited by any logical expression or well-formed formula for which it is possible to assign values to variables in such a way that the expression or formula is true.

See also propositional calculus, predicate calculus, P = NP question.

satisfiability problem *See* P = NP question.

saturation of a transistor. *See* bipolar transistor.

sawtooth waveform A periodic repetitive waveform that is constrained to lie between a maximum and a minimum value. Between these limits the waveform alternately rises and falls linearly with time. The slope of one of the edges of the waveform is made very much steeper than the other, and the waveform thus appears as a repetitive series of linear ramps. *Compare* triangular waveform.

scaling The adjustment of values to be used in a computation so that they and their resultant are within the range that can be handled by the process or equipment. The scaling factor is reapplied to correct the result before output or – if this is not possible – it is output as a qualifier with the result.

scanner 1. A device that can capture an image and convert it into a unique set of electrical signals. The image scanned may be a pattern that is directly related to a code, such as *bar codes on retailed products, or it may be a picture, page, or portion of text. *See also* holographic scanner, bar code scanner, document scanner.

2. *Another name for* lexical analyzer.

scatter read A process in which data from a single record may be collected into (or for the process of *scatter write* written into) several noncontiguous areas of memory.

scheduled maintenance Periodic *preventive maintenance.

scheduler The code responsible for controlling use of a shared *resource.

Access to a shared resource must be subject to two requirements. It is essential to ensure that any *process about to be granted use of a resource will not itself suffer damage, and that it will not cause damage to other processes. This can be thought of as establishing the correctness of the scheduling. Quite separately from this, where it is feasible to allow any of several processes to access a resource, then it is necessary to make a choice between them. This choice will generally have a bearing on the efficiency with which system resources are utilized, and is determined by the *scheduling algorithm.

When used without further qualification, the word scheduler refers to controlling the use of the processors. Scheduling of jobs is usually carried out in two stages. The *high-level scheduler* collects together a particular job mix that is to be executed at any one time, according to criteria that are thought to allow the system to be optimally used. The scheduling among these jobs on a very fine time scale is the province of the *low-level scheduler* (or *dispatcher*), which thus allocates processors to processes.

scheduling algorithm The method used to determine which of several *processes, each of which can safely have a *resource allocated to it, will actually be granted use of the resource. The algorithm may take into account the priority of the user associated with the process, the requirement to maintain high utilization of system resources, and deadlines for the job.

For example, in a priority *time-slicing system, the processes awaiting execution are organized in several queues with the higher-priority queues having a smaller time *quantum. Whenever a processor becomes available for scheduling, the oldest process that is free to run in the highest-priority queue is started.

If this process runs to the end of its quantum without generating an interrupt then it will be rescheduled into a lower-priority queue with a larger quantum. If, before the quantum has expired, the process generates an interrupt then it will be returned either to the same queue or possibly to a higher-priority queue with a shorter quantum. If the process is itself interrupted by some external event that allows the rescheduling of a higher-priority process (with a shorter quantum) then again the interrupted process is returned to the queue from which it originated.

The net effect is that low-priority processes, with long quanta, are likely to be interrupted by the completion of input/output transactions on behalf of higher-priority processes, which will thus be freed for further processing.

schema *See* data description language.

SCHEME A dialect of *LISP, used particularly in teaching computer science.

Schmitt trigger A discrete or integrated circuit whose output has two stable states, i.e. two sustainable values of output voltage, to which it is driven by the movement of its input voltage past two well-defined trigger values. A rise in input voltage above one trigger level causes the output to switch to one state. A fall in input voltage below the other trigger level causes the output to switch to the other state.

Logic signals become corrupted as they travel through a system; the switching edges become *exponentials, *ringing can occur, and *noise may be added. Feeding such a signal through a Schmitt trigger restores the rising and falling edges to a fast transition between the voltages corresponding to the 0 and 1 logic states.

Schonhage algorithm An algorithm that multiplies large numbers very rapidly,

based on the ideas of *modular arithmetic. *See* Chinese remainder theorem.

Schonhage–Strassen algorithm A development of the *Strassen algorithm that was published in 1970 and avoids the explicit use of complex numbers. It multiplies two n-bit numbers in steps of

$$O(n \log n \, \log \log n)$$

Schottky TTL A relatively fast bipolar *logic family, normally produced in integrated-circuit form, whose internal configuration is similar to normal *TTL except that *Schottky transistors* are used. These transistors can be considered as equivalent to a normal *bipolar transistor with a *Schottky diode* connected across the base-collector junction. The Schottky diode is a semiconductor-metal diode that has a low cut-in voltage (*forward bias voltage drop), typically 300 millivolts, compared with 600 mV for other common semiconductor diodes. It also has a relatively high switching speed. In Schottky TTL the low cut-in voltage of the diode limits the base-collector voltage to about 400 mV, which prevents the transistor falling into saturation. This results in faster switching times for the transistors constructed in this way.

scissoring (windowing) Processing the stored data of a large image so that part of it can be displayed. The visible *frame* or *window* formed by the process can be moved to allow examination of the entire stored image. Some graphics terminals have hardware "frame scissoring", but this is only effective when the complete image can be contained in the display file.

scope *Short for* nested scope. *See* block-structured languages. *See also* declaration.

scratchpad A type of semiconductor memory that usually has small capacity but very fast access. It is used for temporary storage of intermediate results or other information that is required during the course of a computation.

screen 1. *Short for* visual display screen. The surface of a cathode-ray tube on which information can be displayed. The word is used more specifically than *display, which can also refer to devices using panel technologies such as plasma, electroluminescent, and liquid crystal displays.
2. To select and display information in response to an instruction or an inquiry.

screen dump A way of transferring the entire graphical or textual contents of a display screen to a printer. Each *pixel of the display appears as a dot of suitable density on the printer. Color screens can be dumped to color printers.

screen editor *See* text editor.

scroll To move the information displayed on a screen or panel in a vertical or horizontal direction: as information disappears at one edge new information becomes visible at the other edge, or alternatively space is provided for the entry of new data. The scrolling action is perceived as a smooth movement. In some displays the movement is in discrete increments of one line pitch and this is referred to as *racking*. Scrolling is technically more difficult to achieve but eases simultaneous reading.

SCSI *Acronym for* small computer systems interface. A standard way of connecting peripheral devices, such as disk storage units, to small and medium-sized computers. It is specified in a document from the ANSI committee X3.31. Up to seven disk units and one computer can be connected to each SCSI.

SDLC *Abbrev. for* synchronous data link control. A *data link control protocol developed and used by IBM, and based on the use of *frames to delimit message boundaries. Only link-layer func-

tions are provided; there is no dependence upon characteristics of data structures of the devices that are communicating.

The frame format consists of an 8-bit flag, an 8-bit address, an 8-bit control field, a variable-length information field, a 16-bit frame check sequence, and another 8-bit flag. The information field carries "user" data and may be any length, although implementations of the protocol often limit it to a multiple of 8 bits in length.

The flag character is

01111110

*Bit stuffing is used to provide data transparency. Whenever a contiguous string of five 1 bits is encountered in the outgoing user data, the sender inserts a 0 bit. When the receiver encounters five contiguous 1 bits in the incoming bit stream, it examines the next one or two bits. If the first bit following (i.e. the 6th bit) is a 0 then it is removed and the user data is accepted. If the 6th bit is a 1 and the 7th bit is a 0, then a flag is accepted and the frame terminated. If both the 6th and 7th bits are 1, then a protocol violation has been detected and the frame is aborted. In the idle state, continuous 1s are sent for 15 bit times.

The address field permits 254 station addresses. Address 0 is reserved for testing, and address 1 means that the frame is directed to all stations on the link.

The link endpoints (stations) are assigned primary or secondary roles. A primary station initiates link activation, directs link use among multiple stations, performs error recovery, and directs link deactivation. The secondary stations may share receiving addresses but have unique sending addresses.

The control field is used by a primary to carry control information and acknowledgments, and to poll receivers. The control field is used by secondaries for the same functions as for primaries, and also to indicate "final frame", i.e. to return control to the primary. In addition there is a special mode in which stations may be configured on a single unidirectional loop.

Positive *acknowledgments are used with retransmission in the case of link errors. Acknowledgments are encoded modulo-8. ACKs may be piggybacked; a single frame may acknowledge up to seven previous frames in the reverse direction, as well as carrying user data in its own direction.

SEAC *Acronym for* Standards Eastern Automatic Computer. The first stored-program electronic digital computer to become operational in the USA, in 1950. (*Compare* Manchester Mark I, EDSAC, EDVAC.) It was one of two different pioneer machines developed by the National Bureau of Standards: SEAC was installed in Washington, and the other, called SWAC (Standards Western Automatic Computer), in Los Angeles. Like EDSAC and EDVAC, SEAC used mercury *delay line memory.

search and insertion algorithm *See* searching.

searching The process of locating information in a *table or *file by reference to a special field of each record, called the *key*. The goal of the search is to discover a record (if any) with a given key value. There are many different algorithms for searching, principally depending on the way in which the table or file is structured.

If a record is to be inserted in the file, and it is important to ensure that keys are unique, then a search is necessary: the insertion may take place as soon as the search has discovered that no existing record has the new key. Such an algorithm is known as a *search and insertion algorithm*.

See also table look-up, sequential search algorithm, binary search algorithm, breadth-first search, depth-first search, trie search.

search tree *See* binary search tree, multiway search tree.

secant method An *iterative method for finding a root of the *nonlinear equation $f(x) = 0$. It is given by the formula

$$x_{n+2} = x_{n+1} - (x_{n+1} - x_n)[f(x_{n+1})/(f(x_{n+1}) - f(x_n))]$$
$$n = 0, 1, 2, \ldots$$

where x_0 and x_1 are given starting values. This formula is derived by replacing $f(x)$ by a straight line based on the last two iterates. Convergence is ultimately less rapid than for *Newton's method, but it can be overall more efficient on some problems since derivatives are not required.

SECDED *Abbrev. for* single error correction/double error detection. An error-processing scheme based on work by R. W. Hamming (1950). If a single bit of a data word passed in the computer is altered, the single error is automatically corrected. If two bits are altered, the double error is detected but not corrected. If more than two bits are altered, the results are ambiguous.

secondary index *See* indexed file.

secondary memory *Another name for* backing store.

second generation of computers. Machines whose designs were started after 1955 (approximately) and are characterized by both vacuum tube (valve) and discrete transistor logic. They used magnetic core main memory. By this time a wider range of input/output equipment was beginning to be available, with higher-performance magnetic tape and the first forms of on-line storage (magnetic drums and early magnetic disks). Models of such on-line storage devices include magnetic drums in the UNIVAC LARC and 1105, and early disks in the IBM 1401–1410. During the second generation, initial efforts at *automatic programming produced B0, Commercial Translator, FACT, FOR-

TRAN, and Mathmatic as programming languages, these in turn influencing the development of the *third generation languages – COBOL and later versions of FORTRAN. *See also* Atlas.

second-order logic *See* predicate calculus.

sector A subdivision of a track on a magnetic disk that represents the smallest portion of data that can be modified by overwriting. Each sector has a unique address, which contains the location of the track and the sector number. In order to read an address or data the drive decoding electronics must be synchronized to the data stream. To achieve this a special pattern, the *preamble*, is written. Following the preamble comes the *address mark or data mark as appropriate.

A disk may be *soft-sectored* or *hard-sectored*. In soft-sectoring the size and position of the sectors is determined by the control electronics and software: disk drives generate an index signal once per revolution of the disk, and when this is received from the drive unit all the sectors of a track are written in one continuous operation. On a hard-sectored disk the start of each sector is related to a sector signal generated by the disk drive and is positively related to the position of the disk. Hard sectoring can achieve higher packing of sectors since it is not necessary to have large intersector gaps to accommodate speed variations.

security Prevention of or protection against (a) access to information by unauthorized recipients or (b) intentional but unauthorized destruction or alteration of that information. Security may guard against both unintentional as well as deliberate attempts to access sensitive information, in various combinations according to circumstances. The concepts of security, integrity, and privacy are interlinked. *See* integrity.

security accreditation Formal authorization that a particular computer installation or network can be used operationally in recognition that all features of the *security policy have been implemented.

security certification A statement by a recognized authority that a *security evaluation has been undertaken competently and in accordance with appropriate regulations.

security classification A classification of the sensitivity of information, e.g. "secret" or "medical records to be inspected only by doctors".

security clearance A categorization associated with a subject, e.g. a user, to describe the *security classification of information to which he is entitled to have access.

security evaluation The examination of a system to determine its degree of compliance with a stated *security model, *security standard, or specification. The evaluation may be conducted (a) by observing the functional behavior of the system, (b) by attempting to penetrate the system using techniques available to an "attacker", or (c) by analyzing the detailed design, especially of the software, often using *verification and validation.

security kernel A *trusted process that mediates all information flows within a system in accordance with a specified *security model. *See also* kernel.

security label A representation of the *security classification directly associated with the information to which it relates, e.g. as part of a transmitted protocol.

security model A formal statement of the intrinsic security features to be provided by a system. The statement usually includes a detailed specification, often in mathematical notation, of the allowed and prohibited relationships between subjects and objects according to their respective *security clearance and *security classifications. It may furthermore specify the events that must be recorded in the *audit trail.

security policy A statement of the measures, especially operational, to be taken in order to defend a system against the postulated *threats. The policy may specify the *security processing mode together with the *security model and their relationship with physical and personnel security controls. For example, the security policy will usually specify the way in which *passwords will be allocated and the arrangements for audit, etc.

security processing mode A description of the *security clearances of the entire set of users of a system in relation to the classification of all the information to be stored or processed by the system. *See* system high, dedicated, multilevel security.

security standard 1. A statement of the extent of evaluation necessary before a particular security feature can be considered for *security certification as *trusted.

2. A set of security features to be provided by a system before it can be deemed to be suitable for use in a particular *security processing mode, or in accordance with a generalized *security policy.

seeding (error seeding; bug seeding) The deliberate addition of errors to a program. Normally the errors seeded are semantic rather than syntactic, and are usually selected and located in a way that is representative of the normal distribution of error type and positioning. For example, a variable name spelling could be altered, or a branching statement condition changed from "less than" to "less than or equal". The pro-

gram is then subjected to test and the errors revealed in the test are analyzed into seeded and nonseeded forms. A test or series of tests should successfully reveal all the seeded faults: the technique has been used as a means of checking the effectiveness (and efficiency) of various test strategies.

It is however difficult to be certain that the seeded errors are truly representative both of the occurrence and the effect of real errors. It is particularly difficult to seed nontrivial errors.

seek time The time taken for a particular track on a storage disk or drum to be located. Typical seek times are in the range 10–30 milliseconds. *See also* latency.

segment 1. Originally, a clearly identifiable set of data, or code, that was moved between backing store and main memory under the control of the user. Later the term was applied to a set of data, still clearly visible to the user, that was managed by the operating system as part of the *virtual-memory system. A segment differs from a *page in that its size is not fixed, and the user has a measure of direct control over its management.

2. Part of a program. The word is usually used in the context of storage allocation, as in code segment, data segment.

select 1. To initiate an action or enable a data path.

2. To choose one of several possible control paths at a particular point in a program. The selection is usually made by a *case statement, though if there are only two alternatives an *if then else statement can be used.

selector 1. A device that can switch a signal path or initiate some other action on receipt of a predetermined signal. The actioning signal can be on the path to be switched or from a separate path.

2. *Short for* selector channel. *See* channel.

selector channel *See* channel.

self-adapting process (self-learning process) An *adaptive process that can be "trained" on representative data to provide a best model for that data and that can "recognize" similar data. *See also* artificial intelligence.

self-checking code *Another name for* error-correcting code *or* error-detecting code.

self-compiling compiler A compiler that is written in the language it compiles. Such a compiler makes it relatively easy to transfer a language to another machine, since the compiler can be compiled on a machine on which it has already been implemented.

self-defining A term applied to a programming language, implying that the compiler for the language can be written in the language. *See* self-compiling compiler.

self-documenting program A program whose function and working can be obtained from a reading of the program text, without additional documentation. Structured design, the use of a high-level language, careful choice of identifiers, and judicious use of comments all contribute to this end.

self-dual *See* duality.

self-extending A term applied to a programming language, denoting the ability to add new features to the language by writing programs in that language.

self-learning process *Another term for* self-adapting process.

self-organizing system A computing system that is capable of developing information and structure out of sets of nat-

ural data that are presented to it. *See also* artificial intelligence.

self-referent list *Another name for* recursive list.

self-relative addressing *See* relative addressing.

semantic analysis *See* static analysis, symbolic execution.

semantic error A programming error that arises from a misunderstanding of the meaning or effect of some construct in a programming language. *See also* syntax error, error diagnostics.

semantic net (or network) A means of representing relational knowledge as a labeled directed *graph. Each vertex of the graph represents a concept and each label represents a relation between concepts. Access and updating procedures traverse and manipulate the graph. A semantic net is sometimes regarded as a graphical notation for logical formulae.

semantics That part of the definition of a language concerned with specifying the meaning or effect of a text that is constructed according to the *syntax rules of the language. *See also* denotational semantics, operational semantics, axiomatic semantics, interpretation.

semaphore A special-purpose *data type introduced by Edsger Dijkstra (1965). Apart from creation, initialization, and annihilation, there are only two operations on a semaphore: *wait* (*P operation* or *down operation*) and *signal* (*V operation* or *up operation*). The letters P and V derive from the Dutch words used in the original description.

A semaphore has an integer value that cannot become negative. The signal operation increases the value by one, and in general indicates that a resource has become free. The wait operation decreases the value by one when that can be done without the value going negative, and in general indicates that a free resource is about to start being used. This therefore provides a means of controlling access to *critical resources by cooperating sequential processes.

semiconductor A material, such as silicon or germanium, whose electrical conductivity increases with temperature and is intermediate between metals and insulators. In pure semiconductors this effect is due to the thermal generation of equal numbers of negative charge carriers (electrons) and positive charge carriers (holes). These materials are called *intrinsic* or *i-type semiconductors*.

The introduction of specific types of impurity atoms into a pure semiconductor can significantly increase its conductivity: *donor impurities*, which belong to group 5 of the periodic table, greatly increase the number of conduction electrons and produce an *n-type semiconductor*; *acceptor impurities*, which belong to group 3, greatly increase the number of holes and produce a *p-type semiconductor*. These materials are called *extrinsic semiconductors*. The conductivity of an extrinsic semiconductor depends on the type and the amount (or *doping level*) of impurity present.

Semiconductors of different conductivity – n-type, p-type, highly doped n- and p-type, i-type – can be brought together to form a variety of *junctions, which are the basis of semiconductor devices used as electronic components. The term semiconductor is frequently applied to the devices themselves.

semiconductor memory (solid-state memory) Any of various types of cheap memory device, normally produced in *integrated-circuit form, that are used for storing binary data patterns in digital electronic circuits. They consist internally of arrays of *latches constructed of semiconductor devices such as *bipolar transistors or *MOSFETs. The memory *capacity of a single chip is increasing by a factor of four every few years:

the 4-megabit chip of dynamic *RAM is now (1989) on the market.

semicustom A technique used for the design of *integrated circuits that is based on the use of fully characterized libraries of circuit elements produced by the manufacturer of the device. The designer is therefore not concerned with low-level details of semiconductor material electrical properties, and can instead concentrate on the functional behavior of the design. Most *ASIC circuit designs (for instance *gate arrays) are produced by this method. *See also* full custom.

semidecidable *See* decision problem.

semidecision procedure *See* decision problem.

semigroup A very simple *algebraic structure comprising a *set S on which there is defined an *associative operation denoted by ∘ (*compare* group). The operator ∘ is assumed to take operands from the set and produce results that are also in S. When the set S is finite a semigroup can be described by giving the *Cayley table of the operation ∘; otherwise it can be described by giving a rule for ∘.

Examples of semigroups include: strings with the operation of *concatenation (joining together); the set of $n \times n$ matrices together with the operation of multiplication; the integers and the operation of choosing the maximum (or minimum) of two elements. The set of integers together with subtraction does not constitute a semigroup.

Semigroups play a major role in the theory of *sequential machines and *formal languages. If M is a sequential machine then any input string induces a function over the state-set of M. The set of all such induced functions forms a *semigroup of the machine* under function *composition (*see* Myhill equivalence, Nerode equivalence). Semigroups are also used in certain aspects of computer arithmetic. *See also* free semigroup, transformation semigroup, monoid.

semiring A *set S (containing a 0 and a 1) on which there are defined two *dyadic operations that are defined by $+$ and $\cdot$ and that obey certain properties: the set S, regarded as a set with a zero on which the operation $+$ is defined, is a *monoid; the set S, regarded as a set with a unit on which $\cdot$ is defined, is a monoid; the operation $+$ is *commutative; the operation $\cdot$ is *distributive over $+$. A semiring is said to be *unitary* if the operation $\cdot$ possesses a unit. A semiring is *commutative* if the operation $\cdot$ is commutative.

The set of polynomials in x whose coefficients are nonnegative integers constitutes an example of a semiring (which is not a ring), the two operations being addition and multiplication. Other uses of semirings occur in *fuzzy theory. *See also* ring, closed semiring.

semi-Thue system An important concept in formal language theory that underlies the notion of a *grammar. It was defined and investigated by Axel Thue from about 1904. A semi-Thue system over the alphabet Σ is a finite set of ordered pairs of Σ-words:
$$\{<l_1,r_1>, \ldots, <l_n,r_n>\}$$
Each pair $<l_i,r_i>$ is a rule, referred to as a *production*, with *left-hand side* l_i and *right-hand side* r_i; it is usually written
$$l_i \rightarrow r_i$$
Let u and v be Σ-words, and $l \rightarrow r$ be a production, then the word ulv is said to *directly derive* the word urv; this is written
$$ulv \Rightarrow urv$$
So w directly derives w' if w' is the result of applying a production to some substring of w. If
$$w_1 \Rightarrow w_2 \Rightarrow \ldots \Rightarrow w_{n-1} \Rightarrow w_n$$
then w_1 is said to *derive* w_n; this is written
$$w_1 \Rightarrow w_n$$

So w derives w' if w' is obtained from w by a sequence of direct derivations.

As one example, let Σ be $\{a,b\}$ and let the productions be
$$\{ab \rightarrow ba, \; ba \rightarrow ab\}$$
then *aabba* derives *baaab* by the sequence
$$aabba \Rightarrow ababa \Rightarrow baaba \Rightarrow baaab$$
It is clear that w derives any permutation of w.

As a second example, with productions
$$\{ab \rightarrow ba, \; ba \rightarrow \Lambda\}$$
w derives Λ (the empty word) if and only if w has the same number of as as bs.

The question of whether w derives w' is algorithmically undecidable.

sender-receiver terminal A term applied to teletype terminals, defining whether the teletype was a receive only (RO), a keyboard-driven terminal that could both send and receive (KSR), or a terminal that was also equipped with paper-tape reader and punch for automatic send-receive (ASR).

sense To determine the condition or content of a signal or storage location. When used in reference to a storage location the word has the same meaning as read.

sensitivity analysis Investigation of the degree to which the behavior of a system is affected by a change in the value of some (explicit or implicit) parameter or variable, or by a combination of changes. For example, a simple analysis might determine how the performance of a system is impacted by changing the number and sizes of the storage buffers that are allocated to that system.

sentence *See* predicate calculus.

sentence symbol (start symbol) *See* grammar.

sentential form *See* grammar.

sentinel A *datum that indicates some important state, usually in the context of input or output. For example, an end-of-data sentinel means all the data has been read.

separator A symbol that separates statements in a programming language, e.g. the semicolon in Algol-type languages.

sequence 1. A *function whose domain is the set of positive integers (or sometimes the set of nonnegative integers). The image set can thus be listed $s_1, s_2,$ ... where s_i is the value of the function given argument i. A *finite sequence* (or *list*) is a function whose domain is
$$\{1, 2, \ldots, n\} \text{ for } n \geqslant 1$$
and hence whose image set can be listed
$$s_1, s_2, \ldots, s_n$$
2. The listing of the image set of a sequence. Hence it is another name for *string.

sequence control register A part of the *control unit that causes the steps of the fetch and execute processes to occur in the correct sequence/timing.

sequence generator A digital logic circuit whose purpose is to produce a prescribed sequence of outputs. Each output will be one of a number of symbols or of binary or *q-ary *logic levels. The sequence may be of indefinite length or of predetermined fixed length. A binary *counter is a special type of sequence generator. Sequence generators are useful in a wide variety of coding and control applications.

sequencer A logic circuit that produces outputs that are intended to provide coordination stimuli for other logic circuits. The exact timing and sequence of these control outputs is dependent on the sequencer circuitry and may depend on a set of input control signals provided by external devices.

sequencing 1. The procedure by which ordered units of data (octets or

messages) are numbered, transmitted over a communications network (which may rearrange their order), and reassembled into the original order at their destination.
2. Proceeding through a program in its ordinary order, normally from sequential memory locations. *See also* loop.

sequency The number of positive-going zero crossings (and therefore half the total number of zero crossings) that the amplitude of a *signal makes per unit time, or, in the case of a spatial signal (a picture), per unit of distance. The term is used mainly with regard to signals capable of taking only one positive and one negative value of amplitude, especially the simple case of $+1$ unit and -1 unit. Although the amplitude is usually discrete, the time (or space) coordinate may be regarded as discrete or continuous, depending on the application and the mathematical methods to be employed.

The term was originally applied to *Walsh functions. In the case of Walsh functions, or any similar functions which are periodic but in which there are several zero crossings per period at unequal intervals, the number of zero crossings per period is called the *normalized sequency*.

Many concepts such as *bandwidth, and processes such as *filtering, which were originally defined in terms of *frequency, can equally well be defined in terms of sequency. The sequency formulation is often handled more simply and more rapidly by discrete devices such as computers.

See also discrete and continuous systems.

sequential (serial) Involving the occurrence of two or more events or activities such that one must finish before the next begins. If one event or activity immediately follows another then they are said to be *consecutive*.

sequential access A method of access to a *file (especially a data file) or a *database: a file or database is said to be sequentially accessed if the sequence of transactions presented to it matches a sequence in which *records are organized.

sequential algorithm In general, any algorithm executed sequentially, but, specifically, one for decoding a *convolutional code.

sequential circuit (sequential machine) A *logic circuit whose outputs at a specified time are a function of the inputs at that time, and also at a finite number of preceding times. In practice, any physically realizable sequential circuit will have a finite transit time, or delay, between the inputs changing and the outputs changing (one or more of these inputs may be clock signals); the intention of the term sequential is to include not only *combinational circuits but also (explicitly) *memory elements such as flip-flops. Analysis and synthesis of sequential circuits is facilitated by *state diagrams.

sequential cohesion *See* cohesion.

sequential file A file organized to support *sequential access.

sequential function Let I and O be alphabets. A function f from I^* to O^* (*see* word) is sequential if it is the response function of a *sequential machine. Often, though not always, there is the implication that the machine has finitely many states. In this sense therefore sequential function is to function as *regular language is to language, since the regular languages are those recognized by finite-state automata.

sequential machine 1. A *finite-state automaton with output (in some contexts including machines with infinite state-set). Thus there is a function f from the *Cartesian product $I \times Q$ to

the product $Q \times O$, with Q a set of states and I, O finite sets of input and output symbols respectively. Suppose, for example,

$$a, q_0 \longmapsto q_1, x$$
$$b, q_1 \longmapsto q_1, y$$
$$c, q_1 \longmapsto q_2, z$$

Then, if the machine is in state q_0 and reads a, it moves to state q_1 and outputs x, and so on. Assuming the starting state to be q_0, it can be seen for example that the input string $abbbc$ is mapped to the output string $xyyyz$. This mapping from the set of all input strings to the set of all output strings, i.e. I^* to O^*, is called the *response function* of the machine. The function f comprises a *state-transition function* f_Q from $I \times Q$ to Q and an *output function* f_O from $I \times Q$ to O.

What is described here is sometimes called a *Mealy machine* to distinguish it from the more restricted *Moore machines*. In a Moore machine, the symbol output at each stage depends only on the current state, and not on the input symbol read. The example above is therefore not a Moore machine since

$$f_O(b, q_1) = y$$

whereas

$$f_O(c, q_1) = z$$

Any Moore machine can be converted to an equivalent Mealy machine by adding more states.

A *generalized sequential machine* is an extension of the notion of sequential machine: a string of symbols is output at each stage rather than a single symbol. Thus there is a function from $I \times Q$ to $Q \times O^*$. *See also* gsm mapping.

2. *Another name for* sequential circuit.

sequential search algorithm The most simple searching algorithm in which the keys are searched sequentially from the top of the file until a match is found.

sequential transducer A nondeterministic version of a generalized *sequential machine.

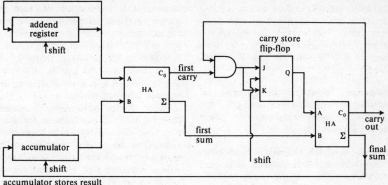

accumulator stores result
Serial adder

serial 1. Involving the sequential transfer or processing of the individual parts of a whole, such as the bits of a character. *Compare* parallel.

  2. *Another word for* sequential.

serial access A method of access to data in which blocks are read from the storage medium in the physical order in which they occur, until the required item is reached.

serial adder A binary *adder that is capable of forming sum and carry outputs for addend and augend words of greater than one bit in length. The individual bits of the addend and augend, starting with the least significant bit, are presented in sequence, together with a carry, to the adder, which then forms sum and carry outputs. The carry must then be stored so that it can be used with the next most significant pair of input bits. The overall result of the summation is stored in, for example, a *shift register, at the completion of each stage of addition. The diagram shows a typical circuit with the addend and augend initially loaded into the addend and accumulator registers.

A serial adder affords a saving in component count when compared with a *parallel adder, but is generally slower.

serial arithmetic Operation upon one bit or digit of a number at a time.

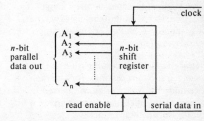

Serial in parallel out

serial in parallel out (SIPO) A term used to describe a class of digital device that can accept serial sequential n-bit data streams and convert them into parallel n-bit data words. These devices often consist of an n-bit *shift register that is serial loaded with n bits of data from the input stream under the control of an external clock (*see* diagram). The n-bit data word can then be read in

413

parallel form from the shift register. *Compare* parallel in serial out.

serial input/output (SIO) A method of communicating data between devices, typically a computer and its peripherals, the individual data bits being sent sequentially. Integrated-circuit devices known as *UARTs can be used to implement the transmitter and receiver required for such a scheme. *See also* parallel input/output.

serial in serial out (SISO) A term used to describe a *shift register that, by implication, cannot be loaded in parallel and cannot be read in parallel: data can only enter or leave the device serially.

serial interface A connection point through which information is transferred one digital bit at a time. The rate may be high, e.g. 10 megabits per second as in Ethernet, or as slow as 110 bits per second via an RS232C interface. The term is sometimes applied to interfaces such as the RS232C and RS422 in which the data is transferred serially via one path, but some control signals can be transferred simultaneously via parallel paths. *Compare* parallel interface, serial-parallel.

serial-parallel A combination of serial and parallel processing; for example, a decimal string is often processed as 4 bits in parallel, and successive 4-bit units are processed serially.

serial printer A printer that prints one character at a time in the sequence in which they appear in the line of text. The sequence may be taken from left to right, or it may be in alternate directions for alternate lines thus avoiding an unproductive carriage-return movement. All serial printers have an arrangement in which a print head moves parallel to the paper and along the line to be printed. The print may be formed by impacting an inked ribbon against the paper, as in the case of *dot matrix and

*daisywheel printers, or by one of the nonimpact marking technologies such as *ink jet or *thermal printers. In some designs the productivity is increased when printing other than complete lines by arranging for the head to move at high speed when passing blank areas. The direction in which the line is to be printed is also optimized.

The speed of a serial printer appears slow compared to the equivalent character per second rate for a *line printer printing full lines. However, the serial printer's ability to print short lines more quickly improves its performance on applications with short lines, such as addresses and amounts on preprinted forms. A 200 cps serial printer can print some types of consumer bills at a rate equivalent to 300 lines per minute.

serial process A *process in which stages in the process are executed in a strictly serial manner, one stage completing before the next starts, and with only one stage active at any one instant.

serial programming *See* single threading.

serial transfer To transmit information as sequential units. For example, if two computers connected by a single wire wish to communicate an 8-bit unit of information, the sending computer would transmit each of the eight bits in sequence over the wire, while the receiving computer would reassemble the sequential bits into the original 8-bit units. Thus an 8-bit serial transfer would have occurred. *Compare* parallel transfer.

serpentine recording A method of recording on magnetic tape (usually in cartridge form) where each track is recorded separately and alternate tracks are recorded in opposite directions, so that it is not necessary to rewind the tape after recording each track.

server A node on a network, usually a *local area network, that provides service to the terminals on the network through managing an expensive shared resource. The following are examples.

A *file server* manages a set of disks and provides storage and archival services to computers on the network that may not have their own disks;

A *printer server* provides printing in hard copy – often high-quality printing at very high speed – so that each terminal or computer on the network need not have its own printer;

A *communication server* provides connection to other communications media, including other local area nets or the public networks, i.e. it is a *gateway.

service bit A bit in an *X.25 *packet that indicates whether the packet is formatted to contain primarily data or control information.

service engineering Any maintenance, *preventive or *remedial.

service routines *Obsolete term for* runtime system.

servosurface *See* disk pack, disk cartridge, actuator.

session layer of network protocol function. *See* seven-layer reference model.

set 1. A collection of distinct objects of any sort. The objects in the set are called its *members* or *elements*. An element can occur at most once in a set and order or arrangement is unimportant. If x is a member of the set S it is customary to write

$$x \in S$$

If x is not a member of S this can be expressed as

$$x \notin S$$

and is equivalent to

$$\text{NOT } (x \in S)$$

i.e. $\in$ and $\notin$ can be regarded as operators. When any element in set S is also in set T, and vice versa, the two sets are said to be *identical* or *equal*.

A *finite set* has a fixed finite number of members and a notation such as

$$\{\text{Ada, Algol, Cobol, PL/I}\}$$

is possible; the members are separated by commas and here are just the names of various programming languages. When the number of elements is not finite, the set is said to be *infinite* and explicit enumeration of the elements is not then possible.

Infinite and finite sets can be described using a *predicate or statement such as $p(x)$ that involves x and is either true or false, thus

$$\{x \mid p(x)\}$$

This is read as "the set of all elements x for which $p(x)$ is true", the elements being characterized by the common property p. Examples of sets described in this way are (letting R be the set of real numbers):

$$\{(x,y) \mid x \in R, y \in R$$
$$\text{and } x + y = 9\}$$
$$\{n \mid n \text{ is a prime number}\}$$
$$\{l \mid l \text{ is the name of a language}\}$$

There is an implicit assumption here that there is some algorithm for deciding whether $p(x)$ is true or false in any particular case.

The idea of a set is fundamental to mathematics. It forms the basis for all ideas involving *functions, *relations, and indeed any kind of *algebraic structure. Authors differ considerably in the way they define sets. A mathematical logician will distinguish carefully between classes and sets, basically to ensure that paradoxes such as *Russell's paradox cannot occur in sets. However, the informal definition is adequate for most purposes.

See also operations on sets.

2. Any data structure representing a set of elements. One example is a *characteristic vector.

3. (of records) *See* CODASYL, def. 2.

4. To cause the condition or state of a switch, signal, or storage location to change to the positive condition.

set algebra The *algebra that consists of the *set of *subsets of some *universal set U together with the associated operations of *union, *intersection, and *complement. The set of subsets associated with set algebra is sometimes described as the *power set of U.

set difference The *dyadic operation between two sets S and T, say, resulting in the set $S - T$ consisting of those elements that are in S but not in T. Formally

$$S - T = \{s \mid s \in S \text{ and } s \notin T\}$$

Set difference is a generalization of the idea of the *complement of a set and as such is sometimes called the *relative complement* of T with respect to S. The *symmetric difference* between two sets S and T is the *union of $S - T$ and $T - S$.

set-up time The period of time during which binary data must be present or "set up" at the input to a digital device before the device enters or samples the data. It is commonly specified for memory devices.

seven-layer reference model The model for communications *protocols that is formally approved by the *International Standards Organization acting in concert with the *CCITT.

The goal is to achieve *open systems interconnection between computer systems and data communications systems without regard to its manufacturer or to the proprietary standards to which the equipment may conform.

The ISO approach is based on the provision of the reference model, which identifies the functionality required in terms of seven separate layers, as summarized in the table. At the ends of the communication path the lowest, physical layer, provides the means of moving a signal between the two separate systems; all communication between the two systems passes over this lowest layer. Above this lowest layer, each layer at each end can communicate only with the layers immediately above and below, by means of an *interface. However, by passing a message down through the layers at the transmitting end, across the physical link, and up through the layers at the receiving end, each layer can communicate with the corresponding layer in the remote system.

The objective of the model is to provide a framework capable of modeling a very wide range of applications, rather than to provide a universal set of protocols. The process of reaching international agreements that not only satisfy the (often conflicting) interests of suppliers and consumers but are also technically sound is slow, often taking several years. Once agreement on a *protocol stack conforming to the model has been reached, the development of commercially viable products conforming to the protocols is again time-consuming. Finally, the methods of testing for conformance, and for resolving cases where apparently conforming implementations are incapable of interworking, is again long drawn out. Despite this, products conforming to the model are now in use for networks themselves (X-25 for packet networks, ISO 8802.3 for CSMA/CD, ISO 8802.7 for slotted rings, ISO 8802.5 for token rings, and ISO 8802.4 for token bus), for internetwork connection (X-75), electronic mail (X-400), file transfer, access, and manipulation (*FTAM), office documentation (*ODA), and manufacturing automation (*MAP and *TOP).

seven-segment display See LCD, LED display.

S-gate *Another name for* ternary threshold gate.

SGML *Abbrev. for* standard generalized markup language. A family of ISO standards for labeling electronic versions of text, enabling both sender and receiver

Layer	Layer Name	Functional Description
1	Physical Layer	Provides mechanical, electrical, functional, and procedural characteristics to establish, maintain, and release physical connections.
2	Data Link Layer	Provides functional and procedural means to establish, maintain, and release data lines between network entities (e.g. terminals and network nodes).
3	Network Layer	Provides functional and procedural means to exchange network service data units between two transport entities (i.e. devices that support transport layer protocols) over a network connection. It provides transport entities with independence from routing and switching considerations.
4	Transport Layer	Provides optimization of available communication services (supplied by lower-layer implementations) by providing a transparent transfer of data between session layer entities.
5	Session Layer	Provides a service of "binding" two presentation service entities together logically and controls the dialogue between them as far as message synchronization is concerned.
6	Presentation Layer	Provides a set of services that may be selected by the application layer to enable it to interpret the meaning of the data exchanged. Such services include management of entry exchange, display and control of structured data. The presentation layer services are the heart of the seven-layer proposal, enabling disparate terminal and computer equipment to intercommunicate.
7	Application Layer	Provides direct support of application processes and programs of the end user and the management of the interconnection of these programs and the communication entities.

ISO/OSI seven-layer reference model

of the text to identify its structure (e.g. title, author, header, paragraph, etc.).

Shannon–Fano coding (Fano coding) *See* source coding.

Shannon–Hartley law *See* channel coding theorem.

Shannon's diagram of a *communication system. A diagram illustrating *Shannon's model of such a system, embodying the source, encoder, channel, noise source, decoder, and destination of information.

Shannon's model of a *communication system. A widely accepted model, set down by Claude Elwood Shannon in 1948, that has an *information source* sending a *message* to an *information destination* via a medium or mechanism called the *channel*. According to Shannon, "the fundamental problem of communication is that of reproducing at one point either exactly or approximately a message selected at another point."

In general, the channel will distort the message and add *noise to it. In order to avoid the distortion, and to reduce the effect of the noise to any desired degree, an *encoder is placed between the source and the channel, and a *decoder is placed between the channel and the destination. Now, the source sends the *transmitted message*, which is encoded as the *transmitted signal*; this is sent through the channel. It emerges as the *received signal*, which is decoded to give the *received message*; this arrives at the destination.

The channel is considered to have a *noise source* that inputs "information" in addition to that in the transmitted signal. The aim of the encoder and decoder is to make the received message resemble, as closely as required, the transmitted message, in spite of the "information" from the noise source.

See also source coding theorem, channel coding theorem.

Shannon's theorems *See* source coding theorem, channel coding theorem.

Shannon text A short standardized text often used for specifying or comparing the performance of document quality printers. It is believed to have the characteristics of "average English text" and is taken from work done by Claude Shannon on the *Mathematical Theory of Communication*. The text consists of 128 characters, including spaces, as follows: The head and in frontal attack on an english writer that the character of this point is therefore another method for letters

shared logic system A term sometimes used to refer to a system where several terminals share a CPU simultaneously.

shared memory The use of the same portion of memory by two distinct *processes, or the memory so shared. Shared memory is used for interprocess communication and for purposes, such as common subroutines, that lead to compactness of memory. *See also* multiport memory, concurrency.

Sheffer stroke *See* NAND operation.

shell A program that provides the *user interface of an *operating system and is often considered to be part of it. The main inner part of the operating system, the *kernel, is thus enclosed by the shell, as in a nut. Some operating systems have a choice of shells.

Shell's method (diminishing increment sort) A sorting algorithm proposed by Donald Shell in 1959 and published as *shellsort*. It is a variant of *straight insertion sort that allows records to take long leaps rather than move one position at a time. It does this by sorting each group $G^{(i)}_j$ of records a distance h_i apart within the file. (The $G^{(i)}_j$ are *disjoint and together contain all the information in the file.) This is repeated for a decreasing sequence of values h_i, and consequently increasing number of groups $G^{(i)}_j$, finally ending with $h_i = 1$.

shellsort *See* Shell's method.

shift 1. To change the interpretation of characters. The term is commonly met on normal typewriters as a change from lower to upper case.

2. Any complete set of characters obtainable without shifting. Hence *change shift* is a synonym for shift (def. 1).

3. The movement of a bit pattern in a bit string. A *left shift* of m ($<n$) bits will move the bit pattern in a string

$$b_1b_2 \ldots b_n$$

leftward, giving

$$b_{m+1} \ldots b_n ? \ldots ?$$

Similarly, a *right shift* of m bits converts

$$b_1b_2 \ldots b_n$$

to $? \ldots ? b_1 b_2 \ldots b_{n-m}$

The bits that are introduced (shown here as question marks) and the use of the bits that are shifted off the end of the string depend on the kind of shift: *arithmetic*, *logical*, or *circular*. In an arithmetic shift the bit strings are regarded as representations of binary integers; if the leading m bits that are lost are all zero, a left shift of m bits is equivalent to multiplication by 2^m and a right shift can be interpreted as integer division by 2^m. In logical shifts the bits introduced are all zero. In circular shifts the bits shifted off at one end are introduced at the other.

shift character Any character used in a stream of characters to change *shift. *Compare* escape character.

shift counter A *synchronous counter that consists of clocked *flip-flops arranged as a *shift register. Data is propagated from left to right (or from right to left) between the flip-flops by the application of a clock or count pulse. Counting is achieved by setting the contents of the shift register to logic 0 (or logic 1) and loading the

leftmost (rightmost) flip-flop with a logic 1 (logic 0). An m-bit counter, which has m flip-flops, will then require m clock pulses to shift this 1 (or 0) to the rightmost (leftmost) flip-flop. The position in the register of the 1 (or 0) thus acts as a count of the number of pulses received since application of the load.

The counter may be made to count continuously by arranging that the output of the rightmost (leftmost) flip-flop sets the input of the leftmost (rightmost) flip-flop. The counter is then known as a *ring counter*.

shift instruction An instruction specifying that the contents of a shiftable register (occasionally concatenated registers) are to be shifted either to the left or to the right a specified number of register positions. *Shifts can be circular or they can be open at both ends. In the latter case there is usually a specification of what happens to bits being shifted out of the register (often they are discarded) and what bits are to be shifted into the register (most often 0s).

shift keying *See* modulation, frequency shift keying, phase shift keying.

shift-reduce parsing *Another name for* bottom-up parsing.

shift register A *register that has the ability to transfer information in a lateral direction. It is an n-stage clocked device whose output consists of an n-bit parallel data word (*see* diagram). Application of a single clock cycle to the device causes the output word to be shifted by one bit position from right to left (or from left to right). The leftmost (or rightmost) bit is lost from the "end" of the register while the rightmost (or leftmost) bit position is loaded from a serial input terminal. The device may also be capable of being loaded with parallel n-bit data words, these then being shifted out of the device in serial

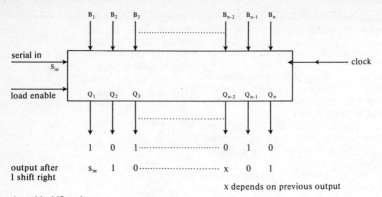

An n-bit shift register

form. *See also* serial in parallel out, parallel in serial out, parallel in parallel out, serial in serial out.

Shift registers with parallel outputs, and with combinational logic fed from those outputs (*see* combinational circuit), are of great importance in *digital signal processing, and in the encoding and decoding of *error-correcting and *error-detecting codes. Such registers may be implemented in hardware or in software, and may be binary or *q-ary. (Hardware implementation is usually convenient only for binary and sometimes ternary logic.) *See* feedback register, feed-forward (shift) register, Good–de Bruijn diagram.

shooting method An iterative method for the solution of boundary-value problems in *ordinary differential equations. Consider the problem
$$y'' = f(x,y,y'), \ y(a) = \alpha, \ y(b) = \beta$$
Let $y(x;t)$ denote the solution of this differential equation from initial conditions
$$y(a) = \alpha, \ y'(a) = t$$
This solves the above problem if $F(t) = 0$ where
$$F(t) = y(b;t) - \beta$$
The equation $F(t) = 0$ is solved iteratively, usually by some variant of

*Newton's method. Each iteration therefore requires the numerical integration of an initial-value problem.

The method is applicable to all types of boundary-value problems, whatever the form of the boundary conditions. Apart from the problem of obtaining good estimates to start the iteration, difficulties can arise due to severe *error propagation in the integration of the initial-value problem. A useful improvement is to guess the missing conditions at both ends of the range, matching the two solutions so defined at an interior point. In difficult cases estimates and matching can be used at several interior points to reduce error propagation; this is known as the *parallel-shooting method*.

shortest-path algorithm An algorithm that is designed essentially to find a *path of minimum length between two specified vertices of a *connected *weighted graph. A good algorithm for this problem was given by E. W. Dijkstra in 1959.

sibling (brother; sister) Either of two nodes in a *tree that are both children of the same parent.

side effect An effect of a *program unit that is not apparent from its *parameters, for example altering a nonlocal variable or performing input/output.

sieve benchmark A program that calculates the prime numbers within a specified range in order to obtain a *benchmark timing to complete execution. It is easy to use and is often employed to tune the optimization algorithms in compilers; however its coverage of language features is limited to arrays, simple variable types, looping, and comparison.

sifting technique *Another name for* straight insertion sort.

sigma algebra (Σ-algebra) *See* signature.

sigma language (Σ-language) *See* formal language.

sigma tree (sigma term; Σ-tree; Σ-term) *See* tree language, term.

sigma word (Σ-word) *See* word.

sign A means used to distinguish between positive and negative numbers. In a computer there are a number of ways of representing the sign of a number, each of which makes use of a single bit called the *sign bit*. The most obvious way of representing positive and negative integers in computer words is by means of the *signed-magnitude* (or *sign-and-magnitude*) *representation*. Here, the leftmost bit in a word is used to denote the sign (0 for + and 1 for −) and the remaining bits in the word are used to represent the magnitude of the integer. It is more usual, however, for a computer to use the two's complement representation of integers. *See* radix complement, complement number system.

signal A form of data that is usually envisaged as a sequence of values of a scalar quantity – the *amplitude* – rec-

orded (i.e. measured, tabulated, or plotted) against time. The amplitude is most often, but by no means always, an electric potential. *See also* discrete and continuous systems, space domain.

signal conditioning *Filtering a continuous signal.

signal operation *See* semaphore.

signal processing The processing of *signals by means of hardwired or programmable devices, the signals being regarded as continuous or discrete and being approximated by analog or digital devices accordingly (*see* discrete and continuous systems). *Filtering and *picture processing are examples of signal processing. *See also* digital signal processing.

signal-to-noise ratio The ratio of the *signal power to the *noise power in a physical transmission channel; it is often measured in decibels (dB). The definition is best applied to statistically well-behaved noise such as *white *Gaussian noise. *See also* channel coding theorem.

signature A collection of symbols, intended to be associated with *functions. Signatures arose originally from the mathematical study of *algebras but are now central to the precise treatment of many computer science issues, including *abstract data types and *algebraic specifications.

In its simplest form a signature is a set of symbols Σ with, for each $\sigma \in \Sigma$, a natural number $\rho(\sigma)$. The significance of this definition is seen in conjunction with algebras: a *Σ-algebra* consists of a set A (called the *carrier* of the algebra) together with, for each $\sigma \in \Sigma$, an n-argument function over A, where $n = \rho(\sigma)$. As an example,

suppose $\Sigma = \{$'zero', 'one', 'plus', 'times'$\}$

with $\rho($'zero'$) = \rho($'one'$) = 0$

and $\rho($'plus'$) = \rho($'times'$) = 2$

421

Then one Σ-algebra results from taking the set of all integers as carrier, and associating the number 0 with 'zero', 1 with 'one', addition with 'plus', and multiplication with 'times'. As indicated by ρ, addition and multiplication are 2-argument functions while 0 and 1, being constants, expect no arguments.

It is important to realize that the above example describes only one possible Σ-algebra. For example, the carrier could be the real numbers, or multiplication could be associated with 'plus' and addition with 'times'; equally sets could be considered instead of numbers, associating, say, *union and *intersection with 'plus' and 'times'. The point is that an algebra can involve arbitrary sets and arbitrary functions: any choice is as much an algebra as any other and it need not reflect in any obvious way the names chosen for the symbols. Indeed the whole point of signatures is to make a distinction between the symbols and their possible interpretations.

In computer science the more complex notion of *many-sorted signature* is often used. This allows algebras to have multiple carriers. A signature now, in addition to function symbols, includes a set of *sorts*. These are symbols that, in an algebra, are associated with carrier-sets. Instead of a natural number, $\rho(\sigma)$ is a sequence of sorts indicating which sets the arguments come from, together with an additional sort giving the set in which the result lies.

signature analysis A method of determining the location and/or nature of a fault in a digital system by input of test sequences and inspection of the resulting output sequences (signatures). The theory is that of *sequential circuits. See also* convolution, sequence generator.

sign bit *See* sign digit.

sign digit (signed field) A single digit used to indicate the algebraic sign of a number. If the binary system is being used, the sign digit is called a *sign bit*. *See also* sign, floating-point notation.

signed field *Another name for* sign digit.

signed-magnitude representation *See* sign.

significance test A statistical procedure whereby a quantity computed from data samples is compared with theoretical values of standard *probability distributions. Formally it is a comparison between a *null-hypothesis*, H_0 (for example that there is no difference between the means of two *populations), and an *alternative hypothesis*, H_1, (that a real difference exists). If H_0 is assumed to be true, the probability distribution of the test statistic can be computed or tabulated. If the test statistic exceeds the *critical value* corresponding to a probability level of α per cent, the null-hypothesis is rejected at the α per cent significance level. The most commonly used levels of significance are 5%, 1%, and 0.1%. Care must be taken to specify exactly what alternative hypothesis is being tested. Tests involving both tails of the probability distribution are known as *two-tailed tests*; those involving only one tail are *one-tailed tests*. *See also* analysis of variance, goodness-of-fit tests, Student's t distribution, chi-squared distribution, multiple-range tests.

sign off *Another term for* log off.

sign on *Another term for* log in.

SIL devices *Short for* single in-line devices. *Integrated circuit devices in which the terminal pins lie in a single line, typically of 0.1 inch pitch. This is in contrast for instance to the layout used for many ICs where the pins lie on two parallel lines – so called dual in-line (*DIL) devices.

silicon chip *See* chip.

SIMD processor *Short for* single instruction (stream), multiple data (stream) processor. *See* concurrency.

similar trees Trees that have the same structure or shape. More formally, two trees are similar if they both comprise exactly one node or, if not, the corresponding subtrees of the two roots are equal in number and are pairwise similar. For ordered trees, the pairwise correspondence is that given by the ordering imposed upon the subtrees of the two trees.

SIMM *Acronym for* single in-line memory module. A memory IC (*integrated circuit) whose pin-out corresponds to the *SIL format. Because the pins lie along one edge of the device package, it can be mounted on a PCB in a vertical plane, minimizing the board area occupied and maximizing the packing density.

simple parity check (simple parity code) *See* cyclic redundancy check.

simplex 1. Denoting or involving a connection between two endpoints, either physical or logical, that can carry data in only one direction with no possibility of data flow in the opposite direction. *See also* duplex, half duplex.
2. A finite graph of k points (the vertices), or a geometric figure, in which every vertex is connected to every other vertex (e.g. a triangle or tetrahedron).

simplex codes A family of *linear *error-correcting or *error-detecting *block codes, easily implemented as *polynomial codes (by means of *shift registers). Considered as (n, k) codes (*see* block code), they have codeword length
$$n = q^k - 1$$
Binary simplex codes have a minimum *Hamming distance equal to 2^{k-1}. They can be regarded as *Reed–Muller codes shortened by one digit, and are identical with the *m-sequences of length $2^k - 1$, together with the *zero word. They are so-called because their codewords form a *simplex in *Hamming space.

simplex method *See* linear programming.

Simpson's rule The approximation
$$\int_{x_i}^{x_{i+2}} f(x)\mathrm{d}x \simeq \tfrac{1}{3}h\,(f(x_i) + 4f(x_{i+1}) + f(x_{i+2}))$$
where $h = x_{i+1} - x_i$
It is used in *numerical integration.

SIMULA A programming language based on Algol 60, with extensions to make it suitable for writing *simulation programs. The major innovation in SIMULA was the concept of the *class*, which was a precursor of the *abstract data type.

simulation Imitation of the behavior of some existing or intended system, or some aspect of that behavior. Examples of areas where simulation is used include communication network design, where simulation can be used to explore overall behavior, traffic patterns, trunk capacity, etc., and weather forecasting, where simulation can be used to predict likely developments in the weather pattern. More generally, simulation is widely used as a design aid for both small and large systems, and is also used extensively in the training of people such as airline pilots or military commanders. It is a major application of digital computers and is the major application of analog computers.

From an implementation viewpoint, a simulation is usually classified as being either discrete event or continuous. For a *discrete event simulation* it must be possible to view all significant changes to the state of the system as distinct events that occur at specific points in time; the simulation then achieves the desired behavior by modeling a sequence of such events, treating each individually. By contrast, a *continuous simulation* views changes as occurring gradually over a period of time and tracks the progress of these gradual changes. Clearly the choice between these two in any particular case is determined by the nature of the system to be simulated and the purposes that the simulation is intended to achieve.

Although the distinction between simulation and emulation is not always clear, an emulation is normally "realistic" in the sense that it could be used as a direct replacement for all or part of the system that is emulated. In comparison, a simulation may provide no more than an abstract model of some aspect of a system.

simulation language A programming language that is specialized to the implementation of simulation programs. Such languages are usually classified as either discrete event simulation languages or continuous simulation languages. *See* simulation.

simulator Any system that performs a *simulation. It is normally a system dedicated for some period to performing a specific simulation, as distinct from, say, the case where a simulation program is executed as a normal job on some general-purpose computer. Simulators often employ either special-purpose hardware or hardware components from the system that is simulated.

simultaneous equations A set of equations that together define an unknown set of values or functions. The term is normally applied to *linear algebraic equations.

single-address instruction An instruction that makes reference to only one operand location. *See also* instruction format, addressing schemes.

single-assignment languages A class of programming languages. These languages have the appearance of traditional *imperative languages in that they incorporate the *assignment statement and typical control flow constructs such as if statements and loops. They impose the limitation, however, that no variable may be assigned a value more than once. (Special provision must be made for assignment statements within loops.) This limitation significantly alters the nature of the assignment statement, which can then be viewed as statically associating a name with a value rather than as a dynamic destructive operation. This static nature allows the normal ordering restrictions of imperative languages to be relaxed, and assignment statements can be executed as soon as the expression on the right-hand side can be evaluated. Because of this property, single-assignment languages are closely associated with dataflow computing (*see* dataflow machine).

single in-line devices *See* SIL devices.

single-step operation Proceeding through the execution of a program either by single instructions or by single steps (clock times) within an instruction. This method is used during program and/or hardware debugging.

single threading A property of a body of code that activates more than one processor, but does so in such a way that at any one time no more than one processor is active. This results in what is termed *serial programming*. For example, code that initiates peripheral transfers may be so written that while a transfer is in progress the processor will not be active, and vice versa. *See also* multithreading, threading.

singly linked list (one-way linked list) A *linked list in which each item contains a single link to its successor. By following links it is possible to access the entire structure from the first item.

singular matrix A square matrix, A, of numbers whose *determinant is zero. A is singular if and only if it is not invertible (*see* inverse matrix).

sinking technique *Another name for* straight insertion sort.

SIO *Abbrev. for* serial input/output.

SIPO *Abbrev. for* serial in, parallel out. *See also* shift register.

SISD processor *Short for* single instruction (stream), single data (stream) processor. *See* concurrency.

SISO *Abbrev. for* serial in, serial out. *See also* shift register.

sister *Another name for* sibling, rarely used.

sizing Preparing an estimate of the likely size of a program or software system. This estimate may subsequently be used, for example, to determine the amount of memory required on a computer system that is to execute the program.

Sketchpad *See* computer graphics.

skew In a *sequential circuit, the arrival of a signal at two or more places at significantly different times, when it should have arrived at more nearly the same time. Skew is said to be present when the difference in arrival times is great enough to cause or threaten malfunction of the circuit; this difference (usually measured in nanoseconds) is called the amount of skew. Most commonly, concern is expressed about *clock skew*, which is the skew in *clock signals (for which the phenomenon has usually the most serious consequences). Skew may be caused by component malfunction, or bad physical construction, but most often by bad logic design of the circuit. *See also* race condition.

skewed tree (unbalanced tree) Any tree that is not *balanced.

skew-symmetric matrix A square matrix, A, such that

$$a_{ij} = -a_{ji}$$

for all a_{ij} in A.

slave machine (direct-coupled machine) A large processor used to handle large jobs in a *master-slave system.

slice of an array of dimension n. **1.** The array of lower dimension that is obtained by fixing one or more of the indices of the n-dimensional array. For example, if A is a 3×4 two-dimensional array then the slice $A[2,]$ denotes the one-dimensional row vector comprising the second row of A while $A[,3]$ denotes the column vector comprising the third column.

2. (trim) The array that is obtained from a larger array of dimension n by restricting the range of an index. For example, if A is a 3×4 two-dimensional array then the 2×4 two-dimensional array comprising the first two rows only of A is a slice of A.

slice architecture *See* bit-slice architecture.

slot reader *See* card reader.

slotted ring *See* ring network.

Smalltalk *Trademark* An *object-oriented language, an object-oriented programming development environment, and a library of objects. Smalltalk was the first language to bring together all the features that characterize an *object-oriented programming system. The language was developed at the Xerox Palo Alto Research Center as a project within the Learning Research Group. It went through many versions during the 1970s (Smalltalk-74, Smalltalk-76, Smalltalk-78) and finally matured as Smalltalk-80. Until recently it was only implemented on Xerox workstations, but a version of Smalltalk-80 is now available for Sun workstations, and PC versions (Smalltalk V and Smalltalk V/286) can be purchased.

smart card *Informal name for* chip card.

smart terminal *Informal name for* intelligent terminal.

smoothing A means by which a table of values $f(x_0)$, $f(x_1)$, ..., $f(x_m)$ at the distinct points x_1, x_2, ..., x_m, can be approximated (represented) by a function, say

$$\sum_{i=1}^{n} c_i \phi_i(x),$$

where $\phi_i(x)$, $i = 1, 2, \ldots, n$, are chosen, and the coefficients c_i, $i = 1, 2, \ldots, n$, are to be determined. Typically $m > n$. The objective is to choose a fit that reduces the effect of random errors in the data combined with producing a curve that is smooth (no rapid changes or oscillations) between the data points. This is generally referred to as smoothing. The smoothing is often achieved by using low-degree polynomials (with suitable $\phi_i(x)$) and the coefficients c_i are frequently determined by the least-squares criterion (*see* approximation theory). *Compare* interpolation.

SNA *Acronym for* systems network architecture. A *network architecture developed by IBM for use with large mainframe computers.

snapshot dump A *dump that shows the state of a program at some particular point in its execution. It is usually obtained during testing or debugging and indicates the point in the program that has been reached and the values of some subset of the program variables.

SNOBOL A programming language designed primarily for the manipulation of textual data. It incorporates powerful pattern-matching and string-searching operators. The current version, SNOBOL IV, also includes facilities for processing other kinds of data, and is in fact a general-purpose language with a special capability in text manipulation.

soft copy A nondurable form of data output, such as text or graphical information on a VDU or the output from an audio response unit.

soft keyboard A keyboard in which the function or code to be generated by each key can be allocated and changed by program control. Keyboards on terminals for applications such as industrial data collection or point-of-sale applications frequently have keyboards in which some keys – usually the numeric and certain essential functions – are hardwired and the others are soft keys. The soft keys may have a meaning that is allocated to them at the time of initial installation and remains unchanged, or they may have their meaning changed during the course of a single transaction.

soft-sectored disk *See* sector.

software A generic term for those components of a computer system that are intangible rather than physical. It is most commonly used to refer to the programs executed by a computer system as distinct from the physical hardware of that computer system, and to encompass both symbolic and executable forms for such programs. A distinction can be drawn between *systems software, which is an essential accompaniment to the hardware in order to provide an effective overall computer system (and is therefore normally supplied by the manufacturer), and *applications programs specific to the particular role performed by the computer within a given organization.

software engineering The entire range of activities used to design and develop software, with some connotation of "good practice". Topics encompassed include *requirements analysis and specification, *program specification, program development using some recognized approach such as *structured programming, systematic *testing techniques, *program correctness proofs, *software quality assurance, software project management, documentation, performance and timing analysis, and the development and use of *software engineering environments. Further, software engineering is generally expected to address the practical problems of software development, including those encountered with large or complex systems. Thus, while there is some emphasis on formal methods, pragmatic techniques are employed where necessary. In its entirety, software engineering addresses all aspects of the development and support of reliable and efficient programs for the entire range of computer applications.

software engineering environment A computer system that provides support for the development, repair, and enhancement of software, and for the management and control of these activities. A typical system contains a central database and a set of *software tools. The central database acts as a repository for all information related to a project throughout the lifetime of that project. The software tools offer support for the various activities, both technical and managerial, that must be performed on the project.

Different environments vary in the general nature of their databases and in the coverage provided by the set of tools. In particular, some encourage (or even enforce) one specific software engineering methodology, while others provide only general support and therefore allow any of a variety of methodologies to be adopted. All environments, however, reflect concern for the entire *software life-cycle (rather than just the program development phase) and offer support for project management (rather than just technical activities). These two features normally differentiate a software engineering environment from a *program development system. *See also* PSE (def. 1).

software house A company whose primary business is to produce software or assist in the production of software. Software houses may offer a range of services, including hiring out of suitably qualified personnel to work within a client's team, consultancy, and a complete system design and development service.

software library *Another name for* program library.

software life-cycle The complete lifetime of a software system from initial conception through to final obsolescence. The term is most commonly used in contexts where programs are expected to have a fairly long useful life, rather than in situations such as experimental programming where programs tend to be run a few times and then discarded. Traditionally the life-cycle has been modeled as a number of successive phases, typically:

    system requirements
    software requirements
    overall design
    detailed design
    component production
    component testing
    integration and system testing
    release
    operation and maintenance

Such a breakdown tends to obscure several important aspects of software production, notably the inevitable need for iteration around the various life-cycle activities in order to correct errors, modify decisions that prove to have been misguided, or reflect changes in the overall requirements for the system. It is also somewhat confusing to treat operation and maintenance as just another life-cycle phase since during this period it may be necessary to repeat any or all of the activities required for initial development of the system. There has therefore been a gradual movement toward more sophisticated models of the software life-cycle. These provide explicit recognition of iteration, and often treat the activities of the operation and maintenance period simply as iteration occurring after rather than before release of the system for operational use. *See also* spiral model, V-model, waterfall model.

software maintenance The process of modifying a software system or component. There are three classes.

Perfective maintenance incorporates changes demanded by the user; these may, for example, be due to changes in requirements or legislation, or be for embedded applications in response to changes in the surrounding system. *Adaptive maintenance* incorporates changes made necessary by modifications in the software or hardware (operational) environment of the program, including changes in the maintenance environment. *Corrective maintenance* is the successful repair of faults discovered in the software.

Maintenance for software always involves a change in the software. This may be effected at the coding level, or may require significant changes in design. *Regression testing of the software follows maintenance as part of a reverification and revalidation activity. Software maintenance is a prodigious source of new software faults, so good quality control through software engineering is essential.

software monitor *See* monitor (defs. 2 and 3).

software package *Another name for* application package.

software prototyping Development of a preliminary version of a software system in order to allow certain aspects of that system to be investigated. Often the primary purpose of a prototype is to obtain feedback from the intended users; the requirements specification for the system can then be updated to reflect this feedback, and so increase confidence in the final system. Additionally (or alternatively) a prototype can be used to investigate particular problem areas, or certain implications of alternative design or implementation decisions.

The intention with a prototype is normally to obtain the required information as rapidly as possible and with the minimum investment of resources, and it is therefore common to concentrate on certain aspects of the intended system and completely ignore others. A prototype may for example be developed with no concern for its efficiency or performance, and certain functions of the final system may be entirely omitted. It must however be realistic in those aspects specifically under investigation.

software quality assurance (SQA) The process of ensuring that a software system and its associated documentation are in all respects of sufficient quality for their purpose. While a quality assurance team may be involved in all stages of a development project, there is typically a recognized quality assurance activity following completion of development and prior to release of the system for operational use.

The checks performed by the quality assurance team (which should be independent of the development team) vary between organizations and also depend on the nature and purpose of the software system. However they typically include functional testing of the software, checks that *programming standards have been respected, that the program documentation is complete and of an adequate standard, and that the user documentation for the system is of the desired quality. The team would also probably explore the reliability of the software system, and attempt to ensure that the software system and its associated documentation are so organized as to promote system maintainability.

A *quality management system* is the framework surrounding all the activities in quality assurance and quality assessment.

software reliability A measure of the extent to which a software system can be expected to deliver usable services when those services are demanded. Software reliability differs considerably from program "correctness" (*see* program correctness proof). Correctness is the static property that a program is consistent with its specification, while reliability is related to the dynamic demands that are made upon the system and the ability to produce a satisfactory response to those demands.

A program that is "correct" may be regarded as unreliable if, for example, the specification against which the program is shown to be correct does not capture all of the users' expectations of the program. Conversely, a program that is not completely correct may be regarded as reliable if the errors are insignificant, occur infrequently at non-critical times, or can simply be avoided by the users.

software specification A precise statement of the effects that the software component of a system is required to achieve. When developing a system, production of the *system specification is typically followed by a period of preliminary investigation and high-level design. It is then possible to identify any necessary hardware components of the system and to produce the software specification for the software component.

A software specification should be detailed, focusing on what the software is to do rather than how this is to be done. The traditional use of natural language for this purpose is gradually being superseded by use of more formal notations. *See also* program specification, module specification, review.

software tool A program that is employed in the development, repair, or enhancement of other programs or of hardware. Traditionally a set of software tools addressed only the essential needs during program development: a typical set might consist of a *text editor, *compiler, *link loader, and some form of *debug tool. Such a set concentrates solely on the program production phase and is that normally provided by a *program development system.

It is now recognized that software tools can assist in all activities of all phases of the *software life-cycle, including management and quality-assurance activities. Thus a comprehensive set would address such issues as requirements specification, design, validation, configuration control, and project management. Such tools would frequently form part of an integrated *software engineering environment.

solid-font printer Any type of *impact printer in which the complete shape of each character of the repertoire is engraved or molded onto a font carrier. The font carrier may be one of a number of forms including a molded ball or wheel, as in a *daisywheel printer, an etched band of metal, as in a *band printer, or a train of separate type slugs that are driven around a track, as in a *train printer. *Compare* matrix printer.

solid-state In general, formed on (or concerned with circuitry formed on) a single chip of semiconductor material, usually silicon, and therefore comprising *bipolar or *field-effect transistors.

solid-state memory *Another name for* semiconductor memory.

solvable problem *See* decision problem.

SOP expression *Short for* sum of products expression.

sort generator *See* generator.

sorting The process of rearranging information into ascending or descending order by means of *sortkeys. Sorting may be useful in three ways: to identify and count all items with the same identification, to compare two files, and to assist in searching, as used in a *dictionary. An *internal sorting* method keeps the information within the computer's high-speed random-access memory; an *external sorting* method uses backing store.

There are a wide variety of methods: *see* bubble sort, bucket sort, cocktail shaker sort, comparison counting sort, distribution counting sort, heapsort, list sort, max sort, merge exchange sort, oscillation sort, polyphase merge sort, quicksort, quickersort, radix exchange sort, radix sort, shellsort, straight insertion sort, straight selection sort, tree selection sort.

sortkey (key) The information, associated with a record of information, that is to be compared in a *sorting process. It follows that the sortkeys must be capable of being ordered, i.e. two keys k_1 and k_2 are such that

$$k_1 < k_2, \quad k_1 = k_2, \quad \text{or} \quad k_1 > k_2$$

sort merge *See* merge exchange sort.

soundex code A method of encoding words that sound alike. An application is surnames that are spelled differently but pronounced virtually the same. All names with similar sounds are given the same *key, while some secondary algorithm is used to match the names. A soundex code for a name is in the form *addd* where *a* is the initial character of the name and *ddd* are three digits derived from the remaining consonants. For example, "Johnson" becomes J523 while "Johnstone" is J525.

source alphabet (source set) *See* code.

source code The form of a program that is input to a *compiler or *translator for conversion into equivalent object code.

source coding (compression coding; source compression coding) The use of *variable-length codes in order to reduce the number of symbols in a message to the minimum necessary to represent the information in the message, or at least to go some way toward this, for a given size of alphabet. In source coding the particular *code to be used is chosen to match the source (i.e. the relative probabilities of the symbols in the source alphabet) rather than any channel through which the message may ultimately be passed.

The main problem in source coding is to ensure that the most probable source symbols are represented by the shortest *codewords, and the less probable by longer codewords as necessary, the weighted average codeword length being minimized within the bounds of *Kraft's inequality. The most widely used methods for ensuring this are *Huffman coding* and *Shannon–Fano coding*; the former is more efficient for a given *extension of the source but the latter is computationally simpler. In either case, a large extension of the source may be necessary to approach the limiting compression factor given by the *source coding theorem.

See also Shannon's model. *Compare* channel coding.

source coding theorem In *communication theory, the statement that the output of any information source having *entropy H units per symbol can be encoded into an alphabet having N symbols in such a way that the source symbols are represented by codewords having a weighted average length not less than

$$H/\log N$$

(where the base of the logarithm is consistent with the entropy units). Also, that this limit can be approached arbitrarily closely, for any source, by suitable choice of a *variable-length code and the use of a sufficiently long *extension of the source (*see* source coding).

The theorem was first expounded and proved by Claude Elwood Shannon in 1948.

source compression coding *Another name for* source coding.

source compression factor The ratio of message lengths before and after *source coding (which is generally intended to make messages shorter). *See also* source coding theorem.

source language The language in which the input to a *compiler or *translator is written.

source-level compatibility *Compatibility that exists when a program may be executed on two or more different computer systems by moving the *source code and recompiling it on each system without any changes. *See also* binary-level compatibility.

source listing *Another name for* program listing.

source program The original high-level language program submitted to a *compiler.

source set *Another name for* source alphabet. *See* code.

space complexity *See* complexity measure, polynomial space.

space-division switch Any switching mechanism that is based on the through connection of a set of input lines selectively to a set of output lines. Space division switches are implemented either by electromechanical means or by electronic means. Prior to the advent of time-division switching, all telephone and telegraph switching machines were implemented using a variety of space-division switching techniques, particularly Strowger (step-by-step) switches and crossbar switches.

space domain A term used to refer to a situation in which the amplitude of a *signal varies with position (usually in two dimensions, as in a picture) rather than with time. *See also* time domain, picture processing, filtering.

space quantization (pixelization) *See* quantization. *See also* picture processing, discrete and continuous systems.

spanning subgraph *See* subgraph.

spanning tree A *subgraph of a *connected graph G; this subgraph is a *tree and includes all the nodes of G. A *minimum-cost* spanning tree is a weighted spanning tree, formed from a *weighted graph, such that the real numbers assigned to each edge, when summed, total not greater than the corresponding sum for any other weighted spanning tree.

sparse matrix A matrix usually arising in the context of *linear algebraic equations of the form $Ax = b$ in which A is of large order and has a high proportion of zero elements (greater than, say, 90%). Special techniques are available that exploit the large number of zeros and reduce considerably the computational effort when compared to a general full matrix. Examples of such methods are variants of Gaussian elimination (*see* linear algebraic equations) and *iteration methods. Large sparse systems can arise in the numerical solution of *ordinary and *partial differential equations. *See also* numerical linear algebra.

SPDL *Abbrev. for* standard page description language. Currently (1988) a draft within the *ODA standard that will make it possible to map to and from the leading *page and *document description languages.

special character *See* character set.

specification (requirements specification) The elicitation, capture, and *expression of requirements for a system comprising hardware, software, and people. It is usually the first phase in a *software life-cycle model. The expression of the specification may be in text in a natural language (e.g. English), in a *specification language, which may be a formal mathematical language, and by the use of specification stages of a methodology that includes a *diagrammatic technique. Characteristics of a good specification are that it should be unambiguous, complete, verifiable, consistent, modifiable, traceable, and usable after development.

See module specification, program specification, software specification, system specification, axiomatic specification, constructive specification.

specification language A language, often a formal mathematical language, that is used in expressing a *specification. Examples include *Estelle, *SADT, *RSL, *VDM, and *Z. *See also* module specification.

spectral analysis *See* time series.

speech generation device A means for producing spoken messages in response to signals from a data processing or control system. The selection of messages is produced by assembling speech sounds from a set of fundamentals that may be artificial in origin or may have been extracted by processing human speech.

speech recognition The process of interpreting voice input to determine its data content. *See also* voice input device.

speech understanding The process of using *speech recognition to perform some task making use of speech. *See also* voice input device.

speed of a computer. A rather vaguely defined term that is often used to indicate the relative processing power of a given computer system, since the power of a computer is largely governed by the ability of the central processing unit to execute instructions rapidly. The CPU's speed is itself dependent on numerous factors such as word length, instruction set, technology of implementation, and memory access times. In general large mainframe computers are very much faster and hence more powerful than small minicomputers, which are in turn faster than microprocessors.

speedup theorem A theorem in complexity theory that, like the *gap theorem, can be expressed in terms of abstract complexity measures (*see* Blum's axioms) but will be more understandable in the context of time:

given any *total *recursive function r (n), there exists a recursive language L such that for any Turing machine M recognizing L, say within time bound S (n), there exists another Turing machine M' that also recognizes L but within a time bound $S'(n)$ that satisfies

$$r(S'(n)) \leqslant S(n)$$

for all but a finite number of values of n. Thus for this language there can be no fastest program.

spelling checker A program, often a component of a word processing system, that will check any or all of the words in a document against a set of dictionaries; this set consists of a base dictionary and optional extra dictionaries specific to the subject of the document or created by the user. On finding a word not known to it the spelling checker may suggest alternative spellings and ask if the word is to be added to the dictionary. Spelling checkers cannot of course detect errors that are themselves valid words, while their attempts to find alternatives to proper names can be distinctly amusing.

sphere-packing bound *Another name for* Hamming bound.

spiral model A *software life-cycle model devised by Barry Boehm that

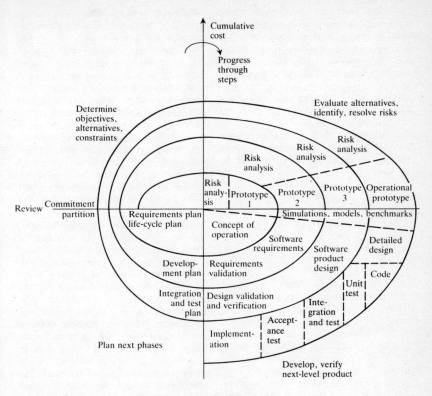

Cumulative cost

Progress through steps

Determine objectives, alternatives, constraints

Evaluate alternatives, identify, resolve risks

Risk analysis

Risk analysis

Risk analysis

Risk analysis

Review Commitment partition

Prototype 1

Prototype 2

Prototype 3

Operational prototype

Requirements plan life-cycle plan

Simulations, models, benchmarks

Concept of operation

Software requirements

Software product design

Detailed design

Development plan

Requirements validation

Code

Integration and test plan

Design validation and verification

Unit test

Implementation

Acceptance test

Integration and test

Plan next phases

Develop, verify next-level product

Spiral model [from *Computer*, May 1988, page 62. © 1988 IEEE]

encompasses a management strategy, a life-cycle development model, and *risk assessment. The model takes its name from the spiral representation as shown in the diagram. Beginning at the center of the spiral, where there is limited detailed knowledge of requirements and small costs, successive refinement of the software is shown as a traverse around the spiral, with a corresponding accumulation of costs as the length of the spiral increases. Interaction between phases is not shown directly since the model assumes a sequence of successive refinements coupled to decisions that project risks associated with the next refinement

are acceptable. Each 360° rotation around the center of the spiral passes through four stages: planning, seeking alternatives, evaluation of alternatives and risks, and (in the lower right quadrant) activities equivalent to the phases represented in *waterfall or *V-models.

spline In its simplest form a spline function (of degree n), $s(x)$, is a piecewise polynomial on $[x_1, x_N]$ that is $(n - 1)$ times continuously differentiable, i.e.

$$s(x) \equiv \text{polynomial of degree } n$$
$$x_i \leqslant x \leqslant x_{i+1}, \ i = 1, 2, \ldots, N-1$$

These polynomial "pieces" are all matched up at points (called *knots*):

$$x_1 < x_2 < \ldots < x_N$$

in the interior of the range, so that the resulting function $s(x)$ is smooth. The idea can be extended to functions of more than one variable. Cubic splines provide a useful means of approximating data to moderate accuracy. Splines are often the underlying approximations used in *variational methods.

split One of the basic actions applicable to a set S on whose elements a *total ordering $\leqslant$ is defined; when applied in the form

$$split(a, S)$$

where a is a member of S, S is partitioned into two *disjoint sets S_1 and S_2: all the elements in S_1 are less than or equal to a and all those in S_2 are greater than a. See also operations on sets.

split screen A visual display screen in which the top and bottom areas of the screen face may be treated as separate screens for the purpose of data manipulation. The split is usually into two parts, not necessarily equal, but there may be more. One part may be used for entering data from the attached keyboard while the other part displays instructions or prompts. The entered data may be manipulated by *scrolling or erasing without affecting the other part of the screen. See also window.

spoofing A deliberate attempt to cause a user or resource to perform an incorrect action. See also threat.

spool 1. The reel or former on which magnetic tape, paper tape, or printer ribbon is wound.

2. To transfer data intended for a peripheral device (which may be a communication channel) into an intermediate store, either so that it can be transferred to the peripheral at a more convenient time or so that sections of data generated separately can be transferred to the peripheral in bulk. Spooling is

therefore a method of handling virtual input and output devices in a *multiprogramming system.

For simplicity consider the case of output. Normally a program wishing to output to a line printer will claim a printer, use it to produce its results, and then release the printer. In a multiprogramming environment this is a potent source of delay since the speed at which a printer operates is typically slow compared with the speed of the process driving the printer; it would therefore be necessary to provide a number of printers approximately equal to the number of processes active in the system.

Spooling is commonly used to overcome this problem. Output destined for a printer is diverted onto backing store. A *process wishing to use a printer will be allocated an area of backing store, into which the results destined for the printer are written, and a *server process, which acts as a virtual printer and transfers information destined for the printer into the backing store area. When the process has no more data to send to the printer, it will inform the server process, which will terminate the information written into backing store. Subsequently a system utility will be used to copy the contents of the backing store for this process onto the printer. Similar arrangements can be established for dealing with the input to processes.

spread See measures of variation.

spreadsheet (spreadsheet program; spreadsheet calculator) A program that manipulates tables consisting of rows and columns of *cells*, and displays them on a screen; the cells contain numerical information and formulae, or text. Each cell has a unique row and column identifier, but different spreadsheets use different conventions so the top left-hand cell may be A1, 1A, or 1,1. The value in a numerical cell is either typed in or is calculated from a formula in the cell; this formula can involve other cells. Each time the value of a cell is changed by typing in a new value from the keyboard, the value of all other cells whose values depend on this one are recalculated. The ability of the cells to store text is used to annotate the table with column headings, titles, etc.

The spreadsheet is particularly suited to the microcomputer since it requires the fast and flexible display handling that is a feature of microcomputer systems. The common characteristic of all spreadsheets is the way the display screen of the computer acts as a *window onto the matrix of cells; if there are more rows and columns than will fit on the screen, then the spreadsheet can be scrolled horizontally or vertically to bring into view previously hidden rows or columns. To change a value it is only necessary to move the cursor into the required cell displayed on the screen and type in the new value.

Spreadsheets can be used for storing and amending accounts, "what if?" financial projections, and many other applications involving tables of numbers with interdependent rows and columns. A spreadsheet is often a component of an *integrated office system.

spread-spectrum modulation *See* modulation.

sprite A user-definable pattern of *pixels that can be moved about as an entity on a display screen by program commands. For example, the screen cursor in a *windows system that takes on different appearances in different situations is a sprite.

SQA *Abbrev. for* software quality assurance.

SQL *Abbrev. for* standard query language. A high-level language for writing routines to query *relational databases. Originally developed by IBM in 1973, it

is now much augmented by IBM and others. An *ANSI standard of 1986 defined the database query language and an *ISO standard was published in 1988. SQL does not currently cater for *referential integrity, but this is planned with other extensions known collectively as *SQL2*.

SQL/DS *Trademark* A *database package marketed by IBM, one component of which is a *relational database system. This system grew directly out of a research project, *system R*, at the San Jose Laboratory of IBM. *System R** is a *distributed database version of system R.

square matrix A matrix in which the number of rows is equal to the number of columns. An $n \times n$ matrix is sometimes called a matrix of *order n*.

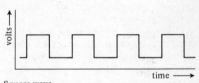

Square wave

square wave A signal consisting of alternate binary ones and zeros. The diagram shows how such a signal, when displayed on an *oscilloscope, may appear. A square wave can be considered as a *pulse train in which pulse separation is equal to pulse duration. When such a waveform is used to operate an electronic switch, it is described as a *switching waveform.

SR flip-flop *Another name for* RS flip-flop. *See* flip-flop.

SSADM *Abbrev. for* structured systems analysis and design method. The standard UK government analysis and design methodology, originated by

*CCTA. SSADM covers the data (information), processing (function), and events (logical) views of a system. The methodology has six phases covering analysis, requirements specification, logical design, and physical design of data and processes down to the program specification. Notations provided are for entity life history diagrams, dataflow diagrams, and process outline specifications. Tools support is available. SSADM is also compatible with the PROMPT II project management methodology.

SSI *Abbrev. for* small-scale integration, i.e. integration of generally less than 100 transistors on a single chip. *See* integrated circuit.

stability A multidiscipline term with a variety of (related) meanings. In *numerical analysis it is used with what appears to be a bewildering array of possible prefixes. There are, however, two important basic usages.

Given a well-defined numerical procedure it is important that roundoff errors do not seriously influence the accuracy of the results. This is referred to as *numerical stability* and depends on the *error-propagation properties of the procedure.

*Discretization methods for the solution of integral and differential equations are based on a subdivision of the region in which the solution is required. Stability here means that perturbations in the data (initial or boundary conditions) have a bounded effect on the solution obtained (ignoring roundoff error) for a given subdivision. The existence of a uniform bound on this effect over all sufficiently fine subdivisions is a necessary condition for the convergence of the method as the subdivision is refined.

In the solution of *ordinary differential equations much of the stability theory has been developed in the study of stiff systems of equations. Of great

importance to this development was the concept of *A-stability* introduced by Dahlquist in 1963. A method is A-stable if it produces bounded solutions for the test problem

$$y' = qy, \; y(0) = 1 \quad \mathrm{Re}(q) < 0$$

for *all stepsizes*. The trapezoidal rule (*see* ordinary differential equations) is an example of an A-stable method. Much of the later theory has investigated similar properties for more general test problems.

stable sorting algorithm A sorting algorithm that preserves the relative ordering of records with equal sortkeys.

stack 1. (pushdown stack; pushdown list; LIFO list) A linear *list where all accesses, insertions, and removals are made at one end of the list, called the *top*. This implies access on a last in first out (LIFO) basis: the most recently inserted item on the list is the first to be removed. The operations *push* and *pop* refer respectively to the insertion and removal of items at the top of the stack. Stacks occur frequently in computing and in particular are closely associated with *recursion.

2. Loosely, a linear *list where accesses, insertions, and removals are made at one end or both ends of the list. This includes a pushdown stack, described above. When the earliest inserted item on the linear list is the first to be removed (first in first out, FIFO), it is a *pushup stack*, more properly known as a *queue. When insertions and deletions may be made at both ends, it is a double-ended queue, or *deque.

A stack may be implemented in hardware as a specialized kind of addressless memory, with a control mechanism to implement any of the insertion/removal regimes. *See also* stack processing.

stack algorithm In general, any algorithm that employs a *stack, but, specifically, one for decoding a *convolutional code.

stack architecture An architecture in which *stack processing is used.

stack frame In a *block-structured language, storage required by a block (procedure) is allocated on entry to the block and is de-allocated at the exit from the block. Since blocks are nested, storage can be allocated on a last in first out basis on a *stack, and the area of the stack containing data for a particular block is called the stack frame for the block.

stack manipulation *Another name for* stack processing.

stack processing (stack manipulation) Use of (almost always) a pushdown *stack implemented in hardware as memory for programs and data. This permits zero-address instructions to be employed and makes programs more compact. Stack mechanisms are also used to provide a way of keeping track of multiple interrupts in which the stack serves as a way of "nesting" the interrupts so that those of lesser priority are pushed down until those of higher priority can be attended to.

staging A form of *spooling associated with the use of magnetic tape. The contents of a tape that is to be operated upon by a process may be staged onto magnetic disk. In this form, tape-winding time is virtually eliminated since it is possible to locate a particular part of the "tape" much more rapidly if it is entirely held on disk.

staircase waveform A waveform that is generally constrained to lie between maximum and minimum voltage values. Between these extremes the waveform can only take on discrete and constant values of voltage for fixed periods of time. The waveform thus consists of a number of small step changes in voltage

level, hence the term staircase. The height of each step will normally be made constant but may be variable, as may the period of time over which the waveform resides at a given voltage level.

stand-alone Denoting hardware or software that is capable of performing its function without being connected to any other component.

standard 1. A publicly available definition of a hardware or software component, resulting from international, national, or industrial agreement.
2. A product, usually hardware, that conforms to such a definition.

standard deviation *See* measures of variation.

standard error *See* measures of variation.

standard function A *function provided as part of a programming language, in particular to evaluate the standard mathematical functions (sin, cos, exp, etc.). The term is sometimes used more generally as a synonym for library program (*see* program library).

standard interface A point of interconnection between two systems or parts of a system, e.g. that between a processor and a peripheral, at which all the physical, electrical, and logical parameters are in accordance with predetermined values and are collectively used in other instances. An interface may be classed as standard on the basis of manufacturer, industry, or international usage. The I/O channels of a processor may be classed as standard interfaces because they are common to all processors of that type, or common to more than one type of peripheral – but they may be specific to a manufacturer. Some interfaces are de facto industry standards and can be used to connect devices from different vendors. The Centronics parallel interface for printers is an example of a manufacturer's interface for which compatible interfaces are available from a number of other printer manufacturers.

Some interfaces are standardized by agreement within trade associations or international committees. The *RS232C interface is used for connecting many types of relatively slow peripherals to processors or modems: the specification is published by EIA of Washington DC but it is also in close agreement with the series of recommendations issued by CCITT of Europe (*see* V.24).

standardization 1. The establishment of an international, national, or industrial agreement concerning the specification or production of components – electrical, electronic, or software – or equipment in general, or of procedures for the use or testing of equipment or software.

2. The act of committing an organization to use specific standards to meet particular needs whenever they arise within the organization. Typically an organization might standardize upon use of a specific compiler for some language, some specific application package, or a particular database management system.

standard product of sums One of the two canonical (i.e. standard or normal) forms of a *Boolean function, useful in comparing and simplifying functions. This form contains one *standard sum term, or maxterm, for each "zero" (false) entry in the *truth table for the expression. This form can be represented as the AND (product) of a group of ORs (the sum terms) of Boolean variables, uncomplemented or complemented. It can also be shown to be the NOR of a group of NORs of the identical variables. *Compare* standard sum of products.

standard product term (minterm) A product (AND) of *n* Boolean variables, uncomplemented or complemented but not repeated, in a function of *n* variables. With *n* variables, 2^n different standard product terms are possible. The complement of any standard product term is a *standard sum term, or maxterm.

standard subroutine *Obsolete term for* a component of a *program library.

standard sum of products One of the two canonical (i.e. standard or normal) forms of a *Boolean function, useful in comparing and simplifying functions. This form contains one *standard product term, or minterm, for each "one" (true) entry in the *truth table for the expression. This form can be represented as the OR (sum) of a group of ANDs (the product terms) of Boolean variables, uncomplemented or complemented. It can also be shown to be the NAND of a group of NANDs of the identical variables. *Compare* standard product of sums.

standard sum term (maxterm) A sum (OR) of *n* Boolean variables, uncomplemented or complemented but not repeated, in a function of *n* variables. With *n* variables, 2^n different standard sum terms are possible. The complement of any standard sum term is a *standard product term, or minterm.

standby time *Another name for* idle time. *See* available time.

STAR One of the early *vector processors, manufactured by CDC and unique on several grounds: it is one of the large machines built by CDC that was not designed by Seymour Cray (the architect was Jim Thornton); it was noted for having very wide words that can be processed in parallel; it was the first machine marketed that was aimed at very rapid processing of vectors.

star closure *See* Kleene star.

star-height The maximum depth to which the *Kleene-star operator is nested in a given *regular expression. The star-height of a *regular language L is the smallest star-height of any regular expression for L. There is no known algorithm for determining the star-height of a regular language. It is however known that there are regular languages of arbitrary star-height.

If complement and intersection are allowed, the class of *generalized* regular expressions is obtained. For these it is not known if there are languages of star-height greater than one.

star network A simple network topology with all links connecting directly to a single central *node. Star networks work well when traffic consists of multiple secondary nodes communicating with a single primary node, e.g. computer terminals connected to a time-sharing host.

The main disadvantages of a star network are:

(a) central switch failure disrupts the entire network;

(b) circuit failures between the central switch and the terminals result in loss of user communication (no alternate paths);

(c) the cost of having every user directly connected to the central site may be very high for geographically distant (dispersed) nodes;

(d) total communication capacity is often limited by the speed of the central switch.

The main advantage of a star network is that the design of the end terminals may be very simple. *See also* network architecture.

STARTS A UK initiative, begun in 1982, to promote best practice in *software engineering. It is funded by the Dept. of Trade and Industry, operated by the National Computing Centre, and widely supported by the IT (*information technology) user and supply industry. The initiative has published information and evaluations of software engineering methods and tools, best practice for IT and real-time systems developers, together with purchasing practice and advice to industry and users.

start symbol (sentence symbol) *See* grammar.

start time *Another name for* acceleration time.

starvation 1. *Jargon* A situation occurring when the rate at which a *process can proceed is sharply reduced by its inability to gain access to a particular resource.

2. A situation arising in a *Petri net when the time between successive entries to a state can become indefinitely long.

state assignment The assignment of combinations of *state variables to the stable internal conditions – *states* – of a *sequential circuit in the synthesis (realization) process.

state diagram A graphical version of a *state table. *See also* finite-state automaton.

statement The unit from which a high-level language program is constructed: a program is a sequence of statements. It is analogous to an *instruction at the machine-code level. *See also* declaration.

statement label *See* label.

statement testing A test strategy in which each statement of a program is executed at least once. It is equivalent to finding a *path (or set of paths) through the *control flow graph that contains all the nodes of the graph. It is a weaker testing strategy than *path testing or *branch testing because it (usually) requires the least number of test cases.

state table 1. A table describing the behavior of a *sequential circuit as a function of stable internal conditions –

states – and input variables. For each combination of these, the next state of the circuit is specified together with any output variables.

2. *See* finite-state automaton.

state transition function, table, diagram *See* finite-state automaton.

state variable A (generally) binary variable describing the state of each memory element within a *sequential circuit.

static Not changing, incapable of being changed, or unable to take place during some period of time, usually while a system or device is in operation or a program is running. *Compare* dynamic.

static allocation An allocation that cannot be changed while a process is running.

static analysis Analysis of a program that does not require the program to be executed as in dynamic *testing. A *software tool is used to check syntax and to construct one or more of

a *control flow graph,

a *dataflow graph,

an information flow graph.

Information flow analysis identifies the relationships between outputs and the input variables, and a *semantic analysis* provides formulae for these relationships. Comparing the results of semantic analysis with a formal *program specification reveals inconsistencies between specification and implementation.

Early work (1975–76) led to analyzers (DAVE, AUDIT, FACES) for single languages such as FORTRAN. Later work led to analyzers for C (e.g. LINT, 1978). There are now analysis tools (e.g. MALPAS, SPADE) that are multi-language and have facilities for comparing specification and code.

static data structure A data structure whose organizational characteristics are invariant throughout its lifetime. Such structures are well supported by high-level languages and familiar examples are *arrays. The prime features of static structures are

(a) none of the structural information need be stored explicitly within the elements – it is often held in a distinct logical/physical header;

(b) the elements of an allocated structure are physically contiguous, held in a single segment of memory;

(c) all descriptive information, other than the physical location of the allocated structure, is determined by the structure definition;

(d) relationships between elements do not change during the lifetime of the structure.

Relaxation of these features leads to the concept of a *dynamic data structure.

static dump A dump, usually of the workspace of a *process, taken at a time when the process can be guaranteed to be inactive, such as at the end of a job step.

static RAM *See* RAM.

station in a communication network. *Another name for* node.

stationery The paper used in *printers. It is one type of *data medium and is available in a number of forms.

Continuous stationery consists of an unbroken length of paper that has transverse perforations dividing the length into identical sheets. The perforations allow the paper to be provided in fanfold form and to be easily separated into shorter lengths or single sheets after printing a job. There are sprocket holes at $\frac{1}{2}''$ pitch, $\frac{1}{4}''$ from both edges, by which the stationery is driven accurately through a printer by a *tractor or pinwheel mechanism. Continuous stationery may be up to 20″ wide and may have additional transverse or longitudinal perforations to enable the sheets to be separated into smaller forms.

Roll stationery is provided in roll form for applications where ease of filing the *printout is not important. It is commonly friction-fed through the printer, but some rolls have sprocket holes as on continuous stationery. Printers that use roll stationery usually have a tear-off facility. Rolls may be typically 2″–3″ wide as used on *point of sale terminals, or 8″–10″ as used on other printers.

Single-sheet stationery consists of a pack of identical separate sheets that may be fed manually into a printer, or may be loaded as a pack into a printer attachment – a *cut sheet feed* – designed to feed them automatically one sheet at a time.

Single-part stationery has only one layer of paper passing through the printer. *Multi-part stationery* consists of two or more layers of paper crimped together to pass through the printer so that multiple simultaneous copies of printout can be obtained on an *impact printer. The papers may be interleaved with carbon to form the copies, or *NCR* (*no carbon required*) paper may be used. NCR paper has a coated surface that under pressure releases ink locally. Multi-part stationery can be in continuous, roll, or single-sheet form.

Label stationery consists of a suitable backing in continuous single-part form on which are mounted self-adhesive labels. These are used to print addresses, for example, the labels being subsequently removed from the backing and applied to envelopes.

Stationery is provided in a number of special forms, e.g. *carrier stationery*, which has custom-designed forms or envelopes mounted onto a backing, which in turn may be single-sheet or continuous form. Stationery can also be *pre-printed* according to the needs of the user.

Stationery specifications consist of two main parts. There is the specification of the paper, which states the characteristics required of the paper in order to withstand the stresses of the types of printer for which it is intended and to give the required printing performance; such characteristics include strength, thickness, porosity, smoothness, density, and material content. A coating may also have to be defined for use with certain printer types, e.g. *thermal printers. There is also the specification of the conversion requirements, which state what form the finished stationery must take, including dimensions, pre-printing, and any special requirements. Stationery is subject to international standards.

statistical analysis *See* statistical methods.

statistical methods Methods of collecting, summarizing, analysing, and interpreting variable numerical data. Statistical methods can be contrasted with *deterministic methods, which are appropriate where observations are exactly reproducable or are assumed to be so. While statistical methods are widely used in the life sciences, in economics, and in agricultural science, they also have an important role in the physical sciences in the study of measurement errors, of random phenomena such as radioactivity or meteorological events, and in obtaining approximate results where deterministic solutions are hard to apply.

Data collection involves deciding what to observe in order to obtain information relevant to the questions whose answers are required, and then making the observations. *Sampling involves choice of a sufficient number of observations representing an appropriate population. Experiments with variable outcomes should be conducted according to principles of *experimental design.

Data summarization is the calculation of appropriate *statistics (def. 2) and the display of such information in the form of tables, graphs, or charts. Data may also be adjusted to make different samples more comparable, using ratios, compensating factors, etc.

Statistical analysis relates observed statistical data to theoretical models, such as *probability distributions or models used in *regression analysis. By estimating *parameters in the proposed model and testing hypotheses about rival models, one can assess the value of the information collected and the extent to which the information can be applied to similar situations. *Statistical prediction* is the application of the model thought to be most appropriate, using the estimated values of the parameters.

More recently, less formal methods of looking at data have been proposed, including *exploratory data analysis.

statistical multiplexing A technique of *time division multiplexing of a number of subchannels onto a common wider-bandwidth channel, where the total *bandwidth required by the individual subchannels exceeds the bandwidth of the multiplex channel. Since the maximum rate required by any one channel is seldom used, due to breaks in transmission, this technique is possible through judicious use of buffering. In this system bandwidth is not allocated permanently to each subchannel but only as required.

statistical prediction *See* statistical methods.

statistics 1. Numerical data relating to sets of individuals, objects, or phenomena. It is also the science of collecting, summarizing, and interpreting such data.

2. Quantities derived from data in order to summarize the properties of a sample. For example, the mean of a sample is a statistic that is a *measure of location, while the standard deviation is a *measure of variation.

status of a process. *See* process descriptor.

status register *See* program status word, processor status word.

status signal A *busy signal or *ready signal.

Steffenson iteration An *iterative method to find the root of a nonlinear *polynomial. It is an improved version of *Aitken's Δ^2-process.

stepper motor *See* actuator.

stepsize *See* finite-difference method.

stepwise refinement An approach to software development in which an initial highly abstract representation of some required program is gradually refined through a sequence of intermediate representations to yield a final program in some chosen programming language. The initial representation employs notations and abstractions that are appropriate for the problem being addressed. Subsequent development then proceeds in a sequence of small steps. Each step refines some aspect of the representation produced by the previous step, thus yielding the next representation in the sequence. Typically a single step involves simultaneous refinement of both data structures and operations, and is small enough to be performed with some confidence that the result is correct. Refinement proceeds until the final representation in the sequence is expressed entirely in the chosen programming language. The approach is normally associated with N. Wirth, designer of the *Pascal and *Modula languages. *Compare* structured programming.

stiff equations *See* ordinary differential equations.

stochastic matrix A matrix, much used for example in simulation, modeling, and communication theory, in which every row is a probability distribution, i.e. every element lies between 0 and 1, and the sum of the elements of each row is unity. A *doubly stochastic matrix* is a stochastic matrix whose transpose is a stochastic matrix.

stochastic process A set of *random variables whose values vary with time (or sometimes in space). Examples include populations affected by births and deaths, the length of a queue (*see* queuing theory), or the amount of water in a reservoir. *Stochastic models* are models in which random variation is of major importance, in contrast to deterministic models. Stochastic processes give theoretical explanations for many *probability distributions, and underly the analysis of *time-series data.

storage (memory, store) A device or medium that can retain data for subsequent retrieval. *See* storage device. *See also* memory.

storage allocation 1. The amount of storage allocated to a *process.
2. The act of allocating storage to a *process. In a multiprogramming system it is necessary to control the use of storage to ensure that processes do not interfere with one another's workspace, except where they do so intentionally in order to cooperate. This represents one instance of the resource control activities within the system.

storage device A device that can receive data and retain it for subsequent retrieval. Such devices cover a wide range of capacities and speeds of access. The semiconductor devices used as the *main memory for the processor may take only a few nanoseconds to retrieve data but the cost of storing each bit is very high by comparison with the devices used as *backing store, which may take milliseconds or even many seconds to retrieve data. *See also* memory hierarchy, memory management.

storage element *See* memory element.

storage hierarchy *See* memory hierarchy.

storage matrix of magnetic tape. *See* automated tape library.

storage oscilloscope An instrument that is used to measure fast nonrepetitive signals. It does this by capturing the signal on demand and continuing to display it until reset. This can be achieved in two ways: a digital storage oscilloscope samples the incoming signal, stores these samples, and displays them; other storage oscilloscopes use a special storage *cathode-ray tube that retains the image by mapping it as a charge pattern on an electrode behind the screen; the pattern then modulates the electron beam to give a picture of the captured signal.

storage pool Those areas of storage that are not allocated to *processes and are used by the storage allocation system as the source from which to meet requests. When a process releases storage it will be returned to the pool for subsequent reallocation.

storage protection The mechanisms, both hardware and software, ensuring that *processes access storage in a controlled manner. For storage in the high-speed levels of the *memory hierarchy, protection is implemented by hardware in order to maintain speed; for slower devices the protection may be entirely by software. In all cases, the intention is to ensure that the type of access made by a process to the storage is in accordance with that indicated when the storage was allocated to the process. For example, in a system with paged memory management a process may be granted access to an area of memory, but only for the purpose of executing the code in that page. Attempts to read from the page or to write to it would be prohibited by the (hardware) protection mechanism.

storage structure A mapping from one representation of a data item to another.

Thus a date may be represented as a vector of three integers (with six permutations to choose from), directly as a string of characters, or, in more recent high-level languages, as a record with three selectors – day, month, and year. A good choice of storage structure permits an easy and efficient implementation of a given *data structure.

storage tube A vacuum tube that can receive and retain information. The data can be erased and new data entered as required. The data may be graphical and visible on the face of the tube or it may be retrieved as an electrical signal. *See also* electrostatic storage device.

store 1. *Another name for* storage, or memory, used especially in the UK.
2. To enter or retain information for subsequent retrieval.

store and forward A method in which information is passed from node to node in a communication network, pausing in each node until sufficient resources (bandwidth, buffer pools, etc.) are available for the next leg of the journey – called a *hop*. In computer networks the information being passed may be *messages or *packets, and may be self-contained with regard to the store-and-forward network (*datagrams), or may depend upon the maintenance of state information (*flow control, *routing paths, etc.) from previous messages or packets. A store-and-forward network is based upon the tradeoff between the cost of memory and computational resources in the store-and-forward nodes, and the cost of the transmission lines between the nodes. *See also* message switching, packet switching.

stored program A *program that is stored in the *memory of a computer. The execution of the program then requires the use of a *control unit – to read instructions from the memory at appropriate times and arrange to carry them out.

The memory used to store the program may be the same as or different from memory used to store the data. There are advantages in using the same (read-write) memory, allowing programs to be modified, but there are greater advantages in limiting opportunities for program modification, either by using physically read-only memory or by restricting access to the part of the memory containing programs.

The concept of program and data sharing the same memory is fundamental to what is usually referred to as a *von Neumann machine or a von Neumann architecture. Although there is some disagreement as to whether the stored-program concept was originated by John von Neumann or by the team of John W. Mauchly and J. Presper Eckert, the first documentation was written by von Neumann in 1945 in his proposal for the *EDVAC.

straight insertion sort (sifting technique; sinking technique) A sorting algorithm that looks at each sortkey in turn, and on the basis of this places the record corresponding to the sortkey correctly with respect to the previous sortkeys.

straight selection sort A sorting algorithm based upon finding successively the record with the largest sortkey and putting it in the correct position, then the record with the next largest key, etc.

Strassen algorithm An algorithm developed in 1968 by V. Strassen to multiply large numbers. It uses the properties of *Fourier transforms. *See also* Schonhage –Strassen algorithm.

stream 1. A flow of data characterized by relatively long duration and constant rate. When the rate is known ahead of time then communication resources may be reserved for the stream. For example, stream traffic may be carried using low-overhead synchronous *time division multiplexing (TDM), while other traffic on the same channel is carried by higher-overhead asynchronous TDM. This is particularly important in satellite transmission systems, where overhead differences between synchronous and asynchronous traffic are very great. It is also important in applications, such as packet speech, that require a low variation in *network delay.

2. To operate a tape transport in *streaming mode.

streamer *Informal name for* streaming tape transport.

streaming A mode of operation of a tape transport, introduced in 1978 by IBM, in which the length of magnetic tape passing the head while stopping and restarting exceeds the length of the interblock gap. After a stop, therefore, the tape has to be *repositioned* (i.e. backed up) in order to be in the correct position for the next start. The alternative to streaming mode is start/stop mode.

Streaming allows a tape transport with only moderate acceleration to handle tape at a considerably higher speed than it could in start/stop mode. However, the average data rate is only improved if substantial quantities of data (typically tens to thousands of kilobytes) are transferred between stops, because of the considerable repositioning time (typically 0.1–2 seconds). The most common application is disk *backup.

Streaming also allows the interblock gap to be very short, increasing the amount of data that can be stored on a given length of tape; this is not compatible with the currently used international format standards for open-reel tape, but most cartridge tape standards define a short or zero interblock gap.

streaming tape transport A tape transport capable of operating in *streaming

mode, and of automatically repositioning the magnetic tape when it stops. Some versions are also capable of operating in start/stop mode at a lower tape speed (or with extended interblock gaps).

Streaming tape transports can use simpler, and hence cheaper and more reliable, mechanisms than those designed for start/stop mode at similar tape speeds. In particular, they usually operate without the *capstan and tape *buffers (tension arm or vacuum column) of conventional tape transports, tape motion and tension being controlled entirely from the reels. Most cartridge tape transports operate only in the streaming mode.

Stretch A monster computer chartered by the US Government and built in the late 1950s by IBM as their IBM 7030; it was designed to "stretch the technique of computer building to its limits." It had a pipelined instruction unit with address lookahead, and a 64-bit word length with double precision arithmetic if required. Addressing was down to the bit over a two-million word memory. It was capable of variable word length working and, in fact, almost anything that could be expected of hardware. A limited number of 7030s were built for atomic energy and similar research establishments.

strictness A term applied to functions. A function that always requires the value of one of its arguments is said to be *strict* in that argument. *See also* lazy evaluation.

stride *See* dope vector.

string 1. A *flexible one-dimensional array, i.e. a flexible vector, of symbols where the lower bound of the vector is fixed at unity but the upper bound, i.e. the string length, may vary.

2. Any one-dimensional array of characters.

445

In formal language theory a string is often referred to as a *word. *See also* sequence.

string manipulation The action of the fundamental operations on strings, including their creation, *concatenation, the extraction of *string segments, *string matching, their comparison, discovering their length, replacing *substrings by other strings, storage, and input/output.

string matching Searching within a string for a given substring.

string segment A *substring of a character string that can usually only be replaced by an array of the same size.

strongly connected *See* connected graph.

strong typing A feature of some programming languages that requires the type of each data item to be declared, precludes the application of operators to inappropriate data types, and prevents the interaction of incompatible types.

structural induction The principle of *induction defined as follows. Let S be a set on which the *partial ordering $\prec$ is defined and which contains no infinite decreasing sequences (where decreasing is defined by the ordering relation). If P is some *predicate and if the following two conditions hold:

(a) let a be a smallest element of S, i.e. there is no x in S such that $x \prec a$, then $P(a)$ is true,

(b) for each element s in S, if $P(x)$ is true for each x in S with $x \prec s$, and from this it follows that $P(s)$ is true,

then $P(s)$ is true for all s in S. Structural induction tends to be used in proving properties of recursive programs.

structure 1. of a program. *See* program structure.

2. *See* data structure, control structure, storage structure.

structured analysis 1. *See* structured systems analysis.

2. *See* SADT.

structured coding *See* structured programming (def. 2).

structured English A form of process logic representation, similar to *pseudo-language, used in *structured systems analysis.

structured programming 1. A method of program development that makes extensive use of *abstraction in order to factorize the problem and give increased confidence that the resulting program is correct. Given the specification of a required program, the first step is to envisage some "ideal" machine on which to implement that program. This ideal machine should offer both an appropriate set of *data structures and an appropriate set of operations on those data structures. The required program is then defined as a program for the specified ideal machine.

By this means the original problem has been reduced to one of implementing the specified ideal machine, and this problem is itself tackled in the same way. A second ideal machine is envisaged, this machine being ideal for implementing the data structures and operations of the first machine, and programs are produced to effect the implementation. This process continues until eventually a level is reached at which the specified data structures and operations of the ideal machine can conveniently be implemented directly in the chosen programming language. Thus the eventual program is based upon "levels of abstract machine", where the top-level machine is ideally suited to the specific application and the lowest-level machine directly executes the chosen programming language. The development process is not, however, simply one of "subroutinization", since both operations and data structures are refined simultaneously at each level.

The overall method of structured programming, which is largely due to E. W. Dijkstra, is heavily influenced by a concern for *program correctness. The intention is that at any level the implementation machine should be so well suited to the problem at hand that the programs for that machine will be small and simple. It should therefore be possible at each level to provide a convincing rigorous argument that the programs are correct.

2. (structured coding) An approach to *coding in which only three constructs are employed for governing the flow of control through the program. These three constructs allow for sequential, conditional, and iterative control flow. Arbitrary transfer of control (i.e. the *GOTO statement) is expressly forbidden. As a direct result, for each compound statement within the program there is precisely one entry point and one exit point, and reasoning about the program is thereby made easier.

structured systems analysis A specific technique for *systems analysis that covers all activities from initial understanding of the problem through to specification and high-level design of the software system. The technique embodies four main concepts: *dataflow diagrams*, a *data dictionary*, *data store structuring*, and *process logic representations*.

The dataflow diagrams show the various processing elements in the system, the *dataflows between these processing elements, and the major stores of data within the system. The processing elements are described in nonprocedural terms, typically using natural language, and a processing element from one diagram may be decomposed onto further diagrams to show greater levels of detail. A *data dictionary is used to record all the various data items in the system, the constraints upon these data items, and the processing elements by which they are accessed. As the decomposition proceeds so both the data stores and the actions of the processing elements are defined in more detail. The data store structuring techniques are based upon the relational model of data and show how each data store is accessed and organized. The algorithms employed by the processing elements are defined by use of process logic representations, typically *program design languages, *decision tables, or "structured" natural language.

Two similar versions of structured systems analysis were developed separately by Gane and Sarson and by De Marco. The technique is intended primarily for use in traditional DP system development.

structured variable (record) A variable in a programming language that is a composite object, being made up of components that are either simple data items or are themselves structured objects; these components are identified by *names.

stub 1. A substitute component that is employed temporarily in a program so that progress can be made, e.g. with compilation or testing, prior to the genuine component becoming available. To illustrate, if it is required to test the remainder of a program before a particular procedure has been developed, the procedure could be replaced by a stub. Dependent upon circumstances, it might be possible for this stub always to return the same result, return values from a table, return an approximate result, consult someone, etc.

2. *See* decision table.

Student's t distribution An important *probability distribution used instead of the *normal distribution when the standard deviation is estimated from data. Discovered by W. S. Gosset ('Student') in 1908, the t distribution gives wider *confidence intervals than the *normal distribution because of the uncertainty in the estimate of the standard deviation (*see* measures of variation). The probability values depend on an integer f, the number of *degrees of freedom, which is the number associated with the estimate of the standard deviation. Tables of the t distribution are widely available, but algorithms for direct computation are relatively lengthy.

The most common applications are

(1) testing differences between *means of two samples;

(2) testing differences from zero of estimated parameters in *regression analysis and *experimental design;

(3) evaluation of *confidence intervals for means and other estimated quantities.

subgraph A portion of a *graph G obtained by either eliminating edges from G and/or eliminating some vertices and their associated edges. Formally a subgraph of a graph G with vertices V and edges E is a graph G' with vertices V' and edges E' in which V' is a subset of V and E' is a subset of E (edges in E' joining vertices in V').

If V' is a proper *subset of V or E' is a proper subset of E then G' is a *proper subgraph* of G. If all the vertices of G are present in the subgraph G' then G' is a *spanning subgraph* of G. See also spanning tree.

subgroup A subset T of a *group G on which the dyadic operation $\circ$ is defined; T contains the identity, e, of G, the inverse x^{-1} for any x in T, and the quantity $x \circ y$ for any x and y in T. For any group G the set consisting of e alone is a subgroup; so also is the group G itself. All other subgroups are *proper subgroups* of G.

sublist See list.

submatrix of a given matrix, A. Any matrix derived from A by deleting one or more of its columns and/or one or more of its rows.

subnet *Short for* communication subnetwork.

sub-Nyquist sampling See Nyquist's criterion.

subprogram Part of a program that may be executed by a *call from elsewhere. The term covers *subroutines, *procedures, and *functions.

subrecursive hierarchy See hierarchy of functions.

subroutine A piece of code that is obeyed "out of line", i.e. control is transferred to the subroutine, and on its completion control reverts to the instruction following the *call. (The instruction code of the CPU usually provides *subroutine jump* and *return* instructions to facilitate this operation.) A subroutine saves space since it occurs only once in the program, though it may be called from many different places in the program. It also facilitates the construction of large programs since subroutines can be formed into libraries for general use. (The same concept appears in high-level languages as the *procedure.)

In the early days of programming, what is now called a subroutine was known as a *closed subroutine*. This was in contrast with the *open subroutine*, which was a piece of code that appeared in several places in a program, and was substituted "in line" by the assembler for each call appearing in the program. The open subroutine was just a convenient shorthand for the programmer: the same facility is now known as a *macro.

subschema See data description language.

subscript A means of referring to particular elements in an ordered collection of elements. For example, if R denotes such a collection of names then the ith name in the collection may be referenced by R_i (i.e. R subscript i). This printed form is the origin of the term but it is also used when the "subscript" is written on the same line, usually in parentheses or brackets:

R(i) or R[i]

See also array.

subsemigroup A *subset T of a *semigroup S, where T is *closed under the dyadic operation ∘ defined on S. Let x be an arbitrary element of S. Then the set consisting of

$$x, \; x \circ x, \; x \circ x \circ x, \; \ldots$$

i.e. all powers of x, is a subsemigroup of S.

subsequence 1. A *function whose domain is a subset of the positive integers and hence whose image set can be listed:

$$s_{i1}, s_{i2}, \ldots s_{im}$$

where $i1 < i2 < \ldots < im$

2. The listing of the image set of a subsequence. Hence a subsequence of a string $a_1 a_2 \ldots a_n$ is any listing of the form

$$a_{i1}, a_{i2}, \ldots a_{im}$$

where $1 \leqslant i1 < i2 \ldots < im \leqslant n$
See also sequence.

subset of a *set S. A set T whose members are all members of S; this is usually expressed as

$$T \subseteq S$$

A subset T is a *proper subset* of S if there is some element in S that is not in T; this is expressed as

$$T \subset S$$

substitution A particular kind of mapping on *formal languages. Let Σ_1 and Σ_2 be alphabets. For each symbol, a, in Σ_1 let $s(a)$ be a Σ_2-language. The function s is a substitution. A *homomorphism occurs where each $s(a)$ is a single word. s is Λ-*free* if no $s(a)$ contains the empty word.

The function s can be extended to map Σ_1-words to Σ_2-languages:

$$s(a_1 \ldots a_n) = s(a_1) \ldots s(a_n)$$

i.e. the *concatenation of the languages $s(a_1), \ldots, s(a_n)$. s can then be further extended to map Σ_1-languages to Σ_2-languages:

$$s(L) = \{s(w) \mid w \in L\}$$

$s(L)$ is called the *substitution image* of L under s.

substring of a string of symbols, $a_1 a_2 \ldots a_n$. Any string of symbols of the form

$$a_i a_{i+1} \ldots a_j$$

where $1 \leqslant i \leqslant j \leqslant n$

The *empty string is regarded as a substring of any string.

substring identifier Let $\alpha = a_1 a_2 \ldots a_n$ denote a string in Σ^* and let $\# \notin \Sigma$. The substring identifier for position i in $\alpha\#$ is the shortest substring in $\alpha\#$ starting at position i that identifies position i uniquely. The existence of such a substring is guaranteed since

$$a_i a_{i+1} \ldots a_n \#$$

will always identify position i uniquely. *See also* position tree.

minuend	0	0	1	1
subtrahend	0	1	0	1
difference	0	1	1	0
borrow	0	1	0	0

Modulo-two subtraction

subtractor An electronic *logic circuit for calculating the difference between two binary numbers, the minuend and the number to be subtracted, the subtrahend (*see* table). A *full subtractor* performs this calculation with three inputs: minuend bit, subtrahend bit, and borrow bit. It produces two outputs: the difference and the borrow. Full subtractors thus allow for the inclusion of borrows generated by previous stages of subtraction when forming their output signals, and can be cascaded to form *n*-bit subtractors. Alternatively the subtract operation can be performed using two *half subtractors*, which are simpler since they contain only two inputs and produce two outputs.

Neither of these devices is commonly encountered since modulo-two subtraction is more conveniently accomplished using two's complement arithmetic and binary *adders.

subtree *See* tree.

subtype A *subset of a *data type, obtained by constraining the set of possible values of the data type. The same operations can be applied to subtype as to type.

successive over-relaxation *See* iterative methods.

successor function 1. The *function *SUCC* that occurs in programming languages such as Ada or Pascal and produces the next element of an enumeration type. Typically

$$SUCC(4) \text{ produces } 5$$
$$SUCC('A') \text{ produces } 'B'$$

2. The *function

$$S : N \rightarrow N$$

for which $S(n) = n + 1$ where N is the nonnegative integers. S plays a crucial role in recursive function theory, particularly in the definition of *primitive recursive functions.

suffix of a string α. Any string β where α is the *concatenation $\gamma\beta$ for some string γ. *Compare* prefix.

suffix notation *Another name for* reverse Polish notation.

suite A set of programs or modules that is designed as a whole to meet some specified overall requirement, each program or module meeting some part of that requirement. For example, a single program suite might contain a program to initialize some database, a program

that permits normal access to that database, a program that performs periodic major updates (such as at the end of each month), and a program that can recover the database after failure.

sumcheck *See* checksum.

sum of products expression (SOP expression) A *Boolean function expressed as a sum of product terms, i.e. as an OR of AND terms containing uncomplemented or complemented variables. An example is

$$f = (x \wedge y') \vee (x' \wedge z)$$

The function is also realizable as the NAND of a group of NAND terms. *See also* standard sum of products, product of sums expression.

sum term A sum (OR) of Boolean variables, uncomplemented or complemented. *See also* product of sums expression.

Sun A US manufacturer of high-performance *workstations that can easily be networked using various protocols. Sun and similar machines are widely used for CAD (*computer-aided design), *CASE, and similar applications requiring high-quality graphics and powerful processors.

supercomputer A class of very powerful computers that have extremely fast processors, currently capable (1988/89) of performing thousands of millions of floating-point operations per second (*see* flops); most are now multiprocessor systems. Large main-memory capacity – tens or hundreds of thousands of words – and long word lengths – typically 64 bits – are the other main characteristics. Supercomputers are used, for example, in meteorology, engineering, nuclear physics, and astronomy. Several hundred are in operation worldwide at present. Principal manufacturers are *Cray Research, *CDC, and NEC, Fujitsu, and Hitachi of Japan.

superconducting memory A memory made up of components whose function depends on the phenomenon of superconductivity. *See also* Josephson (junction) technology.

superconducting technology A logic construction technique depending on the phenomenon of superconductivity. *See also* Josephson (junction) technology.

superconductivity The physical phenomenon that causes some materials to have zero electrical resistance when held at very low temperatures. Superconductivity is of interest to computer engineers since it points to the possibility of great computing power with little or no heat generation. This is especially so since the recent demonstration of superconductivity in certain complex metallic oxides at relatively high (liquid nitrogen) temperatures.

supermini A medium-sized multiuser computer whose systems and architecture have evolved from the minicomputers of a few years ago. A supermini may have as much or more power than a small *mainframe, but it has a different ancestry.

super-Nyquist sampling *See* Nyquist's criterion.

supervisor (monitor; executive) The permanently resident part of a large operating system, dealing most directly with the physical components of the system as distinct from the virtual resources handled by most *processes. Within the supervisor different parts handle different physical components (*see* kernel, memory management, I/O supervisor).

The term has also been used as another name for the entire operating system.

supervisor call (SVC) *See* interrupt.

supervisor state (executive state) *See* execution states.

support programs Programs that do not make a direct contribution to performing the primary function of a computer system but rather serve to assist in the operation of the system. A typical example is a program that serves to archive the contents of a filing system. *See also* software tool.

suppress To prevent the output or sensing of selected data or signals. *See also* zero suppression.

surface mount technology A form of IC (*integrated circuit) packaging where the pins are bent so that they lie in approximately the same plane as the bottom of the IC package. This means that the pins lie along the surface of PCB tracks leading up to the IC and this removes the need to drill holes in the PCB to accept the pins, as is necessary in other forms of packaging. The pins are usually spaced more closely together and along all edges in surface mount devices, enabling a more compact PCB layout.

surjection (onto function) A *function whose *range and codomain coincide. If
$$f : X \rightarrow Y$$
is a surjection then for each y in the codomain Y there is some x in X with the property that
$$y = f(x)$$
A function that is not surjective is sometimes said to be *into*.

suspended *See* process descriptor.

swapping A method of handling main memory by writing information to backing store during periods when it is not in use, and reading it back when required. *See also* paging, roll-in roll-out.

SWCI *Abbrev. for* software configuration item. *See* configuration item.

SWIFT *Acronym for* society for worldwide interbank financial transmission. A cooperative effort to provide a network for *electronic funds transfer. The first product, SWIFT 1, connected 2900 financial institutions in 60 countries and handled one million transactions a day. In 1988 it was approaching saturation and work was in hand for a successor.

swipe reader *US; informal term for* slot reader. *See* card reader.

switch 1. An electronic or electro-mechanical device that is used to connect or disconnect an electric current to an electrical circuit. An electronic switch can present either an effective open circuit or closed circuit depending on the status of an applied "select" signal. These switches are often used to provide isolation between low- and high-voltage switching circuits or to allow remote control of electrical systems.

The word is also used as a verb, followed by a suitable preposition.

2. A type of branch with a choice of many places to which control may be passed. The destination of the branch is determined by the value of some variable. Most high-level languages have a means of doing this: Algol 60 has switch variables, FORTRAN has computed GOTOs, and several other languages, such as Algol 68, Pascal, and Ada, have case statements.

3. To undergo or cause to undergo *switching.

switching Any of various communication techniques that provide point to point transmission between dynamically changing data sources and sinks. *See also* packet switching, message switching, circuit switching.

switching algebra A term that is virtually synonymous with *Boolean algebra when applied to the analysis and synthesis of *logic (switching) circuits.

switching circuit *Another (largely obsolete) name for* logic circuit. Before the availability of low-cost electronic components, logic circuits were commonly

implemented using relays and other switching devices. An AND function was implemented using a series connection of two switches; an OR function used a parallel combination of two switches.

switching speed (toggling speed) A measure of the rate at which a given electronic logic device is capable of changing the logic state of its output in response to changes at its input. It is a function of the delay encountered within the device, which in turn is a function of the device technology.

switching theory The theory of and manipulative methods for *switching algebra. It includes *Boolean-algebra and *state-table or *state-diagram methods of description, as well as *minimization methods.

switching waveform A waveform or signal that is capable of exhibiting one of two possible distinct states, often corresponding to logic 1 and logic 0, and that may be used to change the status of an active switching element between two distinct conditions such as on and off or open and closed.

Sylvester matrices *See* Hadamard matrices.

symbol 1. One of a disjoint set of distinct elements in the alphabet of a *formal language. *See* signature, word.

2. An *identifier in a program.

symbolic addressing An addressing scheme whereby reference to an address is made by some convenient symbol that (preferably) has some relationship to the meaning of the data expected to be located at that address. It serves as an aid to the programmer. The symbolic address is replaced by some form of computable/computed address during the operation of an assembler or compiler.

symbolic execution A form of semantic analysis/proof of a program in which symbols are used as input variables. The program is viewed as having an input state determined by the input data and the initial state of the program. For each line of the program a test is made to see if the state has changed. Each state change is recorded. A logical path through the program is converted into an ordered set of state changes. The final state for each path should be an output state or program termination. The program is proved correct if each sequence of inputs generates only the required output states.

The technique has been automated, but the size of program that can be handled is limited and manual assistance may be needed to handle loops correctly and efficiently. *See also* static analysis, program correctness proof.

symbolic language An obsolete term, now replaced by the term *high-level language.

symbolic logic The treatment of *formal logic involving the setting up of a formalized language. The *propositional calculus and *predicate calculus are two of the more common areas of interest.

symbol manipulation The manipulation of characters rather than numbers, as occurs in symbolic mathematics, text preparation, and finite-state automata simulation. *SNOBOL is a programming language that can be used for writing such programs.

symbol table A list, kept by a language *translator, of *identifiers in the source program and their properties. Before the translator processes any of the source program, the symbol table contains a list of predeclared identifiers; for example, the value of π or the largest integer that a system can hold might be associated with particular names by the translator. As translation proceeds, the trans-

lator will insert and remove symbols from the table as necessary. The properties of entries in the symbol table vary with both language and implementation.

symmetric difference *See* set difference.

symmetric function A *function $f(x_1, x_2, \ldots x_n)$ whose value is unaltered by any *permutation of its n variables. Such functions arise repeatedly in *switching theory.

symmetric group *See* permutation group.

symmetric list *Another name for* doubly linked list.

symmetric matrix A square matrix A such that $a_{ij} = a_{ji}$ for all a_{ij} in A. Thus a symmetric matrix is equal to its *transpose.

symmetric order traversal (inorder traversal) A tour of the nodes of a binary tree obtained by using the following recursive algorithm: visit in symmetric order the left subtree of the root (if it exists); visit the root of the tree; visit in symmetric order the right subtree of the root (if it exists). *Compare* postorder traversal, preorder traversal.

symmetric relation A *relation R defined on a set S and having the property that
$$\text{whenever } x \ R \ y$$
$$\text{then } y \ R \ x$$
where x and y are arbitrary elements of S. The relation "is equal to" defined on the integers is symmetric. *See also* antisymmetric relation, asymmetric relation.

symmetry group A *group consisting of all those *functions that transform a rigid plane figure into itself; the *dyadic operation on the elements of the group is that of *composition of functions. The larger and more complex a symmetry group the greater the symmetry associated with the underlying geometric figure.

synchronization A relationship between *processes such that one process cannot proceed beyond a particular point until another process has reached a particular point. For example, when one process is writing data in a buffer to be read by another process, the two processes must be synchronized so that the reading process does not attempt to read the buffer beyond the point at which the writing process has written data in the buffer. Synchronization can be achieved by using a *semaphore.

synchronizer A storage device with a wide range of operating speeds that is used in an intermediate capacity when transferring data between devices that cannot operate at the same rate.

synchronous Involving or requiring a form of computer control operation in which sequential events take place at fixed times. This requires predetermination of the length of time required by each class/set of events; it requires no acknowledgment that preceding events have been completed. *Compare* asynchronous.

synchronous circuit An electronic logic circuit in which logical operations are performed under the control of and hence in synchronism with an externally generated clock signal.

synchronous counter A *counter consisting of an interconnected series of *flip-flops in which all the flip-flop outputs change state at the same instant, normally on application of a pulse at the counter input. These counters have advantages in speed over asynchronous *ripple counters, in which the output must propagate along the chain of flip-flops after the application of a pulse at the count input. *See also* cascadable counter, shift counter.

synchronous TDM *See* time division multiplexing.

syndrome In coding theory, a symbol vector (ordered set of symbols) generated at an intermediate stage of the decoding algorithm for an *error-correcting code. The syndrome depends only on the error pattern and not on the transmitted codeword. A further stage of the decoding algorithm will use the syndrome to correct the errors in the received message. The details of how the syndrome is found and how it is used, and indeed whether all the errors can be corrected, will depend on the particular error-correcting code that is being employed. If no errors occurred, the syndrome will usually be the *zero word.

syntactic error *See* syntax error.

syntactic monoid of a formal language *L*. The *semigroup of the *minimal machine for *L*.

syntax The rules defining the legal sequences of elements in a language – in the case of a programming language, of characters in a program. The syntax rules define the form of the various constructs in the language, but say nothing about the meaning of these constructs. *See also* parsing.

syntax analysis *Another name for* parsing.

syntax analyzer (parser) *See* parsing.

syntax diagram A diagrammatic representation of the *syntax rules of a programming language; a pictorial equivalent of *BNF.

syntax-directed compiler A compiler that works from the *syntax rules of the language explicitly, and is therefore capable in principle of compiling another language if different parse tables are provided. In practice, syntax is less than half the story, and most of the work of the compiler writer goes into dealing with the *semantics, i.e. in defining the actions to be taken after a particular construct has been recognized in the program.

syntax error A programming error in which the grammatical rules of the language are broken. Syntax errors can be detected by the compiler, unlike *semantic errors, which do not become apparent until run-time. *See also* error diagnostics.

syntax tree *Another name for* parse tree.

system Anything we choose to regard (a) as an entity and (b) as comprising a set of related components. In computing the word is widely used with many shades of meaning. Most commonly, however, it may refer to a related set of hardware units, or programs, or both. The hardware contents of a computer room may be spoken of as "the system", and so may a range of manufacturer's equipment; in each case, the term may be broadened to include the basic software such as operating systems and compilers. A set of programs for a particular application (independently of the hardware and basic software on which it runs) may be referred to as a system; in this case the term may be broadened to include such things as documentation and manual procedures.

system accounting Recording the use of system *resources. On a *multiprogramming system the apportioning of the use of system resources among the active *processes can only be done by the system. For resources such as processors, which are allocated in their entirety to an individual process for a large number of short intervals of time, the appropriate measure is found by recording the real time at the start and finish of each interval to give the length of each interval; accumulating these through the life of the process yields the processor time.

For resources such as memory, in which a number of subunits is allocated

to the process (which will subsequently return them to the *resource allocation mechanism), the usually accepted measure is to determine the elapsed time for which the subunits are allocated to the process and to charge a "rent" for each subunit. For nonreusable resources the normal practice is to charge on a unit-cost basis for the amounts used.

In a bureau, which relies for its revenue on real money charges made to clients, the implementation of the accounting system is a nontrivial problem, especially in regard to decisions concerning spoilt work, or delays experienced by one client because of other clients' activities.

systematic code An (n, k) *block code in which every codeword can be separated into k *information symbols* and $(n - k)$ *check symbols*. The information symbols are identical with those of the source message before encoding. Thus the process of encoding a systematic code involves the insertion of $(n - k)$ check symbols into (i.e. among, before, or, most usually, after) the information symbols. The insertion positions must be the same for all the codewords in the code. Every *linear code can be arranged to be systematic.

system crash *See* crash.

system definition The document, or set of documents, that gives the most authoritative available description of some existing or envisaged system. The nature of the system definition document can vary considerably from project to project, or even during the lifetime of a single project. For example, a system definition prepared early in a development project (prior to system design) might contain an *expression of requirements for the system, the current development plan, estimates of development cost, and a cost/benefit analysis. By contrast, once development is complete, the system definition delivered with the system would be expected to contain a precise description of the actual behavior of the implemented system.

system design The activity of proceeding from an identified set of requirements for a system to a design that meets those requirements. A distinction is sometimes drawn between *high-level* or *architectural design*, which is concerned with the main components of the system and their roles and interrelationships, and *detailed design*, which is concerned with the internal structure and operation of individual components. The term system design is sometimes used to cover just the high-level design activity. *See also* review.

system dictionary *See* data dictionary.

system generation The construction of a version of an operating system. Any large system is almost invariably constructed from a number of separate modules of code, each dealing with specific aspects of the system or with specific types of device. Where it is known that a facility or device will not be supported, it is possible to omit the corresponding modules and to generate a version of the system that contains only modules that are known to be required. This is achieved during system generation.

system high A *security processing mode in which all users have a *security clearance that permits access to all information in a system, even though different parts of the database may have different *security classifications. Output from the system is not necessarily correctly labeled and may be treated as if classified to the highest level of information within the system until manually reclassified.

system life cycle The phases of development through which a computer-based system passes. The term is primarily used in the context of *information sys-

tems, and gained common currency during the 1970s. Life cycle phases have been defined in very many different ways and in varying degrees of detail. Most definitions, however, recognize broad phases such as initial conception, requirements definition, outline design, detailed design, programming, testing, implementation, maintenance, and modification. Some include additional activities such as manual procedures design and staff training.

Most life cycle definitions arose as a result of analysis of the tasks of system development, with the objective of making those tasks more amenable to traditional techniques of management planning and control. In some cases, elaborate planning and control systems have been designed on the basis of the life cycle analysis, with highly formalized documentation and clearly defined managerial decision points.

system R, system R* *See* SQL/DS.

systems analysis The analysis of the role of a proposed system and the identification of a set of requirements that the system should meet, and thus the starting point for *system design. The term is most commonly used in the context of commercial programming, where those involved in software development are often classed as either systems analysts or programmers. The systems analysts are responsible for identifying a set of requirements (i.e. systems analysis) and producing a design. The design is then passed to the programmers, who are responsible for actual implementation of the system.

system security An (operating) system is responsible for controlling access to system resources, which will include sensitive data. The system must therefore include a certain amount of protection for such data, and must in turn control access to those parts of the system that administer this protection. System security is concerned with all aspects of these arrangements.

systems engineering The application of the systems approach in engineering; the management of complexity in product and process. The term is both of general use throughout engineering and of specific use for systems involving computers and software. Systems engineering considers the relationships between the systems being built, the process (itself a system) by which it is developed, and the system(s) in which it will operate. In each of those systems, it considers how behavior emerges from structure, and the relationship between "hard" issues (such as function and performance) and "soft" issues (such as human factors, management, economics, social and political concerns, law, and ethics). In terms of technical design, systems engineering addresses requirements and architectural solutions at the level of the whole system, prior to decisions about tradeoffs between specific technologies.

system software *See* systems software.

system specification A precise and detailed statement of the effects that a system is required to achieve. A good system specification gives a complete statement of what the system is to do without making any commitment as to how the system is to do it. Thus for these purposes the system is treated as a "black box" and the system specification constrains only the externally observable behavior, not the internal implementation.

A system specification is normally produced after an *expression of requirements, and is then used as the basis for *system design. The system specification typically differs from the expression of requirements in both scope and precision: the latter may cover both the envisaged system and the environment in which it will operate, but may leave many broad concepts unrefined.

Traditionally system specifications have taken the form of natural language documents. However both the need for precision and problems with the increasing size of specification documents are leading to the development of more formal notations.

systems programmer A person who specializes in *systems programming and low-level *software, such as *operating systems, *compilers, *communication systems, and *database management systems. *Compare* applications programmer.

systems programming Work carried out by systems programmers, i.e. the production of systems software. The boundary between systems programming and users' programming depends on the circumstances. For example, the writer of a compiler will be regarded as a user by the author of the nucleus, but is likely to be regarded as a systems programmer by the writer of a subroutine for locating the minimum of a function. The user of the minimization routine may regard all these three as systems programmers.

systems software (system software) The totality of software required to produce a system acceptable to end users.

systems theory The study of *systems per se, usually to find characteristics common to all systems or to classes of systems. Systems theorists may be most concerned with the development of theory for its own sake (most often called *general systems theory*), or they may be more concerned with the applications of systems ideas within particular disciplines or problem areas in order to solve problems that are not amenable to traditional "reductionist" approaches. Systems theory has been called the study of organized complexity.

There have been a number of attempts to categorize systems. Perhaps the simplest and most useful is by P. Checkland, who proposes four categories: natural systems, designed physical systems, designed abstract systems, and human activity systems. He also proposes four concepts that are central to systems thinking:

"the notion of whole entities which have properties as entities (emergent properties . . .); the idea that the entities are themselves parts of larger similar entities, while possibly containing smaller similar entities within themselves (hierarchy . . .); the idea that such entities are characterized by processes which maintain the entity and its activity in being (control . . .); and the idea that, whatever other processes are necessary in the entity, there will certainly be processes in which information is communicated from one part to another, at the very minimum this being entailed in the idea 'control'."

system tables The data that collectively defines the status of all *resources and all *processes within the system. Although such data may be represented as tables, it may be more conveniently represented internally as linked lists with pointers back to associated semaphore variables in some cases.

system testing *See* testing.

T

T A dialect of LISP, similar to *SCHEME.

T²L *See* TTL.

tab *Short for* tabulate, i.e. to lay out data, *and for* tabulation character, a control character used when laying out

data to control the movement of a print or display mechanism.

table A collection of *records. Each record may store information associated with a key by which specific records are found, or the records may be arranged in an *array so that the index is the key. In commercial applications the word table is often used as a synonym for matrix or array.

table-driven algorithm An algorithm that uses *table look-up.

table look-up (TLU) A fast method of transforming one set of data values into another. The target data is stored in the form of a *table. In order to perform the transformation, a source datum is used to index into or search the table of target data. The resulting target datum is the result of the table look-up. *See also* hashing.

tablet *Short for* data tablet.

tag 1. To mark in some distinctive fashion any node in a data structure that has been traversed. Using this technique precautions can be taken against revisiting nodes, e.g. in a circular list.

2. *Short for* tag field. A field that is used to discriminate between variants of the same type.

tagged architecture A computer architecture in which extra data bits are attached to each word to denote the *data type, the function of the word, or both. Tagged architecture can represent a powerful form of *memory protection, and has formed a foundation for certain secure computer systems based on *hardware security.

tail of a list. **1.** The last item in a *list.

2. The list remaining when the *head has been removed.

take-up reel *See* magnetic tape.

tape Either *magnetic tape or *paper tape, now normally the former if unspecified.

tape-bounded Turing machine *See* multi-tape Turing machine.

tape cartridge *Short for* magnetic tape cartridge (generally).

tape deck *Another name for* tape transport. *See* magnetic tape.

tape drive *Another name for* tape transport. *See* magnetic tape.

tape file A file recorded on magnetic tape.

tape format The format of information recorded on magnetic tape, allowing a system to recognize, control, and verify the data. There are two levels at which formats are defined.

(a) The format presented by the host system to the *magnetic tape subsystem. This consists of data, usually preceded and followed by *labels, and divided into sections (generally corresponding to files) by *tape marks and sometimes by additional labels; the sections of data are themselves divided into *blocks, although this is done for physical convenience and need have no logical significance.

(b) The format actually recorded, as a pattern of reversals of magnetization, on the tape by the magnetic subsystem.

To the magnetic tape subsystem, "data" means all the information – both logical data and labels – transferred to or from the host. Most magnetic subsystems require tape marks to be distinguished from the data stream. To this data the subsystem adds its own information block by block – often in a preamble to aid synchronization, a postamble to serve a similar purpose when reading in reverse, and check digits, though this varies between one standard format and another. The subsystem inserts an interblock gap (an area with no reversals of magnetization) between blocks, and writes tape marks where directed by the host; in many formats it precedes the first block on the tape by an *identity burst*, i.e. a special pattern of signals that tells the subsystem which of a number of possible formats is in use, and may also help the tape transport to optimize certain of its physical parameters.

A number of different formats (in the second sense) have been standardized as magnetic tape subsystems have developed: those currently used for data interchange use 9 tracks on $\frac{1}{2}''$ tape. Three formats are in common use, all defined by ISO standards (and by corresponding ANSI and ECMA standards). They are as follows.

Nonreturn to zero (NRZ): the particular form standardized is *nonreturn-to-zero mark*, which is properly abbreviated *NRZ1* but much more widely known as *NRZI*. The density is 800 bits per inch (bpi) which, with typical block lengths, allows about 20 megabytes to be recorded on a 2400 foot reel of tape. Error detection is adequate but error correction facilities are crude, and the format, introduced in the 1950s, is now obsolescent.

Phase encoded (PE) format, introduced in the 1960s. The density currently standardized is 1600 bpi, and allows about 40 megabytes on a 2400 foot reel. Logical error detection is less powerful than for NRZ but electrical checks on signal waveforms are also used and a measure of on-the-fly error correction is possible. This format is reasonably simple to implement and is widely used for data interchange; a 3200 bpi version has been proposed to ANSI as an additional standard.

Group code recording (GCR) format, introduced in the 1970s. The density standardized for 9-track $\frac{1}{2}''$ tape is 6250 bpi: this refers to the density in terms of bits of logical data, but as this data is translated by the subsystem into a redundant code the actual density recorded on tape is higher. The format permits about 140 megabytes to be stored on a 2400 foot tape and the redundant coding allows excellent error detection and on-the-fly error correction. The redundant coding does however need complex hardware.

There are further standard formats for ¼" cartridge tape, with higher density standards under discussion, and also for cassette tape (though where personal computers use cassette tape it is generally not to this rather old standard). For all types of tape, further standards giving higher density are likely to be defined as the state of the art develops.

tape header A *header label written at the beginning of a volume of magnetic tape. *See also* label.

tape label *See* label.

tape library 1. An area in which reels of magnetic tape are stored when not actually in use on a tape transport. Each reel is normally stored in a protective case and is visibly labeled, in addition to any *label that may be recorded on the tape.

2. An *automated tape library.

tape mark A signal recorded on magnetic tape that does not represent data but is used to delimit sections of data – usually individual files, hence the alternative term *file mark*. The tape mark is written at the direction of the host system but its form is determined by the magnetic tape subsystem in accordance with the standard for the relevant *tape format. Most formats allow the tape mark to be recorded as a separate *block, but in formats that provide for the insertion of block headers by the subsystem it is usual for the tape mark to take the form of a flag in one of these headers.

If the subsystem encounters a tape mark during a read operation, the host system is informed. In most magnetic tape subsystems there is a *skip to tape mark* (or *tape-mark search*) command that causes the tape to be run to the next tape mark without transferring any data to the host; sometimes there is also a *multiple-skip* command containing a parameter *n*, which causes the tape to skip to the *n*th tape mark. Skip operations are sometimes performed at a higher speed than that used for reading.

It is conventional to write a double tape mark after the last file in a volume.

tape marker *See* BOT marker, EOT marker.

tape punch *See* paper tape I/O.

tape reader *See* paper tape I/O.

tape transport (tape drive; (magnetic) tape unit; tape deck) A peripheral device that moves magnetic tape past sensing and recording heads. *See* magnetic tape. *See also* streaming tape transport, autoload, autothread.

tape unit *Another name for* tape transport. *See* magnetic tape.

target alphabet *See* code.

target computer *See* host computer.

target program *Another name for* object program, now rarely used.

task 1. *Another name for* process.

2. *Another name for* job.

When each job consists of only one process, the above difference is not significant. The concurrent execution of a number of tasks is referred to as *multitasking*. *See also* parallel processing.

tautology A law of logic, in the form of a proposition, that describes a universal truth; no matter what values are assigned to the variables in the proposition the result is always true. An example from the *propositional calculus is

$$(P \lor Q)' = P' \land Q'$$

where $\vee$ and $\wedge$ are the *or* and *and* operators and P' is the negation of P. In the *truth table for a tautology the final result column contains only the value true. If the final column contains only the value false, then a *contradiction* has been identified.

TCP *Abbrev. for* transmission control protocol. The reliable connection-oriented protocol used by DARPA for their *internetworking research. TCP uses a three-way *handshake with clock-based sequence number selection to synchronize connecting entities and to minimize the chance of erroneous connections due to delayed messages. TCP uses positive acknowledgment with retransmission (*PAR), byte sequencing, and sliding window *flow control to provide duplex, ordered, error-free, guaranteed data transfer over established connections. It is usually used in conjunction with *internet protocol (IP), the combination being known as TCP/IP.

t distribution *See* Student's t distribution.

TDM *Abbrev. for* time division multiplexing.

TDS *Abbrev. for* tabular data stream. A data format *protocol that refers to messages between an *SQL client and an SQL server.

tear-off menu A *pull-down menu that can be moved from the place where it was first displayed to another part of the screen that may be more convenient, and from where any of its options may be selected at a later time.

TECO A powerful but difficult to use *text editor at one time much favored by systems programmers on DEC machines.

Telecom Gold A UK national *electronic mail system operated by British Telecom.

teleconferencing A computer-based system enabling users to participate in an activity, such as the management of a complex project, despite being separated in space and/or time. Users will typically be provided with access to a computer terminal, which will allow them to communicate with other members of their team, often but not necessarily simultaneously. Data communication lines are used to transmit the conference information between participants. The system is controlled by a "manager" whose function is to organize the participants and allow them access to the conference and to transmit their inputs to other members.

Some teleconferencing systems enable conference participants to "see" each other via television cameras and monitors connected to the system, but other systems use very simple terminals and can only communicate using the written word. Additional facilities may be provided to allow participants to vote on an issue, the votes being recorded automatically and tabulated. A conference log will be maintained by the system to keep a record of all activity in the conference, and can be displayed for reference by the participants.

Telenet A *public packet network that is owned by General Telephone & Electronics Corp. (GTE) and has been in operation since 1975. It is available in the US and some other countries and provides access to a large number of computer-based services. Telenet was developed from *ARPANET technology and has since evolved.

telesoftware Programs *downloaded onto a computer via a suitable adapter from *videotex, *teletext, and similar services.

teletex A means of medium- to high-speed text transmission, from keyboard to printer, over public switched data networks. Transmission speeds can range from 2.4K bps (using *circuit switching) to 48K bps (using *packet switching), as against 50 bps for telex. It permits a more extensive character set than telex, and permits line and paragraph formatting as in normal correspondence. Teletex standards are the responsibility of CCITT. Teletex was expected to replace telex by about 1990 but has so far had limited market acceptance; its future is in some doubt because of the rapid spread of facsimile transmission (fax).

teletext A system for one-way broadcast transmission of information, primarily in text form but with primitive graphics capability, using spare television channel capacity and adapted domestic TV receivers. On a channel offering teletext, a number of "pages" of information (up to about 100) are transmitted in a continuous cycle, concurrently with the normal TV signal and leaving it unaffected while the receiver is used for normal viewing. Having selected teletext mode on the control pad, it is then possible to select any page number; when the selected page next arrives in the transmission cycle, it is stored in local memory in the set and displayed indefinitely (until the user selects another page or exits from teletext mode).

Among countries in which teletext services are available are Australia, France (Didon and Antiope), West Germany (Bildschirmzeitung and – confusingly – Videotext), UK (Ceefax and Oracle), and US (Closed Captioning).

Compare videotex.

teletypewriter (typewriter terminal) A device that is similar to an electric typewriter but also has a signal interface by means of which it can communicate with a computer: it can receive messages for printing or can send messages that are generated on its keyboard. There may be a paper tape punch and reader attached or integrated into the unit. Teletypewriters were once extensively used as interactive *terminals but have been superseded by *VDUs.

Telidon A Canadian *videotex system.

TELNET *Acronym for* teletype network. The protocol developed for the *ARPANET to allow users on one host computer to connect to the time-sharing resources of another host. The TELNET protocol specifies a standard terminal type, the *network virtual terminal (NVT)*, including its character set (a modified form of ASCII) and standard control sequences for terminal functions such as "move to the next line". Standard control sequences are also defined for host functions such as "interrupt process". It is the responsibility of the programs at each end of the TELNET connection to perform a suitable mapping between the NVT's character set and control functions, and the conventions of the local system. Many of the parameters of the NVT can be modified through option negotiation, in which both ends of the TELNET connection must agree to a proposed change before it can take place.

The name TELNET is also used for similar protocols in networks other than the ARPANET.

template A structure specification. The term is a convenient means of differentiating the structure specification from the declaration of individual instances of the structure. The provision of template facilities allows a programmer to build his own data types.

temporal cohesion *See* cohesion.

temporal logic A *modal logic in which the modal operators express notions of time such as "always", "sometimes", "strong next", "weak next", "next-time", "last-time", "interval chop", "since", "until", and "while".

ten's complement *See* radix complement.

tension arm *See* buffer (def. 2).

tera- (symbol: T) A prefix indicating a multiple of one million million, 10^{12}, or, when the binary system is used, as in computing, a multiple of 2^{40}, i.e.

1 099 511 627 776

term An expression formed from functions, constants, and variables. An example is

$$f(a,g(h(b),c,d))$$

The parentheses must match in the proper way. This can be expressed by defining terms recursively as follows: a term is either a single symbol ϕ, or else has the form $\phi(\tau_1, \ldots, \tau_k)$, where each of $\tau_1, \ldots, \tau_k$ is itself a term. The example above thus has the overall form $f(\tau_1, \tau_2)$: in this case $\phi = f$ and $k = 2$. Another usual constraint is that different occurrences of the same ϕ cannot occur with different values of k, i.e. each ϕ must have a fixed *arity* (number of arguments). Thus

$$f(a,f(h(b),c,d))$$

would not be a term since the first f has arity 2 while the second has arity 3; neither would

$$f(a,g(h(b),c,h)),$$

since the first h has arity 1 while the second has arity 0.

A Σ-*term* is a term in which each ϕ used is in a *signature Σ, and has the arity associated with it by Σ and, if Σ is a many-sorted *signature, all the sorts match properly. Sometimes a Σ-term is allowed to contain variables (of arity 0) in addition to symbols in Σ. Terms can also be viewed as *trees (*see* tree language). Terms (whether as expressions or as trees) are important in the construction of *initial algebras. Terms as defined here are sometimes called *first-order terms*, to distinguish them from the *higher-order terms* involved in *lambda calculus. *See also* predicate calculus.

terminal 1. A data input and/or output device that is connected to a controlling processor to which it is subservient and usually remote. There are a very wide range of terminal types. The *VDU is frequently used as a terminal by which a user can input queries or instructions and receive instructions. The information may be in the form of text or it may be mainly graphical. Terminals designed for a particular environment and business activity come under a general heading of *application terminals. If the terminal has a built-in capability to store and manipulate data it is classed as an *intelligent terminal; without this capability terminals are classed as dumb.

2. (terminal symbol) *See* grammar.

terminal node *Another name for* leaf node.

terminal symbol *See* grammar.

termination The end of execution of a *process. A process that reaches a successful conclusion terminates normally by issuing a suitable supervisor call to the operating system. *See also* abnormal termination.

termination, proof of *See* program correctness proof.

terminator 1. A symbol that marks the end of a statement in a programming language (frequently a semicolon).

2. *Another name for* rogue value.

term language *Another name for* tree language.

ternary logic *See* multiple-valued logic.

ternary selector gate (T-gate) A *combinational ternary logic gate that is important as a building block in the synthesis of ternary logic circuits (*see* multiple-valued logic). A T-gate has four inputs

$$\{a_0, a_1, a_2, s\}$$

and one output $\{t\}$, all of which can take values represented by elements of the set:

TERNARY THRESHOLD GATE

$$\{0, 1, 2\}$$

The function of the T-gate is given by $t = a_s$. It thus acts as a ternary selector, the choice from

$$\{a_0, a_1, a_2\}$$

being selected by the value taken by the s input.

ternary threshold gate (S-gate) A *combinational ternary logic gate that is important as a building block in the synthesis of ternary logic circuits (*see* multiple-valued logic). An S-gate may have any number of inputs $\{a_i\}$ and one output $\{s\}$, all of which can take values represented by elements of the set $\{0,1,2\}$. The function of the S-gate is given by

$$\left.\begin{array}{l} s = 0 \\ s = 1 \\ s = 2 \end{array}\right\} \text{ iff } \sum_i (a_i - 1) \left\{\begin{array}{l} < 0 \\ = 0 \\ > 0 \end{array}\right.$$

The reason for the name S-gate is because the French for threshold is *seuil*. The S-gate should not be confused with the *ternary selector gate (T-gate). More complicated versions of the S-gate have been defined in various ways. *See also* threshold element.

test and set A single indivisible instruction that is capable of testing the value of the contents of a register and altering them. The instruction is used to implement more powerful indivisible operations (such as *lock, *unlock, or *semaphore operations) when the process executing the operation is capable of being interrupted and where the servicing of the interrupt may cause another process to be restarted.

test bed Any system whose primary purpose is to provide a framework within which other systems can be tested. Test beds are usually tailored to a specific programming language and implementation technique, and often to a specific application. Typically a test bed provides some means of simulating the environment of the system under test, of test-data generation and presentation, and of recording test results.

test coverage An estimate of the thoroughness of *testing of a program, usually measured as the proportion of the total actually tested by one or more of *path testing, *branch testing, *statement testing. *See also* LCSAJ.

test data *See* testing.

test-data generator Any means for the automatic or semiautomatic production of data for use in the *testing of some system. Typically both valid and invalid input data for the system under test will be generated in order to test responses to both valid and erroneous inputs. Some generators effectively produce a pseudorandom data stream, recognizing only constraints on the formats of the data. More advanced generators might attempt to produce data that will give good test coverage.

testing (dynamic testing) Any activity that checks by means of actual execution whether a system or component behaves in the desired manner. This is achieved by one or more *test runs* in which the system is supplied with input data, known under these circumstances as *test data*, and the system's responses are recorded for analysis.

Tests can be categorized according to the conditions under which they are performed and the purposes they serve. *Module testing* (or *unit testing*) is performed on individual components in isolation. At the time that components are brought together to form complete subsystems or systems, *integration testing* is performed in order to check that the components operate together correctly. Integration testing typically pays particular attention to the interfaces between components. By contrast, *system testing* normally treats the complete system as a "black box" and investigates its behavior without concern for individual components or internal interfaces. *Acceptance testing* is normally under the control of the procurers of the system, and is designed to ensure that the system is suitable for operational use.

See also beta test, branch testing, path testing, performance testing, regression testing, statement testing, black-box testing, glass-box testing. *Compare* static analysis.

test run *See* testing.

TEX (pronounced tek: the letters are Greek) A computer typesetting system designed by Donald E. Knuth that aims to produce results as good as "hot metal" setting when using a modern raster-image laser typesetter. Knuth was particularly concerned to produce high-quality setting of mathematical material, but TEX is equally suited to textual material. The system includes many innovative techniques, particularly its algorithm for breaking paragraphs into lines in an optimal manner. The source code for TEX is in the public domain, and as a result it is widely used in academic institutions throughout the world.

The input language of TEX provides a very low-level control over the placing of marks on the printed page, and it is generally used via an intermediary macro language. The "Plain TEX" macros provided as part of the system are still at quite a low level, and many users employ higher-level packages such as AMS-TEX and *LATEX.

The output from TEX is in a device-independent form, and separate drivers are required to convert this into the appropriate code for a particular printer. While output normally goes to a laser printer or phototypesetter, it is possible to write a driver for a dot-matrix printer operating in graphics mode. Knuth designed a whole new family of typefaces called Computer Modern Roman to go with TEX using his *METAFONT system, but these do not reproduce well at low resolutions; many users therefore prefer to use *PostScript fonts, using a conversion program to translate the device-independent output from TEX into PostScript code.

text editor A program used specifically for entry and modification of data that is in a textual format. Such data may be a program written in a high-level language or a report or book written in a natural language.

Text editors form an essential part of the user interface of all interactive systems. They may be *line-oriented*, where the text is considered to be a series of lines separated by end-of-line markers, *character-oriented*, where the text is considered to be a stream of characters with any end-of-line or page markers counting as characters, or *screen editors*. With screen editors, the display screen forms a movable *window into the text, within which the cursor may be positioned at points where insertions, deletions, and other editing functions are to be performed.

There is a considerable overlap in function between text editors and *word processing systems.

text formatter *See* formatter.

text processing *Another name for* word processing.

T flip-flop A clocked *flip-flop whose output "toggles", i.e. changes to the complementary logic state, on every active transition of the clock signal (*see* clock). The device acts as a divide-by-two *counter since two active transitions of the clock signal generate one active transition of the output. It can be considered as being equivalent to a *JK flip-flop whose J and K inputs are held at logic 1.

T-gate *Another name for* ternary selector gate.

theorem proving The formal method of providing a proof in *symbolic logic. Each step in the proof will (a) introduce a premise or axiom; (b) provide a statement that is a natural consequence of previously established results using only legitimate rules of inference.

Such formal proofs are often long and tedious. Sophisticated programs known as *theorem provers* can be used to automate much of the process. *See also* mechanical verifier.

theory of types *See* hierarchy of functions.

thermal ink jet *Another name for* bubble jet.

thermal printer A type of printer in which the image is produced by localized heating of paper that has a very thin thermosensitive coating containing two separate and colorless components. When heated the color former melts and combines with the previously colorless dyestuff to make a visible mark. Various colors are possible but blue and black are the most common. Blue toning paper allows higher print speeds but the image fades with time and is not compatible with some photocopiers. Black toning paper requires higher temperatures and pressure at the print head – thus causing greater wear – but fades less quickly and has a longer shelf life. The printers can be either *serial or *line printers. *See also* thermal transfer printer, electrothermal printer.

thermal transfer printer A printer in which thermoplastic ink is transferred to paper from a donor roll or thin backing material by localized heating. This type of printer, introduced in 1982, is very quiet in operation, produces a good contrast image, and is mechanically simple in design. The print head is similar to that used in the earlier *thermal printers that use sensitized paper, but the heating elements are usually smaller and thus allow the formation of a better character shape.

The printers may be *serial or *page printers. A speed of 100 characters per second has been achieved for good-quality serial printers and 4 pages per minute for line printers. The page printer can have a print head with as many as 3200 elements spanning an 8″ width. A donor film, the same size as the page to be printed, is laid over the paper and they are passed beneath the print head. Successive donor films of different colors can be used to print full-color pictures.

thesaurus A feature of word processing systems whereby similes and synonyms may be displayed on screen and incorporated into the text. *Full text retrieval systems may have *thesaurus searching* as an option whereby terms similar in meaning to those sought will also be located.

thin-film memory A memory device whose individual elements are formed by evaporating a thin film of a magnetic material onto a glass substrate. The status of each element may be interrogated (read) or changed (written to) by the application of a d.c. magnetic field parallel to the surface of the device. Large-capacity memories having many thousands of elements can be formed in a single operation using this process.

third generation of computers. Machines whose design was initiated after 1960 (approximately). Probably the most significant criterion of difference between *second and third generations lies in the concept of computer *architecture. Generally, second generation machines were limited to what the engineers could put together and make work. Advances in electronic technology – the development of *integrated circuits and the like – made it possible for designers to design an architecture to suit the requirements of the tasks envisaged for the machines and the programmers who were going to work them. With the development of the experimental machines – the IBM *Stretch and the Manchester University *Atlas – the concept of computer architecture became a reality. Comprehensive *operating systems became, more or less, part of the machines. *Multiprogramming was facilitated and much of the task of control of the memory and I/O and other resources became vested in the operating system or the machine itself.

third-party maintenance *See* TPM.

thrashing A phenomenon that may arise in *paging or other forms of *virtual-memory system. If the page-turning rate for a paging system becomes high, usually because the amount of real memory available for holding pages is small compared with the total *working set of all the *processes currently active, then each process will find itself in a situation in which, on attempting to reference a page, the appropriate page is not in memory. In trying to find space to hold the required page, the system is likely to move out onto backing store a page that will very shortly be required by some other process. As a consequence the paging rate rises to very high levels, the fraction of CPU cycles absorbed in managing page-turning overheads becomes very high, processes become blocked as they wait for page transfers to complete, and system throughput falls sharply.

One method by which thrashing may be alleviated is by an increase in the bandwidth between main memory and backing store, i.e. by providing sufficient interchange capacity to allow the thrashing to take place without inducing unduly long waits for paging-drum transfers. A more effective cure is to reduce the ratio between the total working-set size and the amount of space available for holding the active pages, thus increasing the hit rate on pages in memory, either by reducing the size of

the working set or by increasing the amount of memory on the system.

threaded list A list in which additional linkage structures, called *threads*, have been added to provide for traversals in special orders. This permits bounded workspace, i.e. read-only traversals along the direction provided by the threads. It does presuppose that the list and any sublists are not recursive and further that no sublist is shared.

threading A programming technique used in some code generators in which the "code" consists of a sequence of entry points of routines. The threaded code is interpreted by executing an unconditional branch to the destination indicated by a word of the code; on completion the routine thus activated terminates by again executing an unconditional branch to the entry point indicated by the next code word. *See also* single threading, multithreading.

threat Any action intended to breach the *security of information stored in a system by (a) gaining unauthorized access to that information usually without alerting the authorized user, (b) *denial of service to the authorized user, (c) *spoofing, which aims to confuse the user by introducing false information without alerting the authorized user. Some threats are with premeditated malicious intent but others are opportunistic, e.g. *browsing, or occur during a *crash. *See also* vulnerability.

three-address instruction *See* instruction format. *See also* multiple-address machine.

three-dimensional array *See* array.

three-state output *Another name for* tri-state output.

threshold element (threshold gate) A *logic element whose output is determined by comparing a weighted sum of inputs with a predetermined/prescribed threshold value. If the threshold is exceeded, the output is a logic 1; if not, the output is logic 0. If the number of inputs is odd, if the weights are all equal, and the threshold is equal to half of the number of inputs, then the threshold element behaves as a *majority element.

A system of threshold elements is described by or as *threshold logic. See also* ternary threshold gate.

throughput A figure-of-merit for a computer system in which some description of operating rate such as instructions-per-minute, jobs-per-day, etc., is used.

Thue-system A *semi-Thue system in which, for each production $l \rightarrow r$, the reverse production $r \rightarrow l$ is also present (as in the first example under semi-Thue system). Clearly then

$$w \Rightarrow w' \text{ iff } w' \Rightarrow w$$

time-bounded Turing machine *See* multi-tape Turing machine.

time complexity *See* complexity measure, P = NP question.

time division multiplexing (TDM) A method of sharing a transmission channel among multiple sources by allocating specific time slots to each source. Both synchronous and asynchronous TDM is used.

Synchronous TDM does not require identity bits to be included in a message since the receiving device knows which device is transmitting at all times. The two main methods used in synchronous TDM to identify when a device's time slot occurs are *polling and *clocking. Polling requires a central device to interrogate each sending device when its time slot occurs. Clocking requires each device to have a synchronized clock and a prearranged sending sequence known to all devices. Polling and clocking waste time slots if a device has no data to send. More refined methods require

devices to reserve their time slots ahead of time or allow devices to use time slots of other devices if they were unused on the previous cycle.

Asynchronous TDM allows devices to send data as it is ready, without a prearranged ordering. Data must carry with it the identity of the sending device. Since devices may send data at the same time, collisions may occur, making the messages unreadable. Many networks that utilize asynchronous TDM use *CSMA/CD (carrier sense multiple access with collision detection) to sense when messages have collided and must be retransmitted.

TDM is used in *baseband networking, and may also be used on channels of a *broadband networking system.

See also multiplexing, frequency division multiplexing.

time division switch An all-electronic switching system based on *time division multiplexing principles: an input digitized signal from a source is connected to an output trunk by assigning a group of bits from the input data stream to a time slot in a high-speed time division multiplexed output data stream. Time-division switches are commonly also used as tandem switches where time slots from an input time division multiplexed trunk are selectively connected to time slots in an output time division multiplexed trunk.

time domain A term used to refer to a situation in which the amplitude of a *signal varies with time. *See also* space domain.

time-of-day clock A digital device that provides time-of-day information. It is typically used as a means of scheduling control applications or data collection activities.

timeout A condition that occurs when a process which is waiting for either an external event or the expiry of a preset time interval reaches the end of the time interval before the external event is detected. For example, if the process has sent a message and no acknowledgment has been detected at the end of the preset time period, then the process may take appropriate action, such as retransmitting the message.

The word is also used as a verb.

time quantization (sampling) *See* quantization, discrete and continuous systems.

timer clock A timing device that can generate a *timeout signal after a fixed period of time. These devices are often made programmable, i.e. presetable, so that various timing durations can be obtained. In addition the timeout signal may be generated continuously, i.e. after every timing period, or on a one-shot basis.

time response of a linear channel. *See* convolution.

time series A set of observations ordered in time and usually equally spaced; each observation may be related in some way to its predecessors. Time-series problems arise in economics, commerce, industry, meteorology, demography, or any fields in which the same measurements are regularly recorded.

Time-series analysis is based on models of the variability of observations in a time series, by postulating trends, cyclic effects, and short-term relationships, with a view to understanding the causes of variation and to improving forecasting (*see also* periodogram).

Autoregression is the use of *regression analysis to relate observations to their predecessors. *Moving-average methods* use the means of neighboring observations to reveal underlying trends. Autoregression and moving averages are combined in *ARMA* (or *Box-Jenkins*) forecasting techniques.

Cyclic influences may be of known period (months in a year or days in a week) and data may be seasonally adjusted on the basis of long-term means. Cyclic influences of unknown period may be studied by *spectral analysis*.

Analogous techniques may be used for data regularly ordered in space rather than time.

time sharing A technique, first advocated by Christopher Strachey, for sharing the time of a computer among several jobs, switching between them so rapidly that each job appears to have the computer to itself. *See also* multiaccess system.

time slicing Process scheduling in which a *process is allowed to run for a predefined period of time, now called a *quantum, before rescheduling. *See also* scheduling algorithm.

timing analysis The use of structural information of a program and a knowledge of the processor instruction or module execution times to synthesize the temporal behavior of a software system. For sequential systems this is a simple analysis. For highly concurrent systems the use of simulation techniques or queuing models may be necessary, and system performance/time response becomes stochastic rather than deterministic. *See also* performance testing.

timing diagram A graphical description of the operation of a *sequential circuit; the state(s) of all the relevant variables (inputs, internal memory, and outputs) are shown as functions along the time dimension.

TIP *Acronym for* terminal interface processor. *See* IMP.

tip node *Another name for* leaf node.

TLU *Abbrev. for* table look-up.

TM *Abbrev. for* Turing machine.

toggling speed *Another name for* switching speed.

token 1. One of the meaningful units (names, constants, reserved words, etc.) in the input to a compiler. The *lexical analyzer breaks up the input, which is a stream of characters, into a sequence of tokens.

2. A unique sequence of bits granting send permission on a network. *See* token ring, token bus.

3. *See* Petri net.

token bus A form of network (usually a *local area network) in which access to the transmission medium is controlled by a *token. The network stations (nodes) are interconnected by a *bus, i.e. signals are placed on the transmission medium by one station and can be read by all the other stations. If the signal is a token, indicating that the station that was last transmitting has now finished, the token is passed from station to station in a strict sequence. In a *token ring this sequence is determined by the order in which stations are physically connected to the transmission medium. A station wishing to transmit will start to do so by removing the token from the bus and replacing it with the data to be transmitted; when transmission is complete, the transmitting station will reinitiate the token passing process.

A token bus system has the advantage that the priority of stations can be redefined by redefining the order in which stations are permitted to acquire the token.

token ring A *ring network architecture configured on the basis that each station (node) on the ring awaits the arrival of a *token from the adjacent upstream node, indicating that it is allowed to send information toward the downstream node. The network is configured in a manner that ensures that only a single token is present on the ring at one time. When a sending node intercepts the token, it first sends its message to the downstream node followed by the token, which is then passed to each succeeding node until it is again intercepted by a node with a message awaiting transmission.

tool *See* software tool.

toolbox A set of *software tools, probably from several vendors, not necessarily as closely related or providing as full coverage of the *software life-cycle as a *toolkit.* The set of tools in a toolkit is usually from a single vendor. *See also* PSE, CSSE, IPSE, software engineering environment.

toolkit *See* toolbox.

TOP *Acronym for* Technical Office Protocol. A project that operates in a similar field to the *MAP set of protocols but concentrates on the management of the design process and the associated activities such as costing inventory, rather than on the automation of the machining and assembling of components.

top-down development An approach to program development in which progress is made by defining required elements in terms of more basic elements, beginning with the required program and ending when the implementation language is reached. At every stage during top-down development each of the undefined elements from the previous stage is defined. In order to do this, an appropriate collection of more basic elements is introduced, and the undefined elements are defined in terms of these more basic elements ("more basic" meaning that the element is closer to the level that can be directly expressed in the implementation language). These more basic elements will in turn be defined at the next stage in terms of still more basic elements, and so on until at some stage the elements can be defined directly in the implementation language.

In practice, "pure" top-down development is not possible; the choice of more basic elements at each stage must always be guided by an awareness of the facilities of the implementation language, and even then it will often be discovered at a later stage that some earlier choice was inappropriate, leading to a need for iteration. *Compare* bottom-up development.

top-down parsing A strategy for *parsing sentences of *context-free grammars that attempts to construct a *parse tree from the top down. The term includes techniques that may or may not involve backtracking.

Beginning with a parse tree consisting of just the start symbol of the *grammar, a top-down parser attempts to expand those leaf nodes labeled by nonterminals from left to right using the productions of the grammar. As leaves labeled by terminals are created they are matched against the input string. Should the match fail, new alternatives for the interior nodes are tried in a systematic way until the entire input string has been matched or no more alternatives are possible. A top-down parser without backtracking uses the information contained in the portion of the input string not yet matched to decide once and for all which alternatives to choose. The *LL parsing technique is the most powerful such technique.

Top-down parsing is often implemented as a set of recursive procedures, one for each nonterminal in the grammar, and is then called *recursive descent parsing*.

topological sort A sorting process over which a partial ordering is defined, i.e. ordering is given over pairs of items but not between all of them. An example is given by a dictionary. If a word v is defined in terms of word w, we denote this by $w < v$. Then a topological sort of the dictionary implies an ordering of the terms so that there will be no forward references.

topology 1. The study of those properties of *sets that are shared by all images (homeomorphic images) of the sets under certain mappings that might be described as deformations. Topology is sometimes described as geometry done on a rubber sheet; this sheet can be pulled or stretched into different shapes. Topological properties are unaltered by distortions of this kind. Topological properties can be attributed to *graphs, *grammars, and even *programs themselves.

2. **(interconnection topology)** *See* network architecture.

TOPS *Trademark, acronym for* terminal operating system. One of the multiprogramming systems available on Digital Equipment Corporation's larger machines, the DEC–10 and DEC–20 systems.

total correctness, proof of. *See* program correctness proof.

total function A *function
$$f : S \to T$$
whose value is defined for all elements x in the set S; thus for each x, $f(x)$ produces some value in T. *Compare* partial function.

totally ordered structure *Another name for* linear structure.

total ordering A *partial ordering with the added property that there is always order between any two elements. The usual "less than" ordering between integers is a total ordering. The relation "is a subset of" defined on the *algebra of sets is not.

touch screen *See* touch-sensitive device.

touch-sensitive device A flat rectangular device that responds to the touch of, say, a finger by transmitting the coordinates of the touched point to a computer. The touch-sensitive area may be the VDU screen itself, in which case it is called a *touch screen*; alternatively it may be integral with the keyboard or a separate unit that can be placed on a desk. In the first case the computer user can, for example, make a selection from a number of options displayed on the screen by touching one of them; in the latter two cases movement of the finger across the so-called *touchpad* can cause the cursor to move around the screen. *See also* light pen, mouse.

tournament A directed *graph in which there is precisely one directed edge between any pair of *vertices.

tournament method A method of finding a specific element in some set (e.g. largest of a set of numbers), so called because it involves pairing elements and comparing them to find which one goes through to the next stage, leaving just one element at the end that has not lost.

TPM *Abbrev. for* third-party maintenance. Any maintenance carried out by an organization that is neither the supplier nor the owner of equipment. An advantage of TPM is that systems consisting of items from different suppliers can be maintained from a single point. However, expertise and access to spares and manuals may not be as good as when the originator of the equipment does the work.

TP monitor *Abbrev. for* transaction processing monitor. *See* transaction processing.

trace program A program that monitors the execution of some software system and provides information on the dynamic behavior of that system in the form of a *trace*, i.e. a report of the sequence of actions carried out. Typically a trace program will offer several options as to the kind of trace produced. For example, there may be options to produce a statement-by-statement trace, or to trace just those statements that alter the flow of control, or to trace changes to the value of a specific variable.

track 1. The path followed by the *head over the surface of a recording medium (usually magnetic or optical). The tracks on magnetic disks are circular and concentric. On optical disks they may be similar but are more often turns of a continuous spiral path. Most magnetic tapes carry several tracks running the length of the tape; these may be written or read simultaneously (parallel recording) or, for other tape formats, one at a time (serial recording, or *serpentine recording if alternate tracks are recorded in opposite directions). In *helical scan recording the tracks run diagonally across the axis of the tape.

On *CD-ROM optical disk, the word track is also used (as it is on compact audio disk) to define an item of the contents, of variable length, which may occupy many turns of the spiral path.

2. The portion of a *paper tape that may be punched with holes.

trackerball (trackball) A device for generating signals that can cause the cursor or some other symbol to be moved about on a display screen. It consists of a ball supported on bearings so that it is free to rotate in any direction but is restrained within a socket so that less than half of its surface is exposed. In use, the ball is rotated by the operator's fingers and sensors on two of the support bearings generate trains of pulses related to the rotation of the ball about two axes at right angles. The relationship between the angle of rotation of the ball and the pulses is not calibrated and control is achieved by observing the resulting movement on the screen. In the late 1970s such devices were expensive and were only used in applications such as Air Traffic Control; by the mid-1980s they had reduced significantly in price and become popular for personal computer applications.

tractor A device for moving continuous *stationery through a printer and maintaining good registration relative to the page boundaries. The technique by which this is achieved is known as *tractor feed*. The tractors are used in pairs and consist of loops of light chain or bands on which are mounted pegs (also known as pintles or sprockets) that engage with holes that have been punched along both edges of the stationery. The tractors are usually driven by a d.c. servo or stepper motor that is controlled by the printer electronics. In high-speed printers there may be pairs of tractors above and below the print line but in lower-speed devices there is usually only one pair and friction is relied upon to keep the paper tensioned. In printers for transaction documents the tractors are arranged immediately below the print line so that the document may be torn off close to the last line of print.

trade secrets Pieces of confidential information given in circumstances of confidence that enable the recipient to short-circuit an otherwise necessary course of development. Thus a source listing containing debugged code for one or more algorithms, if given in circumstances of confidence, may be protected by the law as a trade secret and the recipient (and any person who knowingly received the information) barred from using the algorithms in programs of his own. Like *privacy, the law on trade secrets is not at all clear. *See also* copyright, patent.

traffic A measure of the quantity of data or other messages taking place between points of a communication network.

traffic control A term sometimes used in reference to the control of input and

output. It covers both the hardware (channels and interrupts) and software (resource allocation and process synchronization) necessary to achieve the orderly and correct movement of data in a multiprogramming system.

trailer label A *sentinel that occurs at the end of data organized in sequential form, e.g. on magnetic tape. Trailer labels typically include summary statistics of the data, e.g. the total number of records in the file.

trailer record A record that follows a group of related records and contains data relevant to those records. For example, a trailer record may appear at the end of a file and contain a total of monetary fields held on that file, which may be used as a security check.

train printer A type of *impact *line printer in which the type font is etched or engraved upon metal slugs that are pushed around a guide track. It was introduced by IBM in 1965 to supersede the *chain printer. The slugs of the train printer generally have three characters on the face and a gear form at the back. The track guides them around a loop, one section of which runs parallel to the line to be printed. The character set is repeated a number of times to ensure that the track is full. The use of slugs in a track enables greater accuracy of print to be achieved and also yields flexibility of character repertoire. Heavily used characters can be easily replaced and special symbols can be substituted for other characters. Speeds of up to 3000 lpm are achieved.

Train printers dominated the high-speed printer market up to 1982, when the *band printer offered superior performance at lower cost and nonimpact printers with superior print quality and versatility became financially viable.

transaction 1. A single input message to a system (irrespective of whether the message is submitted whole or assembled by means of a dialogue). A transaction reflects some "real-world" event.

2. The *file updating or database updating process initiated by a single input message, i.e. by a transaction. In a *multiaccess system, transactions that are processed concurrently can give rise to problems in maintaining file or *database integrity.

transaction file (movement file) A file, especially a *data file, containing transaction records, prior to the updating of a *master file. Transaction files are only used in *batch processing systems. Once updating has been carried out, the transaction file may be kept in order to permit subsequent recovery of the master file (*see* file recovery).

transaction processing A method of organizing a *data processing system in which *transactions are processed to completion as they arise. A *transaction processing monitor* (*TP monitor*) is a software system that facilitates the handling of transactions in such circumstances. *Compare* batch processing.

transborder dataflow The most complex legal topic yet to be created by the use of computers in society. When a person in Germany contacts an Irish database, combines the information with information extracted from a Swiss reference manual stored in digital format on a computer in France, and sends the output to Australia, Zambia, and Taiwan where it is recorded on disk with no eye-readable copies produced, he creates a literary work that falls outside any conventions that at present exist concerning *copyright. He also may have breached the *data protection legislation of several countries. With the growth in the use of satellites and wideband communication facilities, the importance of transborder dataflow will grow in the 1990s and hence new conventions will have to be drafted.

transceiver *Acronym for* transmitter and receiver. A device that can both transmit and receive signals on a communication medium. Many communication devices, including *modems, *codecs, and terminals, are transceivers.

transducer 1. Any device that converts energy in the form of sound, light, pressure, etc., into an equivalent electrical signal, or vice versa. For example, a photoconductor converts light and ultraviolet radiation into electrical energy, a piezoelectric device converts mechanical stress into electrical energy (and vice versa).

2. In formal language theory, any *automaton that produces output.

transfer rate *See* data transfer rate.

transformation 1. *Another name for* function, used especially in geometry.

2. of programs. *See* program transformation.

3. of statistics data. A change of scale used to improve the validity of statistical analyses. For data in which small values have smaller *variance than large values a logarithmic or square-root transformation is often recommended. For data in the form of proportions, a transformation from the scale (0,1) to an infinite scale is advisable before performing *analysis of variance or *regression analysis. Several transformations exist for proportions, such as the *logistic or log-odds-ratio that is used in the analysis of *generalized linear models. Appropriate transformations may be suggested by studying *residuals in a regression analysis.

transformational semantics *See* program transformation.

transformation matrix An $m \times n$ matrix of numbers used to map vectors with n elements onto vectors with m elements.

transformation monoid *See* transformation semigroup.

transformation semigroup A *semigroup consisting of a collection C of transformations of a *set S into itself (*see* function), the *dyadic operation ∘ being the *composition of functions; it is essential that the set C should be *closed with respect to composition, i.e. if c_1 and c_2 are in C then so is $c_1 ∘ c_2$.

If the identity transformation (*see* identity function) is included in the transformation semigroup, a *transformation monoid* results. Every monoid is isomorphic to a transformation monoid.

transform domain *See* filtering.

transient error An error that occurs once or at unpredictable intervals. *See also* error rate.

transistor A semiconductor device having, in general, three terminals that are attached to electrode regions within the device. Current flowing between two of these electrodes is made to vary in response to voltage or current variations imposed on the third electrode. The device is capable of current or voltage amplification depending on the particular circuit implementation employed. It can also be used as a switch by driving it between its maximum and minimum of current flow.

The transistor was invented in 1948 by Shockley, Brattain, and Bardeen at Bell Telephone Labs. As performance and manufacturing techniques improved, there was a huge growth in computer technology.

See also bipolar transistor, field-effect transistor, MOSFET.

transistor-transistor logic *See* TTL.

transitive closure of a *transitive *binary relation R. A relation R^* defined as follows:

$$x \ R^* \ y$$

iff there exists a sequence

$$x = x_0, x_1, \ldots, x_n = y$$

such that $n > 0$ and

$$x_i \ R \ x_{i+1}, \ i = 0, 1, 2, \ldots, n-1$$

It follows from the transitivity property that

$$\text{if } x \ R \ y \text{ then } x \ R^* \ y$$

and that R is a subset of R^*.

Reflexive closure is similar to transitive closure but includes the possibility that $n = 0$. Transitive and reflexive closures play important roles in parsing and compiling techniques and in finding paths in graphs.

transitive relation A *relation R defined on a set S and having the property that, for all x, y, and z in S,

$$\text{whenever } x \ R \ y \text{ and } y \ R \ z$$
$$\text{then } x \ R \ z$$

The relations "is less than" defined on integers, and "is subset of" defined on sets are transitive.

translation (protocol translation) *See* internetworking.

translation table A table of information stored within a processor or a peripheral that is used to convert encoded information into another form of code with the same meaning. There are a variety of codes used within the field of computing and sometimes more than one code may be used within a single system. For output devices such as printers the *ASCII code is widely used but the code used within the processor may be *EBCDIC. A translation table is used to make the required conversion.

translator A program that converts a program written in one language to the equivalent program in another language. A *compiler is a specific example of a translator: it takes a program written in a high-level language such as FORTRAN or Algol and converts it into machine code or assembly language.

translator writing system A set of *software tools that are designed to aid the production of new language translators. A *compiler-compiler is an example of one such tool.

transmission channel *See* channel.

transmission control unit *See* communication processor.

transmission rate The speed at which information may be transferred from a device or via a circuit. The unit used is usually related to the amount of information transferred per cycle, e.g. characters per second or bits per second. With data transmission circuits the *baud rate is sometimes used.

Transpac The French PTT's *public packet network. It started operation in 1978 after testbed development of the *RCP network. Transpac provides an X.25 interface.

transparent 1. Denoting a property or a component of a computer system that provides some facilities without restrictions or interference arising from the way it is implemented. For example, if a machine with 32-bit wide words has an 8-bit wide ALU yet performs correct 32-bit arithmetic, then the ALU size is transparent in such use.
2. Denoting or using a transmission path that passes a signal, or some particular feature of a signal, without restricting or changing it. Note that nontransparent systems would not allow particular signals to be transmitted as data, reserving them for special purposes. *See also* data transparency.

transport 1. A mechanism for transporting an information storage medium past an access station. The word is most frequently used to refer to either a tape transport (*see* magnetic tape) or a document transport.
2. A service provided by a (local or wide area) communication network, or the architectural layer or interface with this service.

transportable *See* portable.

transport layer of network protocol function. *See* seven-layer reference model.

transpose of an $m \times n$ matrix A. The $n \times m$ matrix, symbol A^T, given by interchanging rows and columns. Thus the i,jth element of A^T is equal to the j,ith element of A.

transputer A high-performance microcomputer, devised and manufactured by the UK company INMOS, designed to facilitate interprocess and interprocessor communication. The transputer comprises a 32-bit *RISC processor with 2 or 4 kilobytes of fast on-chip static *RAM, process scheduling in hardware with a submicrosecond context switch, external memory controller, and four high-speed serial links. The T800 transputer also provides an on-chip floating-point *coprocessor capable of 1.5 megaflops and high-performance graphics support.

A single transputer is a powerful processor in its own right: the serial links allow an architecture in which transputers are arranged in an array, each communicating with its four nearest neighbors. With suitable algorithms this permits very high performance on complex numerical problems.

The transputer is programmed in *occam: the program architecture of processes communicating through channels can be implemented by time-slicing a single computer, or by using multiple transputers, when the serial links provide the channels. Applications of the transputer in pipelines and arrays have demonstrated that it is a successful low-cost approach to achieving a high parallel-processing rate.

trap A system state similar to that caused by an *interrupt but synchronous to the system rather than asynchronous as in the case of an interrupt. There are a variety of conditions that can cause a trap to occur. Examples of such conditions include the attempted execution of an illegal instruction, or an attempt to access another user's resources in a system that supports multi-user protection. The attempted operation is detected by the hardware and control is transferred to a different part of the system, usually in the operating system, which can then decide on what action to take.

trapezium rule The approximation

$$\int_{x_i}^{x_{i+1}} f(x)\,dx \simeq \tfrac{1}{2}h(f(x_i)+f(x_{i+1})),$$

$$h = x_{i+1} - x_i$$

used as the basis for an *extrapolation method in *numerical integration.

trapezoidal rule *See* ordinary differential equations.

traveling salesman problem A well-known *graph-searching problem. In practical terms the problem can be thought of as that of a salesman who wishes to perform a circular tour of certain cities, calling at each city once only and traveling the minimum total distance possible. In more abstract terms, it is the problem of finding a minimum-weight *Hamiltonian cycle in a *weighted graph. The problem is known to be NP-complete (*see* P = NP question).

traversal A *path through a *graph in which every vertex is visited at least once. Traversals are usually discussed in connection with special kinds of graphs, namely *trees. Examples include *preorder traversal, *postorder traversal, and *symmetric order (or inorder) traversal. When parse trees for arithmetic expressions are traversed, these tree traversals lead to prefix (*Polish) notation, postfix (*reverse Polish) notation, and *infix notation respectively.

tree 1. Most commonly, short for *rooted tree*, i.e. a finite set of one or more

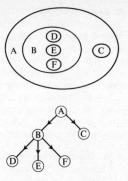

Sample tree represented as a Venn diagram (top) and as a directed graph

*nodes such that firstly there is a single designated node called the *root* and secondly the remaining nodes are partitioned into $n \geqslant 0$ *disjoint sets, T_1, T_2, ..., T_n, where each of these sets is itself a tree. The sets T_1, T_2, ..., T_n are called *subtrees* of the root. If the order of these subtrees is significant, the tree is called an *ordered tree*, otherwise it is sometimes called an *unordered tree*.

A tree can be represented as a *graph with the root node represented by a vertex connected by (directed) arcs to the vertices representing the root nodes of each of its subtrees. An alternative definition of a (*directed*) *tree* can thus be given in terms from graph theory: a tree is a directed *acyclic graph such that firstly there is a unique vertex, which no arcs enter, called the root, secondly every other vertex has exactly one arc entering it, and thirdly there is a unique path from the root to any vertex.

The diagram shows different representations of a tree.

2. Any *connected acyclic graph.

3. Any data structure representing a tree (def. 1 or 2). For example, a rooted tree can be represented as a pointer to the representation of the root node. A representation of a node would contain

pointers to the subtrees of the node as well as the data associated with the node itself. Because the number of subtrees of a node may vary, it is common practice to use a *binary-tree representation.

The terminology associated with trees is either of a botanic nature, as with *forest, *leaf, root, or is genealogical, as with *ancestor, *descendant, *child, *parent, *sibling. *See also* binary tree.

tree automaton A generalization of the notion of a *finite-state automaton, applying to trees rather than strings (*see* tree language). There are two versions. A *top-down* machine begins at the root of the tree; having read the symbol at a node it changes state accordingly and splits into n machines to process separately the n descendants. A *bottom-up* machine begins with several separate activations of itself – one at each leaf node of the tree. Whenever all the subtrees of a particular node have been processed, the machines that have processed them are replaced by a single one at that node. Its state is determined by the symbol at the node and the final states of the descendant machines.

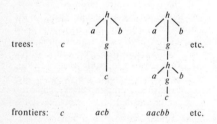

trees:

frontiers: c   acb   aacbb   etc.

Language generated by a tree grammar

tree grammar A generalization of the notion of *grammar, applying to trees (often called *terms* in this context) rather than strings (*see* tree language). A *regular tree grammar* is the corresponding generalization of the notion of *regular grammar. Productions have the form

$$A \rightarrow t,$$

where A is a nonterminal and t a term, e.g.

$$S \rightarrow h(a,g(S),b) \mid c$$

These productions generate the *regular tree language* shown in the diagram. Note that the *frontiers* of these trees are the strings shown below each tree in the diagram. A set of strings is *context-free if and only if it is the set of frontiers of the trees in a regular tree language.

The notion of *context-free grammar can be similarly generalized. This time nonterminals can themselves be function symbols having an arbitrary number of arguments, e.g.

$$F(x_1,x_2) \rightarrow$$
$$f(x_2,F(x_1,g(x_2))) \mid h(x_1,x_1,x_2)$$

This means, for example, that $F(a,b)$ could be rewritten to

$$f(b,F(a,g(b))),$$

and then to

$$f(b,f(g(b),F(a,g(g(b))))),$$

and then to

$$f(b,f(g(b),h(a,a,g(g(b)))))$$

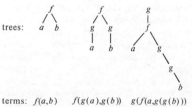

trees:

terms: $f(a,b)$ $f(g(a),g(b))$ $g(f(a,g(g(b)))$

Examples of Σ-trees and Σ-terms

tree language (term language) In *formal language theory, a generalization of the notion of language, applying to trees (often called *terms* in this context) rather than strings. Alphabets are extended to give each symbol an *arity*, the arity of each symbol dictating the number of subterms, or descendants in the tree, that it has.

For example, let Σ be the alphabet $\{f,g,a,b\}$ and give arities 2,1,0,0 to f,g,a,b respectively. Then examples of Σ-*trees* and their equivalent representations as Σ-*terms* (or *well-formed expressions over* Σ) are shown in the diagram. A Σ-language is now any set of Σ-terms. *See also* tree grammar, tree automaton.

tree search Any method of searching a body of data structured as a tree. *See* breadth-first search, depth-first search.

tree selection sort A refinement of *straight selection sort that makes use of the information gained in the first step to save on the subsequent number of comparisons required. It was proposed in 1956 by E. H. Friend and modified by K. E. Iverson in 1962. *See also* heapsort.

tree walking *Traversal of a tree.

trial function *See* finite-element method.

triangular matrix A square matrix in which every element lying to one side of the main diagonal is equal to zero. Thus for a *lower triangular matrix*, L,
$$l_{ij} = 0 \text{ if } i < j$$
and for an *upper triangular matrix*, U,
$$u_{ij} = 0 \text{ if } i > j$$
If, in addition,
$$l_{ii} = 0 \text{ or } u_{ii} = 0$$
then L or U is said to be *strictly lower* or *strictly upper triangular* respectively. The inverse of a lower (or an upper) triangular matrix, if it exists, is easy to calculate and is itself lower (or upper) triangular.

triangular waveform A periodic repetitive waveform that takes on its peak positive and negative excursions at fixed points in time. Between these peaks the waveform alternately rises and falls linearly with time. The rates of rise and fall determine the repetition rate or frequency of the waveform and in general are made equal. *Compare* sawtooth waveform.

tridiagonal matrix A band matrix A in which
$$a_{ij} = 0 \text{ if } |i - j| > 1$$

trie search A searching algorithm that examines data stored in a *trie* (name derived from information re*trie*val). A trie is essentially an *n*-ary tree with nodes that are *n*-place vectors, the components of which correspond to digits or characters.

trigger To initiate the operation of an electrical circuit or device. Thus a signal supplied to the trigger input of a circuit may cause the circuit's output signal to be synchronized to this input.

trim of an array. The array obtained by constraining the subscripts to lie in some specified subrange. For example, the trim of a vector
$$v = (v_1 \ v_2 \ \ldots \ v_{10})$$
obtained by constraining the index i so that $3 \leqslant i \leqslant 7$ is the vector
$$(v_3 \ v_4 \ v_5 \ v_6 \ v_7)$$
See also slice.

triple precision The use of three times the usual number of bits to represent a number. It is seldom required. *See also* double precision.

tri-state output (three-state output) An electronic output stage consisting of a logic gate, commonly an inverter or buffer, that exhibits three possible *logic states, namely logic 1, logic 0, and an inactive (high-impedance or open-circuit) state. The inactive state allows the device outputs to be combined with other similar outputs in a busing structure such that only one device is active on the bus at any one time.

trivial graph A *graph with just one vertex.

Trojan horse (trojan) A form of program designed to circumvent the security features of a system. The usual method of introducing a Trojan horse is by donating a program, or part of a program, to a user of the system whose security is to be breached. The donated code will ostensibly perform a useful function; the recipient will be unaware that the code has other effects, such as writing a copy of his username and password into a file whose existence is known only to the donor, and from which the donor will subsequently collect whatever data has been written.

Trojan horses can be particularly effective when offered to systems staff who can run code in highly privileged modes. Two remedies are effective: no code should be run unless its provenance is absolutely certain; no code should be run with a higher level of privilege than is absolutely essential. *See also* virus.

Tron *Acronym for* the real-time operating-system nucleus. A project commenced in 1984 at Tokyo University to create a framework for the design of microprocessor systems for *workstations, *personal computers, and industrial embedded applications. The project has developed Tron architectures on silicon, now manufactured by Hitachi, and three operating systems: *BTron*, *CTron*, and *ITron*.

BTron is a business-oriented operating system for personal computers with English, Japanese, and other character set capabilities. CTron is a (network) communications-oriented operating system. ITron is a real-time operating system, designed to give rapid response to external events and intended for applications ranging from automatic bank teller machines to aircraft landing systems.

trouble shooting The resolution of a particular problem associated with a project or system. This activity is exceptional rather than part of the planned life of the project or system.

true complement *Another name for* radix complement.

truncation *See* roundoff error.

truncation error *Another name for* discretization error.

trunk *Another (US) name for* bus.

trunk circuit An interconnecting transmission channel between a switching machine in one location and a switching machine in an adjacent node.

trusted Having, involving, or denoting a security feature that is necessary to uphold a *security policy. Such features, when granted *security certification, may be considered "trustworthy". A trusted computer base is the totality of the security features within a system including hardware, firmware, and software.

truth table 1. A tabular description of a *combinational circuit (such as an *AND gate, *OR gate, *NAND gate), listing all possible states of the input variables together with a statement of the output variable(s) for each of those possible states.
2. A tabular description of a *logic operation (such as *AND, *OR, *NAND), listing all possible combinations of the truth values – i.e. *true* (T) or *false* (F) – of the operands together with the truth value of the outcome for each of the possible combinations.

TSR *Short for* terminate and stay resident program. A type of program normally found on single-tasking microcomputer systems. After the program has been loaded into memory and executed it does not release the memory but remains there, ready to be reactivated when required, often by a single keystroke (*see* hot-key). The advantage is that it is not necessary to terminate one program before starting another; however, the maximum amount of memory available for other programs is reduced.

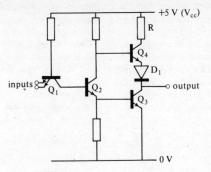

TTL NAND gate

TTL *Abbrev. for* transistor-transistor logic. A widely used family of logic circuits that is produced in integrated-circuit form and whose principal switching components are *bipolar transistors. It is available in low power and high switching speed versions (*see* Schottky TTL), in addition to the standard form.

The diagram shows the equivalent circuit of a TTL two-input *NAND gate. The basic circuit uses a multiemitter bipolar transistor, Q_1, which is easily fabricated in integrated-circuit form. Each base-emitter junction of Q_1 effectively acts as a *diode, in a similar manner to a *DTL input stage. Thus if all inputs are at a high voltage (logic 1), all input "diodes" are reverse biased; the collector voltage of Q_1 rises to V_{cc}, turning on Q_2 (which acts as a phase splitter). The emitter voltage of Q_2 rises while its collector voltage falls, turning Q_3 on and Q_4 off. The output thus falls to logic 0, i.e. zero volts.

If any one of the Q_1 inputs is returned to logic 0, 0 volts, then Q_1 is turned hard on, turning off Q_2 whose collector voltage rises; this turns on Q_4. No current is available via Q_2 for Q_3's base, and so Q_3 turns off. The output thus increases to $+5$ volts, i.e. logic 1. Diode D_1 is included to establish the correct bias conditions for Q_4. The out-

put stage, consisting of Q_3, D_1, Q_4, and R, acts as a power amplifier and is often termed a *totem-pole output*.

TTL is the most commonly used technology for SSI and MSI devices due to its low cost, high speed, and ready availability.

T-type flip-flop *See* T flip-flop.

Turbo languages Implementations of popular programming languages by Borland Inc. for the IBM PC and equivalents (and in some cases for the Apple Macintosh). They include Turbo Basic, Turbo C, Turbo Pascal, and Turbo Prolog. They are characterized by extremely fast compile speed and an integrated environment comprising editor, compiler, and debugger; in addition, the language as implemented includes many enhancements over the "standard" language. The Turbo languages are very popular and have sold in large numbers, making the version of the language they implement a de facto standard.

Turing computability *See* Turing machine.

Turing machine (TM) An imaginary computing machine used as a mathematical abstraction by Alan Turing to make precise the notion of an effective procedure (i.e. an algorithm). There are many

481

equivalent ways of dealing with this problem; the first was Turing's version, published in 1936.

A Turing machine is an *automaton that includes a potentially infinite linear tape (in both directions) divided into boxes or cells and read by a read-head that scans one cell at a time. Symbols written on the tape are drawn from a finite alphabet:

$$s_0, \ldots, s_p$$

The control or processing unit of the machine can assume one of a finite number of distinct internal states:

$$q_0, \ldots, q_m$$

The "program" for a given machine is assumed to be made up from a finite set of instructions that are quintuples of the form

$$q_i s_j s_k X q_j$$
where X is R, L, or N

The first symbol indicates that the machine is in state q_i while the second indicates that the head is reading s_j on the tape. In this state the machine will replace s_j by s_k and if $X = R$ the head will move to the right; if $X = L$ it will move to the left and if $X = N$ it will remain where it is. To complete the sequence initiated by this triple the machine will go into state q_j.

A function f,

$$f : N^k \to N$$
where $N = \{0,1,2, \ldots \}$,
$$N^k = N \times \ldots \times N \; k \text{ times}$$

is (*Turing*) *computable* if for each x in N^k, when some representation of x in N^k is placed on the tape (the N machine in the initial state of q_0 say), the machine halts with a representation of f (x) on the tape. *See also* effective computability.

It is customary in the study of abstract computation models to make a distinction between deterministic and nondeterministic algorithms. In a *deterministic Turing machine* the overall course of the computation is completely determined by the Turing machine (program), the starting state, and the initial tape-inputs; in a *nondeterministic Turing machine* there are several possibilities at each stage of the computation: it can execute one out of possibly several basic modes. The class of problems solvable by deterministic Turing machines in *polynomial time is the class *P*; the class of problems solvable by nondeterministic Turing machines in polynomial time is the class *NP*. *See also* P = NP question.

turnaround document *See* document processing.

turnaround time (turnround time) 1. The time that elapses between the submission of a job to a computing facility and the return of results.

2. In data communications, the time taken to reverse the direction of transmission on a channel.

turnkey operation The delivery and installation of a complete computer system plus application programs so that the system can be placed into immediate operational use.

turtle graphics A method for translating information from a computer into pictures or patterns. The original drawing device was a simple pen-plotter known as a *turtle*, a motorized carriage carrying one or more pens and connected to its controller and power source by a flexible cable. The drive wheels of the carriage can be precisely controlled to steer it in any direction across a floor or other flat surface covered in paper or similar material; the pens can be raised and lowered by control signals.

The action of the turtle can now be simulated by graphics on the display of a small computer: the *screen turtle* usually has the form of a triangular arrow that may or may not produce a line as it is made to move across the screen. *See also* LOGO.

two-address instruction *See* instruction format. *See also* multiple-address machine.

two-dimensional array *Another name for* matrix. *See also* array.

two-level grammars (VW-grammars, van Wijngaarden grammars) A generalization of *context-free grammars that enables non-context-free aspects of a language to be specified. They were developed by A. van Wijngaarden and used in the formal definition of Algol 68. The productions of a two-level grammar are split into two parts: those in the first part are called *hyperrules* and act as templates for context-free productions; those in the second part are called *metaproductions*. The metaproductions are context-free productions and they define the set of nonterminals to be used in the hyperrules. The power of two-level grammars comes from the fact that the hyperrules can be templates for an infinite set of productions. It is in this way that they are used to define non-context-free aspects of a language.

two-level memory A memory system with two memories of different capacities and speeds. *See* multilevel memory, memory hierarchy.

two-norm (Euclidean norm) *See* approximation theory.

two-plus-one address *See* instruction format.

two's complement *See* radix complement.

two-way linked list *Another name for* doubly linked list.

two-way merge An algorithm that merges two ordered files into one single sorted file. It may be viewed as a generalization of sorting by insertion, and was proposed by John von Neumann in 1945.

Tymnet The US public packet-switching carrier that developed from Tymshare Inc.'s internal terminal network used by their public time-sharing service. Net-work switches are interconnected by voice-grade lines. A central supervisor creates a *virtual connection route for each call at call initialization. Flow control is performed on a link-by-link basis for each virtual connection. Messages between nodes contain data for up to 20 different calls, packed into 66-byte frames. Data is repackaged at each node into new blocks for the next hop.

type *Short for* data type, used especially in combination, as in logical type (or type logical) and integer type (or type integer).

type 0 (1, 2, 3) language (or **grammar**) *See* Chomsky hierarchy.

type-insensitive code A program for the numerical solution of *ordinary differential equations that attempts to be efficient, irrespective of whether the problem is stiff or nonstiff. This is usually achieved by switching automatically in the code between different classes of methods.

typewriter terminal *Another name for* teletypewriter.

U

UART *Acronym for* universal asynchronous receiver/transmitter. A *logic circuit, usually an integrated circuit, that will convert an asynchronous serial data stream into a byte-parallel form and vice versa. The normal application is in the interfaces for data transmission lines and peripherals.

UCSD Pascal A version of *Pascal developed at the University of California San Diego, and later marketed by Softech Inc. UCSD Pascal was developed as a portable system to run on a variety of microcomputers; this was achieved by compiling into *p-code, an interpretive code for a hypothetical machine that could be implemented on many target systems. The same technique is applied to other languages in the p-system software. UCSD Pascal introduced a number of extensions to the language, particularly in the areas of string handling and independent compilation (*see* interface); it is thus not compatible with the ISO Standard for Pascal. UCSD Pascal has been superseded by *Turbo Pascal.

UI *Abbrev. for* user interface.

ULA *Abbrev. for* uncommitted logic array.

ULTRIX A version of *UNIX designed and implemented by *DEC to run on their VAX series of processors.

unary operation (monadic operation) defined on a set S. A *function from the domain S into S itself. The *identity function is unary. Other examples are the operations of *negation in arithmetic or logic and of taking *complements in set theory or in *Boolean algebra. Although basically functions, unary operations are frequently represented using a special notation, e.g. $\neg A$ or A'. When the set S is finite, a *truth table can be used to define the meaning of the operation.

unbundling The separation of system software charges from hardware charges in the marketing of computer systems. Historically, when system software was minimal and represented a small part of total system cost, it was included without additional charge. Unbundling was a natural result of system hardware becoming less expensive while software was becoming a much larger proportion of the cost.

uncertainty 1. The uncertainty about a piece of knowledge in a *knowledge base can be represented in a variety of ways. The most popular is to attach a number to the fact or rule, e.g. 1 for complete truth, 0 for complete falsity, ¾ for likely. Sometimes these numbers are intended to be the probability of the knowledge being true. Reasoning systems must assign an inferred uncertainty value to an inferred piece of knowledge.

2. *See* entropy.

uncommitted logic array (ULA) A form of programmable logic array. *See* PLA.

unconditional jump (unconditional branch) A *jump that causes the program sequence to start at a new address; the instruction address becomes the contents of the *program counter.

undecidable *See* decision problem.

undefined *See* partial function.

underflow The condition that arises when the result of an arithmetic operation is smaller than the allowable range of numbers that can be represented, or the result so obtained.

undetected error of magnetic tape. *See* error rate.

undirected graph *See* graph.

unfolding *See* folding.

Unibus *Trademark* A minicomputer *bus structure devised by DEC and used in their PDP 11 series of computers. It is a single bus structure that has 56 bidirectional lines and is common to peripherals, memory, and the processor. The maximum transfer rate is one 16 bit word every 750 nanoseconds. All transfers are initiated by a master device and acknowledged by the receiving or storage device. The allocation of the role of master device is dynamic and the processor can grant control of the bus in response to a request from a peripheral.

unification An operation on well-formed formulae, namely that of finding a *most general common instance*. The formulae can be *terms or atomic formulae (*see* predicate calculus). A *common instance* of two formulae A and B is a formula that is an *instance* of both of them, i.e. that can be obtained from either by some consistent substitution of terms for variables. As an example let A and B be the following:

$$A = p(f(u),v)$$
$$B = p(w,g(x))$$

Let u, v, w, x, y, z be variables, and c, d constants. Consider the substitution that replaces u, v, w, x respectively by the terms y, $g(z)$, $f(y)$, z. This substitution, when applied to A and B, transforms them both into the same formula I_1, where

$$I_1 = P(f(y), g(z))$$

Hence the above is a common instance of A and B. It is however only one of infinitely many: other common instances of A and B include

$$I_2 = P(f(z),g(y))$$
$$I_3 = P(f(y),g(y))$$
$$I_4 = P(f(f(y)),g(g(z)))$$
$$I_5 = P(f(c),g(d))$$

Note that I_2, I_3, I_4, I_5 are themselves instances of I_1. In fact any common instance of A and B is an instance of I_1 and therefore I_1 is called a *most general common instance* of A and B. Of the formulae above, the only other one that is a most general common instance is I_2. I_5 would also be one if c and d were variables rather than constants; indeed the y and z of I_1 could be any two distinct variables. In some cases A and B have no common instance; two examples of this are

$$A = P(f(u),v)$$
$$B = P(g(w),x)$$

and

$$A = P(f(u),u)$$
$$B = P(w,f(w))$$

If A and B do have a common instance however, they must have a most general one. There are algorithms (the original one being Robinson's,

1965) for deciding whether a given A and B have a common instance, and if so finding a most general one. Robinson's motivation for describing unification was its role in *resolution theorem proving. Resolution was at one time associated with "general problem-solving" techniques in artificial intelligence. More recently it has provided the conceptual basis for the *logic programming language *PROLOG. Another use of unification is in compile-time type-inference, especially for *polymorphic types.

unilaterally connected graph *See* reachability.

uninterruptible power supply (UPS) A power supply that is guaranteed to provide correct working voltages to the circuits of a computer in spite of interruptions to the incoming electrical power supply from the grid. Short-duration interruptions may be dealt with by an electric motor driven from the main power supply and driving an alternator that provides the electrical energy as input to the computer power supply. For longer-duration interruptions other means, including accumulators or an internal-combustion engine motor to drive the alternator, may be employed.

union 1. of two *sets. The set that results from combining the elements of two sets S and T, say, usually expressed as

$$S \cup T$$

$\cup$ is regarded as an *operation on sets, the *union operation*, which is *commutative and *associative. Symbolically

$$S \cup T =$$
$$\{x \mid x \in S \text{ or } x \in T\}$$

The union of S and the *empty set is S. *See also* set algebra.

2. of two *graphs, G_1 and G_2. The graph that includes all the vertices and edges of G_1 and G_2, i.e. that contains the union of the two sets of vertices and

of the two sets of edges as its vertices and edges.

unipolar signal A signal whose signaling elements are constrained to lie either between zero volts and some arbitrary positive voltage or less commonly between zero volts and some negative voltage. Unipolar signals are used in data-communication systems. *Compare* bipolar signal.

uniquely decodable (uniquely decipherable) A term usually applied to *variable-length codes: unique decodability ensures that codewords can be recognized unambiguously in the received signal so that the decoding process is the exact inverse of the encoding process.

Unisys A US corporation formed from Sperry and Burroughs in 1987 and one of the world's top five computer companies in terms of revenue (1988 figures). It manufactures a full range of computer products.

unitary semiring *See* semiring.

unit matrix *Another name for* identity matrix.

unit testing (module testing) *See* testing.

universal flip-flop *See* flip-flop.

universal quantifier *See* quantifier.

universal set A *set that, in a particular application, includes every other set under discussion. Such sets give a more definite meaning to notions like *complement and *membership: in asking whether or not x is in S, where S is some set, it is assumed that x is a member of some universal set.

universal Turing machine A *Turing machine M that, given any two numbers n and m as input – one of them a suitable encoding of a Turing machine K – outputs the result of applying K to m. A universal Turing machine therefore

serves as an executive program for the class of Turing machines.

UNIX *Trademark* An operating system originally introduced by Bell Laboratories in 1971 for DEC PDP 11 minicomputers. It was intended to provide a simple uniform environment in which relatively small numbers of users, with considerable shared interests over and above the fact that they were all using the same computer system, could collaborate on a shared project. UNIX has become very popular and has been implemented on a very wide range of systems, from stand-alone personal computer systems, through workstations and minicomputers, to mainframes and supercomputers. There has been some divergence between a number of competing versions, and there is now movement toward an internationally agreed definition of a UNIX standard.

unlock (unlock primitive) An indivisible operation by which a process indicates that it has completed its access to a particular resource. *See also* lock, semaphore.

unordered tree *See* tree.

unpack To convert from a packed format to a form in which individual items are directly accessible. *See* pack.

unsolvable *See* decision problem.

up *Informal* Denoting a system or component that is operational and in service and either busy or idle; it has passed all its tests and is in a condition during which random faults may be predicted to give an *MTBF.

UPC *Abbrev. for* Universal Product Code. *See* bar code.

updating *See* file updating.

upline The direction from a remote node toward a central or controlling node in a hierarchical network. The word may also be used as a verb: to upline or to *upline load,* i.e. to send programs or data from a remote node to a more central or controlling node. Upline loading may be used for the storage of programs or data that were created or modified at the remote node, but cannot be stored there permanently. Upline loading may also be used to transmit data collected at a remote node to a more central node for further processing. *Compare* downline.

up operation *Another name for* V operation. *See* semaphore.

upper bound of a set *S* on which the *partial ordering < is defined. An element *u* with the property that *s < u* for all *s* in *S*. Also *u* is a *least upper bound* if, for any other upper bound *v*, *u < v*.

Since numerical computing demands the truncation of infinite arithmetic to finite arithmetic, the computation of least upper bounds of real numbers, indeed of any limit, can only be achieved to a machine tolerance, usually defined to be machine precision: the smallest epsilon eps, such that
$$1.0 + \text{eps} > 1.0$$
See also array, lower bound.

UPS *Abbrev. for* uninterruptible power supply.

uptime The time or percentage of time during which a computer system is actually operating correctly.

upward compatibility *See* compatibility.

user agent The entity in the X 400 electronic mail *protocol with which the human user communicates. Its function is to offer services to the user as both a sender and a receiver of mail messages. When preparing to send a mail message, the user agent allows the user to construct the message. An X 400 mail message contains two distinct components: one contains only information relating to the delivery of the message, such as the address(es) of the recipient(s) and information about the confirmation of delivery; the other contains only the message proper. Once the message has been constructed, it is passed by the user agent to the *MTA (message transfer agent), which is responsible for passing the message to the recipient. At the point of delivery, the user agent allows the user to determine what messages await collection. The user agent may also be able to access a *message store, which can act as a buffer for incoming mail.

user area The part of the main memory of a computer that is available for use by the users' programs. A significant portion of the main memory may be dedicated to the operating system and the facilities that it requires, e.g. buffers.

user-friendly A qualitative term applied to *interactive systems (hardware plus software) that are designed to make the user's task as easy as possible by providing feedback. Ways that help to make a system user-friendly include:

(a) list of valid commands available on request;

(b) *menu-driven routines used;

(c) errors entered by the user traced and diagnosed;

(d) commands in upper or lower case accepted;

(e) a *help system whereby information appropriate to the current situation is always available at the touch of a key.

As an example of (c), consider a microcomputer running a *Basic program that reaches a line it cannot interpret. The processor is likely to stop running the program and return control to the user. It may then output a code corresponding to the error, for the user to trace in his manual. A more user-friendly system would output the type of error, e.g. SYNTAX ERROR, indicate the place in the program where the syntax was incorrect, and enter a mode whereby it could be corrected.

As computers and terminals become available to many more people with no previous experience in the computer industry, it becomes important that only the simplest interactions should be necessary for them to start making practical use of the systems.

The term user-friendly is acquiring a wider ranging application, e.g. to other types of man-machine interfaces, catalogues, and training manuals.

user interface (UI) The means of communication between a human user and a computer system, referring in particular to the use of input/output devices with supporting software. Examples include the use of a *mouse with *bit-mapped graphics and the use of *windows. *See also* command-driven user interface.

user manual (user guide) *See* documentation.

user state *See* execution states.

utility programs The collection of programs that forms part of every computer system and provides a variety of generally useful functions, including file copying and deleting, text preparation, and program cross-referencing.

uvwxy lemma *Another name for* the *pumping lemma for context-free languages.

V

V.24 A standard electrical interface defined by the CCITT for interconnecting *DTE (data terminal equipment) to a *modem. The interface includes definition of control signals as well as clocking and data signaling standards. It is essentially equivalent to the *RS232C

interface standard developed by the EIA in the US.

V.35 A standard electrical interface defined by the CCITT for interconnecting *DTE (data terminal equipment) to a line-unit. The interface is specifically intended to support higher-speed digital communications at up to 64 K bps, and includes definitions of control signals and clocking signals as well as data signals.

vacuum column *See* buffer (def. 2).

validation *See* verification and validation.

validity check Any check that some entity respects the constraints applying to that entity. For example, when the value of a data item is input by a program, a validity check is normally performed to ensure that this value is within the acceptable range.

value-added *See* VAN, VAR.

VAN *Abbrev. for* value-added network. VANs form a class of business that adds value to telephone and data networks by providing additional services such as information.

V & V *Short for* verification and validation.

van Wijngaarden grammar *Another name for* two-level grammar.

VAR *Abbrev. for* value-added reseller. VARs form a class of business operation that adds value to basic PCs and other computing equipment by configuring it with additional hardware and/or software.

variable 1. A string of characters that is used to denote some value stored within the computer and may be changed during execution. Thus when a program reads the value of a data object, that object is said to be a variable or variable if the value read changes on subsequent reads or can be modified by the program. A variable may be internal to the program, in which case it is held in memory, or external if the program must perform an input operation in order to read its value. *See also* name.

2. *See* parameter.

variable-length code A *code in which a fixed number of source symbols are encoded into a variable number of output symbols. This variable number (the *code length) may be made to depend on some property of the source symbols input to the encoder, often their relative frequency of occurrence. If a variable-length code is to be instantaneously decodable (i.e. a *prefix code), it must obey *Kraft's inequality. *See also* source coding theorem. *Compare* fixed-length code.

variable-length vector A *vector, i.e. a one-dimensional array, that usually has a fixed lower bound but its upper bound may vary according to values assigned to the array. *See also* string.

variable word length computer A computer that does not have a *fixed word length but operates on data of different word lengths; this may also apply to instruction sizes. The lengths of data words that can be handled are usually in units of *characters or *bytes, so that the computer handles strings of characters or bytes. It is then known as a *character machine* or *byte machine* respectively. A variable word length computer is particularly important where data is itself of varying lengths (e.g. strings of characters) as well as cases where natural data lengths do not fit word (hardware-restricted) boundaries.

variance *See* measures of variation.

variant field An optional part of a *record.

variation 1. *See* measures of variation.

2. (contractual variation) The process of changing a contract to supply goods or services, and the results of any change to the contract as represented in a contract amendment.

variational method A technique for the solution of certain classes of *ordinary and *partial differential equations that involves the use of a *variational principle*. That is, the solution of the differential equation is expressed as the solution of a minimization problem that involves an integral expression. The equation is then solved by carrying out an approximate minimization. Variational principles arise naturally in many branches of physics and engineering. As an example, the solution of

$$y'' + q(x)y = f(x),\ 0 \leqslant x \leqslant 1$$
$$y(0) = y(1) = 0$$

is also the solution of the problem

$$\underset{v\, \varepsilon\, V}{\text{minimize}} \int_0^1 \{v'(x)^2 - q(x)\, v(x)^2 - 2f(x)\, v(x)\}\, \mathrm{d}x$$

where V is a class of sufficiently differentiable functions that are zero at $x = 0$ and $x = 1$. An approximate minimization can be carried out by minimizing over the subspace of functions

$$\sum_{j=1}^{n} c_j \phi_j (x)$$

When the trial functions $\phi_j(x)$ are *splines, the resulting method is an example of the *finite-element method.

VAX *See* DEC.

VAX/VMS *Trademark* The operating system offered by DEC as the standard system for their VAX range of processors. The system functions by producing a *virtual machine for each user of the VAX hardware.

VDI *Abbrev. for* virtual device interface. *See* CGI.

VDM *Abbrev. for* Vienna Development Method. A notation and methodology for writing formal specifications, based on the Vienna Definition Method developed at the IBM Laboratory in Vienna in the 1960s for the definition of programming languages. *See* constructive specification.

VDU *Abbrev. for* visual display unit. An output device that can temporarily display information, and can be used in conjunction with an integral or separate keyboard to form a *terminal. The information can be both alphanumeric and graphical, and can be erased or changed under the control of a processor that may be remote or part of the unit. In alphanumeric mode there are most commonly 24 rows of 80 characters. In graphics mode using standard TV technology the resolution is typically 640 by 240 *pixels, although much higher resolutions are possible.

The display is generally achieved via a *cathode-ray tube but other technologies are in use (*see* display). In most cases the image is formed from a raster of horizontal lines similar to a television picture, but for displays that may be used for prolonged periods by a single operator the quality and stability of the image has to be significantly better than can be achieved on a domestic TV.

Most devices have a selection of display attributes that can be used to emphasize or differentiate items of information, e.g.

(a) blink or flash – in which the items are intermittently displayed at a rate that can be readily perceived;

(b) brilliance – in which a noticeable difference in illumination is applied in a steady state;

(c) reverse video – in which the character is displayed in the opposite contrast to the surrounding information; in a display that has bright characters on an apparently black screen the reverse video characters appear as black characters within a bright character-sized rectangle;

(d) underline – in which a line, usually displayed at the same brilliance or blink rate as the associated character, is drawn beneath the character;

(e) color – the color of the item and its background may be controlled individually.

vector A one-dimensional *array. In computing, vectors are widely used since the memory is essentially a vector of words. The notation for vectors is determined by the programming language. In mathematics (and in this dictionary), the conventional notation is to use a bold italic lower-case letter, e.g. v, to denote a vector in its entirety, and the corresponding plain italic lower-case letter indexed by a subscript, e.g. v_i, to denote an element of the vector.

A vector may also be used to express a deficient *matrix, in which case it is necessary to distinguish between a row vector and a column vector.

vectored interrupts An efficient method implemented in hardware for dealing with many different devices, each of which is capable of interrupting and each different type of device requiring a unique *interrupt handler. The *interrupt vector* is an array of interrupt handler locations. When a device successfully interrupts the processor, it supplies the processor with a reference to its entry in the interrupt vector. The processor then uses this to transfer control to the appropriate interrupt handler.

vector-mode graphic display (vector graphics) A method of presenting graphical or pictorial images in which the pen of a plotter or the spot on a VDU moves along the path of the line to be drawn. *Compare* raster-mode graphic display.

vector norm *See* approximation theory.

vector processing Processing of sequences of data in a uniform manner, a common occurrence in manipulation of matrices (whose elements are vectors) or other arrays of data. This orderly progression of data can capitalize on the use of *pipeline processing. *See also* array processor.

Veitch diagram *Another name for* Karnaugh map.

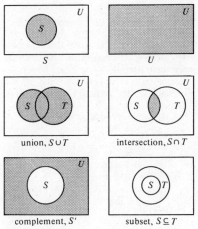

union, $S \cup T$ intersection, $S \cap T$

complement, S' subset, $S \subseteq T$

Venn diagrams

Venn diagram A schematic representation of a *set, first used in the 19th century by John Venn. A universal set U will typically be represented by a rectangle, and a subset S of U by the interior of a circle (or another simple closed curve) lying wholly within the rectangle. Some examples are shown in the diagram. Where appropriate, the shaded areas represent the sets indicated beneath each figure.

verification The process of checking the accuracy of transcription of information. It is generally applied to data that has been encoded via a data-preparation machine by an operator reading from a document. The documents are subsequently read by another operator and entered into a machine that compares the input with that prepared by the first operator. Any differences are signaled and a correction or confirmation action is made by the second operator.

Data may also be verified when it is copied to a storage peripheral from the main store or another storage peripheral. In this case the data is normally coded in a way that allows *error detection, and verification only involves checking the written data for consistency: it is not compared with the source data.

verification and validation (V&V) A generic term for the complete range of checks that are performed on a system in order to increase confidence that the system is suitable for its intended purpose. This range might include a rigorous set of functional tests, performance testing, reliability testing, and so on. Although a precise distinction is not always drawn, the verification aspect normally refers to completely objective checking of conformity to some well-defined specification, while the validation aspect normally refers to a somewhat subjective assessment of likely suitability in the intended environment.

verification condition *See* program correctness proof.

version control Control of the creation and usage of the various versions of a given entity. For a recognizable entity, e.g. a software component, there may be various reasons for developing several distinct versions of the entity. A later version may represent an improvement over an earlier one, in that certain errors have been corrected or new capabilities added, or it may employ an alternative approach to meeting the same requirements.

Version control promotes correct usage of the various versions, perhaps by restricting access to existing versions and creation of new versions. For example, the "current release" version of some software component may be protected against modification or deletion, while access to (or even knowledge of) a version under development may be limited to the development team.

vertex An element of the set of points that underlies the concept of a *graph. Edges are obtained by joining together pairs of vertices.

vertical check *See* cyclic redundancy check.

vertical format unit (VFU) The part of the control electronics of a printer that governs the vertical format of the document to be printed. Information about the desired format may be encoded into a loop of paper tape, sometimes called a *carriage control tape*, or it may be sent via the interface from the host system to which the printer is connected. The paper tape loop may be formed from standard 1″ paper tape or it may be a special tape with provision for 12 channels. The number of character positions in the tape loop is arranged to be the same as the number of lines on the form to be processed, or for short forms may be a multiple of the lines. The paper tape may be moved in synchronism with the document to be printed. Each channel of the tape represents a selectable tab stop, and the printer can be instructed to move paper continuously until a punching is detected in a designated channel.

In more recent designs of printer the reliability problems involved with the repeated cycling of the tape loop have been overcome by an *electronic VFU (EVFU)*. The information about the format may still be encoded on paper tape but prior to starting the print operation the printer cycles the tape twice: during the first cycle the information is read into a memory and during the second cycle the information is checked. During the printing operation the stored information is scanned in synchronism with the movement of the printing paper. This type of VFU usually has a facility to allow the host system to transmit the format data over the interface and directly into the printer memory. Many modern designs of printer now rely on *downloading the format information and do not provide an alternative.

vertical microinstruction *See* microprogramming.

vertical recording *See* magnetic encoding.

very large-scale integration *See* VLSI, integrated circuit.

VFU *Abbrev. for* vertical format unit.

VGA *Abbrev. for* video graphics array. A color *graphics adapter that is available for some models of the IBM PS/2 series. Adapters to the VGA standard are produced by other manufacturers to fit into non-IBM computers. The VGA can generate a 640 × 480 16-color screen in addition to all the modes of the *EGA and *MCGA. Multiple graphics pages are available so that a range of animation techniques are possible. VGA is analog in composition: each of the three colors that constitute the image can take on a range of intensities between zero and a maximum value.

VHDL A *CHDL (computer hardware description language) developed as part of the very high speed integrated circuit (VHSIC) project. It embodies many of the principles of *CONLAN and is becoming the accepted standard CHDL.

videodisk (or (UK) **videodisc**) A form of *read-only optical disk, devised for recording TV programs but also used for education and training. A write-once version is also available. Videodisks have been used for recording data, particularly when it is in image form, for computer systems; *CD-ROM is now preferred for most such applications.

video terminal A *VDU that displays information on a cathode-ray tube and generally has an associated keyboard. Normally the image is formed by a raster of horizontal lines similar to a television picture.

videotex A system that enables a keyboard to be used in conjunction with an ordinary television receiver and a telephone, forming a terminal that provides interactive dial-up access to one or more remote services providing information. The information-providing capacity of a videotex service is limited only (a) by the amount of on-line file store that the operator of the service can provide with reasonable response times, and (b) by the effectiveness of the indexing facilities provided to enable users to find the information they want.

Although initially conceived as a domestic service, the take-up of videotex has been mainly by businesses; in some cases, companies use it as a straightforward means of providing a data communication network linking geographically dispersed locations.

Among countries in which public videotex services are available are Australia, Canada (Telidon and Vista), France (Tictac and Titan), West Germany (Bildschirmtext), Japan (Captain), UK (Prestel), and US (Qube). *Viewdata* was an early generic name for videotex, and also an early name for the UK Prestel service, and it is still sometimes encountered.

Compare teletext.

Vienna Development Method *See* VDM.

viewdata *See* videotex.

VIPER A 32-bit validated computer implemented in silicon on sapphire, originally devised by the Royal Signals and Research Establishment, UK. The top-level design was simulated in *Algol 68 and was formally proven between two levels of *HOL specifications using pencil and paper algebra and a HOL theorem prover. The major state-design level was simulated in the *CAD toolset ELLA, and was also formally proven using the HOL theorem prover. A block-level model was also simulated in ELLA. The gate and chip levels were tested, and conventional *VLSI CAD checks were performed. It is believed that the VIPER microprocessor has been proved correct to the highest level practicable in the late 1980s.

virgin medium Material such as a magnetic tape or disk or paper tape that is suitable for the recording of data, but has not been used or preformatted for that purpose. *Compare* empty medium.

virtual call service In a *packet switching network, a technique of setting up a *virtual connection between terminals prior to the transmission of user data.

virtual connection A logical connection between two network terminating points that appears to the end equipment as a physical connection (generally with some transport delay). The use of virtual connections has found application in both voice and data transmission as a means of increasing utilization of trunking facilities where the physical facility is time-shared between a multiplicity of terminating equipments.

virtual machine A collection of resources that emulates the behavior of an actual machine. The virtual machine concept originated in Cambridge, Mass., in the late 1960s as an extension of the *virtual memory system of the Manchester Atlas computer.

A *process is defined in its totality by the contents of the workspace to which it has access. Provided that the behavior of the workspace is consistent with the expected behavior, there is no means by which a process can determine whether a resource that it manipulates is realized by a physical resource of that type, or by the cooperative actions of other resources that jointly present the same changes in the contents of the process' workspace. As an example, a process cannot determine whether its output is passed directly to a printer or is sent via some form of *spooling system. Similarly it cannot determine whether it has sole use of a processor or is *multi-programming with other processes. In a virtual machine environment no particular process has sole use of any system resource, and all system resources are regarded as being potentially sharable. In addition, use of virtual machines provides *isolation between multiple users of a single physical computer system, giving some level of computer security.

The virtual machine approach forms the basis of a number of commercially produced operating systems, especially of IBM's VM/CMS and of DEC's VAX/VM products.

virtual memory A system in which a *process' workspace is held partly in high-speed memory and partly on some slower, and cheaper, backing-store device. When the process refers to a memory location the system hardware detects whether or not the required location is physically present in memory, and generates an interrupt if it is not; this allows the system supervisor to transfer the required data area from backing store into memory. For this purpose the address space is subdivided into *pages typically holding 4 kilobytes of data. Addresses within a page are defined by the 12 low-order bits in the address. The high-order bits can be thought of as the page number; they are used to search an *associative memory that shows either the physical location within memory of word zero of the page, or indicates that the page is not present in memory – at which point an interrupt is generated. The system supervisor then locates the page on backing store and transfers it into memory, updating the associative memory as it does so.

virtual terminal A nonphysical terminal that is defined as a superset of characteristics of a class of physical terminal types. The virtual terminal idea is analogous to defining a non-real-world language into which some set of real-world languages can be translated bilaterally.

In some *packet switching networks, attempts have been made to use the virtual terminal concept as a means of performing protocol translation between dissimilar terminals. At the input node the message is translated into the virtual terminal format, and at the output node it is retranslated into the receiving terminal's protocol. The generality of the concept is somewhat limited because of nontranslatable characteristics of certain types of terminals with respect to others.

virus A self-replicating program. A serious virus could breach the *security policy of a system especially by absorbing system resources, often at some predetermined future date, thereby leading to *denial of service. A virus in combination with a *Trojan horse can "infect" files of an installation into which it is introduced and their subsequent transfer to another installation can spread the "infection". Although a virus requires the services of a specific type of host system to replicate, an entirely self-replicating program, called a *worm*, can replicate spontaneously.

VisiCalc *Trademark* An early innovative *spreadsheet program developed by VisiCorp for the *Apple microcomputer system.

visual display unit *See* VDU.

Viterbi decoding The decoding of a *convolutional code by Viterbi's algorithm.

VLIW *Abbrev. for* very long instruction word. A VLIW machine is one in which the instruction is hundreds of bits long.

VLSI *Abbrev. for* very large-scale integration, i.e. integrated-circuit fabrication technology that allows over 100 000 transistors to be integrated on a single chip. *See* integrated circuit.

VM/CMS *Trademark, acronym for* virtual machine, conversational monitor system. An operating system originally produced in Cambridge, Mass. (On its first introduction the C stood for Cambridge.) The original system ran on a specially modified IBM 360/44, and was the first to make formal use of the concept of a *virtual machine, as distinct from a *virtual memory. The basis of the system is a supervisory level that creates a number of virtual machines (VMs); in each of these VMs a user can run his own program, using his terminal to control the VM and also to provide the route by which he passes input to, or receives output from, his VM. Most users run a copy of CMS, the monitor system, which in turn actually controls the running of the jobs.

VME 29 *Trademark, acronym for* virtual machine environment for 2900 series. One of the operating systems offered by ICL for use with their 2900 range of computer systems.

V-model A *software life-cycle model that is a development of the *waterfall model. The diagram shows the STARTS V-model in which successive phases are displayed in a V formation with square-corner boxes representing the activities performed in a phase and with rounded-corner boxes representing the outputs from a phase. Outputs become the inputs to the next phase. The left leg of the V includes phases in which the detail of the design and the implementation of the software are gradually increased. In ascending the right leg of the V, the software is progressively assembled from its modules and testing proceeds from single modules through to the full system and eventual acceptance of the system.

Across-phase activities such as project and quality management are included; some links to contractual procedures are also included, for example invitation to tender (ITT). The model shares the weakness of waterfall-type models in omitting a diagrammatic representation of iteration between life-cycle phases. *See also* spiral model.

VMS *See* VAX/VMS.

voiceband *See* bandwidth.

voice coil *See* actuator.

voice input device A device in which speech is used to input data or system commands directly into a system. Such equipment involves the use of *speech recognition processes, and can replace or supplement other input devices.

Some voice input devices can recognize spoken words from a predefined vocabulary, some have to be trained for a particular speaker. When the operator utters a vocabulary item, the matching data input is displayed as characters on a screen and can then be verified by the operator. The speech recognition process depends on the comparison of each utterance with words appearing in a stored vocabulary table. The table is created or modified by using the voice input equipment together with a keyboard. A data item or system command is typed and the related spoken word is uttered, several times. The spoken word is then analyzed and converted into a particular bit pattern that is stored in the vocabulary table.

void set *Another name for* empty set.

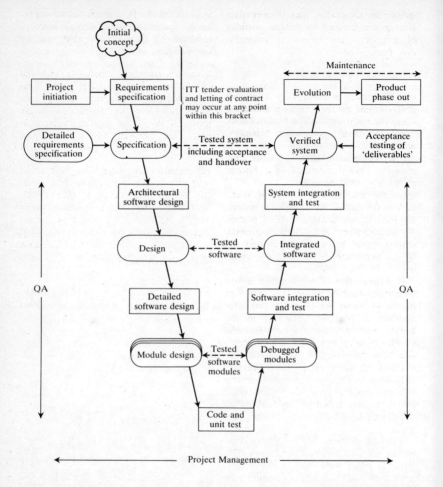

V-model [Reproduced from the STARTS Guide 1987, by permission of the Department of Trade and Industry, with acknowledgments to the National Computing Centre and for help given by representatives of UK industry]

volatile memory A type of memory whose contents are destroyed on the removal of power to the memory. When volatile memories are used for crucial applications, they can be backed up with temporary battery-power supplies. *Compare* nonvolatile memory.

Volterra integral equation *See* integral equation.

volume A removable unit of any data storage medium, e.g. a reel or cartridge of magnetic tape or an exchangeable disk pack.

volume label *See* label.

von Neumann machine Any computer characterized by the following concepts:

(a) the main units are a *control unit, *arithmetic and logic unit, a *memory, and input and output facilities;

(b) programs and data share the same memory, thus the concept of a *stored program is fundamental;

(c) the control and arithmetic units, usually combined into a *central processor (which may contain internal storage – accumulators and other registers), determine the actions to be carried out by reading instructions from the memory.

It follows that a program for a von Neumann machine consists of a set of instructions that are examined one after another; a "program counter" in the control unit indicates the next location in the memory from which an instruction is to be taken. It also follows that the data on which the program operates may include variables: storage locations can be named so that the stored value may be subsequently referenced or changed during execution of the program.

The vast majority of present-day computers are von Neumann machines. The name is taken from that of the American, John von Neumann. *Compare* non von Neumann architecture.

V operation (up operation) *See* semaphore.

voting logic *See* comparator.

VSAM *Acronym for* virtual storage access method. An *access method for *data files, supporting both *sequential access and indexed access (*see* indexed file), and based on primary indexes that are structured as B+ trees (*see* B–tree).

It is specific to IBM machines and operating systems using *virtual memory techniques, and is intended as an improvement on *ISAM.

V-series Interfaces defined by the *CCITT. In general, CCITT specifications that refer primarily to analog communications, or to the lowest layers (physical layers) of digital communications, are prefixed by 'V'. Examples include V.24 and V.35. *See also* X.

vulnerability Any mechanism that could lead to a breach of the security of a system in the presence of a *threat. Vulnerabilities may arise unintentionally due to inadequacy of design or incomplete debugging. Alternatively the vulnerability may arise through malicious intent, e.g. the insertion of a *Trojan horse.

VW-grammar *Short for* van Wijngaarden grammar, *another name for* two-level grammar.

W

wait list A list of the processes that are awaiting the completion of some activity before they can again run on a processor. Typically the activity is associated with input or output, but may in theory be associated with any activity that can cause a process to be suspended while awaiting the freeing of a *semaphore (or an equivalent mechanism that may be in use to control process synchronization).

wait operation *See* semaphore.

walk through A product review performed by a formal team. A number of such reviews may be held during the lifetime of a software project, covering, for example, requirements specification, program specifications, design, and implementation. The review is formally constituted; there is a clear statement of the contribution that each member of the review team is required to make, and a step-by-step procedure for carrying out the review. The person responsible for development of the product under review "walks through" the product for the benefit of the other reviewers, and the product is then openly debated with a view to uncovering problems or identifying desirable improvements.

Walsh analysis One of the many forms of orthogonal analysis (especially of *signals); it employs the *Walsh functions as its orthonormal basis. Walsh analysis is especially suited to *digital signal processing since the Walsh functions themselves, and the operations based upon them, are easily represented and rapidly carried out by simple digital systems. The analysis of a signal in terms of Walsh functions is called its *Walsh transform*. See also discrete and continuous systems, filtering, sequency, bandwidth.

Walsh functions A complete set of functions that form an *orthonormal basis for *Walsh analysis: they take only the values $+1$ and -1, and are defined on a set of 2^n points for some n. For purposes of computer representation, and also for their use in coding, it is usual to represent "$+1$" by "0", and "-1" by "1". As an example, the 8-point Walsh functions are then as follows:

$$\text{wal}(8,0) = 00000000$$
$$\text{wal}(8,1) = 11110000$$
$$\text{wal}(8,2) = 00111100$$
$$\text{wal}(8,3) = 11001100$$
$$\text{wal}(8,4) = 10011001$$
$$\text{wal}(8,5) = 01101001$$
$$\text{wal}(8,6) = 01011010$$
$$\text{wal}(8,7) = 10101010$$

Note that the Walsh functions (usually denoted *wal*) consist alternatively of even and odd functions (usually denoted *cal* and *sal* by analogy with *cos* and *sin*).

Furthermore, within the set of 2^n functions there is one function of zero *sequency, one of (normalized) sequency 2^{n-1}, and one pair (odd and even) of each (normalized) sequency from 1 to $2^{n-1} - 1$.

A set of Walsh functions corresponds, with some permutation of columns, to a *Reed–Muller code and, with a column deleted, to a *simplex code. See also Hadamard matrices.

Walsh transform See Walsh analysis.

WAN *Abbrev. for* wide area network.

wand A small hand-held device that can be used to read printed *bar codes or characters. The device may have a shape similar to a pen, but is usually larger in diameter or may be designed to be grasped in the palm of the hand. In use it is stroked over the surface of the printing at a steady speed and an audible and/or visual signal is actioned to indicate if a satisfactory sensing of data was achieved. The wand usually only contains the sensors and the minimum of electronics and is connected to the control electronics by a flexible cable. In some devices the wand is only a plastic enclosure and handle for guiding the end of an array of optical fibers.

Warshall's algorithm An algorithm for *transitive closure that saves computational time or storage space by doing computations in a particular order.

waterfall model A *software life-cycle model that represents the successive phases as boxes and the onward progression of partially worked software as connecting arcs. Typically the first phase, whatever its name, is shown as the highest box, and the outputs of this and other phases appear to flow into the subsequent phases. Sometimes the flow is only shown from first phase toward the last phase and no iteration around phases is conceived. Other versions of

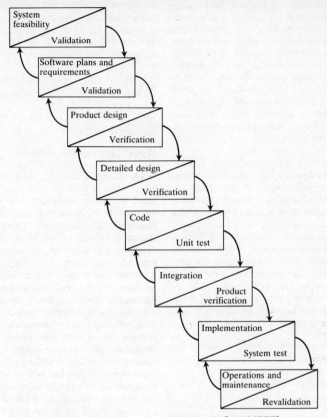

Waterfall model [from *Computer*, May 1988, page 62. © 1988 IEEE]

the model show a reverse flow as in the example shown in the diagram.

It is rare for the waterfall style of model to show the various activities that occur across all life-cycle phases. For example, the diagram omits important activities such as project management, quality management, and configuration control. A further weakness of many waterfall models is the treatment of maintenance. Maintenance in this example is shown as a single box: this is the view of a system as perceived by the supplier, and particularly a supplier who has no responsibility for software maintenance. In reality each maintenance action will follow the full life-cycle from feasibility through to implementation.

See also spiral model, V-model.

WATFIV An improved version of *WATFOR.

WATFOR A fast load-and-go *FORTRAN compiler developed at the University of Waterloo in Canada (hence WATerloo FORtran) and widely used for the teaching of programming in the FORTRAN era.

weakest precondition For some given program statement S and some *postcondition R there is a (possibly empty) set of program states such that if execution of S is initiated from one of these states then S is guaranteed to terminate in a state for which R is true. The weakest precondition of S with respect to R, normally written

wp (S,R)

is a predicate that characterizes this set of states. Use of the adjective weakest explicitly indicates that the predicate must characterize all states that guarantee termination of S in a state for which R is true.

The term was introduced by Dijkstra in 1975 in conjunction with a calculus for the derivation of programs; this provides for development of a program to be guided by the simultaneous development of a total correctness proof for the program. *See* program correctness proof, predicate transformer.

weakly connected graph *See* connected graph.

WEB *See* literate programming.

weighted code A *block code in which a weight has been assigned to each of the symbol positions in a codeword. *See also* 8421 code, excess-3 code.

weighted graph A *graph that has weights associated with the edges of the graph. The weight can be regarded as a *function from the set of edges into some appropriate codomain. This function is sometimes called a *cost function*. For example, in graphs with geographical origins, weight might represent distance or cost of travel.

weighted least squares *See* least squares, method of.

weighted mean *See* measures of location.

well-formed formula (wff) *See* propositional calculus.

well-founded relation A particular kind of *partial ordering, used in termination proofs (*see* program correctness proof). A well-founded relation on a set S consists of a partial ordering

$$R \subseteq S \times S$$

such that there does not exist any infinite sequence $x_1, x_2, x_3, \ldots$ of members of S for which each pair $\langle x_i, x_{i+1} \rangle$ belongs to R. As an example, if S consists of the natural numbers, then the "greater than" relation, containing all pairs $\langle m,n \rangle$ such that $m>n$, is well-founded, since there are no infinite descending sequences of natural numbers. On the other hand "greater than or equal to", and "less than" are not well-founded. On the set of integers, none of these relations are well-founded. As another example, if S is the set of all finite sets of natural numbers, then "proper superset of" is well-founded.

In the application to terminate proofs it is shown that, whenever a certain point in the program is visited during execution, the current value of some quantity lies within S and also that, if x is the value of that quantity at one such visit, and x' its value at a later visit, the pair $\langle x,x' \rangle$ belongs to R. It then follows that that point in the program cannot be visited infinitely often. By considering enough such points it can be concluded that any execution must have finite length.

well-ordered set A set S on which the relation $<$ is defined, satisfying the following properties:

(a) given x,y,z in S,
if $x < y$ and $y < z$, then $x < z$

(b) given x,y in S, then exactly one of the following three possibilities is true:

$$x < y, \ x = y, \text{ or } y < x$$

(c) if T is any nonempty subset of S, then there exists an element x in T, such that

$$x = y \text{ or } x < y, \text{ i.e. } x \leqslant y$$

for all y in T
This relation $<$ is said to be a *well ordering* of the set S.

wff *Short for* well-formed formula. *See* propositional calculus.

W grammar *Another name for* two-level grammar.

whetstone benchmark A *benchmark program built up from a carefully selected mix of computer instructions and data types selected to be "typical" for scientific calculations. The whetstone metric obtained has been widely used to measure comparative processing performance of hardware/software systems.

while loop *See* do-while loop.

Whirlwind The first real-time computer, built at the Massachusetts Institute of Technology and capable of calculating at high speed. The Whirlwind project had its origins in wartime defense and was officially launched in December 1944. The first version, operational in 1950, used electrostatic storage tubes but a ferrite core store was in use (its first appearance) by 1953.

white-box testing *Another name for* glass-box testing.

white noise Noise occurring in a channel and regarded as continuous in time and continuous in amplitude, the noise being uniform in energy over equal intervals of *frequency. (Note that, by contrast, white light is uniform in energy over equal intervals of wavelength.) *Compare* impulse noise.

Whitney read/write head *See* read/write head.

wide area network (WAN) A communication network distinguished from a *local area network (of which it may contain one or more) because of its longer-distance communications, which may or may not be provided by a

*common carrier or *PTT. The term is sometimes used as another name for the *public packet network of a particular country or region.

wideband (broadband) *See* bandwidth.

width of a bus. The number of signal lines in the *bus.

Williams-tube store *See* electrostatic storage device.

wimp *Acronym for* windows icons menus pointers. A type of *user interface commonly encountered on *microcomputers and *workstations. Separate tasks are each represented by a rectangular portion of the screen called a *window. A window may display a *menu, and an option on a menu may be selected by using a *mouse or other *pointing device. Windows not currently required may be overlaid by other windows or reduced to a small symbol or *icon representing the function of the window. For example, a window that had been used for word processing might have a picture of a pencil for its icon.

Winchester technology The name given to the design approach used in the IBM 3340 disk drive, which was introduced in 1973. It demonstrated a significant advance in technology, allowing an increase in recording density to 300 tracks per inch and 5600 bits per inch. The technology has been adopted by many manufacturers.

The read/write heads and the carriage assembly that supports them are enclosed with the disks in a hermetically sealed enclosure called a *data module*. When the data module is mounted in the drive unit it is automatically coupled to a system that supplies it with filtered cooling air. An entirely new head design was introduced having a trimaran structure with two outriggers supporting a much narrower "hull" that carries the read/write head. The surface of the disk has an oxide coating of only 1.12

micrometers, compared to 4.7 μm of previous designs, and a lubricant coating to prevent damage during head take-off and landings. When the disk is rotating the film of air drawn around with it provides an air bearing that causes the head to fly at a height of only 0.5 μm. In earlier drives, e.g. IBM 2311, the heads flew at 3.05 μm.

The head used in the Winchester technology has a very low mass and is loaded toward the disk with a force of only 10 grams compared to the 350 grams used in earlier designs. To prevent damage to the data through repeated landing and take-off of the heads, an area of the disk is usually reserved for this purpose. The low mass and loading force are such that if as a result of malfunction – or by intention in some designs – the heads do land on a data area, the probability of the data being corrupted is very low.

Most recent designs using aspects of Winchester technology have the disk pack permanently fixed within the drive. The capacity of these disks ranges from a few tens of megabytes to approaching a gigabyte.

window 1. A rectangular area on a display screen inside which part of an image or file is displayed. A windows system is a means of presenting users with views of the state of a number of separate *processes, each carrying out a task for the user. The user is able to initiate, monitor, and terminate processes, each process having an associated window. The window for each process is assigned to a specific area of the display by the user and it may overlap or be overlapped by the windows associated with other processes (i.e. more than one window can be displayed at once). As each process runs, it updates the contents of its window, and the user can direct input to the process by placing his cursor in the window and typing or otherwise generating input. This is of value where a user with a workstation is

managing a number of different related activities.

The windows system was originally conceived at Rank Xerox and was first used commercially on the Apple Macintosh computer. *See also* windowing, X-Windows.

2. An allocation of messages, data units, or both, given by a receiver to a sender in a data communication protocol. It controls how much data the sender may transmit before it receives an *acknowledgment from the receiver. The window is used for *flow control by the receiver, to prevent the sender from transmitting more rapidly than the receiver can process. The window is also used for *error management, by establishing the range of data that is unacknowledged and thus may need to be retransmitted. The selection of a proper window size is dependent upon the properties of the path between the sender and receiver: bandwidth, delay, and network congestion are important factors.

windowing (scissoring) Processing the stored data of a large image so that part of it can be displayed. The visible *window formed by the process can be moved to allow examination of the entire stored image. Some graphics terminals have hardware windowing, but this is only effective when the complete image can be contained in the display file.

Winograd's algorithm A method, due to S. Winograd, for multiplying matrices that requires fewer multiplications than a straightforward calculation as a result of "pre-processing" the two matrices concerned. This involves storing vectors that are used several times in the calculation.

wired logic A form of digital logic in which some logic functions are implemented by directly connecting together the outputs of one or more logic gates.

The success of this technique depends on the electronic characteristics of the gates involved. The technique is commonly used in bus communication systems with *tri-state output or with *open-collector devices.

wired-program computer A digital computer, usually a special-purpose one, in which the sequence of operations is fixed and cannot be self-altered. The sequence may take different paths in accordance with data-dependent conditions. Speed of operation is gained at a decrease in flexibility.

wire printer *See* dot matrix printer.

wire wrapping A technique for connecting components into *circuit boards by tightly wrapping wires around specialized terminals instead of soldering wires to them.

word 1. (machine word; computer word) A vector of bits that is treated as a unit by the computer hardware. The number of bits, referred to as the *word length* or *word size*, is now usually 16 or 32. The memory of a computer is divided into words (and possibly subdivided into *bytes). A word is usually long enough to contain an *instruction or an integer.

2. (string) In *formal language theory, a finite sequence of *symbols* drawn from some set of symbols Σ. This is then a *word over the alphabet* Σ or a Σ-*word*. The elements of Σ are also called *letters*. Common notation includes:

$|w|$ – the length of the word w,

w_i – the ith symbol in w,

Λ, the *empty word* – the unique word of length 0,

Σ^* – the set of all Σ-words.

Σ^* is infinite unless Σ is empty, in which case

$$\Sigma^* = \{\Lambda\}$$

See also concatenation.

word algebra *See* initial algebra.

word length (word size) *See* word.

word processing (text processing) A facility that enables users to compose documents using a computer with facilities to edit, re-format, store, and print documents with maximum flexibility. A typical word processing system consists of a microcomputer system possibly modified for word processing applications, and an associated printer capable of producing high-quality output at least comparable with that from an electric typewriter.

The systems available today fall into three main categories: stand-alone systems supporting one operator; clustered systems enabling several operators to share printers and files; hybrid systems attached to a central mainframe or minicomputer and able to perform additional functions. The following features are generally provided.

Document creation and editing, including the ability to (a) insert, delete, copy, and move text around in a document; (b) include text and/or graphics from other files; (c) search for and replace strings in the document.

Checking of spelling according to general and specialist dictionary files.

Document formatting and printing using a choice of paper sizes and formats with multiple copies as required.

Text justification to specified margins with automatic hyphenation.

Ability to create a document from a standard template, e.g. one containing a company letter heading.

Use of alternative character sets such as bold, italic, underlined.

Layout of tables, figures, etc.

Substitution of variable information when printing the document for easy production of form letters, etc.

word processor A system designed specifically for word processing.

word size (word length) *See* word.

Wordstar *Trademark* A popular *word processing program for microcomputers from the MicroPro International Corporation.

work area *Another name for* workspace.

work file *See* file.

work function The *complexity function of an algorithm.

working set The set of *pages currently in use by a process. A process running in a *virtual memory environment can be regarded as having a subset of its total address space actually in use over any short period of time. The objective of the *memory management system is to ensure that for each process those pages, and only those pages, that are actually in use are retained in memory, thus maximizing the *hit rate for these pages.

workspace (work area) A block of locations within the main memory that are used for the temporary storage of data during processing.

workstation A position for an operator that is equipped with all of the facilities required to perform a particular type of task. It is often a powerful computer system that has excellent graphics and a very fast processor, is highly interactive, and is usually part of a network. Such systems are much used in engineering, electronics, energy, and aerospace industries, and in universities. Applications include *CAD, *desktop publishing, and *AI research. In data processing and office systems the basic electronic equipment would normally be a visual display and keyboard; however there may also be ancillary electronic equipment such as magnetic storage devices, printer, OCR or bar code scanner.

worm 1. (or **WORM)** *Acronym for* write once, read many times. A class of storage device in which information, once written, cannot be erased or overwritten. *See* optical storage.

2. *See* virus.

worst-case analysis *See* algorithm.

worst fit A method to map *segments to holes (spaces) in *virtual memory. It selects the largest available hole in memory that can fit a needed segment, so as to leave a large hole for other segments.

wp or **WP** *Abbrev. for* word processing or word processor.

wrap around A facility of a VDU, allowing it to display lines of text that would otherwise be too long to be displayed completely: the line appears on the screen as two or more successive lines. This division into shorter lines that can fit within the available screen size is a function of the VDU electronics and there is no need for a format character to be included in the data stream.

write (often followed by *to*) To cause data to be recorded in some form of storage. The word is often used to qualify the meaning of a noun, as in write head.

writeable control store (WCS) *See* microprogramming.

write error *See* error rate. *See also* write error recovery.

write error recovery An *error recovery process used if an error is detected when data is being written to a storage peripheral or is being verified (*see* error detection). The first step is to check that it is not simply a reading error. If the error persists, it is usual either to overwrite the block or else to write the data again in another location. Often several attempts are made, and both methods may be used in turn. Some devices, such as certain optical disk drives, use such powerful *error-correcting codes that

write error recovery is considered unnecessary.

write head *See* head.

write instruction A program instruction
that causes an item of data to be recorded in some form of storage.

write-once Denoting optical media on
which the user can write data, which is
then permanent: the media cannot be
erased and reused. It is often called
worm media, standing for *write once
read many times*, or *read-mostly* media.
See optical storage.

write ring (write-permit ring) A ring that
is attached to the hub of a reel of magnetic tape to permit its content to be
overwritten or erased. When the reel is
mounted on a tape transport the ring
actuates a switch that permits the writing process. An interrupt is normally
sent to the system if writing is
attempted without the write ring.

write time The elapsed time during
which a given amount of data is being
recorded in some storage device. It does
not include any latency or check read
time.

wysiwyg *Acronym for* what you see is
what you get, used to describe a computer program that allows the transfer
of textual, graphical, or other images
from screen to printer, preserving all
characteristics such as aspect ratio,
color, character size, font, and line spacing. The screen therefore shows what
will be obtained on the printer.
Wysiwyg (or better: many printers have
higher definition than the screen) is considered to be a desirable feature of
*word processing, *desktop publishing,
and other programs where the appearance of the final printed product is
important.

X

X The *CCITT issues a large number of
standards documents; these are identified by an initial letter and a serial
number. Those that refer to data transmission are prefixed with the letter X,
and some of the more important are
listed below.

X 3   the functional definition of a
*PAD (packet assembler/
disassembler). This definition
needs to be read in conjunction
with X 28 and X 29.

X 21   defines the physical signaling
and the details of the
communications protocol
between a *DTE (data terminal
equipment) and a *DCE (data
communications equipment).
This forms the basis of most
connections to data networks.

X 25   defines the method of
interworking between a
customer's equipment and a
*packet switching network, when
these are connected by a
dedicated circuit.

X 28   the definition of the *protocol
between a terminal operating
with an *RS232 interface and a
*PAD.

X 29   the definition of the *protocol
between a *packet switching
network and a *PAD.

(The three protocols X 3, X 28,
and X 29 are often referred to
as XXX or triple-X.)

X 31   describes the support of a
packet mode terminal by an
*ISDN.

X 32   defines the method of
interworking between a
customer's equipment and a
packet switching network, when
these are connected by a public
switched network.

X 75   defines the method of establishing a *virtual circuit that traverses more than one X 25 packet switching network. In many respects X 75 is identical to X 25, and in some cases networks interwork using X 25 rather than X 75.

X 121   defines the international numbering plan for public data networks.

X 137   availability objectives for international packet switched networks.

X 300   overview of interworking between public networks for the provision of data transmission services.
(A number of other working documents in the X series provide further details of these internetwork services.)

X 400   overview of mail services provided by data networks.
(A number of other working documents in the X series give details of aspects of the overall mail facilities.)

X 500   overview of the directory services to be provided in conjunction with other services on data networks.

X-ON/X-OFF A method of *flow-control based on the exchange of specific control characters over a *duplex channel. The sending device will assume that the receiver is able to accept characters at any time, and will transmit on that basis. If the receiver is unable to accept further characters it will transmit an 'X-OFF' character to the sender, which must then cease transmission until an 'X-ON' character is transmitted by the receiver.

X-OPEN A joint initiative by some of the world's leading computer manufacturers to endorse and integrate evolving standards in order to encourage applications *portability, and to give a seal of approval to conforming products. Common standards have been defined for UNIX System V (specification commands, utilities, system calls, and libraries), languages (C, COBOL, FORTRAN, Pascal), and data management (ISAM, SQL). Coverage of standards by X-OPEN is being extended to include networking, *X-Windows, and the *POSIX user interface.

XOR or **xor** *See* exclusive-OR operation.

XS3 code *Short for* excess-3 code.

X-series *See* X.

X-Windows *Trademark* A precisely defined form of windowing mechanism, developed by MIT, that is anticipated will ultimately form the basis of an international standard for window management systems (*see* window). The definition of X-Windows is controlled by *X-OPEN in order to ensure that it cannot be changed by unilateral action on the part of a supplier or implementer.

Y

YACC *Acronym for* yet another compiler-compiler. A widely used *compiler-compiler provided as part of the *UNIX operating system environment.

yellow book The *coloured book defining the *transport service within the UK academic community.

Yourdon A proprietary software design method devised by E. Yourdon. The method has diagram notations for *ERA diagrams, *dataflow diagrams, structure charts (module calls), and *state (transition) diagrams. Also supported are *review techniques such as structured walkthrough, and guidelines for analysis and design that include qualitative assessment of the good and bad characteristics of a design. The method is supported by tools and is used both for real-time and data-processing applications.

Z

Z A formal notation, based on *set algebra and *predicate calculus, for the specification of computing systems. It was developed at the Programming Research Group, Oxford University. Z specifications have a modular structure. *See also* constructive specification.

Z3 An electromechanical programmed calculator built in Berlin by Konrad Zuse and fully operational in 1941. Like the earlier (nonprogrammed) calculators, Z1 (mechanical) and Z2 (electromechanical), constructed by Zuse, it did not survive the war. An improved machine, the Z4, was completed by 1945.

zero-address instruction An instruction that contains no address fields. It may for example enable *stack processing: a zero-address instruction implies that the *absolute address of the operand is held in a special *register that is automatically incremented (or decremented) to point to the location of the top of the stack.

zero function The *function whose value is zero for every element in its domain. The term is usually applied more specifically to the function

$$Z : N \to N$$

for which $Z(n) = 0$

for all n in N, the set of nonnegative integers. This function is basic to the theory of *recursive and *primitive recursive functions.

zero matrix *Another name for* null matrix.

zero suppression The elimination of nonsignificant zeros. While numerical data is being processed it may be expanded to a uniform number of digits by the addition of nonsignificant zeros to the left of the most significant digit. For printout or display these nonsignificant zeros are suppressed.

zero-trip loop *See* do-while loop.

zero word In coding theory, a word consisting entirely of zero digits. It lies at the origin of *Hamming space. *See also* Hamming weight.

ZIF socket *Short for* zero insertion force socket. A *chip socket into which it is possible to place a chip with no downward force. Electrical contact is then made by moving a small lever that causes each leg of the chip to be firmly gripped. A ZIF socket is used where chips are regularly moved in and out of a socket, e.g. in a *PROM programmer.

UK Data Protection Legislation

The UK has now enacted the Data Protection Act 1984 to comply with the Council of Europe Convention. The Act establishes an independent public register, and is concerned only with "personal data" as defined in the Act.

The definitions are as follows:

data means information recorded in a form in which it can be processed by equipment operated automatically in response to instructions given for that purpose.

personal data means data consisting of information that relates to a living individual who can be identified from that information (or from that and other information in the possession of the data user), including any expression of opinion about the individual but not any indication of the intentions of the data user in respect of that individual.

data subject means an individual who is the subject of personal data.

data user means a person who holds data.

The Act came into effect in stages:

● **From 12 September 1984:** Under sections 23 and 24(3) an individual has been entitled to compensation from a data user for any damage or distress suffered by reason of the loss, damage, destruction, disclosure, or access to his personal data, provided the damage has been suffered after 12 September 1984. It is a defence to an action of this kind if the data user can prove that he had taken such care as in all the circumstances was reasonable to prevent the damage or distress.

This is in effect a right of action for damages caused by inadequate computer security.

● **From 11 November 1985:** Data users have been able to register their activities with the Data Protection Registrar.

The registration form requires the data user to give:

● its name and address;

● a description of the personal data it holds and the purpose or purposes for which the data is held;

● a description of the source or sources from which it intends or may wish to obtain the data or the information to be contained in the data;

● a description of any person or persons to whom it intends or may wish to disclose the data;

● the names or a description of any countries or territories outside the UK to which it intends or may wish directly or indirectly to transfer the data;

● one or more addresses for the receipt of requests from data subjects for access to the data.

The Registrar is using a classification system to assist data users in filling in the registration forms so that, in most cases, a small business would be able to indicate by the use of code numbers the type of data it holds, the type of sources it uses, and the type of person to whom it intends to disclose the data. Registration forms and notes concerning registration are available from Post Offices.

● **From 11 May 1986:** If a data user who is holding personal data fails to register then under Section 5 of the Act the data user will be guilty of the new criminal offence of failing to register. A data user is also not entitled to process personal data after registration except in accordance with the terms of its registration.

● **From 11 November 1987:** Under Section 24 of the Act if a court is satisfied on the application of a data subject that personal data held by a data user concerning him is inaccurate it may order the rectification or erasure of the data. Additionally it may order the rectification or erasure of any data held by the data user that contains an expression of opinion that appears to the court to be based on the inaccurate data. However the section contains provisions that will, alternatively, allow the data user, in certain circumstances, to supplement the data by a statement of true facts as approved by the court.

● **From 11 November 1987:** Under Section 11 the Registrar is allowed to strike a data user off the register. Additionally prior to that date he was entitled to take action against a data user relying on information on misuse of data having taken place since September 1984 and was entitled to indicate to a data user his intention to strike a data user off the register the moment his powers to do so came into effect.

In practice he has to indicate specific requirements to a data user and failure to comply will lead to an "enforcement notice" requiring the data user to take within a time limit particular steps to comply with the Data Protection Principles (see below). Only as a last resort will the Registrar issue a de-registration notice.

● **From 11 November 1987:** A data subject has been entitled to obtain a printout from a registered data user of any personal data held by him. The details and the consequences of this provision are referred to in Subject Access Provisions (below).

It is now possible for a person to apply for and, on payment of a fee, obtain copies of any criminal convictions recorded against him on the UK Police National Computer. Standard forms are available to do this from Scotland Yard. No prosecutions have been brought under the Act and little use has been made of it by legal practitioners in the UK.

Data Protection Principles

The eight principles of data protection legislation are fundamental statements of good practice that have behind them the criminal and civil penalties of the Data Protection Act 1984. They are:

1. The information to be contained in personal data shall be obtained, and personal data shall be processed, fairly and lawfully.

2. Personal data shall be held only for one or more specified and lawful purposes.

3. Personal data held for any purpose or purposes shall not be used or disclosed in any manner incompatible with that purpose or those purposes.

4. Personal data held for any purpose or purposes shall be adequate, relevant, and not excessive in relation to that purpose or those purposes.

5. Personal data shall be accurate and, where necessary, kept up to date.

6. Personal data held for any purpose or purposes shall not be kept longer than necessary for that purpose or those purposes.

7. A data subject shall be entitled

(a) at reasonable intervals and without undue delay or expense

(i) to be informed by any data user whether he holds personal data of which that individual is the subject; and

(ii) to access to any such data held by a data user; and

(b) where appropriate, to have such data corrected or erased.

8. Appropriate security measures shall be taken against unauthorized access to, or alteration, disclosure, or destruction of personal data and against accidental loss or destruction of personal data.

OXFORD

MORE OXFORD PAPERBACKS

Details of a selection of other Oxford Paperbacks follow. A complete list of Oxford Paperbacks, including The World's Classics, Twentieth-Century Classics, OPUS, Past Masters, Oxford Authors, Oxford Shakespeare, and Oxford Paperback Reference, is available in the UK from the General Publicity Department, Oxford University Press (RS), Walton Street, Oxford, OX2 6DP.

In the USA, complete lists are available from the Paperbacks Marketing Manager, Oxford University Press, 200 Madison Avenue, New York, NY 10016.

Oxford Paperbacks are available from all good bookshops. In case of difficulty, customers in the UK can order direct from Oxford University Press Bookshop, 116 High Street, Oxford, Freepost, OX1 4BR, enclosing full payment. Please add 10 per cent of the published price for postage and packing.

MEDICINE IN OXFORD PAPERBACKS

Oxford Paperbacks offers an increasing list of medical studies and reference books of interest to the specialist and general reader alike, including The Facts series, authoritative and practical guides to a wide range of common diseases and conditions.

CONCISE MEDICAL DICTIONARY

Third Edition

Written without the use of unnecessary technical jargon, this illustrated medical dictionary will be welcomed as a home reference, as well as an indispensible aid for all those working in the medical profession.

Nearly 10,000 important terms and concepts are explained, including all the major medical and surgical specialities, such as gynaecology and obstetrics, paediatrics, dermatology, neurology, cardiology, and tropical medicine. This third edition contains much new material on prenatal diagnosis, infertility treatment, nuclear medicine, community health, and immunology. Terms relating to advances in molecular biology and genetic engineering have been added, and recently developed drugs in clinical use are included. A feature of the dictionary is its unusually full coverage of the fields of community health, psychology, and psychiatry.

Each entry contains a straightforward definition, followed by a more detailed description, while an extensive cross-reference system provides the reader with a comprehensive view of a particular subject.

Also in Oxford Paperbacks:

Drugs and Medicine   Roderick Cawson and Roy Spector
Travellers' Health: How to Stay Healthy Abroad 2/e
Richard Dawood
I'm a Health Freak Too!
Aidan Macfarlane and Ann McPherson
Problem Drinking   Nick Heather and Ian Robertson

SCIENCE IN OXFORD PAPERBACKS

Oxford Paperbacks offers a challenging and controversial list of science and mathematics books, ranging from theories of evolution to analyses of the latest microtechnology, from studies of the nervous system to advice on teenage health.

THE AGES OF GAIA
A Biography of Our Living Earth
James Lovelock

In his first book, *Gaia: A New Look at Life on Earth* (OPB, 1982), James Lovelock proposed a startling new theory of life. Previously it was accepted that plants and animals evolve on, but are distinct from, an inanimate planet. Gaia maintained that the Earth, its rocks, oceans, and atmosphere, and all living things are part of one great organism, evolving over the vast span of geological time. Much scientific work has since confirmed Lovelock's ideas.

In this new book, Lovelock elaborates the basis of a new and unified view of the earth and life sciences, discussing recent scientific developments in detail: the greenhouse effect, acid rain, the depletion of the ozone layer and the effects of ultraviolet radiation, the emission of CFCs, and nuclear power. He demonstrates the geophysical interaction of atmosphere, oceans, climate, and the Earth's crust, regulated comfortably for life by living organisms using the energy of the sun.

'Open the cover and bathe in great draughts of air that excitingly argue the case that "the earth is alive".' David Bellamy, *Observer*

'Lovelock deserves to be described as a genius.' *New Scientist*

'He is to science what Gandhi was to politics.' Fred Pearce, *New Scientist*

Also in Oxford Paperbacks:

What is Ecology?   Denis Owen
The Selfish Gene 2/e   Richard Dawkins
The Sacred Beetle and Other Great Essays in Science
Chosen and introduced by Martin Gardner

SCIENCE IN OXFORD PAPERBACKS

Oxford Paperbacks' expanding science and mathematics list offers a range of books across the scientific spectrum by men and women at the forefront of their fields, including Richard Dawkins, Martin Gardner, James Lovelock, Raymond Smullyan, and Nobel Prize winners Peter Medawar and Gerald Edelman.

THE SELFISH GENE
Second Edition
Richard Dawkins

Our genes made us. We animals exist for their preservation and are nothing more than their throwaway survival machines. The world of the selfish gene is one of savage competition, ruthless exploitation, and deceit. But what of the acts of apparent altruism found in nature—the bees who commit suicide when they sting to protect the hive, or the birds who risk their lives to warn the flock of an approaching hawk? Do they contravene the fundamental law of gene selfishness? By no means: Dawkins shows that the selfish gene is also the subtle gene. And he holds out the hope that our species—alone on earth—has the power to rebel against the designs of the selfish gene. This book is a call to arms. It is both manual and manifesto, and it grips like a thriller.

The Selfish Gene, Richard Dawkins's brilliant first book and still his most famous, is an international bestseller in thirteen languages. For this greatly expanded edition, endnotes have been added, giving fascinating reflections on the original text, and there are two major new chapters.

'learned, witty, and very well written . . . exhilaratingly good.' Sir Peter Medawar, *Spectator*

'Who should read this book? Everyone interested in the universe and their place in it.' Jeffrey R. Baylis, *Animal Behaviour*

'the sort of popular science writing that makes the reader feel like a genius' *New York Times*

Also in Oxford Paperbacks:

The Extended Phenotype Richard Dawkins
The Ages of Gaia James Lovelock
The Unheeded Cry Bernard E. Rollin

OXFORD REFERENCE

Oxford is famous for its superb range of dictionaries and reference books. The Oxford Reference series offers the most up-to-date and comprehensive paperbacks at the most competitive prices, across a broad spectrum of subjects.

THE CONCISE OXFORD COMPANION TO ENGLISH LITERATURE

Edited by Margaret Drabble and Jenny Stringer

Based on the immensely popular fifth edition of the *Oxford Companion to English Literature* this is an indispensable, compact guide to the central matter of English literature.

There are more than 5,000 entries on the lives and works of authors, poets, playwrights, essayists, philosophers, and historians; plot summaries of novels and plays; literary movements; fictional characters; legends; theatres; periodicals; and much more.

The book's sharpened focus on the English literature of the British Isles makes it especially convenient to use, but there is still generous coverage of the literature of other countries and of other disciplines which have influenced or been influenced by English literature.

From reviews of *The Oxford Companion to English Literature Fifth Edition:*

'a book which one turns to with constant pleasure . . . a book with much style and little prejudice' Iain Gilchrist, *TLS*

'it is quite difficult to imagine, in this genre, a more useful publication' Frank Kermode, *London Review of Books*

'incarnates a living sense of tradition . . . sensitive not to fashion merely but to the spirit of the age' Christopher Ricks, *Sunday Times*

Also available in Oxford Reference:

The Concise Oxford Dictionary of Art and Artists
edited by Ian Chilvers
A Concise Oxford Dictionary of Mathematics
Christopher Clapham
The Oxford Spelling Dictionary   compiled by R. E. Allen
A Concise Dictionary of Law   edited by Elizabeth A. Martin

LAW FROM OXFORD PAPERBACKS

Oxford Paperbacks's law list ranges from introductions to the English legal system to reference books and in-depth studies of contemporary legal issues.

INTRODUCTION TO ENGLISH LAW
Tenth Edition

William Geldart
Edited by D. C. M. Yardley

'Geldart' has over the years established itself as a standard account of English law, expounding the body of modern law as set in its historical context. Regularly updated since its first publication, it remains indispensable to student and layman alike as a concise, reliable guide.

Since publication of the ninth edition in 1984 there have been important court decisions and a great deal of relevant new legislation. D. C. M. Yardley, Chairman of the Commission for Local Administration in England, has taken account of all these developments and the result has been a considerable rewriting of several parts of the book. These include the sections dealing with the contractual liability of minors, the abolition of the concept of illegitimacy, the liability of a trade union in tort for inducing a person to break his/her contract of employment, the new public order offences, and the intent necessary for a conviction of murder.

Other law titles:

Freedom Under Thatcher: Civil Liberties in Modern Britain
Keith Ewing and Conor Gearty
Doing the Business   Dick Hobbs
Judges   David Pannick
Law and Modern Society   P. S. Atiyah